"Jackson is one of t
all of us to emul
—Chris Hedges, jou
and Princeton University lecturer; author of
War Is a Force That Gives Us Meaning

"*Jackson Rising* is the rarest of things: a real strategic plan. You will not find a simple wish list that glosses over the hard questions of resources, or some disembodied manifesto imploring the workers forward, but a work in progress building the capacity of people to exercise power."
—Richard Moser, author of *The World the Sixties Made*

Jackson Rising Redux

Lessons on Building the Future in the Present

Edited by Kali Akuno and Matt Meyer

PM

Jackson Rising Redux: Lessons on Building the Future in the Present
Edited by Kali Akuno and Matt Meyer

ISBN: 978–1–62963–928–4 (paperback)
ISBN: 978–1–62963–864–5 (hardcover)
ISBN: 978–1–62963–952–9 (ebook)

Library of Congress Control Number: 2020947299

Cover by John Yates / www.stealworks.com
Interior design by briandesign

10 9 8 7 6 5 4 3 2 1

PM Press
PO Box 23912
Oakland, CA 94623
www.pmpress.org

Printed in the USA.

Contents

II EMERGENCE

III BUILDING SUBSTANCE

VI RADICAL MUNICIPALISM

VII TOWARD THE GENERAL STRIKE AND DUAL POWER

VIII GOING FORWARD: ECOSOCIALISM AND REGENERATION

Acknowledgments

We would like to thank each and every author who made a contribution to this publication. We would like to give thanks to all those authors who provided new or updated versions of already published works and all those who contributed new works or interviews that appear in print in this volume for the first time. We would like to acknowledge all of the journals, newsletters, websites, and movement spaces that are helping to bring everyone's full attention to the important words and work spotlighted here and give those literary and organizing spaces all the recognition and support they are due.

We would like to highlight with special gratitude the work of Firoze Manji and Daraja Press, publisher of *Jackson Rising: The Struggle for Economic Democracy and Black Self-Determination in Jackson, Mississippi* (2017). This book would not be possible without the steadfast solidarity and professionalism behind that earlier effort. Ajamu Nangwaya was coeditor of that book, so we give special thanks for his work both there and in his writings that reappear here.

We must also acknowledge the many contributions of the membership and staff of Cooperation Jackson toward the completion of this work. A special shout-out to Sabrina Howard for the extraordinary art found on the cover and to Shambe Jones for his design assistance in that effort.

Last, we have to acknowledge the historic contributions of the people of Jackson, Mississippi—without whom this experiment in radical social transformation would not be possible.

Please note the following citations for previously published work:

1. Kali Akuno's "*The Jackson-Kush Plan: The Struggle for Black Self-Determination and Economic Democracy*" was originally published in part as "The Jackson Plan" on the Malcolm X Grassroots Movement website and in full on Kali's blog, *Navigating the Storm*, https://mronline.org/wp-content/uploads/2020/07/Jackson-KushPlan.pdf.

2. Kali Akuno's "The People's Assembly Overview: The Jackson People's Assembly Model" was first published on the Malcolm X Grassroots Movement website and Kali's blog, *Navigating the Storm*, November 17, 2014, https://navigatingthestorm.blogspot.com/2014/11/peoples-assemblys-overview-jackson.html.

3. "The Jackson Rising Statement: Building the City of the Future Today," which was written by Kali Akuno for the administration of the late Mayor Chokwe Lumumba was first published on the Jackson Rising: New Economy Conference website, https://jacksonrising.wordpress.com/ local/jackson-rising-statement.

4. Ajamu Nangwaya's "Seek Ye First the Worker Self-Management Kingdom: Toward the Solidarity Economy in Jackson, MS" was first published by Pambazuka News, September 18, 2013, https://www.pambazuka.org/governance/seek-ye-first-worker-self-management-kingdom.

5. Carl Davidson's "Jackson Rising: An Electoral Battle Unleashes a Merger of Black Power, the Solidarity Economy and Wider Democracy" was first published on the website of RIPESS the Intercontinental Network for the Promotion of Social Solidarity Economy, and Carl's blog, *Keep on Keepin' On*, May 9, 2014, https://carldavidson.blogspot.com/2014/05/jackson-rising-electoral-battle.html?m=0.

6. Bruce Dixon's "Jackson Rising: Black Millionaires Won't Lift Us Up but Cooperation and the Solidarity Economy Might" was first published on Black Agenda Report, May 7, 2014, https://tinyurl.com/4sr6k7th.

7. Kali Akuno's "Casting Shadows: Chokwe Lumumba and the Struggle for Racial Justice and Economic Democracy in Jackson, Mississippi" was first published as a study for the Rosa Luxemburg Stiftung—New York Office, February 24, 2015, https://rosalux.nyc/casting-shadows.

8. Katie Gilbert's "The Socialist Experiment: A New-Society Vision in Jackson, Mississippi" was first published in the Fall 2017 issue of the *Oxford American*, with support from the Economic Hardship Reporting Project, https://main.oxfordamerican.org/magazine/item/1296-the-socialist-experiment.

Foreword

Richard D. Wolff

I

Every economic system in human history displays this pattern: it is born out of a prior system, it evolves, and then it dies, giving way to the next system. Modern capitalism, the dominant system in today's world, was born in England in the seventeenth century, spread globally, has changed over time, and is now declining. In its uneven process of dying away, capitalism is also giving birth to new and different systems. Cooperation Jackson is one of those.

Capitalism often grew out of the declines of the slave and feudal systems that preceded it. The master-and-slave economic systems usually lasted for centuries, but then unevenly broke down. Sometimes, when breaks happened in particular places and at particular times, some masters and/or slaves could not or would not stay within that system. Instead, they struggled to survive by finding or inventing and then developing some new economic system. In one possible outcome, those refugees from slavery became instead employers and employees in a system we call capitalism. The same story applies to feudalism. Its lord-and-serf system declined and eventually broke down unevenly in different places and at different times. Then ex-lords and ex-serfs sometimes groped their ways into the capitalist system as employers and employees.

Now it is capitalism's turn to decline slowly and unevenly. That process has already been underway for some time in the old centers of capitalism (Western Europe, North America, and Japan). In particular moments and at particular places, people caught in capitalism's deep economic and social difficulties struggled, found, and developed an alternative noncapitalist economic system, one that was not capitalist in the precise sense of not organizing the production of goods and services in enterprises characterized by a small minority, the employers, who owned and operated them. Unlike capitalism, the alternative system did not position the majority within enterprises, the ex-employees, as nonowners and pure order-takers. Instead, the alternative system effectively democratized enterprises. It made them into democratically operated workplaces. In them, all were workers, each with one vote, who made all the basic decisions: what, how, and where to produce and how to dispose of the output. Collectively, the workers became their own employers.

Such a transition from capitalism to what we can call a worker cooperative–based economic system was the modern analogue of the various transitions from feudalism to capitalism in earlier times and places. So for example, in poverty-stricken northern Spain during the 1950s, a Catholic priest and his parish rediscovered and repurposed an old idea into a new economic system. They experimented with democratic worker cooperatives as the determinedly noncapitalist workplace organization grounding a new economic system. The Mondragon Cooperative Corporation (MCC) came to be its name as it moved from an initial six-person worker co-op to the huge corporation that it is today. Encompassing many diverse worker co-ops, MCC is now one of Spain's ten largest corporations.

Different worker co-ops developed elsewhere in different conditions of capitalist difficulties and declines. A third of the economy of the Italian Emilia-Romagna region is constituted by worker co-ops that have coexisted with capitalist enterprises for decades. The co-ops are networked in ways that provide both mutual support and an effective mechanism for growth. An example in the United States saw the Cheeseboard in Berkeley, California, start as a worker co-op in 1971 and grow into six worker co-ops in the San Francisco Bay area today. The United States Federation of Worker Cooperatives, formed in 2004, was a milestone, furthering the development of worker cooperatives across the country. There are many more examples that reflect both capitalism's deepening problems and crises and the rising attraction of worker co-op–based economies as the alternative being born out of capitalism's decline.

Cooperation Jackson is one of these key historic pioneering experiments. Cooperation Jackson has founded and is constructing a better economic system and a better society out of the failures, breakdowns, and decline of capitalism. Because of the US's particular mix of a capitalist economy and systemic racism targeting the African American community, Cooperation Jackson is a unique experiment in worker co-op–based economic and social development. It aims both to overcome the racist victimization of African Americans and the economic victimization that capitalism imposes on employees. It is a quiet social revolution underway to move the African American community forward: economically, politically, and culturally. In so doing, it models crucial learning and leadership for all other employees in the US—the vast majority—who need likewise to find a way out of and beyond capitalism, one that is better.

II

It is understandably difficult for many living in a dying system to understand or admit what is happening. History provides us with countless examples of people denying the declines of the Greek, Roman, and British empires, and now the US empire. Those past imperial systems had looked so powerful and so invincible for so long. Yet all of them disintegrated and gave way.

Modern capitalism arose in Europe out of the disintegration of feudalism, signaled by the black death pandemic of the fourteenth century. The violent French and American Revolutions were feudalism's end and capitalism's birth. Yet contemporaries rarely recognized the signs. Likewise, in today's decline of capitalism, few see them.

The beneficiaries of ongoing systems are usually the most blind. Feudal lords thought the system would go on forever. The wealth and power they amassed provided the props they needed to believe their own hype. Capitalists today are blind in just the same ways. Their accumulated wealth and power—from mansions and yachts to nuclear missiles—comforts them into imagining that their system will not disintegrate like all former systems did.

The COVID-19 pandemic ought to suggest a historical parallel to world capitalism. What the black death signaled about feudalism, COVID-19 signals about today's capitalism. With all its wealth, power, and nuclear missiles, capitalism was far more vulnerable to, unprepared for, and deeply damaged by the pandemic than capitalists imagined it would be. Systemic, deep, and recurring flaws and weaknesses were exposed. Millions began to grasp—emotionally, ideologically, and practically—that capitalism had become a failed system.

When systems decline, their victims usually feel and then see it before their beneficiaries do. That is one reason the beneficiaries devote so much of their wealth and energies to persuading the victims that criticisms of the system are wrong, and that decline is definitely *not* happening. The beneficiaries denounce critics of the system as evil, perverse, disloyal, and deserving punishment by the police and army. Those atop the system seek to convince everyone, themselves included, that the system is the best humanity can achieve. It is likewise too strong and solid to ever be undone.

Systems last so long as the mass of their victims accept their beneficiaries' views. When slaves, serfs, and employees stop accepting what masters, lords, and employers say about the system, decline sets in. How long the decline lasts, what particular forms it takes, and what sparks its final collapse depend on the particular conditions and traditions of each decline's time and place.

US capitalism's decline is now well underway. Its basic economic institutions, corporations, are in greater debt than at any time in the system's history. The US government owns more of that debt now than ever before. More of the purchasing power of consumers, on which corporations depend, likewise depends on the US government doling out tax breaks, welfare payments, mortgage loans, guarantees, forbearance, rent moratoria, student loans, and so on. The US government now imposes tariffs, bans, and sanctions on countries and corporations to shape and control world trade. Its central bank floods the economy with trillions in new money to lubricate a capitalism now on state life support.

The myth of private capitalism's invincibility is smashed. Its corporations and its working class are as desperately reliant on government support as the poor are on welfare. As people see that, the inevitable question will arise: If we are *all* on government support, why are some so much richer than others? The government is a social institution that dispenses society's money. We should all have a say in how that is accomplished. Why should private individuals, unaccountable to society, make key decisions (what to produce, what technology to use, where to produce, and what to do with the output) when society as a whole makes production possible. At first, such questions arise unconsciously. The decline eventually brings them to consciousness, which in turn deepens the decline. When victims of the system's decline become the system's conscious critics, the decline accelerates.

Private US capitalism has failed to cope with its economic problems. All capitalisms have, for centuries, experienced downturns (crashes, recessions, depression, busts, etc.) on average every four to seven years. The US had the dot.com crash in 2000, the subprime mortgage crash in 2008, and the COVID-19 crash in 2020: three crashes in twenty years. Each crash was worse than the one before: more workers unemployed, more businesses reduced or destroyed, more public budgets and services undermined. The latest crash began in February 2020, *before* the pandemic hit. No real solution to capitalism's instability and its immense social costs has been found. As we go through this latest one, more and more of us see the systemic problem.

US capitalism has failed to correct its ever-deepening inequality of income, wealth, and power. Even during the COVID-19 pandemic—a crisis we "all had to get through together"—the richest got much richer, while over fifty million US citizens filed unemployment compensation claims. The inequalities that helped bring about the three crashes of this new century were worsened by those crashes. The problem is the system.

US capitalism's economic failures are now reigniting its long-accumulated social failures. Chief among these are the systemic racism, sexism, and ecological destruction that have characterized US capitalism from its beginnings. It is becoming ever harder to deflect oppositions to them, to deny or rationalize them, or to postpone solutions. Capitalism's decline also expands a majority's sympathies for real solutions to those social failures.

The critics of capitalism are growing in number, in organization, and in self-confidence. These are all effects as well as signs of system decline. Opposition to capitalism as a system is slowly but steadily displacing the Cold War fetish of thinking only piecemeal reforms were needed or possible (itself an ideological concession to capitalism). Equally important, the critics of capitalism are finding ways to engage and share with the system's victims. The victims can and do develop the critics' understanding, and vice versa. Their growing alliance both reflects and deepens capitalism's decline.

III

Regarding the birth of a new or next system from the decline of the old: What comes after capitalism? To answer that question underlines the enormous importance of Cooperation Jackson today: its achievements and its promise. Cooperation Jackson is one birth of the next system within a declining capitalism. It gives not only hope for capitalism's victims and critics, it also provides an intense social laboratory for everyone, participants and observers, to learn what to do and what to avoid in making such births successful.

Of course, capitalism always had, from its beginnings, victims and critics. But during the system's long ascendancy in replacing feudalism, slavery, and other prior systems, victims and critics were successfully suppressed, deflected, or absorbed. This was true both in capitalism's early years and in its later, more recent times. The most important tradition of criticism and opposition has proven to be socialism. First, socialists were the dominant movements of critical opposition within national capitalisms and even of opposition to capitalism internationally. After the short-lived Paris Commune of 1871, when many crucial lessons were learned, socialists in the Soviet Revolution of 1917 began a several-decade-long experiment in birthing a new postcapitalist system *as they understood it.* Beside the Soviet Union, those experiments included many Eastern European nations, the People's Republic of China, Cuba, Vietnam, and others.

Like the earlier Paris Commune, those experiments also yielded crucial lessons, and Cooperation Jackson's program learned them. That is one important reason why it can counter a declining capitalism and escape from its repeated failures to bring genuine economic development to the Jackson, Mississippi, area.

Thus, Cooperation Jackson builds its economic development strategy around raising the economic, political, and cultural level of life *for the whole of society*. It does not prioritize an employer minority as capitalist development projects do. Likewise, Cooperation Jackson is determined not to repeat or allow the statism of the early socialist experiments. Cooperation Jackson is relentlessly democratic. Its economic basis is *not* enterprises divided into employers and employees: the capitalist model. The economic base for Cooperation Jackson is the worker cooperative, the deliberately democratized enterprise.

For Cooperation Jackson, the democratized enterprise, the worker co-op, becomes the economic partner for democratized politics and culture. The point is to mobilize democratic participation across the entire community. Where the socialist experiments over the last century focused on government, the ownership of property in means of production (social versus private), and the means of distributing resources and products (market versus planning), Cooperation Jackson concentrates elsewhere. The "social relations of production" inside the enterprise become one key focus. Those have finally to change from the patterns of the past: the master versus the slave, the lord versus the serf, and the employer versus the employee. Instead, Cooperation Jackson prioritizes enterprises in which all are individually employees but also collectively their own employer. The workers have no masters, lords, or employers over them. Unlike the socialist models, state officials have not replaced private citizens as employers (that only changes *who* the employer is). Cooperation Jackson changes much more than that "who." It alters the relationship inside the enterprise itself. No minority owns or controls the enterprise. Instead, it has become a democratic workplace community.

Cooperation Jackson aims to ground its community's democratic politics and culture on a genuine economic democracy. What people experience in their co-op workplaces is one person, one vote, and majorities decide the what, how, and where of production, as well as the uses to be made of the outputs produced. That daily training in real democracy strengthens the demand for parallel democracies in politics and culture. This will enable not only the blocked and long delayed economic development of the African American community, it will build African American communities into models for the economic development in the capitalist US and beyond.

What Cooperation Jackson is doing widens the space for a worker co-op sector of the US economy. As Cooperation Jackson grows and builds mutual support networks with other worker cooperatives, the US will become economically diverse. It will include democratic worker co-op enterprises alongside and interacting with top-down hierarchical capitalist enterprises. All Americans will, thus, be able for the first time to directly observe and compare the alternative types of enterprises. All will be able to buy from, sell to, and work in both types, or they will have family and friends who do. Real knowledge and real comparisons will inform Americans and, thereby, give them real freedom of choice. All Americans will then be able to choose what mix of the two types of enterprises they prefer for the US.

The leadership and model that Cooperation Jackson can provide will stimulate workers, and some employers too, inside capitalist enterprises to convert them into worker co-ops. Mutual support among them will facilitate the sector's growth and, thus, the entire economy's diversity.

Worker co-ops will inevitably discover that their prosperity and growth are hampered by all sorts of existing laws, regulations, and customs. Most of those need to be changed. They were developed and revised continuously over the last two centuries by capitalist enterprises seeking to make them serve their interests. Capitalist enterprises supported those parties and politicians that best served their interests. Capitalists funded them, supported their projects, and provided vital links to voters and their communities. As worker co-ops gain a foothold within economies where capitalism long prevailed (as in the US today), they will encounter laws, regulations, and customs that do not help worker co-ops prosper and grow. Some directly prevent and others threaten worker co-ops and their growth.

What worker co-ops need now is what capitalist enterprises already have: new or changed laws, regulations, and customs that support forming, running, and growing worker co-ops. To get them, worker co-ops will need a political movement active in their communities' politics and culture. Worker co-ops will need political parties to achieve for them what today's major parties (Republican and Democratic) have long achieved for capitalist enterprises. New political parties responsive to worker co-ops' needs and aspirations will need to work out compromises with the old parties (Republican and Democratic) and the capitalism they represent. They will also need to renegotiate those compromises when needed to accommodate the shifting balance between capitalist and worker co-op sectors of the national economy.

IV

Cooperation Jackson represents a bold, courageous commitment *to not* be taken down with capitalism's decline, *to not* resign a community's hopes and dreams to poverty and hopelessness. Cooperation Jackson dares to build an altogether different and far better system than what the capitalist US offers and has always offered. That is what the people of Jackson need. It is also what so many other Americans need.

It is an honor for me to write this introduction to a book devoted to one of our best hopes today for a new and better postcapitalism and the genuine economic and social development it can bring.

INTRODUCTION

Building Economic Democracy to Construct Ecosocialism from Below

Kali Akuno and Sacajawea "Saki" Hall

In a small corner of Jackson, Mississippi, a scrappy little project is striving to make a big impact in the prefigurative development of the next socioeconomic system that will help guide humanity's continuing evolution and transcend the oppressive and exploitative capitalist social order now threatening humanity, and all complex life on our precious planet, with extinction. This project aims to synthesize the practices and institutions of the social and solidarity economy in combination with permacultural design, digital fabrication, and energy democracy, thus establishing economic democracy on a municipal level to inspire and help build ecosocialism from below on a national and international level. The name given to this scrappy little project is the Jackson-Kush Plan, and the organization leading its advancement is Cooperation Jackson.

What, you might ask, is "ecosocialism," and why is Cooperation Jackson aiming to build it? Loosely defined, ecosocialism describes a classless socioeconomic system in which humans live in balance with nature. Exchange value would be subordinated to use value by organizing production primarily to meet social needs and the requirements of environmental protection and ecological regeneration. To build an ecologically rational society along these lines requires the collective ownership of the means of production, democratic planning to enable society to define the goals of production and investment, and a new technological production structure that meshes with society's plans and stays within the Earth's ecological carrying capacity. In turn, building such a democratic culture necessitates the transformation of social relations, particularly those of production and reproduction, through deliberate and intentional struggles to eliminate white supremacy, settler colonialism, imperialism, patriarchy, heterosexism, speciesism, and all systems of domination, oppression, hierarchy, extraction, and exploitation.[1]

However, before we get to ecosocialism and the overarching challenge ahead, we must first establish concrete examples of economic democracy. So what is economic democracy? In short, it is the democratization of our economy's basic production structures. This transformation starts with the democratization of our workplaces, the institutions of finance and investment, and the distribution of goods and services within the market. More specifically, economic democracy calls first and foremost for transforming our workspaces into worker cooperatives; we must break capital's stronghold on the institutions of finance and investment by establishing capital controls and creating such institutions as public community banks. At the same time, we must struggle to bring investment institutions under democratic control, particularly on the local level through practices like participatory budgeting in the public arena. Economic democratization also entails expanding the practices and institutions of the solidarity economy and the commons—whether through community land trusts, time banking, community currencies, solidarity markets, or other means.[2]

With these basic definitions and parameters in mind, the question becomes how to move from our immediate, short-term democratic economic pursuits toward our comprehensive long-term pursuit of economic democracy. Making Jackson a comprehensive *transition city* through the agency of our Jackson Just Transition Plan is our strategy—one we hope also speaks to other communities trying to make this historical transition.

To fully grasp our program and strategy, it is critical to understand Cooperation Jackson's reason for being and our emerging structure. Over the course of our first five years, from May 2014 through May 2019, Cooperation Jackson has endeavored to create four interconnected and interdependent institutions:

- *A federation of emerging local cooperatives and mutual aid networks.* Our emerging federation is growing to comprise a number of interconnected and interdependent worker, consumer, and community cooperatives cooperating as one overall, coherent, and democratic body. We are also constructing various mutual aid institutions and practices to reinforce the federation's solidarity and provide multiple ways to exchange value, labor, and time to improve the quality of life of all federation and community members.

- *A cooperative incubator.* Our incubator is Cooperation Jackson's start-up training and development center. The incubator aids new cooperators with basic training, feasibility studies, business plan development, financing, training in democratic management, and more.
- *A cooperative school and training center.* We are currently aiming to open our economic democracy school in 2022. Our aim is to ensure that Cooperation Jackson serves as a center of social transformation by continually broadening the social consciousness of all its cooperators and enhancing their skills, abilities, and overall capacities to act as conscious actors in improving their social context and environment.
- *A cooperative financial institution.* We are working to build a set of financial institutions that will be used to start and strengthen all of Cooperation Jackson operations and serve as a means of self-capitalization and democratic investment to expand the initiative.

All of Cooperation Jackson's programs and strategy are presently executed through five intentionally interlocked and interdependent focal points, including various campaign initiatives, projects, and programs. These include:

- The development of self-managed green worker cooperatives and an extensive network of mutual aid and social solidarity programs, organizations, and institutions, such as community land trusts. This programmatic approach is translated into transformative policy aimed at making Jackson a *solidarity city*.
- The development of an eco-village, community energy production, and sustainable methodologies and technologies of production and ecologically regenerative processes and institutions. This programmatic approach is translated into transformative policy aimed at making Jackson a *sustainable city.*
- The development of a network of 3D print factories that anchor community production cooperatives and institutions. This

programmatic approach is translated into transformative policy aimed at making Jackson a *fab city* (or digital fabrication laboratory city).

- The development of an all-embracing, class-oriented union cooperative to build genuine worker power from the ground up, in Jackson. This programmatic approach is translated into transformative policy aimed at making Jackson a *workers' city*.
- The development of a human rights institute to craft a human rights charter and commission for Jackson. This programmatic approach is translated into transformative policy aimed at making Jackson a *human rights city*.

The transformative policy components attached to each of the focal points are critical since none of the system(s) change processes described here can be sustained in a nonrevolutionary context unless the state supports and reinforces them. Such support means providing legal justification, incentives, and resource allocation to various initiatives. It also entails aggressive monitoring and enforcement from municipal government in response to strong social movements and civilian institutions that pressure government.

All these transformative policy components are fundamentally articulations of "nonreformist reforms." The notion of nonreformist reforms was formulated by the French socialist André Gorz in the 1960s. Gorz posed the formulation to bridge short-term engagements for social justice in everyday life with the longer-term vision for an anti-capitalist world.[3] Gorz's formulation centers on struggling for demands and reforms that improve conditions in people's immediate lives while subverting the logic of the capitalist system, upending its social relations, and diluting its strength. Nonreformist reforms seek to create new logic, new relations, and new imperatives that create a new equilibrium and balance of forces to weaken capitalism and enable the development of an anti-capitalist alternative. This aim is exactly what Cooperation Jackson's transformative policy components seek to accomplish.

Green Worker Cooperatives, Mutual Aid Network, and Solidarity Economy Institutions

No one practice or form associated with the solidarity economy alone can transform the capitalist economy and build economic democracy as a transitional alternative. In our view, we must develop and employ several complementary and reinforcing practices and forms of solidarity economics at once to subvert the dynamics of the capitalist system, its logic, and its imperatives.[4] Accordingly, Cooperation Jackson is currently building or aiming to build these complementary solidarity institutions and practices:

- *Community land trust (CLT).* A CLT is a democratic nonprofit corporation that stewards and develops land and other community assets on behalf of a community. Cooperation Jackson's primary objective in developing this institution is to acquire and decommodify as much land as possible in Jackson, to take it off the capitalist market.
- *Community saving, lending, and investing.* This practice includes community-controlled financial institutions ranging from lending circles to credit unions. We are creating new grassroots funds in our community and supporting several existing ones; the need is to create our own finance capacity, given that few "traditional" financial institutions will lend to poor Black people with little, no, or bad credit. We have borrowed ideas heavily from Spain's Mondragon, prioritizing the work of creating a self-reinforcing financial institution to gain maximum control over capital and its deployment for Jackson's collective benefit.[5]
- *Price-based mutual credit.* Mutual credit is a form of barter in which a network of creditors and debtors lend to and borrow from each other through various forms of direct exchange and account for the goods and services exchanged. Our model draws heavily on the experiences of the Mutual Aid Network (MAN) in Madison, Wisconsin, in creating a credit system denominated in either the national currency (US dollar) or our local alternative currency (as described below).[6] Our Mutual Credit system—transferable and practical to the community's working-class people—operates within standard capitalist-oriented firms that willingly participate in the practice.
- *Time banking.* Time banking is a method people can use to exchange services using time as currency instead of money. This practice of valuing everyone's time equally, no matter the task, allows everyone to help produce value in the community and assures that typically undervalued or unappreciated skills and services get their

due. Our main aim in building this practice is to elevate women's often unpaid work and to allow those presently excluded from the monetary economy to join the emerging solidarity economy on an equal footing, so they can access the goods and services needed to improve their overall quality of life.

- *Poshterity budgeting.* Poshterity is personal and community budgeting that explores ways to design and utilize various value exchange options to replace monetary need. This practice helps people to improve their standard of living and quality of life by identifying where, when, and how to use their limited resources to maximum effect. Broadly utilized, this practice helps end poverty's stranglehold on the vast majority of Jackson's residents.
- *Alternative currency.* An alternative currency is any form of currency used as a substitute for the national currency, in our case the US dollar. In the United States, private individuals, corporations, or nonprofit community institutions create such currencies to counterbalance the standard currency's use. Alternative currencies enhance the market mobility and access of those who—lacking jobs and other sources of income—have limited access to standard currency. Pursuing this practice buttresses our cooperatives and financial institutions and helps our city amid budgetary crisis to support the struggle to retain the Black majority and Black political power against the pressing threats of gentrification, displacement, and privatization.
- *Tool lending and resource libraries.* Tool libraries allow community members to check out or borrow tools, equipment, and "how-to" instructional materials, either free of charge (with community norms and conditions) or for a rental fee (also with norms and conditions). Pursuing this practice eliminates aspects of oversaturation and overconsumption in our community (like having too many construction companies and trucks, etc.) and gives more people access to critical tools to engage in critical work projects and improve their quality of life.
- *Participatory budgeting.* According to social scientists Mike Menser and Juscha Robinson: "Participatory budgeting consists of a process of democratic deliberation and decision-making in which ordinary city residents decide how to allocate part of a public budget through

a series of local assemblies and meetings. . . . Community members determine spending priorities and elect budget delegates to represent their neighborhoods, budget delegates transform community priorities into concrete project proposals, public employees facilitate and provide technical assistance, community members vote on which projects to fund, and the public authority implements the projects." When citizens direct municipal budgets and set investment priorities, documented benefits include "more equitable public spending, higher quality of life, increased satisfaction of basic needs, greater government transparency and accountability, increased levels of public participation (especially by marginalized residents), and democratic and citizenship learning."[7] In Jackson, we are developing this practice to humanize governance and to institutionalize equity processes through governance.

- *Community energy production.* Community energy is the cooperatively owned and democratically managed production and distribution of energy from such renewable sources as sunlight, wind, geothermal, and biophotovoltaics (which produce energy directly from plants).[8] Renewable energy can be used for direct consumption and production or can be exchanged on the public energy utility grid for compensation or a financial return to the community. In Jackson, we are developing this practice to reduce our community's carbon footprint, to contribute concretely to the development of sustainable energy systems, and to create energy self-reliance and self-determination in our community.

All of these solidarity institutions and practices are in very rudimentary stages of development. As of mid-2019, our main priorities are building three interrelated and interconnected initiatives to incorporate all of these practices and advance economic democracy in Jackson.

First is expanding our Community Production Cooperative, our light manufacturing digital fabrication factory and education center. Second is creating a model of off-grid sustainable housing—the Ewing Street Eco-Village Pilot Project. Third is laboring, through People's Grocery and Food Security Complex, to end food apartheid in our community and boost food security in West Jackson.

Hard work and ambitions aside, this work to construct economic democracy in Jackson is at best a small step toward an ecosocialist future.

Reaching that will take the agency and collective power of the multinational working class on a global level—building worker-owned and community-owned self-managed cooperatives, organizing worker-led labor unions that own and control their workplaces, and forming people's assemblies in communities or municipalities to deepen democracy.

Part of this larger program must be a plan to reduce the production and consumption of various consumer goods. The program should also eliminate the planned obsolescence built into the life cycle of all modern consumer products from cars to cell phones, a practice that enriches corporations and drives resource extraction.

This larger program must also expand the production of public goods and services held in common, ending the false scarcities that capitalism produces. Designing cities around mass transit could reduce the need for individual cars. Collective urban farms and edible lawns could ensure greater local food sovereignty, while drastically reducing emissions for food transport and storage.

We must also implement "regenerative production" standards, replacing extractivist logic with regenerative logic. For every resource we extract and use, we must either replace it or create conditions for it to regrow or regenerate itself. This could mean, for example, planting three trees for every tree cut, rehabilitating damaged habitats, and reintroducing species harmed by extractive industries.

Given the capitalist system's expansive drive, restoring Earth's natural habitats will be no small feat. In practice, restoration will involve regenerating our soils, massive reforestation, and ocean-cleaning projects.

The transition to waste-free methods of production, distribution, consumption, and recycling must be front and center in any program of constructing ecosocialism. This shift will be easier if accompanied by local material sourcing, local production, and localized supply and value chains. We must ramp up recycling, reuse, and composting while reducing downstream waste in landfills and incinerators, both of which release greenhouse gases.

We need comprehensive zero-waste and recycling processes for all nonperishable products, and producers must bear primary responsibility for compliance. One option is requiring corporations to invest in the production of fully recyclable or reusable products and to fully internalize the costs of including disposable components—say, plastic or cardboard wrappings—rather than passing them on to consumers and the public.

Some new production methods will require new technology. We need massive public funding for open-source research into the development of carbon-neutral production techniques for the industrial and consumer goods needed to ensure a high quality of life for billions of people. Several young technologies are headed in the right direction. For instance, digital fabrication—in which computers direct production—allows for decentralized manufacturing and uses far less material than traditional processes.

This larger shift—in Jackson and the rest of the world—will necessitate learning and incorporating a mixture of Indigenous and sustainable methods of production drawn from precapitalist cultures. Far from a call to return to precapitalist production, this is a call to press forward with the full range of scientific knowledge that humanity has accumulated—for example, drawing on the more durable and sustainable methods of concrete production used in ancient Rome or on ecologically sound food cultivation methods from the Incas and Aztecs.

To stop runaway climate change and save the species and habitats that can still be saved, we must now fully open our imaginations and dig deep into the reservoirs of our accumulated knowledge to enact comprehensive systems change over the next ten to fifteen years.

Given the tremendous obstacles our ancestors have overcome over the past two hundred thousand years—from extreme ice ages through super-volcanic eruptions to the genocidal spread of global capitalism—we know we have the capacity to cope and flourish, but will we develop the necessary will and organization? Cooperation Jackson believes we can and must, and we are working as hard as we can to play our part in our small little corner of this precious Earth.

Notes

1 Aspects of this definition are drawn from Michael Löwy, *Ecosocialism: A Radical Alternative to Capitalist Catastrophe* (Chicago: Haymarket Books, 2015); Victor Wallis, *Red-Green Revolution: The Politics and Technology of Ecosocialism* (Toronto: Political Animal Press, 2018).

2 Aspects of this definition are drawn from Tom Malleson, *After Occupy: Economic Democracy for the 21st Century* (New York: Oxford University Press, 2015).

3 For more information, see André Gorz, *Strategy for Labor: A Radical Proposal* (Boston: Beacon, 1964); Eric Shragge, *Activism and Social Change: Lessons for Community Organizing* (Toronto: University of Toronto Press, 2013).

4 For more information, see Erik Olin Wright, *Envisioning Real Utopias* (London: Verso, 2010); Robin Hahnel and Erik Olin Wright, *Alternatives to Capitalism: Proposals for a Democratic Economy* (London: Verso, 2016).

5 See Mondragon's website, accessed July 1, 2022, http://www.mondragon-corporation.com/eng; Carl Davidson, *New Paths to Socialism: Essays on the Mondragon Cooperatives and Workplace Democracy, Green Manufacturing, Structural Reform and the Politics of Transition* (Pittsburgh, PA: Changemaker Publications, 2011).

6 See Mutual Aid Networks, accessed June 25, 2022, http://www.mutualaidnetwork.org/gears.

7 This definition came from Mike Menser and Juscha Robinson,"Participatory Budgeting: from Puerto Alegre, Brazil to the US," accessed July 1, 2022, https://www.academia.edu/266607/Participatory_Budgeting_From_Porto_Alegre_Brazil_to_the_US.

8 See Biophotovoltaics, accessed May 9, 2022, https://biophotovoltaics.wordpress.com.

I

GROUNDINGS

Build and Fight: The Program and Strategy of Cooperation Jackson

Kali Akuno

The fundamental program and strategy of Cooperation Jackson is anchored in the vision and macrostrategy of the Jackson-Kush Plan.[1] The Jackson-Kush Plan, as you will read later in this book, was formulated by the New Afrikan People's Organization and the Malcolm X Grassroots Movement between 2004 and 2010, to advance the development of the New Afrikan Independence Movement and hasten the socialist transformation of the territories currently claimed by the United States settler-colonial state. As noted in several articles throughout the book, Cooperation Jackson is a vehicle specifically created to advance a key component of the Jackson-Kush Plan, the development of the solidarity economy in Jackson, Mississippi, to advance the struggle for economic democracy as a prelude toward the democratic transition to ecosocialism.

Although Cooperation Jackson is rooted in an ideological framework, vision, and macrostrategy, it is not a static organization. Like any dynamic organization, we do our best to center our practice on addressing the concrete conditions of our space, time, and conditions and to align our theory with our practice. As such, our program and strategy are constantly adapting and evolving to address new challenges and seize new opportunities. And it will continue to do so.

End Pursuits

The program and strategy of Cooperation Jackson is intended to accomplish *four fundamental ends*:

- To place the ownership and control over the primary means of

production directly in the hands of the Black working class of Jackson.
- To build and advance the development of the ecologically regenerative forces of production in Jackson, Mississippi.
- To democratically transform the political economy of the City of Jackson, the State of Mississippi, and the southeastern region.
- To advance the aims and objectives of the Jackson-Kush Plan, which are to attain self-determination for people of African descent and the radical, democratic transformation of the State of Mississippi (which we see as a prelude to the radical decolonization and transformation of the United States itself).

Controlling the Means of Production

We define the means of production as labor power and the physical, nonhuman inputs that enable humans to transform the natural world to provide sustenance for themselves. The inputs in question are arable land, access to water, natural resources (wood, metals, minerals, etc.), and the tools and facilities that enable the cultivation of food and the transformation of raw materials into consumable goods and services and the production or capturing of energy to power the tools and facilities. We also add control over processes of material exchange and energy transfer to our definition to give it greater clarity and force of meaning in line with our commitment to sustainability and environmental justice. The processes we feel are, therefore, necessary to control are the processes of distribution, consumption, and recycling and/or reuse. Without assuming some responsibility for these processes, we merely perpetuate the dynamics of externalization that are inherent in the capitalist mode of production, particularly the production of pollution and the stimulation of waste from overproduction.

A population or people that does not have access to and control over these means and processes cannot be said to possess or exercise self-determination. The Black working-class majority in Jackson does not have control or unquestionable ownership over any of these means or processes. Our mission is to aid the Black working class in Jackson, and the working class overall, to attain them.

Building the Productive Forces

On the question of building the productive forces in Jackson, it should be noted that while Jackson is the largest city in the state of Mississippi, and arguably the most industrialized city in the state, it is not and never has been a major center or hub of industrial production. Like most of the Deep South, Mississippi's development as a settler-colonial state has fundamentally been contingent upon the extraction of natural resources, such as timber for colonial and antebellum era ship building, and cash crop agriculture, such as cotton, tobacco, sugarcane, and rice, which were primarily sold as international commodities (see the "Exploiting Contradictions" section below). Mississippi, like most of the South (North Carolina, Florida, and Texas being unique exceptions each in their own right), has not been able to break out of its historic position within the US and world capitalist system as a site of resource extraction and the superexploitation of labor.[2] One of our primary tasks is to break this structural relationship by playing a leading role in industrializing Jackson, first and foremost, then the Kush District, and eventually the whole of Mississippi.

In many respects, we are positioning ourselves to act as a "developer," which is normally a role that is exclusively played by the bourgeoisie, i.e., the capitalist class, or the state. We are aiming to upend this paradigm on many levels and in several strategic ways. One, we are seeking to negate the role of capital being the primary determinant of the social development of Jackson (see the point about exploiting the dynamic of uneven development within the capitalist system below) by situating this role in the hands of the working class through the agency of its own autonomous organizations and its control over the municipal state apparatus. But we are not seeking to replicate the dynamics of *development* in the standard capitalist sense. The central dynamic in our quest is to upend the old aims, norms, processes, and relationships of capitalist development, which have little to no regard for the preservation of the environment and ecology, and replace them with new norms that are fixed first and foremost on repairing the damage done to our environment and ecosystems and creating new systems that will ultimately regenerate the bounty of life on our planet in all its diversity. This will be possible by strategically incorporating, utilizing, and innovating the technologies of the third and (emerging) fourth waves of the Industrial Revolution, which will enable the elimination of scarcity but within ecological limits (see more on this point below). What we aim to do is make Jackson a hub of community production, which is anchored by 3D print manufacturing for community consumption, i.e., direct use value consumption and commodity production to exchange value in consumer markets. How we plan to advance this initiative will be discussed in more detail below.

Democratically Transforming the Economy

To democratically transform the capitalist world-economy, we have to transform the agent central to this process, the working class, into a democratic subject. This transformation starts with the self-organization of the working class itself. Although not foreign to the working class historically by any means, particularly to the Black working class in the United States (which was often left solely to its own ends for self-defense and survival), worker self-organization is not a common feature of the class at present. This is a dynamic that we must change in Jackson (and beyond).

Now, to be clear on terms, "self-organization" means first and foremost workers directly organizing themselves through various participatory means (unions, assemblies, etc.), primarily at their places of work or points of production but also where they live, play, pray, and study. The point of this self-organization is for workers to make collective, democratic decisions about how their labor is used, when, and to what ends and about how to take action collectively to determine the course of their own lives and the intention of their actions.

We will not and cannot accomplish any of the core ends described above without stimulating the self-organization of the Black working class in Jackson on a mass scale. While Cooperation Jackson, the Malcolm X Grassroots Movement, and the broad forces aligned with the Jackson-Kush Plan have made some significant social and political advances and demonstrated our capacity to reach the masses, particularly in the electoral arena, we still haven't stimulated the self-organization of the Black working class on a mass scale. More work—profoundly more—must be done to accomplish the main tasks in this regard, which are to elevate and strengthen the class consciousness of the community, foster and cultivate new relationships of social solidarity among the working class, and co-construct and advance new social norms and values rooted in radical ecological and humanitarian principles. In effect, what we are aiming to do is develop a new transformative culture.

In order to reinforce the development of this new culture within the present confines of Mississippi and the overall capitalist world-system, we have to harness the power of the Black working class and utilize it politically to eliminate the structural barriers blocking the "legal" development of the solidarity economy within the state. One of the main things we have to eliminate are Mississippi's legal statutes that presently restrict cooperatives to farming businesses, utilities, and credit unions. We have to create a new legal framework and paradigm that will enable any form of productive endeavor to become a cooperative or solidarity enterprise.

In the Jackson context, it is only through the mass self-organization of the working class, the construction of a new democratic culture, and the development of a movement from below to transform the social structures that shape and define our relations, particularly the state (i.e., government), that we can conceive of serving as a counterhegemonic force with the capacity to democratically transform the economy. Again, we have taken some baby steps in this direction with the election of Chokwe Lumumba as mayor in 2013 and the founding of Cooperation Jackson in 2014, but we have a long way to go to get where we desire and need to be.

Advancing the Jackson-Kush Plan

"Politics without economics is symbol without substance." This old Black Nationalist adage summarizes and defines Cooperation Jackson's relationship to the Jackson-Kush Plan and the political aims and objectives of the New Afrikan People's Organization and the Malcolm X Grassroots Movement in putting it forward. Without a sound economic program and foundation, the Jackson-Kush Plan is nothing more than a decent exposition of revolutionary nationalist politics. Cooperation Jackson is the vehicle we have collectively created to ensure that we do not just espouse good rhetoric but also engage in a concrete struggle to create a democratic economy that will enable Black and other colonized, oppressed, and exploited people to exercise self-determination in Mississippi (and beyond).

We have to be clear—crystal clear—that self-determination is unattainable without an economic base, and not just your standard economic base, meaning a capitalist-oriented one, but a democratic one. Self-determination is not possible within the capitalist social framework, because the endless pursuit of profits that drives this system only empowers private ownership and the individual appropriation of wealth by design. The end result of this system is massive inequality and inequity. We know this from the brutality of our present experience and the nightmares of history demonstrated to us time and time again over the course of the last five hundred years.

We strive to build a democratic economy, because that is the surest route to equity, equality, and ecological balance. Reproducing capitalism, either in its market-oriented or state-dictated forms, will only replicate the inequities and inequalities that have plagued humanity since the dawn of the agricultural revolution. We believe that the participatory, bottom-up democratic route to economic democracy and ecosocialist transformation will be best secured through the anchor of worker self-organization, the guiding structures of cooperatives and systems of mutual aid and communal solidarity, and the democratic ownership, control, and deployment of the ecologically friendly and labor-liberating technologies of the Fourth Industrial Revolution.

As students of history, we have done our best to try and assimilate the hard lessons from the nineteenth- and twentieth-century national liberation and socialist movements. We are clear that self-determination expressed as national sovereignty is a trap if the nation-state does not dislodge itself from the dictates of the capitalist system. Remaining within the capitalist world-system means that you have to submit to the domination and rule of capital, which will only empower the national bourgeoisie against the rest of the population contained within the nation-state edifice.

However, we are just as clear that trying to impose economic democracy or socialism from above is not only a very problematic and antidemocratic endeavor, it also doesn't dislodge capitalist social relations, it only shifts the issues of labor control and capital accumulation away from the bourgeoisie and places it in the hands of the state or party bureaucrats. We are clear that economic democracy and the transition to ecosocialism have to come from below, not from above, that workers and communities have to drive the social transformation process through their self-organization and self-management, not be subjected to it. This does not mean that individuals, organizations, and political forces shouldn't try to intervene or influence the development of the working class and our communities. We believe that we should openly and aggressively present our best ideas, programs, strategies, tactics, and plans to the working class and to our communities in open forums, discussions, town halls, assemblies, and other deliberative spaces, and debate them in a principled democratic fashion to allow the working class and our communities to decide for themselves whether they make sense and are worth pursuing and implementing.

Confronting and Defeating Black Disposability

Above and beyond all of the lofty goals and ambitions mentioned above, there is one aim that we have above all others, and that is to counter the escalating threat of disposability confronting the Black working class.[3] The US economy no longer needs the labor power of the Black working class, and as a result the Black working class constitutes a growing problem for the economic and social order of the empire, a problem in need of a solution.

Once the driving force behind the US economy, constituting (as chattel) and producing over half of the country's wealth during the antebellum period, the Black working class is now a surplus population, one confronting ever greater levels of exploitation, precariousness, and material desperation as a direct result of the processes and forces of globalization and automation.[4] At the same time, the agricultural sectors where the Black working class were concentrated until the early twentieth century have been largely mechanized or require even cheaper sources of super-exploited labor from migrant workers to ensure profits.[5]

To deal with the crisis of Black labor redundancy the US ruling class has responded by creating a multipronged strategy of limited incorporation, counterinsurgency, and mass containment. The stratagem of limited incorporation sought to and has partially succeeded in dividing the Black community by class, as corporations and the state have been able to take in and utilize the skills of sectors of the Black petty bourgeoisie and working class for their own benefit. The stratagem of counterinsurgency crushed, divided, and severely weakened Black organizations, particularly Black revolutionary organizations. And the stratagem of containment resulted in millions of Black people effectively being re-enslaved and warehoused in prisons throughout the US empire.[6]

This three-pronged strategy exhausted itself by the mid-2000s, as core dynamics of it (particularly the costs associated with mass incarceration and warehousing) became increasingly unprofitable and, therefore, unsustainable. Experiments with alternative forms of incarceration (like digitally monitored home detainment) and the spatial isolation and externalization of the Black surplus population to the suburbs and exurbs currently abound, but no new comprehensive strategy has yet been devised by the ruling class to solve the problem of what to do, and what politically can be done, to address the Black surplus population problem. All that is clear from events like the catastrophe following Hurricane Katrina and the hundreds of Black people being daily, monthly, and yearly extrajudicially killed by various law enforcement agencies is that Black life is becoming increasingly more disposable. It is becoming more disposable because in the context of the American capitalist socioeconomic system, Black life is a commodity rapidly depreciating in value, but it still must be corralled and controlled.

The capitalist system is demonstrating, day by day, that it no longer possesses the capacity to absorb dislocated and displaced populations into productive endeavors, and it is becoming harder and harder for the international ruling class to sustain the provision of material benefits that have traditionally been awarded to the most loyal subjects of capitalism's global empire, namely the "native" white working classes of Western Europe and the "whites" of the settler-colonial projects of the United States, Canada, Australia, and New Zealand.

When the capitalist system can't expand and absorb it must preserve itself by shifting toward "correction and contraction"—excluding and, if necessary, disposing of all the surpluses that cannot be absorbed or consumed at a profit.[7] We are now clearly in an era of correction and contraction that will have genocidal consequences for the surplus populations of the world if left unaddressed. The Black working class is now confronting this genocidal threat. At its heart, this program and strategy, by attaining the four ends stated above, will create a model that provides a means to counter the escalating threat of disposability confronting the Black working class and provides some practical know-how pertaining to how to build a solid base of anti-capitalist transformation.

Exploiting Contradictions

To concretely attain our four stated ends, we are seeking to exploit *three critical contradictions* within the capitalist world-system as a whole and the political economy of Mississippi and the United States in particular.

One of the primary contradictions we are trying to exploit is the *dynamic of uneven development*. Uneven development speaks to the fact that capitalism as a global system transforms the world through the concentration of human labor and human ingenuity (i.e., the production tools, industrial manufacturing, carbon-based energy manipulation, advanced communications) to alter the physical environment for the pursuit of profit. Capitalism tends to concentrate the development of the productive and social forces in limited areas, while simultaneously restricting and distorting development and growth in other areas as part of the same process. Like the various modes of production that have preceded it, capitalism does not, and cannot, develop or transform the physical environments that humanity operates within and depends upon, uniformly. Meaning, in simple terms, that you can't build factories, power plants, freeways, strip malls, and grocery stores everywhere. Any serious attempt to do so would eliminate the limited concentration of surpluses the system extracts from workers and the Earth itself.[8]

How Cooperation Jackson plans on exploiting this particular contradiction is by capitalizing on Mississippi's position as a weak link in the chain of capitalist production within the United States. Mississippi, like most of the southeastern portion of the United States, is grossly underdeveloped in comparison to the northeastern seaboard, the midwestern region, and the West Coast. Since its colonial occupation by European settlers, the southeastern region, and Mississippi in particular, have primarily functioned as a site of resource extraction (like timber for ship building during the antebellum period) on the one hand, or cash crop production (like "King Cotton") for international manufacturing and consumer markets, on the other. Since the dominance of hydrocarbon-dependent (oil) industrial production within the capitalist system from the early nineteenth century onwards, regions that concentrated on resource extraction and mono–cash crop production got locked into a position of relative dependency within the system that restricted their development.[9] As a site of dependent development, Mississippi has not been infused and developed by capital to possess advanced infrastructure outlays and networks (i.e., railways, highways, ports) or production clusters (factories, warehouses, logistic networks). As we note in "Casting Shadows," the weak and relatively sparse concentration of capital in Mississippi creates a degree of "breathing room" on the margins and in the cracks of the capitalist system within which a project like ours can maneuver and experiment in the quest to build a viable anti-capitalist alternative.[10]

We harness this breathing room by exploiting the fact that there is minimal competition in the area to serve as a distraction or dilute our focus, a tremendous degree of pent-up social demand waiting to be fulfilled, and a deep reservoir of unrealized human potential waiting to be tapped.

The second critical contradiction we are trying to exploit is the *ecological limits of the capitalist system*. The capitalist system is a system bent on self-destruction. You cannot have limitless growth on a planet with finite resources. Something has to give. As it now stands, the capitalist system is rapidly destroying all of the vital, life-giving and sustaining systems on our planet. Hydrocarbon dependent industrial production has forever altered our atmosphere. There is now more carbon in our atmosphere than at any time over the last three million years![11] Carbon dioxide, methane, and other climate altering gases induced by human production are beginning to cook the climate, with each year being progressively hotter than the previous one. The polar ice caps are disappearing right before our very eyes. The oceans are becoming more and more acidic, harboring ever-greater dead zones each year. Just as importantly, ocean currents, which regulate the flow of heat energy and weather patterns on the planet, are collapsing. And the constant resource extraction and drive to urbanize at the heart of the capitalist system are eliminating essential ecosystems and habitats on which complex life depends, resulting in the quickening of the sixth great extinction event, which might result in the loss of over 90 percent of the species currently living on the planet—including us.

As awkward and problematic as it may sound, we plan on exploiting this contradiction by getting out in front of the issue of climate change as much as we can politically and turning the economic strategies being proposed herein to address the climate crisis on their head. Our aim, as you will read in greater detail later, is *not* to foster and reinforce so-called green capitalism.[12] Our aim is to help fashion and create a *regenerative economy*, one that not only restores and replenishes the resources its extracts from the earth but aids in the actual restoration of our earth's ecosystems. We aim to do this by building a set of reinforcing institutions—such as green worker cooperatives, community land trusts, eco-villages, and centers of community production—that generate and redistribute both use values via mutual aid practices and exchange values via the production of commodities, from the effort to recycle, reclaim, and reuse between 80 and 90 percent of essential resources and materials currently consumed and to introduce new zero-emission and zero-waste production methods on a large scale, starting with our municipality. We believe this regenerative orientation, coupled with sound solidarity economy practices, can and will be the basis for the development of economic democracy as an alternative to capitalism, and a prelude toward the democratic transition to ecosocialism.[13]

The third and final contradiction we are trying to exploit pivots on transcending the *productive limits of the capitalist system* that center on the conflict between the industrial, hydrocarbon dependent version of capitalist accumulation versus the emerging productive methods and technologies of the Third and Fourth Industrial Revolutions. These new methods and technologies potentially enable the development of a new mode of production and a society defined by social relationships radically different than those we have known over the past five hundred years. These emerging technologies and new social relationships lean toward the development of what some are calling a *postcapitalist* society, a potential equivalent of what we call economic democracy. One of the chief proponents of this view, Paul Mason, holds that "post-capitalism is possible because of three major changes information technology has brought about."[14] Mason outlines three key components central to this contradiction, which enable a tremendous amount of maneuverability. He summarizes them thus:

> First, it has reduced the need for work, blurred the edges between work and free time and loosened the relationship between work and wages. The coming wave of automation, currently stalled because our social infrastructure cannot bear the consequences, will hugely diminish the amount of work needed—not just to subsist but to provide a decent life for all.
>
> Second, information is corroding the market's ability to form prices correctly. That is because markets are based on scarcity while information is abundant. The system's defense mechanism is to form monopolies—the giant tech companies—on a scale not seen in the past 200 years, yet they cannot last. By building business models and share valuations based on the capture and privatization of all socially produced information, such firms are

> constructing a fragile corporate edifice at odds with the most basic need of humanity, which is to use ideas freely.
>
> Third, we're seeing the spontaneous rise of collaborative production: goods, services and organizations are appearing that no longer respond to the dictates of the market and the managerial hierarchy. The biggest information product in the world—Wikipedia—is made by volunteers for free, abolishing the encyclopedia business and depriving the advertising industry of an estimated $3bn a year in revenue.
>
> Almost unnoticed, in the niches and hollows of the market system, whole swaths of economic life are beginning to move to a different rhythm. Parallel currencies, time banks, cooperatives and self-managed spaces have proliferated, barely noticed by the economics profession, and often as a direct result of the shattering of the old structures in the post-2008 crisis.[15]

These remarkable technological and productive advances are the product of the Third and Fourth Industrial Revolutions.[16] As noted, they are rapidly changing civilization, for better or worse depending on one's position, and making a dramatic new orientation to work and labor possible.

The Third Industrial Revolution, also known as the digital revolution, started in the 1960s but exploded in the late 1980s and 1990s and is still expanding today. This revolution refers to the advancement of technology from analog electronic and mechanical devices to the digital technologies we have now. The main technologies of this revolution include the personal computer, the Internet, and advanced information and communications technologies like our cell phones.

The Fourth Industrial Revolution, also known as the cyber-physical revolution, is marked by technological and knowledge breakthroughs that build on the digital revolution and are now fusing the physical, digital, and biological worlds (including the human body). The main technologies of this revolution include advanced robotics, computer numeric control (CNC) automation, 3D printing, biotechnology, nanotechnology, big data processing, artificial intelligence, and autonomous vehicles.

These new technologies are not only changing everything in the world around us, they are also changing our social relationships and culture(s). In and of themselves, these technologies are somewhat value neutral—meaning neither good nor bad. Their value and intent will be determined by humanity. They will either aid humanity in our collective quest for liberation, or they will help further our species' inhumanity toward itself and Mother Earth. One thing is painfully clear, and that is that if these technologies remain the exclusive property of the capitalist class and the transnational corporations they control, these technologies will not be used for the benefit of the majority of humanity but to expand the methods of capital accumulation and further consolidate the power of the 1% that rule the world. Under their control, these technologies will lead to a crisis of global unemployment on a scale unseen in human history. The end result will be global dystopia, that is, a social nightmare predicated on massive poverty, lawlessness, and state repression, rather than the potential utopia these technologies have always foreshadowed.[17]

The only way we are going to come anywhere close to attaining anything like the utopia these technologies promise is to democratize and subject them to social production for the benefit of all, rather than continuing to allow them to be controlled and appropriated by the few. The democratization of the technologies of the Third and Fourth Industrial Revolutions, which we denote as #TechDemocracy, is one of the primary demands and areas of focus of Cooperation Jackson. We struggle for #TechDemocracy first and foremost by educating our members and the general public about the promises and perils of the technology, so that people can make informed decisions. Our next course of action is self-organization to acquire as much of this technology as we can, with the explicit purpose of controlling these means of production and utilizing them for the direct benefit of our organizations and our community. We call this self-organization *community production*, and, to this end, we are currently building our own Center for Community Production.[18]

Our third course of action is organizing our community for political and economic power to expand and reinforce our self-organization, or community production, efforts to gradually make them ubiquitous or ever present in our community, with the explicit intent of gradually replacing the exploitative and environmentally destructive old forms of production. Our fourth general course of action is to utilize our self-organization and political power to make demands on the government, the capitalist class, and transnational corporations to remove the controls they have on the technology, such as exclusive patents, to free it, and for government to make massive investments in these technologies and turn them into public utilities, and to ensure that the capitalists and corporations make restorative investments in these utilities for the public good.

These are the core elements of our transformative program to utilize and participate in the development of the Fourth Industrial Revolution for the benefit of our community and the liberation of the working class and all of humanity.

Our Concrete Program

This is the basic outline of our transition city vision. These are the components we are organizing to get the City of Jackson to adopt.

Despite the limited capacity, experience, and resources of our organization, we dream big and plan big. There are some, friend and foe alike, who maintain that our program and strategy constitute an extreme case of overreach. There is undoubtedly some truth in this statement, but we make no apologies for our approach. We firmly believe that we must demand the impossible, both of the world and of ourselves, in order to change both subjects. With effective organizing and sound strategy that capitalizes on exploiting the contradictions cited above, we believe our program will enable us to transform Jackson, Mississippi, the Deep South, and beyond.

To reiterate the general public framing of our mission and program, we state:

> Cooperation Jackson is an emerging network of cooperative enterprises and supporting social solidarity institutions based in Jackson, MS. Our aim is to transform Jackson's economy and social order by building a vibrant local social and solidarity economy anchored by worker and community owned enterprises that are grounded in sustainable practices of production, distribution, consumption and recycling/reuse. Through these enterprises and institutions, we aim to produce quality living wage jobs for our community; create sustainable and regenerative productive systems that affirm the life of our community; protect our community from the ravages of climate change; and to respect, protect and

fulfill the human rights and human potential of all the residents in our community.[19]

The Concrete Programmatic Activities Cooperation Jackson Is Currently Working on to Advance the Transition City Vision

To fully grasp our program and strategy, it is critical to understand what Cooperation Jackson is on a structural basis. Cooperation Jackson is the sum total of four interconnected and interdependent institutions.

- *A federation of emerging local cooperatives and mutual aid networks.* The federation is and will be composed of a number of interconnected and interdependent worker, consumer, and community cooperatives cooperating as one overall, coherent, but democratic body. This body is and will be supported by various mutual aid institutions and practices that reinforce the solidarity of the federation and provide various means to exchange value, labor, and time to improve the quality of life of all of the members of the federation and the community in general.
- *A cooperative incubator.* The incubator is the start-up training and development center of Cooperation Jackson. The incubator aids new cooperators with basic training, feasibility studies, business plan development, financing, training in democratic management, etc.
- *A cooperative school and training center.* The primary purpose of our economic democracy school is to ensure that Cooperation Jackson serves as an instrument of social transformation by constantly broadening the social consciousness of all its cooperators and continually enhancing their skills, abilities, and overall capacities to act as conscious actors in improving their social context and environment.
- *A cooperative credit union and bank.* The credit union and bank and other financial institutions will be used to start and strengthen all of the operations of Cooperation Jackson and serve as a means of self-capitalization and democratic investment to expand the initiative. At present, our efforts in this arena are being conducted through the Southern Reparations Loan Fund (SRLF), which was formally established by the Southern Grassroots Economies Project (SGEP), in 2016. Cooperation Jackson is a founding member of SRLF and a board member of SGEP.[20]

All of Cooperation Jackson's programs and strategies are dependent upon and conducted through the aforementioned structures. However, our practical program and strategy is presently oriented around five intentionally interlocked, interconnected, and interdependent focal points of execution. These focal points of execution include various campaign initiatives, projects, and programs that you will read about in greater detail below. The five focal points are:

- The development of green worker-managed cooperatives and an extensive network of mutual aid and social solidarity programs, organizations, and institutions. This programmatic approach is translated into transformative policy as our effort to make Jackson a *solidarity city*.
- The development of an eco-village, community energy production, sustainable methodologies and technologies of production, and ecologically regenerative processes and institutions. This programmatic approach is translated into transformative policy as our effort to make Jackson a *sustainable city*.
- The development of a network of 3D print factories that anchor community production cooperatives and institutions. This programmatic approach is translated into transformative policy as our effort to make Jackson a *fab city* (meaning a digital fabrication laboratory city).
- The development of an all-embracing, class-oriented union cooperative to build genuine worker power from the ground up in Jackson. This programmatic approach is translated into transformative policy as our effort to make Jackson a *workers' city*.
- The development of a human rights institute to craft a human rights charter and commission for Jackson. This programmatic approach is translated into transformative policy as our effort to make Jackson a *human rights city*.

Each of the transformative policy components attached to each of the focal points is critical, because none of the system(s) change processes we aim to make can or will be sustained in a nonrevolutionary context without structural support and reinforcement from the state. The structural support and reinforcement in question entails legal justification, incentives, resource allocation, and monitoring and enforcement from operatives of the state and civil society, meaning civilian institutions that monitor the conduct and performance of government. These transformative policy components are fundamentally articulations of *nonreformist reforms*. The notion of nonreformist reforms, although conceptually far older than its articulation, was first concretely formulated by André Gorz, a French socialist, who posed the formulation as a bridge from our short-term engagements for social justice in everyday life to our longer-term vision for an anti-capitalist world.[21] The formulation centers on waging struggle for demands and reforms that improve conditions in people's immediate lives in ways that don't strengthen the capitalist system but subvert its logic, upend its social relations, and dilute its strength. These reforms seek to create new logics, new relations, and new imperatives that create a new equilibrium and balance of forces to weaken capitalism and enable the development of an anti-capitalist alternative. This is exactly what our transformative policy components seek to accomplish.

Green Worker Cooperatives, a Mutual Aid Network, and Solidarity Economy Institutions

No one practice or form associated with the solidarity economy in and of itself is sufficient to transform the capitalist economy and build economic democracy as a transitional alternative. We subscribe to the theory that we have to simultaneously develop and employ several complementary and reinforcing practices and forms of solidarity economics in mutual relationship with each other to subvert the dynamics of the capitalist system and its logic and imperatives.[22]

The complement of solidarity institutions and practices that we are either currently building, with varying degrees of present implementation, or aiming to build are as follows:

- *Community land trust* (CLT). A CLT is a democratic nonprofit corporation that stewards and develops land and other community assets on behalf of a community. Our primary objective in developing this institution is to acquire and decommodify as much land as possible in Jackson to take it off the capitalist market (learn more about our CLT below in the "Sustainable Communities Initiative" section).
- *Community saving, lending, and investing*. This practice includes a range of community-controlled financial institutions ranging from lending circles to credit unions. We are working to create and/or support existing community financial institutions (as there are

several grassroots funds in our community with which we are linked and related) to create our own financing capacity, given that most of the "traditional" financial institutions will not lend to poor Black people with little, no, or bad credit. We have borrowed heavily from Mondragon's approach in this regard in prioritizing the work of creating a self-reinforcing financial institution to give us maximum control over capital and how we deploy it for our collective benefit.[23]

- *Price-based mutual credit*. Mutual credit is a form of barter, where creditors and debtors constitute a network of people lending to each other through various forms of direct exchange and accounting for the goods and services exchanged. In developing our model, we are drawing heavily from the experiences of the Mutual Aid Network in Madison, Wisconsin, in working to create a system that employs credit denominated by either the national currency (US dollar) or our local alternative currency (see below for more details).[24] This will enable our mutual credit system to be transferable and practical for working-class people in the community working within standard capitalist-oriented firms that willingly participate in the practice.
- *Time banking*. Time banking is a method for people to exchange services using time as currency instead of money. This practice allows everyone to contribute to the production of value in the community, enables skills and services that are not valued or are undervalued in the capitalist economy to be valued equally by valuing everyone's time equally, no matter the task. We are working on building this practice primarily to revalue women's work and to allow those presently excluded from the monetary economy to engage in the emerging solidarity economy on an equal footing in order to access the goods and services they need to improve their overall quality of life.
- *Poshterity budgeting*. *Poshterity* is individual and community budgeting that explores how to design and utilize the varieties of value exchange options available to replace monetary need. This practice helps people to improve their standard of living and quality of life by demonstrating where, when, and how to utilize their limited resources to maximum effect. We are exploring the broad utilization of this practice to end the strangulation of impoverishment that afflicts the vast majority of Jackson's residents.

- *Alternative currency*. An alternative currency is any form of currency used as a substitute to the national currency, in our case the US dollar. In the United States private individuals, corporations, or nonprofit community institutions create these types of currencies to serve as a counterbalance to the standard currency. Alternative currencies enable greater market mobility and connection to those with limited access to standard currency who lack jobs and other sources of income. We are pursuing this practice to buttress our cooperatives and various financial institutions and to aid our city with its critical budgetary crisis to support the struggle to retain the Black majority and Black political power against the pressing threats of gentrification, displacement, and privatization (see the "Sustainable Communities Initiative" section below for more details on our fight against gentrification and displacement).
- *Tool lending and resource libraries*. Tool libraries allow community members to check out or borrow tools, equipment and "how-to" instructional materials, either free of charge (with community norms and conditions) or for a rental fee (also with norms and conditions). We are pursuing this practice to eliminate aspects of overconsumption in our community and to enable more people to have access to necessary tools to engage in critical work projects and improve their quality of life.
- *Participatory budgeting*. According to Mike Menser and Juscha Robinson:

  > Participatory budgeting consists of a process of democratic deliberation and decision-making in which ordinary city residents decide how to allocate part of a public budget through a series of local assemblies and meetings. It is characterized by several basic features: community members determine spending priorities and elect budget delegates to represent their neighborhoods, budget delegates transform community priorities into concrete project proposals, public employees facilitate and provide technical assistance, community members vote on which projects to fund, and the public authority implements the projects. Various studies have suggested that participatory budgeting can lead to more equitable public spending, higher quality of life, increased satisfaction of basic needs, greater government transparency

and accountability, increased levels of public participation (especially by marginalized residents), and democratic and citizenship learning. Most of the well-known examples of participatory budgeting involve city administrations that have turned over decisions over municipal budgets, such as its overall priorities and choice of new investments, to citizen assemblies. Other examples involve school budgets, housing project budgets, and the budgets of cooperatives and nonprofit organizations.[25]

We are developing this practice to humanize governance in Jackson and to institutionalize equity processes through governance.

- *Community energy production*. Community energy is the production and distribution of energy from renewable sources, i.e., solar, wind, geothermal, and biophotovoltaics (producing energy directly from plants) that are cooperatively owned and democratically managed.[26] This energy can be utilized for direct consumption and production or can be exchanged on the public energy utility grid for wider distribution for some form of compensation or return to the community. We are developing this practice to reduce our community's carbon footprint, to make a concrete contribution toward the development of sustainable energy systems, and to create energy self-reliance and self-determination in our community.

All of the abovementioned solidarity institutions and practices are still emerging and in very rudimentary stages of development. As of April 2017, we made a priority of building three interrelated and interconnected green cooperatives. These are: (1) Freedom Farms, an urban farming cooperative; (2) Nubia's Place Café and Catering Cooperative; and (3) the Green Team, a landscaping and organic waste gathering and composting cooperative.

Freedom Farms is an urban worker-owned farming cooperative, based in West Jackson. Freedom Farms currently produces on two acres of land in the emerging Fannie Lou Hamer Community Land Trust, held by Cooperation Jackson. Freedom Farms specializes in organic vegetables and is in the process of expanding production into fruits and fish. Freedom Farms' produce is primarily being sold and consumed at Nubia's Place Café and Catering Cooperative.

Nubia's Place Café and Catering Cooperative is a health-oriented café and catering worker-owned cooperative that operates out of the

Lumumba Center. It is designed to fight the chronic obesity and diabetes-related afflictions that threaten the lives of many of our community's residents. Organic waste from Nubia's Place is handled and processed by the Green Team.

The Green Team is a yard care and composting worker-owned cooperative. It focuses on gathering and processing organic yard waste into compost to keep it from the landfill and water drainage systems. It also gathers organic materials from grocery stores and restaurants and turns this organic waste into compost that is sold to gardeners, farmers, and hardware and home supply stores.

We are very intentional about creating a cooperative ecosystem that reinforces and builds upon itself. With these three cooperatives, we have created a reinforcing value chain wherein Freedom Farms produces food that is sold and consumed at Nubia's Place Café, the waste from which is utilized by the Green Team to create organic compost that nourishes the crops produced by Freedom Farms. This is an example of the types of sustainable and regenerative enterprises and productive systems that we are intentionally constructing. In addition, we are working to develop green cooperatives in other fields including housing, recycling, construction, childcare, and solar installation and green retrofitting.

However, these three green cooperatives are not enough to create a truly reinforcing and self-sustaining economy of scale that can transform our local economy. Given both the existing political economy in our region and the new economy we are trying to develop, we have to build our own supply and value chains.[27]

Value chains are the decision-making processes by which cooperatives, or any form of business, receive and process raw materials, add value to the raw materials through various labor and technical processes to create a finished product, and then sell and/or exchange the end product to customers and communities through effective distribution and marketing.

A supply chain is the entire network of entities (directly or indirectly) interlinked and interdependent in serving the same customer base or market. It comprises vendors who supply raw materials and natural resources, producers who convert these materials and resources into finished products, warehouses that store the products, distribution centers and networks that deliver the products to retailers, and retailers who present the products to communities and sell them to consumers.

Supply chains underlie value chains, because without them no producer has the ability to give customers what they want, when and where they want it, at prices that they want and/or can afford. In standard capitalist market dynamics, producers compete with each other only through their supply chains, reducing the degree of value increase from improvements on the producers' end, which cannot make up for deficiencies in the supply chain that reduce the producer's ability to compete.[28]

To foster the development of a noncapitalist alternative, we have to socialize every step of the productive process required to create, distribute, and recycle a product to collective ownership and democratic management to increase the effective scale and scope of the solidarity economy. It is only by creating solidarity-oriented value chains and supply chains that we can and will effectively displace and replace the capitalist economy. Our emphasis on intentionally creating mutually interconnected and interdependent cooperatives and solidarity networks is fundamental to how we will ensure the attainment of our end pursuits locally, regionally, and beyond.

Sustainable Communities Initiative

To improve the quality of life in our city and for the sake of our children, grandchildren, and great-grandchildren, we can and must end the overlapping environmental, climatic, and human rights crises confronting us. Cooperation Jackson believes that we can solve these crises by organizing our communities to execute a comprehensive program that will protect our environment, curb our carbon emissions, stimulate employment, and democratically transfer wealth and equity.

We call this comprehensive program a Just Transition Program, which is premised on ending our systemic dependence on the hydrocarbon industry and the capitalist driven need for endless growth on a planet with limited resources, while creating a new democratic economy that is centered around sustainable methods of production, distribution, consumption, and recycling that are more localized and cooperatively owned and controlled.[29] Cooperation Jackson's specific contribution to a just transition program is our Sustainable Communities Initiative, which has four primary components:

- green worker cooperatives (see above);
- building an eco-village;

- developing food sovereignty;
- just transition policy reform.

The Sustainable Communities Initiative was the first major initiative launched by Cooperation Jackson. At this stage in the organization's development and the execution of this initiative, our Sustainable Communities Initiative is primarily a neighborhood-based strategy that centers on transforming a key neighborhood in West Jackson by creating a living, working *eco-village*. The eco-village will be anchored by a community land trust (CLT) and a network of interlocking and interdependent institutions that will help stabilize rents, provide affordable green housing, create quality high-paying jobs, and lay a foundation for the sustainable transformation of Jackson's economy through cooperative enterprise and solidarity economics.

We are targeting West Jackson because it is the working-class gateway to Downtown Jackson, which is the heart of the state government of Mississippi and the economic engine of Jackson, and because it is critical to stopping the advance of gentrification and maintaining Jackson's Black working-class majority, which is essential to the Jackson-Kush Plan as a comprehensive political project. Over the past thirty-plus years, West Jackson has suffered from rapid capital flight and divestment, driven in large part by white flight. Since the late 1970s, West Jackson has become a Black working-class community, with a high concentration of poverty. Since the late 1980s, large parts of West Jackson have become dilapidated and abandoned. It is now estimated that there are over 1,832 vacant lots and 832 abandoned structures out of a total of 6,748 lots in the community (it is estimated that 41 percent of the parcels in the community are unused). The community has an estimated 13,890 people, the vast majority of whom are Black (an estimated 92 percent).[30]

Four major real estate and so-called economic development initiatives adjacent to West Jackson are driving speculative pressures on the community, which is confronting it with the threat of gentrification and race- and class-based displacement. The four development initiatives are the Midtown-based Medical Corridor initiative (being driven by the University of Mississippi and funded by the state government), the Downtown–One Lake Redevelopment initiative (being driven by the Greater Jackson Chamber of Commerce and proposed and outlined in "Plan 2022"), the development of a sports and entertainment complex in

Downtown Jackson (being driven by the destruction of the old stadium in the Medical Corridor development area and Jackson State University's desire for a larger stadium), and the Capitol Complex Bill, or Downtown Annexation Bill (being driven by some neocolonial forces that aim to create an exclusive zone of political control and economic development controlled by the governor and big developers within the very heart of the capitol city).[31] Each initiative is at a different stage of development, but all have committed financial streams and widespread support among local and state elites.

The primary force driving the encroaching gentrification is the Medical Corridor. The Medical Corridor was approved after Hurricane Katrina and capitalized primarily by the federal relief funds secured for the State of Mississippi by former governor Haley Barbour, who was and is a very adept politician and a close friend of then president George H.W. Bush. The corridor's secure capitalization provides the economic conditions that enable and drive the other developments. Over the course of the next decade, the corridor's expansion will provide hundreds of short-term construction jobs and thousands of long-term medical and medical support jobs. All of these new doctors, nurses, technicians, pharmacists, and other support and spin-off workers will need places to live, shop, dine, play, and worship. Many will want to avoid long suburban commutes and have easy access to various living amenities and various types of entertainment. To fulfill these needs, and anticipating the long-term profits that can be drawn from them, speculators and developers have literally consumed most of Fondren, Midtown, and Central City and are rapidly encroaching on the northern borders of West Jackson due to its strategic location, accessibility, and cheap real estate values.

None of the aforementioned development initiatives are designed to incorporate the existing population living in West Jackson in their long-term plans. This is where Cooperation Jackson and the Sustainable Communities Initiative come into the picture. Our first task is to stop gentrification and displacement, which we are trying to contain at what we call the Fortification Line. The Fortification Line is our line in the sand. It is the point we are declaring to the forces of gentrification "you cannot pass." Fortification Street defines the line, which is one of the main horizontal east-west thoroughfares in West Jackson that separates the northern section of the community from the central heart of the community. As noted before, there are parts of the northern section of

West Jackson, those directly adjacent to Midtown and Central City, that are already being bought up by real estate speculators, and there are parts of the community below the Fortification Line that are already in contest between our forces and the forces of gentrification.

One of the stated gentrification projects below the Fortification Line is the Capitol Street Corridor project. This project is being defined and pushed by the Greater Jackson Chamber of Commerce and is aimed at developing West Capitol Street.[32] Their aim is to acquire as much of the depressed value real estate on and around West Capitol Street as possible, to turn into market rate "middle-income" housing whose residents will be catered to by a new commercial district that will be directly linked to the Jackson Zoo and a renovated golf course adjacent to Hawkins Field Airport.[33] We are working diligently to counter this gentrification move by purchasing as much of the available real estate as we can afford and holding it in our community land trust. This blocks the capitalist forces pushing gentrification from getting a consolidated hold on the street, as we will never sell our property, nor will we consent to their plans, which would inevitably lead to the displacement of the Black working-class community, either through higher real estate values, higher taxes, or higher rents. Holding the forces of gentrification and displacement at the Fortification Line is central to maintaining a Black working-class majority in Jackson.

As the Medical Corridor develops and expands, Midtown, Central City, and Fondren and adjacent neighborhoods are going to become majority non-Black areas. The forces behind the gentrification of Jackson are deliberately trying to dilute the numerical strength of the Black working class in Jackson to change the political character of the city. The Black working class is the social base for the radical politics that have been expressed in the city. Without this base, Chokwe Lumumba, a revolutionary New Afrikan nationalist, would never have been elected to office.

Jackson is presently over 80 percent Black.[34] The political calculation of the reactionary forces pushing for displacement and seeking to profit from gentrification is that to break the bloc of radical political forces in Jackson, they have to reduce the Black population considerably. Based on deductions from the last two municipal elections, they have to get the Black numbers below 60 percent of the overall population.[35] If they can accomplish this, they will ensure that no one politically comparable to Chokwe Lumumba will get elected again. This is why we are trying to hold the Fortification Line, as we need to ensure that the city retains at least 70 percent of its present Black working-class population to sustain the radical political orientation of the city. That said, Cooperation Jackson is not averse to "economic development," of which West Jackson and many other Black working-class communities throughout the city are in desperate need. However, we are for *sustainable, community driven and controlled development without displacement*. We firmly believe that the existing community must equitably benefit from the new developments that are being planned and that the community must self-determine and execute its own community revitalization and wealth-building initiatives.

The Sustainable Communities Initiative is one of the few bottom-up development initiatives in Jackson. The project is being driven by the membership of Cooperation Jackson through extensive community outreach, but its foundations were laid by the long-standing organizing efforts of the Malcolm X Grassroots Movement and the Jackson People's Assembly. The Sustainable Communities Initiative's success will neutralize the attempt to displace the Black working-class community of West Jackson and create an array of eco-friendly and worker-and community-owned cooperative businesses and institutions that will be accessible to the long-standing and potentially new residents of West Jackson.

The anchor of our grand vision for a sustainable city is the West Jackson Eco-Village. The eco-village is being organized in the heart of the Downtown Gateway section of West Jackson. This community is situated in municipal Wards 3 and 5 and is primarily populated by Black working-class residents.

The community is almost exclusively a bedroom community with few employment opportunities at present. The largest employers in the community are Jackson State University and Jackson Public Schools. Vast tracts of this community, as previously noted, are either vacant or dilapidated and abandoned. The community is also in an extensive food desert. Residents of the community typically have to travel two to three miles to access quality produce, fruits, and meats.

The eco-village seeks to radically alter the quality of life in West Jackson over the next several years by increasing and improving the housing stock, creating quality living-wage jobs, and servicing essential energy, food, and entertainment needs. The base of the eco-village is quality cooperative housing that is green, off the utility grids, and extremely affordable. In its broad dimensions, the eco-village will contain a significant portion of the Freedom Farms Urban Farming Cooperative, which will provide a significant number of quality jobs through the green worker cooperatives listed earlier, in addition to a multistakeholder grocery cooperative and a comprehensive arts and culture entertainment complex owned and managed by our emerging Revolutionary Resonance Arts and Culture Cooperative.

The ecological component of the community is centered on creating a "living-systems" integrated community anchored by a solar-thermal, recycling, and composting network that will provide extremely affordable and sustainable energy and green jobs that will help fight ecological degradation and climate change. Per the terms of "cooperative living" that we are adopting, adapting, and developing, all of the residents of the housing cooperative will participate in the village's recycling and composting programs that will create a protected market for our urban farming cooperative, as well as our emerging composting and recycling cooperatives. In addition, all of our houses will primarily operate on solar energy and be connected to an internal community energy production grid that will foster energy efficiency and sustainability throughout the village. The exercise of collective land, home, and energy ownership and the provision of permanent affordability will enable us to fight the encroachment of gentrification and displacement threatening the predominantly Black working-class community of West Jackson.

We are currently pursuing several strategies to acquire a significant number of vacant lots and abandoned homes in West Jackson. At this point, we possess over forty properties in our target community, including the Lumumba Center for Economic Democracy and Development, and have applied for several properties currently owned by the State of Mississippi, the City of Jackson, and the Jackson Redevelopment Authority. We are also seeking to acquire several vacant lots and abandoned homes that are privately owned.

Following our land acquisition drive, the second major step in developing the eco-village is the Ewing Street Initiative. We currently own 90 percent of Ewing Street between Robinson and Central Streets, and are actively in the process of acquiring the remaining 10 percent. We are targeting these properties because they are the most contiguous properties we presently have, and they are zoned in a manner that will give us the greatest organizing and operational flexibility. The first step of the Ewing Street Initiative is cleaning and clearing the lots. Remediating the soils on the lot will lead the expansion of our agricultural production and provide a higher level of food security to our members and the West Jackson community. The next step is creating our first community energy production unit on the block, which will then be followed by the introduction of off the grid, digitally fabricated houses. We plan on this phase of the development coming into fruition over the course of the next three years. The successful implementation will provide us with a model to replicate on a broader scale throughout Jackson that will demonstrate the benefits of a new way of living to our community and effectively combat the gentrification and displacement threatening it.

The broader just-transition component of our overall initiative focuses on instituting policies that curb ecological destruction and climate change and incentivize the creation of sustainable jobs and cooperative enterprises in our city. We are committed to helping the city realize the vision of the Lumumba administration of making Jackson the most "sustainable city" in the South (if not the country), by committing the city government to institute policies that will enable Jackson to become a zero-emissions and zero-waste city by 2025.[36]

Our zero-emissions program calls for the following:

- *Weatherization and energy efficiency retrofitting*. We want to push the City of Jackson to retrofit and weatherize all of the buildings that it owns and operates, so that they conserve heat in the winter and naturally cool the facility in the summer. We also want the city to incentivize this type of retrofitting in the private and nonprofit sectors of the economy with grants, low-interest loans, tax-credits, etc.
- *Solar-thermal energy production*. We want to encourage the City of Jackson to place solar panels on all of the buildings and facilities it possesses that have the capacity to host the equipment. We also want to encourage the city to install solar-thermal converters in all of the facilities it controls that have the capacity to regulate their energy use via this technology, as well as to incentivize private solar-thermal energy conversion and production and enable residents and businesses to supply excess energy to the main power grid to aid the energy company in eliminating its dependence on fossil fuels.

- *Zero-emissions fleet.* We want to push the City of Jackson to gradually replace its entire operating fleet, including all police vehicles, with electric vehicles. We also want to encourage the city to incentivize the purchasing of electric cars and to create publicly owned and operated electric fueling stations throughout the city to accommodate this transition.
- *Expanded and sustainable public transportation.* We want to push the City of Jackson to gradually acquire a fully electric public transportation fleet and to expand its public transportation vehicles, routes, and hours to accommodate more efficient and accessible transportation throughout the city and the metro region.

Our Zero-Waste Program calls for the following:

- *Comprehensive recycling.* We want to encourage the City of Jackson to create a comprehensive recycling program that includes mass public education and a system of inducements and rewards for residents, businesses, and civil institutions in the city to recycle all that can be recycled to reduce the burden on the city's landfill and create more private and public-sector jobs in waste management and recycling.
- *Comprehensive composting.* We want to encourage the City of Jackson to create a comprehensive composting program that gathers all of the organic refuse produced by households, businesses, and civil institutions and includes the requisite public education necessary to encourage individuals, families, businesses, and institutions to participate and to adhere to all of the necessary sanitary standards.
- *Comprehensive oil reuse.* We want to encourage the City of Jackson to create a comprehensive cooking oil gathering program that calls for all restaurants and food service businesses and institutions producing mass amounts of used cooking oils for their food production, such as schools, colleges, universities, and hospitals, to recycle these materials so they can be reused for other energy and production needs and help eliminate the need for their extended production and disposal at public expense.
- *Local food production.* We want to encourage the City of Jackson to create a local food and production charter, to encourage and incentivize local food production and distribution to create more jobs

and reduce carbon emissions by eliminating the need for extended transportation systems and refrigeration. The incentive program should focus exclusively on supporting producers who reside in Jackson and are drawn from the communities historically discriminated against and capital deprived.

A critical component of our just-transition work is *food sovereignty*. Food sovereignty is critical to our mission and the realization of our end goals.

Food sovereignty is defined as "the right of peoples to healthy and culturally appropriate food produced through ecologically sound and sustainable methods, and their right to define their own food and agricultural systems. It puts the aspirations and needs of those who produce, distribute, and consume food at the heart of food systems and policies rather than the demands of markets and corporations."[37]

Despite the overabundance of food in the United States, which is largely produced by heavily subsidized transnational corporations utilizing the most extreme and unsustainable industrial agricultural methods, most Black working-class communities are confronted with various types of food access deprivations, what many are calling food apartheid.[38] These deprivations range from food deserts, offering little to no access to fresh and healthy foods, to super exploitative overpricing. All of these deprivations are the direct result of white supremacy and the exploitative efficiencies inherent to capitalism. To become self-determining subjects, we have to be able to securely provide our communities with the food and nutrients needed to sustain healthy and productive lives.

We have to do it sustainably, because industrial agriculture is one of the leading contributors to climate change and a driving force of the sixth great extinction event through which we are living. Industrial agriculture is eviscerating our ecosystems and destroying our soils and the ability of humanity to provide sustenance sustainability. According to the United Nations Food and Agriculture Organization, humanity only has sixty years of topsoil remaining (as of 2014). The organization further states that "unless new approaches are adopted, the global amount of arable and productive land per person in 2050 will be only a quarter of the level in 1960, due to growing populations and soil degradation."[39]

To attain a modicum of food sovereignty in Jackson over the course of the next five to ten years, we have to create our own comprehensive, interconnected, and interdependent network of cooperative farms, processing centers, food hubs, compost and soil generators, food processors, canneries, shipping and trucking cooperatives, grocery stores, etc. Our first major initiative to actually realize food sovereignty in Jackson starts with our People's Grocery Initiative. The People's Grocery Initiative is the effort to transform a previously Black-owned grocery store in West Jackson into a multistakeholder community cooperative that will serve, in part, as a food bank, a farmers' market, a community supported agricultural provider, a market aggregator, and an anchor of our first eco-village.[40]

The proposed site of the People's Grocery is within our eco-village zone, situated at the intersection of West Capitol and Rose Streets, and is central to our effort to hold the Fortification Line discussed above. This initiative is being launched with the support of the Mississippi Association of Cooperatives and a network of Black farmers throughout Mississippi. The first step is to work with this initial network to build a level of food security as a first step toward attaining food sovereignty. With Freedom Farms being the anchor, we aim to create an interconnected and interdependent network of urban farms that links with rural Black and organic farmers throughout the state and region who are willing to strategically coordinate and practice sustainable zero-waste methods of production, distribution, pricing, and aggregate consumption and gathering for composting. Starting from here and collectively making a plan of gradual expansion based on the statewide and regional integration of producers, workers, and consumers (see the "Regional Considerations, Plans, and Aspirations" section below) dedicated to the solidarity economy and the struggle for economic democracy, we can create a value chain with enough significant scale and scope to attain food sovereignty for our community that will help us realize our Just Transition and self-determining goals.

As these points illustrate, there are viable and attainable solutions that we can implement now that will help our city work its way out of its health, human rights, environmental, and climate change–contributing crisis. We want to encourage everyone in Jackson to support us in advancing this cause by becoming a member or supporter of Cooperation Jackson. This course of action would help us build and execute the Sustainable Communities Initiative to engender our collective power and advance a just transition to a new economy and social horizon.

Community Production Initiative

As noted earlier in this essay, Cooperation Jackson has launched a critical initiative to own and control the means of industrial production called the Community Production Initiative. Community production is industrial manufacturing based on a combination of third- and fourth-generation industrial technologies, namely the combination of digital technology and automated production with 3D printing and quantum computing, that is collectively owned and democratically operated by members of geographically and/or intentionally defined communities. The Community Production Initiative is centered on building the Community Production Cooperative, and the Center for Community Production.

The Community Production Cooperative is an emerging multi-stakeholder cooperative specializing in 3D print/digital fabrication manufacturing. The stakeholders involved include Cooperation Jackson, our tech operators who operate as worker-owners, and a class of community owners and investors.

The Center for Community Production will serve as a fab academy training center, a coding and digital programming innovation hub, a community makerspace, and a workforce development entry point.[41] A *fab lab* is defined as "a technical prototyping platform for innovation and invention, providing stimulus for local entrepreneurship."[42]

Combined, the Community Production Cooperative and the Center for Community Production have three fundamental divisions of production:

- the education division;
- the commercial manufacturing division;
- the community production division.

The education division will primarily, but not exclusively, focus on training members and the community on how to use the 3D printing machines and other Fourth Industrial Revolution technologies, in part through the fab lab network. It will also teach members, students, and the community how to code. Finally, this division will partner with various workforce development programs throughout Jackson and the region to aid workers to create their own jobs or secure high-paying jobs in the dog-eat-dog capitalist system.

The Commercial Manufacturing Division will primarily focus on providing built-to-order, high-quality, high-volume 3D printed products.

It will also aid businesses with designing and prototyping new products. The commercial division will also produce its own specialty products, ranging from toys to medical aids and tools. In addition, the commercial division will also provide precision laser and water jet cutting services.

The Community Production Division will focus on providing a range of makerspace services to the community, where members and customers can work individually or collaboratively to produce products for their own use or for the market. However, the primary aim of our community production division is to produce directly for community need. Utilizing this technology as a democratically governed public good or public utility will help us address several essential production needs in our community, like the need to create sustainable or green manufacturing businesses and our need for quality, affordable off-the-grid green housing, which digital fabrication makes possible. But, that is not all. 3D printing will also enable us to produce everything from recyclable consumer goods and services, advanced medical aids and tools, and the next generation(s) of 3D printing machines on the road to advancing the means of production to noncommodified forms as witnessed in futuristic sagas like Star Trek.

The Community Production Initiative is a critical investment in the liberation of our community and its emancipation from the terrors of scarcity and the agonies of hard labor that Black people have been subjected to in the US empire. Democratizing the fourth generation of industrial innovation and technology from the bottom up is central to humanizing the new social relationships that will be fostered by the new "robot era" and defeating the rapid genocidal advance of capitalism's disposable age.

The Jackson Union-Cooperative Initiative

The Union-Cooperative Initiative is a long-term initiative to organize the working class in its totality—meaning unionized and nonunionized workers, cooperators, the underemployed, and the unemployed—throughout Jackson to address their common needs and interests, build genuine worker power from the ground up, and serve as the core transformative force to democratize the local economy and society. The objective is to create a class- and community-oriented syndicate,[43] one big union, with multiple autonomous divisions that would democratically introduce and enforce economic, social, and cultural rights,[44] norms, and standards in Jackson via workers' and people's assemblies, and other democratic institutions and processes (see the connection to the Jackson Human Rights Institute below).

The primary objectives of this initiative are to:

- train the future generation of working-class militants in Jackson and throughout Mississippi;
- create a new dynamic model of community unionism in Mississippi;
- build militant class-consciousness in Jackson and throughout Mississippi;
- change social relations between class forces in Jackson and throughout Mississippi;
- win collective bargaining rights and overturn the Taft-Hartley "right-to-work [for less] regime" in Mississippi.

The five aforementioned objectives will be accomplished by building the following institutions:

- The Mississippi Organizing Institute will:
  - train workers in participating unions in the arts of union and community organizing;
  - train various sectors of the community in the arts of union and community organizing.
- The Mississippi Workers Union will:
  - serve as a class-based community union that will embrace all workers, regardless of trade and/or occupation;
  - engage in campaigns to protect workers in all trades and occupation;
  - engage in campaigns that challenge the various laws that exploit and/or limit the rights of workers and organized labor.
- Union Cooperatives will work to:
  - build democratic unions in the cooperatives that develop in Jackson and throughout Mississippi and help the worker-owners fortify their democratic practice and sustain ongoing relations with workers in noncooperative enterprises;
  - convert existing businesses into union-shop cooperatives;
  - create union initiated and supported worker cooperatives.

To help build its base and its transformative potential, the Jackson Union-Cooperative Initiative will support and advance the following initiatives aimed at building working-class power and transforming social relationships in Mississippi to create economic democracy, a regenerative economy, and the fulfillment of human rights. These core initiatives include:

- The Jackson Just Transition Plan, which puts workers in the lead of a municipal process to create a regenerative local economy grounded in sustainable development and provides real, worker-owned green jobs. (For more details see the "Green Worker Cooperatives, Mutual Aid Network, and Solidarity Economy Institutions" section above.)
- The Human Rights Charter Initiative, which aims to radically transform municipal governance by having Jackson adopt human rights norms, standards, and procedures and adhere to them in its governing and administrative processes and activities. This initiative will enable many progressive things, but key among them are enabling policies that will protect workers, guarantee collective bargaining rights, and support worker ownership and workplace democracy. (For more details see the "Jackson Human Rights Institute" section below.)

The Jackson Human Rights Institute

The Jackson Human Rights Institute is a project of Cooperation Jackson. The human rights institute is a human rights training and organizing institute that is focused on fulfilling one of the key policy planks of the Jackson-Kush Plan, which was and is making Jackson a *human rights city*. In December 2014, Cooperation Jackson and the Malcolm X Grassroots Movement initiated and led a progressive coalition that pressured the city council to pass a resolution committing it to make Jackson a human rights city.[45]

Making Jackson a *human rights city* entails creating a human rights charter for the City of Jackson that is enforceable by law and based on the major covenants, conventions, and treaties of the United Nations that define international law. It also entails creating a human rights commission, which will be governed by specially elected officials who will enforce the charter and its statutes and work to ensure that our municipal government respects, protects, and fulfills the entire complement of our human rights, particularly the complement of positive rights so vehemently denied in the United States, like the right to water, food, housing, education, and health care, encompassed in economic, social, and cultural rights (ESCR).[46]

The commission will have several divisions that address areas of social concern beyond the standard measures of remediation addressed through the limited scope of law enshrined in the US Constitution or the constitution of the State of Mississippi, which are predominantly oriented around the protection of negative rights. Negative rights are fundamentally what we call civil and political rights that require that the state or private entities abstain from coercing or interfering with an individual's activities. These types of rights constitute things such as freedom of speech, freedom of religion, the right to a fair trial, habeas corpus, etc.[47]

One of the primary divisions of the commission will center on protecting and enforcing the economic, social, and cultural rights of the people of Jackson. This division is necessary to help aid the people of Jackson relieve the grinding impoverishment they are subjected to by the capitalist system and the forces that control and wield it to serve their own narrow interests of capital accumulation. By enforcing and protecting economic, social, and cultural rights, we are helping the workers of Jackson overcome the racist limitations of the Taft-Hartley regime and the right to work laws, that is the "right to work for less," which have defined the relations between capital and labor in Mississippi.[48] In striving to protect these rights, we are also reinforcing the imperatives of democracy, solidarity, equity, and justice that underlie our work to build economic democracy in Jackson.

Regional Considerations, Plans, and Aspirations

The vast majority of what you have read so far primarily focuses on our operations within Jackson and our aims to transform it. Jackson isn't our only focus. We have a vision, program, and strategy to transform Mississippi and our greater region. Our drive in this regard is driven by necessity. The supply chains and value chains that we need to create cannot be created exclusively in Jackson. While we have learned a lot from studying numerous efforts around the world that focus on the importance of going local and building "municipal socialism," [49] we do not believe that socialism or economic democracy can be built in isolation on a local level, as it is neither economically viable nor ecologically sustainable. You have to have wider relationships and links to other areas to access the resources you need to survive and, ultimately, thrive.

What is presented below is an outline of our southern regional organizing vision, program, and strategy. Our mission is to create a more democratic and equitable economy in the South through the fostering of sustainable solidarity economics and the development of a network of interconnected cooperative enterprises throughout the region.

Although the economy of the southeastern region is diversifying—including more manufacturing, technological research and development, biomedical expansion, and tourism—it is still largely dependent on agricultural production and the extraction of natural resources. The existing cooperative infrastructure in the region reflects this reality, as the vast majority of cooperatives are either agricultural or service the needs of agriculture or agricultural (rural) areas, such as the rural utility cooperatives or credit unions.

In order to build a more dynamic, democratic, sustainable, and transformative economy in the region, we will have to simultaneously build upon, strengthen, and expand the existing cooperative enterprises and infrastructure *and* diversity, and expand into new areas, economic niches, and markets. The new areas we will focus on are the expanding metropolitan areas in the region. The new niches will primarily be in the manufacturing, recycling, new energy, distribution, and service industries. The new markets will, of necessity, be emerging markets, expanded local and regional markets, and greater entrée into national and international markets.

In order to execute this strategy, we will have to create a broad multiracial and multiclass alliance. This alliance will be rooted in cooperative principles, promote the self-determination of historically oppressed peoples and communities, and encourage sustainability and a just transition to a new economy and society. This alliance will prioritize organizing working-class communities in the South, in both urban and rural areas, to accomplish its mission. Organizing youth and students, particularly high school and college students, will also be a priority. In addition to organizing workers, youth, and students to build cooperative enterprises, this alliance will also campaign to create a comprehensive policy regime that will support cooperative development and sustainable methods of production, distribution, and consumption throughout the South. It will also campaign for divestment from extractive industries, particularly hydrocarbon-based industries, and for community reinvestments that will help democratize public and private finance on a regional, global, and international scale.

To reach our constituents and move the mission and agenda, these are some of the concrete steps and means we will undertake.

Core Cities

To diversify and transform the regional economy on a whole, the southern cooperative movement will have to make some critical inroads in creating dynamic cooperative ecosystems in key metropolitan areas. These metropolitan based ecosystems should include a mix of worker, producer, and consumer cooperatives that mutually reinforce and support each other by dedicating themselves to engaging in cooperative business planning, production, and purchasing to create our own protected markets, security, and operating leverage in our local markets.

We should also seek to create one or two cooperatives of scale in each core city over the course of the next ten years. We should use a number of strategies to get us to scale up in each locale, based on the opportunities present. One strategy is to engage in extensive community- and worker-led campaigns to move anchor institutions (i.e., place-based major institutions with considerable purchasing power) to localize their supply chains and procurement to serve the wealth-building needs of oppressed and marginalized communities by partnering with cooperatives built by and based in these communities. This strategy may enable us to create a number of relatively large-scale cooperatives that employ fifty or more people, all of whom receive living-wage incomes. Large-scale cooperatives that could potentially emerge via this strategy include health-care workers (nurses and other direct health service providers), laundries, food management and distribution, transportation, alternative energy installation and servicers, urban farming, and waste management, to name but a few. Another likely strategy entails creating innovative cooperatives to address new market needs, particularly those pertaining to climate change and environmental sustainability. This strategy might entail creating comprehensive recycling cooperatives that not only gather and sort through recyclable materials to be reused or repurposed but also create new products out of recycled materials.

Rural/Urban Production Networks

The existing infrastructure that connects agricultural cooperatives with credit unions not only needs to be maintained but also expanded. We can effectively expand upon it by creating a series of interconnected rural/

urban production networks that link our core cities with agricultural cooperatives that are adjacent (or relatively near) to these metropolitan areas. The production networks will be based on creating protected markets for the agricultural cooperatives through the collective purchasing of the urban cooperatives and by creating cooperative restaurants, food hubs, food processing centers, food manufacturing enterprises (producing canned goods, dried goods, fish and poultry cuts, etc.), and food distribution and transportation companies. We will work with the various credit unions that service these urban areas and the agricultural enterprises that are a part of this network to create special investment funds and portfolios that support and reinforce these productive networks and link them directly to the regional and climate reinvestment funds.

New Energy Production and Transition

Per our commitment toward ending the extractive economy and creating sustainable methods of production, we have to strategically invest in the infrastructure that will enable this transition. We have to get the rural energy utilities to transition to solar and wind energies and divest from coal, natural gas, and oil. We also have to encourage the urban utilities to make this transition and allow solar producers to sell power back to the grid. Both orientations will require popular campaigns to create the policy shifts needed.

While we are pushing for new policy regimes, we should start by developing incipient, small-scale infrastructure to lay the groundwork for the transition by creating new energy installation and production cooperatives that will create low-scale solar energy markets in our rural/urban productive networks. By converting all of our cooperative enterprises into solar power users and distributors—and by recruiting businesses, public and private institutions, and homeowners to also convert to being solar power users and distributors—will create this new energy market. The objective is to slowly create and grow the new energy market infrastructure that over time, ideally a period of five to ten years, will compel the utilities and the legislatures to make the necessary policy changes that will support a just transition.

By Way of Conclusion

So here, dear readers, are snapshots of the comprehensive programmatic and strategic vision of Cooperation Jackson. Please note that we have taken great risk in presenting this information. Parts of what have been laid out in this essay will give fodder to our many enemies and detractors in the State of Mississippi and beyond. We know it can and will be used against us and may in fact be a factor in aiding our enemies to get a few steps ahead of us. However, we are taking this risk because we think it is essential that other progressive forces understand what we are doing, why, and how we are thinking about it and planning on achieving it. We think this is critical, because, even if we should fall short or utterly fail in our efforts, we hope that there is enough laid out here for others to be inspired by and learn from to be able to pick up the mantle and continue to run forward with it in the pursuit of liberation.

We also put this out to elicit the solidarity and mutual aid of you the reader. We can't accomplish all of this on our own. We need your help. We need nonextractive, patient capital to move on many fronts, like the Community Production and Community Land Trust initiatives and to defeat gentrification and displacement. We need cooperation and mutual aid between cooperatives and social enterprises to build the necessary value and supply chains needed to create and sustain a viable alternative. We need technical assistance in numerous areas, particularly in how to develop anti-capitalist business plans and models. And we are going to need political support. We need forces throughout the US empire and the world to provide us with various forms of political support to keep the reactionary state and federal governments off our backs and to help advance our efforts to enact the nonreformist reforms we are campaigning to enact.

As our actions in Jackson, Mississippi, over the past decade demonstrate, we can change the world for the better by working together in solidarity. We ask that you join us in this effort by offering whatever mutual aid and support you can provide and by organizing a Cooperation wherever you live that is directly linked with grassroots efforts to build bottom-up democratic people's and by forming mutual bonds with us and formations like ours throughout the US and the world. This is how we will give birth to the new world waiting to be born.

Notes

1 See Kali Akuno, "The Jackson-Kush Plan and the Struggle for Black Self-Determination and Economic Democracy," May 23, 2012, accessed May 4, 2022, http://navigatingthestorm.blogspot.com/2012/05/the-jackson-kush-plan-and-struggle-for.html.

2 See Eugene R. Dattel, "Cotton in a Global Economy: Mississippi, 1800–1860," October 2006, accessed May 4, 2022, https://www.mshistorynow.mdah.ms.gov/issue/cotton-in-a-global-economy-mississippi-1800-1860; Max Grivno, "Antebellum Mississippi," July 2015, accessed May 4, 2022, https://www.mshistorynow.mdah.ms.gov/issue/antebellum-mississippi.

3 For more information on our "disposability thesis," see Kali Akuno, "Until We Win: Black Labor and Liberation in the Disposable Era," September 4, 2015, accessed May 4, 2022, http://www.counterpunch.org/2015/09/04/until-we-win-black-labor-and-liberation-in-the-disposable-era.

4 See Edward E. Baptist, *The Half Has Never Been Told: Slavery and the Making of American Capitalism* (New York: Basic Books, 2016); Sven Beckert, *Empire of Cotton: A Global History* (New York: Vintage, 2015).

5 See Douglas A. Blackmon, *Slavery by Another Name: The Re-Enslavement of Black Americans from the Civil War to World War II* (New York: Anchor, 2009)..

6 See Christian Parenti, *Lockdown America: Police and Prisons in the Age of Crisis* (London: Verso, 2008); Ruth Wilson Gilmore, *Golden Gulag: Prisons, Surplus, Crisis and Opposition in Globalizing California* (Berkeley: University of California Press, 2007); Kevin "Rashid" Johnson, "Racialized Mass Imprisonment: Counterinsurgency and Genocide," *Socialism and Democracy* 28, no. 3 (September 2, 2014): 57–63; Jordan T. Camp, *Incarcerating the Crisis: Freedom Struggles and the Rise of the Neoliberal State* (Oakland: University of California Press, 2016).

7 See William I. Robinson, *Global Capitalism and the Crisis of Humanity* (New York: Cambridge University Press, 2014); William I. Robinson, *A Theory of Global Capitalism: Production, Class and State in the Transnational World* (Baltimore: Johns Hopkins University Press, 2004); Samir Amin, *The Implosion of Contemporary Capitalism* (New York: Monthly Review Press, 2013).

8 See Neil Smith, *Uneven Development: Nature, Capital, and the Production of Space*, 3rd rev. ed. (Athens: University of Georgia Press, 2020).

9 See Samir Amin, *Uneven Development: An Essay on the Social Formations of Peripheral Capitalism* (Sussex, UK: Harvester Press, 1973), accessed May 4, 2022, https://tinyurl.com/2p8ek8zh; Donald Tomaskovi-Devey and Vincent J. Roscigno, "Uneven Development and Local Inequality in the US South: The Role of Outside Investment, Landed Elites, and Racial Dynamics," *Sociological Forum* 12 (December 1997): 565–97.

10 Kali Akuno, "Casting Shadows: Chokwe Lumumba and the Struggle for Racial Justice and Economic Democracy in Jackson, Mississippi," February 24, 2015, accessed May 4, 2022, http://www.rosalux-nyc.org/casting-shadows.

11 See Phillip Bump, "There's More Carbon Dioxide in the Air Now than Any Time in 3 Million Years," May 10, 2013, accessed May 4, 2022, https://tinyurl.com/2p82c8n5.

12 See Daniel Tanuro, *Green Capitalism: Why It Can't Work* (Halifax, NS: Fernwood Publishing, 2014).

13 See John Bellamy Foster, Brett Clark, and Richard York, *The Ecological Rift: Capitalism's War on the Earth* (New York: Monthly Review Press, 2011); Michael Löwy, *Ecosocialism: A Radical Alternative to Capitalist Catastrophe* (Chicago: Haymarket Books, 2015); Joel Kovel, *The Enemy of Nature: The End of Capitalism or the End of the World* (London: Zed Books, 2008).

14 See Paul Mason, "The End of Capitalism Has Begun," *Guardian*, July 17, 2015, accessed May 4, 2022, https://www.theguardian.com/books/2015/jul/17/postcapitalism-end-of-capitalism-begun.

15 Ibid.

16 See Klaus Schwab, *The Fourth Industrial Revolution* (London: Penguin Random House, 2017).

17 See Peter Frase, *Four Futures: Life After Capitalism* (London: Verso, 2016); Gerd Leonhard, *Technology vs. Humanity: The Coming Clash between Man and Machine* (Zürich: Futures Agency, 2019).

18 We are establishing the center of community production on West Capitol Street, across the street from our Chokwe Lumumba Center for Economic Democracy and Regenerative Development. The official name of our center for community production is the Imari Abubakari Obadele Center for Community Production in honor of the late Imari A. Obadele who was a contemporary and partner of Malcolm X and a founder of several major Black Liberation organizations and institutions including the Group on Advanced Leadership (GOAL), the Republic of New Afrika (RNA), and the National Coalition of Blacks for Reparations in America (NCOBRA).

19 See Cooperation Jackson, accessed July 28, 2022, https://cooperationjackson.org/intro.

20 See Southern Grassroots Economies Policy, accessed May 4, 2022, https://f4dc.org/ARCHIVES/sgeproject.org/about/index.html.

21 See André Gorz, *Strategy for Labor: A Radical Proposal* (Boston: Beacon, 1964); Eric Shragge, *Activism and Social Change: Lessons for Community Organizing* (Toronto: University of Toronto Press, 2013).

22 See Erik Olin Wright, *Envisioning Real Utopias* (London: Verso, 2010); Robin Hahnel and Erik Olin Wright *Alternatives to Capitalism: Proposals for Democratic Economy* (London: Verso, 2016).

23 See Mondragon, accessed May 4, 2022, https://www.mondragon-corporation.com/en; and Carl Davidson, *New Paths to Socialism: Essays on the Mondragon Cooperatives and Workplace Democracy, Green Manufacturing, Structural Reform and the Politics of Transition* (Pittsburgh: Changemaker Publications, 2011).

24 Mutual Aid Networks: Website of the Humans Global Cooperative, accessed May 4, 2022, http://www.mutualaidnetwork.org/gears.

25 This definition was taken from Mike Menser and Juscha Robinson, "Participatory Budgeting: From Puerto Alegre, Brazil to the US," 2008, accessed May 4, 2022, https://www.academia.edu/266607/Participatory_Budgeting_From_Porto_Alegre_Brazil_to_the_US.

26 See "Bio-photovoltaics – producing green electricity from algae and moss," i-Teams, accessed May 9, 2022, https://biophotovoltaics.wordpress.com/ and https://iteamsonline.org/bio-photovoltaics.

27 For more information on value and supply chains, see Evan Tarver, "Value Chain vs. Supply Chain: What's the Difference?" Investopedia, updated August 2, 2021, accessed May 4, 2022, https://www.investopedia.com/ask/answers/043015/what-difference-between-value-chain-and-supply-chain.asp.

28 This definition of supply chain was adapted from "Supply Chain," Business Dictionary, accessed May 4, 2022, https://businessdictionary.info/definition/supply-chain.

29 For the definition of "just transition" closest to ours, see "Movement Generations Just Transition Zine," Movement Generation Justice and Ecology Project, accessed May 4, 2022, https://movementgeneration.org/justtransition.

30 For more about West Jackson, see "West Jackson Master Plan," Duvall Decker, accessed May 4, 2022, https://www.duvalldecker.com/project/west-jackson-master-plan.

31 See Jimmie E. Gates, "Jackson Pushes Health Care Corridor," *Clarion Ledger*, September 28, 2015, accessed May 4, 2022, https://www.clarionledger.com/story/news/2015/

09/28/jackson-pushes-health-care-corridor/73012020; Geoff Pender, "One Lake Bill Moves Forward; Fed Money, Approval Pending," *Clarion Ledger*, February 21, 2017, accessed May 4, 2022, https://www.clarionledger.com/story/news/politics/2017/02/21/one-lake-bill/98214952; Adam Ganucheau, "Gov. Bryant Unexpectedly Revives Talk of New Jackson State Stadium," *Mississippi Today*, March 30, 2016, accessed May 4, 2022, https://mississippitoday.org/2016/03/30/gov-bryant-unexpectedly-revives-talk-of-new-jackson-state-stadium-2; Tim Summers Jr., "Capitol Complex Would Fund (Parts of) Jackson," accessed May 4, 2022, https://www.jacksonfreepress.com/news/2016/mar/09/capitol-complex-district-would-fund-parts-jackson.

32 See Jimmie E. Gates, "Hinds County Helping to Pave West Capitol Street," *Clarion Ledger*, November 29, 2015, accessed May 4, 2022, http://www.clarionledger.com/story/news/2015/11/29/hindscounty-help-pave-west-capitol-st/76451412.

33 See Roslyn Anderson, "Could Capitol Street Corridor Transformation Stabilize Zoo?" WLBT3, updated March 9, 2017, accessed May 4, 2022, https://www.wlbt.com/story/29948444/could-capital-street-corridor-transformation-stabilize-zoo.

34 See "Population Demographics for Jackson, Mississippi in 2020, 2019," *Clarion Ledger*, April 23, 2014, accessed May 4, 2022, https://suburbanstats.org/population/mississippi/how-many-people-live-in-jackson.

35 See "Jackson Mayor Election Results by Precinct," *Clarion Ledger*, April 23, 2014, accessed May 4, 2022, http://www.clarionledger.com/story/news/local/2014/04/23/jackson-mayor-electionresults-by-precinct/8062809.

36 See Kali Akuno, "Jackson Rising Statement," docshare.tips, May 2016, accessed May 4, 2022, https://docshare.tips/jackson-rising-policy-statement-mayor-chokwe-lumumba-_574da309b6d87f1a2d8b5a4b.html.

37 This definition is from the first global forum on food sovereignty, the "Declaration of Nyéléni, Mali," 2007; see US Food Sovereignty Alliance, accessed May 4, 2022, http://usfoodsovereigntyalliance.org/what-is-food-sovereignty.

38 See Tracy, "Food Apartheid: The Silent Killer in the Black Community," *Atlanta Black Star*, June 16, 2015, accessed May 4, 2022, https://atlantablackstar.com/2015/06/16/food-apartheid-the-silent-killer-in-the-black-community; Christopher Cook, "Covering Food Deserts: Tips for Bringing Context to a Complex Story," University of Southern California Center for Health Journalism, accessed May 4, 2022, https://centerforhealthjournalism.org/resources/lessons/covering-food-deserts.

39 See Chris Arsenault, "Only 60 Years of Farming Left if Soil Degradation Continues," *Scientific American*, December 5, 2014, accessed May 4, 2022, https://www.scientificamerican.com/article/only-60-years-of-farming-left-if-soil-degradation-continues.

40 The People's Grocery name is intentional. There is the obvious association of the name with the working masses of Jackson but the deeper meaning is historical. The deeper meaning is drawn from the People's Grocery Cooperative operated and managed by Thomas Moss, in 1888, in Memphis, Tennessee, that was burned to the ground, and where Thomas Moss, along with two others, were lynched in 1892. The lynching was documented and presented to the world by Ida B. Wells, who was a friend of Thomas Moss. Ms. Wells's reporting on this case was the start of our critical antilynching campaign and career; see "The People's Grocery... and Ida B. Wells," accessed May 4, 2022, http://historic-memphis.com/biographies/peoples-grocery/peoples-grocery.html; Linda A. Moore, "125th Anniversary of People's Grocery Lynching Remembered," *Commercial Appeal*, updated March 9, 2017, accessed May 4, 2022, https://tinyurl.com/mpd9vmzf.

41 A "makerspace" is a physical location where people gather to share resources and knowledge, work on projects, network, and build; see "7 Things You Should Know about Makerspaces," EDUCAUSE, April 9, 2013, accessed May 4, 2022, https://library.educause.edu/resources/2013/4/7-things-you-should-know-about-makerspaces.

42 See "Getting Started with Fab Labs," fabfoundation, accessed May 4, 2022, https://tinyurl.com/38cucwxv.

43 On syndicalism, see Daniel De Leon, "Syndicalism," 1909, accessed May 4, https://www.marxists.org/archive/deleon/works/1909/3.htm; Rudolf Rocker, "Anarcho-syndicalism: Theory and Practice," 1939, accessed May 4, 2022, https://theanarchistlibrary.org/library/rudolf-rocker-anarchosyndicalism; "The Relevance of Anarcho-Syndicalism: Noam Chomsky Interviewed by Peter Jay," July 25, 1976, accessed May 4, 2022, https://chomsky.info/19760725.

44 See "International Covenant on Economic, Social and Cultural Rights," United Nations Human Rights Office of the High Commissioner, December 16, 1966, accessed May 4, 2022, http://www.ohchr.org/EN/ProfessionalInterest/Pages/CESCR.aspx.

45 See "Historic Human Rights City Resolution Passed in Jackson, MS to Create 1st Human Rights Charter and Commission in the South," Cooperation Jackson, December 17, 2014, accessed May 4, 2022, https://tinyurl.com/2p962tec.

46 See "Introduction to Economic, Social, and Cultural Rights," ESCR-Net, accessed May 4, 2022, https://www.escr-net.org/rights.

47 On the concept of "negative rights," see globalization101.org, http://www.globalization101.org/negative-vs-positive-rights.

48 See David Macaray, "Labor Unions and Taft-Hartley," *Counterpunch*, January 2, 2008, accessed May 4, 2022, http://www.counterpunch.org/2008/01/02/labor-unions-and-taft-hartley; Nelson Lichtenstein, "Taft-Hartley: A Slave-Labor Law?" *Catholic University Law Review* 47, no. 3 (Spring 1998): 763–89, accessed May 4, 2022, http://scholarship.law.edu/cgi/viewcontent.cgi?article=1478&context=lawreview.

49 On the notion of "municipal socialism," see Murray Bookchin, *Social Ecology and Communalism* (Oakland: AK Press, 2007); Ellen Leopold and David A. MacDonald, "Municipal Socialism Then and Now: Some Lessons for the Global South," *Third World Quarterly* 33, no. 10 (2012): 1837–53, accessed May 4, 2022, https://tinyurl.com/dpcu756j.

Toward Economic Democracy, Labor Self-Management, and Self-Determination

Kali Akuno and Ajamu Nangwaya

"To recapitulate: we cannot follow the class structure of America; we do not have the economic or political power, the ownership of machines and materials, the power to direct the processes of industry, the monopoly of capital and credit. On the other hand, even if we cannot follow this method of structure, nevertheless we must do something. We cannot stand still; we cannot permit ourselves simply to be the victims of exploitation and social exclusion."
—William Edward Burghardt Du Bois, *Dusk of Dawn: An Essay Toward an Autobiography of a Race Concept*

"The new militancy on the part of Blacks and many young whites have caused, not only in the Deep South but the North as well, to realize that racism is an unnecessary evil which must be dealt with by 'men and governments' or by 'men and guns.' If survival is to be the name of the game, then men and governments must not move just to postpone violent confrontations, but seek ways and means of channeling legitimate discontentment into creative and progressive action for change.

Politics will occupy the attention of the nation in the 1970s as the Black man makes his reentry into the political arena. Step by step he will achieve many victories as we have seen in our northern big cities. While this is important, I believe that the key to real progress and the survival of all men, not just the Black man, must begin at the local, county, and state levels of governments.

While politics will not cure all of our ills, it is the first step toward erecting a representative and a responsive government that will deal with the basic needs.

Land, too, is important in the 1970s and beyond, as we move toward our ultimate goal of total freedom. Because of my belief in land reform, I have taken steps of acquiring land through cooperative ownership. In this manner, no individual has title to, or complete use of, the land. The concept of total individual ownership of huge acreages of land, by individuals, is at the base of our struggle for survival. In order for any people or nation to survive, land is necessary. However, individual ownership of land should not exceed the amount necessary to make a living. Cooperative ownership of land opens the door to many opportunities for group development of economic enterprises, which develop the total community, rather than create monopolies that monopolize the resources of a community."

—Fannie Lou Hamer, "If the Name of the Game Is Survive, Survive"

"The revolution can accomplish the emancipation of labor only by gradual decentralization, by developing the individual worker into a more conscious and determining factor in the processes of industry by making him [or her] the impulse whence proceeds all industrial and social activity. The deep significance of the social revolution lies in the abolition of the mastery of [humans over humans], putting in its place the management of things. Only thus can be achieved industrial and social freedom."

—Alexander Berkman, "The Pattern of Life under Decentralized Communism"

Part 1. Introduction and Reasoning: Short Narrative of an Experiment

For many people in Jackson, Mississippi, Tuesday, February 25, 2014, will forever be remembered as a day of infamy. On this day, Jackson Mayor Chokwe Lumumba died without warning or clear explanation. With Chokwe's untimely death, the hope and promise he embodied for Jackson was nearly extinguished, for when he died the vision of liberation he projected and the transformative plan he offered to attain it were almost buried with him.

Some of what was concretely lost is best illustrated by outlining what Mayor Lumumba was intending on doing on this fateful day to help advance some of the objectives of the Jackson-Kush Plan. February 25, 2014, was the day of a regularly scheduled city council meeting, and at this particular meeting the Lumumba administration was set to launch three critical items. The first was to secure the formal approval of the council for the administration's choice of director for the department of public works. The second was to secure the council's approval of the Jackson Rising: New Economies Conference. The third was to lay out his administration's plans to facilitate the building of a vibrant social and solidarity economy in Jackson to improve the overall quality of life and transform the social relationships in the community.

Unfortunately, none of these items were ever presented to or considered by the council. When Chokwe died, the council delayed engaging or initiating any critical action for months to concentrate on the special election that was called to determine who his successor would be. This was further complicated by the fact that two members of council ran in the special election for mayor.[1] Chokwe Antar Lumumba, the youngest son of Chokwe Lumumba, also ran for mayor during the special election. However, he finished second in the race, losing the mayoral seat to former councilman Tony T. Yarber. It should be noted that Chokwe Antar won the majority of the Black vote during the special election, but lost the election on account of two interrelated factors: a historically high white voter turnout in support of Councilman Yarber and a relatively low Black voter turnout.

In many people's minds, this electoral defeat was interpreted as the death of the Jackson-Kush Plan. Many equated the plan with Chokwe Lumumba and electoral politics and did not think there was more to the work in Jackson other than Chokwe's notoriety and popularity. As time has demonstrated, nothing could be further from the truth. There should be no doubt about it, Chokwe's death was a hard blow to the New Afrikan People's Organization, the Malcolm X Grassroots Movement, the People's Assembly, and progressive forces in Jackson overall, as the accumulated experience, knowledge, skill, and leadership capacities developed by Chokwe were fundamentally irreplaceable. But what turned out to be the fundamental saving grace for the revolutionary forces in Jackson was the Jackson-Kush Plan, which has served as our guiding light, our North Star.

The Jackson-Kush Plan is grounded in over forty years of community organizing and base building by forces like the Provisional Government of the Republic of New Afrika, the New Afrikan People's Organization, and the Malcolm X Grassroots Movement. It is not a fly-by-night idea. It is a vision and plan with an organic base that has long been committed to the politics of revolutionary transformation and is far beyond being dependent upon one man or one organization.

After Chokwe's death, the forces guided by the Jackson-Kush Plan rallied to fulfill many of the uncompleted or half completed tasks central to the plan. The New Afrikan People's Organization and the Malcolm X Grassroots Movement rallied to get Chokwe Antar Lumumba elected in the immediate months following Chokwe's death. The People's Assembly successfully held a session just days after Chokwe's passing and played a key role in launching the Coalition for Economic Justice, in January 2016, to fight a series of policy threats that were hostile to Jackson's municipal sovereignty and Black political control.[2] The motion to advance the Jackson-Kush Plan was certainly stunted by Chokwe's death, but it was not halted.

The first clear indication that the plan did not die with Chokwe was the hosting of the Jackson Rising Conference and the launch of Cooperation Jackson. Cooperation Jackson was launched on Thursday, May 1, 2014, and the Jackson Rising Conference was held Friday, May 2 through Sunday, May 4, 2014. Both events indicated that the forces associated with the Jackson-Kush Plan still possessed the will, fortitude, and capacity to move forward with the expansion of the plan as designed.

The Jackson Rising Conference was originally planned and conceived as a joint initiative of the Lumumba administration and the Malcolm X Grassroots Movement. It was supported by the Southern Grassroots Economies Project, which included Cooperation Texas, the Federation of Southern Cooperatives, the Fund for Democratic Communities, and the Highlander Research and Education Center. However, upon Chokwe's death, the conference lost support from the city government, and became the exclusive province of the Malcolm X Grassroots Movement and the conference planning committee. The conference was originally planned and designed to roll out the Lumumba administration's plans to foster the growth of a vibrant, locally grounded solidarity economy.

Some of the things that the administration was planning on rolling out were:

- the creation of a unit within the city's economic development department that would focus on promoting cooperative development and supporting new cooperative enterprises with technical assistance;
- the creation of a loan fund that would be jointly capitalized by the city and several local, regional, and national credit unions;
- the introduction of new municipal policies and procedures that would incentivize the development of cooperatives and allow the city to serve as an anchor institution in advancing their development.

However, given the absence of governmental support, the Jackson Rising Conference was utilized to launch the next phase of the Jackson-Kush Plan's execution: the development of a strong, autonomously oriented social and solidarity economy. Cooperation Jackson was created to execute this pillar of the Jackson-Kush Plan, and in the three intervening years since Chokwe's passing it has worked diligently to build a dynamic and integrated solidarity economy in Jackson anchored by a growing network of worker cooperatives, a community land trust, a growing network of urban farms, along with the steady incorporation of a number of mutual aid practices. Cooperation Jackson has a long, long way to go to reach the scale and scope of the development of the solidarity economy envisioned in the Jackson-Kush Plan or even attain some of its mid-term goals, such as making cooperatives responsible for over 10 percent of Jackson's gross domestic product. However, the initiative has been launched, and we are indeed "making the road while walking it," as is demonstrated in the "Build and Fight" chapter in this volume, written by Kali Akuno.

Cooperation Jackson it trying to make cooperative economics, labor self-management, ecological sustainability, and the democratization of new technologies central to the project of revitalizing the Black liberation movement, establishing the collective ownership of the means of production, and the emancipation of the working class. White supremacy, settler colonialism, capitalist exploitation, and patriarchal domination have prevented the Black working class from exercising substantive control over their lives for centuries. To counter these systems of oppression, Cooperation Jackson maintains that its preferred path of "build and fight" development is a necessity to transform the oppressive social relations conditioned by the advance of late capitalism in its neoliberal form. This orientation draws on a long tradition of self-help, mutual aid, collective entrepreneurship, and group economics practiced by Black people in the United States. A snapshot into the depth of this history is captured in the book *Entrepreneurship and Self-Help among Black Americans: A Reconsideration of Race and Economics.*[3] The harsh reality of American apartheid in the South and de facto segregation in the North forced Blacks to depend on their collective resources in the pursuit of self-determination and collective liberation.

Cooperation Jackson is promoting cooperative economics as an alternative to capitalism and not just as a way to pragmatically get by in an anti-Black economic, social, and political environment. Cooperation Jackson embraces cooperative economics because it is primarily centered on putting people before profits and the promotion of democracy at work. These are necessary practices to facilitate worker control, ownership, and management of the economic enterprise and support the practice of self-reliance among workers that underscores the quest for self-determination long pursued by the forces of the Black liberation movement.

From its inception as an idea in a Malcolm X Grassroots Movement study group, the organizers of Cooperation Jackson have identified labor self-management, that is workers exercising the intellectual, strategic, and operational control of the workplace, as central to the project of building economic democracy through the social and solidarity economy. Under labor self-management, the workers own, manage, and control their workplace and make all of the decisions around matters like the level of employment, introduction of technology, the level of profit to set aside for distribution, making hiring decisions, and determining the level of investment. Essentially, the workers make all the decisions in a worker cooperative or labor self-managed firm. We must never forget that it was capitalism's need for a servile, available, and dependable source of plantation labor that was the driving force behind the importation and enslavement of millions of Afrikans in the Americas. Cooperation Jackson's commitment to cooperative economics and labor self-management is an effort to eliminate the dynamic of labor exploitation that is at the heart of capitalism. It also addresses the need to create workplaces that give workers control over how their labor is used and how the value created from this labor is disbursed or shared.

The Focus of This Work

The purpose of *Jackson Rising: The Struggle for Economic Democracy and Black Self-Determination in Jackson, Mississippi*, is to share some of the collective experience that has been accumulated by the forces advancing the Jackson-Kush Plan over the last decade. The collection of essays assembled in this work represent the best summations of the struggle in Jackson in the humble opinion of the editors. The book covers a broad range of subjects and experiences, including reflections on the Jackson-Kush Plan itself; the organizing work leading to the election of Chokwe Lumumba as councilman of Ward 2, in 2008 and 2009; the campaign to elect Chokwe Lumumba as mayor, in 2012 and 2013; experiences from the mayoral administration of Chokwe Lumumba, from July 2013 through February 2014; and numerous reflections on the social and political impact of Chokwe's death and what organizers in Jackson did in response to sustain and advance the Jackson-Kush Plan.

However, we have placed a particular focus on the effort to advance cooperative economics and build economic democracy. Why this emphasis? As the old saying goes, "Politics without economics is symbol without substance." We think that economic transformation is central to the project of dismantling the capitalist and imperialist systems and creating new transformative relationships that heal society and foster harmony with the life-generating and life-sustaining systems of our planet. Unfortunately, in our view, too much emphasis has been placed on electoral politics in reference to the Jackson-Kush Plan, both by the mainstream capitalist press and in left and progressive media circles. This emphasis reflects a deep, manufactured bias in bourgeois societies that orients the public toward paying more attention and giving more credence to the illusions of alleged "democratic governance," rather than the real contests for political and social power reflected in the movement of capital and the perpetuation of capitalist social relationships that the sham of democratic governance enables in these societies (even with reforms or moderations in the case of left or social democratic governments in bourgeois states). We aim to re-center every reader's gaze on the challenges to the "free" movement of capital (meaning the domination of capital over labor and the natural world) and the rejection of capitalist social relationships represented by the thought, strategy, and work of Cooperation Jackson.

Part 2. The Necessity of Cooperative Economics, Labor Self-Management, and the Struggle for Economic Democracy

Compelling Reasons for Cooperative Economics and Labor Self-Management

A compelling reason for us to embrace cooperative economics and labor self-management is the simple fact that capitalism is not working for hundreds of millions of people across the globe. It is creating chronic joblessness, underemployment, poverty, homelessness, limited access to educational opportunities, the exploitative and insecure work-life that is closely mimicking the nasty and brutish experience of nineteenth-century capitalism, and concentrating income, power, and wealth in the hands of the ruling class and their enablers (the bourgeoisie). On the latter issue of wealth and concentration of income in the hands of the economic elite, the United States leads the pack with the top 20 percent of income earners capturing over 50 percent of its national income on an annual basis.[4] In 2012, the top 10 percent of the households in the United States commandeered 77 percent of its net worth, while the bottom 40 percent of households had a negative or zero net worth.[5] In countries such as Austria, the Netherlands, and Germany, the top 10 percent of households grabbed over 60 percent of the net worth in 2012, while in Portugal, Luxembourg, Norway, and France, over 50 percent of the net worth is controlled by the top 10 percent of households.[6] Even Sweden, which is often seen as a socialist paradise by some political liberals in North America, had the second highest Gini coefficient score for wealth inequality in 2014, which stood at 79.90, while that of the United States came in at 80.56.[7] Since capitalist societies encourage selfish, individualistic, and self-regarding values and behaviors, this level of wealth hoarding in the hands of a class that is hostile and antagonistic to the interest and well-being of the laboring class cannot be a positive development.

In capitalist societies across the globe, the operational logic and practice of the old adage "he (or she) who pays the piper calls the tune" is in effect. Given the fact that getting elected is a very expensive affair and deep-pocketed donors are essential to campaign financing, this state of affairs has enabled the bourgeoisie to get its preferred laws and policies in the realm of liberal capitalist democracy. In the article "Why 21st Century Capitalism Can't Last," the editor and publisher of the socialist magazine *Jacobin*, Bhaskar Sunkara, shares his perspective on the corrosive mixture and unholy alliance of money and power in society:

> It isn't that the rich are getting richer; it's that they're also getting more powerful. Across the world, inroads against economic democracy—collective bargaining rights and robust social welfare programs—since the 1970s have undermined political democracy, and that's going to make mere policy shifts even more difficult to achieve. Workers aren't pushing for wealth redistribution anymore; in fact, they're actually losing battles to preserve gains won in past generations. No longer threatened at the grassroots, the ability of the world's wealthiest citizens to shape politics is nearly absolute.
>
> Developments in the United States, such as the Citizens United and McCutcheon rulings eliminating limits on campaign fundraising restrictions, have made the connection between financial wealth and political influence even more apparent. But despite public outrage—almost 90 percent of Americans think there's too much money in politics—reform appears to be a faint hope.[8]

Cooperative economics and labor self-management provide the members of the laboring classes, who experience class exploitation and domination and nonclass forms of oppression, with practical economic tools to challenge the economic and political power of the economic and political elite. The oppressed are in a position to build a counterhegemonic practice that mirrors the embryonic values and institutions of the future socialist society, while living within the existing capitalist, patriarchal, and racist social order.

It was not an accidental occurrence or for flippant reasons that Karl Marx and Mikhail Bakunin saw cooperative economics and labor self-management as useful tools in the struggle for socialism and the undermining of capitalism. In 1864, Marx made the comment below on cooperative economics and labor self-management of production:

> But there was in store a still greater victory of the political economy of labor over the political economy of property. We speak of the cooperative movement, especially of the cooperative factories raised by the unassisted efforts of a few bold "hands." The value of these great social experiments cannot be overrated. By deed, instead of by argument, they have shown that production on a

> large scale, and in accord with the behest of modern science, may be carried on without the existence of a class of masters employing a class of hands; that to bear fruit, the means of labor need not be monopolized as a means of dominion over, and of extortion against, the laboring man himself; and that, like slave labor, like serf labor, hired labor is but a transitory and inferior form, destined to disappear before associated labor plying its toil with a willing hand, a ready mind, and a joyous heart.[9]

Marx saw the labor self-managed factories as spaces that prepared the workers for life in communist society. Further, the practice of labor self-management provides proof of the capabilities of workers to self-organize without the oppressive overlordship of capital or its representatives.[10]

Bakunin viewed the cooperatives as preparatory arenas of struggle for the stateless, self-managed and classless (anarchist communist) society: "Let us, whenever possible, establish producer-consumer cooperatives and mutual credit societies [credit unions] which, though under the present economic conditions they cannot in any real or adequate way free us, are nevertheless important in as much as they train workers in the practice of managing the economy and plant the precious seeds for the organization of the future."[11]

Bakunin was quite perceptive in his understanding that within the institutional environment of capitalism, which would be the operational context of the producer, consumer, and financial cooperatives would not by themselves emancipate the laboring classes and other oppressed groups. There must be a political struggle to wrest power from the ruling class and start the process of creating the classless, stateless, and self-managed socialist society. The initiative to create a solidarity economy in Jackson cannot divorce itself from social movement activism and the class struggle. To do so would be tantamount to conceding that capitalism is the only game in town.

The collapse of the former Soviet Union and, with it, its version of socialism has led many members of society to believe that there is no viable alternative to capitalism. The proponents of capitalism have used all available means to reinforce the preceding perception, even while conceding that there are problematic behaviors among certain agents of this economic system:

> The revival of anti-capitalist rhetoric owes much to the financial crisis of 2008 and its aftermath. The crisis was merely the latest example of the inherent stability of capitalism, a process that, while allowing the economy to benefit from "creative destruction," causes a lot of collateral damage along the way. The real problem is that capitalism has become associated with high finance, rather than the heroic entrepreneurship of Thomas Edison, whose inventions still surround us. It is not just that few people can see the benefits of complex financial products like credit default swaps. He adds that "bankers have undoubtedly done their best to give capitalism a bad name. The extraordinary scale on which big banks have been rigging interest rates and foreign-exchange markets and ripping off their customers is almost beyond comprehension." [12]

Contrary to the propagandistic claim about capitalism being the only game in town, there are alternatives to this system. One example that demonstrates in practice elements of a postcapitalist practice is the Mondragon cooperative experiment in the Basque region of Spain. Some key lessons from this experiment are documented in *Making Mondragon: The Growth and Dynamics of the Worker Cooperatives Complex* and *Values at Work: Employee Participation Meets Market Pressure at Mondragon*.[13] The Mondragon Corporation is a network of cooperatives and other organizations, with worker cooperatives at its center. In 2015, the Mondragon Corporation generated €12.11 billion [approximately $13.44 billion US] in income, provided 74,335 jobs, invested €317 million [approximately $352 million US] in its operation, with 43 percent of the worker members being women and worker-owners constituting 81 percent of the cooperatives' workforce.[14] The Jackson-Kush Plan and the emerging cooperative experiment in Jackson are heavily influenced by the Mondragon experiment and its interrelationship with the Basque movement for self-determination and sovereignty. In these movements, we have found many parallels with our struggle for self-determination and economic democracy in Mississippi and throughout the Black Belt region of the US South.

The history of Basque people organizing for self-reliance, as reflected in the Mondragon experiment, is a compelling argument for the need to embrace cooperative economics in general and labor self-management in particular. Cooperative economics is based on organizing and meeting the needs of your members or community and doing so with the strategic objectives of satisfying self-determined human needs and social bonding, not the generation or pursuit of profits. In the process of the people reflecting on why the institutional context in which they are located has prevented them from being able to adequately meet their need for high-quality affordable goods and services, revolutionary or progressive organizers have the opportunity to pose questions that encourage the people to think critically and interrogate the structural shortcomings of capitalism. In other words, as a result of posing questions about the basic features of capitalism and the predictable anti-people or anti-working-class economic, social, and political outcomes that it produces, a critical mass of people might come to the conclusion that capitalism must become history for them to lead decent, just, and ecologically sustainable lives.

The revolutionary organizers ought to predicate their organizing intervention among the oppressed around their self-defined needs. By utilizing the critical problem-posing methodology of the late Brazilian educator Paulo Freire, on the basis that the exploited are and can act as the architects of their own emancipation, we increase the likelihood of turning the people on to a radically transformative approach to relating to the world:

> Critical and liberating dialogue, which presupposes action, must be carried on with the oppressed at whatever stage of their struggle for liberation. The content of that dialogue can and should vary in accordance with historical conditions and at the level at which the oppressed perceive reality. But to substitute monologue, slogans, and communiqués for dialogue is to attempt to liberate the oppressed without their reflective participation in the act of liberation is to treat them as objects which must be saved from a burning building: it is to lead them into the populist pitfall and transform them into masses which can be manipulated.
>
> At all stage of their liberation, the oppressed must see themselves as women and men engaged in the ontological and historical vocation of becoming more fully human. Reflection and action become imperative when one does not erroneously attempt to dichotomize the content of humanity from its historical forms.
>
> The insistence that the oppressed engage in reflection on their concrete situation is not a call to armchair revolution. On the

> contrary, reflection—true reflection—leads to action. On the other hand, when the situation calls for action, the action will continue an authentic praxis only if its consequences become the object of critical reflection. In this sense, the praxis is the new raison d'être of the oppressed; and the revolution, which inaugurates the historical moment of this raison d'être, is not viable apart from their concomitant conscious involvement.[15]

When cooperatives employ a genuine participatory and democratic framework of labor self-management to address the needs of the people for food, housing, employment, childcare services, and other basic necessities, it helps enable people to better compare and contrast the difference between the capitalist system and the postcapitalist systems that are emerging. The first contrast typically emerges in the arena of decision-making and operational control. Democratic, self-managed cooperatives enable workers to have greater control over the decisions that impact their lives as opposed to the authoritarian and alienating organizational structures and processes that are associated with capitalism.

Organizing people around their needs, which include their social and cultural needs for human contact and connection, enables our social movements to make quantum leaps toward the development of a protagonistic consciousness that calls on people to utilize and/or create opportunities to engage in transformative practice. As Amílcar Cabral, the revolutionary, educator, organizer, and military strategist from Cape Verde and Guinea-Bissau, makes clear, our organizing strategy must center on the experiences of the people and address their concrete material needs:

> Always remember that the people do not fight for ideas, for the things that exist only in the heads of individuals. The people fight and accept the necessary sacrifices. But they do it in order to gain material advantages, to live in peace and to improve their lives, to experience progress, and to be able to guarantee a future for their children. National liberation, the struggle against colonialism, working for peace and progress, independence—all of these will be empty words without significance for the people unless they are translated into real improvements in the conditions of life.[16]

The people are likely to make greater sacrifices and commitments to social change projects that respond to their here-and-now daily needs, but which also offer a vision of how to solve the major issues confronting society that limit their freedom and constrain their aspirations. We believe that cooperatives and the practices of democratic self-management, mutual aid, and solidarity present the Black working class in Jackson (and well beyond) with an organizational form and philosophical outlook that literally allows them to take their future into their own hands.

Another compelling reason for cooperative economics and labor self-management is the emphasis that they place on developing the capacities of the members or cooperators to shape the world in their image and interest. When we refer to capacity building, we are highlighting the necessity of equipping the cooperators with the requisite knowledge, skills, and attitude to collectively build the economic and social infrastructure of a humanistic, caring, and participatory democratic present and future. A key principle of the international cooperative movement affirms the need to educate and train cooperative stakeholders and to share information with the public: "Cooperatives provide education and training for their members, elected representatives, managers, and employees so they can contribute effectively to the development of their cooperatives. They inform the general public—particularly young people and opinion leaders—about the nature and benefits of cooperation."[17]

We believe the commitment to "developing the individual worker into a more conscious and determining factor in the processes of industry" will only emerge from the systematic and purposive educational program that must be carried out among the cooperators, or targets of liberation, as noted by Alexander Berkman.[18] Our character and psychological predisposition have been shaped under undemocratic authoritarian relations and processes and our possession of the requisite knowledge, skills, and attitude of self-management and participatory democracy is uneven. As a result, we tend to demonstrate behaviors that are not unlike those of our oppressors and exploiters. Critical education is essential to the process of exorcising the ghosts of conformity within the status quo from the psyche and behavior of the oppressed to enable the development of a cultural revolution. Cultural revolutions typically precede political revolutions, as the former create the social conditions for a critical mass of the people to embrace new social values that orient them toward the possibility of another world. Therefore, training and development programs, the constant dissemination of critical information, and mass educational initiatives are central to the goal of preparing the people for self-management and self-determination.

The abilities and knowledges that worker collectives need to manage their own affairs, or that oppressed people need to exercise self-determination are unevenly distributed and developed. Without education initiatives to intervene, the better skilled and more formally educated members in our collectives and organizations often dominate decision-making and organizational processes. The preceding conditions often unintentionally recreate relations of domination within our cooperative or labor self-managed structures. To be truly effective our educational initiatives have to be fortified by clear accountability and harm-reduction practices that reinforce our democratic practices and strivings for human development.

Another compelling reason to embrace and promote cooperative economics and labor self-management in this period of triumphant neoliberal capitalism is their capacity to serve as antidotes to liberal individualism, selfishness, and rampant competition. On the collectivism/individualism continuum, the United States and its inhabitants are classified as highly individualist. Sadly, Black people tend to score high on individualism in these studies. The article "Cultural Orientations in the United States: (Re)Examining Differences Among Ethnic Groups" provides contextual factors that explain this behavioral phenomenon among Blacks.[19] Economic and social cooperation will encourage and cultivate values like unity, self-determination, collective work and responsibility, collective purpose, solidarity, and in-group trust and faith. It would certainly help in reversing the unacceptably high level of individualism in the Afrikan community and the general society within the United States. The ideological realm is a site of struggle in winning the people over to socialism and away from their commitment to philosophical liberalism, which is the dominant ideology in the United States and other societies in the Global North. The possibility of revolution in capitalist society, in particular this capitalist society, with its settler-colonial foundations and imperialist imperatives, becomes stronger when a critical mass of people embraces the antidote of cooperation, collectivism, solidarity, mutual aid, and sharing in thought and action. This is what we are trying to cultivate and build in Jackson.

Enabling Structures and Supportive Organizations for Cooperative Economics

The act of thinking about the possibility of another world outside of capitalism, white supremacy, and patriarchy meets an untimely demise when it rams into the iceberg of a nonenabling social and economic environment. In other words, the ideas of emancipation that are grounded in the construction of alternative institutions are thrown onto the barren soil of an institutional environment that only nurtures and supports structures that facilitate exploitation and top-down or authoritarian relations with the people. Cooperative economics and labor self-management can only thrive and expand if they have the necessary enabling structures and organizations that will allow them to successfully compete with and challenge capitalist firms for the hearts and souls of the people in their capacity as the purchasers of goods and services. We are not looking to establish an alternative economic practice that is a quaint little infrastructure that exists on the margins of the mainstream economy. Our aim ought to be the development of a counterhegemonic, liberating economic and social infrastructure whose aim is the liquidation of the predatory, exploitative, and alienating economic system that is making the lives of the dispossessed a living hell. Capitalism cannot exist in the absence of the support that it gets from varied institutions and programs abroad in society.

What exactly are we alluding to when we refer to *enabling structures and supportive organizations* for cooperative economics and labor self-management? We are going to attempt to answer the preceding question by illustrating how essential they are to the survival of capitalist firms. The companies that follow the capitalist ownership patterns, method of handling workers, and approach to operating and managing a business benefit from the business education and conventional economics programs that are taught in the primary, secondary, and tertiary levels of the educational system. The taxes from the laboring classes are used to finance the business regime that exploits the workers and make capitalist business ideas and practices second nature in our consciousness. It ought to be clear to the reader that the public education system is an enabling structure that provides the existing economic system with ideologically prepared and technically trained or educated personnel to function in capitalist firms. Most of the students who take high school economics and business management courses are not normally exposed to consumer, financial, and worker cooperatives as viable business forms that promote economic democracy and privilege the needs of their members rather than the making of profits for their stakeholders.

Even at the college and university level, only a few students are trained to work in cooperatives and worker self-managed firms. The educational programs that address the need of the cooperatives for cooperators and staff with the knowledge, skills, and attitude to effectively and efficiently function in these democratic, member-owned and controlled economic enterprises were specifically designed for this purpose. Cooperative economics and labor self-management projects do not have an available pool of prospective cooperators who are trained at taxpayers' expense, or trained at all, as is the case with economic initiatives that are following the orthodox path of capitalist economic development. The Mondragon cooperatives have created their own educational structures over the years to meet their need for trained cooperators at the shop floor, technical, and administrative levels of the cooperative workforce.[20]

The Mondragon University was created in 1997 and offers undergraduate and graduate degree programs. The university is in effect the training and research-and-development arm of a wider network of interlocking cooperatives, and it is governed by the students, members, and the stakeholders in the other cooperatives. Mondragon has other training and development entities within its Knowledge Group such as the Politeknika Ikastegia Txorierri, the Lea Artibailkastetxea, and the Otalora, as well as research and development organizations. We cannot exaggerate the importance of educating the members in Cooperation Jackson and the community at large for this developing economic democracy and self-determination project.

The conservative path to creating or running businesses finds a much more enabling environment in the area of access to start-up and working capital than cooperatives. Conventional businesses, especially large corporations, have supportive financial structures such as the stock exchange and venture capital funds, and institutions, such as commercial and investment banks, to finance their projects. The Rochdale-style cooperatives have been around (in one form or another) since the 1840s but are still viewed in both mainstream and alternative economic circles as strange organizational creatures, with their collectivistic pattern of ownership and control, especially worker cooperative and labor self-managed firms. In the modern era, almost all businesses need loans to survive and grow. Consumer and worker cooperatives are at a distinct disadvantage in this respect. Small businesses, which constitute the vast majority of cooperatives worldwide, are usually undercapitalized. The problem is quite severe for cooperatives because of the orientation of most banks and financial institutions, which were constructed to fortify capitalism, capitalist social relations, and firms that adhere to capitalist logic. Most banks and other financial institutions are not comfortable or willing to support social enterprises structured around collective ownership. They view them as extremely risky investments. Throughout its history, the cooperative movement has created its own financial institutions to address this problem. However, most have been grossly inadequate to address the comprehensive needs of the movement. But there are several successful models that are worth noting, studying, and emulating based on critical assessments of one's space, time, and conditions.

Mondragon's credit union, the Caja Laboral Popular Cooperativa de Crédito, is perhaps the most instructive. The Caja Laboral Popular is the provider of financial services and technical assistance, advice, and promotion to the Mondragon cooperatives. The Caja Laboral Popular was instrumental in establishing the insurance and social security infrastructure of the Mondragon cooperative confederation, the Seguros Lagun Aro. With respect to the supportive financial structures of the Mondragon cooperatives, Ramon Flecha and Ignacio Santa Cruz illuminate the indispensable role these financial and technical assistance institutions play in the success of the Mondragon cooperatives:

> The creation of the Mondragon Corporation and its financial group, organized through Caja Laboral Popular and the Lagun Aro, allowed the cooperatives to develop a wide range of reciprocal and mutually supportive mechanisms. These included knowledge transfer, the reallocation of capital and workers (when required) between cooperatives, shared support services, the creation of common funds, a shared strategy for new entrepreneurial projects, and a specific strategy to cover basic needs, such as health assistance.[21]

The Caja Laboral Popular is a major mobilizer of capital for the cooperatives by way of the savings of the people in the Basque Country and the rest of Spain. It is one of the largest financial institutions in the country. In addition to the Mondragon experience, there are two additional large-scale experiences that are worth citing. These include the Desjardins Group of financial institutions, mainly credit unions, in Quebec (and beyond), and the cooperative Banca Popolare dell'Emilia Romagna S.C. in Emilia Romagna and throughout Italy (although these have come under serve political attack over the last decade or more by neoliberal political forces).[22] These examples have much to offer, both positive and negative, to Cooperation Jackson and those of us seeking to make another world possible under the constraints of living under the oppressive conditions of the current world-system.

As these examples illustrate, credit unions, as financial cooperatives, will have an important part to play in the development of Cooperation Jackson and the solidarity economy movement in Jackson. Following the example of Caja Laboral Popular, people of a progressive persuasion in Jackson and beyond could start shifting their savings and financial transactions from banks to credit unions or other forms of mutual financial aid to help capitalize cooperatives in the city. They would have to complement this action with being active in running the credit unions and charting a new direction for them as instruments of the class struggle.

As you will read throughout this work, Cooperation Jackson is developing a mutually integrated systems approach to the organizing of the cooperatives it is building and will rely on a high degree of coordination and mutual aid among the cooperatives and supporting organizations to be successful. The cooperatives will have to balance their desire for autonomy with the objective need for integration. A principle of the cooperative movement in general is cooperation among cooperatives, and cooperatives have to develop the structures and organizations that will transform them into a cohesive and integrated system. This type of cooperative development on a large scale would enable democratic enterprises to both defend themselves from capitalist organizations and compete for the hearts and minds of the people in the struggle over how best to balance the delivery of essential goods and services with social justice and ecological balance. As these cooperating cooperatives with their supportive structures bulk up in size, they will be better able to withstand the competitive onslaught of conventional capitalist firms. They would also be able to strategically extract some level of support from the state for various reasons that are relevant to the particular contexts of struggle.

Role of the State in Cooperative Economics and Labor Self-management

At present, the state is a fact of life that the agents of anti-capitalist and postcapitalist struggle are compelled to contend with and address in their strategic pursuit of liberation. In spite of the state being an agent and enabler of the wealthy and other socially dominant groups, the state controls economic resources that are the product of the labor of the working class. The working class must struggle to control these resources and not just surrender them to the capitalists and the dominant operative forces that manage the state to reinforce and reproduce capitalist social relations. These captured and appropriated resources can and should be used to advance the development of the social and solidarity economy. Through working-class struggle on a mass scale, the possibility exists to recapture and redirect the resources controlled by the state in the form of social and income security programs like universal basic income or the provisioning of cooperatives and other social economy projects that may undermine and gradually transform the operative social relationships that presently exist to reinforce capitalism in the long term.

One of the functions of the state in advanced capitalist countries like the United States, Canada, Germany, Sweden, and others with liberal bourgeois democratic political systems is the legitimizing of the social order in the eyes and worldview of the masses. This function is critical to the construction of hegemony in capitalist societies, which is primarily executed through social institutions such as schools, the media, the police, and health and welfare agencies. This legitimation function compels the liberal capitalist state to carry out minimally necessary initiatives that alleviate the lot of the oppressed, often through welfare programs. This action on the part of the state also assists in staving off the masses' receptivity to radical and revolutionary ideas of social movements. This legitimation function often compels the masses to project the fulfillment of their hopes and aspirations onto the same system that is crushing their dreams and systematically exploiting and oppressing them. When the bourgeois state regulates certain outrageous actions of capitalist firms or other power brokers in society, it is done to prevent the system from falling into disrepute and inspiring revulsion against it. Such an act is an expression of the liberal bourgeois state fulfilling its legitimation function to ensure the reproduction of systems of extraction and the private appropriation of socially produced value that define the capitalist system.

History has demonstrated that strong working-class and people's movements can create tremendous tensions within liberal bourgeois states that challenge their legitimation function and apparatus. They do this by creating tension between the function of the state as a facilitator of capital accumulation and a guarantor of "basic" democratic rights. It is by exploiting the structural tensions within the bourgeois state, particularly the legitimation function of its hegemonic apparatus, that interventions can be made by radical activists to compel the state to utilize some of the resources it has extracted from the people to support cooperative economic development. Ajamu Nangwaya's article in this volume speaks to the ways that the state is able to provide cooperatives with valuable support, such as financing, education, technical assistance, and other services.

For cooperatives to be utilized as tools of revolutionary social transformation their members must constantly struggle against being co-opted by the institutions and other instruments of the bourgeois state. To sustain a revolutionary orientation and practice, our cooperatives cannot become dependent upon the concessions or largesse of the bourgeois state or the protected markets the state confers in limited cases. Sadly, however, there is a long history of cooperatives pursuing this route and succumbing to the logic of capitalism and the perpetuation of the system. As a result, many cooperatives simply come to see themselves as one sector in the capitalist political economy alongside the private and public sectors. This political orientation has enabled many cooperatives to be viewed as nonthreatening to the system and relatively safe to the operatives of the state.

However, in most cases where progressive political parties or social forces have employed cooperatives and other types of mutual aid institutions and practices to help advance a socialist or noncapitalist path of development, they were viewed as a dire threat to the established social order by the dominant forces of capital and the state and were often the target of destabilization or repression. This was definitely the case in Jackson when the administration of Chokwe Lumumba promoted cooperatives as an essential plank in its platform for the transformation of the municipality, which is duly noted by Nathan Schneider in "The Revolutionary Life and Strange Death of a Radical Black Mayor."[23]

Outline of the Book

The focus of this book is sharing the story of how the Jackson-Kush Plan emerged, how the forces that are committed to it have planned and worked to bring it to fruition, and what lessons we have learned from our collective successes and failures. As previously noted, the book gives particular focus to the effort to develop the social and solidarity economy pillar of the Jackson-Kush Plan through the work of Cooperation Jackson.

The first section of the book, "Groundings," lays the critical foundation to understand how Cooperation Jackson is expanding the vision of the Jackson-Kush Plan toward fulfilling its mission to build a dynamic social and solidarity economy in Jackson to provide a solid material foundation for the transformation that is being envisioned and struggled for. "Build and Fight," written by Kali Akuno on behalf of Cooperation Jackson, is the most comprehensive statement written to date on the theory and programmatic outline of the work that Cooperation Jackson is pursuing. We think it can and will be instructive to practitioners everywhere.

The second section of the book, "Emergence," provides us with the public write-up of the now famous Jackson-Kush Plan, written by Kali Akuno. It also provides us with several other works that address dimensions of how the Jackson-Kush Plan emerged and was unveiled to the world. The third section of the book, "Building Substance," focuses on the process of organizing the Jackson Rising conference and some of the immediate outcomes that emerged from it. Essays in this section include one from veteran radical organizer and intellectual Carl Davidson, who wrote one of the first insightful articles to correctly grasp the link between our efforts to use electoral politics to build power and to transform the local economy. Another is written by militant journalist and former Black Panther Party member, the late Bruce Dixon, focusing on the centrality of Black working-class organizing to the effort to democratically transform the economy through cooperative economics. It also addresses how this type of self-organization is a necessary heightening of the class struggle within the Black community.

The fourth section of the book, "Critical Examinations," addresses a number of key issues and challenges confronting Cooperation Jackson and the execution of the Jackson-Kush Plan. The essay, "The Centrality of Land and the Jackson-Kush Plan," by renowned housing and human rights activist Max Rameau, addresses the question of land ownership and property relations and how these systems, and how they are controlled, are central to any people's struggle for liberation. The essay "A Long and Strong History with Southern Roots," by Jessica Gordon-Nembhard, the chief intellectual on Black cooperative history and development in our age, attempts to situate the birth and development of Cooperation Jackson in the long thread of Black cooperative development in the South. The chapter "Coming Full Circle: The Intersection of Gender Justice and the Solidarity Economy," is an interview by renowned journalist Thandisizwe Chimurenga with Cooperation Jackson cofounder and executive committee member Sacajawea "Saki" Hall. The interview addresses how Cooperation Jackson is struggling to eliminate the systemic dynamics of sexism, patriarchy, and heterosexism and incorporate a dynamic analysis and practice of intersectionality into its work and worldview.

The fifth section of the book, "Movement Expansions," outlines the effects of the Jackson-Kush Plan outside of Mississippi, including substantive looks at Community Movement Builders in Atlanta, Cooperation Humboldt in California, and the Afrikan Cooperative Union. Section 6 takes us further both conceptually and geographically, as radical municipalism is taken up in the UK by the *Green European Journal* and in the Kurdish struggle in Rojava. Section 7 examines contemporary initiatives toward the general strike and dual power. In addition to reprinting the important work by the Symbiosis Collective, with a special preface, and looking at building the commune in Venezuela, this section includes a dialogue on the COVID-19 formation People's Strike, with commentary from the coeditors, as well as Saki Hall, Rose Brewer, and Wende Marshall.

The final section of this book, "Going Forward: Ecosocialism and Regeneration," provides us with a series of reflections on the overall work to implement the Jackson-Kush Plan and what lessons can and should be drawn from these experiences. Along with two afterwords, we examine some lessons that can be learned from Jackson-Kush, as well as some ways forward, given current material conditions.

Work, Reflect, Study, Improve! And Repeat.

Notes

1 The two council members who ran for mayor during the special election of 2014 were Tony Yarber and Melvin Priester Jr.

2 On the Coalition for Economic Justice, see Kali Akuno, "Countering the Confederate 'Spring': The Assault on Black Political Power in Jackson, MS," Black Agenda Report, March 9, 2016, accessed May 5, 2022, https://blackagendareport.com/black_power_jackson_MS.

3 John Sibley Butler, *Entrepreneurship and Self-Help among Black Americans: A Reconsideration of Race and Economics* (Albany: State University of New York Press, 1991), 79–142.

4 Christopher Ingraham, "If You Thought Income Inequality Was Bad, Get a Load of Wealth Inequality," *Washington Post*, May 21, 2015, accessed May 5, 2022, https://tinyurl.com/2s486edj.

5 Ibid.

6 Ibid.

7 For more information on the Gini coefficient, see "Who, What, Why: What is the Gini coefficient," BBC News, March 12, 2015, accessed May 5, 2022, http://www.bbc.com/news/blogs-magazine-monitor-31847943; Erik Sherman, "America Is the Richest, and Most Unequal, Country," *Fortune*, September 20, 2015, accessed May 5, 2022, https://fortune.com/2015/09/30/america-wealth-inequality.

8 Bhaskar Sunkara, "Why 21st Century Capitalism Can't Last," Al Jazeera America, April 26, 2014, accessed May 5, 2022, http://america.aljazeera.com/opinions/2014/4/thomas-piketty-capitalism21stcentury.html.

9 Bruno Jossa, "Marx, Marxism and the Cooperative Movement," *Cambridge Journal of Economics* 29 (January 2005): 3–18.

10 Ibid. 6.

11 Sam Dolgoff, ed., *Bakunin on Anarchism* (Montréal: Black Rose Books, 1980), 173.

12 "What's the Alternative?" *Economist*, August 15, 2015, accessed May 5, 2022, https://www.economist.com/books-and-arts/2015/08/15/whats-the-alternative; the quote in the excerpt is from John Plender's book *Capitalism: Money, Morals and Markets* (London: Biteback Publishing, 2016).

13 George Cheney, *Values at Work: Employee Participation Meets Market Pressure at Mondragon* (Ithaca, NY: Cornell University Press, 1999); William Foote Whyte and Kathleen King Whyte, *Making Mondragon: The Growth and Dynamics of the Worker Cooperatives Complex* (Ithaca, NY: Cornell University Press, 1988).

14 "All Our History," Mondragon, accessed May 5, 2022, http://www.mondragon-corporation.com/eng/about-us/economic-and-financial-indicators/highlights.

15 Paulo Freire, *Pedagogy of the Oppressed*, 30th anniversary ed. (New York: Continuum, 2000), 65–66.

16 Lar Rudebeck, *Guinea-Bissau: A Study of Political Mobilization* (Uppsala, SE: Scandinavian Institute of African Studies, 1974), 91.

17 "Cooperative Identity, Values and Principles," International Cooperative Alliance, accessed May 5, 2022, https://www.ica.coop/en/cooperatives/cooperative-identity.

18 Alexander Berkman, "The Pattern of Life under Decentralized Communism," in *Patterns of Anarchy: A Collection of Writings on the Anarchist Tradition*, ed. Leonard Krimerman and Lewis Perry (New York: Anchor Books, 1966), 344.

19 Heather M. Coon and Markus Kemmelmeier, "Cultural Orientations in the United States: (Re)Examining Differences Among Ethnic Groups," *Journal of Cross-Cultural Psychology* 32, no. 3, (May 2001): 348–64.

20 Sharryn Kasmir, *The Myth of Mondragon: Cooperatives, Politics, and Working-Class Life in a Basque Town* (Albany: State University of New York Press, 1996) 153–54.

21 Ramon Flecha and Ignacio Santa Cruz, "Cooperation for Economic Success: The Mondragon Case," *Analyse und Kritik* 33, no. 1 (May 2011): 163, accessed May 5, 2022,

https://www.analyse-und-kritik.net/Dateien/5696575a8cb2e_ak_flecha_santa-cruz_2011.pdf.

22 For more on the attacks on the Banca Popolare, see "Not So Popolari: Reform of Italy's Biggest Cooperative Banks Will Help the Sector to Consolidate," *Economist*, January 23, 2015, accessed May 5, 2022, https://www.economist.com/news/2015/01/23/not-so-popolari.

23 Nathan Schneider, "The Revolutionary Life and Strange Death of a Radical Black Mayor," Vice, April 17, 2016, accessed May 9, 2022, https://www.vice.com/en/article/5gj7da/free-the-land-v23n2.

Organizing for Self-Determination and Liberation: Beyond the Basics in the Black Liberation Movement

Sacajawea "Saki" Hall

Living in Jackson, Mississippi, and building Cooperation Jackson has been a huge struggle. Our work here in Jackson is filled with complexities, contradictions, successes, failures, and everything in between. As we continue to document that history it is important that we provide a clear analysis that allows people to see how we moved this project and what the future can hold for its success. This essay is not meant to review our self-criticisms; that important reflection is developed elsewhere. Here I share the unspoken struggles, those less directly dealt with difficulties, which more often than not provide lessons we must glean for building our movements. These are based on life in Jackson over the past decade, and I hope they will contribute to strengthening our people, empowering our community, and informing the wide range of communities and movements reading this book. Based on twenty years of educating and organizing throughout the US, it is intended to pose some critical questions more than provide clichéd answers.

My time in Jackson has often led me to question if all the hard work was worth it. In a much more visceral way than I've experienced before at different points in my life, I wondered whether we had gained as much as we had lost. During one of the most difficult times, between 2017 and 2018, I was separated from my political home—the organization I had joined at the start of what I call my conscious participation in the Black liberation movement, the Malcolm X Grassroots Movement (MXGM). Cooperation Jackson was asked to divorce itself from the family of Chokwe Lumumba and the Lumumba administration led by Chokwe's son. Friendships, comrades, and political relationships were strained and a significant number of them completely lost. Many people declared they would not take sides as a matter of principle and then slowly disappeared.

Moving Beyond

When I first read "Tell No Lies, Claim No Easy Victories: Response to Ultra-Left Attacks on the Lumumba Administration in Jackson, Mississippi" by Akinyele Omowale Umoja for the National Coordinating Committee of the New Afrikan People's Organization (NAPO), I was angry and felt politically and personally attacked. After writing a response that I never published, I honestly reflected on my time in Jackson up until that point. I sat with the "ultra-left sectarian" label. Akinyele wrote: "Cooperation Jackson has not been able to develop a base of support among indigenous Black people in Jackson, particularly Black workers.... This group has failed to mobilize and organize Black workers in a city which is 80% Black and working class." I could concede to this statement three years into Cooperation Jackson. None of us thought we had the membership we could have had or needed to have for the future we envisioned. It did seem a little unfair, though, to charge an organization three years old with having failed to organize some unknown percent that would represent a base of roughly 160,000 people. We thought we were coming into an MXGM base that could be increased and strengthened but soon realized that outside of the mobilization for elections, there was no ongoing campaign work to maintain a minimal base or rebuild a base that had existed decades before. In essence, we had to start from scratch.

One of Akinyele's criticisms required several readings. "Ultra-left politics," he wrote, "is an orientation that overestimates the level of consciousness and organization of the people and capacity of the revolutionary movement, while often engaging in sectarian politics divorced from the people's struggle." This one confused me, and I debated it, tried to fit it on and wear it, and found it particularly hard having been politically trained through MXGM—the NAPO mass-based group. One of my favorite Ella Baker quotes came to mind: "Oppressed people, whatever their level of formal education, have the ability to understand and interpret the world around them, to see the world for what it is, and move to transform it." This is the basis from which I have always operated, and that is enough to give me solace.

While all of the intense critiques stung, this sting may have lasted the longest and echoed the most in my head: "Cooperation Jackson has relied on the legacy and used the name and image of Baba Chokwe and the Lumumba family and the history of NAPO/MXGM organizing in Jackson, to gain and maintain support locally, nationally, and internationally. Cooperation Jackson can no longer undermine the contribution and political commitment of Baba Chokwe Lumumba, while cloaking itself in his political and organizational legacy." We were being accused, here and in less politically eloquent ways, of "pimping" off Baba Chokwe's name…that we had been doing this from the start. Wow!

Another person took it upon himself to wage an ongoing campaign, telling anyone and everyone he could (including funders) that Cooperation Jackson had "no real work," were misusing money, had a "pattern of dishonest and poor leadership," and should not be "artificially" held up or endorsed, because it damages the effort to "build a powerful movement." Now I believe strongly in the practice of criticism/self-criticism and believe that the practice is vital to correcting mistakes and improving practice both individually and collectively. I've learned that it takes being willing to have your ego bruised and requires having trust that a comrade (not any ol' person) is acting in good faith to keep at it. It takes working through differences and struggling for alignment and political clarity. Sometimes it even requires a partway understanding that there are irreconcilable differences, hopefully coming to further understandings that allow for working together in areas where you do agree. Even if it takes some time to get there, the goal should be as much principled unity as possible, when and where possible, to work for the collective good. But some of these attacks seemed beyond principled criticisms.

So we decided from then on till the present—both as an organization and among our leadership, as individuals—that we would not engage in a war of criticism or even self-defense. As a Christian, I've always rejected the idea of an eye for an eye. It has been hard at times to self-censor, and I have found myself in situations where I have had to grit my teeth and nod my head. I also reject the notion of getting smacked in the face and turning the other cheek. But I know what Rev. Martin Luther King Jr. meant. We have been and still are willing to engage in honest struggle, that takes a willingness to say things that are uncomfortable and even at odds, as well as to hear them. At the end of the day, Akinyele Umoja's essay time and time again made me want to respond in a "comradely principled revolutionary struggle" way, even though I do not believe that is the way in which it was offered to me publicly. Even when my grief went from acceptance to rage, I landed on acceptance and never published or circulated my scathing analytical reply.

I realized early on, however, that I *would be* telling lies by being completely silent—and that would not honor Amílcar Cabral (author of the phrase "tell no lies") or Chokwe Lumumba. So I decided that I would be true to my experience and represent myself, my role, and my organization as best I could in the timeline of our existence in the Black radical tradition we were born into. I would, when asked, provide my own and my organization's political analysis about the City of Jackson and our work. I have not thrown stones, shade, or glitter. Our conditions and context are that bad.

The full Cabral quote is necessary in our work. He wrote: "Hide nothing from the masses of our people. Tell no lies. Expose lies whenever they are told. Mask no difficulties, mistakes, failures. Claim no easy victories." Moving beyond solidarity to action, beyond mobilizing to organizing, beyond cultural activity to base building, requires memorizing this full quote, and, more importantly, putting it into practice.

The Future in the Present

Cooperation Jackson as an institution grew out of the Jackson-Kush Plan, the Malcolm X Grassroots Movement (MXGM), and NAPO. The members of MXGM who cofounded Cooperation Jackson, along with a group of nonmembers, were all transplants to Jackson, Mississippi. Long before the organization was even thought of, a phase of our solidarity economy work had begun. For me, the new chapter of my life in Jackson was continuing the story of my life as an activist and organizer in New York and Atlanta, except I was not sure what I would do for an income after my contract as conference coordinator of the Jackson Rising New Economies Conference ended. For all of us, the work included getting ready for hosting a huge conference, studying, and participating in training on solidarity economics and cooperatives (regardless of whether we had studied or lived experience), building relationships in the community, outreach, door knocking, and meetings. This work began before the organization, whose name we borrowed (with permission) from Cooperation Texas. We knew there would need to be an institution to carry out the work and be the container for additional projects, co-ops, and coalition building. What we did not know was that launching the institution would end up getting fast-tracked after the untimely death of Mayor Chokwe Lumumba.

The leadership of Cooperation Jackson decided with limited funds and without nonprofit status to forgo any compensation for our work in order to acquire land in West Jackson. We did this with the explicit understanding that land is a basis for our freedom, independence, and self-determination. None of this work has been done to benefit any one family or small group of people. Our coordinating committee at the time knew we would need to have a core team to work full-time, and we decided to pay five of us $1,000 a month based on need, desire, and capacity. I point this out to say that real sacrifices must be made in our movement-building work. Moving to Jackson, further away from my family, network of supportive friends, and work opportunities, was no easy choice. But is what was needed to add capacity to my former political organization and to start this project. A stipend of $1,000 a month for a family of four (supplemented with food stamps, because Kali refused to get the stipend and worked on a full-volunteer basis!) was what we felt needed to happen at that historic juncture.

We created the nonprofit, in addition to a limited liability corporation, to raise charitable funds, establish a community land trust (CLT), and engage in cooperative and solidarity economy education and training. The majority of the funds raised by Cooperation Jackson have been used to acquire land explicitly to take it off of the speculative market. Short of directly liberating the land, the CLT is a direct way to operationalize the motto, "Free the Land."

Cooperation Jackson's work is anchored in West Jackson, particularly the Poindexter Park and Capital Neighbors sections of West Jackson. These are Black working-class/poor neighborhoods, with a high concentration of homeless individuals, arguably the highest concentration in Mississippi. The leadership of Cooperation Jackson, which includes me, chose this neighborhood for two reasons. First, because of its history. The Poindexter Park neighborhood is home to the original Provisional Government of the Republic of New Afrika; its house was located at 1148 Lewis Street. We wanted to be connected to this history and its living memory in the neighborhood. Also, in analyzing the city, we noted the high concentration of Black homeownership and available land in the neighborhood. This combination is important in our ongoing fight against land speculation and gentrification. We knew then and know even more now that such speculation is on the rise in West Jackson.

My life and work are not divorced from the people's struggle. I live and work within the trenches of my neighborhood. Living here, doing this work, and struggling within and as part of a community has reminded me of my working-class background. It has deepened my anti-capitalist analysis, my commitment to centering our Black poor/working-class community organizing, and the importance of centering Black women. Even though I live under similar conditions as my neighbors, I also fully recognize my privilege and the positionality.

I am willing to commit class suicide, and Jackson has reminded me in very uncomfortable ways that I can and will *have to* if I'm being true to revolutionary politics.

We made a choice to live and work in West Jackson instead of driving in from North Jackson or the surrounding suburbs. We made the choice to be here with our children, despite this being a neighborhood reminiscent of our own childhoods rampant with drugs, violence, and poverty in Los Angeles and New York. We want better for our children, and we want better for all of our people, but knowing the challenges of organizing Black working-class people from our own respective upbringings and experiences, we chose to live and work in this neighborhood, despite the challenges. We chose to develop relationships with other Black working-class people to build a more self-determined future. Many organizers become literally divorced from the people's struggle in both their living conditions and their lack of organizing in poor communities. Outside of holding cultural events or identifying as a "Black organizer," too many live their lives disengaged from the struggle of Black poor, working class, and even so-called middle-class everyday life.

When we moved to Jackson, our organization was in a period of great transition. The successful election of Chokwe Lumumba as the mayor of Jackson was extraordinary. Chokwe was a known entity to the people of Jackson and solidified some possibilities for organizing. However, although the people of Jackson knew Baba Chokwe Lumumba, they did not know MXGM or NAPO, let alone the Jackson-Kush Plan. This meant that it became too easy for a 180-degree shift to take place with an overreliance on electoral politics.

Telling no lies and claiming no easy victories must mean honestly assessing the lack of political education, leadership development, and engagement in the hood, when there is no real campaign or project to engage "the people." Getting out the vote is one thing, but building or rebuilding a base within the community is another. Based on our own work over the years, Cooperation Jackson's leadership knows that we have a long road ahead to become deeply rooted in the community and gain the people's trust. We recognized in 2015 that developing the solidarity economy component locally was more than simply introducing it to the base; we had to start from scratch. We had a relatively strong membership, but, by 2018, after the unfortunate splits, we had to rebuild that base.

While plenty of people want to say and think that this separation was based on personal differences, there were very fundamental differences politically and ideologically. We internally discussed the Kush plan, which was at a crossroads, and understood that as an effort at a coordinated strategy it was, in essence, dead. What then does an organization, an experimental project birthed from a long process that led to the strategy, do in such a situation? We agreed to keep doing what we started out doing and to continue even if whisper campaigns and threats to our work continued. We believe in the idea of letting our work speak for itself; it has to if we truly want to unplug from the nonprofit industrial complex! If we truly believe (as scary as it may feel) that the revolution will not be funded, we have to move forward with deeply grassroots base building in our communities. And despite our plethora of media, social media, and self-made media, the revolution will still not be televised. This is not to say that special funding or media will play no role in our work, but the hard work of building and sustaining radical movements cannot be reliant and dependent on either of these elements if we are to truly organize for people's liberation.

While Cooperation Jackson's mission and aim are to build a solidarity economy and realize economic democracy, we advocated and uplifted the three pillars of economic democracy, participatory democracy via people's assemblies, and electoral politics (including the development of an independent political party). We did not, and do not, uplift simple electoral victories outside of these wider strategic concepts simply because it might be advantageous to "cloak" ourselves in Baba Chokwe's political and organizational legacy. We did create an autonomous Cooperation Jackson People's Assembly, which led to housing justice work, rent relief, an eviction hotline, and rental assistance fairs.

The people have to be prepared to make choices in their own ultimate interests. We hope the redirection of the assemblies will be a vehicle for these choices, and we hope they become truly autonomous from the city's administration in order to exercise their independent agency. A truly independent people's relationship with progressive government will mean criticisms, making demands, and organizing for change. Isn't that the way an inside-outside strategy, one that ultimately works both within and outside of the system, works? Being in government and working with progressive local government is always an inside-outside strategy!

An inside-outside strategy can't keep compromise on the outside for the protection of those on the inside! This was already my frustration with work in international and domestic human rights projects I've engaged in since 2009. From climate justice work to the Decade for People of African Descent (which ends in 2024), my position is that there is not a balance to be forged nor do we try to balance things for comfort's sake. Inside-outside work is needed but it is also a contradiction. It is only okay when we recognize it as such and constantly work to check ourselves on which is the priority tactic or strategy to advance the needs of the people. Which aspect of the inside-outside dynamic, at any given moment, will best shift the balance of power? Most of the time, the outside protest and self-organization is, of course, most able to mobilize for lasting change.

We need to be discussing and heavily debating how grassroots organizations and movements engage in electoral politics. I question if the model I helped implement in Jackson had it right from its inception. I was challenged to think about this even more deeply while in Germany for a housing gathering, after a discussion turned into a fishbowl debate between me and a comrade from PAH (a national housing justice grassroots organization in Spain). The requirement for members of PAH is that they step down from the organizations they've been part of while they hold any elected office. For them, there is no blurred line between the movement and organizations, making demands in the interest of its membership, on the one hand, and, on the other, any elected officials coming out of that same movement while they are in office. I'm not completely sold on this being the only way to approach the potential conflicts that can arise or to protect each side. The premise of their model was taken for granted here though, and it led to major conflict.

Clearly and in general, the level of consciousness and organization of our people needs to be raised. Our strategic and tactical debates and our handling of internal and external contradictions needs to be sharpened. Joining MXGM taught me that it is our role to build what consciousness and organization exist within our communities. As organizers, it is our responsibility to not only meet the people where they are but also to engage in dialogues that will increase their capacity to connect their lived experiences with an analysis of the roots of our oppression. Creating a base of people committed to revolutionary transformation means including language that may not be familiar at first. It also means not assuming that our people aren't ready.

We see in our everyday work that everyday working-class Black people in Jackson are ready to engage with and be introduced to radical ideas. We still maintain that this is why thousands of Black working-class people voted en masse for Chokwe Lumumba and Chokwe Antar Lumumba. Over the decades of Chokwe's public works, particularly as a movement lawyer, the people of Jackson were introduced to his radical ideas and those of the New African Independence Movement (NAIM).

As for Cooperation Jackson's leadership, we have been clear from day one that our views are minority views among the people. We are going to have to win people over to our politics and positions through demonstrated action, not just through the conviction of our arguments. Cooperation Jackson is and always was premised on making revolutionary nationalist rhetoric both material and concrete. From the perspective of the NAIM, clearly the level of consciousness and organization of our people needs to be raised. However, this doesn't mean our communities aren't clear about the conditions they face.

People know all too well their conditions, and our job is to pose solutions based on our collective experience, study, and ideology. Organizing people means supporting their voices to exert power, a force to push for the change they/we want to see in the city. This is a power that needs to exercise its muscles for when we don't have a favorable mayor, a progressive mayor, or even a mayor who comes from local grassroots organizing. The muscle of the community has to be ready when the state government pushes back against our efforts to govern in a transformative way. Together, we must build the new model of sustainable urban living that we envision. Revolutionary organizing is about telling no lies and preparing our people for the struggles ahead. It entails providing leadership that offers a direction. Revolutionary leadership points out our failures, and collectively summarizes our history so we can learn from all of our efforts—the good, the bad, and the ugly.

I wholeheartedly believe in flexibility, but we can't take mass appeal to mean becoming so broad and general that we contradict the fundamental principles that are at the very core of what grounds us. At this moment, with humanity and Mother Earth on the brink of destruction, our call for radical, revolutionary, transformative action must be loud and clear. Beyond revisionism, we must assert unapologetically anti-capitalist, anti-extractivist, and anti-imperialist politics, policies, and processes.

This requires educating the people about the reality of what taking clear stances might mean, choosing to make sacrifices in the short term for the benefits in the long term. We must be clear about the limitations and traps of the system. We've talked at length about how radical movements have been undermined and destroyed in this pursuit, and how the Democratic Party has been the graveyard of social movements in the US. We've been clear and honest about what mayors can do and what the limitations of these positions are, particularly in Mississippi, where municipalities have few rights that cannot be overwritten by the state. This is the reality all over the South.

In my view, we were and are clear—crystal clear. We have a difficult road ahead to make Jackson a successful model that could illustrate how revolutionary nationalist politics can concretely serve our people. If our plan is going to serve the people, the base of Black working-class people, it will have to be led by strong organizations, not a fickle group of petty bourgeois drifters who will turn on us at the drop of a dime. With our understanding of contemporary capitalism and the United States, you can't have it both ways. Making Jackson, Mississippi, a model of revolutionary governance and transformation requires Cooperation Jackson and hopefully other organizations and individuals to step up, be clear about their mission and their means, and prepare our people to fight.

With this clarity and the help of an organization committed to building the future in the present, we can make Ella Baker's words a reality and transform the world through our own liberation.

A Beautiful Struggle (Saki's Continuous Learning in Past, Present, and Future)

Sacajawea "Saki" Hall

Constantly feeling like I'm thrown back to my childhood,
repeatedly,
in the recent past, the present, and when I'm thinking of the future.
Like a great sci-fi movie, book, or song.

Do I want this for my children?
Back on food stamps, except it was paper money then, and now I'm the mom responsible for food shopping and I wouldn't/couldn't send my daughter out to the bodega with the EBT card to get a few things real quick.

Gun shots, yup that's the same too. Except shots in a noisy busy NYC L.E.S./BK/Far Rockaway PJs aren't as loud as on my Jackson quiet streets. Well, not quiet—quieter, our block is lined with houses looking like what I grew up thinking were the nicer neighborhoods in Queens and St. Louis. Don't get it twisted though.

> The block on lock, the trunk stay locked
> Glock on cock, the block stay hot.
> —Erykah Badu, "Danger"

I grew up with gunshots, and people I knew shot,
I was in it, but not of it, in a protective bubble.
We've created that bubble, for now,
who knows what the future holds,
gun culture in the Deep South is on a whole 'nother level.
And my lightweight pacifist self knows the value of self-defense,

increasingly in the US, what feels more and more like the Wild, Wild West.

I vividly remember regularly seeing, sometimes counting, the crack vials with different color
tops on my walk to school. After school, walking home, splitting up, with other latchkey kids.
I went from driving and dropping off one to preschool,
to using the carpool lane to drop off and/or pick up two.
Carpool, mostly reserved for my busiest days,
and the time of day: very early, early, almost late, late, and very late.
The long carpool line, multitasking, documents, conference calls, feeling like such a waste of gas and totally misnamed, still it taught me a lot.
Like how I needed to recognize myself and model for them that, in most cases, multitasking is overrated.
I preferred parking and walking in, when it was my turn, most days it was my only break. Getting steps in, a quiet moment alone, or engaging in the Jackson Public Schools culture, I knew nothing of at the start. The longer I had, and more people I knew, I appreciated having no cell phone signal too.
I could chit chat and get the school scoop.
Not gossip though, I avoid that, didn't have time back then, definitely don't have time for it now.

I had community, I had people looking after us, a village, each place we lived.
A blessing, a feeling that I want to give.
My childhood was *a lot* rougher than A. and T. have had.
So far, I literally think about Armageddon in their lifetime, and I never did as a kid.
And yet they've spent their formative years, like me, living in the hood.
Neglected and divested, burned out, people smoked out, neighborhood.
I hadn't imagined that for them. Not sure what I imagined,
I didn't spend time thinking about it before them.
Really didn't think about it when I had her then him,
until I questioned, what the hell was I doing?
What are we doing to our family with this movement lifestyle?!

Their eight-plus years in Jackson have been drastically different and still similar to me,

in community.
Hearing, seeing, living a variety, and even more than me:
Cooperative housing, Fannie Lou Hamer Community Land Trust, worker cooperatives, solidarity economy, economic democracy, membership meetings, planning meetings, meetings, toys circling up for a kids-only meeting,
actions, farming that's called Freedom, land and liberation, revolution, like Ayiti.
Build and Fight, I hope they get that part faster than me and in that order.
Planting Life, like I planted a tree in NYC, Tompkins Square Park, specifically.

They could reject it at some point,
or get it and still make other choices than me.
I hope it permeates enough though,
so it's in their flesh and bones, and they can't shake it,
like I felt without knowing it,
it's in my bloodline, on both sides.

Using their imaginations to come up with ideas for healing the planet.
2018, the No Littering campaign! Recruiting members to join, planning interviews,
ideas for YouTube.
They took it beyond what I knew.
In middle school/early high school,
I too came up with an idea I thought was brilliant,
only later to find out it was called socialism.
Who knew?
Not the one person, my best friend, I broke down my theory to.

I still feel like Ally McBeal on the daily.
Having moments in the midst of life, where my brain sidetracks briefly as commentary. It could be a brief "huh?" with a confused face. Or a relevant song that I'm dancing to, to silence or censor myself from doing or saying something I may or may not regret.

Except, Ally McBeal was a legal comedy drama.

I gave up my seven-year plan to become a lawyer the second year of college. Honestly, my life has been more like a dark comedy, sci-fi, drama, fantasy, musical. And the songs that randomly come to mind as the soundtrack of my life in the last ten years
are more often than not PG-13 movie soundtracks,
video game soundtracks and anything and everything "lore."
My latest contradiction, Disney's *Encanto*.

The musical is relevant to my little people, my life growing up, my life from then to now, and of course: *love* (in all of its complexities, family, romance, marriage/partnerships/or not, and community). Disney is getting so much better, especially since *Frozen*. And still, I remind them periodically, Disney is evil, as shorthand for conglomerate global capitalist companies that started out racist as all get up, especially coming out of the United States. I can't say that all every single time.

I wasn't feeling the "Surface Pressure" song at first watching the movie, maybe I was in denial as to which character represented me the most. As the soundtrack played over and over again in my house and in the car, this one hit me, a few different times, in multiple ways.

> I'm the strong one, I'm not nervous
> I'm as tough as the crust of the earth is...
> Who am I if I don't have what it takes?
> No cracks, no breaks
> No mistakes, no pressure
> —Lin-Manuel Miranda, "Surface Pressure" (performed by Jessica Darrow)

Ironically, not only does it remind me of my childhood and young adulthood,
and the multiple hoods I lived in during that span of my life.
It is so spot on for the beautiful struggle
within my head and heart in my lifetime, including the last eight years in Jackson.
Trying to be perfect, literally, it did break me, several times.
Now I say to my kiddos and remind myself, no one is perfect all the time.
And practice doesn't make perfect, it makes you better, but people still make mistakes,

there is always room to grow, and we are always learning and need to keep practicing.

I try to do what I call "Parent with My Politics."
It's hard, real hard to do. There are a lot of parallels between my experience parenting the two people I birthed into the world and the political/movement work I've participated in for the last twenty years. Things we've been taught that we need to unlearn, lessons we grew up with that have gotten us through and even saved our lives. Navigating the contradictions of what we now see as unhealthy, even toxic, that we don't want to use, and then sometimes we do to get through. Pushing yourself hard, and then harder than you may have thought you could, for someone/something bigger than you, no matter how small or big they get. All while accepting your limits and capacity as a human being so you can be alive to see another day, and fight another fight, and build what your vision is and what transformative work requires.

Having to be constantly willing to learn something new.
Listening to yourself, your gut, and the training they've put you through, which can mean ignoring what your elders or friends with experience or what the "experts" tell you.
Embracing the sacrifice, even when it doesn't seem fair,
and you need and want a break.
Having to discipline yourself, and being consistent, or trying real damn hard to be.
Being flexible and willing to see through their lens, squat down to their size,
be the child and learner almost as much as the parent and teacher.
I say almost, because given the role you have as a parent requires accepting the responsibility it takes to know the difference.

To me, that is a similar and yet very different dance we play in our personal and political work, having different roles at different times that can change, shift, be the same in a new context, yet hopefully not stay the same for too long.

It feels good to be trusted and challenged and still trusted,

that type of relationship takes a long time to build with people you don't know,
who you work with and/or on behalf of,
A. and T. remind me that it is possible,
and that it's even possible to regain and rebuild trust
when it's been broken on either side,
for what seems small to them and big to me,
or what seemed small to me was big for them.
When you communicate and are intentional
about asking for trust rather than demanding it
and checking in at different points
knowing that love and trust and respect, like other things,
take work,
and grows stronger
the longer
you practice it with a person.

I'll always be a mom, although I am trying to organize my way out of a job. In both roles, there's love, and then there is also compassion, and I think you can have compassion without "love."
I definitely think love is needed; compassion is necessary.

Both so often feel like a tightrope. Or the lined-up dominoes in the "Surface Pressure" song. Mississippi is magical, and it's fucked up too. I love and appreciate my time in Jackson. I'm constantly reminded of things I'm thankful for. I'm also constantly reminded of questions like: How much control do you really have, or try to have, are you willing to let go of? How much control do you need to cling on to, and how important is that? Those questions and reality have made having a family in Jackson and doing this work in Jackson so hard.

At the end of the day, with all the parenting experience I've had with family for decades and the mentoring/teaching I've done *and* this work that I committed to, I have found at the core some basic principles that I try to hold onto, because they have held true for centuries. And I hope and pray and doubt and question and try to trust and keep my faith that I can stay grounded in these principles through my lifetime.

And when I'm at my worst and wonder why I'm doing all of this, I can keep going knowing that I'm doing it for myself and for my children and their great grandchildren seven times over.
For Mother Earth, and my ancestors from this land, across the sea, across the ocean, the full beauty of African peoples. For a time when I will no longer exist physically on this earth. And what I think is my legacy is unseen, and my life's contribution becomes another stepping stone for humanity.

I've thought of Erykah Badu's line, "I chose me," in the song "Me," time and time again over the past five years.

Last year, I wrote: I've had to make some tough choices, damn near impossible choices, and when I feel like quitting instead of Harriet's shotgun on my back, I don't think about turning back, I choose Me. I choose Me, for the We. Yes, Jill Scott, *one is the magic number*. How could I choose self-care so unapologetically that I forget the We? We better struggle and love principally. We better work hard and play hard and work harder. We better heal individually and collectively, and be okay with anger and grief and rage as much as love and joy, pleasure and peace. I can be disappointed with you, and you can criticize me. Emotional ranges we can identify and work through. We all better love me and choose Me, if we all are going to do this together.

I also jotted down,
Wearing a mask, are you?
Not the kind that Fanon spoke of,
the kind that shows I care for my health, and I care for yours too.

I was thinking a lot about the idea of self-care, selflessness, selfishness in relationship to Black people, and even the wider social justice movements prepandemic and during and the American exceptionalism and individualism that permeate our lives. There is a line between practicing self-care and masking, between putting oneself over the well-being of our comrades and being disciplined in this work of self-care. It may not be as thin of a line between wearing a mask in a pandemic or having a Black skin with a white mask, but think about it. Thinking of masks

in different forms even reminded me of a time I journaled when I was a teen
about feeling like I wore a mask of smiles and confidence outside in everything I did
and took it off once I was inside, at home, and, even then, not always fully.

I've been told many times, at different points of my life:
In order to take care of others, you have to take care of yourself.
I believe that, and nine times out of ten it's been true.
And, still, there are some times,
where in order to have the oxygen mask on so I can take a breather, a full exhale,
I've had to get them ready quick and in a hurry.
Do things for them along the way they are more than capable of doing,
do the things I complain about on any other day, to get them up and out, out of the way.
I mean, what if the conditions of a plane that requires those oxygen mask to drop
means you have very little time, and doing what they say not to do,
gives your little person, or people, a higher rate of survival?
I've thought of that in multiple scenarios in my life and work,
and I've chosen (in my head at least) to sacrifice my oxygen mask and hold on tight.

What are you willing to sacrifice?
To make sure life survives
and more than that,
THRIVES
Differently.

Writing has always been a labor of love. I enjoy it, only it feels like my process takes forever. In the range of writing I've done—from academic to radio journalism, social media gigs to my various roles in Cooperation Jackson that all require some degree of writing—I often say that I have a love/hate relationship with writing. This has been true for every type of writing aside from my personal journals. I rarely share this free-flowing form of writing that I do. I'm thankful for everyone who said they'd be down to read it if need be, who stood by waiting to read something and never got anything, who helped me, especially Isa, who embodies feminist politics of the free-flowing imagination and writing and taught me by being, and those who encouraged me, especially my partner Kali, who kept pushing me to contribute to our second book by writing individual pieces.

II

EMERGENCE

The Jackson-Kush Plan: The Struggle for Black Self-Determination and Economic Democracy

Kali Akuno

A major progressive initiative is underway in Jackson, Mississippi. This initiative demonstrates tremendous promise and potential in making a major contribution toward improving the overall quality of life of the people of Jackson, Mississippi, particularly people of African descent. This strategy is the Jackson-Kush Plan, and it is being spearheaded by the Malcolm X Grassroots Movement (MXGM) and the Jackson People's Assembly.

The Jackson-Kush Plan is an initiative to apply many of the best practices in the promotion of participatory democracy, solidarity economy, and sustainable development and combine them with progressive community organizing and electoral politics. The objectives of the Jackson-Kush Plan are to deepen democracy in Mississippi and to build a vibrant, people-centered solidarity economy in Jackson and throughout the State of Mississippi that empowers Black and other oppressed peoples in the state.

The Jackson-Kush Plan has many local, national, and international antecedents, but it is fundamentally the brainchild of the Jackson People's Assembly. The Jackson People's Assembly is the product of the Mississippi Disaster Relief Coalition, which was spearheaded by MXGM in 2005 in the wake of Hurricane Katrina's devastation of Gulf Coast communities in Mississippi, Louisiana, Alabama, and Texas. Between 2006 and 2008, this coalition expanded and transformed itself into the Jackson People's Assembly. In 2009, MXGM and the Jackson People's Assembly were able to elect human rights lawyer and MXGM cofounder Chokwe Lumumba to the Jackson City Council, representing Ward 2.

What follows is a brief presentation of the Jackson-Kush Plan as an initiative to build a base of autonomous power in Jackson that can serve as a catalyst for the attainment of Black self-determination and the democratic transformation of the economy.

Program or Pillars

The Jackson-Kush Plan has three fundamental programmatic components that are designed to build a mass base with the political clarity, organizational capacity, and material self-sufficiency to advance core objectives of the plan. The three fundamental programmatic components are:

- building people's assemblies;
- building a network of progressive political candidates;
- building a broad-based solidarity economy.

People's Assemblies

The people's assemblies that MXGM are working to build in Jackson and throughout the State of Mississippi are designed to be vehicles of Black self-determination and the autonomous political authority of the oppressed peoples and communities in Jackson. The assemblies are organized as expressions of participatory or direct democracy, wherein there is guided facilitation and agenda setting provided by the committees that compose the People's Task Force but no preordained hierarchy. The People's Task Force is the working or executive body of assemblies. The task force is composed of committees that are organized around proposals emerging from assemblies to carry out various tasks and initiatives, such as organizing campaigns and long-term institution building and development work.

Rooted in a History of Resistance

The people's assembly model advanced by MXGM has a long, rich history in Mississippi and in the Black Liberation Movement in general. The roots of our assembly model are drawn from the spiritual or prayer circles that were organized, often clandestinely, by enslaved Africans—to express their humanity, build and sustain community, fortify their spirits and organize resistance. The vehicle gained public expression in Mississippi with the organization of "Negro Peoples Conventions" at the start of Reconstruction to develop autonomous programs of action to realize freedom as Blacks themselves desired it and to determine their relationship to the Union.

This expression of people's power re-emerged time and again in Black communities in Mississippi as a means to resist the systemic exploitation and terror of white supremacy and to exercise and exert some degree of self-determination. The last great expression of this vehicle's power in Mississippi occurred in the early 1960s. It was stimulated by a campaign of coordinated resistance organized by militant local leaders, like Medgar Evers, that drew on the national capacity and courage of organizations like the Student Nonviolent Coordinating Committee and the Congress of Racial Equality. This campaign created the democratic space necessary for Black communities in Mississippi to organize themselves to resist oppression more effectively. Broad-based, participatory people's assemblies were the most common form of this self-organization.[1] One of the most memorable outgrowths of this wave of people's assemblies in Mississippi was the creation of the Mississippi Freedom Democratic Party, which tested the concrete limits of the Voting Rights Act and challenged white hegemonic control over the Democratic Party in the State of Mississippi and throughout the South.

It is this legacy of people's assemblies that MXGM is grounding itself in, and one we encourage others, particularly those in the Occupy movement, to study to help guide our collective practice in the present to build a better future.

A Comprehensive Electoral Strategy: Mounting an Effective Defense and Offense

MXGM firmly believes that at this stage in the struggle for Black liberation the movement must be firmly committed to building and exercising what we have come to regard as "dual power"—building autonomous power outside of the realm of the state (i.e., the government) in the form of people's assemblies and engaging electoral politics on a limited scale with the expressed intent of building radical voting blocs and electing candidates drawn from the ranks of the assemblies. As we have learned through our own experiences and our extensive study of the experiences of others, we cannot afford to ignore the power of the state.

First and foremost, our engagement with electoral politics is to try to negate the repressive powers of the state and contain the growing influence of transnational corporations in our communities. From police violence to the divestment of jobs and public resources, there are many challenges facing our communities that require us to leverage every available means of power to save lives and improve conditions. We also engage electoral politics as a means to create political openings that provide a broader platform for a restoration of the "commons," create more public goods utilities (for example, universal health care, public pension schemes, government financed childcare, and comprehensive public transportation) and the democratic transformation of the economy.[2] One strategy without the other is like mounting a defense without an offense or vice versa. Both are critical to advancing authentic, transformative change.

Fundamental to our engagement with electoral politics is the principle that we must build and employ independent political vehicles that are not bound to or controlled by either of the two monopoly parties in the United States. We are particularly focused on building an independent political force that challenges the two-party monopoly and empowers oppressed people and communities throughout the State of Mississippi. In the effort to build on the legacy of independent electoral engagement by Blacks in Mississippi, MXGM's members are all registered members of the Mississippi Freedom Democratic Party and are starting to work as activists within the party to extend its reach and impact.

It is this combination of building and exercising dual power—building autonomous people's assemblies and critical engagement with the state via independent party politics—that are the two fundamental political pillars of the Jackson-Kush Plan.

To date, some of the accomplishments of this model beyond the 2009 election of Chokwe Lumumba include:

- leading the campaign to elect the first-ever Black sheriff of Hinds County, Tyrone Lewis, in August 2011;[3]
- leading the campaign to free the Scott sisters, which won their release in January 2011;[4]
- successfully campaigning to save the J-Tran city public transportation in Jackson from devastating austerity cuts planned by then mayor Harvey Johnson;
- uniting with the Mississippi Immigrant Rights Alliance and other progressive forces to pass an anti–racial profiling ordinance in

Jackson and to defeat Arizona-style anti-immigrant legislation in Mississippi in 2011 and 2012 respectively.[5]

Building a Local Solidarity Economy

The critical third pillar of the Jackson-Kush Plan is the long-term commitment to building a local solidarity economy that links with regional and national solidarity economy networks to advance the struggle for economic democracy.

"Solidarity economy" as a concept describes a process of promoting cooperative economics that encourage social solidarity, mutual aid, reciprocity, and generosity.[6] It also describes the horizontal and autonomously driven networking of a range of cooperative institutions that support and promote the aforementioned values ranging from worker cooperatives to informal affinity-based neighborhood bartering networks.

Our conception of "solidarity economy" is inspired by the Mondragon Corporation, a federation of mostly worker cooperatives and consumer cooperatives based in the Basque region of Spain, but it also draws from the best practices and experiences of the solidarity economy and other alternative economic initiatives already in motion in Latin America and the United States.[7] We are working to make these practices and experiences relevant in Jackson and to facilitate greater links with existing cooperative institutions in the state and elsewhere to help broaden their reach and impact on the local and regional economy. The solidarity economy practices and institutions that MXGM is working to build in Jackson include:

- a network of cooperative and mutually reinforcing enterprises and institutions, specifically worker, consumer, and housing cooperatives, and community development credit unions as the foundation of our local solidarity economy;
- sustainable, green (re)development and green economy networks and enterprises, starting with a green housing initiative;
- a network of local urban farms, regional agricultural cooperatives, and farmers' markets (drawing heavily from recent experiences in Detroit, we hope to achieve food sovereignty and combat obesity and chronic health issues in the state that are associated with limited access to healthy and affordable foods and unhealthy food environments);

- developing local community and conservation land trusts as a primary means to begin the process of reconstructing the "commons" in the city and region by decommodifying land and housing;[8]
- organizing to reconstruct and extend the public sector, particularly public finance of community development, to be pursued as a means of rebuilding the public sector to ensure there is adequate infrastructure to provide quality health care, accessible mass transportation, and decent, affordable public housing, etc.

In building along these lines, we aim to transform the economy of Jackson and the region as a whole to generate the resources needed to advance this admittedly ambitious plan.

Turning Theory into Action: Organizing Campaigns and Alliance Building

These fundamental program components or pillars of the Jackson-Kush Plan will only be built through grassroots organizing and alliance building. The key to the organizing component of the overall plan is the launching and successful execution of several strategic and synergistic organizing campaigns. The most critical of these organizing campaigns are:

- the Amandla Education Project;[9]
- Take Back the Land;
- Operation Black Belt;
- 2013 Electoral Campaigns.

The Amandla Education Project

The Amandla Project is a youth and community education project specializing in skill building for civic engagement and participation. The project provides training to youth and community members in the people's assembly and the broader civil society in Jackson on community organizing, conflict resolution, critical literacy, media literacy, journalism and media advocacy, political theory, political economy, human rights advocacy, cooperative planning and management, participatory budgeting, the principles and practices of solidarity economy, sustainable economic development, and ecological sustainability. The project also specializes in teaching the rich history of social struggle in

Jackson and Mississippi in general, focusing on the legacy of struggle to deepen and expand democracy in the state and the lessons from this struggle that can be employed today to enhance civic engagement and participation.

In its first year, the Amandla Project will recruit, train, and organize one hundred youth and community organizers. These hundred individuals will serve as the core organizing cadre for the Jackson-Kush Plan. Our objective is to place ten organizers in each of Jackson's seven wards and to utilize the remaining thirty to enhance the overall organizing capacity of progressive forces in the State of Mississippi.

These organizers will be trained by a team of experienced organizers drawn from the ranks of MXGM, the Mississippi Chapter of the National Association for the Advancement of Colored People, the Mississippi Workers Center for Human Rights, and other allied organizations that support the People's Assembly and the Jackson-Kush Plan.

Training one hundred organizers is a critical start, but is in no way sufficient to meet the comprehensive needs of the Jackson-Kush Plan. To develop and train the cohorts and cadre of organizers needed to realize the objectives of this plan, MXGM, the Mississippi Chapter of the National Association for the Advancement of Colored People (NAACP), and the Praxis Project are working in alliance to build a training school by the start of 2013 that will serve as the cornerstone of this long-term educational initiative.

The Take Back the Land Campaign

The Take Back the Land campaign is an initiative to create a network of urban farms and farmers' markets to promote a healthy diet, affordable produce, and food sovereignty in the city. It also aims to create a land trust network cooperative housing, and a workers' cooperative network, to provide a base of employment for many of the unemployed and underemployed residents of Jackson.

The Take Back the Land campaign will focus on occupying vacant land, abandoned homes, and industrial facilities and converting them into usable agricultural land for urban farming, refurbished green housing to establish a cooperative housing network, and community space to establish training facilities, business centers, and recreational spaces.

Aspects of this campaign have already been launched by MXGM with the healthy foods initiative and the Fannie Lou Hamer Gardens

Project. This initiative is also conceptually linked with the National Take Back the Land Movement that was launched in 2009 by the Land and Housing Action Group of the US Human Rights Network, which originally consisted of MXGM, the Survivors Village, the Chicago Anti-Eviction Campaign, and Take Back the Land Miami.[10]

Operation Black Belt

Operation Black Belt is a campaign to expand worker organizing in Jackson and Mississippi overall, concentrating particularly on Black and immigrant workers. The aim is to organize these workers into associations and unions, to provide them with a collective voice and power, and to improve their living standards.

The long-term objective of this campaign is to challenge, and eventually overturn, the "right to work" laws and policies in Mississippi. These laws and polices play a major role in sustaining the extreme rates of poverty and health disparities in the state and must be overturned to improve the living standards of the vast majority of its residents. MXGM and the People's Assembly aim to partner with the Mississippi Workers Center for Human Rights to build and expand this critical long-term campaign.

2013 Electoral Campaigns

For the 2013 city elections in Jackson, the Jackson People's Assembly and MXGM are prepared to run two candidates. One candidate, the attorney Chokwe Lumumba, who currently serves as the city councilman for Ward 2, will run for mayor. The other candidate, June Hardwick, is also an attorney and will run for city council in Ward 7.

The objective of running these candidates and winning these offices is to create political space and advance policies that will provide maneuverable space for the autonomous initiatives of the Jackson-Kush Plan to develop and grow, as well as building more ward-based people's assemblies and task forces in Jackson, base building for the overall plan, and raising political consciousness about the need for self-determination and economic democracy to solve many of the longstanding issues affecting Black people. To create the democratic space desired, we aim to introduce several critical practices and tools into the governance processes of the Jackson city government that will help foster and facilitate the growth of participatory democracy, including:

- *participatory budgeting*, to allow the residents of Jackson direct access and decision-making power over the budgeting process in the city;
- *gender-sensitive budgeting*, to address the adverse impact of policy execution as reflected in budget priorities that negatively impact women and children;
- *human rights education and promotion* that will require all city employees to undergo human rights training to ensure that their policies and practices adhere to an international standard of compliance with the various treaties ratified by the United States government and the results-based norms established by the United Nations.

We also aim to make several critical structural changes to the City of Jackson's governance structure. The most critical change we will propose and fight for is creating a human rights charter to replace the existing city charter as the basis of sovereignty and governance for the city. Finally, we aim to advance several economic and social changes on a structural level in Jackson via the governance process. These include:

- expanding public transportation by increasing transport lines and launching a fleet of green vehicles that utilize natural gas, ethanol, and electric energy;
- creating a network of solar- and wind-powered generators throughout the city to expand and create a sustainable power grid;
- creating a South-South trading network and fair-trade zone that will seek to give rise to trading partnerships with international trading blocs, such as CARICOM (the Caribbean Community and Common Market) and ALBA (the Bolivarian Alliance for the Americas).

Alliance Building

Following the example of Malcolm X and countless Black political strategists and organizers before and after him, MXGM is a major advocate for strategic alliance building and united front politics. We are clear that none of our strategic objectives and demands can be attained simply by the forces we can muster, and few of our transitional goals and objectives can be reached without creating substantive alliances with strategic partners and allies. The Jackson-Kush Plan, as a transitional plan, is no exception to the rule.

Alliance building has been central to the operations of MXGM in Jackson. In many fundamental respects, the roots of the Jackson People's Assembly rest with the principled alliance of Black progressive organizations like the Southern Echo, the Mississippi NAACP, the Mississippi Workers Center, the Nation of Islam, the Mississippi American Civil Liberties Union, the National Coalition of Blacks for Reparations in America, the Mississippi Immigrants' Rights Alliance, the Mississippi Freedom Democratic Party, the National Conference of Black Lawyers, and so forth, assembled in the early 1990s to combat environmental racism, labor exploitation, and various aspects of institutional racism in Mississippi. Some of the key alliances we have formed or helped support over the last twenty-plus years include the Andre Jones Justice Committee, the Mississippi Justice Coalition, the Concerned Citizens Alliance, the Jackson Human Rights Coalition, the Concerned Workers of Frito Lay, the Johnnie Griffin Justice Committee, the Anti-Klan Coalition, the Kwanzaa Coalition, the Chokwe Lumumba Legal Support and Defense Committees, the Workers United for Self Determination, the City Wide Coalition for Selective Buying Campaign, the Grassroots Convention, the Committee to Free the Scott Sisters, and the Full Pardon Committee for the Scott Sisters.

For the Jackson-Kush Plan and its objectives to be realized, we are going to have to build a broad alliance in the city that is aligned with the principal aims of the plan and the initiatives that emerge from the people's assemblies. This alliance will intentionally be multinational in its outlook and orientation but based in and led by Black working-class communities and forces. We assess our strategic allies to be the growing Latino/Latina community and various immigrant populations that are migrating to the state seeking employment in the agricultural, construction, and professional service sectors. The strategic nature of these forces rests in our common interest in eradicating white supremacy and institutional racism. This alliance will also give due focus to building principled relationships with white progressive forces throughout the city and state, which are essential to shifting the current and foreseeable balance of power in the state. Our immediate aim is to win enough of these forces over to our vision and program to weaken, if not altogether neutralize, aspects of white conservative power in the state.

The objectives of the Jackson-Kush Plan require the building of coalitions and alliances that far exceed the borders of Mississippi. We envision the coalitions and alliances we are seeking to build in Mississippi as being an essential cornerstone to the building of a strategic South by Southwest radical people's alliance, rooted in the rebuilding of principled alliances among the primary oppressed peoples in the US, namely Blacks, Xicanos, and Indigenous nations. When and if linked with the growing immigrant population, this grand alliance possesses the potential to transform the United States into an entirely new social project.

What You Can Do to Help Promote and Advance the Jackson-Kush Plan

MXGM believes that for organizing initiatives like the Jackson-Kush Plan to be successful, it will take a balance of self-reliant initiative, will, and resourcing, combined with genuine solidarity and joint struggle on the part of our allies. To help see this initiative to fruition, we are calling on our allies and supporters to build with us in the following concrete ways:

Promotion and Education

The first critical task is to spread the word about the Jackson-Kush Plan. Promote it among your family, friends, and comrades and wherever you live, work, play, rest, or pray. Promote the democratic potential that the plan represents, and educate people about the importance of this initiative, the lessons that can be learned from it, how it can be applied in their context, and how they can support it.

Resource Generation

No major social initiative like the Jackson-Kush Plan can succeed without resources. The Jackson-Kush Plan needs a broad array of resources, but its two most fundamental needs are money and skilled volunteers.

We need money for a great number of things, most specifically to help support and build our organizing drives and campaigns, which includes paying organizers, covering work expenses (transportation, operations, facilities, etc.), and producing and promoting educational and agitation materials. If all of our allies and supporters were to make small individual donations, we firmly believe we could raise millions to support this critical work. In this spirit, we are challenging everyone who supports the Jackson-Kush Plan and the work of MXGM to make a contribution of $5 or more to this work to ensure that it succeeds. You can make a tax-deductible contribution to Community Aid and Development, Inc., our 501c3 fiduciary agent, by visiting http://www.cadnational.org.

The types of skills we need are in the areas of organizing, management, fundraising, and entrepreneurship. Additionally, in the technical fields of social networking, farming, construction, engineering, journalism and media, and health care, we are looking for volunteers to come to Jackson and make commitments to help at strategic times for short-term campaign initiatives, mainly for one or two weeks, and, when and where possible, to make more long-term commitments for several months or years to work under the discipline of MXGM and the people's assemblies.

Solidarity and Joint Campaigns

Political support for the Jackson-Kush Plan and the many initiatives within it is just as essential as resource support. We strongly encourage folks in the South to join us in building and extending Operation Black Belt, as this campaign ultimately needs to be a southern-wide initiative to be successful. The Amandla Project needs book and curriculum donations, pedagogical exchanges, and volunteer trainers to help it get started. We further call on our allies and supporters everywhere to support our 2013 electoral campaigns by joining one of our volunteer brigades, which will start in the summer of 2012 to carry out the will of the People's Assembly. And, of course, make generous financial contributions to the campaign coffers of Chokwe Lumumba and June Hardwick. More critically, however, we would like to encourage our allies and supporters outside of Mississippi to form local and regional Jackson Solidarity Circles to support the plan and relate directly with MXGM and the People's Assembly to support some or all of the aforementioned initiatives. We strongly encourage organizing and organizational development anywhere to enable social transformation to happen everywhere.

We are also looking to inspire, encourage, and support Jackson-like plans in other Black Belt regions of the South. In particular, Black Belt regions with mid-sized cities like Jackson that have similar race and class demographics, as these represent the greatest potential for success, given the current balance of forces in the US, primarily because these cities don't possess the same degree of consolidated transnational capital to contend with as do larger cities. We would hope that over time Jackson-Kush Plan solidarity committees throughout the Black Belt South would take up this call to action and build their own local political bases of support to engage in dual power initiatives that can link with the forces advancing the Jackson-Kush Plan, so as to empower Black and oppressed communities in the South.

If people would like to work more closely with MXGM to build the Jackson-Kush Plan, we strongly encourage people of Afrikan descent to join MXGM. We strongly encourage whites and other non-Afrikan peoples who are committed to antiracist, anti-imperialist, antisexist politics interested in working directly with us to join the Malcolm X Solidarity Committee.

Forward!

The Jackson-Kush Plan is a major initiative in the effort to deepen democracy and build a solidarity economy. To the extent that this plan calls for a critical engagement with electoral politics, we take heed of the lesson and warning issued by Guyanese professor Walter Rodney, who stated:

> I say this very deliberately. Not even those of us who stand on this platform can tell you that the remedy in Guyana is that a new set of people must take over from old set of people, and we will run the system better. That is no solution to the problems of Guyana. The problem is much more fundamental than that. We are saying that working class people will get justice only when they take the initiative. When they move themselves! Nobody else can give (freedom) as gift. Someone who comes claiming to be a liberator is either deluding himself or he is trying to delude the people. He either doesn't understand the process of real life. Or he is trying to suggest that you do not understand it. And so long as we suffer of a warped concept of politics as being leadership, we're going to be in a lot of trouble.[11]

We draw two lessons from this statement and the history associated with it. One, that to engage is to not be deluded about the discriminatory and hierarchal nature of the system or deny its proven ability to contain and absorb resistance or reduce radicals to status quo managers. The lesson we draw from Rodney's statements are that we have to fight in every arena to create democratic space to allow oppressed and exploited people the freedom and autonomy to ultimately empower themselves. The second lesson regards leadership. MXGM believes that leadership is necessary to help stimulate, motivate, and educate struggling people, but that leaders and leadership are not substitutes for the people themselves and for autonomous mass movement with distributed or horizontal leadership. As the legendary Fannie Lou Hamer said, "We have enough strong people to do this. For people to win this election, it would set a precedent for other counties in the state. People need a victory so bad. We've been working here since '62 and we haven't got nothing, excepting a helluva lot of heartaches."[12]

The Jackson-Kush Plan ultimately aims to build a strong people prepared to improve their future and seize their own destiny. We hope you will join us in its building and advancement. *In Unity and Struggle!*

This paper was published in its original form on July 12, 2017, on the website of the Malcolm X Grassroots Movement.

Notes

1 See Charles M. Payne, *I've Got the Light of Freedom: The Organizing Tradition and the Mississippi Freedom Struggle* (Berkeley: University of California Press, 2007); Charles Dittmer, *Local People: The Struggle for Civil Rights in Mississippi* (Urbana: University of Illinois Press, 1995); Aldon D. Morris, *The Origins of the Civil Rights Movement: Black Communities Organizing for Change* (New York: Free Press, 1986); Emilye Crosby, *A Little Taste of Freedom: The Black Freedom Struggle in Claiborne County, Mississippi* (Chapel Hill: University of North Carolina Press, 2005); Francesca Polletta, *Freedom Is an Endless Meeting: Democracy in Action in Social Movements* (Chicago: University of Chicago Press, 2007).

2 The "commons" refers to the resources of the Earth that everyone is dependent upon and must utilize to survive and thrive. The essential "commons" are land, water, and air.

3 See Black Agenda Morning Shot, August 29, 2011, interview with Kamau Franklin by Kali Akuno, accessed July 1, 2022, http://youtu.be/IIJcginZkpw; Elizabeth Waibel, "Lewis Prepares for the Future," JFP.ms, August 31, 2011, https://www.jacksonfreepress.com/news/2011/aug/31/lewis-prepares-for-the-future.

4 See "Lumumba Says Scott Sisters Released because of Supporters," 116 WAPT News Jackson, accessed May 9, 2022, http://youtu.be/oXBm_szT_5E; and Jamilah King, "Scott Sisters Finally Set Free," *Colorlines*, January 3, accessed May 9, 2022, 2011, https://www.colorlines.com/articles/scott-sisters-finally-set-free.

5 See Susan Eaton, "A New Kind of Southern Strategy," *Nation*, August 10, 2011, accessed May 6, 2022, http://www.thenation.com/article/162694/new-kind-southern-strategy.

6 On solidarity economy, see Ethan Miller, "Solidarity Economy: Key Concepts and Issues," in *Solidarity Economy I: Building Alternatives for People and Planet*, ed. E. Kawano, T. Masterson, and J. Teller-Ellsberg, (Amherst, MA: Center for Popular Economics, 2010), accessed May 6, 2022, http://www.communityeconomies.org/index.php/publications/chapters/solidarity-economy-key-concepts-and-issues.

7 See Mondragon, accessed May 6, 2022, https://www.mondragon-corporation.com/en.

8 Decommodifying: rejecting as a *commodity*, that is as something for sale, land, housing, etc., and strengthening the social elements, making citizens less dependent on the market.

9 *Amandla* is a Xhosa and Zulu word for *power*. It is used in the same way as the slogan "Black Power" is used by the Black Liberation Movement in the United States. It is used in call and response form, and the response is *awethu*, which means *to us*. Combined, it means "Power to the People," as made popular in the United States by the Black Panther Party for Self-Defense. This slogan was and remains common in the Azanian (i.e., South African) freedom movement.

10 For more on the National Take Back the Land Movement and its history, see Kali Akuno, "Some Thoughts on What Can Be Done to Withstand the Neo-Confederate/Neo-Fascist Conquest of Power," Navigating the Storm, January 17, 2022, accessed May 9, 2022, http://navigatingthestorm.blogspot.com.

11 This 1976 interview can be seen in Victor Jara Collective, *In the Sky's Wild Noise* (Brooklyn, NY: Autonomedia, 1983), accessed May 6, 2022, https://archive.org/details/XFR_2013-08-07_2A_01.

12 Quoted in Kay Miles, *This Little Light of Mine: The Life of Fannie Lou Hamer* (New York: Plume Books, 1994), 176.

People's Assembly Overview: The Jackson People's Assembly Model

Kali Akuno for the New Afrikan People's Organization and the Malcolm X Grassroots Movement

> "We must practice revolutionary democracy in every aspect of our Party life. Every responsible member must have the courage of his responsibilities, exacting from others a proper respect for his work and properly respecting the work of others. Hide nothing from the masses of our people. Tell no lies. Expose lies whenever they are told. Mask no difficulties, mistakes, failures. Claim no easy victories."
> —Amílcar Cabral, "Tell No Lies, Claim No Easy Victories"

Brief Synopsis

People denied their agency and power and subjected to external authority need vehicles to exercise their self-determination and exert their power. A *people's assembly* is a vehicle of democratic social organization that, when properly organized, allows people to exercise their agency, exert their power, and practice democracy—meaning "the rule of the people, for the people, by the people"—in its broadest terms, which entails making direct decisions about the economic, social, and cultural operations of a community or society and not just the contractual ("civil") or electoral and legislative (the limited realm of what is generally deemed to be "political") aspects of the social order.

What the People's Assembly Is

A people's assembly, first and foremost, is a mass gathering of people organized and assembled to address essential social issues and/or questions pertinent to a community.

"Mass" can be and is defined in numerous ways depending on one's views and position, but per the experience of the New Afrikan People's Organization (NAPO) and the Malcolm X Grassroots Movement (MXGM) in Jackson, Mississippi, we define it as a body that engages at least one-fifth of the total population in a defined geographic area (neighborhood, ward or district, city, state, etc.). We have arrived at this one-fifth formula based on our experience of what it takes to have sufficient numbers, social force, and capacity to effectively implement the decisions made by the assembly and ensure that these actions achieve their desired outcomes.

"Addressing essential social issues" means developing solutions, strategies, action plans, and timelines to change various socioeconomic conditions in a desired manner, not just hearing and/or giving voice to the people assembled.

Second, another defining characteristic of a truly democratic assembly is that it calls for and is based upon "one person, one vote." Agency is vested directly in individuals, regardless of whether the assembly makes decisions by some type of majoritarian voting procedure or by consensus. This aspect of direct engagement, direct democracy, and individual empowerment is what separates a people's assembly from other types of mass gatherings and formations, such as alliances or united fronts, where a multitude of social forces are engaged.

However, given these two basic defining characteristics, it should be noted that there are still different types of people's assemblies. Within NAPO/MXGM we break assemblies down into three essential types.

United front or *alliance-based assembly*. This type of assembly is typically a democratic forum that is populated and driven by formally organized entities (i.e., political parties, unions, churches, civic organizations, etc.) that mobilize their members to participate in broad, open decision-making sessions with members from other organizations and/or formations. What makes this different then from a typical alliance or coalition is that the organizations and their leaders do not make the decisions on behalf of their members in these spaces; members make decisions as individuals within the general body. The main limitation with this type of assembly formation is that it tends to remain "top heavy." That is, the various organizational leaders often to do not disseminate adequate information about meetings or inform their members about decisions and activities of the assembly. And there is the problem that many organizations do not have consolidated members or a base that they can turn out, instead they are legitimated by their history, social position, or the charisma of their leadership.

Constituent assembly. This type of assembly is a representative body, not a direct democratic body of the people in their totality. This type of assembly is dependent on mass outreach but is structured, intentionally or unintentionally, to accommodate the material (having to work, deal with childcare, etc.) and social limitations (interest, access to information, political and ideological differences, etc.) of the people. The challenge with this type of assembly is that if it doesn't continue to work to bring in new people (particularly youth) and struggle and strive politically to be mass in character, then it tends to become overly bureaucratic and stagnant over time.

Mass assembly. The mass assembly is the broadest example of people's democracy. It normally emerges during times of acute crisis, when there are profound ruptures in society. This type of assembly is typically an all-consuming, short-lived entity. Its greatest weakness is that it typically demands that those engaged give all of their time and energy to the engagement with the crisis, which over time is not sustainable, as people eventually have to tend to their daily needs to sustain themselves, their families, and their communities.

The Jackson Assembly Model

At present, the Jackson People's Assembly operates in a space between a constituent and mass assembly. In the main, it operates as a constituent assembly, engaging in a number of strategic campaigns (such as defending the 1 percent sales tax that was voted in by the residents of Jackson, in January 2014) and initiatives to address the material needs of our social base and to extend its power (such as support for Cooperation Jackson). This is based primarily on the material limitations imposed on the base and the members of the People's Task Force (see below for details) by the daily grinds of the capitalist social order (i.e., tending to work, child care, health, and transportation challenges, etc.). There have also been some political challenges confronted over the past year adjusting both to the mayoral term of Chokwe Lumumba and how to relate to it and how to address the sudden loss of Mayor Lumumba and the counterreaction to the people's movement that facilitated the election of Mayor Tony Yarber, in April 2014. However, during times of crisis, the assembly tends to take on more of a mass character, such as in the immediate aftermath of the passing of Mayor Lumumba, in late February 2014, to defend the People's Platform (devised by the assembly) and many of the initiatives the Lumumba administration was pursuing to fulfill it. It should be noted, however, that even though the current practice in Jackson tends toward the constituent model, the aim is to grow into a permanent mass assembly.

The basic outlines of the Jackson people's assembly model can be found in the Jackson-Kush Plan.[1] A synopsis of the model, taken from the plan, outlines it thus:

> The People's Assemblies that MXGM and NAPO are working to build in Jackson and throughout the State of Mississippi, particularly its eastern Black belt portions, are designed to be vehicles of Black self-determination and the autonomous political authority of the oppressed peoples and exploited classes contained within the state. The assemblies are organized as expressions of participatory or direct democracy, wherein there is guided facilitation and agenda setting provided by the committees that compose the People's Task Force but no preordained hierarchy. The People's Task Force is the working or executing body of the assembly. The task force is composed of committees that are organized around proposals emerging from the assembly to carry out various tasks and initiatives, such as organizing campaigns (like Take Back the Land) and long-term institution building and development work (like land trusts and cooperative housing).
>
> The people's assembly model advanced by MXGM and NAPO as a core component of the Jackson-Kush Plan have a long, rich history in Mississippi and in the Black Liberation Movement in general. The roots of our assembly model are drawn from the spiritual or prayer circles that were organized often clandestinely by enslaved Afrikans to express their humanity, build and sustain community, fortify their spirits and organize resistance. The vehicle gained public expression in Mississippi with the organization of "Negro Peoples Conventions" at the start of Reconstruction to develop autonomous programs of action to realize freedom, as Afrikans themselves desired it and to determine their relationship to the defeated governments of the Confederacy and the triumphant government of the Federal Republic.

This expression of people's power re-emerged time and again in the New Afrikan communities of Mississippi as a means to resist the systemic exploitation and terror of white supremacy and to exercise and exert some degree of self-determination. The last great expression of this vehicle of Black people's self-determined power in Mississippi occurred in the early 1960s. It was stimulated by a campaign of coordinated resistance, organized by militant local leaders like Medgar Evers, that drew on the national capacity and courage of organizations like the Student Non-Violent Coordinating Committee (SNCC) and the Congress of Racial Equality (CORE). This campaign created the democratic space necessary for New Afrikan communities in Mississippi to organize themselves to resist more effectively. Broad, participatory-based People's Assemblies were the most common form of this self-organization. One of the most memorable outgrowths of this wave of Peoples Assemblies in Mississippi was the creation of the Mississippi Freedom Democratic Party (MSFDP), which challenged the hegemonic control over the Black vote on a state and local level since the New Deal, and remains a vehicle that serves as a constant reminder of the need for genuine Black equality and self-determination to this day.

Basic Functions of a People's Assembly

Regardless of their type, people's assemblies have two broad functions and means of exercising power:

- *They organize autonomous, self-organized and -executed social projects*. Autonomous in this context means initiatives not supported or organized by the government (state) or some variant of monopoly capital (finance or corporate industrial or mercantile capital). These types of projects range from organizing community gardens to forming people's self-defense campaigns and housing occupations to forming workers' unions and building workers cooperatives. On a basic scale these projects function typically as "serve the people" or "survival" programs that help the people to sustain themselves or acquire a degree of self-reliance. On a larger scale, these projects provide enough resources and social leverage (such as flexible time to organize) to allow the people to engage in essential fight back or offensive (typically positional) initiatives.

- *They apply various types of pressure on the government and the forces of economic exploitation in society.* Pressure is exerted by organizing various types of campaigns against these forces, including mass action (protest) campaigns, direct-action campaigns, boycotts, noncompliance campaigns, policy-shift campaigns (either advocating for or against existing laws or proposed or pending legislation), and even electoral campaigns (to put someone favorable in an office or to remove someone adversarial from office).

How to Carry Out the Functions of the Assembly

To carry out these critical functions, an assembly must organize its proceedings to produce clear demands, a coherent strategy, realistic action plans, and concrete timelines. It must also organize itself into units of implementation, committees, or action groups to carry out the various assignments dictated by the strategy and action plans.

When considering these functions and how they are executed in Jackson, it is critical to note that our model makes a clear distinction between the assembly as an *event*, the assembly as a *process*, and the assembly as an *institution*. In Jackson, the assembly as an event is where we take up general questions and issues and deliberate and decide on what can, should, and will be done to address them. The process of the assembly, where the more detailed questions of strategy and planning, such as setting concrete timelines and defining measurable goals and deliverables, are refined is conducted through the People's Task Force and the assembly's various committees and working groups. The assembly as an institution is a product of the combined social weight of the assembly's events, processes, actions, and social outcomes.

Basic Organizing Assumptions

There are three basic assumptions being made in this chapter that must be clear for anyone thinking of organizing a people's assembly (following this model or any other model in our experience and study). In our experience, forces attempting to organize a people's assembly that don't explicitly address these assumptions tend to struggle and/or outright fail. These assumptions are:

- The social forces organizing the people's assembly must have the ability to mobilize and assemble a significant number of people to participate and engage in a democratic process (review our one-fifth formula above). This typically means that the social force or forces organizing the assembly have already built a significant base and are able to or are committed to scaling up.

- The social forces organizing the people's assembly have experience participating in, and ideally facilitating, broad democratic processes (participating in democratic processes is more important than having experience facilitating a process, as facilitation is a skill that we encourage all to learn but that should not be a prerequisite for participation).
- The social forces organizing the people's assembly are willing to engage, or are experienced in engaging, in broad democratic processes guided by norms established, accepted, and self-enforced by the assembled body.

Key Components of the Assembly as Event

To make sure that the assembly as an event is effective, we recommend that each of the following be clearly articulated and in place:

- *Group norms and codes of conduct*. These should be co-constructed by the participants of the assembly, and should be crafted at the start of an assembly formation. These norms and codes should cover everything from how to facilitate a meeting, how to raise a question, how to raise an objection, how to keep the assembly from being dominated by a few individuals, how to check various forms of privilege and power, and how to arrive at decisions and conclusions. The norms and codes should be visited and/or referenced at each assembly event to ensure that all participants, old and new, know what they are and that they constitute the guiding operating principles of the assembly that ensure that it is productive and truly democratic.
- *Clear agenda*. To the greatest extent possible, everyone who attends the assembly should know the agenda before the meeting. Even when this has been communicated, it is essential that the agenda be reviewed at the beginning of each and every assembly meeting, so that all participants are clear on what it is and what the assembly is seeking to accomplish.
- *Clear goals and objectives*. Each assembly event should be clear about what it is hopes to accomplish. Is it trying to investigate an

issue, is it trying to address an issue (as in trying to solve it), or is it merely sharing information for folks to start investigating and deliberating on a question? This is critical to not wasting people's time and energy.

- *Clear and concise questions*. These are necessary for the assembly to sufficiently address a social question, engage in clear deliberations, and make sound decisions about how to address it. Bad questions can and will lead to run-on discussions and inconclusive deliberations.
- *Strong but even-handed facilitation*. We recommend that each assembly event have multiple facilitators playing mutually supportive roles. The facilitators must be prepared to move the agenda, move the process(es), and intervene when and where necessary to ensure that everyone is abiding by the assembly norms and codes of conduct.
- *Detailed note-taking*. It is critical that detailed notes are taken and disseminated. These are essential not only for detailing what deliberations and decisions have been made but also to hold the assembly as an institution accountable to itself and to the community.
- *Next steps and follow-up procedures*. At the end of each assembly event, the facilitators should reiterate what decisions have been made and which bodies or groups of the assembly are responsible for carrying them out, how, and by when. The facilitators should also move the group to ensure that each committee or working group has the capacity to fulfill its task or help it add to its capacity by recruiting more assembly participants to get involved. The People's Task Force is also tasked with making sure that each committee is clear about what its task is and has the resources it needs to accomplish its task, reiterating the deadline for accomplishing it and organizing more support for the committee, should that be necessary.

Key Components of the Assembly as a Process

Although the authority of the assembly is expressed to its highest extent during the mass "events," the real work of the assembly that enables it to exercise its power is carried out through the organizing bodies and processes of the assembly. The People's Task Force and various committees and working groups are the primary organizing bodies of the assembly. These bodies execute the work of the assembly—the outreach, networking, fundraising, communications, intelligence gathering, trainings, and campaigning.

In our people's assembly model, the People's Task Force serves as the coordinating committee of the assembly. The task force, a body directly elected by the assembly, serves at its will and is subject to immediate recall by the assembly (meaning that it can be replaced, with due process, at any time). The primary function of the assembly is to facilitate the work of the committees and the working groups, which includes ensuring that the committees and working groups regularly meet or meet as often as is deemed necessary; ensuring that each body has a facilitator, an agenda, and notetakers (if not provided by the committee or working group itself); facilitating communication between committees and working groups; ensuring that all of the actions of the committees and working groups are communicated thoroughly to the assembly; and coordinating the logistics for the assembly gatherings.

Committees are standing, meaning regularly constituted, bodies of the assembly that deal with certain functions and/or operations of the assembly. The basics include outreach and mobilization, media and communications, fundraising and finance, and security. Working groups are campaign- or project-oriented bodies. They emerge and exist to execute a decision of the assembly to accomplish certain time-limited goals and objectives. Examples drawn from our experience include working groups that successfully campaigned for the release of the Scott sisters, forced the federal government to provide more housing aid to internally displaced persons from New Orleans and the Gulf Coast after Hurricane Katrina, and successfully organized public transportation workers, in alliance with the assembly, to save Jackson's public transportation (JTRAN) and provide its workers with higher wages. All committees and working groups operate on a volunteer principle and, for the most part, committee and working group members participate on a self-selecting basis.

The Assembly as an Institution

Most people's assemblies are relatively short-lived bodies, existing only for weeks or months, which does not allow or enable them to become social institutions. The Jackson People's Assembly, in its present iteration (NAPO/MXGM organized a people's assembly in the early 1990s that fought the Ku Klux Klan and designated human rights veteran Henry Kirksey to be the first major Black candidate for mayor), has been in continuous operation since 2005. Unlike many other models or examples of people's assemblies, our model is focused on building an ongoing process and an enduring base of power. Sustainability is one thing that makes our assembly an institution, but it is not the only thing. What validates the assembly as an institution more than its staying power is its social weight, which is its ability to act as a "dual power" or counterweight to the policies and actions of the government and local and regional business interests (i.e., capital).

It is the combination of staying power and attained social weight that makes the people's assembly a social institution in its own right. It should be noted that becoming a counterweight or a dual power was not by accident, it was by design and required strategic thought, detailed planning, intensive education, capacity building, trust building, persistence, and determination. We mention this because we want to encourage all those who are considering building a people's assembly to take the task of building an institutional vehicle of dual power seriously, as we think this is the primary reason to build this type of social movement vehicle.

What an Assembly Can Accomplish

When we look at the experiences of various people's and social movements throughout history and throughout the world, we see that people's assemblies can and do wield different types of power (all contingent on factors of space, time, conditions, and the balance of forces). Throughout the world today, people's assemblies have been and are used to revolutionize people's daily lives, change the balance of power in societies, and in some recent instances have toppled governments and ushered in revolutionary change. Some examples include Nepal, Greece, Spain, Tunisia, Egypt, and Burkina Faso to name a few.

What follows is a brief breakdown of what people's assembles have accomplished and can accomplish, based on the aforementioned examples and many other historic examples.

- During periods of stability within the capitalist-imperialist nation-state system, when the markets and the government (i.e., the state) are able to project and maintain the status quo operations of the system, an assembly can push for various "positional" reforms and low- to mid-level autonomous projects. Positional reforms include things like advancing various policy reform campaigns (offensive or defensive), such as the implementation of local citizens' review or police control boards.[2] Examples of low- to mid-level autonomous projects include things like building "self-reliance"-oriented cooperatives, something we are currently working on in Jackson through Cooperation Jackson and initiatives it is pursuing like the Sustainable Communities Initiative.[3]

- During periods of progressive or radical upsurge, an assembly can push for structural reforms and engage in autonomous people-centered projects. One of the best examples of the exercise of this type of power is how the various assemblies in Venezuela were able to both push and enable the progressive administration of President Hugo Chávez to make radical changes to the nation-state's constitution between 1998 and 2010. Venezuela during this period is also a good example of what scalable autonomous projects can look like, such as the numerous cooperatives that were built, the housing developments that were constructed, and the significant land transfers that took place. Argentina during and after the 2001 crisis offers another critical example of how the assemblies there encouraged workers to seize numerous factories and turn them into cooperatives.
- During prerevolutionary periods, an assembly can function as a genuine "dual power" and assume many of the functions of the government (state). Perhaps the best example of this over the past ten years comes from the revolutionary movement in Nepal, where the revolutionary forces stimulated and organized assemblies to act as a direct counterweight to the monarchial government and the military, ultimately resulting in the establishment of a constitutional democracy and a more "representative" legislative body. Another recent example comes from Chiapas, Mexico, from 1994 until the mid-2000s, when the Zapatistas were able create extensive zones of "self-rule" and "autonomous production" that were governed by assemblies.
- During revolutionary periods, an assembly can effectively become the government (state) and assume control over the basic processes

and mechanisms of production. There have been a few experiences or examples of assemblies commanding this much power since the 1980s in places like Haiti, the Philippines, Nicaragua, Burkina Faso, and Grenada. Recent experiences that come closest are Egypt, in the winter of 2011 and the summer of 2013, and Nepal during various periods from 2003 to 2006.

- During periods of retreat, an assembly must defend the people and the leadership that has emerged and developed, fight to maintain as many of the gains it has won as possible, and prepare for the next upsurge. The experiences of the Lavalas movement in Haiti in the early 1990s and mid-2000s is perhaps the best example of how assemblies and other people's organizations can weather the storm of counterrevolutions and defeats.
- The leadership of an assembly should be able to make clear distinctions between these periods and understand how, why, and when to act as a counterhegemonic force during stable and prerevolutionary periods of the current social system, and how, why, and when to act as a hegemonic force during revolutionary periods. It must also be able to make distinctions during each period between acts of positioning (i.e., building allies, assembling resources, and changing the dominant social narratives, etc.) and acts of maneuvering (i.e., engagements of open confrontation and conflict with the repressive forces of the state and capital).

> "Do not be afraid of the people and persuade the people to take part in all of...the decisions which concern them—this is the basic condition of revolutionary democracy, which little by little we must achieve in accordance with the development of our struggle and our life."
> —Amílcar Cabral, "Apply Party Principles in Practice"

> "We're trying to get ourselves organized in such a way that we can become inseparably involved in an action program that will meet the needs, desires, likes or dislikes of everyone that's involved. And we want you involved in it.... We are attempting to make this organization one in which any serious-minded Afro-American can actively participate, and we welcome your suggestions at these

membership meetings.... We want your suggestions; we don't in any way claim to have the answers to everything, but we do feel all of us combined can come up with an answer.... With all of the combined suggestions and the combined talent and know-how, we do believe that we can devise a program that will shake the world."
—Malcolm X, "Afro-American History"

Notes

1 "Navigating the Storm," accessed May 6, 2022, https://tinyurl.com/2d7dw2wt.

2 As promoted by the Every 28 Hours Campaign, unavailable May 9, 2022, https://mxgm.org/the-black-nation-charges-genocide-our-survival-is-dependent-on-self-defense; also see "Operation Ghetto Storm," accessed May 9, 2022, http://www.operationghettostorm.org.

3 See "Sustainable Communities Initiative," Cooperation Jackson, accessed May 9, 2022, http://www.cooperationjackson.org/sustainable-communities-initiative.

The Jackson Rising Statement: Building the City of the Future Today

Kali Akuno for the Mayoral Administration of Chokwe Lumumba

Perspectives and Priorities of Mayor Chokwe Lumumba on the Development of Jackson, Mississippi

Jackson, Mississippi, is a city on the move. On June 4, 2013, the proud City of Jackson elected me to serve as its mayor to bring change to the city in the form of transparency, deep civic engagement, and economic reform and justice. By electing my administration, the people of Jackson made a clear statement that they are desiring fundamental change, are prepared to see it administered and, most importantly, want to play the leading role in implementing it.

Over the next four years, my administration will govern in accordance with human rights principles and standards. Our goal is to create equity for all. Through broad civic engagement, participatory and transparent governance, and sound fiscal management, we will build a sustainable future for Jackson.

This future will be grounded in the highest provision of public services in public works administration, city planning, economic development, education, health care, transportation and public safety. We also aim to build a dynamic new economy rooted in cooperative development and anchored by green jobs, living wages, and strong worker protections. The development of this new economy will be driven by the emerging human rights, workers, youth, immigrant, and green social movements in partnership with my administration and socially responsible businesses, investors, and philanthropies.

Contextualization: Where We Stand

Jackson, like many urban centers, is struggling to overcome decades of economic divestment, deindustrialization, suburban flight, a declining tax base, chronic under- and unemployment, poorly performing schools, and an antiquated and decaying infrastructure.

While addressing all of these interrelated issues is important, the one that will receive the greatest attention during my administration is the infrastructure crisis. In order to ensure the health of our residents and rebuild our infrastructure to revitalize the economic foundations of our city, we must improve our sewage, water treatment, and drainage systems, repave and rebuild our roads and bridges, expand our transportation systems, and modernize our energy systems.

The "Jackson Rising" conference will be held at Jackson State University on May 2–4, 2014. Come be part of participatory democracy. Help Jackson rise!

The most urgent infrastructure needs are our sewer and water treatment systems. In November 2012, the City of Jackson signed a consent decree with the Environmental Protection Agency, the Department of Justice, and the Mississippi Department of Environmental Quality to improve the sewer and water quality systems in the city.

The consent decree gives the City of Jackson seventeen years to overhaul our water treatment and sewage systems. The critical improvements to these systems will require hundreds of millions of dollars to properly address. If the city is unable to make these improvements at scheduled intervals, the consent decree may result in Jackson losing control of its sewage and water treatment systems. My administration is determined to ensure that Jackson will retain its control over these life sustaining systems.

Crises often present new opportunities. Jackson's infrastructure crisis can be a major catalytic opportunity for our city and our residents. Over the course of the next fifteen to twenty years, the City of Jackson will have to spend an estimated $1.2 billion to repair and upgrade its infrastructure. These infrastructure expenditures could potentially generate a short-term economic boom for the city.

However, the challenge is how will we finance these critical infrastructure expenses? The lion's share of the expense will be financed through bonds and other forms of debt financing. But relying on these means of finance alone will place an undue burden on future generations that my administration is determined to avoid.

Privatization is also not an option under any circumstances. Therefore, we are going to have to be very creative and innovative in our approach to solving this critical issue.

How We Will Govern

We believe that the creativity and innovation will come from the genius within our own community. We will stimulate and catalyze this genius by our practice and methodology of participatory and transparent governance. This methodology is grounded in my firm belief and grounding in human rights advocacy and promotion.

Human Rights Implementation

To ensure that the full complement of our residents' human rights are respected, protected, and fulfilled, my administration intends to implement the following policies and programs:

- *Human rights charter*. The charter will establish the legal standing, policy framework and institutional support of our municipality for the promotion and protection of our residents' human rights. We seek to institute the charter with the support and approval of the city council, through the passage of an ordinance establishing its full standing under the law.
- *Human rights commission*. The commission will serve as the implementing, enforcement and monitoring body for the charter and the general programs it commissions. The commission will specifically address issues of compliance, accountability, monitoring, and documentation pertaining to how the government fulfills its human rights obligations. The commission will work in consultative status very closely with civil society and the social movements of the city to fulfill its mission.
- *Human rights institute*. The institute will operate as a quasi-governmental but independent institution dedicated to human rights education and the broad promotion of human rights. The institute will focus on providing human rights education to all city employees and the community at large.

Jackson, Mississippi, made history during the civil rights movement and is making history again today—this time to strengthen, not destroy, human rights.

To design and develop these institutions, policies, and programs, my administration is working closely with various local partners, including the Jackson People's Assembly, the Malcolm X Grassroots Movement, the Mississippi NAACP, One Voice, the Veterans of the Mississippi Civil Rights Movement, the Mississippi Workers' Center for Human Rights, the Mississippi Association of Cooperatives, and the Mississippi Immigrant Rights Alliance, among others. On a national level, we are partnering with the Praxis Project, the Fund for Democratic Communities, the Human Rights Institute of Columbia Law School, the National Economic and Social Rights Initiative, the Human Rights Commission of Eugene, Oregon, and the US Human Rights Network.

Participatory and Transparent Governance

There are numerous ways my administration will strive to elicit the broadest and deepest participation of our residents to resolve the challenges confronting our city. Our aim is to turn our challenges into opportunities for the empowerment of our residents and the revitalization of our city.

Two prominent ways my administration will foster and encourage broad civic participation among our residents are through "participatory budgeting" processes and "people's assemblies."

Participatory budgeting. Participatory budgeting is a process of democratic decision-making that encourages residents to directly deliberate upon and determine budgetary allocations for the municipality. Our objective in engaging the participatory budgeting processes is to place more power in the hands of our residents and to deepen democracy in our community by making governance more participatory.

My administration is beginning to collaborate with organizations like the Fund for Democratic Communities, the Democracy Collaborative, and the Participatory Budgeting Project, preparing to introduce the participatory budgeting process to the city and to educate the government and the community on various ways it can be applied in Jackson. Our objective is to initiate the process in early 2014 to help us determine a portion of our 2014–15 annual budget that will be more directly controlled by our residents via their direct determination of how these resources should be allocated.

People's assemblies. People's assemblies are self-organized instruments of people's agency and power. As a human rights promoter and community organizer, I have always advocated and supported the development of people's assemblies as a means to give voice and power to those who have systematically been denied them in our society.

Over the years, as a member of community organizations like the Malcolm X Grassroots Movement, I have participated in organizing assemblies to elect the first Black mayor of Jackson, to give voice to those internally displaced by Hurricanes Katrina and Rita, and to give voice to the residents of Ward 2 and be directly accountable to them on an ongoing basis.

As mayor I fully intend to support the efforts of the Ward 2 People's Assembly, the People's Task Force, and the Malcolm X Grassroots Movement to build a citywide people's assembly. In addition to supporting people's assemblies, my administration will consistently consult the neighborhood associations and other institutions of civil society in our community as part of my commitment to build a more vibrant and participatory democracy in Jackson.

Good governance through human rights advocacy and protection, we believe, will encourage and mobilize our city to unite as a community and create the long-term solutions needed to solve our critical problems. In addition to human rights implementation and participatory governance, we believe that the implementation of our core campaign agenda will lay the foundation for the long-term revitalization of Jackson.

My Vision for the Future

"Building the city of the future today"—this is the prime directive of my administration. Through the practice of participatory democracy and transparent governance, we will establish the foundations for equity and prosperity that will sustain the city for the generations to come by concentrating on these four fundamental programmatic objectives for the redevelopment of Jackson.

Rebuilding and Redeveloping Jackson's Infrastructure

As noted above, Jackson must overhaul and rebuild its infrastructure if the city is going to revitalize itself. It is imperative that we rebuild our water management and waste treatment systems; become more efficient in our energy consumption; diversify our sources of energy; overhaul our streets, highways, and bridges; and create a comprehensive public transportation system.

Water management and waste treatment. We aim to completely overhaul these systems by removing all of our antiquated pipes, pumps, and refineries and replacing them with the most sustainable equipment and materials that we can access. We also aim to reduce water consumption by installing newer, more accurate and efficient meters, and by engaging in extensive community education campaigns to reduce extraneous consumption. We will also reduce hazardous runoff into our drainage systems by creating more stringent policies and penalties.

Energy efficiency. We aim to simultaneously diversify our energy sources and significantly reduce our consumption. We will start by retrofitting all of the city's buildings and facilities to ensure that they are energy efficient. We will also convert all of the city's light pole fixtures to ensure that they use solar power energy converters and efficient bulbs.

We aim to utilize as much solar and wind power as we can harness by supporting the building of solar power stations in several strategic locations throughout the city that are currently vacant or underutilized. We also aim to utilize several of these spaces to create wind farms to harness electricity. Further, we also aim to develop programs that will incentivize and subsidize the extensive cultivation of solar power in residential areas, businesses, and governmental properties.

Repaving our streets and rebuilding our highways and bridges. We aim to repave all of the major thoroughfares, arteries, and highways of our city (excluding interstate highways) that need repaving. In doing so, we will use the most eco-friendly and sustainable products currently available. We also intend to retrofit all of the bridges in our city, all of which are vital for transportation and trade in our metropolis.

Creating a comprehensive public transportation system. We aim to lay the foundation for the development of a comprehensive public transportation in our city, based on a fleet of clean energy buses, an energy efficient metro-rail system, and a comprehensive system of bike and walking trails.

Making Jackson the Greenest, Most Sustainable City in the Southeast

My administration is fully committed to building a sustainable future for our city and communities. Greening our infrastructure and transforming how we generate and consume energy is the critical first step. But it is only the first step. Additional steps we are committed to taking include creating a comprehensive recycling system, developing a zero-waste management system, eliminating the use of toxins in our community, creating a network of urban gardens and farms, and modernizing the city's policies and codes for procurements, contract bidding, and departmental operations to achieve this overall goal.

- *Recycling and zero waste.* We are going to design and implement a comprehensive recycling program for the city. The program will address not only government facilities but all of the city's residential and commercial facilities. We will also incentivize waste reduction at the source—in our households and businesses—by extensive education campaigns and policy change, such as pay-as-you-throw legislation.
- *Urban gardening and farming.* To effectively utilize our abundance of land, ensure the food security of our community, encourage and promote healthy eating habits, and create long-term employment opportunities in impoverished communities, my administration is promoting the growth and expansion of urban gardening and farming. We are strongly encouraging the development of urban farming cooperatives to produce "to scale" agricultural yields and serve the health and employment needs of our community.
- *Policy alignment.* In order to make Jackson the most sustainable city in the Southeast, we have to align our policies to meet our goals. In collaboration with the city council, my administration intends to overhaul all of our zoning, permitting, procurement, contracting, and bidding processes to ensure they reflect our vision and priorities and establish the means for my administration to accomplish our goals.

Jackson is located on several major trade routes and, with improved infrastructure, has ample opportunity for all its people to enjoy prosperity.

Redeveloping West, South, Northwest, and Downtown Jackson

To build equity in our marginalized and underserved communities, we are committed to concentrating our redevelopment resources in these strategic areas. Our objectives are to rehabilitate considerable portions of the existing housing stock in these communities to make them sustainable structures.

We are also going to develop new green, energy-efficient housing complexes in these communities. We also aim to incubate and attract businesses to provide jobs and serve these communities. To retain and attract more youth and talent to our city, we are committed to building a dynamic network of arts and entertainment venues to enhance and highlight the talents and gifts of Jackson's residents.

- *Housing*. My administration is fully committed to improving the overall housing stock of the city to retain our existing population and attract new, young, creative, and enterprising residents. We aim to create thousands of new affordable housing units in our target communities, utilizing the most sustainable and energy efficient methods and products available. We also aim to rehabilitate a substantial portion of our existing housing stock for historic preservation and affordability.
- *Business incubation and employment*. In order to revitalize our target communities, we have to attract and create new industries to provide employment for the residents in these communities and offer new retail and service businesses to serve their consumer needs. We are strongly encouraging the development of cooperative enterprises to serve these needs but are also aggressively recruiting businesses nationally and internationally.
- *Arts and culture*. Jackson is deeply connected to the Delta Blues and the artistic craftsmanship of the African American community. It is also steeped in the history of African American people for civil and human rights. My administration fully intends to celebrate and promote our culture, and honor the contributions of those who sacrificed for the fulfillment of many of our fundamental human rights, as no Jackson administration ever has. Our aim is to use this cultural capital as an engine to spur economic growth via tourism and the creation of creative zones to support artists and cultural workers and encourage them to produce social and economic value for our community.

Building a Dynamic New Economy Based on Cooperative Development

A central component of the economic development vision and strategy of my administration is the promotion and development of various cooperative enterprises. In alignment with our vision of sustainability and to address our employment and economic equity issues, we are particularly looking to stimulate and incubate green manufacturing industries.

We are also looking to encourage the growth of cooperatives in the health services, recycling, waste management, hauling, warehousing, retail, hospitality, and housing industries. My administration is developing the institutional capacity to promote, incubate, and develop cooperatives by committing a division of our Department of Planning and Development to this task.

We are also creating a strategic cooperative fund and developing technical assistance partnerships with organizations and institutions like the Fund for Democratic Communities, the Democracy Collaborative, the Federation of Southern Cooperatives, the Malcolm X Grassroots Movement, and Mondragon-USA among others.

The broader aspects of our work to develop a *new economy* for Jackson will encourage the growth of the private sector in the manufacturing, retail, and entertainment sectors and foster the development of various public-private partnerships with cooperatives, labor unions, credit unions, private enterprises, socially responsible banks and investors, and philanthropies.

- *Cooperative development.* Cooperatives are rapidly becoming engines of economic growth and employment stabilization in several urban centers struggling with historic divestment and deindustrialization that are comparable to Jackson, such as Cleveland and Cincinnati, Ohio, Reading, Pennsylvania, and Richmond, California. Jackson is in many respects poised to become the Mondragon of the United States, given its industrial infrastructure, strategic location along several trade routes (including I-20 connecting Atlanta to Dallas-Fort Worth and I-55 connecting New Orleans to Chicago), and historic knowledge and association with cooperative development from the mutual aid societies, credit unions, and farmers cooperatives developed in African American communities throughout the state.
- *Cooperative incubator.* As noted, the incubator will be housed in the Department of Planning and Development and will operate in partnership with numerous academic and nonprofit organizations from Jackson and throughout the United States and the world in

order to aid our communities and socially conscious entrepreneurs with the technical support they need to build sound businesses. These technical skills include business planning, market research and analysis, sustainable financing, financial and asset management, and worker-owner management and democracy.

- *Cooperative fund.* My administration is committed to creating this fund utilizing city and community development block grant funds. Given the infrastructural challenges we have noted, these funds will not be as substantial as we would like. However, our aim is to use these funds as strategic leverage to attract additional financial resources from philanthropies, credit unions, banks, socially responsible corporations, various types of capital funds, and individual donors and investors.

One of our first major initiatives promoting cooperative development is the "Jackson Rising: New Economies Conference." The "Jackson Rising" conference will be held May 2–4, 2014, at Jackson State University and will focus on educating our community about cooperative enterprises and how to start and run them effectively, in addition to addressing how cooperative development can benefit the City of Jackson and how we will build cooperatives in our community to build wealth and equity. We encourage all of the participants of the Neighborhood Funders Group Conference to join us at future conferences.

Moving Forward: Developing Strategic Partnerships to Serve Our Needs

To address our infrastructure crisis and accomplish this ambitious vision, broad unity and critical alignment will have to be achieved in our city. As stated before, we believe we can and will achieve the unity and alignment needed through the practice of good governance. Through this, we believe that we will be able to produce the majority of the resources we need to revitalize our community. But we won't secure all of the resources needed on our own.

We are going to have to secure some resources from the State of Mississippi and even more from the federal government. Given the growing political divisions at the state and federal levels, we doubt if we realistically will receive enough resources from these sources to meet our projected expenditures of $1.2 billion for our infrastructure overhaul, let alone the resources needed to redevelop our communities and improve our public education system.

To become the city of the future, the sustainable, cooperative city we envision, the City of Jackson must form strategic partnerships with philanthropies and other nongovernmental entities that promote and support human rights, social responsibility, transparency, civic engagement, participatory governance, community empowerment, sustainability, and cooperative development. We encourage all those who share our commitments and support our vision to join us in a strategic partnership on this trailblazing effort to make Jackson rise!

This article was first published at https://jacksonrising.wordpress.com/local/jackson-rising-statement.

Seek Ye First the Worker Self-Management Kingdom: Toward the Solidarity Economy in Jackson, Mississippi

Ajamu Nangwaya

> "We have to make sure that economically we're free, and part of that is the whole idea of economic democracy. We have to deal with more cooperative thinking and more involvement of people in the control of businesses, as opposed to just the big money changers, or the big CEOs and the big multinational corporations, the big capitalist corporations which generally control here in Mississippi."
> —Chokwe Lumumba, "Jackson, Mississippi, Mayor Elect Chokwe Lumumba on Economic Democracy" (2013)

> "Always bear in mind that the people are not fighting for ideas, for the things in anyone's head. They are fighting to win material benefits, to live better and in peace, to see their lives go forward, to guarantee the future of their children."
> —Amílcar Cabral, *Revolution in Guinea: Selected Texts* (1969)

I am happy to be a participant at the Eastern Conference for Workplace Democracy 2013 and to be in the presence of worker cooperators, advocates of labor or worker self-management, and comrades who are here to learn about and/or share your thoughts on the idea of workplace democracy and workers exercising control over capital.

Worker self-management or the practice of workers' controlling, managing, and exercising stewardship over the productive resources in the workplace has been with us since the nineteenth century. Workers' control of the workplace developed as a reaction to the exacting and exploitative working condition of labor brought on by capitalism and the Industrial Revolution. Many workers saw the emancipation of labor emerging from their power over the way that work was organized and the fruit of their labor distributed.

I believe we are living in a period that has the potential for profound economic, social, and political transformation from below. It might not seem that way when we look at the way that capitalism, racism, and patriarchy have combined to make their domination appear inevitable and unchallenged. But as long as we have vision and are willing to put in the work, we shall not perish. We shall win!

On June 4, 2013, the people of the City of Jackson, Mississippi, elected Chokwe Lumumba, a human rights lawyer and an advocate of the right to self-determination of Africans in the United States, as their mayor. That is a very significant political development. But that is not the most momentous thing about the election of Chokwe Lumumba. The most noteworthy element of Lumumba's ascension to the mayoral position is his commitment to economic democracy, "more cooperative thinking" and facilitating economic and social justice with and for the people of Jackson.

The challenge posed to us by this historical moment is the role that each of you will play in ensuring a robust program of worker cooperative formation and cooperative economics in Jackson. We ought to work with the Jackson People's Assembly, the Malcolm X Grassroots Movement, and other progressive forces to transform the City of Jackson into America's own Mondragon. It could have one possible exception. Jackson could become an evangelical force that is committed to spreading labor self-management and the social economy across the South and the rest of this society—the United States.

The promotion of the social economy and labor self-management could engage and attract Frantz Fanon's "wretched of the earth" onto the stage of history as central actors in the drama of their own emancipation. By promoting the social economy, labor self-management, and participatory democracy by civil society forces and structures (the assemblies), Chokwe and the social movement organizations in Jackson are privileging or heeding Amílcar Cabral's assertion that the people are not merely fighting for ideas.[1] They need to see meaningful change in their material condition. The development of a people controlled and participatory democratic economic infrastructure in Jackson would give concrete form to their material aspirations.

Cabral was a revolutionary from Guinea-Bissau in West Africa and his approach to organizing and politically mobilizing the people could provide insights and direction to our movement-building work. In order to build social movements with the capacity to carry out the task of social emancipation, we need to organize around the material needs of the people. The very projects and programs that we organize with the people should be informed by transformative values, a prefiguring of what will be obtained in the emancipated societies of tomorrow.

As an anarchist, I am not a person who is hopeful or excited by initiatives coming out of the state or elected political actors. More often than not, we are likely to experience betrayal: collaboration with the forces of domination by erstwhile progressives or a progressive political formation forgetting that its role should be to build or expand the capacity of the people to challenge the structures of exploitation and domination. I am of the opinion that an opportunity exists in Jackson to use the resources of the municipal state to build the capacity of civil society to promote labor self-management.

Based on the thrust of the Jackson-Kush Plan, which calls for the maintenance of autonomous, deliberative and collective decision-making people's assemblies and the commitment to organizing a self-managed social economy, which would challenge the hegemony or domination of the capitalist sector, I see an opening for something transformative to emerge in Jackson.[2] As revolutionaries, we are always seeking out opportunities to advance the struggle for social emancipation. We initiate actions but we also react to events within the social environment. To not explore the movement-building potential of what is going on this southern city would be a major political error and a demonstration of the poverty of imagination and vision.

Primary Imperatives or Assumptions

There are four critical imperatives or assumptions that should guide the movement toward labor self-management and the social economy in Jackson. They are as follows:

Build the Capacity of Civil Society

We should put the necessary resources into building the requisite knowledge, skills, and attitudes needed by the people to exercise control over their lives and institutions. In the struggle for the new society, we require independent, counterhegemonic organizational spaces from which to struggle against the dominant economic, social, and political structures.

In any labor self-management and social economy project in Jackson, we must develop autonomous, civil-society-based supportive organizations and structures that will be able to survive the departure of the Lumumba administration. If the social economy initiatives are going to operate independently of the state, they will need the means to do so. Therefore, the current municipal executive leadership in Jackson should turn over resources to the social movements that will empower and support them in their quest to create economic development organizations, programs, and projects.

Be Part of the Class Struggle, Racial Justice, and Feminist Movements

When we talk or think about social and economic change in the City of Jackson, it is not being done outside of a structural context. We are compelled to address the systems of capitalism, white supremacy/racism, and patriarchy and their impact on the lives of the working-class, racialized majority. It is critically important to frame the labor self-management and the solidarity economy project as one that is centered upon seeking a fundamental change to power relations defined by gender, race, and class.

The worker cooperative movement ought to see itself as a part of the broader class struggle movement that seeks to give control to the laboring classes over how their labor is used and the surplus or profit from collective work is shared. The solidarity economy and labor self-management will have to seriously tackle oppression coming out of the major systems of domination and allow our organizing work to be shaped by the resulting analysis.

Develop an Alternative Political Decision-Making Process—an Assembly System of Governance

The system of assemblies that is proposed in the Jackson-Kush Plan is the right approach to creating alternative participatory democratic structures. It is through these political instruments that the people will set the community's priorities and contest with the powers-that-be in the liberal capitalist political system.

As we strive to build the embryonic collectivistic economic structures of the future just society, we need the political equivalent. The latter should be of a scale that allows for direct democratic participation of the people. The federative principle can be used to link the community-based assemblies into a unified citywide, regional, or statewide body, whose role would be a coordinating one. Power must reside at the base where the people are located.

Displace Economic Predators Who Are Currently Located in Racialized, Working-Class Communities

In working-class Afrikan communities across the United States, there are economic predators that exploit and dominate the local business scene. These petty capitalists must be seen for what they are: business operators who do not normally employ the people in the local community. They live—and spend the wealth generated in the community—elsewhere. We do not need to search hard for business ideas or opportunities because the existing capitalists and their businesses should become targets for replacement with worker cooperatives and other solidarity economy enterprises. If these existing owners would like to become worker-cooperators, they are free to join the labor self-managed enterprises.

The City of Jackson could contribute to worker cooperative development in a number of areas. It could make a material contribution in the areas by providing technical assistance, financing, procurement, and contract set-aside for worker cooperatives, and education and the promotion of worker self-management and the social economy.

Be an Evangelical Promoter of Worker Self-Management and the Social Economy

The City of Jackson's Office of Economic Development is the chief organ that facilitates business development. Its mandate is "to maximize the city's potential as a thriving center for businesses, jobs, robust neighborhoods and economic opportunity for everyone in the Capital City.... [It] supports business and the development community within city government and between city agencies. It also partners with other organizations to further economic development." However, the terms of reference should be expanded to specifically state that it "promotes worker cooperatives, consumer cooperatives, and other social economy enterprises as instruments to create economic security, jobs, livable wages, economic development, and economic democracy."

Furthermore, the Office of Economic Development should be empowered to vigorously, strategically, and relentlessly create the enabling conditions for the development of worker cooperatives and other social enterprises in Jackson. A part of its worker or labor self-management agenda should include transforming the City of Jackson into a catalyst for this approach to workplace democracy: workers' control of the means of production and the producers of wealth being the ones who determine how the economic surplus or profit shall be distributed. This new role for the Office of Economic Development will be startling to some and is likely to generate opposition. But Mayor Lumumba ought to borrow a play from the playbook of conservative governments: move with lightning speed in implementing his administration's policies in the first two years and keep the opposition dizzy, disoriented, and playing catch-up. Lumumba has a mandate to include labor self-management by way of worker cooperatives. The economic development plank in the mayor's election platform stated that he is committed to "build[ing] co-ops and green industry" and ensuring "that Jacksonians are well-represented with jobs and business ownership." [3] Labor self-management, cooperatives of all types, and social enterprises are the tools needed to give form to his electoral commitment. Jamilah King also interprets Lumumba's platform in a similar fashion: "In his campaign literature and in news media interviews, Mayor Lumumba stressed that his economic program will incorporate principles of the 'solidarity economy.' Solidarity economy is a[n] umbrella term used to describe a wide variety of alternative economic activities, including worker-owned cooperatives, cooperative banks, peer lending, community land trusts, participatory budgeting and fair trade."[4]

Larry Hales correctly asserts that "Lumumba's political history did not scare away voters, nor did the bold and progressive Jackson Plan, which is reminiscent of the Republic of New Afrika's program of the 1960s, calling for the establishment of an independent, Black-led government in five former confederate states."[5] The City of Jackson should move ahead and start implementing the solidarity economy mandate. Mayor Lumumba should immediately hire a team of solidarity economy and labor self-management personnel, whose principal role would be to bring about the condition for the economic democracy takeoff.

They would be embedded in the Office of Economic Development and at least one of the positions should be a senior leadership/

management one. The latter is needed to communicate Lumumba's seriousness about the social economy thrust of his administration and to give the necessary clout to the economic democracy team to get the work done. Lumumba, the Malcolm X Grassroots Movement, and the Jackson People's Assembly will have to get out into the community and in all available spaces to educate the people about labor self-management and the solidarity economy.

Education and Conscientization for Worker Self-Management

The people have been long exposed to the capitalist approach to economic development and it is quite fair to assert that the ideas of capitalism are dominant on the question of economic efficacy. The people might have a critique of capitalism but it is generally seen as the only game in town, especially with the demise of the former Soviet Union and with it bureaucratic, authoritarian state socialism. In this context, Bob Marley's exhortation to the people to "emancipate yourself from mental slavery/None but ourselves can free our minds" is very instructive.

The preceding verses from Marley's "Redemption Song" implicitly call on us to engage in critical education about oppression and emancipation. As worker self-management practitioners and/or advocates, our educational programs would also provide the necessary knowledge, skills, and attitudes to operate worker cooperatives, other social enterprises, and the enabling labor self-management structures. Therefore, the educational initiatives would be directed at facilitating worker self-management and the social economy and political/ideological consciousness-raising.

In carrying out this educational program, the method of teaching and learning should mimic the democratic economic development method that we are pursuing. We are not seeking to reinscribe authoritarian, leadership-from-above ways of teaching and learning. I believe ancestor Ella Baker, an advocate of participatory democracy and an organizer within the Afrikan Liberation Movement in the United States, was onto something when she declared, "Give people light and they will find a way."[6]

We are not seeking mastery over the people. The goal is to engender in the laboring classes an appreciation and consciousness of the transformative possibilities and to move toward their realization. As Paulo Freire in his *Pedagogy of the Oppressed* reminds us, "Leaders who do not act dialogically, but insist on imposing their decisions, do not organize the people—they manipulate them. They do not liberate, nor are they liberated: they oppress."[7]

One of the admirable features of labor self-management is its commitment to placing the power of economic self-determination in the hands of the worker-cooperators. Education has long been an instrument for igniting the passion for emancipation within the radical or revolutionary sections of the labor self-management movement. Mayor Lumumba is very much aware of the educational task ahead in developing the social economy: "And this will bring about more public education and political education to the population of the city, make our population more prepared to be motivated and organized in order to participate in the changes which must occur in the City of Jackson in order to move it forward. We say the people must decide. 'Educate, motivate, organize.'"[8]

Mayor Lumumba and his civil society allies can carry out the following educational initiatives to advance worker cooperatives and the social economy:

- hire worker cooperative educators and developers to staff the Office of Economic Development;
- execute professional development education of all city personnel with economic and business development responsibilities;
- educate institutional actors such as hospitals, educational institutions, and the city's bureaucracy about the economic virtue of purchasing from worker cooperatives and other social enterprises that are located in Jackson;
- organize labor self-management and social economy workshops for all relevant elected municipal officials and their staff;
- develop a public education campaign to educate the people about worker cooperatives, labor self-management, and the social economy;
- enlist the support of the United States Worker Cooperative Federation, regional worker cooperative federations, and cooperative educators in designing a worker cooperative/labor self-management education training manual and program;
- develop a three-year social economy and worker self-management education pilot project in an elementary, junior high, and high school;

- infuse materials on the social economy and labor self-management in all business and economics courses in the elementary and secondary school curricula;
- engage in dialogue with the colleges and universities in the City of Jackson to add courses and programs on the social economy and labor self-management;
- work with colleges, universities, and the state on workforce-adjustment or retraining programs that prepare workers for cooperative and labor self-management entrepreneurship.

Technical Assistance

Jackson's Business Development Division provides prospective business operations with advice on preparing their business plans, site selection, and access to financial resources. Its role and that of other entities within the city's bureaucracy should be enhanced to provide business formation and development technical assistance to prospective worker cooperatives and other social economy businesses. The City of Jackson's technical assistance provision role could include the following:

- work with civil society groups and the postsecondary institutions in the region to create a civil-society-based technical assistance provider organization that would facilitate the formation and development of worker cooperatives and other social economy businesses;
- sell a city-owned building at the nominal price of $1 to a community-based labor self-management and social economy technical assistance provider;
- aid the technical assistance provider to create a labor self-management and social economy incubator to increase the survival rate of these firms;
- provide assistance and advice on the identification of business creation opportunities and the development of feasibility studies and business plans;
- provide training and development opportunities to social enterprises that would allow them to bid for city contracts.

Financing Labor Self-Management

One of the most serious challenges faced by small businesses is their limited access to investment and working capital. We have to find creative ways to build organizations that are able to mobilize capital for labor self-management and other social economy projects. The City of Jackson currently provides grants and incentives to businesses so as to attract investment dollars. It can expand the criteria to include worker cooperatives, other cooperatives, and social enterprises. Among the financial policies that could be explored, the city could:

- Encourage worker cooperatives and other cooperatives to apply for its matching business grants in the Small Business Development Grant Program and the Storefront Improvement Grant, which provides up to $15,000 to recipients.
- Create a Social Economy Development Grant Program that provides up to $30,000 to worker cooperatives and other social economy firms that employ at least seven employees, invest at least $100,000 (20 percent of which can be sweat equity), and hire at least 75 percent of the workers from within Community Development Block Grant eligible areas.
- Create a Social Economy Feasibility and Business Plan Grant that provides a one-to-one matched funding grant of up to $10,000.
- Create a credit union that is committed to facilitating cooperative entrepreneurship and community economic development.
- Collaborate with credit unions to expand their capacity to serve as agents for cooperative economic development.
- Work with civil society organizations to create a cooperative and social enterprise loan fund. The revolving loan fund Cooperative Fund of New England [now the Cooperative Fund of the Northeast] could be used as a model for the provision of startup and working capital to social economy entities.
- Capitalize the cooperative and social economy loan fund with a $300,000 grant over four years that would be matched at a two-to-one ratio from foundations, trade unions, and other social movement organizations and/or other levels of government.
- Procure funding for a labor self-management and social economy incubator that is operated by a civil-society-based organization.
- Seek funds to support the matched savings instrument called individual development accounts. Prospective worker-cooperators would use their accumulated savings to capitalize their labor self-managed enterprises. This matched-savings program would

enable worker cooperators in developing their business plans through its accompanying educational component.

The city could also support labor self-management and social economy projects through its procurement and equal opportunity programs by taking the following initiatives:

- create procurement opportunities for worker cooperatives and other social economy businesses, including those with only a few worker-cooperators or employees and a small annual turnover;
- establish business or contracting set-asides that are exclusively directed at worker cooperatives and other social economy businesses;
- include worker cooperatives in equal opportunity or affirmative action business program established by the city;
- develop subcontracting opportunities for cooperative businesses on the city's infrastructure development projects;
- develop the creative capacity to ensure that labor self-managed and social economy firms are able to participate in business opportunities with the City of Jackson.

Conclusion

We have to build the road as we travel. All of our organizing work should be directed at developing the capacity of the oppressed to act independently of the structures of domination. The Lumumba administration, the Jackson People's Assembly, and the Malcolm X Grassroots Movement have an opportunity to use the resources of the municipal state to advance labor self-management and the solidarity economy.

The worker cooperative movement and progressive entities across the United States should support the civil society forces in Jackson in their effort to build the supportive organizations and structures to engender labor self-management and the solidarity economy. The labor self-management and social economy work being advanced in Jackson ought to be geared toward the purpose of social emancipation and placing the people in the driver's seat in creating history.

I would like to close with a statement by the Italian anarchist Errico Malatesta who captures the spirit in which we ought to wage struggle and create a participatory-democratic culture within the movement for emancipation:

> We who do not seek power, only want the consciences of [the masses]; only those who wish to dominate prefer sheep, the better to lead them. We prefer intelligent workers, even if they are our opponents, to anarchists who are such only in order to follow us like sheep. We want freedom for everybody; we want the masses to make the revolution for the masses. The person who thinks with [her] own brain is to be preferred to the one who blindly approves everything.... Better an error consciously committed and in good faith, than a good action performed in a servile manner.[9]

This essay was first published on Pambazuka News, September 18, 2013, https://www.pambazuka.org/governance/seek-ye-first-worker-self-management-kingdom.

Notes

1 Amílcar Cabral, *Revolution in Guinea: Selected Texts* (New York: Monthly Review Press, 1969), 86.
2 Malcolm X Grassroots Movement and the Jackson People's Assembly, "The Jackson Plan: A Struggle for Self-determination, Participatory Democracy and Economic Justice," July 12, 2012, accessed June 20, 2022, https://socialistproject.ca/2012/07/b664.
3 Jamilah King, "Solidarity Economy: Jackson Mississippi Goes Radical," Grassroots Economic Organizing, accessed June 27, 2022, https://geo.coop/content/solidarity-economy-jackson-missippi-goes-radical.
4 Jamilah King, "Mayor Chokwe Lumumba Wants to Build a 'Solidarity Economy' in Jackson, Miss," *Colorlines*, July 2, 2013, accessed June 27, 2022, https://www.colorlines.com/articles/mayor-chokwe-lumumba-wants-build-solidarity-economy-jackson-miss.
5 Larry Hales, "The Political, Historical Significance of Chokwe Lumumba Mayoral Win in Jackson, Miss.," *Workers World*, June 25, 2013, accessed June 27, 2022, https://www.workers.org/2013/06/9664.
6 Barbara Ransby, *Ella Baker and the Black Freedom Movement: A Radical Democratic Vision* (Chapel Hill: University of North Carolina Press, 2003), 105.
7 Paulo Freire, *Pedagogy of the Oppressed* (New York: Continuum, 2005), 178.
8 Monica Moorehead, "People's Assembly's Platform Brings Mayoral Victory for Chokwe Lumumba," *Workers World*, June 11, 2013, accessed June 20, 2022,https://www.workers.org/2013/06/9423.
9 Cited in Michael Schmidt and Lucien van der Walt, *Black Flame: The Revolutionary Class Politics of Anarchism and Syndicalism* (Oakland: AK Press, 2009), 184.

III

BUILDING SUBSTANCE

Jackson Rising: An Electoral Battle Unleashes a Merger of Black Power, the Solidarity Economy, and Wider Democracy

Carl Davidson

Nearly five hundred people turned out over the May 2–4, 2014, weekend for the "Jackson Rising" conference in Jackson, Mississippi. It was a highly successful and intensive exploration of Black power, the solidarity economy, and the possibilities unleashed for democratic change when radicals win urban elections.

The gathering drew urban workers and rural farmers, youth and the elderly, students and teachers, men and women. At least half were people of color. About fifty were from the City of Jackson itself and most were from other southern states. But a good deal came from across the country, from New York to the Bay area, and a few from other countries—Canada, South Africa, Venezuela, and Zimbabwe.

The major sponsors included the Malcolm X Grassroots Movement, the Federation of Southern Cooperatives, Praxis Project, Southern Grassroots Economies Project, the US Solidarity Economy Network, and the US Social Forum. Funding came from Community Aid and Development, Inc., the Mississippi Association of Cooperatives, the Coalition for a Prosperous Mississippi, the Fund for Democratic Communities, the Ford Foundation, the Wallace Action Fund, the Surdna Foundation, and the Rosa Luxemburg Foundation.

But to grasp the meaning and significance of this meeting, a step back to see how it began—and why it almost didn't happen—is required.

The conference was the brainchild of Jackson's late Mayor Chokwe Lumumba and one group of his close supporters, the Malcolm X Grassroots Movement (MXGM), soon after he was elected on June 4, 2013, and had placed his people in a few key city positions. They had initiated the conference, which was then endorsed by the city council, to help shape and economic development plan for the city and the outlying Black-majority rural areas, known as the "Kush"—hence the name of the overall project, the "Jackson-Kush Plan."

Chokwe Lumumba was rooted in the Black revolutionary organization, the Republic of New Afrika (RNA), which claimed the Black-majority areas of several states in the Deep South. He was one of its leading members, and a widely respected civil rights attorney. The RNA also had an economic outlook, a form of cooperative economics through the building of "New Communities"—named after *ujamaa*, a Swahili word for *extended family*, promoted by former Tanzanian president Julius Nyerere. The new mayor connected this core idea with the long-standing role of cooperatives in African American history, the experience of the Mondragon co-ops in Spain, and the solidarity economy movement that had emerged and spread from the Third World in recent decades. Together, all these ideas merged in the mayor's project, "Cooperation Jackson."

Lumumba's election had taken Jackson's political elite off guard. Making use of the Mississippi Freedom Democratic Party to run as an independent in the Democratic primary, he defeated the incumbent and forced a runoff. Given that Jackson is an 80 percent Black city, he then won overwhelmingly. So when he died suddenly of heart failure on February 25, 2014, with his supporters in a state of shock, his opposition moved quickly to counterattack. The MXGM, the People's Assembly, and other pro-Chokwe groups now had two tasks, trying to get Chokwe's son, Chokwe Antar Lumumba, elected mayor while continuing to plan the conference, but with city support on hold.

Lumumba, thirty-one years old, lost to Tony Yarber, 46 percent to 54 percent. Chokwe Antar received over 65 percent of the Black vote, but the turnout had dropped. The Yarber team immediately moved to fire all the Choke sympathizers from city government and tried to sabotage the conference. Local right-wing web publications attacked it as "thinly veiled communism."

A Tale of Two Cities

What is behind this antagonism? Jackson is indeed a tale of two cities, on the cusp of two competing visions. Given its demographics, any mayor is likely to be Black, but what that can mean is another matter. Just driving around the city gives you a quick glimpse of the problem. While the largest city in the state and the capitol, replete with major government buildings, the city is eerily quiet and empty. There are a few upscale areas but also large areas of older, wood-framed housing of the unemployed and the working poor. There are huge fairgrounds but little in the way of basic industry.

Two paths emerged. One was neoliberal and aimed at exporting as much of the Black poor as possible in order to open up wider areas for gentrification attracting the better-paid servants of the businesses that served government. The other was progressive, the Cooperation Jackson plan, which aimed at growing new worker-owned businesses and new housing co-ops that worked in tandem with the Black farmers of the "Kush." It also stressed democratized city services, while creating new alternative energy and recycling start-ups and also taking advantage of the city's position as a major regional transport hub. It's a conflict not unique to Jackson and shared by many cities around the country. Here's the four points summing up "Cooperation Jackson":

- Cooperation Jackson is establishing an educational arm to spread the word in their communities about the distinct advantages and exciting possibilities of mutual uplift that business cooperatives offer.
- When Mayor Chokwe Lumumba was still in office, Cooperation Jackson planned to establish a "cooperative incubator" providing a range of start-up services for cooperative enterprises. Absent support from the mayor's office, some MXGM activists observed, a lot of these co-ops will have to be born and nurtured in the cold.
- Cooperation Jackson aims to form a local federation of cooperatives to share information and resources and to ensure that the cooperatives follow democratic principles of self-management that empower their workers. "We've always said 'free the land,'" observed one MXGM activist. "Now we want to 'free the labor' as well."
- Finally, Cooperation Jackson intends to establish a financial institution to assist in providing credit and capital to cooperatives.

The conference project thus found itself in the eye of a storm. But with luck and some judicious tactics one key figure, Jackson State University president Carolyn Meyers, decided to stick with MXGM and allowed the conference to continue its plans on her campus using the huge Walter Payton Center and two classroom buildings. A last-minute fundraising blitz pulled in enough resources to squeeze through and make it happen.

When the hundreds of registered participants poured into the huge hall Friday evening and saw it filling up, one could sense the excitement and rising spirit of solidarity amid diversity. The opening plenary keynote speakers included: Jessica Gordon Nembhard of the US Solidarity Economy Network; Wendell Paris of the Federation of Southern Coops/Land Assistance Fund and Cornelius Blanding, special projects director of that organization; Ed Whitfield of the Southern Grassroots Economies Project based in North Carolina; and Kali Akuno of Jackson's MXGM.

Gordon Nembhard started off. A professor at John Jay College in New York, she recently published *Collective Courage: A History of African American Cooperative Economic Thought and Practice*, a groundbreaking study on the topic. "Courage is a word I had to use," she explained. "Everywhere I turned, from the early efforts of free Blacks to buy others in their family out of slavery to the Underground Railroad to burial societies and other clandestine forms of mutual aid, it took courage to motivate all these cooperative forms of resistance to slavery and white supremacy, from the beginning down to our own times."

She gave the example of Fannie Lou Hamer, well known as a founder of the Mississippi Freedom Democratic Party, who was in the battles in Mississippi in the 1960s: "But do we know her as a co-op member, a group that sustained her when she was denied an income. As Ms. Hamer put it, 'Until we control our own food, land, and housing, we can't be truly empowered.'"

Wendell Paris who, as a young Student Nonviolent Coordinating Committee worker was mentored by Ms. Hamer, continued the theme: "Land is the basis for revolution and it is important for us to hold on to our land base." He described the workings of the Panola Land Buyers Association in Sumter County, Alabama: "Freedom isn't free. In the training to run co-ops successfully, you learn more than growing cucumbers. You learn organizing and administration, the training ground for taking political offices."

At different times during introductions, or even in the remarks of speakers, the chant, "Free the Land!" would rise from the participants, accompanied by raised fists. This came from the RNA tradition, referring to an older battle cry of self-determination for the Black areas of the

Deep South. It clearly still had resonance, and was often followed with "By Any Means Necessary!"

The opening session was closed out by comments from Ed Whitfield and Kali Akuno. "All successful enterprises produce a surplus," said Whitefield, "and our empowerment runs through retaking the surplus we have created and putting it to uses that best serve us. We're not here making excuses. We're here making history. As long as we accept the current economic structures and approaches to development that flow from those structures and paradigms, we can't get out of bondage."

Akuno added:

> It's an uphill climb here in Mississippi. The Republican Tea Party government we have on a state level is not in favor at all of what we're trying to push through cooperative development. There was a bill supporting cooperatives that they killed earlier this year. On a municipal level, we are looking to transform all of the procurement policies of the city, all of the environmental regulations and standard policies within the city, and particularly all of the land-use policies in the city, that will support cooperatives. On the more practical side, we are launching a new organization from this conference called Cooperation Jackson, and it is going to be the vehicle by which all of the follow-through is going to be carried out.

But the municipal battle, Akuno concluded, would be difficult given the neoliberal, repressive, and pro-gentrification policies of the new team in charge. All the items presented by the opening speakers expressed the common theme of the conference organizers—putting political power in the hands of the Black masses and their allies, then anchoring and using that power to shape and grow a cooperative economic democracy that would serve the vast majority. It was both a tribute to Chokwe Lumumba and an expression of his vision. Winning it, however, would not come easy.

The next day, Saturday, was a different story. Here space was opened up for more than thirty diverse workshops, spread out over three time slots, with two more plenary sessions. Topics included the influence of Mondragon, community land trusts, Black workers and the AFL-CIO, the communes in Venezuela, mapping the solidarity economy, co-ops on a global scale, waste management and recycling, working with legislatures, and many more. No one report can cover them all, but here's the flavor of a few.

Mondragon and the Union Co-op Model

What were the nuts and bolts of Spain's Mondragon Corporation and how could unions serve as allies in creating similar enterprises in the US? This was the question posed at an excellent workshop with three presenters: Michael Peck, the US representative of Mondragon; Kristen Barker of the Cincinnati Union Coop Initiative; and Dennis Olson of the United Food and Commercial Workers.

Peck began with a brief overview of the Mondragon Corporation and its 120 co-ops and their accomplishments. The key point: In Mondragon, workers own their labor but rent their capital, rather than the other way around. "But sometimes," he noted, "you can tell more about something by look[ing] at one of its failures than all its successes."

He was referring to the fact that a major Mondragon co-op, Fagor, which made kitchen appliances, recently closed down. "The housing market in Spain and Europe collapsed and without new homes, new appliance sales sank. Plus, there was tough price competition from Asia." The corporation had carried Fagor for several years but could no longer justify it. Despite anger, "the vote of the workers to close it was unanimous." In the regular world, the workers would get their pink slips and be on the street.

But Mondragon was different. "Mondragon first set up a solidarity fund with every worker donating 1.5 percent of their salary, adding up to some fifteen million euros," he explained. "This was to cushion the transition. Then it worked to reassign all the Fagor workers to other co-ops, which it has now accomplished for the large majority." Peck added that Mondragon would continue creating new co-ops both in Spain and around the world, and the true test was not that some would eventually close, which was natural, but what happened when they did.

Kristen Barker then gave the workshop an enthusiastic account of how a small group in Cincinnati, armed with only a few good ideas, had over four years moved to a point where three substantial co-ops were opening in the city and several more were in the works. "We were really inspired when we heard of the agreement between Mondragon and the United Steelworkers," said Barker. "Our effort also stands on the shoulders of the Evergreen Coops in Cleveland. To date, Evergreen has launched three co-ops: Evergreen Laundry, Ohio Cooperative Solar that offers energy retrofits and solar panel installation, and Green City Growers that grows high-end lettuce for hotels and restaurants in

Cleveland. They have dozens of potential cooperatives in the pipeline. We are partnering with the major players of this initiative including the Ohio Employee Ownership Center for our unique project."

The first three co-ops in Cincinnati, Barker added, were Sustainergy, a building trades co-op to retrofit buildings to better environmental standards; the Cincinnati Railway Manufacturing Cooperative, which will make undercarriages for rail cars and has partnered with both the United Steel Workers and the local NAACP; and Our Harvest, a food hub co-op, which starts with local farms and takes their produce to a central site for packaging and marketing. It's partnered with the United Food and Commercial Workers International Union (UFCW) and other agricultural groups. Dennis Olson explained how the UFCW was particularly helpful in connecting growers through the distribution centers to the unionized grocery chains, as opposed to Walmart.

"We only had a small study group to start—some community organizers, some Catholic nuns, a few union people," concluded Barker. "But we did a lot of research, made partners, and got the word out in the media. Soon we had more people calling with more ideas, like co-op grocery stores in 'food desert' areas, jewelry makers' co-ops and so on. We started getting some interest from the city, and now things are taking off."

Starting Co-ops in Jackson and the "Kush"

This session was chaired by John Zippert of the Federation of Southern Cooperatives. He started with an excellent short summary of "Cooperatives 101" but quickly turned to drawing out the workshop participants on their concerns. Most were Black women from Jackson—one was interested in whether an African hair care products and services co-op was possible; another wanted to start a co-op of home health-care workers. One man from Memphis said he had a small business distributing African products to small Black stores in the surrounding states, but he was getting on in years. How could he turn it into a co-op that would live after him? Everyone shared ideas and legal options.

As the session ended, I ran into Ben Burkett, a Black farmer who is locally active in the Indian Springs Farmers Association, part of the "Kush." I knew he was also president of the National Family Farm Coalition, but I asked him more about his local operation. "Well, I don't do cotton anymore, not much cotton in Mississippi these days," he explained. "I do many vegetables, and sweet potatoes are a good crop.

But it's one thing for a farmer to grow and dig sweet potatoes. It's quite another to have the equipment to scrub them, cut them into French fries, and then bag and store them, while getting them quickly to your markets. That's where the value of the co-op comes in. We can pool our resources for these things, and it makes a big difference. We'd be in bad shape without the co-op."

Waste Management, Recycling, and City Politics

The politics of garbage was the main topic here. Chaired by Kali Akuno, this workshop gave the most insight into what was going on in Jackson as a new and backward regime was replacing that of Chokwe Lumumba. "Waste Management serves the city poorly," said Akuno. "It often ignores our neighborhoods. It does no recycling; it dumps the waste in a landfill in a small city to the north of here, gives them a payment, and that's the end of it."

Akuno explained they had a different plan. Since a large part of the city's budget deals with services like these, they wanted to break them into smaller pieces so local contractors or co-ops could bid on them, then recycle the waste into a revenue stream. In addition to helping the environment and employment, it would keep the money circulating locally.

"Another piece was setting up an incubator to foster the development of cooperatives," Akuno added. "The government can't run the co-ops. It won't build them, but it can set the table. For most of the past twenty years, even though there has been a succession of Black mayors, 90–95 percent of contracts go to people who don't live in Jackson. [Our plan, on the other hand], was all about hiring people in Jackson." "Now everything is going to be a fight," he added. "Even if your plan is reasonable and sustainable, it won't matter if it's stepping on the wrong toes."

Saturday also included two mealtime plenary sessions: one at lunch, featuring the diverse organizations taking part, and the other at dinner, giving everything an international dimension.

The lunch plenary included Omar Freilla of Green Workers Cooperatives, Steve Dubb of the Democracy Collaborative, Michael Peck of Mondragon-USA, Ricky Maclin of New Era Windows, Saladin Muhammad of Black Workers for Justice, and MaryBe McMillan, secretary treasurer of the North Carolina AFL-CIO.

"Community cooperatives," said Steve Dubb, "can be considered part of a long civil rights movement that fights for both racial and economic justice. For example, Dr. Martin Luther King in the last year of his life helped launch the Poor People's Campaign for an Economic Bill of Rights. The return of cooperatives to the movement, as illustrated by what's happening here, is a welcome development."

MaryBe McMillan stressed the importance of both labor and the concentration of forces in the South. "Why organize in the South? Because what happens in the South affects the entire nation." Speaking for Black workers, Saladin Muhammed added, 'We need power not just democracy; we need power that shapes what democracy looks like. When plants shut down, workers should seize control and turn them into cooperatives."

The evening session started with a tribute to Chokwe Lumumba by his son, Chokwe Antar Lumumba. "We are victorious because we struggle. I'm not afraid of the term 'revolutionary.' We need to be as revolutionary as the times require. Free the land! The struggle my father started is not over, but only beginning. It continues, by any means necessary." Also featured were Françoise Vermette of Chantier de l'Economie Sociale in Quebec, Pierre Laliberté of the International Labor Organization in Switzerland, Mazibuko Jara of *Amandla!* magazine in South Africa, Elbart Vingwe, Organization of Collective Cooperative in Zimbabwe, Omar Sierra, deputy consul general of Venezuela in Boston, and Janvieve Williams Comrie, Green Worker Coops in the US.

"Freeing the land has given our people a new sense of belonging," said Omar Sierra, of Venezuela. "Chokwe Lumumba extended his solidarity to us in a time of need. Our people are saddened by his passing and will not forget him."

William Copeland, a cultural organizer from Detroit, summed up the spirit of the crowd: "These presentations demonstrate the international significance of the Black Liberation Movement and southern movement building."

On Sunday morning, those who had not needed to leave early for the airport gathered in a large session of the whole that closed out the weekend. One after another, people stood up and testified to how their consciousness had been altered by their discussions and new experiences over the weekend. Emily Kawano of the Solidarity Economy Network made the point of understanding that the projects ahead, while including co-ops, also reached beyond them to other forms, such as participatory budgeting, public banks, and alternative currencies.

Finally, at an auspicious moment, an African American women rose and in a strong church choir voice began singing an old civil rights anthem, "Organize, organize, organize!" Everyone was on their feet, hands clapping, fists raised, and interspersing "Free the Land!" with the chorus. It couldn't have had a better closing moment.

This article was first published on Keep on Keepin' On, May 9, 2014, accessed June 27, 2022, http://carldavidson.blogspot.com/2014/05/jackson-rising-electoral-battle.html.

Jackson Rising: Black Millionaires Won't Lift Us Up but Cooperation and the Solidarity Economy Will

Bruce A. Dixon

For a long time now we've been fed and been feeding each other the story that uplifting Black communities means electing more faces of color to public office and creating more Black millionaires. Those wealthy and powerful African Americans, in the course of their wise governance and their normal business and philanthropic efforts can be counted on to create the jobs and the opportunities needed to largely alleviate poverty and want among the rest of us. The only problem with this story is that it's not working and in fact never really did work.

It was a myth, a fable, a grown-up fairy tale that told us nothing about how the world and this society actually functioned. In the real world, we now have more Black faces in corporate board rooms, more Black elected officials, and more Black millionaires than ever before, alongside record and near-record levels of Black child poverty, Black incarceration, Black unemployment, and the loss of Black land and wealth. The fortunes of some of our most admired Black multimillionaires, like Junior Bridgeman and Magic Johnson, rest firmly on the continued starvation wages and relentless abuse of the workers in their hundreds of fast food and other restaurants.

Over the first weekend in May 2014, about 320 activists from all over the country, including 80 or more from Jackson and surrounding parts of Mississippi, converged on the campus of Jackson State University for "Jackson Rising." They came to seek and to share examples of how to create not individual success stories, but stories of collective self-help, collective wealth-building, collective success, and the power of mutual cooperation.

The hundreds gathered at "Jackson Rising" spent the weekend exploring and discussing how to fund, found, and foster a different kind of business enterprise—democratically self-managed cooperatives. They reviewed future plans for, and current practices of, cooperative auto repair shops, laundries, recycling, construction, and trucking firms. They discussed cooperative restaurants, child and elder care co-ops, cooperative grocery stores, cooperative factories, farms, and more, all collectively owned and democratically managed by the same workers who deliver the service and create the value.

Participants at "Jackson Rising" learned a little of the story of Mondragon, a multinational cooperative enterprise founded in the Basque Country, the poorest and most oppressed part of Spain. That country now has about a 25 percent unemployment rate, but in the Basque Country, where Mondragon cooperatives operate factories, mines, retail, transport, and more, the unemployment rate is 5 percent. When a Mondragon factory or store or other operation has to close because of unprofitability, Mondragon retrains and relocates those workers to other cooperative enterprises. Mondragon's cooperative ethos makes it so different from other enterprises, one representative explained, that they're about to have to offer their own MBA program, to guarantee they can get trained managers without the bloodsucking, predatory mindset taught and valued at most business schools. They heard that Mondragon is now partnering with the United Food and Commercial Workers International Union (UFWC) and local forces to establish cooperative grocery stores and enterprises in Cincinnati. Those attending "Jackson Rising" heard about the concept of a solidarity economy, an economy not based on gentrification or exploitation or the enrichment of a few, an economy based on mutual cooperation to satisfy the needs of the many, to stabilize neighborhoods and communities, and provide needed jobs and services.

Cooperation, or as it's sometimes called, "the cooperative movement" is a model that is succeeding right now in tens of thousands of places for tens of millions of people around the world. It's a model that can succeed in the United States as well. The dedicated core of activists in the Malcolm X Grassroots Movement (MXGM), after deeply embedding themselves locally in Jackson, Mississippi, and briefly electing one of their own as mayor in the overwhelmingly Black and poor city of 175,000 people, are determined to show and take part in a different kind of Black economic development.

To that end, they've formed what they call "Cooperation Jackson," with four short-term objectives:

1. Cooperation Jackson is establishing an educational arm to spread the word in their communities about the distinct advantages and exciting possibilities of mutual uplift that business cooperatives offer.
2. When Mayor Chokwe Lumumba was still in office, Cooperation Jackson planned to establish a "cooperative incubator" providing a range of start-up services for cooperative enterprises. Absent support from the mayor's office, some MXGM activists observed, a lot of these co-ops will have to be born and nurtured in the cold.
3. Cooperation Jackson aims to form a local federation of cooperatives to share information and resources and to ensure that the cooperatives follow democratic principles of self-management that empower their workers. "We've always said 'free the land,'" observed one MXGM activist. "Now we want to 'free the labor' as well."
4. Finally, Cooperation Jackson intends to establish a financial institution to assist in providing credit and capital to cooperatives.

The MXGM activists are serious thinkers and organizers. They conducted door to door surveys of entire neighborhoods in Jackson, complete with skills assessments to discover how many plumbers, plasterers, farmers, carpenters, construction workers, truck mechanics, nurses and people with other health care experience live there and how many are unemployed. You'd imagine any local government that claimed it wanted to provide jobs and uplift people might do this, but you'd be imagining another world. In Jackson, Mississippi, local activists are figuring out how to build that new and better world. The US Census Bureau gathers tons of information useful to real estate, credit, banking, and similar business interests, but little or nothing of value to those who'd want to preserve neighborhood integrity and productively use the skills people already have.

In the short run, new and existing cooperatives in Jackson or anyplace else won't get much help from government. Mike Beall, president and CEO of the National Cooperative Business Association pointed out that the federal budget contains a mere $7 million in assistance for agricultural cooperatives, which the Obama administration has tried to remove the last two years in a row. There was, he said, no federal funding whatsoever to assist nonagricultural business cooperative start-ups or operations.

By contrast, Walmart alone receives $7.8 billion in tax breaks, loophole funds, and public subsidies from state, federal, and local governments every year and, according to one estimate, about $2.1 million more with each new store it opens. Another single company, Georgia Power, is about to receive $8.3 billion in federal loan guarantees and outright gifts for the construction of two nuclear plants alongside its leaky old nukes in the mostly Black and poor town of Shell Bluff. When it comes to oil companies, military contractors, transportation infrastructure outfits, agribusiness, pharmaceuticals, and so on, there are hundreds more that get billions in federal subsidies. Cooperatives get nothing. In the State of Mississippi, according to one "Jackson Rising" workshop presenter, nonagricultural cooperatives are technically illegal. All these traditional corporations have one thing in common. Unlike democratically run cooperatives, which share their profits and power, traditional corporations are dictatorships. Their workers don't, in most cases, have freedom of speech at work or the opportunity to form unions and certainly don't get to share in the wealth their labor creates for their bosses. To normal capitalist corporations, those workers, their families, and their communities are completely disposable. Detroit used to be a company town for the auto industry. When that industry grew and consolidated enough to disperse production to lower-wage areas around the world, it quickly abandoned Detroit and its people leaving a shattered, impoverished, polluted ruin behind.

The new mayor of Jackson, Tony Yarber, who ran with developers' money against the son of the late Chokwe Lumumba and narrowly defeated him, locked a number of city employees affiliated with the old administration out of their offices immediately after the election, before even being sworn in. The city removed all sponsorship and assistance to the "Jackson Rising" conference. There was a campaign in the local press branding its organizers as communists, terrorists, unpatriotic, and unfit to discuss the serious matters of job creation and building local economies. But the conference ran smoothly anyway with invaluable assistance from the Federation of Southern Cooperatives/Land Assistance Fund (an organization that has helped save the land and land rights of more Black farmers over the last forty years than any other), the

Praxis Project, the Fund for Democratic Communities, the Highlander Research and Education Center, and several others.

"This new mayor of ours made a big mistake. What would it cost him, even if he imagines cooperatives cannot succeed, to give his blessing to this gathering?" asked Kali Akuno of Cooperation Jackson. "As an organizer I can now ask why he's against job creation? He's got no answer to that.... It's hindsight of course, but maybe we should have paid attention to this piece first, and the electoral effort only afterward. Who's to say that if we'd done it that way, we would not have been more successful in retaining the mayor's seat."

This past weekend was the fiftieth anniversary of the first freedom rides that kicked off the youth-led phase of the Southern Freedom Movement. Something of similar importance happened in Jackson, Mississippi, last weekend. At "Jackson Rising," hundreds of movement activists from around the country discovered, rediscovered, began to visualize and explore cooperation and the solidarity economy. They met with their peers from North Carolina, Ohio, Zimbabwe, South Africa, and of course Mississippi who were already engaged in pulling it together. It's an economy not based on gentrification as Black urban regimes in Atlanta, New Orleans, and other cities have been and still are doing. It's not based on big ticket stadiums or shopping malls or professional sports teams, none of which create many permanent well-paying jobs anyway. It's not based on fast food and restaurant empires that follow the McDonald's and Walmart model of low wages and ruthless exploitation. It's about democracy and collective ownership of business, collective responsibility, and collective uplift.

It's coming. Jackson, Mississippi, is already rising, and your community can do the same. Black Agenda Report intends to stay on top of this story in the coming weeks and months.

This article first appeared on Black Agenda Report, May 7, 2014, accessed May 16, 2022, http://www.blackagendareport.com/content/ jackson-rising%C2%A0black-millionaires-wont-lift-us-cooperation-solidarity-economy-might.

Coming Full Circle: The Intersection of Gender Justice and the Solidarity Economy

Sacajawea "Saki" Hall Interviewed by Thandisizwe Chimurenga

Thandisizwe Chimurenga: I see in one of your bios you talk about growing up in a solidarity economy, having a cooperative upbringing, what do you mean by that?

Saki Hall: My mother is from Haiti and my father is from St. Louis, Missouri. Since I lived in New York with my mom's side of the family, the Haitian side of my family predominantly raised me. So I have my Haitian family and then my extended family of friends I grew up with living in the Lower East Side of Manhattan. Both were tight-knit communities. In both cases we didn't have a lot of money so folks creatively figured out how to meet their needs. I feel like I was raised in two cultures that actually taught me some of the fundamentals of what it means to care and share with each other, to be a cooperator, as they say in the cooperative world. Caring and sharing is a key dimension of solidarity.

My mom has told me a story several times of when my dad bartered a painting for bread. He had done a small oil painting of a loaf of bread with a wine bottle based on a local bakery. One day they were hungry and had no money, so he went to the bakery and in exchange for the painting the baker gave him the same daily-baked long loaf of bread featured in my dad's painting. At that time, they lived on about $800 a month with only a VA pension and an SSI check.

In New York City during the 1980s, we used subway tokens in place of dollars at bodegas—a corner store—and with street vendors. My best friend and I stretched our resources on Saturdays by going through together with one token each way on the subway, and then we'd have two tokens to use for lunch. So we could share a hot dog and a knish from a hot dog vendor.[1]

Another example that connects me to the work I'm doing now is the apartment building I grew up in on East 9th Street. My mother gave birth to me and my father delivered me in our apartment in 1978 with everyone from the building there pitching in. Our building went through a long co-op conversion process. It was resident self-managed through the 1980s and then formally became a low-income co-op in the early 1990s. I had always known we had a tenant association that governed and managed the buildings. I did not learn that I lived in a "shared-equity cooperative" until two years ago at a community land trust conference I went to for Cooperation Jackson. After college I learned of the strong housing, homesteading, and squatting movements that the Lower East Side had, along with other boroughs like the Bronx. My building was a product of the successful actions and organizing. Now I'm learning the details of the process on a deeper level cause I'm one of the people leading our work to develop cooperative housing.

I feel like I've come full circle, and I'm working with Cooperation Jackson to take it to another level. Housing is very important, land is critical. We are developing the Fannie Lou Hamer Community Land Trust. It's a tool that can make housing permanently affordable and put the development process in the hands of the community instead of corporate developers. Ultimately, we want to see land and housing no longer be a commodity to be bought and sold to the highest bidder.

What these personal stories mean for me in terms of our work in Jackson is that I've come to realize, remember really, that I have lived experiences that show what we are aiming for is possible. So it is totally possible for us to have quality, affordable housing, which is a human right. And even more importantly, *we can* collectively own and control the land and our housing. We are asserting that we have a right to the city here in Jackson.

From my childhood to now, I see the creativity of everyday working people and their organic practice of solidarity, especially women of color, immigrant women, single women, the women I grew up with including my mother. So we have a responsibility to: (a) recognize and value that, and (b) tap into the creativity and practices that already exist to strengthen and expand it, and (c) connect it to a movement for transformative liberation.

I think our vision and goals resonate with people. I think a lot of people have a similar experience like I'm describing. So many of us have these roots that have been passed down, in most ways, informally. Black people would not have survived the brutality of chattel slavery and Jim Crow apartheid without practicing solidarity and cooperation in organized formal ways. So it is that sharing, caring, and cooperation from the past, along with the ways we continue to do it now to survive, that we want to very intentionally tap into and make systematic with formal institutions like time banks, skill shares, and bartering and have a dynamic solidarity economy.

TC: You identify as a Black feminist.
SH: Right, a radical Black feminist.

TC: How do Black feminist politics and the struggle for Black women's liberation connect with the work of Cooperation Jackson and the effort to build the solidarity economy?
SH: So growing up in the hood, Black, a child of an immigrant, in a diverse, multinational, working-class neighborhood, I formed a race and class analysis early on, my gender analysis did not get fully shaped until later.

For me, women have to be at the center of our efforts to build a solidarity economy. So when I talk about that organic solidarity I grew up with, the informal ways oppressed people around the world live and work cooperatively, even the so-called informal economy, women are at the center of that.

Again, using an example from my childhood, I remember being sent downstairs to borrow milk, sugar, or some other food on the regular. It's not borrowing 'cause you can't give what you put in some cereal and ate back [laughter]. We didn't have to pay anyone back because they came to our house just the same. And when I think about it, nine times out of ten it had to do with cooking and meals, and the majority of the time it was women doing that cooking. So I took part in that mutual aid. Now, what I didn't know and learned recently when my godmother passed away, was that they shared food stamps. And mind you, I know people exchanged food stamps as a form of currency. When I heard that I was like wow, that's deep. I actually wrote it down on the, you know, the program they have at wakes. Learning that women shared food stamps spoke volumes to me about women. We are creative about how to take care of our families and each other with very little resources.

I'm sharing that example because what I take from it is how central "care work" is to the practice of solidarity. And if we are going to truly build a solidarity economy that is transformative, women have to be at the center of that. In Cooperation Jackson, we recognize this. As an organization we are working toward fully recognizing care work, and to fully center it as much as we center the value of worker-cooperatives in building a solidarity economy.

Women pretty much still take on the primary responsibility for care work. This work holds the social fabric of communities together and labor goes into creating or reproducing this fabric every day, social reproduction. Care work includes maintaining a household, parenting children, taking care of a grandparent, taking care of other people's family, social activities, healing, cooking, emotional support, and even sex. A radical feminist lens recognizes social reproduction as labor and care work is critical to social reproduction. Capitalism and patriarchy separate social reproduction from economic production, it makes a false separation between public and private. Social reproductive labor is not valued, recognized. It's unpaid, in some cases paid, but severely underpaid.

Disconnecting social reproduction from economic production marginalizes the people who do social reproductive labor, making their role invisible and easily exploited.

Any economy relies on social production. Capitalism would not survive without social reproductive labor, the unpaid labor that allows for immense profit. What would profit margins be if a company had to pay the husband for working in the office and his wife for the work she does to run their home? Or had to pay a single mom double for her nine-to-five and her care work? Domestic workers, mostly nonwhite women, mostly immigrants, work for low pay and do unpaid care work at home. And with the sheer amount of hours taking care of someone's family and home, it limits the time they can provide for their family and community. Sex workers are in the public and private sphere, doing paid work that is criminalized because socially, it's for the private sphere, and, morally, only for married hetero men and women.

So social reproduction and the role of women, and some men, is solidarity based, and a solidarity economy can reflect and support the transformation of society. A solidarity economy in and of itself doesn't automatically end gender and sexual oppression, but it does offer an opportunity unlike capitalism.

For Cooperation Jackson, we believe we have to challenge ourselves and each other to actively struggle against patriarchy and heterosexism in our work and in our lives: against the assigned gender roles and norms that dictate who is a woman, what being a man means, even the subtle things like what color is allowed for which gender, pink being for girls and blue being for boys, and against the violence that comes in different forms that is used to enforce these made-up concepts, especially toward people who do not conform to these standards like transgender people.

I see it as my responsibility as a member of Cooperation Jackson, as a mother, as a birth worker, to provide a Black radical feminist analysis for our work and to push us all toward practice that is beyond theory. And that is the hard part: the multiple systems of oppression and how they overlap limit us all.

TC: Cooperation Jackson is working on participatory budgeting. What would it look like if Black women were in charge of the budget or had a say in the city budget? Is fighting for a participatory budget an intentional part of the work of Cooperation Jackson in terms of integrating Black women's knowledge and experiences into how to govern a municipality? Is that part of the plan?

SH: We've been talking about and studying participatory and human rights budgeting, which in simple terms is creating a budget that actually comes out of the community and reflects its needs, as opposed to a budget that is created by government officials and then we all deal with the consequences of it. In Jackson, Mississippi, if Black women, especially Black working-class women, were centered in the process of creating a budget I think it would look very different than the city's typical budget. What I mean by centered is that the development of a budget would be driven by the knowledge, experience, ideas, and participation of Black women. For example, I think education and schools, things like affordable housing, would be prioritized compared to police departments or tourism. So it would be important for families like mine that have a hard time or cannot pay at all for extracurricular activities to have access to free after-school programs, free arts programs. That could be included in a city budget. Going back to housing like I talked about earlier, the priority placed on urban redevelopment often means giving tax breaks to corporate developers. I'm sure for poor and working-class women, bringing in money to help improve the city wouldn't mean displacing them from their homes. Protecting affordable housing with policy and the money to back it up would be my priority if I had a part in the planning.

The City of Jackson is in a budget crisis; so hard decisions have to be made about what gets cut, where money goes and how much goes where. If we were able to do things differently, these decisions would be based on the people most directly impacted. So in our case setting priorities for Jackson's urgent infrastructure repairs would be done in a democratic participatory process seen through the lens of Black and other working-class people, particularly women, and not the contractors and the corporations that typically dominate the process and its outcomes.

The important part is actually how decisions get made, not only about allocating resources through a budget. It is about who is there to make those decisions, how much power do they have and can use in the process. So yeah, there's a lot of things that are needed, that have to be changed on the municipal level for us to get to the goals we set outlined in the Jackson-Kush Plan that relate to human rights or participatory budgeting and more. There are a lot of things that have to change to create a deeply democratic system. Human rights budgeting is just one of the tools that will go a long way toward advancing our goals. That is why we've been studying it and plan to relaunch mass education and trainings on human rights budgeting. Not only is there an opportunity to meet the economic and social needs going unmet when the decision-makers don't have the same interests, imagine the impact of the process with practicing agency and collective power through the process.

TC: When I hear people say women in leadership, it makes me think of a woman, a female figurehead. When I hear about women's participation, what comes to mind are women doing the majority of the work, but not receiving the credit or acknowledgment of their work. So women already participate, women are in leadership. You know to me it's more than women and leadership or women's participation. How is this being practiced in Cooperation Jackson?

SH: Right, women's leadership has to be centered, it is not enough to have us in the room. To me there is a difference between women having roles in an organization and women having power in an organization.

When I say power, I mean decision-making power that sets the agenda and goals of every dimension of the organization.

Audre Lorde is quoted often saying we don't live single-issue lives, and there is no hierarchy of oppression. That highlights the intersectionality framework that informs our work. Cooperation Jackson understands that Black people's self-determination and liberation is not possible without ending heteropatriarchy just like it is not possible without ending capitalism and white supremacy.

Radical feminism recognizes the intersections of heterosexism, patriarchy, capitalism, white supremacy, and other systems of oppression. These systems of oppression privilege men, privilege heterosexuals, privilege whiteness, privilege the ruling class, English as a language, adults, etc. In Cooperation Jackson, we have a vision of a deeply democratic, cooperative, sustainable community. For us that means we have to create a culture free of patriarchy and heterosexism. Our struggles are connected, and our liberation is intrinsically connected, and we are committed to moving us as close as possible in that direction.

Cooperation Jackson specifically, like every organization, at least that I'm aware of, we are struggling to create this liberated space in our organization and we all know we have a long way to go in our communities.

What we *have* done to this point is that we've institutionalized space for women's leadership and queer leadership. I'm excited that our membership and core leadership of the organization represents young queer people and women. That stands out in Jackson, Mississippi [chuckle]. At the same time, that is not enough. Heterosexist views and behaviors have to be struggled with and shifted. We attempt to make tasks nongendered like taking notes at a meeting and cleaning. It is interesting how we all fall into defaults and have to remind ourselves and each other.

Patriarchy is a hell of a…

TC: Well, hell of a drug.

SH: [Laughs] Yeah, and so you know, it rears its ugly head in the personal and political spaces. Even in radical, progressive, women friendly, queer friendly spaces, time and time again. And we've internalized it, so even women and queer folks perpetuate it ourselves.

We have been intentional in actively creating the space and environment that is truly open and conducive to women and queer folks coming in from anywhere and genuinely feeling like they can fully engage and participate in discussing the work and doing the work. And it is in subtle and overt ways—like having a sign on the bathroom door that says, "Gender Is a Universe." We have a banner on our entrance wall outside that says, "All Our Family Welcomed," with the rainbow and gender equality symbols including a combined queer and Black power symbol. We have a room called the Little People's Society named by one of our members. She is a high school student, and her family provides childcare at our gatherings. That little people (children) are welcomed in all spaces is a community agreement.

TC: What do you see going forward?

SH: As a leader of Cooperation Jackson, I have to make sure that we create the time and space to engage in the struggle to dismantle sexism, patriarchy, and heterosexism. Because it takes time, it takes processing. It's about our relationships with each other. So I'm not the only one doing this, but it can't only be a few of us. I do see it as part of my responsibility though, to point out when sexist language or behavior happens or to highlight the impact on women if we are talking about an issue and that gets left out. And that can be uncomfortable and frustrating at times.

Cooperation Jackson has to systematize these things, document this analysis, and integrate it into all of our writing more. We need to document how it is impacting our work and practice, both successes and challenges.

A challenge for me is how to encourage and push the younger women in the organization to be more visible and vocal in our overall work. But I have to check myself sometimes because it can't only be about the way I define active leadership or challenging patriarchy. So I am constantly learning and developing myself, which is a part of the process, unpacking our privilege and unlearning what we've been socialized to accept.

What I think we have done is create the space for this to happen. Instead of sitting back and waiting for them to ask to step into a role, we are encouraging and asking them to facilitate a meeting, do a report back. Collective models of leadership and decision-making can provide a space for everyone to participate fully. But it has to be coupled with principles and practices like men stepping back and not dominating discussions, sharing power overall. So I see us getting stronger in our theory and practice.

Note

1 A knish is an Eastern European snack food consisting of a filling covered with dough that is either baked, grilled, or deep fried. It can be purchased from street vendors in urban areas with a large Jewish population, sometimes at a hot dog stand or from a butcher shop. It was made popular in North America by Eastern European immigrants from the Pale of Settlement (mainly from present-day Belarus, Poland, Lithuania, and Ukraine).

Casting Shadows: Chokwe Lumumba and the Struggle for Racial Justice and Economic Democracy in Jackson, Mississippi

Kali Akuno

In the State of Mississippi, deep down in the heart of "Dixie," a critical democratic experiment is taking place that is challenging the order of institutional white supremacy and paternalistic capitalism that form the foundations of the state's settler-colonial order. This experiment in social transformation is building a radical culture of participatory democratic engagement to gain control over the authoritative functions of governance and to democratize the fundamental means of production, distribution, and financial exchange. It is being led by the New Afrikan People's Organization and the Malcolm X Grassroots Movement. We are building on nearly two hundred years of struggle for Afrikan liberation in the territories claimed by the European settler state of Mississippi. This experiment, the Jackson-Kush Plan, is named after the state's capitol and the name given by members of the Provisional Government of the Republic of New Afrika to the eighteen contiguous majority-Black counties that border the Mississippi river.

The Jackson-Kush Plan has three fundamental programmatic focuses that intend to build a mass base with political clarity, organizational capacity, and material self-sufficiency:

- building people's assemblies throughout the Kush District to serve as instruments of *dual power* to counter the abusive powers of the state and of capital whether regional, national, or international;
- building an independent political force throughout the state, but concentrated in the Kush District, which will challenge and replace the authority of the two parties of transnational capital,

the Democrats and the Republicans, which dominate the arena of electoral politics in the State of Mississippi;
- building a solidarity economy in Jackson and throughout the Kush District anchored by a network of cooperatives and supporting institutions to strengthen worker power and economic democracy in the state.

This experiment is anchored in the rich history of the Black Liberation Movement in Mississippi that extends from Reconstruction to our successful 2013 campaign to elect as mayor of Jackson a human rights attorney and long-time revolutionary organizer, Chokwe Lumumba. It draws on the practices of grassroots struggles to build consensual democracy, such as the autonomous communities led by the Zapatistas in Chiapas, Mexico, as well as solidarity economies that subordinate capital to labor, such as Mondragon in Euskadi, the Basque region of the Spanish nation-state. Our organization extensively studied these and other international movements for years via study groups, international delegations, and international exchanges. We have tried to absorb their best practices and apply them to our particular conditions.

The fundamental aim of this experiment is to attain power for Afrikan, Indigenous, and other oppressed peoples and exploited classes in order to liberate ourselves from the oppressive systems of white supremacy, capitalism, colonialism, and imperialism in the state of Mississippi.

Contextualizing the Initiative: Challenging Poverty, Prisons, and Paternalism

For most people the potential of our democratic experiment runs counter to the common perceptions about Mississippi as a historic standard-bearer for the ruthless enslavement of African people. As the demand for cotton grew worldwide in the nineteenth century, Mississippi became the center of the expanding domestic slave trade. Over one million enslaved Afrikans were transported to the Deep South between 1790 and 1860. The brutal conditions in the Mississippi and Ohio River regions inspired the phrase "being sold down the river." The growth of "King Cotton" also resulted in the expulsion of the Indigenous population and the marginalization of poor whites in the face of plantation economies. The failure of radical Reconstruction to dissolve the plantation system after the Civil War, along with the creation of "Black codes" to enforce segregation, created a triple *P* effect that has affected Mississippi ever since: poverty, prisons, and paternalistic white supremacy.

This paternalist capitalism shifted how Black labor was exploited. Following the collapse of the short-lived Reconstruction government in Mississippi, Black workers were primarily confined to being sharecroppers—farm laborers who worked almost exclusively for the large landowners who were their former owners and their descendants. Wholly dependent on the large landowners for their wages, food, shelter, and medical care, sharecroppers were slaves by another name. This system lasted from the 1870s to the 1960s. It was gradually weakened by the industrialization of large portions of agricultural production, particularly the mechanization of cotton picking. This displaced nearly a million Black workers between the late 1940s and the early 1970s, forcing them to migrate to urban areas throughout the US.

Industrial manufacturing entered the state on a significant scale in the late 1920s. The key industries included shipbuilding, timber cutting and processing, transport and shipping, canning, and later, industrial farming of catfish, chicken, and pigs. Industrial capital created a system of super-exploitation through the manipulation of the existing racial order and the fragmentation of the multinational working class. Black workers were usually relegated to menial positions and those who performed skilled labor in the factories were grossly undercompensated. Capital uses the racial divide to hinder working-class consciousness and organization. Beginning in the late 1890s, regional capital, both agricultural and industrial, was able to build a solid alliance with sectors of the white settler working class to resist unionization and to use the passage of Taft-Hartley to defeat the legislative gains of the National Labor Relations Act. Furthermore, the institutionalization of "right to work" laws designed to privilege white workers became a defining feature of the paternalist capitalism that governs Mississippi labor relations.

Today, Mississippi is the poorest state in the union with a median household income of $37,095. The City of Jackson is one of the poorest metropolitan cities in the US. Between 2008 and 2016 the median household income was $33,434 and the poverty rate 28.3 percent.[1] According to the US Bureau of Labor Statistics, as of August 2013, the city's "official" unemployment rate stood at 8.0 percent. However, its "real" unemployment rate is estimated to be above 25 percent.[2] Mississippi's wealth equity figures are even worse. It is estimated that people of African descent control less than 10 percent of the vested capital in the state. Mississippi is also one of the most repressive states in the union. It has the third highest incarceration rate in the US and the overwhelming number of those incarcerated are people of African descent.[3] It is also noted for being at or near the bottom of every major quality of life indicator, including health measures, quality of housing, transportation, worker rights and protections, and educational access and attainment.

Despite Mississippi's oppressive past and present there is tremendous potential for radical transformation. It is our argument that Mississippi constitutes a "weak link" in the bourgeois-democratic capitalist system that underscores the US's settler-colonial regime.[4] Although capitalism has thoroughly dominated social relations in Mississippi since its inception as a colonial entity, the local practice can best be described as a "contingent" expression of that system because of its overt dependency on paternalist white supremacy. The local capitalist and elite classes attempt to maintain social and political control over the state, its peoples, and its resources by tempering and distorting the profit motive that is central to the capitalist mode of production. This severely restricts agricultural and industrial production, trade, and financial flows in and out of the state. Rather than stimulating growth and maximizing profits through increased production and trade, the local, white ruling class has prioritized a strategy of containment that deliberately seeks to fetter the Black population by limiting its access to capital and decent wages, both of which constitute a critical source of labor power and strength in a capitalist society. As an old saying goes, "In Mississippi, money doesn't talk as loud as race."

This contingent form of paternalist capitalism has produced a number of deep contradictions within the state. Black populations constitute a majority in sixteen western counties in Mississippi, resulting in the highest percentage of Black elected officials in the union. Furthermore, thousands of Blacks are migrating back to Mississippi every year, and, despite all of the xenophobic initiatives of the Republican Party, a growing immigrant population promises to make it a majority nonwhite state over the next twenty years. However, demographics are not the only determining factor. A long memory of white supremacy together with its present manifestations make the majority-Black populations in the Kush District acutely aware of their interests and compels them to act upon them on every front of social life. It is this combination of favorable demographics, elevated political consciousness, and strong political mobilization that have created the preconditions for our political experiment. This is why we characterize Mississippi as a weak link in the chain. Although we cannot limit our activities to these weak links, it is crucial that we identify and utilize them because they provide more space to demonstrate practical alternatives that can galvanize momentum for similar projects in more difficult circumstances.

A Short History of Black Resistance in Mississippi

People of African descent have a long history of resistance against colonization, enslavement, exploitation, and white supremacy in the lands that now comprise the State of Mississippi. One of the earliest acts of resistance was the Natchez rebellion of 1729, when an alliance of enslaved Africans and Indigenous people from the Natchez nation rebelled against French colonists.[5] This was followed by countless numbers of enslaved Africans who liberated themselves and became Maroons in the backwoods of the territory during its early days as a French, Spanish, English, and American colonial possession. There were also numerous slave rebellions during the antebellum period in Mississippi.

After the Civil War, people of African descent organized several independent communities, purchased considerable portions of farmland, started countless businesses, and won a considerable number of political offices in the Reconstruction government. These efforts continued even after the defeat of Reconstruction and the imposition of the brutal Jim Crow apartheid regime established the threat of constant terror. In the three decades following the Second World War, resistance grew to levels unmatched since Reconstruction.

The height of this resistance was in the 1960s during the rise of Medgar Evers and the National Association for the Advancement of Colored People (NAACP), the militant campaigns of the Student Nonviolent Coordinating Committee (SNCC), the Congress of Racial Equality (CORE), the Southern Christian Leadership Conference (SCLC), and their alliance in the Conference of Federated Organizations (COFO).

In the electoral arena, attempts by Blacks to independently challenge and change our social and political status go back to the 1964 creation of the Mississippi Freedom Democratic Party (MFDP) through COFO. The

MFDP famously challenged the Democrat's "Dixiecrat" wing by attempting to seat delegates at the 1964 Democratic National Convention in Atlantic City, New Jersey. Despite its recent emergence on the scene as an organized force, the MFDP immediately carried significant weight in the Black community because of the historic struggles waged by Black activists to enter the party in the mid-1960s and then to assume majority control in the early 1970s.

Ever since, the merits of building an independent political vehicle through the MFDP or an independent political party have been points of contention. The vast majority of political activists in the Black community have argued that it is better for Black people in Mississippi to be linked with the Democratic Party and the multiracial alliance that it has represented since the New Deal. In particular, they contend that alliances with the Democrats are necessary for promoting progressive legislation that serves the interests of the Black community and for repelling attacks from conservatives and racists. During the 1960s and 1970s, the Democratic Party's tepid support for the civil rights movement as well as the policies and programs that emerged therefrom largely incorporated Mississippi's Black community into its "hegemony," the social processes utilized by ruling elites to consolidate, justify, and normalize their social domination. Our challenge is how to address the hegemony of "Democratic tradition" within the Black community, particularly among its "consistent voters" throughout the state and beyond. One reason why Mississippi is a weak link is because its Democratic Party is not particularly strong. The national party leadership takes the Black vote for granted and is reluctant to invest adequate resources because of the Republican Party's firm grip on the overwhelming majority of white voters in the state.

From these struggles a tradition was born and has been nurtured over forty years. Emerging from this tradition are ongoing efforts both to revitalize the MFDP as well as to build an independent party. The work to revitalize the MFDP is the stronger of the two initiatives in large part due to its preexisting infrastructure and credibility. More activists also view it as having greater strategic utility because it enables their work to be distinct from, yet still a part of, the critical Democratic Party primary system in Jackson. Given that Jackson is over 80 percent Black, and that nearly 99 percent of the Black community in the city and the state support the Democrats, the Democratic primary constitutes the "real" election in Jackson, and it has served this purpose since at least 1993, when the split in the Black vote between Henry Kirksey and Harvey Johnson delayed the eventuality of a Black mayor until 1997. For this reason, many activists don't want to jettison the MFDP for something wholly new. Despite this, the initiative is still relatively small and will take some time to come to full and complete resolution within the broader movement.

Our efforts to build an independent political force that could elect Chokwe Lumumba to Jackson's city council and then mayor bridged the history of the MFDP with the radical political objectives that emerged out of the New Afrikan Independence Movement, the Provisional Government of the Republic of New Afrika, and the Revolutionary Action Movement/African People's Party, which collectively gave birth to the New Afrikan People's Organization and the Malcolm X Grassroots Movement.

The Jackson-Kush Plan was key to the rise of Mayor Lumumba, but electoral work is only one aspect. The plan is a movement for economic, political, and cultural self-determination that emerged out of the Jackson People's Assembly in 2005 as a response to the crisis of displacement and disenfranchisement in the aftermath of Hurricane Katrina. The idea was to first build a solid base in Jackson, the center of commerce and mass media in Mississippi, which will then enable us to branch out to allies in the Kush.

There are three interlocking components of the Jackson-Kush Plan: (1) the People's Assembly, (2) an independent political vehicle that can win political office, and (3) worker cooperatives and a solidarity economy. Tremendous strides have been made in each of these initiatives, but as we will now see, they have developed unevenly.

Building and Sustaining the People's Assembly

The key to this experiment in direct democracy is building a social movement that can successfully use the favorable socio-material conditions in Jackson and throughout the Kush District to transform oppressive and exploitative social relations. The vehicle most critical to this transformative process is the people's assembly because it allows the people of Jackson to practice democracy, by which we mean "the rule of the people, for the people, by the people," in its broadest terms. This entails making direct decisions not only in the limited realm of what is generally deemed the "political" (the contractual, electoral, and legislative aspects of the social order), but also the economic, social, and cultural operations of our community. The New Afrikan People's Organization and the Malcolm X Grassroots Movement started organizing assemblies in the late 1980s to allow Black people to exercise self-determination and exert their power.

A people's assembly is a mass gathering of people organized and assembled to address essential social issues that are pertinent to a community. We define a body as a "mass" body when it engages at least one-fifth of the total population in a defined geographic area, whether it is a neighborhood, ward, city, or state. We have arrived at this formula after nearly twenty years of experience of what it takes to amass sufficient social forces and capacities to effectively implement the decisions made by the assembly.

The Jackson People's Assembly is based on a "one person, one vote" principle. We emphasize that agency must be vested directly in individuals, regardless of whether the assembly makes decisions through a voting process or some form of consensus. This aspect of direct engagement and individual empowerment distinguishes a people's assembly from other types of mass gatherings in which a multitude of social forces are engaged. For example, alliances and united fronts tend to reinforce hierarchal structures because their leaders make the decisions on behalf of the people they claim to "represent," often without their knowledge and direct consent. On the scale of organizing millions of people, we acknowledge that it is often impossible to avoid at least some representational processes. On the population scale of Jackson, however, we can engage in more direct and participatory forms of democratic decision-making and governance.

At present, the Jackson People's Assembly operates at an oscillating midpoint between what we describe as a "constituent assembly" and a "mass assembly." A constituent assembly is a representative body that is dependent on mass outreach but it is structured, intentionally or unintentionally, to mitigate material and social obstacles to participation, such as having to work, caring for children, lacking access to information, and political and ideological differences. The challenge with this type of assembly is that it tends to become overly bureaucratic and stagnant if it doesn't continue to bring in new people, especially youth, and if it is unable to maintain the struggle on a mass scale. A mass assembly is the purer example of a people's democracy. It normally emerges during times of acute crisis when there are profound ruptures in society. These types of assemblies are typically all-consuming, short-lived entities. Their greatest weakness is that they usually demand that participants give all of their time and energy to engaging the crisis, which is unsustainable because people eventually have to tend to their daily needs.

Due to these circumstances, the Jackson People's Assembly operates principally as a constituent assembly that engages in a number of strategic campaigns to address the material needs of our social base and to elevate its economic power. Nevertheless, during times of crisis the assembly tends to adopt more of a mass character. This occurred, for example, amid the untimely death of Mayor Lumumba in late February 2014. This meant that the people's assembly had to defend many of the initiatives of the Lumumba administration that were based in the People's Platform devised by the assembly. Even though the current practice in Jackson tends toward the constituent model, the aim is to grow into a permanent mass assembly of a "new type." This more permanent mass assembly would be built by diffusing the assembly deeper into the neighborhoods. These neighborhood assemblies will anchor the program of the Jackson People's Assembly by addressing the specific community-level economic and social needs, such as the program of digital fabrication and computer numerical control manufacturing being designed and implemented by Cooperation Jackson. These neighborhood assemblies will form the basis of overlapping "all city" task force structures that would coordinate the productive and social activities of the assembly while maintaining its coherent municipal character.

More broadly, our assembly has two broad functions and means of exercising power. The first is to organize "autonomous" social projects not supported by the government or some variant of monopoly capital, whether financial, corporate, industrial, or mercantile. These types of projects include organizing community gardens, people's self-defense campaigns, and housing occupations, as well as forming unions and worker cooperatives. On a basic scale these projects function as serve-the-people survival programs that help our community to sustain itself and acquire a degree of self-reliance. On a larger scale, these projects provide enough resources and social leverage (such as flexible time to organize) to allow people to engage in essential resistance and/or offensive (typically positional) initiatives.

The second means of exercising power is to apply pressure on the government and the forces of economic exploitation in society. We exert pressure by organizing various types of campaigns including mass action protests, direct-action campaigns, boycotts, noncompliance campaigns, and policy-shift campaigns that either advocate for or against existing, proposed, or pending laws.

In order to carry out these critical functions, an assembly must produce clear demands, a coherent strategy, realistic action plans, and concrete timelines. It must also organize itself into committees or action groups that can carry them out. Our model makes clear distinctions between the assembly as an "event," a "process," and an "institution." The assembly as an event is where we deliberate on general questions and issues and decide what can be done to address them. The assembly as a process is where the various committees and working groups refine the more detailed questions of goals, strategy, and timelines. The assembly as an institution is a product of the combined social weight of the assembly's events and processes as well as its actions and outcomes. Although the authority of the assembly is expressed to its highest extent during the mass "events," the real work of the assembly that enables it to exercise its power is carried out by its committees and working groups.

The coordinating committee of the assembly is the People's Task Force. It is a body directly elected by the assembly, serves at its will, and is subject to its immediate recall, which means that its members can be replaced, with due process, at any time. Its primary function is to facilitate the work of the committees by ensuring that they meet regularly or as often as is deemed necessary; that each body has as a facilitator, an agenda, and notetakers if these are not provided by the committees; that there is open communication between the committees; that all of the actions of the committees are communicated thoroughly to the rest of the assembly; and that they coordinate the logistics for the assembly gatherings.

Committees are regularly constituted bodies of the assembly whose functions include outreach and mobilization, media and communications, fundraising and finance, intelligence gathering, trainings, and security. Working groups are campaign- or project-oriented bodies that execute the time-limited goals of the assembly. Our working groups have successfully campaigned for the release of the Scott sisters;[6] for the federal government to provide more housing aid to internally displaced persons from New Orleans and the Gulf Coast after Hurricane Katrina; and for an alliance between the assembly and public transportation workers, which saved Jackson's public transportation system and won its workers higher wages. All committees and working groups are comprised of volunteers who, for the most part, choose where to focus their energies on a self-selecting basis.

In various social movements throughout the world, people's assemblies wield different types of power depending on local conditions and the balance of forces. In the last five years, in places like Nepal, Greece, and Spain, they have revolutionized people's daily lives and have even played significant roles in altering public discourse, shifting the balance of power within nation-states, and in a few cases have led to the toppling of governments in Tunisia, Egypt, and Burkina Faso.[7]

What follows is a brief explanation of what people's assemblies can accomplish in different historical circumstances and conditions.

1. During periods of stability, when capitalist governments and markets can maintain the status quo, assemblies can push for various "positional" reforms like the implementation of police control boards or local citizens' review boards, such as the Every 28 Hours Campaign.[8] Assemblies can also engage in projects with low- to mid-scale autonomy like "self-reliant" worker cooperatives, such as Cooperation Jackson's Sustainable Communities Initiative, which I will describe below.
2. During periods of radical upsurge, assemblies can push for structural reforms and engage in projects for mid- to large-scale autonomy. For example, between 1998 and 2010, assemblies in Venezuela were able to push the Chávez administration to make radical changes to the constitution, form numerous cooperatives, construct affordable housing, and engage in significant land transfers to poor people.
3. During prerevolutionary periods, assemblies can become parallel institutions that assume some of the functions of the government. Over the last ten years, the revolutionary movement in Nepal organized assemblies to act as a direct counterweight to the monarchy and the military, which resulted in the founding of a constitutional democracy and a more "representative" legislative body. In another recent example, from 1994 until the mid-2000s, the Zapatistas in Chiapas, Mexico, were able create extensive zones of "self-rule" and "autonomous production" that were governed by assemblies.
4. During revolutionary periods, assemblies, when buttressed by revolutionary political parties, can effectively become the government

and assume control over the basic processes and mechanisms of production. In the 1980s, assemblies commanded this much power in Haiti, the Philippines, Nicaragua, Burkina Faso, and Grenada.[9] The most recent examples are Egypt, in the winter of 2011 and summer of 2013, and Nepal, during stretches between 2003 and 2006. In the case of Burkina Faso and Grenada, the assemblies were often fostered and organized by the revolutionary political party.

5. During periods of retreat, assemblies can defend their people and leaders, fight to maintain their gains, and prepare for the next upsurge. The experiences of the Lavalas movement in Haiti in the early 1990s and mid-2000s are perhaps the best example of how assemblies and other people's organizations can weather the storm of counterrevolutions and defeats.

The driving forces of an assembly, and in particular, its organic intellectuals, organizers, and cultural workers, should be able to distinguish clearly between acting as a "counterhegemonic" force during stable and prerevolutionary periods and acting as a "hegemonic" force during revolutionary periods. This means distinguishing between, on the one hand, acts of positioning, such as building allies, assembling resources, and changing the dominant social narratives, and on the other hand, acts of maneuvering, such as open confrontation and conflict with the repressive forces of the state and capital.[10]

As for the Jackson People's Assembly, our effort to expand its scale and scope has been consistent. The greatest challenge to the assembly has been the almost nonstop run of electoral campaigns in which our movement has been engaged since 2009. For considerable periods, significant sections of the assembly's base have served as the organizing force driving the electoral campaigns. At times this has challenged the standard operations of the assembly and in some moments created tensions regarding its role. On more than one occasion the strategic question has been raised, is the assembly primarily a vehicle to build "dual power" or is it a vehicle to nurture and support progressive political candidates? The affirmative answer from the vast majority of the assembly's base is consistently that it must be a vehicle to exercise political power outside of elected office. Nevertheless, as we will now see, the challenge to act in a manner contrary to the hegemonic sway of electoral politics is a constant struggle.

Engaging Power: The Administration of Mayor Chokwe Lumumba

To date, the most critical experience we have accumulated in the realm of engaging power is the brief administration of the late Mayor Chokwe Lumumba, which lasted almost seven months, from July 1, 2013, until his untimely death on February 25, 2014. Chokwe first moved to Mississippi in 1971 to support the project of the Provisional Government of the Republic of New Afrika to establish its capitol in the state of Mississippi. This effort was brutally suppressed by the US government in August 1971 when eleven of its leaders and activists became prisoners of war. Chokwe became a lawyer in large part to defend and free these organizers, who became known nationally and internationally as the RNA-11. After spending some years in the late 1970s and early 1980s in Detroit and New York City, Chokwe returned to Mississippi permanently in the mid-1980s to build the New Afrikan People's Organization and advance the development of a mass movement through the Malcolm X Grassroots Movement, which was founded in Jackson in 1990.

The decades of base-building and forging strategic alliances among various forces in the city and state enabled us to start seriously considering Chokwe for political office in the mid-2000s. The catalyst for this consideration was our analysis of the weakening of Black people's power, especially in the Gulf Coast region, following the devastation and displacement wrought by Hurricane Katrina. After careful deliberation and planning, our organizations devised the Jackson-Kush Plan and in the spring of 2009, we were able to elect Chokwe to the Jackson City Council representing Ward 2. This was followed by the successful election of Hinds County's first Black sheriff, Tyrone Lewis in 2011. In June 2013, we were able to elect Chokwe mayor. Although we were only able to move a mere fraction of our electoral agenda during his time in office, we did gain a tremendous amount of experience about how to better "engage state power."

We say "engaging state power" rather than "wielding state power" for two reasons. First, the capitalist and imperialist nature of the American constitutional framework limits the agency of any individual officeholder at every level of government. We often try to drive this point home to the broader movement by saying, "It should be clear that, at best, we won an election, a popularity contest. We did not win the ability to control the government, just the temporary ability to influence its tactical affairs on a municipal level."

Second, we are an organization that is part of a radical movement for New Afrikan or Black liberation whose strategic aim has historically been and continues to be the decolonization of the southeastern portion of the US. Therefore, pursuing an elected office within the US government has been viewed by many of our historic allies as a means of legitimizing the powers that be. In remaining consistent with the pursuit of self-determination and national liberation, our campaigns for any elected office within the US constitutional framework are assessed and conducted on a case-by-case basis according to the potential for that office to either create more democratic space or advance policies that test the limits of structural change.

Given these limitations, our electoral initiatives are "temporal," meaning short- to mid-term engagements that attempt to bring to light various social contradictions by making every critical issue a mass issue. In so doing, we ask the people to demand structural solutions, what many call "transitional demands,"[11] that attempt to address the contradictions at their root. Doing this is easier said than done, but under the leadership of the New Afrikan People's Organization and the Malcolm X Grassroots Movement, our electoral work has been able to move consistently in this direction by engaging in three key strategies: mass education, preparatory battles, and operational fronts.

Mass Education

The key to our ability to make transitional demands on a consistent basis is to constantly engage in mass education work that makes direct causal and structural links between local realities and national and international issues. It is much easier to raise transitional demands when there is widespread understanding that our local issues are expressions of systemic issues. The people's assembly is the primary vehicle of mass education. We use instruments such as community outreach, forums, radio, newsletters, editorials in local allied newspapers, and social media. It has taken nearly two decades of consistent mass education work to build the level and depth of social consciousness that exists presently in Jackson.

Preparatory Battles

One of the keys of our electoral success has been transferring victories from social justice struggles to the electoral arena. This requires picking key pre-electoral fights that highlight the essence of our political platform and distinguish us from other candidates and political forces. From our vantage point, these preparatory battles must not only help bring together and build broad sectors of the community. They must also have the ability to educate the masses by raising consciousness and preparing them for future struggles by building the capacity and organizational strength necessary to become transformative agents. There were two key battles in the period between 2009 and 2013 when Chokwe served as a city councilperson.

The first issue was fighting to save Jackson's public transportation system, expand its services, and increase the wages of its workers. This was not only a fight against neoliberal austerity, but a battle to address an ongoing structural weakness in Jackson. Like a lot of midsized southern cities, Jackson has an inadequate public transportation system. Most people must own vehicles to get around. In a city with high concentrations of poverty, transportation costs can be exorbitant for an average worker making minimum wage or less. This struggle also aided the elderly, who constitute a high percentage of the population, as well as people with disabilities. Fighting a proposed cut of a public good with a proposed expansion resonated with broad sectors of the working class and highlighted key material differences in our approach and concerns.

The second issue was putting forth and passing an anti-racial-profiling ordinance. This ordinance was intentionally designed to address, on the one hand, policing strategies that would further criminalize and imprison Black people, and on the other hand, proposed xenophobic measures on a municipal and state level to detain and deport undocumented immigrants. Proposing our ordinance forced a conversation about the repressive nature of the state and the need for common unity of various communities, especially "Black and brown unity," in fighting the forces of white supremacy. The ordinance passed because of how it was framed. It galvanized working and professional sectors in the Black, Latino, white, and immigrant communities by demonstrating that they had common interests and common enemies.

Operational Fronts

Since the early 1990s, with the emergence of the Jackson People's Assembly, the New Afrikan People's Organization has built coalitions that are as operational as they are political. By "operational" we mean that each organization in the front plays a designated role, not just in the coalition, but in the broader arena of social struggle against white supremacy, economic exploitation, and state violence. Building a coalition in this manner helps to avoid unproductive competition within the movement and advances a division of labor that builds interdependent and vested relationships. It also enables us to develop long-term and deep political commitments to move beyond the "least common denominator" platforms that are typical of coalitions. The clearest expression of the depth of these relationships is the People's Platform, which was developed in 2009 under the leadership of the people's assembly and adopted by all of the strategic allies in our various operational fronts.

A key to our operational fronts approach has been the construction of three different but fundamentally interrelated bodies: the popular front, the united front, and the national liberation front. Although these are often regarded as mutually exclusive strategies, we buck the trend. We conceive of the popular front as a big tent in the fight against white supremacy, fascist aggression, and other forms of economic and social reaction. It is intentionally constructed as a multiclass, multiracial, and multinational front that seeks to address broad social issues on the basis of the highest level of unity possible. Meanwhile, the purpose of the united front is to build and maintain strategic fields of engagement with various social forces with bases in the working class. It focuses on working class struggles for jobs, higher wages, and better working conditions, and to counter the mass repression and incarceration of the working class. It is critical to note that in Mississippi most of these social forces are not unions or worker centers, although both are represented in the front. Rather, it is primarily composed of churches and community organizations. Finally, the national liberation front is a multiclass front of New Afrikan or Black forces focusing on the broad and multifaceted struggle for self-determination for people of African descent.

In terms of policy, since we assumed that we would occupy the mayoral office for at least one term, we prioritized transformative policies because we thought that their impact would be the most enduring legacy of our administrative term. These policies include the following:

- make Jackson a sustainable city centered on the production and use of renewable energy sources and "zero-waste" production and consumption methods;

- support cooperatives and cooperative development in the city, including but not limited to the creation of a cooperative incubator in the city's department of planning and development, as well as the creation of a cooperative startup loan fund;
- mandate strict local hiring policies for city contract awards to ensure greater equity;
- enforce strong community benefit agreements and reinvestment requirements for corporations, commercial retailers, and developers wanting to do business in Jackson;
- expand and modernize public transportation systems in the city, including the support for rail projects and renewable energy fleets;
- expand public health services and guarantee access for residents to join the programs of the Affordable Health Care Act that have largely been rejected by the state government;
- expand the democratic scope of public education, and in particular, change policy to make school board positions elected rather than appointed by the mayor;
- create strong community oversight of the police through a control board with the power to subpoena, indict, and fire officers for misconduct or human rights violations. We also sought to implement policies that decriminalized the possession and use of marijuana in order to end one aspect of the "war on drugs," which has largely served as a war on the Black working class and produced the largest carceral state on earth;
- create policies to institutionalize participatory budgeting in order to be fully transparent, better allocate resources, and deepen democracy on a significant scale;
- institutionalize a human rights charter and human rights commission to require the city to abide by international norms and standards of conduct and policy outcomes.

All of these policies sought to institutionalize certain aspects of the People's Platform. We believed that we could pass this entire legislative agenda because of the momentum of the people's assembly together with the overall balance of power between the mayor and the city council. Jackson has seven electoral wards and seven city councilpersons. During the Lumumba administration, there were five Black councilpersons and two white councilpersons. Four of the Black councilpersons were solidly aligned with the administration and the fifth generally fell in line to avoid looking obstructionist. One white councilperson was a member of the Democratic Party and is viewed as liberal within the Jackson context. She supported and voted for our agenda as long as it didn't overtly threaten the power of developers who were key to her electoral success. The other white councilperson was affiliated with the Tea Party faction of the Republican Party and typically voted against anything we proposed on ideological grounds. Despite Chokwe's untimely death, his short administration accomplished a number of significant things. It passed a 1 percent sales tax to raise revenues to fix the city's crumbling infrastructure and keep its water system from being regionalized or privatized, which would have diluted Black political control. It published the "Jackson Rising Policy Statement," the administration's most concrete translation of the People's Platform into public policy recommendations. Finally, it introduced participatory democratic practices into Jackson's municipal government.

The Lumumba administration attempted to govern the city as an open book by allowing the city council to engage in all departmental planning sessions, participate directly in budgeting sessions, and by having weekly one-on-one meetings with all seven council members. These practices had never been done in Jackson and have not been followed by Chokwe's successor. We also turned all major policy decisions into "mass questions" and "mass engagements." On two major occasions the Lumumba administration organized processes for the general public to decide on a major issue: the passage of an "infrastructure repair budget" in October 2013 and the 1 percent sales tax referendum in January 2014, which passed with 94 percent of the ballots. As part of the political project of democratizing American democracy, this process elicited mass support, built a public culture of participatory engagement, and shifted the balance of political power toward the Black working class. The more the class was engaged and actually exercised decision-making power, the less governance was an elite affair ruled by technocrats and the servants of capital.

Our administration's main constraint, which ultimately occupied much of our time in office, was a threatening consent decree forced on the city by the Environmental Protection Agency (EPA) in late 2012 to address its water quality issues. Jackson has some of the worst water quality of any midsize city in the country. The problem is Jackson's antiquated water delivery system. In the "historic section" of Jackson built before the early 1960s, most of the pipes are made of copper and lead and are over a hundred years old. The EPA decree stipulates that, from 2012, the city has seventeen years, with strict intermittent timelines of three, five, and ten years, to complete an entire overhaul of the water delivery system or face severe penalties and the possibility of losing control over the ownership and management of the system. It was estimated in 2013 that the overall cost of this overhaul would be at least $1 billion.

The questions this threat posed to our administration were, first, how to generate the revenue to cover this expense and retain control of the water system, and second, how to do it without sacrificing other standard expenditures and critical programs, policies, and our overall agenda. The truth is that we did not have an adequate answer to these questions. The population at large and our social base in particular were adamant about not losing control over the system. But there were divisions within and between the administration and our social base about how to save it and how to generate the resources to do so. These problems were exacerbated by members of the Tea Party in the state legislature who introduced an emergency management bill modeled on a Michigan law that would have allowed the state to take over troubled municipalities.

Our differences of opinion and lack of clarity on these issues, coupled with our general inexperience in governing, resulted in our administration enacting a set of contradictory policies. One set of policies resulted in raised water rates while another led to a 1 percent sales tax increase. It also compelled a faction of our administration to engage forces outside of our standard theory and framework of practice in alliance-building. On the advice of Frank Biden (brother of then–vice president Joe Biden) and the Blue Green Consultant Group (an engineering and sustainable energy consulting firm tied to Biden and to various transnational corporations) some members of our administration started to appeal to, and entertain advice and offers from, transnational corporate engineering firms to repair and finance our consent decree operations. The reasoning for this deviation was to explore creative ways to finance the water system overhaul in order to retain the city's control over it.

The end result of this confusion was that our policies and actions alienated a critical portion of our base, particularly the elderly on fixed incomes for whom the increased water rate created a degree of hardship without sufficient explanation or enough relief. This confusion and alienation proved costly for our next attempt to engage with electoral politics.

When Mayor Lumumba suddenly died, the city council followed the protocols of the city's charter by appointing an interim mayor and scheduling a special election for the mayor's seat in mid-April 2014, barely a month and a half after Chokwe's death. In order to continue advancing our agenda, the base of our movement compelled Chokwe's youngest son, Chokwe Antar Lumumba, to run for mayor. However, the movement did not have enough time to reflect on the lessons learned from Mayor Lumumba's term, let alone collectively internalize them to refine its practice. As a result, we did not adequately address all of the contradictions that had developed during the Lumumba administration. This led to the demobilization of a critical part of our base. Although Chokwe Antar made it to the runoff round of the special election and won a solid majority of Black voters (officially 67 percent), he lost the election to City Councilman Tony Yarber by nearly 2,500 votes.

In a city that is nearly 80 percent Black, facts generally dictate that the person who wins the Black majority's vote wins the elections. The 2014 special election was an exceptional case in that Tony Yarber only won 32 percent of the Black vote but secured an overwhelming 90 percent of the city's white minority vote, which turned out at a record-breaking rate of 75 percent. Although the historic white voter turnout was crucial, the decisive factor was actually the low Black voter turnout. Plain and simple, the base did not turn out. They sent us a clear message and we are now in the process of internalizing these lessons so that we can continue to advance our critical experiment. The key takeaways are as follows:

1. The process of mass education and instructional struggle is more important than holding office. During our brief period in office, we believed that the act of governing was just as important as mass education. We now believe decisively that mass education and instructional struggle must be primary. We have to constantly engage the base on all critical questions throughout the entire process of any decision so that they understand all of the choices and their implications and can make sound collective decisions.
2. Our practice has to be as sound as our theory. Our practice of governance did not always equate to our previous work of building

an independent base of political power rooted in a democratic mass movement. Capacity was our most critical challenge in this regard. Key members in the administration who had been crucial to building the mass base of our democratic experiment often did not have the capacity to fully participate in the people's assembly or in other areas of the mass work because they were preoccupied with learning their new positions and the limits they entailed.

3. Since 2009, our broad efforts have developed scores of new organizers, both young and old, but our plans to systematically train and develop these new organizers have not been as intentional as we desired. Securing adequate resources to develop a school and training program we call the Amandla Project has been a challenge. Many of the organizers who have the experience, training, and skill to serve as dynamic educators and trainers have had to give priority to other critical areas of work on our agenda. After the passing of Mayor Lumumba, the Jackson People's Assembly and the organic leadership of the Jackson-Kush Plan initiative determined that being intentional about the development of new cadres should be made a top priority. Since Chokwe's experience and skill as a leader could not be replicated and replaced, we would have to "raise hundreds of new Chokwes," not only to sustain but to advance the initiative. Along with the Jackson Human Rights Institute, we are now conducting ongoing trainings at the Chokwe Lumumba Center for Economic Democracy and Development.
4. The united front and the national liberation front must take precedence over the popular front. To pass legislative initiatives like the 1 percent sales tax we overemphasized appeals to the popular front to the detriment of the other fronts. The small-business faction of our base cringed at the notion of taxing corporations and the wealthy to pay for the system's redevelopment, primarily out of fear of "scaring away" the few industrial and commercial employers that remain in the city. This produced friction within the united front because many workers felt that we were privileging middle-class interests and concerns over the concrete needs of the working class. This contributed to the demobilization experienced during the April 2014 special election. Even a relatively well-organized and mobilized mass movement is seriously constrained by the structural limits of

capitalism, particularly in its neoliberal form. This taught us the extent to which we have to avoid the many pitfalls of neocolonialism that are centered in unprincipled alliances among oppressed peoples as well as between the leaders of the oppressed and the forces of the oppressor.

5. We have learned the extent to which governing in the neoliberal era is a ruling class project of "accumulation by dispossession" that generates private wealth by plundering public goods on all levels of government.[12] Under present dynamics there is intense economic compulsion to govern the city as if it were a business, especially midsize cities like ours with a declining tax base and diminishing job opportunities. Rather than providing essential services, politicians ravenously search for savings like capitalists seeking profits. This encourages privatizing and outsourcing services, consolidating and downsizing government departments, depressing wages, and breaking unions and other forms of worker solidarity. Since there are fewer profitable ventures in the real economy, various forces of capital view the municipal state as a depository bank that they must politically capture in order to survive. This is true especially of small-business owners who are the only real faction of capital in the Black community in Jackson. The Black elite is a driving dynamic in Jackson's politics. This poses deep challenges for a radical project ultimately trying to transform the capitalist social order on a local level, but which remains dependent in part on alliances with "petty bourgeois" or small-capital social forces in order to win elections and govern effectively. We, along with left forces engaging in similar initiatives elsewhere, have to figure out how to win elections and govern without relying on the resources and skills of these vacillating social forces.

We are now recalculating and rebuilding our operational fronts in the wake of the new conditions and regional alliances that have been created by the forces of capital in response to our success in 2013. The main issue is how to build a new and more reliable popular front in light of capital's clear aim to split our previously existing alliances over questions of economic development. In light of our mixed experiences engaging state power, we are now focusing our work on revitalizing the People's Assembly and initiating economic transformation through cooperative development in the form of Cooperation Jackson. This is to better prepare us for the next round of mayoral and city council elections in 2017 when we intend to again run Chokwe Antar Lumumba for mayor together with several other candidates for city council as determined by the People's Assembly.[13]

We have prioritized building Cooperation Jackson during this next period to strengthen the organization of the working class, expand production in our city and region, and to build a more coherent movement for economic democracy.

Cooperation Jackson and the Struggle to Create Economic Democracy

Cooperation Jackson is an emerging vehicle for sustainable community development, economic democracy, community ownership, and resistance to gentrification. It will consist of four interdependent institutions: an emerging federation of local worker cooperatives, a developing cooperative incubator, a cooperative education and training center, and a cooperative bank or financial institution. The broad mission of Cooperation Jackson is to advance economic democracy by promoting universal access to common resources. In defiance of the culture of cutthroat competition, this network of worker-owned and self-managed cooperatives will create a "solidarity economy" based in shared values of social responsibility and equity. Cooperative businesses are unique from other types of commercial enterprises in that they exist to meet the needs of people, not to maximize profits. They are often formed as a way to expand economic opportunity, promote sustainability, and build community-wealth by creating jobs with dignity, stability, living wages, and quality benefits. Rather than making working people subservient to capital, cooperatives put capital in the service of working people by:

- democratizing the processes of production, distribution, and consumption;
- equitably distributing the surpluses produced or exchanged;
- creating economies of scale;
- increasing bargaining power;
- sharing costs of new technology;
- gaining access to new markets;
- reducing individual market risks;

- creating and obtaining new services;
- purchasing in bulk to achieve lower prices;
- providing credit under reasonable terms.

Cooperatives and community collectives have a long history in Mississippi, particularly within the Afrikan community. In particular, Cooperation Jackson draws from Fannie Lou Hamer and her work to build the Freedom Farms Cooperative and the Federation of Southern Cooperatives/Land Assistance Fund, which helped lay the foundations for the broader initiative to build a dynamic democratic economy in Jackson.[14]

We want to accomplish a major breakthrough for the cooperative movement in the South by becoming the first major network of predominately worker cooperatives to be established in an urban area. While it will undoubtedly take years, if not decades, we believe we possess the potential to transform the lives of working-class Jacksonians by becoming the Mondragon or Emilia-Romagna of the United States.[15] We hope to create a model that will encourage and enable workers throughout the US to implement their own initiatives to promote economic democracy, solidarity economics, and cooperative development.

Cooperation Jackson's primary focus is the Sustainable Communities Initiative. It is a place-based strategy to transform a neighborhood in West Jackson, the working-class gateway to Downtown Jackson. For more than thirty years, West Jackson has suffered from rapid capital flight and divestment that are driven in large part by white flight. Since the late 1970s, West Jackson has become a Black working-class community with high concentrations of poverty. Since the late 1980s, large parts of West Jackson have become dilapidated and abandoned. It is now estimated that there are over 1,832 vacant lots and 832 abandoned structures out of a total of 6,748 lots in the community with approximately 41 percent of total parcels in the community unused. The community has an estimated 13,890 people of which 92 percent are Black.[16]

In Municipal Ward 3, the primary focus of the Sustainable Communities Initiative, there is an estimated eight thousand people, the overwhelming majority of whom are Black working-class people. The community is almost exclusively a bedroom community with few employment opportunities at present. The largest employers in the community are Jackson State University and Jackson Public Schools. Vast tracts of this community are either vacant or dilapidated and abandoned. The community is also in a food desert. Residents typically have to travel two to three miles to access quality food.

Four major real estate and economic initiatives developing adjacent to West Jackson are driving speculative pressures on the community and confronting it with the threat of gentrification through race- and class-based displacement. The four development initiatives are the Medical Corridor being driven by the University of Mississippi and funded by the state government, the One Lake Redevelopment initiative being pushed by the Greater Jackson Chamber of Commerce and proposed in "Plan 2022," the development of a new sports stadium for Jackson State University athletics through the destruction of the old stadium in the Medical Corridor development area, and downtown real estate speculation fueled by various petrochemical companies seeking to expand their lobbying and business operations in the state capitol. Each initiative is in a different stage of development, but all have dedicated and committed funding streams and widespread support among local elites.

The primary force compelling this speculation is the Medical Corridor. Its expansion provides the economic conditions that enable the other developments. Over the course of the next decade the corridor's expansion will provide hundreds of short-term construction jobs and thousands of long-term jobs in the medical and medical support fields. All of these new doctors, nurses, technicians, and other support and spin-off workers will need places to live. Many will want to avoid long suburban commutes and have easy access to various living amenities and opportunities for entertainment. Knowing these needs and anticipating the long-term profits that can be drawn from them, speculators and developers are rapidly moving in on West Jackson due to its strategic location, accessibility, and cheap real estate values.

None of these elite-driven developments are designed to incorporate the existing population living in West Jackson. This is where Cooperation Jackson and the Sustainable Communities Initiative come into the picture. Cooperation Jackson is not averse to economic development, of which West Jackson and many other Black working-class communities throughout the city are in desperate need. However, we are committed to sustainable, community-driven and controlled development without displacement. We firmly believe that the existing community must equitably benefit from the new developments and should be able to determine and execute its own community revitalization and wealth-building initiatives.

The Sustainable Communities Initiative is one of the few bottom-up development initiatives in Jackson. It is being driven by the membership of Cooperation Jackson through extensive community outreach, but its foundations were laid by the long-standing organizing efforts of the Malcolm X Grassroots Movement and the Jackson People's Assembly. The initiative's success will mitigate the displacement of the Black community of West Jackson and create an array of eco-friendly and community-owned cooperative businesses and institutions that will be accessible to both the longstanding and new residents of West Jackson.

We will accomplish this by establishing the following institutions:

- *Community land trust* (CLT). Cooperation Jackson will create a nonprofit corporation that develops and stewards affordable housing, community gardens, civic buildings, commercial spaces, and other community assets. We will purchase a number of vacant lots, abandoned homes, and commercial facilities primarily in West Jackson that are currently owned by the State of Mississippi, the City of Jackson, and private owners. We will organize them into a community land trust to ensure that they are removed from the speculative market and dedicated to sustainable communal endeavors.
- *Community development corporation*. Cooperation Jackson will create a community development corporation to help create new low-income housing to sustain working-class communities and affordable commercial facilities to support the development of cooperative enterprises in Jackson.
- *Housing cooperative*. Cooperation Jackson will turn a significant portion of the land and properties acquired and held by the CLT into an "eco-village" housing cooperative. This will provide quality affordable housing and stable rents to help sustain and build vibrant working-class communities in Jackson. It will also create a significant degree of its own energy and waste management infrastructure to ensure that it can more effectively utilize alternative sources of energy and eliminate waste by creating a comprehensive "zero-waste" recycling program.
- *Cooperative education and training center*. The Lumumba Center for Economic Democracy and Development will promote broad

> public understanding of economic democracy, the foundations of solidarity economics, the principles of cooperatives, and how worker-owned and self-managed enterprises benefit workers, their families, and their communities. It will also educate and train working people to successfully start, finance, own, democratically operate, and self-manage a sustainable cooperative enterprise.

The eco-village seeks to radically alter the quality of life in West Jackson over the course of the next decade by increasing and improving housing that is green and permanently affordable, creating high quality, living wage jobs, and servicing essential needs for energy, food, and entertainment. With the support of some of the other cooperatives in Cooperation Jackson, our housing cooperative will start by ensuring that each house in the cooperative is LEED (Leadership in Energy and Environmental Design) approved and draws 50 percent or more of its energy from solar energy. Each house will also have water catchment and efficiency systems and will be integrated into a zero-waste resource recycling and regeneration program. We are also in the process of creating a "clean energy" division of our construction cooperative that will specialize in building and installing solar panels for affordable community use. The eco-village will also provide affordable operational space for several cooperative enterprises, which will create a mutually reinforcing and self-sustaining market ecosystem, supply chain, and network of associated worker-owners. In its broadest dimensions, the eco-village will also be an integrated "living-systems" community based on principles of "cooperative living" whereby all of the residents of the housing cooperative will participate in the village's recycling and composting programs, which will create a stable protected market for recycling and urban farming cooperatives.

Our Freedom Farms Urban Farming Cooperative plans to build a network of farming plots throughout Jackson, but primarily concentrated in West Jackson, to create a comprehensive urban farming operation that will provide and sustain dozens of living wage jobs over time. The farming operation will start with hoop house and raised bed production and hydro, aquaponic, and aeroponic farming in some of the commercial facilities held in the CLT in West Jackson. The urban farming cooperative will establish several neighborhood-based farmers' markets to supply transportation-challenged residents in low-income communities with affordable and high-quality foods (vegetables, fruits, fish, and poultry). This will end our food deserts and address the chronic health issues that particularly plague Black people, such as obesity, diabetes, hypertension, and chronic heart disease. We will also become a primary supplier of quality organic produce to the Jackson public school system as well as to the grocery and convenience stores that serve low-income communities. Freedom Farms will also house our child-care cooperative and a worker and consumer grocery cooperative.

These efforts are combined with a number of campaigns that will make Jackson one of the most sustainable cities in the world and a localized attempt to transition the city away from the extractive economy. We are currently engaged in a public education campaign to get the municipal energy company, Entergy, to follow through on preliminary agreements it made with the Lumumba administration to institute a broad program of solar conversion. We are also engaged in a campaign to have the City of Jackson take the lead on the creation of clean energy by dedicating its buildings and vacant lands toward the production and distribution of solar energy. We are working with the Mississippi Association of Cooperatives (MAC) and the Federation of Southern Cooperatives/Land Assistance Fund (FSC/LAF) on a campaign to get the numerous utility cooperatives in Mississippi to institute a broad program of solar energy conversion and production in the rural portions of the state. Furthermore, a joint study group of Cooperation Jackson and the People's Assembly is developing a strategy and campaign to challenge and end fracking in the state of Mississippi, which is being aggressively pursued by Governor Phil Bryant and a host of state-based and transnational petrochemical companies.[17] Finally, we are also engaging in joint ecosystem stewardship initiatives. In particular, we are supporting work to protect the wetlands in and around Jackson by launching a citywide campaign to end the presence of organic refuse in the city's antiquated storm drain system. Eliminating this type of dumping will help the city to clean the sludge that currently clogs and contaminates the drainage system. The leaves, grass, and organic waste that are currently dumped into the system by numerous inhabitants can be recycled and reused as organic compost to support local farmers and restore the depleted topsoil of the Mississippi Delta region.

Our anchor point for all of this is the Lumumba Center for Economic Democracy and Development, located at 939 West Capitol Street, Jackson,

MS 39203, in the heart of the West Jackson community. It will serve as the organizing base for the Sustainable Communities Initiative and the overall administrative operations of Cooperation Jackson. The Lumumba Center has close to six thousand square feet, possesses a restaurant-grade kitchen, and is accompanied by a back lot of over three-fourths of an acre of land for the urban farming and recycling cooperatives. As part of our commitment to developing "new and sustainable" forms of economic activity and social living that will enable and support a just transition from the extractive economy, the Lumumba Center will be one of the greenest buildings and business operations in Jackson. In line with our vision of sustainability, we will utilize as much of the surface area of the building as possible for the production of solar energy and will also weatherize and retrofit it to reduce energy and water consumption.[18]

The Lumumba Center will also serve as the base of operations and production for the Nubia Lumumba Arts and Culture Cooperative, which grounds the cultural work of Cooperation Jackson, including the mass communications, issue-framing, and popular education that are key to social movements creating transformative counterhegemonic narratives. The Arts and Cultural Cooperative conducts regular programming out of the Lumumba Center, including cultural events (public lectures, hip-hop, spoken word, and art exhibits), production sessions (films, music, and visual arts), and art and wellness trainings (production classes, art trainings, physical fitness, martial arts, and yoga).

Cooperation Jackson has made some significant advances in its relatively brief history because of the foundations laid by the People's Assembly and the Lumumba administration. Next to the People's Assembly, it is now the tip of the spear in our offensive engagements to advance the Jackson-Kush Plan.

By Way of Conclusion

We started this essay by noting that the fundamental aim of this experiment is to attain power. We have had and continue to experience small "tastes of power." In our movement's most recent victory, in early December 2014, a critical resolution was passed by the city council to make Jackson a human rights city with a human rights charter and commission. Nevertheless, the road to social liberation is long and often treacherous. Following the electoral defeat of Chokwe Antar Lumumba in April 2014, we shifted toward building Cooperation Jackson and a network of cooperatives. Our major foreseeable challenge is securing enough resources, grants, and capital to build the organization and to finance our initial start-ups. Although this is a challenge for all cooperatives, it is a special one for us because our movement does not have the backing of any of the local or regional sources of finance capital. Virtually all of these sources are opposed to major aspects of our platform and avidly supported our opponent. By all indications, the harder we push and the more we advance, the more determined they become to hinder if not arrest our development.

A lot is currently riding on the success of Cooperation Jackson. Even if it only launches two or three viable cooperatives within the next two years, it will prove that our vision is attainable and worth fighting for. Should it seriously struggle or fall short it will likely reinforce the capitalist narrative that "there is no alternative." After decades of combating self-hate, individualism, consumerism, and the ethos of "get rich or die trying," we cannot afford to go one step backwards. So the pressure is on. We are stuck between a rock and a hard place because our base doesn't have the financial resources to support multiple cooperative start-ups on its own. And we do not yet have any extensive contacts with progressive financers and investors, either nationally or internationally, willing to support cooperative enterprises and green alternatives. So we must be extremely innovative to survive, not to say thrive. We are looking for allies and we are encouraged by how much national and international attention our work has received.

The "Jackson Rising: New Economies Conference" that we organized and hosted in May 2014 has been noted as one of the most influential and inspirational conferences about solidarity economics and economic democracy in the US in decades. Our people's assembly model, our people-centered human rights agenda, and our demand for a national plan of action for racial justice and self-determination have been adopted by many of the forces involved in the growing Ferguson resistance and Black Lives Matter movements. Our challenge is to transform all of this interest and enthusiasm into a national and international network of support that will help us advance the Jackson-Kush Plan and continue to build the transformative movements of our age from Occupy to the Movement for Black Lives.

Unfortunately, we do not possess a crystal ball to indicate where we will ultimately land. Nevertheless, our collective confidence has grown through this experience as we have witnessed time and time again something that Chokwe Lumumba often stressed: "A movement that secures the love and confidence of the people has no bounds." We are still very much making the road by walking, but we are certain that we are still headed down the right path. We believe that our experiences and contributions are worth learning from and we hope that others engaged in the struggle to liberate humanity will welcome them in the spirit of unity and struggle in which they are shared.

Stay tuned!

This is a substantially revised and updated version of a study that was originally published by the Rosa Luxemburg Stiftung–New York Office (https://rosalux.nyc) and is republished here with their permission.

Notes

1 United States Census Bureau, accessed May 16, 2022, https://www.census.gov/quickfacts/fact/table/jacksoncitymississippi,US.

2 Kimberly Amadeo, "What is the Real Unemployment Rate?" Balance, updated June 3, 2022, accessed June 20, 2022, https://www.thebalance.com/what-is-the-realunemployment-rate-3306198.

3 Analyzing data from the Bureau of Justice Statistics, the Prison Policy Initiative concludes that per 100,000 population in Mississippi, 1,645 Blacks are incarcerated compared with only 399 whites. Prison Policy Initiative, accessed May 16, 2022, https://www.prisonpolicy.org/graphs/MS_incrates2001.html. See also Jerry Mitchell, "Miss. Locks Up More Per Capita than China and Russia," *Clarion-Ledger*, updated October 21, 2014, accessed May 23, 2022, https://www.clarionledger.com/story/news/2014/10/18/miss-incarceration-rate-one-highest-nation/17468129.

4 This notion of the "weakest link in the chain" is borrowed from Lenin; see V.I. Lenin, *Imperialism: The Highest Stage of Capitalism*, in *Lenin's Selected Works* (Moscow: Progress Publishers, 1963), 1:667–766.

5 Jaime Boler, "Resistance by Enslaved People in Natchez, Mississippi (1719–1861)," *Mississippi History Now* (February 2006), accessed May 16, 2022, https://www.mshistorynow.mdah.ms.gov/issue/slave-resistance-in-natchez-mississippi-1719-1861.

6 Jamie and Gladys Scott were convicted of armed robbery in 1994 in Scott County, Mississippi. They allegedly stole from two men in Forrest, Mississippi. The Scott sisters were given double-life sentences. After three failed appeals over a sixteen-year period, the Scott sisters were granted clemency by Governor Haley Barbour on December 29, 2010. The actual perpetrators of the robbery served no more than three years in jail. The campaign to free the Scott sisters was led by the People's Assembly and adjudicated by attorney Chokwe Lumumba; see Micah Smith, "The Scott Sisters," *Jackson Free Press*, August 7, 2015, accessed May 19, 2022, http://www.jacksonfreepress.com/news/2015/aug/07/scott-sisters; Ward Schaefer, "The Tragic Case of the Scott Sisters," *Jackson Free Press*, November 3, 2010, accessed May 19, 2022, https://www.jacksonfreepress.com/news/2010/nov/03/the-tragic-case-of-the-scott-sisters.

7 Shubhanga Pandey, "The Next Nepali Revolution," *Jacobin*, January 3, 2016, accessed May 19, 2022, https://www.jacobinmag.com/2016/01/nepal-liberal-constitution-maoists-protests-monarchy; Gerassimos Moschonas, "A New Left in Greece: PASOK's Fall and SYRIZA's Rise." Dissent (Fall 2013), accessed May 19, 2022, https://www.dissentmagazine.org/article/a-new-left-in-greece-pasoks-fall-and-syrizas-rise; Sten Hagberg, "The Legacy of Revolution and Resistance in Burkina Faso," Stockholm International Peace Research Institute, February 22, 2016, accessed May 19, 2022, https://www.sipri.org/commentary/essay/2016/legacy-revolution-and-resistance-burkina-faso.

8 Malcolm X Grassroots Movement, "The Black Nation Charges Genocide! Our Survival Is Dependent on Self-Defense!" (2014), unavailable May 20, 2022, https://mxgm.org/the-black-nation-charges-genocide-our-survival-is-dependent-on-self-defense. See also Arlene Eissen, "Operation Ghetto Storm: 2012 Annual Report on the Extrajudicial Killing of 313 Black People by Police, Security Guards and Vigilantes," updated November 24, 2014, accessed May 23, 2022, http://www.operationghettostorm.org.

9 Alison Roseberry-Polier, "Haitians Overthrow Regime, 1984–1986," Global Non-Violent Action Database, accessed May 19, 2022, https://nvdatabase.swarthmore.edu/content/haitians-overthrow-regime-1984-1986; Jose Maria Sison, "It Was a Convergence of Various Forces," *Philippine Daily Inquirer*, February 26, 2006, accessed May 19, 2022, https://news.google.com/newspapers?nid=2479&dat=20060224&id=FFg1AAAAIBAJ&pg=1930,4044246; Hagberg, "Burkina Faso"; Ken I. Boodhoo, "Grenada: The Birth and Death of a Revolution (Dialogue #34)," LACC Occasional Papers Series, Paper 36 (1984), accessed May 20, 2022, https://digitalcommons.fiu.edu/laccopsd/36.

10 The concepts of "war of position," "war of maneuver," and "hegemony" are drawn from the work of Italian Marxist Antonio Gramsci. The term *hegemony* describes the social processes utilized by ruling elites to consolidate, justify, and normalize their social domination; see Antonio Gramsci, *Selections from the Prison Notebooks*, ed. Quintin Hoare and Geoffrey Nowell Smith (New York: International Publishers, 1971): 229–39; also see Valeriano Ramos, "The Concepts of Ideology, Hegemony, and Organic Intellectuals in Gramsci's Marxism," *Theoretical Review* 27 (March–April 1982), accessed May 20, 2022, https://www.marxists.org/history/erol/periodicals/theoretical-review/1982301.htm.

11 The notion of "transitional demands" or a "transitional program" is largely adopted from the works of Leon Trotsky; see Leon Trotsky, *The Age of Permanent Revolution: A Trotsky Anthology*, ed. Isaac Deutscher (New York: Dell, 1964), 254–59; Leon Trotsky, "The Transitional Program" (1938), accessed May 20, 2022, https://www.marxists.org/archive/trotsky/1938/tp/transprogram.pdf.

12 The notion of "accumulation by dispossession" is drawn from the work of David Harvey. It describes the ongoing process of primitive accumulation or accumulation through wholesale plunder and theft; see David Harvey, "The New Imperialism: Accumulation by Dispossession," in *Socialist Register 2004: The New Imperial Challenge*, eds. Leo Panitch and Colin Leys (London: Merlin Press), 63–87, accessed May 20, 2022, http://socialistregister.com/index.php/srv/article/view/5811/2707#.WIYculNrjIU.

13 Chokwe Antar Lumumba was elected mayor of the City of Jackson and sworn into office on July 3, 2017.

14 Kay Mills, "Fannie Lou Hamer: Civil Rights Activist." Mississippi History Now (April 2007), accessed May 23, 2022, https://www.mshistorynow.mdah.ms.gov/issue/fannie-lou-hamer-civil-rights-activist.

15 See the website of Mondragon, accessed May 23, 2022, https://www.mondragon-corporation.com/en; also see People's Food Co-op, "People's History," accessed May 23, 2022, https://www.peoples.coop/peoples-history.

16 For more information on these statistics, see Duvall Decker Architects, "West Jackson Master Plan," accessed May 23, 2022, http://www.duvalldecker.com/west-jackson-master-plan. Please note that the section of West Jackson on which we are concentrating does not reflect the entire region analyzed in this document.

17 Global Energy Monitor Wiki, "Mississippi and Fracking," updated April 30, 2012, accessed May 23, 2022, https://www.gem.wiki/Mississippi_and_fracking.

18 The concept of a "just transition" emerged out of the labor left in the 1980s to demand that workers in the coal and petrochemical energy industry be given job training to prepare them for newer, more climate-friendly occupations in the wake of the downsizing of jobs in the industry. Cooperation Jackson uses an expanded definition of this concept drawn from the Climate Justice Alliance and the Our Power Campaign, which it also helped to construct. According to the expanded definition, a "just transition" is a worker- and community-driven process of transitioning from a petrochemical dependent economy to a restorative, carbon-neutral economy. See "Our Power Campaign: Communities United for a Just Transition," accessed May 23, 2020, https://tinyurl.com/4nz4vxna.

The Socialist Experiment: A New-Society Vision in Jackson, Mississippi

Katie Gilbert

Chokwe Lumumba had been the mayor of Jackson, Mississippi, for five months when, in November 2013, he stood behind a lectern and addressed a group of out-of-towners with a curious phrase he would soon explain with a story: "Good afternoon, everybody, and free the land!"

On his tall, thin frame he wore a bright blue tie and a loosely fitting suit, extra fabric collecting around the shoulders of his jacket. Wire-rimmed glasses rested over a perpetually furrowed brow on his narrow, thoughtful, frequently smiling face. A faint white mustache grazed his upper lip.

In welcoming the attendees of the Neighborhood Funders Group Conference, a convening of grantmaking institutions, Mayor Lumumba was conversational and at ease, as he tended to be with microphone in hand. His friends had long teased him for his loquaciousness in front of a crowd.

Lumumba informed the room that on the car ride over he'd decided he would tell them a story. He explained that big things were happening in Jackson—or, were about to happen—and his story would offer some context. It was one he had recounted many times. Polished smooth, the story was like an object he kept in his pocket and worried with his thumb until it took on the sheen of something from a fable, though the people and events were real. "It was March of 1971 when I first came to the State of Mississippi," Lumumba began. "It was several months after the students at Jackson State had been murdered," he said, referring to the tragedy at the city's predominantly Black college, which left two dead and twelve injured after police opened fire on a campus dormitory in May 1970, less than two weeks after the Kent State shootings.

Lumumba had traveled to Mississippi with a group called the Provisional Government of the Republic of New Afrika (PG-RNA). He was twenty-three at the time and was taking a break from his second year of law school in Detroit. He had put his training on hold for the work of new-society building. After the assassination of Martin Luther King Jr., Lumumba had been increasingly drawn to what he considered the radical humanism of the Provisional Government's plan to create a new, majority-Black nation in the Deep South. The PG-RNA planned to peacefully petition the United States government for the five states where the concentration of Black population was largest: Mississippi, Louisiana, Alabama, Georgia, and South Carolina. Leaders framed their demand for this transfer as a reparations payment after centuries of enslavement and degradation that Black people had experienced in America. As part of a symbolic effort to break with a painful past and announce a new way forward, the PG-RNA encouraged New Afrikans to shed names with European origins in favor of African ones. Edwin Taliaferro became Chokwe Lumumba: Chokwe, he said, for one of the last tribes to successfully resist the slave trade and Lumumba for Patrice Lumumba, who led Congo to independence and became its first democratically elected prime minister. The Republic of New Afrika's Declaration of Independence announced that its socialist society, arranged around cooperative economics, would be "better than what we now know and as perfect as man can make it."

By March of 1971, when the mayor's story began, Lumumba was an officer in the Provisional Government. The organization had made an oral agreement to buy twenty acres of land from a Black farmer in Bolton, Mississippi, a small town about twenty miles west of Jackson. They had hired a contractor to build a school and dining hall on the property. The site would be named El Malik after the name Malcolm X had taken for himself: El-Hajj Malik El-Shabazz. March 28, a Sunday, had been chosen as Land Celebration Day, when the group would inaugurate the site at El Malik.

Lumumba was in the caravan's lead vehicle as they approached Bolton that afternoon. Forty-two years later, he described to the conference attendees in Jackson how the Klan drove up and down the road in their trucks, brandishing weapons, and how state, local, and federal police formed a barricade across the road. Mississippi's attorney general, A.F. Summer, had declared that there would be no Land Celebration Day. Akinyele Omowale Umoja, an African American Studies professor at Georgia State University, writes in his book *We Will Shoot Back: Armed Resistance in the Mississippi Freedom Movement* that the day before the scheduled event, PG-RNA leaders had seen a hand-painted sign near the property that the KKK had posted: "Niggers, there will be no meeting here Sunday. Free six-foot holes."

Mayor Lumumba paused, and when he spoke again his voice had moved up a register. "This was a different day about to break," he said. "And even though sometimes we break our days somewhat recklessly, it was certainly going to break. There were five hundred of us"—other records say there were one hundred fifty—"and we said, 'We come in peace, but we come prepared.' We had old people, we had young people, we had babies. We were praying. Hard revolutionaries, driven back to prayer!" He laughed. "Looking for God wherever we could find Him."

The day might well have combusted. What happened instead, Lumumba told the audience, was something that seemed, even as it unfolded, like a miracle best left unexamined. "I know it's hard for a lot of you to believe this—that roadblock opened up. Just like the Red Sea."

Past the barricade, the New Afrikans traveled five miles. They had arrived. Two months later, the Bolton farmer would renege on his agreement to sell, and support for the PG-RNA and its efforts would wane over the next few years, as FBI and state and local police pushed successful counterintelligence programs to undermine the group's efforts. But in looking back, Lumumba focused on the energy of that Sunday, when the people around him fell to the ground in such profound joy that they began to eat the dirt, he recalled, out of a spontaneous desire to take into their bodies the freedom they believed they'd found. "That's where that slogan came from," Lumumba said. "'Free the land.'"

In Lumumba's successful campaigns for city council in 2009 and for mayor in 2013, "Free the land" had been a common refrain of his supporters. His platform, too, echoed the vision he and his fellow New Afrikans had harbored for their new society on Land Celebration Day. He pledged that his office would support the establishment of a large network of cooperatively owned businesses in Jackson, often describing Mondragon, a Spanish town where an ecosystem of cooperatives sprouted half a century ago. In debates and interviews, he promised that Jackson, under the leadership of a Lumumba administration, would flourish as the "Mondragon of the South"—the "City of the Future."

As Mayor Lumumba neared the end of the story of Land Celebration Day, his voice faltered. He turned his head and squeezed his eyes closed to regain composure. The memory of Land Celebration Day was still a live wire running through him and through his plans as mayor of Jackson.

"The reason I started off with that little prelude," he told the Neighborhood Funders Group Conference attendees, "is that I wanted to say that what has not changed is the vision of that new society, that new way of thinking. That new way of engineering and governing a society, where everyone would be treated with dignity. Where there would be no class, no gender, or color discrimination. Even though it didn't happen in that little community which we called El Malik, now it's about to happen in Jackson, Mississippi. And would you believe it?"

As a child, Chokwe Lumumba's son Chokwe Antar sometimes wished for another name, one that sounded more like those of his friends. But Antar also trusted his parents, and he looked up to them. He knew his father's work as a civil rights–oriented lawyer was important, and he used to sneak out of his bed at night to lie on the floor of his parents' room and listen as they discussed his father's cases. He shared his father's name, and he would grow up to share his profession.

After Land Celebration Day in 1971, Chokwe Lumumba returned to Detroit and finished his law degree. In 1976, he joined the Detroit Public Defenders Office, and two years later he opened his own law firm. In 1986, Chokwe and his wife, a flight attendant born Patricia Ann Burke who changed her name to Nubia Lumumba, moved their family to Brooklyn so Chokwe could better represent his high-profile clients there, including Black nationalist Mutulu Shakur and his stepson, Tupac Shakur. Even after the PG-RNA dissolved, Lumumba had never stopped thinking about how a group of determined activists could build a new society where Black people could escape racism, racist violence, and deprivation. Lumumba cofounded two organizations to keep working toward versions of the PG-RNA goal: the New Afrikan People's Organization (NAPO) in 1984, and, later, the Malcolm X Grassroots Movement (MXGM). According to Professor Umoja, NAPO's members still oriented themselves toward the goal of a Black nation. MXGM was slightly different—members advocated self-determination for Black communities using a variety of means, including independence, but also sought other paths that would lead toward empowerment and liberation. In 1988, when the couple's daughter, Rukia, was nine, and their son, Antar, was five, the Lumumbas relocated to Jackson, Mississippi. In the following years, Chokwe and Nubia would often tell Rukia and Antar that they'd come to the South because there was work to be done there and because they wanted to give their children the struggle.

Lumumba's work as a lawyer invited renown to the family, but also occasional vitriol. Antar and Rukia spent one afternoon hiding in a closet with a knife clutched between them after a death threat was breathed over the phone while their parents were away. In high school, on the phone with a girlfriend, Antar would wrap up by saying, "Okay, goodbye to you, too, FBI!" His parents always said that the house's phones were tapped. Years later, among the hundreds of pages of documents that emerged from a Freedom of Information Act request for FBI reports on Chokwe Lumumba, Antar saw his high school graduation photo. The sight of it there didn't unsettle him because it confirmed what he'd always been told.

After Antar's freshman year at Murrah High School, his father judged that basketball was too prominent a priority in his son's life and decided that Antar would transfer from his school and its championship team. Chokwe offered him a list of new high schools to choose from. Antar entered his sophomore year at Callaway High as a D-average student and went on to graduate in the top 10 percent of his class.

Antar recalls that his mother used to joke, with an edge of seriousness, that her children had better not pursue that "same old boring lawyer thing" that took so much of her husband's time without bringing in as much money as it should. She hoped her children would pursue careers that would allow them the finer things in life. She noted that Antar loved drawing street plans and hearing her talk about Benjamin Banneker's designs for Washington, DC, and that math seemed to come easy to him. She pushed him to consider becoming an engineer or an architect. Most of all, she seemed to want to ensure that her son didn't choose a career just because it was his father's.

But once Antar entered college at Tuskegee University in Alabama, he never seriously considered anything but a path to law school. After he earned a Juris Doctor from the Thurgood Marshall School of Law at Texas Southern University, he returned home in 2008 to help run his father's law practice. Within the year, he was watching his FBI-surveilled activist father wade into the quagmire of Jackson city politics. Chokwe had been tapped as the public face of a long-brewing effort to continue working toward the PG-RNA's vision of an egalitarian, Black-led society—or at least some version of it.

In the early 2000s, MXGM's leadership formed a think tank to plot out a twenty-first-century strategy to realize the new-society dream. After some discussion, at the organization's annual ideological conference in 2005, MXGM's national membership determined that Mississippi was the best staging ground for the experiment in society building—the same conclusion the PG-RNA had come to in the 1970s. The eighteen contiguous counties that run along the Mississippi River on the state's western edge are all majority-Black (except one, which is 47.8 percent Black). The MXGM new-society drafters referred to this line of counties along the Mississippi Delta as the Kush District, as PG-RNA leadership had, named after the ancient civilization built along the banks of the Nile, in what is now Egypt and Sudan. MXGM members began moving to Jackson from all across the country. In 2012, after roughly ten years of refining their blueprint, the think tank posted a draft of its Jackson-Kush Plan to the MXGM website. The document detailed steps to build a socialist, majority-Black, eco-focused model society within Mississippi's shrinking capital city, as well as initiatives to mobilize communities in the Kush District, and expand from there.

The society described in the Jackson-Kush Plan was a close descendant of the one envisioned by the PG-RNA, with some tweaks based on lessons learned and the interests of the drafters three decades after Land Celebration Day. Like the PG-RNA vision, a central pillar of the new society would be economic democracy based in cooperative ownership. Another would be the embrace of fully participatory democracy through the organization of self-governing organs called people's assemblies, which would be the loci of real decision-making power in the communities where they operated.

The starkest difference between the PG-RNA's and the Jackson-Kush Plan's new-society visions was in the stance on engaging with the country's established system of electoral politics. The PG-RNA's leaders had based their call for a new society on the argument that the federal, state, and local governments were illegitimate, since they had long relied on broad disenfranchisement to amass their power. MXGM revised this stance: A central goal described in the Jackson-Kush Plan was the development of progressive political candidates who, if elected, could support the goals of economic democracy and self-governing people's assemblies from that elected office.

In 2008, two of the drafters of the Jackson-Kush Plan approached Chokwe Lumumba about running as one of those candidates. They also approached Antar, then twenty-five, about running for a city council seat. Antar demurred. The idea of running for office wasn't practical in his mind or, frankly, all that appealing. He'd just returned to the city after seven years away at school; outside of family and friends, not many people knew him in Jackson, and, beyond that, he had little interest in electoral politics as a form of public service.

Antar tried to dissuade his father from running, too—Chokwe Lumumba may have been a highly respected lawyer in the community, but that didn't make for a political profile prominent enough to run a successful campaign. His father agreed; mayor would be too much just then. He'd run for city council instead. But he made it clear that he disagreed with his son on the broader point: Antar needed to consider running for office someday. Sometimes, he told his son, the movement requires that we give of ourselves and do something we didn't envision.

In 2012, as Chokwe was finishing his term on the council and shifting his attention to his run for mayor, MXGM pressed Antar to run to fill his father's vacated council seat. He declined again. Antar had just married his longtime girlfriend, Ebony, an English professor at Tougaloo College, and months later, they'd learn she was pregnant. But he dedicated himself fully to his father's campaign, serving as its official spokesperson as he helped to draft the platform on which Chokwe Lumumba would squeak into a runoff election after a second-place finish in the Democratic primary—and go on to win the mayorship. Still, Antar harbored absolutely no interest in becoming a politician himself, and he couldn't imagine what would ever change his mind.

It wouldn't be long before he'd find out.

On a Tuesday morning in late February 2014, not quite eight months into Chokwe's term, the mayor called his son complaining of chest pains. Antar left court and rushed to Chokwe's house to drive his father to the emergency room at St. Dominic's Hospital. Mayor Lumumba told the hospital staff that he thought he might be having a heart attack. According to a 2016 lawsuit filed by the family against St. Dominic's,

Chokwe waited hours at the hospital before he received any treatment. According to the lawsuit, a cardiologist recommended a blood transfusion. Just before 5 p.m., Chokwe died suddenly. The cause of death was later determined to be a heart attack.

Shock and grief coursed through Jackson with the news that the mayor was dead. Many Jacksonians were still nursing the morale boost that had come with Lumumba's election. They had faith that their city was about to figure out new ways to address longstanding problems: crumbling streets and dangerously outdated water infrastructure, a depleted tax base, and a lack of jobs. During his brief tenure, the late mayor had asked the city to vote on a new 1 percent sales tax to help begin to pay for the infrastructure fixes the city desperately needed. He'd helped organize people's assemblies to provide forums to answer Jacksonians' questions about the proposal. Voters approved the new tax with 90 percent in favor.

"There was a sense of loss greater than just his passing," Antar told me later. "People said to me, 'We felt like we were on the right track. What do we do now?'"

At Chokwe's funeral, former Mississippi governor William Winter, a Democrat, admitted that during the mayoral campaign, he'd feared that as mayor Lumumba would divide the capital city. "I could not have been more wrong," he said, adding, "The strong leadership of Chokwe Lumumba has opened the door to a bright future for us."

On the night that Chokwe died, Antar was the only family member present. His mother had passed away ten years before from a brain aneurysm, and Rukia was rushing to Jackson from her home in New York. As he waited for Rukia and extended family in Detroit to arrive, Antar asked the friends who had gathered in the hospital room to give him some time alone with his just-deceased father. In that quiet moment, before the shock of Lumumba's death had spread through Jackson, Antar resolved to run for mayor. He would keep the decision to himself until he told his wife the next morning, giving himself the night to turn it over in his head. But as soon as the idea came to him in that hospital room, he knew he wouldn't separate himself from it again. He thought of his father's mandate: Sometimes the movement requires that you give of yourself and do something you didn't envision as part of your plan. A more practical concern was bearing down on him, too. The new-society vision needed a new protector, a new vessel. Who else could it be but him?

Chokwe Antar Lumumba was thirty at the time, and he looked younger. In his public appearances he shifted between a lawyerly, knitted-brow seriousness, often repeating the last few words of a sentence to underline his point, and a readiness to amiably tease a friend or fellow candidate and break into his boyish laugh. I would come to learn that with strangers and familiars alike his charisma takes the form of a warm accessibility, the sense that he has time for everyone, and doesn't begrudge anyone who asks for it.

I traveled to Jackson for the first time in March 2016, two years after Chokwe Lumumba died. In Chicago, where I live, the protracted winter still lingered, but I found Jackson was already in full leaf, deep into spring. My hotel on North State Street was across from a middle school whose grounds included space for a modest football field, faded tennis courts, and a scuffed soccer field. Across the street to the north was the sprawling campus of the University of Mississippi Medical Center, the city's largest employer after the State of Mississippi, with about ten thousand employees. Up the road was the Fondren District, the site of a dedicated revitalization effort led over the past two decades by nearby residents, where coffee shops' signs bore thoughtful fonts and a tapas restaurant and oyster bar made new use of a shuttered public school. Antar met me in the lobby of my lodge-themed hotel on one of my first evenings in town. He strode in wearing a black hoodie and a flat-brimmed Detroit Tigers ball cap. He had waves for the people he knew behind the front desk and a handshake for me. We sat at one of the lobby's round wooden tables and Antar told me about the last couple of years, affirming his continued dedication to the work his father had left unfinished. His wedding ring clanged against the table's glass top when he struck it to emphasize his points, which he did when he brought up cooperatives. "What we have to establish are businesses that are in the business of making money but *also* have an interest in serving the community—not in picking up and moving out," he said. He laid out an analysis of why the solutions delineated in the Jackson-Kush Plan were still necessary, quoting Malcolm X, Gandhi, and his father. He spoke of the importance of oppressed people leading self-determined lives, resurrecting the parlance of the Republic of New Afrika. But other parts of his analysis were more current, like when he talked about mass incarceration and the proliferation of prisons as a Band-Aid over the US's industrial decline and stagnant economy. "On many levels, this economic experiment that we have in this country is a *failed model,*" he said with another strike to the glass. "And it's a failed model in particular for oppressed people."

Six weeks after his father's death, Antar ran in the April 2014 special election for mayor. He lost in a runoff to Tony Yarber, founder and pastor of the majority-Black Relevant Empowerment Church. As mayor, Yarber had scrapped the most notable parts of the Lumumba administration's agenda, including plans for the city-supported cooperative businesses, the people's assemblies, and the goal to turn Jackson into a zero-waste city.

Antar's loss was another setback for the new-society goal, so the MXGM members most connected to the Jackson-Kush Plan shifted their route forward yet again. That May, members of Lumumba's former administration and MXGM went ahead with what had been planned as a city-supported event called the "Jackson Rising: New Economies Conference." The three-day summit sought to provide an educational foundation for attendees in building the pieces of a democratic, cooperative economy. At the end of the conference, a few core members of MXGM announced a new organization called Cooperation Jackson to continue the co-op-building goal.

In late 2015, I had emailed Cooperation Jackson and a few days later I was on the phone with Sacajawea Hall, a cofounder of the organization who had moved to Jackson from Atlanta in December 2013. I'd been doing some traveling, guided by an interest in alternative economic models inside the United States. The prehistory of this interest might be traced to 2006 when, at twenty-two years old, I took a job as a researcher for *Institutional Investor's Alpha,* a magazine that analyzes hedge funds, which I knew next to nothing about. I was to help coax information from secretive hedge fund managers about the billions of dollars under their management. I had no idea that I'd taken the job on the eve of the strangest moment in nearly a century to be covering the financial industry. By 2008, I was reporting for *Alpha*, and that year the public, US-based pension funds I covered collectively lost more than one-fourth of their value after the collapse of the global financial market. Suddenly, knowing nothing became our shared national condition as we watched our economic system flail in the precise ways we were told it never would. The revoking of this system's untouchable status granted us permission to peer into our enormous, tangled economic apparatus and ask: In what ways has this system long been failing us? And, more crucially:

What might we build that's better? Radical economic experiments have proliferated in the US since the 2008 collapse—but then, they feel radical only if you've lived your life, as most of us have, believing that profit maximization, endless economic growth, and the individual's mandate to consume are circumstances as intrinsically human as hunger and childbirth. I count myself among those who struggle to imagine living within any other economic arrangement, but by the time I called Saki Hall I was starting to understand that other people's imaginations have granted them more leeway, and some were living out economic experiments that embody alternatives. At the end of our conversation, Saki invited me to come see for myself what Cooperation Jackson was doing.

The month before my trip, I spent a week living and working at Twin Oaks Community in Louisa, Virginia. Twin Oaks is a fifty-year-old fully egalitarian mini-society of roughly one hundred members, where labor and governance systems are modeled from the utopia described in B.F. Skinner's novel *Walden Two.* At Twin Oaks, I hauled soil on a vegetable farm, snipped strawberry bushes, and hosed down equipment in the tofu factory. I helped two affable men named Tony and Ezra prepare a Sunday dinner of split pea soup, smoked pork belly, and baguettes. I was apprised of the joys of polyamory, the necessity of requiring the group's permission for pregnancy in a community where children are supported by the whole, and the freedom in not being defined by a lifetime in a single job or role. During my week at Twin Oaks, the pebble I couldn't lose from my shoe was the place's overwhelming whiteness. It was also true that the preponderance of people at Twin Oaks came from middle- and upper-class backgrounds. Here was a vision for a drastically new way of thinking about our economic arrangement, and yet its population lacked representation from the racial minorities who had for so long been kept away from the levers of economic control in our country. I didn't know if this constituted a failure of Twin Oaks's model—but it made me less interested in the experiment being run there.

In the course of my research, I had never heard Chokwe Lumumba or any member of MXGM or Cooperation Jackson describe the Jackson-Kush Plan as a utopian vision. Still, when I arrived in Mississippi, a line from utopian scholar Ruth Levitas rattled in my head: "Utopia's strongest function, its claim to being important rather than a matter of esoteric fascination and charm, is its capacity to inspire the pursuit of a world transformed, to embody hope rather than simply desire." If I wanted to plot for myself the coordinates of the line between fantastical and real societies, between unheard-of ambitions for change and perfectly familiar ones, between a fable told for comfort and a plan for real change on the ground somewhere, I felt that I needed to better understand what was happening in Jackson. I hoped being there would offer some insight into how those lines are drawn, and how fixed they really are.

Toward the end of our conversation in the hotel lobby, Antar departed from the scholarly analysis and made a declaration that struck me as uncharacteristically dramatic: He saw Jackson, Mississippi (and he never said the city without the state), as a last chance. This was a place where long-marginalized Black communities could build a new economy for themselves, a democratic and fair society, a foundation for good lives to grow from. In his mind, this Black-majority city that sat in the middle of the state with the highest concentration of Black people in our country *had* to be the staging ground for this particular experiment in moving past economic and governance systems that weren't working for so many. Antar told me he was grateful he hadn't won the special election in 2014. He wasn't ready then, he'd realized. But now he was. Though he hadn't publicly announced it, he said he would run for mayor of Jackson again in 2017.

An abundance of deep, wide potholes was my first indication that something wasn't quite working in Jackson. After an earlier rainstorm, the pockmarks dotting the capital city's streets shimmered with mock placidity. "I was trying to miss that one!" Saki exclaimed after her car lurched through a pothole pond spanning two lanes, throwing us against our seat belts and jostling the car seats embracing her five-year-old daughter and two-year-old son in the back seat. A red plastic plate dotted with the crumbs from her daughter's breakfast hopped from Saki's lap to her feet.

Saki wanted to talk about the potholes: Did I see all of them? See that one there, how deep it is? To Saki, the potholes stood for something more than a threat to her car's underbody. To Saki, and, I would soon learn, to many other Jacksonians, the proliferation of unfilled potholes was a clear sign of a downward spiral in full effect.

Saki had picked me up from my hotel on my first day in town with an offer of a driving tour of Jackson. I enthusiastically accepted. We trundled southward over the potholes until we reached downtown. Well-maintained grounds studded with magnolias and tupelos spread out around the grand, Greek Revival State Capitol, Governor's Mansion, and City Hall. These were interspersed with muted, modern, concrete and steel buildings housing government agencies like the Mississippi Gaming Commission and the Parole Board. A few local restaurants operated out of the downtown storefronts, but many of the storefronts stood tenantless. Faded signs indicated the businesses that had since departed or dissolved, imparting a feeling that the past remained cloyingly close by.

In the decades before the Civil War, the newly crowned capital city had prospered as cotton made Mississippi a wealthy state. That changed in 1863 when Union armies destroyed Jackson; its skeletal remains allegedly earned it the nickname "Chimneyville." The city has been struggling to claw back to its former economic abundance ever since.

During Mississippi's eleven years of Reconstruction, the Freedmen's Bureau established by the US Congress helped lay the foundation for the state's public school system. Black citizens' participation in democracy was higher than in any other southern state—more than two hundred Black people were elected to public office during the period. But a concerted effort to alter the trajectory of societal reshaping, called the Mississippi Plan, was devastatingly successful. Developed in 1875 by the conservative Democrats desperate to eject Reconstruction-supporting Republicans from office, the Mississippi Plan employed organized violence to intimidate and kill those working toward a society in which races were equal. Democrats had regained political power by 1876; in 1890, they passed a new state constitution that concretized the exclusion of Black citizens from the democratic process. In two years, the number of Black Mississippians registered to vote fell from 142,000 to 68,117. Generations later, Mississippi's public schools managed to delay real desegregation for sixteen years after the *Brown v. Board of Education* decision in 1954. According to the Mississippi Historical Society, one-third of the districts in the state had achieved no desegregation by 1967 and less than 3 percent of the state's Black children attended classes with white children. It took another Supreme Court decision, in 1969, to force real desegregation in Mississippi.

Jackson was 60 percent white in 1970, and by the 2010 census, 18 percent white. The city's population decreased from nearly 200,000 in 1990 to under 170,000 in 2016. As the majority-white suburbs expanded, they turned into a kind of sticky ring around the city center, pulling economic development out of Jackson. The Mississippi Department of Revenue reports that the City of Jackson brought in approximately $117 million in gross sales tax in fiscal year 1990 and $177.6 million in fiscal year 2016—worse than stagnant when accounting for inflation. And as the tax base has crumbled, so has the city's infrastructure. The *Clarion-Ledger* wrote in March 2017 that a report from an engineering firm in 2013 found that more than 60 percent of Jackson streets had four years or less of serviceable life left. In 2017, that life is about spent.

Saki steered us a few blocks west of downtown, to a silent stretch of streets lined with one- and two-story buildings. These were more like memories of buildings, with empty window frames, unkempt overgrowth outside, and encroaching wilderness inside. Saki told me we were in the middle of the Farish Street Historical District.

Farish Street was built by slaves and after emancipation it came to be used primarily by the formerly enslaved. A new business district emerged during Reconstruction, and it thrived in Jim Crow's "separate-but-equal" South as an alternative to the Capitol District blocks away, where Black Jacksonians weren't welcome. Farish Street was one of the largest African American districts in the South; it held legal firms, doctors, dentists, jewelers, banks, retail stores, and hospitals.

In the 1950s, Black activists mobilized Black and white protesters to put pressure on white-owned businesses across the city to allow access to Black customers. A sit-in at a Jackson Woolworth's turned violent. When the Civil Rights Act passed in 1964, mandating the desegregation of public places, many African Americans in Jackson celebrated their victory by taking full advantage of it, bringing their spending to previously inaccessible white businesses. The African American business owners on Farish Street suffered. Integration didn't work both ways; as Black people moved into previously white spaces, white spending failed to flow into Farish Street. Integration hadn't happened between two groups with equal economic footing and control, a fact for which Farish Street's slow implosion offers lingering evidence. Businesses closed like falling dominoes, and new ones stayed away as the area became known as a magnet for drugs and prostitution. Revitalization efforts of various kinds were killed by infighting and funds insufficient to the area's growing needs. What I saw outside of Saki's car window in March 2016 was the result of this history: an abandoned community, a failure on the part of the city.

Saki rattled over the train tracks that bisect the capital, and we passed into West Jackson, another part of the city entirely. The population here is almost completely Black, and, according to the Hinds County Economic

Development Authority, unemployment in West Jackson is double both the county and state averages. In 2014, Duvall Decker, a local architecture firm, worked alongside neighborhood residents and eighteen Jackson-based organizations to compile a "West Jackson Planning Guidebook" for a section of West Jackson around Jackson State University; according to their findings, residents in the area had a choice of three grocery stores in comparison to sixteen check-cashing businesses, and almost half of the properties were officially vacant. In the past year, the number of grocery stores dropped to just two. On this side of the tracks, Capitol Street—which originates in front of the Old State Capitol on the east side—is a quiet, winding road, flanked by rows of abandoned structures.

Saki's daughter announced from the backseat that she had to go to the bathroom, and Saki pulled a U-turn. We were just a few minutes from Cooperation Jackson.

In the spring of 2015, Cooperation Jackson moved into the building now dubbed the Chokwe Lumumba Center for Economic Democracy and Development. A group of volunteers set to work renovating the building, a former daycare center, to better fit its new purpose. Pastel murals were painted over and mildewed carpeting ripped out, and a fresh paint job brightened the building's exterior. The color was the deep green of the kale and collards that would soon populate a cooperatively owned farm in the backyard.

We parked in a long driveway, and I helped Saki unload the children. From the outside, the single-story structure looked like it had been snapped from a strip mall and dropped into its grassy one-acre lot. Saki pressed a doorbell and a young man wearing a lip ring and a light brown cap to hold his dreadlocks opened the door. He led us across a linoleum floor into the cool darkness of the Lumumba Center. Saki and her daughter headed for the bathroom, which had a hand-drawn sign on the door: "Gender Is a Universe."

The man who had let us in introduced himself as Brandon King. He was another cofounder of Cooperation Jackson and a member of MXGM. Brandon had moved to Jackson a little over a year ago, a month before Chokwe Lumumba died. I would soon learn that, like Brandon and Saki, many of Cooperation Jackson's twenty cofounders had moved to Jackson from cities outside of Mississippi.

Saki had recently decorated the beige cinder block walls of the Lumumba Center with photo collages. One featured Chokwe. She showed me the industrial kitchen where the group planned to open a cooperatively owned café called Nubia's Place. In the center's biggest room, she pointed to the areas that would eventually hold a stage for open mic nights, seating for the café, and couches. A door led to the wide backyard, where seedlings of cooperatively owned Freedom Farms were pushing upward under the soil.

Typing at a desk in a small office off the main room I recognized Kali Akuno, another founding member of Cooperation Jackson and its apparently tireless de facto spokesperson. He was also Saki's partner. I'd seen videos of him speaking about their work at conferences around the world. Kali had drafted the public version of the Jackson-Kush Plan and, I would later learn, he had been one of the first to approach Chokwe Lumumba about running for office.

A year after my first visit to the Lumumba Center, Antar would run again for the mayor's seat. As had been the case for his father's bids for office and Antar's previous run in the special election, the campaign's messaging and platform would be developed with input from members of MXGM. One of his most regularly invoked campaign slogans—"When I become mayor, you become mayor"—would be rooted in the Jackson-Kush Plan's vision of self-determination and self-governance. In his debates and speeches, Antar would regularly seize opportunities to champion cooperatives as part of the prescription for the city's economic malaise. He would also mention the Lumumba Center, a place where that work of establishing economic democracy was slowly getting started.

The Jackson-Kush Plan had reached a moment in which it had an established base in the former daycare center on Capitol Street and a charismatic young attorney seeking to offer more support for the plan from inside City Hall. But for something to come of this moment, so long in the making, Antar would need to convince voters that his vision—especially his economic vision—was the one they should vote for at a desperate moment for their city, despite the more familiar solutions competing for the role.

The first big showdown between Jackson's top mayoral candidates was in March 2017—two months before the primary election and a year after my initial trip to Jackson. (Antar had officially announced his candidacy on May 19, Malcolm X's birthday, with a press conference on the steps of Jackson's City Hall, where the assembled crowd had chanted: "Free the land! Free the land! Free the land!") Grace Inspirations Church, in West Jackson, hosted the forum on a Sunday evening and the roughly two hundred attendees who gathered in the sanctuary were still dressed in their Sunday best. I noticed men in suits with matching ties and pocket squares, and women in long dresses, a few in swooping hats.

It was a welcome occasion for civic sociability and also for indulging in some lofty plans to fix Jackson. The city's infrastructure problems continued to nose their way into the lives of every Jacksonian. Many of the forum's attendees had come from houses that were under notices to boil tap water before it was safe to drink; the next day, city officials would announce that water in a large swath of the city would be turned off for forty-eight hours the following weekend in order to replace pipes in a portion of Jackson's out-of-date water distribution system.

The church's pastor, Danny Ray Hollins, opened the forum with a word of prayer. As it turned out, it was a prayer for Jackson. "It's our home," he said. "It's a city that we love—a city with a myriad of issues. Problems. Problems not brought about as a result of any one man, or one administration. We have *sent out the call!* To those who would be *mayor!* And we've invited them here—to church." His tongue delivered that last word to the room like it was wrapped in silk. "And we're here to hear them share their vision for this city."

The five most popular candidates among the sixteen running for the mayor's seat had been invited to participate in the forum. All five were Democrats, and all five were Black. On Grace Inspirations' altar stage, six empty chairs were arranged in a semicircle. The moderator, Pastor C.J. Rhodes, took a seat toward the center and called the candidates to the stage one by one. Along with his brief introductions, he noted each person's placement in the polls—Antar was in the lead—until a woman of grandmotherly age in one of the front pews called for him to stop it with the polls. "Yes, thank you, ma'am," Rhodes said, admonished, and followed her directive as he welcomed the last three men.

A poll released a few days after the debate would confirm that Antar stood comfortably in first place. His support was sharply racialized, and despite his overall favorable numbers, he had garnered a net negative impression among the white Jacksonians polled. But the white contingent was small enough and his favorability among Black voters was high enough that his lead in the race was a stable one. Brad Chism, a white political analyst in Jackson, declared that his own polling data indicated it was Antar's race to lose.

Antar's biggest competition was John Horhn, a veteran state senator. Horhn had run for mayor twice before, and both times he failed to garner enough support to qualify for a runoff. This year, he had refined his argument. "We're at a point in our city where we've got to make sure we get it right the next time," he said at one point during the forum. "We're only going to get one more bite at the apple in my opinion." I'd heard people speak with similar finality about Jackson in recent months (including other references to near-finished apples). They usually meant the same thing: If the city's finances didn't take a few steps back from the edge of potential bankruptcy, if crime didn't abate and the schools didn't improve their outcomes, Jackson was vulnerable to takeover from the State of Mississippi. Though Horhn presented state takeover as an implicit threat, he also positioned some level of help from the state as Jackson's last possible saving grace—and himself, with a twenty-four-year tenure in the Senate, as the one person who could broker that salvation.

Another close contender for the likely Democratic primary runoff was Robert Graham, who spent most of his speaking time on litanies of his own experience as Hinds County supervisor and his thirty-five years as a civilian employee of the Jackson Police Department. He stressed his involvement in a deal to bring a Continental tire plant to the Jackson area, slated to open in 2018 with twenty-five hundred jobs on offer.

Ronnie Crudup Jr. was a long shot, in fourth place. He was the only candidate who didn't register particularly strong opinions among those polled, in a positive or negative direction. His father, Bishop Ronnie Crudup Sr., is senior pastor of a church serving over three thousand in South Jackson.

Incumbent mayor Tony Yarber was a distant fifth in the polls, the only candidate in the top five with a net negative favorability rating, at -39.2 percent. A perception of mismanagement along with a spate of sexual harassment cases had pulled his reputation into a sharp downward plunge over the course of his three years in office.

In one of his first questions to Antar, Rhodes bored directly into the discomfort that plenty of Jacksonians still felt about the Lumumbas, pointing to the history of the PG-RNA and the sense that Antar's platform had been born out of some sort of bigger plan—or "agenda," as the more suspicious tended to put it. "One of the concerns that came up in the last election," Rhodes said, his eyes on Antar, "was about whether or not, for lack of a better way of saying it, Antar Lumumba is going to be an antiwhite mayor, and push away white folks, and is going to bring in nationalists, and it's going to be *Jafrica* and all these kinds of things." Some murmuring and laughter broke out around the room.

"I appreciate you asking that question, Pastor Rhodes," Lumumba began. In his job as a criminal defense attorney, he said, he worked with many people who don't look like him, and had plenty of success. But his voice was climbing stairs, building up to something higher. "I've been labeled as a radical," he continued. "My father was labeled as a radical. You were told that he would divide the city, and what was demonstrated was something entirely different." Antar would tell me later that he and the MXGM members helping to run the campaign had made the concerted decision to embrace the loaded "radical" descriptor that had been hurled at his father and at him in his previous campaign. His pace quickened a few steps, riding on its own momentum. "Honestly, when people call me a radical, I take it as a badge of honor. Because Martin Luther King was radical." Applause spread through the room. "Medgar Evers was radical." The applause intensified, and so did Antar. "*Jesus Christ* was radical." The applause didn't break, so he spoke louder to be heard. "The reality is that we have to be prepared to be as radical as circumstances dictate we should be. If you look outside these doors and you see a need for a change, then you should all be radical." I heard shouts of "Amen!" He went on, "And the reality is that we haven't found ourselves in the condition we're in because someone has been too *radical* for us." He inflected these last few words. "I would argue we haven't been radical enough." The applause carried on like an unbroken wave.

The audience's response made me think about a question that had been posed during Chokwe Lumumba's campaign: Was it possible for a person to be both a revolutionary and a politician? Throughout the debate, the candidates piled on the Yarber administration's apparent inaction in fixing the streets, and the mayor's responses tangled into long paragraphs explaining the technical details that had complicated the solutions. I found myself wondering if the mundane, full-time job of running a city with long-neglected infrastructure could leave any room for helming a revolution. Because Chokwe Lumumba's tenure was so truncated, it remained an open question.

Still, it was true that the people in the church that afternoon became most animated when Antar shifted from the role of knowledgeable attorney into that of revolutionary. And he didn't withhold his more progressive ideas—rooted in the Jackson-Kush Plan—for reimagining how economic revitalization could happen in Jackson. "Oftentimes we find ourselves engaged in merely a discussion of how we entice businesses to come here. We have to also consider where there is a need that we can fill, where we can develop the businesses ourselves. And look at *cooperative business* models where the people who live in the community own the business, and the people who work in that business not only determine what their labor will be, but they have a say-so in what the fruits of the labor will be."

In addition to being central to the PG-RNA's new-society ideal, cooperatives had been an important part of other visions for true racial equality in the state. In 1969, in Sunflower County, Mississippi, the voting rights activist Fannie Lou Hamer helped develop the Freedom Farms Cooperative—the namesake of the beds behind Cooperation Jackson. In her 2014 book *Collective Courage: A History of African American Cooperative Economic Thought and Practice,* Jessica Gordon Nembhard, a political economist who researches African American collective economies, argues that co-ops have existed as a necessary counterweight to this country's economic violence against Black communities from the beginning of slavery here. "There seems to be no period in US history where African Americans were not involved in economic cooperation of some type," she writes. Cooperatives, though never a critical mass, have offered an alternate mindset, a means of insulating the economic participation of a group pushed out of the dominant system.

Cooperatives are a main tenet of the Jackson-Kush Plan. The framers of this new-society experiment viewed them as a way to help people unlearn the lessons their economy taught them and train them to be democratic in every aspect of their lives. They knew that the individual, foundational work of building buy-in for a whole new type of economy would be even harder than winning an election.

A few days after the mayoral forum at Grace Inspirations Church, I stopped by the Lumumba Center for a class. It was a Wednesday at noon, just in time for that week's installment of the Economic Democracy Learning Series, led by Kali Akuno. In a large room with a wall of street-facing windows, eight folding tables were arranged in a rectangle. The ten or so attendees took their seats around it with the ease of people who had done this many times before. Saki sat at the front of the room next to Kali, who clicked final preparations into his laptop. Slides lit up a projector screen on the wall behind him as students unwrapped sandwiches, flipped open Styrofoam containers of chicken wings, and forked fruit salad out of Tupperware.

In Kali's mind, Cooperation Jackson is an experiment; his hypothesis is that living and working in fully democratic communities will change the people involved. One of the experiment's first steps, he believes, is for people to realize how capitalism has shaped them and to recognize how alternatives could refresh their perspectives.

He picked up on this week's slide and began. The class was continuing its guided tour through Marx's *Capital*. Under discussion today was Marx's concept of exchange-value. Kali asked if someone would volunteer to read the first slide. After a silence, a woman wearing a green cloth headband over graying dreadlocks and strings of beads around her neck complied. She read:

> *The exchange value of a commodity is what one receives in exchange for this commodity.*
> *Statement A: One chair is the exchange-value of two pairs of pants.*
> *Statement B: Two pairs of pants are the exchange-value of one chair.*

When she had finished reading, her brow didn't unfurrow and her mouth kept silently working. Kali waited. "How will we, in this new environment we're creating, fairly determine exchange-value?" the woman asked. She pointed to the woman next to her, half of a young white couple dividing their attention between the front of the classroom and their two small children playing behind them. The young woman was a skilled seamstress. If a seamstress has been developing her skill for twenty years, the woman in the green headband reasoned, a pair of pants she produces would be worth more than one chair, wouldn't it?

Kali shook his head and turned the question back to her. "Is that just profit in your thinking?"

She considered this and eventually nodded once, her brow still knitted.

Kali continued through the slides. Before moving to Jackson, Kali had worked as a high school teacher, and he knew when to slow down, reword something, and expand where it might help. The overriding question he returned to again and again, in different forms, was: See how this capitalist economic system has shaped you when you weren't looking?

As the class passed its second hour, eyes fell downward. I noticed a glow of cell phones nestled in many laps. It was a clear, sunny day, but through the thick sheets of adhesive window tint lining the windows onto Capitol Street, the view of outside was abstracted, a soupy blue. After an afternoon with this view, the laborious deconstruction of exchange-value made the city outside seem blank and theoretical—like an empty place requesting something to be built in it.

Toward the end of the three-hour class, Kali paused and looked around, noting the man next to me who'd finished his chicken wings and laid his head on the table. Kali acknowledged the denseness of the material and admitted that it had taken him three passes through *Capital* before he really started to grasp it. He recited the socialist dictum stripped down to its simplest articulation: From each according to their ability, to each according to their need. "No democracy has achieved that yet," he added. It was clear that he didn't share this anecdote to caution anyone in the room against working toward the achievement. After all, he labored for three hours every Wednesday afternoon to make his lessons understood. The implicit challenge was to figure out a way to do what no one else had done.

Kali had been brought up in Los Angeles during the tumultuous 1970s and 1980s. His parents were active in the Black Power movement, and he grew up going to the movement's meetings and reading its literature. Most of his parents' peers ascribed to a Marxist-socialist orientation. As a young boy, Kali told his mother, in all earnestness, that he wanted to know everything. He read hungrily, and as a teenager he particularly looked forward to packages in the mail from an uncle who wrote for Black newspapers and music journals in Toronto. In these publications, he read about people like Maurice Bishop and groups like the People's Revolutionary Government of Grenada. His political education came, too, from what was happening around him in LA. Starting from the early eighties, the crack epidemic pummeled Kali's neighborhood with a force he didn't understand. It hit most of the families in his neighborhood, and eventually his own, and its effects were devastating. When Kali saw how, in preparation for the 1984 Olympics, the city cleaned up much of the drug trade, he concluded that they could have stopped the destruction of his community much earlier and had chosen not to. He began to notice a ruthlessness in the various systems around him.

Kali joined MXGM's Oakland chapter in 1996, just six years after Lumumba had cofounded it. By the time the organization began to discuss plans to stage an experiment in Mississippi, he was MXGM's national organizer. He moved to Jackson permanently in 2013 to devote his life to the Jackson-Kush Plan. He would go on to serve in Chokwe Lumumba's administration as its director of special projects and external funding.

Talking with Kali after the Economic Democracy class, I learned that his thinking has shifted in subtle ways over the last decade, as Jackson's economic and infrastructure problems have continued to mount. He's seen that elections can, in his opinion, become a distraction from the real work of transforming society. "I'm sure Antar doesn't want to be mayor forever," he said. "So, what are we setting up for beyond that? And beyond that, in my mind, is not just making sure we have someone in office for the next fifty years. If that's the best we can do, then we've failed, in my opinion."

"Because I think we're ultimately trying to get to the point where we've changed the rules of society—both formally and informally—where we've created a more democratic society, a more equitable society. And if there's a fully engaged citizenry, then the need for a city council and a mayor starts to become fairly moot."

I asked him what the movement stood to gain if Antar were indeed elected mayor in the fast-approaching election. After all, MXGM had decided as a body to run Antar as the face of the Jackson-Kush Plan. He pushed back in the metal folding chair and leaned his wide upper body onto the table. "That is a good question," he said. His head rested heavily in his hand, and his knee bobbed as he thought. "Woo. That's a good question." I realized I'd expected he'd have his thoughts on the topic crafted and close at hand, given his involvement both in the campaign and in the building of the Jackson-Kush Plan. He sighed. "Honestly," he admitted, "I'm a minority voice who didn't want Antar to run this time."

Kali's conception of a successful realization of the plan goes far beyond four years of Antar in the mayor's office. He imagines people's assemblies—the bodies open to all citizens that drive self-government and undergird the fully democratic society described in the Jackson-Kush Plan—coming together to, for example, defy the state's orders against sanctuary cities for undocumented immigrants, and training people in Jackson to protect immigrants from ICE raids. He imagines the creation of an alternative currency in Jackson, so that the city government could use the US dollar to pay off its debts and pay city workers part of their salaries in a "soft" currency to use at the corner grocery. For each part of this vision, the stakes would rise higher with Antar's election. I had figured that two subsequent electoral losses might have been a fatal blow to the current version of the Jackson-Kush Plan. But now I saw that, if Antar did win, it would be the next four years that would become the high-stakes last chance.

Kali then ticked off Jackson's problems and listed the municipal operations facing privatization or takeover by the state: the water system, the schools, the whole of downtown. "We're setting ourselves up to administer the most severe austerity the city's seen probably since the Civil War.... We have to be clear that if we fail, that's not just MXGM failing, or Chokwe Antar failing. That's a failure for the Left in this country."

Kali's fears are not without precedent. In a 1992 article, "Black Mayors: A Historical Assessment," historian Roger Biles explained a trend: Simultaneous with the changing laws and demographic shifts that finally made possible the election of Black mayors in major cities around the United States, white flight and the decline of industry were draining those cities' wealth and resources. These factors conspired to make Black mayoral victories, as Biles quotes from H. Paul Friesema, "a hollow prize." Biles writes: "As the tax base available to big city governments shrank, the same could not be said of the demand for public services. Rising costs for welfare, law enforcement, and maintenance of an aging infrastructure exacerbated the problems awaiting neophyte Black mayors." An embattled Kenneth Gibson, mayor of Newark, concluded resignedly: "Progress is maintaining the status quo."

Biles, who is completing a book on Harold Washington, the first Black mayor of Chicago, told me that the hollow-prize problem persists to this day. The problem is most pointedly felt, he observed, by leaders who come into the mayor's office on a wave of expectations that are, perhaps, "unrealistically high."

During Chokwe Lumumba's truncated term, the combination of Jackson's tight municipal resources and massively expensive problems created rifts within his administration. The Environmental Protection Agency had served the city with a consent decree in 2012 to force it to fix the antiquated sewage system that was spilling into the Pearl River. A 2013 estimate put the cost of the infrastructure fix at around $1 billion.

Infighting festered over how to raise the revenue. Eventually, the city increased water rates and passed a 1 percent sales tax—a regressive tax, in that it could burden low-income Jacksonians more than high-income earners. In a report reflecting on Chokwe's eight-month tenure, Kali wrote: "The most critical lesson we learned is that our practice has to be as sound as our theory. While in office, our practice of governance did not always equate to our previous work of building an alternative base of political power rooted in a democratic mass movement." The very real problem of insufficient resources highlighted a central rub inherent in the Lumumba administration: Were they aiming to capably govern a city, or to altogether reimagine it? Insiders didn't agree on the answer.

In the week leading up to the primary election on Tuesday, May 2, Jackson was crackling with the full focus of the competing campaigns. Yard signs bearing the faces of the main candidates—Lumumba, Horhn, Graham, and Yarber—clustered in abandoned lots like weeds competing for sunlight. It was the primary, not the general election in early June, that came freighted with the suspense of determining the city's next mayor. In the thoroughly blue city, a Democratic candidate was guaranteed to win the final race, and the only serious contenders fell on that side of the ballot. Antar ran in a crowded field of nine Democratic candidates, and pollster Brad Chism was certain that their support would be too divided for any one person to earn more than 50 percent of the vote. A runoff between the two top Democratic candidates was all but inevitable. By the weekend the local papers had unveiled their endorsements like the sharing of long-guarded secrets. All three publications endorsed Lumumba, even the long-running, conservative-leaning daily the *Clarion-Ledger*.

On Saturday morning, I stopped by Cooperation Jackson, where I found Brandon King in the backyard, working on Freedom Farms. From the gate, I saw him near the far edge of the fence, plunging a hoe into the ground, alone. When he noticed me approaching, he rested his hoe in the soil and smiled a hello. He was dressed like a farmer, but one who had gone to art school. Layers of necklaces strung on leather bands rested their shells and stones above his sternum, and a solid tattoo band wrapped around his left arm, opening into the shape of a star on his elbow.

The day hadn't yet unleashed its full heat, but Brandon was sweating from the work of turning a grassy patch into a new bed. He indicated another fifteen feet along the fence and told me it would be a bed for sweet peas. In the grass beside us lay a coil of chain-link fencing that he planned to install against the wooden fence so the pea shoots could climb and curl their way up toward the sun.

"How's it going?" I asked, lifting my hands to indicate, how's it *all* going—the farming, but also the mounting of the new-society experiment which had brought him here to Jackson. Brandon grabbed the hoe, lifted it high, and drove it down into the soil. He knew what I meant, and he answered for all of it. "Oh, you know me!" He let out a laugh, tinged with exasperation. "I'm impatient."

In our conversations over the previous year, Brandon had never struck me as impatient. His voice had a soft edge of something like shyness, and he always revealed a willingness to be deeply introspective and an ability to rest in the contradictions he noticed in himself, in other people, and in circumstances.

Brandon had lived in New York before moving south, and he had moved to Jackson to live in the City of the Future that Chokwe Lumumba had described. He'd never stopped wanting to live in that place. Here in the backyard, perspiring as he lifted and pulled his hoe, he was still working toward it.

Brandon's mother was one of the first Black women to work as a machinist in the Norfolk Naval Shipyard near Chesapeake, Virginia, the town where Brandon and his brothers had grown up. She frequently confronted racism and sexism on the job. At home, she introduced her children to radical Black thinkers like Malcolm X and Marcus Garvey. When Brandon was sixteen, she put down those books in favor of a Bible and became a devout Christian. He picked up her books and fell deeper into them. He respected his mother, but he didn't want her life. The nine-to-five grind was anathema to him. In every conversation I had with Brandon, he repeated his insistence that he hopes to never become a "status quo manager," like an incantation that can keep that life away. He fears the numbness, the existential stuckness—and the resigned acceptance of society the way it is.

During college—Brandon studied sociology and art at Hampton University in Virginia—he took two trips to New Orleans to provide support for the survivors of Hurricane Katrina. While there, he met members of the Malcolm X Grassroots Movement. After graduating, he moved to New York to work as a union organizer and DJ, and he joined the local MXGM chapter. In the three years since Brandon had moved to Mississippi, the Jackson-Kush Plan had seen some progress—in the founding of Cooperation Jackson, for example, and the securing of the land on which we stood—but it had also slammed up against obstacles. Nubia's Place had struggled to obtain the food license necessary to serve food out of its space in the former daycare center, though it had been catering for local organizations and events for two years. City worker furloughs, instituted under Mayor Yarber to save the city from bankruptcy, have made for a lean city staff and the resulting interminable wait times for securing business licenses.

In December 2016, Brandon, Kali, Saki, Antar, and Rukia traveled to Barcelona to observe, in a more fully developed form, elements of the society they were working toward in Jackson. Barcelona's deputy mayor took them on a tour of the city's cooperatives, including stops at a cooperatively owned bar and a cooperatively owned bookstore. They also visited the Green Fab Lab, a place to tinker and research new ways to produce renewable energy and use 3D printers, laser cutters, and other machines to make all manner of stuff. It was a chance for Brandon and the others to see an on-the-ground, functioning version of some of the plans struggling to move past dream-stage in Jackson.

A boarded-up building across the street from the Lumumba Center was meant to be the location of Jackson's own fabrication laboratory, where collectively owned 3D printers and other machines would turn out items the community needs: everything from car chassis, piping, copper wire, and insulation for houses, to dishware and utensils for Nubia's Place. But Cooperation Jackson's purchase of the building was being held back by legal snafus, and the organization was struggling to raise the money for the 3D printer and other technology. A fifteen-minute walk away on Ewing Street, Cooperation Jackson owned a grassy lot where Brandon pictured an affordable eco-village, with housing built in the fab lab and a collection of cooperatively tended farms. The first step was establishing the urban farm that would provide food to residents. But that work had been held back, too. The empty lot had long been used as a dumping ground, and the soil was poisoned with the old paint, garbage, and construction debris of the society Brandon is trying to move away from.

On the eve of Jackson's mayoral primary, Brandon was suffering these various mundane hindrances pointedly. It was all just moving so slowly, and the new society they were building wasn't feeling sufficiently set apart from the old one. "I didn't move here to help build a bunch of big cooperative businesses," he said. "When are we going to break off and do our own thing?" He leaned on his hoe, and the dreams tumbled from him: When will we be making and distributing products from the fab lab? When will we have a self-feeding network of cooperatives? When will we have an alternative currency mediating our new economy?

I told Brandon I'd help with the farming while we talked, and he grabbed another hoe. I asked if he'd been helping with Antar's campaign. A bit, he said. "But I'm not going to vote," he added. When I didn't hide my surprise, he explained that he didn't want to participate in what he considered to be an "illegitimate system." While Kali was anxious about the pressure the election could impose, Brandon was skeptical of the entire enterprise. A system relying on people's assemblies to select the next mayor, he offered, would do a better job of bringing more voices and perspectives into the democratic process.

A few hours later, we put away the gardening equipment and shifted to loading subwoofers, folding tables, and eight crates full of records into Brandon's pickup truck. He had been asked to DJ a community cookout at Antar's campaign headquarters that afternoon. The parking lot in front of the A&D Tax Services office that housed the campaign's daily operations was taken over by a bouncy castle, grills, and tables of food. Antar and Ebony moved among their friends and supporters, laughing and teasing. They seemed eager and excited about the potential that the next few days would usher in. Under fast-moving clouds, dozens of Jacksonians mingled in the lot, holding their plates of grilled meat and fresh fruit, or they sat in folding chairs along the building's front windows. I watched people form lines to do the Cha Cha Slide in front of the table where Brandon stood, lining up his tracks. It wasn't the work of new society building, but it might turn out to be related.

Three days later, Chokwe Antar won ten thousand more votes in the primary than his father had. His 55 percent support in the Democratic primary meant there was no need for a runoff in a Jackson mayoral race for the first time in twelve years. In the general election the next month, he secured 93 percent of voters' support.

Around the country, pockets of attention snapped toward this decisive win of the young mayoral candidate running on a plan to establish a society with socialist roots in the Deep South. Antar's landslide primary win came on the heels of President Trump's one-hundred-day mark. A post-election analysis released by Millsaps College and Chism Strategies noted that the "Trump Factor" might have helped mushroom support for Antar late in the race: "To the extent undecided voters wanted to express a protest vote against the status quo, Lumumba was that vessel."

Antar indicated on a national stage a willingness to accept the role when, in early June, he appeared as a speaker at the People's Summit in Chicago alongside Bernie Sanders, author Naomi Klein, and environmental activist Bill McKibben. With his speech, Antar made headlines in Jackson and in a smattering of national publications by declaring that his administration would make the capital of Mississippi "the most radical city on the planet." He called for other cities to join him, name-checking Washington, DC; Gary, Indiana; and Chicago.

Inauguration Day was July 3, a hot and sunny Monday in Jackson. Museums and city offices were closed for Independence Day. The people who streamed into one of downtown's newest structures, the hulking Jackson Convention Complex, for the swearing-in ceremony wore Lumumba-for-mayor t-shirts, suits, dashikis, and sundresses. After he had laid his hand on a Bible and sworn to protect the constitutions of the United States and Mississippi, Chokwe Antar Lumumba took to the podium and asked the hundreds of Jacksonians present to look past the inevitability of the present society with him.

"This is the building of the *new* society," he said, adding later: "For so long Mississippi has been known as the symbol of limits. It has been known as a haven for oppression, for some of the most horrible suffering in the history of the world. So it is only fitting that we should become the leaders of that change." The inaugural address was an opportunity to posit a possible future, and Antar embraced it. What would happen next with Jackson's roads and water systems, with the people's assemblies, with the cooperatives and the fab lab, wasn't certain. But on this Inauguration Day just before Independence Day, Antar was helping a city and a country to see past the present, and that, in itself, was radical.

"Free the land!" he called out three times as he concluded his address, raising his right fist high above the rose boutonniere pinned to his lapel.

"Free the land!" the City of Jackson called back to him.

This article was originally published the Fall 2017 issue of the *Oxford American*, with support from the Economic Hardship Reporting Project.

Casting Light: Reflecting on the Struggle to Implement the Jackson-Kush Plan

Kali Akuno

> "Our agenda includes topics whose importance and acuteness are beyond doubt and in which one concern is predominant: The Struggle. We note, however, that one type of struggle we regard as fundamental is not explicitly mentioned in this agenda, although we are sure that it was present in the minds of those who drew it up. We are referring to the struggle against our own weaknesses. We admit that other cases may differ from ours. Our experience in the broad framework of the daily struggle we wage has shown us that, whatever the difficulties the enemy may create, the aforenamed is the most difficult struggle for the present and the future of our peoples. This struggle is the expression of the internal contradictions in the economic, social and cultural (therefore historical) reality of each of our countries. We are convinced that any national or social revolution which is not founded on adequate knowledge of this reality runs grave risks of poor results or of being doomed to failure."
>
> —Amílcar Cabral

When navigating treacherous waters or dimly illuminated paths, it is necessary to have a stable mind, a steady hand, and clear vision. And when trying to help others navigate out of similar journeys, it is necessary to provide clear and concise lessons and instructions.

Politics anywhere and everywhere has always been complicated and tricky. The electoral dimension of "modern" politics is no different.

The electoral systems that we've been subjected to and institutionalized within over the last two hundred–plus years of the US settler colonial project are treacherous, particularly for the colonized and subjugated peoples in this colonial empire, and those drawn from its laboring and exploited classes. These sectors of society have been forced to "perform" for power and influence in the main, and contest for power on rare occasion, within a rigged game, wherein the very limited choices on offer merely allow one to engage in symbolic gestures centered on regulating aspects of the capitalist economy, making minor adjustments to who reaps the most benefits from the system and how those benefits will be disbursed. On occasion, we've been able to raise our voices regarding whether to expand or contract the repressive mechanisms and institutions that reinforce the systems of white supremacy and heteropatriarchy, and to adjust the degrees of pollution and waste we are subjected to by the capitalist social order of extreme extraction and exploitation.

It is within this oppressive and undemocratic social order that those of us seeking liberation are constantly searching for pathways to emancipation. The Jackson-Kush Plan was and is one of these pathways. The broad and multifaceted effort to execute this plan, euphemistically called the J-K Plan for short, has recently been the subject of some public controversy and come under some scrutiny, primarily by its own author—myself. Statements I made on October 21, and widely broadcast to the world on October 25 via the Black Agenda Report prompted much of the controversy. But this was only kindling apparently, as the main controversy was stirred up by Bruce Dixon's article in the Black Agenda Report on November 1, entitled "Democratic Party Affiliation in Mississippi a Compromise Made in Error Says Cooperation Jackson's Kali Akuno."

Unfortunately, comrade Bruce Dixon missed the mark in providing a clear and concise rendering of the lessons I was trying to provide about the ongoing struggle to implement the Jackson-Kush Plan and realize its promise and potential toward making a substantive contribution to the social transformation of the US empire. Now, before going too deep into this essay, let me say unequivocally that I support Bruce Dixon's cause of trying to educate people, most particularly a younger generation of Black activists and organizers, about the treachery of the Democratic Party, in the hope of dissuading them from joining it or aligning with it in any form or fashion. But it is essential that I correct some mischaracterizations of the struggle in Jackson that have been advanced by Bruce Dixon over the course of the last several weeks. These mischaracterizations only serve to distort the contradictions at play in the ongoing struggle in Jackson, and in my view hinder folks from learning the critical lessons I was trying to convey on October 21.

Let it also be known that while I disagree with many of the policy and programmatic priorities articulated by the mayoral administration of Chokwe Antar Lumumba thus far, as well as Mayor Lumumba's increasing public alignment with the Democratic Party (particularly the so-called Bernie wing of the party), I have a vested interest in doing all that I can to help the Lumumba administration succeed. I am committed to struggling with the administration, internally where possible and externally when necessary, to stay the course of pursuing radical social transformation as articulated in the Jackson-Kush Plan. However, the central question that must be addressed is how is "success" being defined and assessed, and by whom? These are critical questions that will be returned to shortly, to help everyone clearly understand what the fundamental "compromise made in error" was (and is) that I referenced in October.

Since the release of the Jackson-Kush Plan in 2012, thousands of people throughout the US empire and the world have stated that the plan, and the work that has emanated from its pursuit, have been a major source of inspiration for those seeking a more democratic and equitable future in general, and those on the left seeking to build political and social power more particularly. In short, the plan rests on three pillars: (1) the construction of a dual power in the form of a people's assembly to build collective power (power with as opposed to power over) from the ground up to build a new society and to nullify the power of the settler-colonial state; (2) to build an independent political party (originally stated as a political force in the document as a result of an internal compromise) to serve the will of the people's assembly; and (3) to initiate the process of constructing socialism by building a comprehensive solidarity economy from the ground up through the autonomous, self-managed initiatives of the organized community to build the local productive forces and provide an alternative to capitalism and its forced impositions, which force the vast majority of us to work for wages and pay rent (or mortgages) in order to survive.

It must be noted, for the sake of clarity and transparency, that there was a political organization behind the development of this plan, and until fairly recently, its coordinated execution. The political organization is the New Afrikan People's Organization (NAPO) and its mass association, the Malcolm X Grassroots Movement. Both organizations are partisans of the New Afrikan Independence Movement (NAIM) and highly influenced by the democratic-centralist organizations of the twentieth century that fought for national liberation and state power as the primary means to advance the development of socialism and emancipate New Afrikan people. The J-K Plan was not and could not be a spontaneous development. It took years to formulate, and it was built on decades of hard work and experimentation that was synthesized through years of study and reflection. So there was a conductor, as it were, driving its advance, which is critical to note as a lesson for anyone trying to pursue a similar strategy. Knowing what went into its development and execution cannot be ignored or overlooked.

That said, of all the things that the J-K Plan conveys, the component of it that has far and away drawn the most attention has been its electoral component. Like it or not, this has been the primary source of inspiration engendered by this document. Given how the media is focused in this society, and how power is too often narrowly understood, this sadly is what the overwhelming majority of people focus on in reference to the radical work in Jackson. In our specific case, it would seem that the J-K Plan provides a straightforward rationale for the city council victory of Chokwe Lumumba in 2009, and justifies the pursuit of the mayoralty of Jackson by Chokwe Lumumba in 2013 and Chokwe Antar Lumumba in 2014 and 2017, and seems to provide a road map to building municipal and eventually regional (i.e., the Kush) and state level power in Mississippi. And while there undoubtedly is some truth to this perception, it should be noted that it fails to grasp the deeper meanings and pursuits of the strategy. For instance, the electoral component of the strategy was originally intended to be an adjunct component of a broader objective, which was to build a transformative, anti-colonial power from the ground up through the people's assembly as an autonomous vehicle of self-governance that would engage in a developmental process of socialist construction by building a dynamic social and solidarity economy on the local level to create new social relations and means of production (which is the mission of Cooperation Jackson). Building a new independent political party that would engage in electoral politics, but not be bound by its pursuits, was just one component of this radical strategy. Sadly, this understanding has been lost or ignored, and even more disappointing, has not really been pursued by the forces claiming adherence to the J-K Plan over the past ten years. Why this is so brings us to the heart of the contradiction or "compromise made in error."

When I and my comrade Kamau Franklin first conceived of the idea and advanced the proposal to NAPO and MXGM that Chokwe Lumumba run for mayor in 2008, our primary objective was to use the campaign to: (a) gather concrete information about who and how many people in Jackson believed in and would openly support the pursuit of New Afrikan (Black) self-determination and sovereignty, and (b) use the data gathered from this social experiment to advance our base-building work in the city (and beyond) to build power. The power we were focused on building was the enhancement of the capacity of a self-organized community to collectively exercise its will by transforming the social means to meet its material and social needs. The focus was on changing social relationships from below, by moving people to pool their resources, skills, and intellectual capacities to more effectively utilize what they have to improve their lives and to struggle to either build or appropriate the resources (land, capital, and social institutions) needed to suit this end. It should be noted, that we did not rule out the notion that Chokwe should win the election, but this was not our initial focus.

However, in the process of agreeing to pursue this course of action, comrades in the Jackson chapter (keep in mind that neither I nor Kamau lived in Jackson in 2008) stated that they did not want to engage in a "symbolic action," that they wanted to "win," meaning actually attain the office (which as it turns out became focused on the Ward 2 council seat, as the initial proposal to run for mayor was modified based on commitments the chapter had already made to an existing candidate). Given that we had done some preliminary research on the possibility of winning an election that was favorable, I initially offered no resistance to this notion. For my part, I went along with this notion because I thought that we all agreed with the power building objectives stated above. As it turns out, we did not. The *problem* was that we failed to collectively define what we meant by "winning" beyond this point, and herein was the fundamental "compromise made in error." We did not agree on whether the victory was defined as building power, or winning and holding office.

Or, if the answer was both/and, how would this advance the liberation of Black people within the US in the short- and medium-term? How would this victory support the building of the New Afrikan Nation, the decolonization of Turtle Island, and the dismantling of the US government? We moved forward on the basis of assumptions, not on the basis of concrete clarity. And moving forward on this basis is what has led us to the impasse that we find ourselves in today.

For this, I have to be very self-critical and address my own failings. For my part, I had assumed that as a result of working closely with comrades in the Malcolm X Grassroots Movement for well over a decade and a half, that we had fundamental clarity and agreement on these and many other central questions. I didn't heed a warning issued by Amílcar Cabral decades earlier about always struggling for the utmost clarity when attempting to move forward strategically, primarily to overcome the underdevelopment of our political forces and our movements overall. I didn't do this at this critical juncture. Struggles for clarity were made in earnest down the road, and proposal after proposal was sent to press for clarity. But most fell on deaf ears, particularly when they challenged the notion of why we were continuing to engage in electoral politics if it wasn't serving the primary function of building power.

As a result of this compromise, winning elections became the primary focus of the "on the ground" work in Jackson from 2009 on. In practice this election-centered focus has translated into downplaying the politics of the New Afrikan Independence Movement, limiting public discussion of the Jackson-Kush Plan, crafting a more "popular" political platform called the "people's platform" that orientated itself toward the restitution of a welfare state as opposed to the construction of socialism, and making public overtures to appease capital expressed in statements that "Jackson is open for business" and "we want corporations to come here and get rich." All of these moves were made to enable the candidates to become more "electable." These actions and orientations are in contradiction with the focus and pursuits of the original campaign proposal. This development sadly repeats a timeworn pattern of revolutionaries throughout the world over the past two hundred–plus years who turn to electoral politics to allegedly transform the system from within, who along the way get transformed by the system and step-by-step become revisionists, reformers, and agents of neocolonial subjugation and neoliberal social destruction.

Therefore, the choice of which electoral vehicle to employ in pursuit of the original proposal's aims was and is a secondary contradiction, not a primary one. Bruce's article mistakenly makes the vehicle question the primary contradiction, i.e., whether we should have engaged in electoral politics at all given the objectives being pursued, which is an error. Radicals and radical movements must seriously interrogate when and where to engage in electoral politics. For my part, I see electoral politics as a field of struggle that revolutionaries cannot ignore, given the balance of forces in society as a whole. But I don't think we need to give much of our limited time and energy toward this pursuit. Rather, I argue that we need to put the majority of our time and energy into building working-class organizations that are focused on enhancing the productive capacities of the class in its comprehensive composition (meaning those who are employed, underemployed, structurally unemployable, those who labor in the fields, and those who labor in prison) and amassing the skills and resources to transform society and defeat the corrosive powers of capital.

However, this does not negate the fact that one of the original pursuits of the J-K Plan was to build a new political party, one that would engage in electoral politics but be more of a facilitator of the political pursuits of the social movements than a traditional "American" political party. That such a party has not been built after ten years of this experiment is, without question, one of the critical failings of the project thus far. But, when "winning" elections under the present social conditions becomes the primary objective, the primary contradiction we've confronted negates the pursuit of autonomous power, the execution of a radical program, and the building of a revolutionary vehicle all at the same time.

But, in reference to the vehicle question itself, there are a few mischaracterizations comrade Bruce has made that must be clarified. The first notion is that we, particularly those of us in Cooperation Jackson, broke with the Democratic Party. On this point, it must be noted that it is hard to break with something that you never joined. Cooperation Jackson has never been associated with the Democratic Party, nor have I. In fact, over the past twelve years as it relates to electoral politics I worked hard to build new electoral vehicles, like the Reconstruction Party (ReconP) while situated in New Orleans from 2006 to 2008, or supported Green Party (GP) candidates like the McKinney/Clemente

(2008) and Stein/Baraka (2016) tickets in particular, or helped rebuild the Mississippi Freedom Democratic Party (MFDP), which still exists and generally poses as a left alternative to the Democratic Party in the state of Mississippi. Further, it should be noted that when Chokwe Lumumba ran for office in 2008/2009 and then again in 2012/2013 he did so as a member of the MFDP, which won access to the Democratic Party primary in 1968 as a part of an effort to empower Black voters in Mississippi (the vast majority of whom only gained access to the ballot in 1965). In addition, NAPO and MXGM, to my knowledge, have never made a formal decision to join the Democratic Party, here in Mississippi or anywhere else. That said, the organizations' unofficial slide into the orbit of the Democratic Party and all its open and discrete machinery has progressively gotten worse since 2008, when neither organization chose to support the Reconstruction Party or the campaign efforts of an MXGM member, Rosa Clemente, who was then running for vice president under the Green Party ticket. The primary reason being that the vast majority of the members of these organizations at that time did not want to isolate the organizations or themselves from the Black masses who were overwhelmingly rallying to the Obama campaign. So yes, there is a lesson here again about the need to be clear, centered, and focused in one's strategic pursuits, but it centers more on strategic focus then it does on questions of tactical implementation (which in the case of the J-K Plan is what an electoral apparatus would be).

So if there is a fundamental lesson to be learned from the struggle to implement the Jackson-Kush Plan over the last ten years, as noted, it is the need to be clear, and to constantly struggle with yourself, with your comrades, and with the social actors and movements you are engaged with for clarity and consensus. In my honest view, the New Afrikan People's Organization, the Malcolm X Grassroots Movement, the Jackson People's Assembly, the Lumumba administrations, and Cooperation Jackson have all contributed a fair amount toward the reinvigoration of the Left over the last ten years, particularly in the realm of providing those on the left with a sense of hope—albeit misplaced hope in many respects because it is sadly being employed to prop up liberal notions about the utility of electoral politics to the left (as can be seen by recent efforts of the Movement for Black Lives, MoveOn.org, and others). But as it relates to the advance of the Jackson-Kush Plan, we could have and should have done a lot more toward the realization of its objectives over this span of time. As it stands, the forces publicly aligned with the J-K Plan (which truth be told is not altogether clear anymore to this author) are now (objectively and subjectively) fortifying (intentionally and unintentionally) several misleading narratives that are being widely promoted by liberal and revisionist forces to justify their reformist worldview and politics. The primary danger is that our labors will be utilized to uphold and promote the false notion that capitalism can be tamed and reformed through electoral politics. It cannot. And connected with this, there is the danger of reinforcing the false notion that the state is or can be a neutral arbitrator of various conflicting social interests. The state is not neutral in any form, but most particularly in its settler-colonial form, which we are subject to in the US. The state is a historic vehicle that exercises power over society that must be transgressed through human action. This requires democratic vision, the self-organization of the working class and oppressed peoples, and radical practices of material production (the goods and services we need to live) and social reproduction (nurturing and caring for each other and our children and grandchildren) over generations to create a new society.

The aims and objectives of the Jackson-Kush Plan are still a viable radical pursuit. Despite the mounting resistance to the program being mounted by reactionary forces in Mississippi, there is still enough time and political space to fully implement the strategy and realize its aims. However, it requires a major course correction in my view that demands a realignment of the constituent forces related to the J-K Plan that focuses on building a transformative power from the ground up, breaks with the politics of reform and accommodation with neoliberalism, and fortifies the position of the radical social movements within Jackson. The "success" that I spoke to earlier, would for its part, include the Lumumba administration being a part of this realignment and entail it centering on processes of social transformation, and the struggles this would inevitably invite, over and above merely serving as an instrument of "good governance." Focusing on transformation means advancing the final goals of self-determination and the construction of socialism through the agency of the working class and fortifying these constructions with every decision the administration makes executing the functions of state governance within the municipality.

For my part, I will continue to struggle for the realization of the Jackson-Kush Plan through the work and contributions of Cooperation

Jackson and the construction of a new political organization to help fill in some critical gaps that exist in the movements for revolutionary social transformation in the US. It is my sincere hope that the New Afrikan People's Organization, the Malcolm X Grassroots Movement, and the administration of Chokwe Antar Lumumba will make the course corrections suggested herein. Our movement has nothing to gain by pursuing the path of collaboration and compromise. If anything, without a major course correction, the Lumumba administration is structurally poised to reenact an American version of the neoliberal tragedy currently being executed and administered on the Greek people by Syriza. It is only by pursuing a revolutionary path, however difficult it may appear in the short term from the perspective of having to be a "responsible" administrative force, that we, as a movement, will gain. This would entail pursuing things like a comprehensive food sovereignty program, with the aid of working-class vehicles like Cooperation Jackson and the People's Assembly, to eliminate the threat of food being used as a weapon, that would require converting most, if not all, of the city's vacant properties into urban farms. This would entail creating administration supported people's markets and distribution centers, and support for a local alternative currency or token, to help facilitate the exchange of this community produced value.

The Syriza trap is not completely inevitable. Clear leadership, with a clear plan, and uncompromising will can still go another route. I say this because I know all conscious political actors make mistakes and we all have the ability to learn from them, and most importantly, correct them. It is in this light that I note that despite our present differences, we have to be cognizant of the fact that in the face of the concentrated power of our enemies, none of our differences ultimately rise above those posed to us collectively by the systems of capitalism, imperialism, colonialism, white supremacy, and heteropatriarchy, and their conscious and willing agents and enablers. The process of "unity-struggle-unity" is still applicable on the level of alliances, fronts, and blocs. When and where possible, I look forward to allying with the Lumumba administration, NAPO, MXGM, and many other organizations in the common struggle to dismantle the systems of hierarchy, alienation, and oppression and construct a new world, beginning in Jackson, but in no way limited to it.

Much more could and will be said in due time on the subject of sharing some hard lessons from the ongoing struggle for radical social transformation in Jackson. However, it is my hope that this short essay helps to illuminate a path of struggle just a bit more, and helps to inform those who have been inspired by the collective works in Jackson to not repeat our critical mistakes.

> "Policy is the starting-point of all the practical actions of a revolutionary party and manifests itself in the process and the end-result of that party's actions. A revolutionary party is carrying out a policy whenever it takes any action. If it is not carrying out a correct policy, it is carrying out a wrong policy; if it is not carrying out a given policy consciously, it is doing so blindly. What we call experience is the process and the end-result of carrying out a policy. Only through the practice of the people, that is, through experience, can we verify whether a policy is correct or wrong and determine to what extent it is correct or wrong. However, people's practice, especially the practice of a revolutionary party and the revolutionary masses, cannot but be bound up with one policy or another. Therefore, before any action is taken, we must explain the policy, which we have formulated in the light of the given circumstances, to Party members and to the masses. Otherwise, Party members and the masses will depart from the guidance of our policy, act blindly and carry out a wrong policy."
>
> —Mao Zedong

Reflections on 2018: A Year of Struggle, Lessons, and Progress

Cooperation Jackson Executive Committee

> "If it was easy, it would have been done already."

2018 has been a year of growth and growing pains for Cooperation Jackson. We've experienced some significant advances and some setbacks. Over the last four years of our organization, we have learned a lot that we aim to build upon to improve our practice and advance our work in 2019 and beyond.

When launching Cooperation Jackson in 2014, we knew we were taking on an ambitious project. In the effort to establish an economic foundation to realize the Jackson-Kush Plan we knew we had a lot to both learn and unlearn. To this end, we are attempting to learn from successful solidarity economy systems from around the world and apply them here in Jackson, along with innovating new methods of sustainable production in order to make a concrete contribution toward a just transition and social transformation.

Accomplishments

After several years of trial and error, our Lawn Care Cooperative (the Green Team) is becoming a fully self-sustaining entity. The co-op, which is currently composed of two worker-owners and one employee, has secured several contracts and is earning a profit. The Green Team is looking to expand its overall operations in 2019 by returning to the composting operation that was not sustainable in its first iteration due to lack of facilities, sufficient staffing, and distributed knowledge.

Freedom Farms Cooperative faced a major setback in early 2018 due to a record winter freeze and challenges with capacity, experience, and staff turnover. This past spring and summer, Freedom Farms made substantial progress with an increase in production. Produce has been sold to our membership, the neighboring West Jackson community, the Mississippi Farmers Market, Rainbow Grocery Cooperative, Cash and Carry Grocery, and several restaurants in town. This summer's neighborhood outreach included produce giveaways and the start of an herb garden and Black healing space. Although limited, in 2018 we experimented with time-banking in exchange for produce. In 2019, the farm will primarily explore permaculture-based designs and growing methods, establish a fruit orchard as part of the Ewing Street Eco-Village, and experiment with high-yield specialty crops and added-value products by farming on the additional, previously uncultivated plots of our community land trust.

The Community Production Center faced several delays in finalizing the center's purchase and renovations. We are excited to announce the center is opening in January 2019 and the Community Production Cooperative will start a second round of Fabrication Laboratory training. To create an immediate revenue source, the co-op will start producing t-shirts, memorabilia, and signs while it builds its capacity to produce space-efficient furniture and affordable housing for our community land trust.

Our Fannie Lou Hamer Community Land Trust (CLT) presently has over forty parcels of land. Land that otherwise would either be vacant or up for speculation. This includes the Kuwasi Balagoon Center, the new Community Production Center, a small apartment building we will soon be renovating, two houses presently being rented to members, and one house that will be available for rent. In 2019, our goal is to rehab two additional houses we presently have for further housing. We will expand our CLT with more property in 2019 as resources permit.

We are extremely proud of our hard-won accomplishments. But we can always do better. And do better we shall. Check out "2018 Year in Review" to learn more about our work and view our photo slideshow.

> We aim to transform the economy of Jackson and the region as a whole to create the material base needed to support and build the autonomous politics we are pursuing. But we see that Solidarity Economy, if developed to its own logical conclusions, represents

the limit of economic reform possible within a capitalist framework of social production governed by a bourgeois social order. We are clear that in order to build socialism that something more than just the principles and institutions of economic and social solidarity will be needed. What we believe will be needed are new political and social identities crafted on the transformation of consciousness produced in part by engaging in the practices associated with Solidarity Economy and radical participatory and horizontal democracy. Solidarity Economy when pushed to its limits as a means of heightening contradictions within the capitalist system we believe is a transitional strategy and praxis to build 21st century socialism and advance the abolition of capitalism and the oppressive social relations that it fosters. (Jackson-Kush Plan, 2012)

"This Isn't Heaven, and We Aren't Angels."

2018 was also a year of transition for Cooperation Jackson. Many of these transitions were intentional and explicitly designed to strengthen our organization and improve its overall practice. However, some of the transitions we experienced were not intentional, but the outcome of divisions within our organization, our movement network, and the local and national social movements we have been and/or are a part of.

Some of the intentional transitions made include:

- realigning and restructuring our organization to correct the undisciplined, inefficient, and unaccountable practices that emerged as a result of differences regarding how to implement and uphold our mission and vision;
- severing our organizational relationship with the Malcolm X Grassroots Movement (MXGM) and the New Afrikan People's Organization (NAPO);
- disassociating ourselves from the administration of Chokwe Antar Lumumba and its policies and orientation to governance;
- structuring a new board that did not include members of the groups mentioned above.

Some of the unintentional transitions we experienced included:

- the resignation of a founding member and former codirector Iya'Ifalola Omobola;

- severing our relationship with the café and catering business we helped to start and finance.

To be clear, both the intentional and unintentional transitions we have experienced and are moving through are reflections of the growing pains that all organizations and social movements aiming at social transformation experience. As the saying goes, "You can't make an omelet without breaking a few eggs." And in our efforts to create a transformative organization, we have ruffled a few feathers in and beyond our community in the effort to upend unequal power relations and transform various problematic views and behaviors, including our own. Despite our best efforts to move forward with all the forces that started this transformative journey with us, we have now arrived at some forks in the road that make this no longer possible. As a result of the transitions that have occurred, we now have our fair share of detractors and supporters, enemies, and allies. This comes with the territory. In our view this indicates that we are in fact doing some things right—and there is always room for improvement.

We have learned a great deal in 2018, about ourselves, our commitments, our principles, our politics, our limits, and the strengths and weaknesses of our plans and strategies. We remain determined to utilize this learning to correct the many errors we have made in the past four years. We fully understand that many don't and won't agree with some or any of the conclusions and resolutions we arrive at. We respect everyone's democratic right to their opinion. We have the obligation to uphold and realize the vision we were constructed to fulfill to the best of our ability, and that is what we aim to do.

Organizational Realignment and Restructuring

In the effort to build a culture of radical participatory democracy and stimulate and encourage worker self-organization and self-management we intentionally decided not to "over structure" the organization at its founding. This experiment produced mixed results over the course of our first four years, with various discipline (attendance, punctuality, preparedness, substance abuse, etc.) and underperformance (not completing tasks, not meeting deadlines, not studying, not communicating with fellow cooperators, etc.) challenges. In the effort to correct many of our shortcomings and improve our overall practice, our executive committee, which serves as the vision holder and coordinating body of the organization, outlined a program to reorganize and realign the organization starting in the spring of 2017 to address the undisciplined and unaccountable culture that our initial experiment enabled.

Now, in hindsight, many of our early errors were rather inevitable. Although our organization started with a remarkable assemblage of volunteers, it did not start with the full complement of the thinkers, planners, and resource persons who envisioned it and the Jackson-Kush Plan overall. Unfortunately, many of these leaders left the City of Jackson and/or the Malcolm X Grassroots Movement before Cooperation Jackson was officially launched in 2014. We therefore started with some critical gaps, particularly in terms of background knowledge, political alignment, and various skills and competencies that these individuals would have been in a position to help the organization more adequately address.

Over time, these gaps and insufficiencies caught up with us. Where they have expressed themselves most significantly has been in the inconsistent orientation and onboarding of new staff and members, who received varying degrees of grounding in our history, politics, principles, aims, objectives, commitments, strategies, plans, structures, and theory of change as a result of our inadequate capacity in this regard. In addition to this shortcoming, we often spread ourselves too thin the first three years of our development, trying to serve as an incubator, a school, a network, and a radical community organization (in the effort to fill in various social movements gaps left open by the then grieving and depleted Jackson Chapter of the Malcolm X Grassroots Movement in the wake of Chokwe Lumumba's sudden passing in 2014).

We also struggled with how to balance the demands of our trying work with building quality interpersonal relationships, how to deal with the level of self-exploitation that we strategically adopted, how to balance our various health needs with our overextended workloads, how to build trust and resolve conflicts, how to establish a collective definition and practice of restorative justice, and how to build the collective knowledge, skill, and capacity to operate horizontally.

In the effort to prioritize this critical interpersonal work, the executive committee elicited the help of various advanced practitioners in the fields of restorative justice, effective communication, and semantics drawn from our movement networks to help us deal with the challenges of accountability, reevaluate our structures, and create collective tools for building a healthy and sustainable culture that can acknowledge tensions and resolve conflict. Several committees were formed to address these challenges and create new systems and practices to strengthen our work. In addition to committee work, we also held two retreats over the past two years toward this end that had mixed results. We are continuing this core work and giving it high priority in our development over the course of the next two years.

To be clear, not all of our shortcomings were due to structural issues. A considerable portion of our failings were due to the lack of sufficient political alignment and the struggles to attain it. Several of the staff who have left the organization did so either directly or indirectly because they did not agree with the explicit commitments of our organization toward a just transition and the construction of ecosocialism, to the study of critical anarchist and Marxist thinkers and practitioners, to internationalism and the need for multinational/multiracial alliances, and to the construction of a genderless society. Many do not agree that these principles, ideas, and commitments align with the struggle for Black self-determination and liberation. We do! And further our organization was explicitly founded to extend these principles, ideas, and practices, and make them applicable in the here and now in our specific time, space, and context. We respect that not everyone holds these views; this is their democratic right. But it is our obligation to uphold these ideas, principles, and practices to advance the mission of the organization, and we fully intend to do so to the best of our ability.

We are fully committed to learning from our shortcomings over the past four and a half years, and to applying the lessons learned to improve our practice. This is particularly true in the area of cooperative development. Since our founding, we have pursued the development of a number of cooperatives that did not pan out for various reasons. Some of these projects include a gas station and convenience store cooperative, a recycling cooperative, an industrial scale composting cooperative, and an arts and culture cooperative.

The gas station and convenience store experiment was challenged by the various restrictions the US government placed on CITGO, which is owned by the Venezuelan government, that hampered the ability of this initiative to move forward. However, we ultimately made the decision to jettison it because it was not compatible with our commitment toward a just transition away from fossil fuels.

The recycling cooperative suffered from trying to grow too large too fast. We initially envisioned it working on a small neighborhood scale, then tried to seize upon a major opportunity that presented itself when we started to pursue a merger with an existing Black-owned recycling company to pursue the municipal recycling contract. This initiative was undercut by the maneuvers of the powerful corporate magnet, Waste Management, and how it manipulated the city's waste hauling contract under the administration of Mayor Tony Yarber. Unfortunately, our recycling working group has been unable to fully regroup and recover from this blockage (which included the Black-owned recycling firm sadly going out of business in 2017, due to the world-scale recycling glut). The industrial scale composting cooperative we pursued was not able to find a suitable, properly zoned facility from which to operate. It was further hampered by the indiscipline of its anchors and uneven skill development and knowledge between and among them. Despite these challenges, we attempted to maintain a composting operation in a pared down fashion through 2017. The arts and culture cooperative was challenged with finding a viable product and business focus. However, it should be noted, that other than the gas station, we remain committed to trying to develop cooperatives to address these strategic needs in the years to come.

Without question, we remain a work in progress. We still have some major work ahead regarding how to better onboard new staff and general members to better ensure alignment, to better balance the distributions of power and responsibility, and to address the systemic dynamics of heteropatriarchy and how they manifest in our thinking and practice. But we have strengthened the foundations of our organizing model over the course of the past year through the realignment and reorganization efforts that we have made. We are reassured by our level of increased productivity over the last six months that our particular organizing model is sound. Per our model: we remain committed to building a network of interconnected and interdependent solidarity economy institutions and practices that includes, but is not limited to, a federation of multistakeholder cooperatives, a cooperative incubator, a cooperative education and training center, a community land trust, cooperative financial systems, and a range of solidarity practices like time banking, mutual aid provisioning, local currencies, etc. We are further reaffirmed in our development model, which seeks to use the collective resources either secured or procured by the organization to provide our various start-ups with deeply affordable (often rent-free) facilities from which to operate and conduct business that are provided through our community land trust holdings. These are bolstered with the no-interest capital investments our nonprofit makes to enable our cooperatives to start as debt-free as possible, along with providing stipends to their anchors to enable them to have dedicated quality time for study, training, experimentation, and business development. Given the overall hostility to Black entrepreneurs and businesses by the financial institutions in our area, we believe the small gains we have made over a very short period of time demonstrate the efficacy of our organizing strategy and development model.

On Severing Key Relationships

After years of internal struggle with and within formerly fraternal organizations, several relationships originally meant to be strategically interconnected became impossible to maintain due to the emergence of a number of irreconcilable political differences and mounting antagonistic actions toward our organization by key figures within these organizations. The irreconcilable differences sadly emerged over varying interpretations of the Jackson-Kush Plan and how to implement and advance it. After years of intense deliberation and struggle, we decided to formally separate ourselves from the New Afrikan People's Organization, the Malcolm X Grassroots Movement, and the administration of Chokwe Antar Lumumba in the winter of 2017–18.

These were not easy or lighthearted decisions. Several of us invested decades of our lives fostering, building, and supporting these organizations, and wanted nothing short of seeing them accomplish their historic missions. The same goes with our various individual and collective efforts as social justice organizers to help elect Chokwe Antar Lumumba. Without a doubt, we want his administration to succeed and to serve as a strategic instrument to advance the Jackson-Kush Plan. We still hold out hope that the administration and the aforementioned organizations will pursue an independent course relative to electoral politics, transcend the limitations of social-democratic thinking, turn away from neoliberal compromises and prescriptions of governance, and play a historic role in executing the Jackson-Kush Plan to the fulfillment of its radical potential in a manner that we can fully unite with.

We also knew that these decisions would not come without consequence. We knew that they would confuse many in the community and within our membership. We calculated that this confusion would create degrees of distance and isolation from some forces in town who would take a partisan position against us, either because they don't know us (as many of us are not "native" to Jackson, but organizers who intentionally moved here to serve the Jackson-Kush Plan), haven't heard our story, or don't agree with our politics and positions. And, without a doubt we have experienced varying degrees of distance and isolation from various forces. However, we have not and will not ask anyone to take a partisan position on our behalf to counter the intentional efforts to isolate us.

Our aim is to encourage people to think critically for themselves and to analyze the politics, policies, and actions of all the social actors in our community to determine whether they align with your own principles, values, and interests, and act on that basis. Beyond that, we are primarily concentrating our energy on "showing and proving" in 2019 and beyond.

What also complicated the severing of these relationships was the fact that a majority of our second board, which was installed in 2016, was deliberately constituted by individuals from the Malcolm X Grassroots Movement and/or the New Afrikan People's Organization. This was done intentionally to cement the relationships between Cooperation Jackson and these organizations, based on our presumed alignment around the execution of the Jackson-Kush Plan. Unfortunately, these board members conflated the business of Cooperation Jackson with that of the Lumumba administration. These forces wanted Cooperation Jackson to serve as an extension of the Lumumba administration, therefore elevating political struggle in the electoral arena over political struggle in the economic arena. This is a critical juxtaposition of priorities in the struggle to implement the Jackson-Kush Plan in our view—although we do not deny that they should be related in certain strategic ways. However, in trying to make Cooperation Jackson a programmatic arm of the Lumumba administration they were jeopardizing our 501(c)3 status in key ways by having it become a partisan instrument of the Democratic Party, with whom they are aligned. After an intense and deeply regrettable period of struggle over the latter half of 2017 and the beginning of 2018, we gradually had to come to terms with how counterproductive the relationship between Cooperation Jackson and MXGM, NAPO, and the Lumumba administration had become and assumed responsibility for changing these dynamics.

This entailed making several deliberate attempts to find common ground, develop some shared understanding, and find ways to work together despite our deepening differences. Unfortunately, our differences by this point were too great to overcome. In short, our differences centered on: (a) the centrality of the Jackson-Kush Plan toward the governance of the City of Jackson, (b) how to promote and raise awareness of the Jackson-Kush Plan within the Black working-class and poor majority of Jackson, (c) their advocacy and promotion of capitalist oriented solutions, including efforts to recruit ruthless transnationals like Amazon to the city, (d) their negation of the social and solidarity economy as a primary means to transform and transition the local economy toward the construction of ecosocialism, and (e) our contrasting views on the question of governance, with our insistence on a protagonistic methodology to governance that intentionally favors advancing the interests of the working class and the oppressed, versus their insistence on a more liberal methodology of governance that favors class collaboration and incremental alterations to the status quo.

As part of the effort to resolve some of these differences with the Lumumba family and the Lumumba administration, our executive committee came to a mutual agreement with Rukia Kai Lumumba and Chokwe Antar Lumumba to disassociate Cooperation Jackson from both in early January. This agreement also included Rukia stepping down from the board and the board chair position of her own accord, the removal of Mayor Chokwe Lumumba's name from our center and his likeness from the next printing of our *Jackson Rising* book, as well as the removal of Nubia Lumumba's name from our café and catering cooperative (with which we are no longer aligned or connected as you will read).

Following this meeting, our executive committee, then including Brandon King, Iya'Ifalola Omobola, Kali Akuno, and Sacajawea Hall, sadly came into open conflict with the MXGM and NAPO representatives on the board. Our collective efforts to create clear lines of distinction between these organizations, which Sacajawea and Brandon were still a part of at this time, and respect their protocols regarding group security and public disclosure were not respected, and were in many ways manipulated in the course of this struggle. After several failed attempts to de-escalate tensions, avoid repeating highly unproductive interpersonal exchanges, and enable various parties to fully express themselves without conflict or interruption, our ability to engage this board in a productive manner ceased in early February. This occurred after the board threatened the funding of the organization if it did not comport itself to the dictates of the Lumumba administration and submit to its program. And further, this was while it tried to silence and censure Kali Akuno, then our codirector, for making public statements in an individual capacity that offered constructive criticism to the Lumumba administration, MXGM, and NAPO regarding their execution of the Jackson-Kush Plan. Following this, our executive committee called for the resignation of this board. Our objective was to protect the organization from their course deviations and to ensure that it remained true to its mission and purpose. The full board resigned on Thursday, February 8. Following this, we then seated an interim board of directors in April that was and is aligned with our organization's mission and vision relative to the execution of the Jackson-Kush Plan and the implementation of our unique organizing strategy and development model.

To honor our agreement with the Lumumba family, we removed Mayor Lumumba's name from our primary operating facility in March. We proudly renamed our primary operating center in July 2018. The new name of our center is the Kuwasi Balagoon Center for Economic Democracy and Sustainable Development. Kuwasi Balagoon was a queer revolutionary New Afrikan anarchist freedom fighter, who passed away from AIDS-related causes while in prison custody in 1987. Kuwasi was also ahead of his time in his opposition to environmental racism and his concern for the ecology and the overall well-being of our planet and its life-giving systems.

We take inspiration from Kuwasi's unflinching political commitment, his vision, and his courage.

Sadly, in the course of these struggles, it became painfully clear that our former codirector, Iya'Ifalola Omobola, was deeply conflicted about the politics of Cooperation Jackson and our separation from the Lumumba family and administration (to be clear, Iya was the only member of our executive committee who was not a member of MXGM or NAPO). In the effort to remain "neutral" as she defined it, she resigned her position this past March and left the organization. Unfortunately, her actions since that time have demonstrated anything but neutrality in our view. But she has a right to her positions and her alignments, as do all of the individuals that have left the organization for similar reasons over the past two years, and we respect that.

The last critical transition, as briefly noted above, was Cooperation Jackson severing its relationship with and financial support of the café and catering cooperative start-up we had been working to build for several years. This officially occurred in September, after two years of struggle with its anchors over alignment and accountability. Despite our differences, we wish them well as they continue to pursue their development independently.

Despite all of these transitions, our organization has become more aligned, focused, and strengthened. To this end, our interim board is working diligently to help us realize two critical, but as of yet unfulfilled, structural commitments to advance our work and practice as a critical part of our realignment and reorganization to strengthen the organization. The first item is expanding our new board, which will be seated in 2019, to include representatives from all of our emerging cooperatives, our community land trust, and our general membership. The second item is laying the groundwork to have our first general member assembly in early 2020. The interim board is also helping the organization revise and strengthen its bylaws and think through how to create new structures that will help it transcend the many limitations of the nonprofit or 501(c)3 form we currently employ to conduct most of our business.

Where We Stand, Where We Are Going, and How We're Going to Get There

"The future belongs to those who prepare for it."

It is safe to say that the social movement forces that relate or related to the Jackson-Kush Plan, either now or in the past, are at a crossroads. Sadly, the social movements in Jackson have been in retreat since 2014, despite many efforts to revitalize them. We argue that this retreat was prompted by the many unresolved social issues that crystallized into immediate crisis during the short administration of Mayor Chokwe Lumumba, which lasted from July 2013 through February 2014. Some of the major crises included how to deal with projected revenue shortfalls for the city, the budget deficits these shortfalls created, and the threat of furloughs of city employees that emerged as a result, in addition to how to address the consent decree the EPA placed on the city to address its long-standing water quality issues. We have also encountered numerous threats to the autonomy of the municipal government from the neo-Confederate dominated state government, and major capital advances by developers and transnational corporations in the city accelerating the threats of gentrification and displacement of Black working-class communities. With the wane of movement institutions like the People's Assembly to address these issues in a comprehensive and coordinated fashion, many of the key organizations in the radical social movement in Jackson fractured, pursued their own individual courses of action, and reformulated their alliances and allegiances. The political conflicts underscoring the transitions mentioned herein have helped to foster some of confusion in the community that has led to degrees of disengagement and apathy among many, but particularly among the radical social forces in Jackson, which we are still grappling with.

In the midst of this social dynamic, the founding and guiding forces driving the development of Cooperation Jackson played a vital role in keeping the Jackson-Kush Plan alive after Mayor Lumumba's untimely transition in February 2014. Since January 2014 and the hosting of our first community education session about the solidarity economy, Cooperation Jackson played the leading role in propagating the Jackson-Kush Plan, both in word and programmatic deed. However, over the years, our disagreements with many of our former partners over strategy, alignments, priorities, tactics, platform development, and policy orientation has led us on a different path, one centered on maintaining the integrity of the Jackson-Kush Plan as envisioned as a radical program of social transformation that centered the self-emancipation of the Black working class and the construction of ecosocialism. We reject the stated and implied notions by many of our former allies that the Black working class in Jackson can't be organized, or that its interests must be subordinate to those of the Black professional classes and the dominant white business interests in the region. We similarly reject the notion that we should not be engaged in protagonistic politics that explicitly advocate and advance the interests of the Black working class. The Black working class is the primary protagonist of the Jackson-Kush Plan, and its interests must be elevated and fought for without compromise in our view. Upholding this position has created several rifts and distinctions on the ground in Jackson, particularly over the last two years. All sides have suffered declines in community participation and engagement, and we are no exception.

We agree with some of the detractors of our work that have come forward of late, in noting that we don't have an adequate base at present to fully implement and advance our "Build and Fight" program. We don't shy away from this criticism in the least. The forces that launched the Jackson-Kush Plan were never sufficient to see it fully implemented to its conclusion on their own. That these forces, when combined, were strong enough to win a few elections and start an initiative like Cooperation Jackson over the past ten years does not mean that any of them should be overly glorified. Being able to touch, move, and mobilize 20 percent of the city's population, as exhibited through the electoral campaigns that have been carried out in the name of the Jackson-Kush Plan, is significant, but not sufficient.

What we have learned the hard way over these last two years is that we are going to have to build our own base. We cannot rely on the old alliances and the social forces that accompanied them, because of the confusion, political differences, and disengagement noted above. To achieve our aims and objectives we have to become a majoritarian movement, which in our context means that we have to go further and deeper into organizing the Black working class in order to fulfill the promises and potential of the Jackson-Kush Plan.

We have to do the long, hard, patient, and often inglorious work of building our own base in the Black working-class communities of Jackson. As a relatively young organization, with a heavy concentration of "out-of-towners" who moved to Jackson to work explicitly on advancing the Jackson-Kush Plan, and who live and work in some of the most economically depressed communities in the city, we know this is going to be a major, long-term task and challenge. A challenge we are game for.

What follows are some of the adjustments we have and are making to our program in order to meet this challenge over the course of the next several years:

We are reducing our field of action. This means restricting the number of cooperatives and solidarity institutions we strive to build. It also means limiting the core of our work to West Jackson over the next several years to address the concrete needs in this community and sufficiently organize within it.

We will be limiting our business development activities to concentrate on expanding the operations of Freedom Farms Cooperative and the Green Team Lawn Care Cooperative (including the effort to reestablish a small-scale industrial composting operation) and launching the Community Production Center and gradually building the Community Production Cooperative.

We are consolidating the operations of our community land trust. We are going to expand the board of the CLT, renovate our current housing stock, fix several of the abandoned homes we presently own to make them habitable cooperative housing units for more of our members, and host an education series on CLT's and cooperative housing. We will continue to expand the trust as noted, to the extent our fundraising efforts and resource mobilization enables it.

We are currently looking to make one major expansion in 2019, and that is to acquire the West Park Shopping Center and turn it into the Ida B. Wells Plaza.

We are deepening the interconnection and inter-reliance of our institutions and activities. In order to meet our primary objectives, we are going to ensure that all of our activities reinforce each other more coherently, with the intent being to create our own supply and value chains and be more efficient with the time and energy of our members.

We are concentrating on the development of our first model eco-village pilot on our Ewing Street properties to fortify and enhance the joint work of our four core entities: our emerging Community Production Cooperative, Freedom Farms Cooperative, the Green Team, and our community land trust.

We are going to concentrate more heavily on "capacity" raising among our members. In reducing the size and scope of our operations, we are restructuring our time to do more structured education among our staff, members, and community around the concrete skills needed to create and facilitate democratic institutions.

We will be conducting a new orientation and training program for all of our members. This will be structured around our new membership manual (which we are still in the process of completing as of this statement's release) and the new *Worker-Owner Workbook* produced by the Cincinnati Union Co-Op Initiative.

Like all young social justice organizations, particularly those attempting to transcend the logic of capitalism, we have confronted a number of critical challenges and taken some lumps in the process, but we continue to learn, grow, and advance and we hope that all those interested and committed to constructing ecosocialism through a just transition and the development of a regenerative economy will join us in this effort.

"We make the road by walking."

IV

CRITICAL EXAMINATIONS

The Jackson-Kush Plan: The Struggle for Land and Housing

Max Rameau

> "Revolution is based on land. Land is the basis of all independence. Land is the basis of freedom, justice and equality."
> —Malcolm X, "Message to the Grassroots," November 10, 1963

While the land relationships that dominate this society have implications for every relation in society, the recent crisis of gentrification and forced removal in low-income Black communities, along with the volatile boom-bust real estate cycles, has made the struggle for adequate housing the most pronounced battleground in an increasingly intense war over the vision for the future of how we relate, prioritize, and manage access to land.

The current regime of land relationships renders housing and community development fatally flawed in at least two respects: first, houses serve dual social functions in this society, but those functions are contradictory and at odds with each other. And second, decisions about land use are fundamentally undemocratic, rendering people unable to make basic decisions about how to improve their own communities. Left unresolved, these two contradictions conspire to perpetuate poverty, destabilize societies, and provoke social unrest.

As things stand, a house simultaneously serves two starkly dissimilar functions: the first function is housing as the shelter required for human survival: a place to live, rest, raise a family and contemplate the meaning and direction of one's life. The second function is housing as an investment. Generally speaking, real estate is regarded as a solid investment specifically because human beings cannot survive without it. The quality of that investment improves as housing prices increase beyond the reach of low- and middle-income people. That is to say, the more difficult it is for average people to access basic housing they can afford, the greater the likelihood of a substantial return on investment.

This dual function, housing as both shelter and investment, creates a perverse incentive for banks, corporations, developers, and individual investors to support gentrification, which constitutes in essence the forced removal of low-income people from targeted communities. The aforementioned actors profit directly from this economic phenomenon, setting the stage for an inherent conflict of interest that pits two opposing rights directly against each other.

It is easy to see how those rights—the right to housing and the right to make profit—can come into conflict with one another: if the right to housing means everyone gets a home they can afford, then how do banks, developers, and landlords make a profit? Conversely, if banks, developers, and landlords have the right to profit maximization by increasing prices, how do the human beings who do not have a lot of money access housing?

When the economic stakes are sufficiently high—such as during a housing "boom" where hundreds of millions of dollars in profit are on the line—the drive to expand the supply of housing and increase profit margins intensifies, making the competition even more cutthroat. At this point, the core issues of land and housing exceed the corrective powers of regulation or other types of legislation. At this point, a house can no longer effectively function as both a home, to which every human being has a right, and an investment vehicle, through which investors have a right to derive profit, which might come at the expense of human beings seeking life sustaining shelter. At this point, the fundamental role of land and housing in that society is in full contradiction.

The second fatal flaw in the current regime of land relationships is the undemocratic nature of decisions made about land usage. Under the existing economic order, residents of a racialized low-income neighborhood may collectively decide, in a democratic manner, that their community is in great need of decent and affordable housing, access to fresh food, local shops, playgrounds and activity areas for children, space for public meetings, and access to internet-connected computers. In order to meet these needs, the community may identify local land—the land upon which they have lived their lives, worshipped, worked, and been educated—to set aside as space for housing, farmland, commercial activities, recreational areas, and the commons. Residents may determine such land usage will improve their individual and collective lives, allowing them to build a sustainable and thriving community.

Instead, however, the land is converted into high-end lofts, a high-end art gallery specializing in postmodern impressionistic sculptures, and a chain shop offering $5 cups of coffee while pimping the stylistic renderings of white artists providing their own interpretations of Black music genres.

The difference between the vision and the reality is not rooted in best practices but in the dominance of those who have money—even if they lack good ideas—over those who endure marginalized social and economic real-life conditions. This situation—where people with a deep stake in the outcome of their long-time neighborhood have less of a voice in how their community is developed than someone who has never visited and whose interests primarily lie in extracting dollars from that community—is an insurmountable contradiction that is incapable of developing human beings and more closely resembles a colonial relationship than a functioning democracy.

Of course, contradictions exist in every system and their existence alone is not necessarily indicative of systemic failure or crisis. Contradictions escalate to the level of crisis not only when the contradictions are sufficiently deep but also when the areas of contradiction are central to the survival of the group involved.

For example, a family might be forced to confront the contradictions associated with limited resources and prioritization when, at a particular time on a specific night, the single television set in the home is tasked with the triple functions of simultaneously broadcasting a presidential debate, a high-stakes playoff game, and a troupe of stuffed animals who sing, dance, and recite a series of base-10 integers in correct sequence. While this contradiction is real, it is not rooted in an issue area that is central enough to challenge that family's very existence in the same way as contradictions over access to food or housing. Therefore, even though contradictions themselves are inherent in any system, the depth and issue areas of those contradictions determine if the situation devolves into full-blown crisis.

During the so-called real estate boom, from approximately 2003 to 2007, land and housing prices across the country skyrocketed to unprecedented levels at breakneck speeds. While rapidly rising real estate prices resulted in tremendous profits for banks, developers, and other speculators, the underbelly of the "boom" was nothing short of devastating for Black communities. Long-time residents—who were only residents because they were segregated into those neighborhoods in the first place—found themselves forced out by a combination of rapidly rising prices, a sudden interest in the government in enforcing housing codes resulting in huge fines, changes in the local support system (a cheap corner store replaced with a less centrally located and higher priced organic food store), and stepped up harassment by local police interested in protecting the new residents from the natives.

The gentrification and forced displacement of low-income Black communities is always a devastating process and, given the nature of finance capital during the era of neoliberalism, an entirely predictable consequence of the predominant land relationships in this society. The preceding outcome in 2007–8 highlighted to a new generation the way the investment function of houses squeezed out the housing function. This state of affairs exposed the undemocratic nature of housing and community development.

As the real estate boom turned into a bust, middle-class whites were, often for the first time, forced to confront the impacts of some of those same contradictions, albeit in entirely different ways. Even as the "home" aspect of millions of houses was undamaged by storms, fires, or even the ravages of time, millions of middle-class whites lost that home because the "investment" aspect of the house was adversely impacted by the real estate bust.

Even when there was nothing wrong with the "home," tens of millions of people faced foreclosure-related eviction because of the house's function as an investment. In order to maximize those investments, financial institutions designed and implemented complex and risky financing mechanisms that maximized profit when it worked but led to a full collapse of the house of cards as foreclosures increased.

Consequently, the number of families without homes, due to gentrification and foreclosure, skyrocketed, while simultaneously the number of vacant houses—each representing a failed investment—also skyrocketed. Due to the risky investment schemes employed, the foreclosures had a multiplier effect, triggering even more investment losses and causing an economic recession.

The only way to prevent a full global economic collapse was to force low- and middle-class people to use their future earnings to bail out a handful of financial institutions that made and lost billions by defrauding the same low- and middle-income people who were now bailing them out.

In order to realize proper levels of profit, big banks and other speculators asserted their right to use the investment function of a house, not just as a priority over the home function of the same house but also at the very expense of that home function.

Equally as bad, house investors, even the demonstrably fraudulent ones, rather than the residents of the house or the impacted communities, had full authority to determine what to do with all of those vacant foreclosed homes as well as the hundreds of billions of dollars the banks received in exchange for them.

In case the point has not been adequately underscored, the contradictions associated with land relationships—particularly how the investment function of a house is incompatible with the housing function of a house—directly cause gentrification and other displacement and have reached full crisis level.

In response to the growing crisis, an aggressive and robust social movement emerged to defend families from forced removal, whether in the form of gentrification or foreclosure-related eviction, and redesign the system in order to resolve the underlying contradiction.

One of the early entrants in that movement was Take Back the Land, which was formed in Miami, Florida, in 2007. Take Back the Land helped create a national, Black-led Land and Housing Action Group in the fall of 2009, that was initiated and anchored by the US Human Rights Network, and consisted originally of the Malcolm X Grassroots Movement, Survivors Village in New Orleans, the Chicago Anti-Eviction Campaign, and Picture the Homeless, a full two years before Occupy Wall Street took over Zuccotti Park in New York City. In 2010, the Land and Housing Action Group initiated the national Take Back the Land campaign, which became a national network in early 2011.[1]

The national Take Back the Land campaign made at least three major contributions to the burgeoning movement: first, as a Black-led and populated organization, it came with a clear line on the importance of Black self-determination, political leadership, and perspective on common social issues. Second, the Take Back the Land campaign modeled a form of civil disobedience—called Positive Action (after the theory and practice developed by Kwame Nkrumah and the Convention People's Party)—that was appropriate for this particular issue and historical moment.[2] And, third, the national Take Back the Land campaign developed a political theory that framed the underlying contradiction as one of land and land relationships, not just gentrification or foreclosures.

The theory and framing proved critical in distinguishing the way in which the Take Back the Land campaign analyzed the underlying contradiction at the root of the crisis.

For example, the primary argument adopted by most organizations engaged in anti-foreclosure work was that foreclosure was caused by high mortgages (the result of the real estate boom) and, therefore, families should benefit by getting new mortgages that reflected the housing prices of the real estate bust, not the boom.

The demand inherently cultivated a base limited by two essential factors: income and status. While a reduced mortgage could prove helpful to an individual family in an "underwater" property—where the amount of the mortgage is greater than the market value of the house—the broader economic recession significantly swelled the ranks of the unemployed. Consequently, dropping the mortgage by $50,000, $100,000, or even $200,000 had little practical value to a family with no income.

Potential movement members were also limited by historic social and economic realities. While roughly 58 percent of whites live in a family-owned home, in the history of the United States, the number of Black people living in a home owned by a family member has never exceeded 49 percent. For those organizing in Black communities that meant that even if their anti-foreclosure campaign succeeded beyond their wildest imaginations and helped 100 percent of homeowners, it would still fail to help the majority of Black people.[3]

A movement fighting for the human right to housing cannot be based on economic distinctions such as homeowners, renters, squatters, and people without homes.

Additionally, campaigns designed to win mortgage principal reduction for a single homeowner proved too transactional in nature to serve as the basis on which to organize over the long term. Without a broader vision, members left after the "victory" of a new mortgage. The campaign failed to include a mechanism through which members would remain engaged over the long term. Most importantly, winning a new mortgage, based on the investment function of the market value of a house, did nothing to change the underlying causes of either gentrification or foreclosures. In fact, giving everyone new and lower mortgages only increases the chance that prices will skyrocket again soon, repeating the entire cycle in record time.

So while most anti-foreclosure campaigns framed the issue of foreclosure in terms of...foreclosure, the limitations of that framing were quickly revealed in practice. Ending foreclosures by only looking at foreclosures was a logical dead end.

Take Back the Land ventured to answer the fundamental question facing all social movements: How do we resolve the underlying contradiction that gave rise to this movement in the first place?

The Malcolm X Grassroots Movement (MXGM) played a central role in organizing the national Take Back the Land campaign and developing the political theory and analysis that informed the movement's groundbreaking work.

While we were clear that the only way to end gentrification and foreclosure-related displacement was to look beyond gentrification and foreclosure and fundamentally reimagine and restructure land relationships, we struggled to clarify what that meant in terms of which campaigns could be built.

In an early campaign document, Kali Akuno of MXGM argued the recent boom-bust cycle demonstrated the unsustainability, danger, and inhumanity of the investment function of housing. Therefore, Akuno argued that housing can only serve a single function: that of a home. In order to advance this bold vision, our general strategy must be to end the investment function of housing by protecting housing from the forces of the market forces. In short, because it is an essential human need, housing cannot be a commodity subject to profiteering.[4]

As long as housing remained a commodity subject to the whims of market forces, we can never realize either the human right to housing or democratic control over resources owned by corporations or individuals. In order to ensure the human right to housing and democratic control over land in our communities, we must ensure that housing is a protected public good, not just another commodity. Akuno called this "the decommodification imperative."[5] From that moment onward, Take Back the Land's clarion call was the decommodification of land and housing.

In a direct and congruent way, the initiatives of the Land and Housing Action Group and the national Take Back the Land campaign paved the way for the land-centered organizing of Cooperation Jackson. Pursuant to the Jackson-Kush Plan, over the past three years, Cooperation Jackson has secured nearly forty properties in West Jackson, which constitute over four noncontiguous acres of land. The land is not individually owned for the purpose of resale at profit but collectively controlled for the purpose of sustainable development with equitable benefit.

And while the dual crises of gentrification and foreclosures have focused attention on housing, Cooperation Jackson has clearly understood that housing is but one function of land. As such, land has been set aside for farming, commercial space, recreational space, nature conservancy, natural resource exploration, and the development of a new "commons" in Jackson.

At a time when economies of scale are causing the displacement of Black families and communities from their farms, out of their homes, and from their long-standing neighborhoods, Cooperation Jackson's fulfillment of the decommodification imperative through the collective acquisition of land is protecting those areas from the next round of land speculation because these properties are being held in a community land trust (CLT), dubbed the Fannie Lou Hamer Community Land Trust, and per the organization's covenant agreements will not and cannot be put up for sale and, therefore, will not be directly subject to market forces.

As decommodified land, those properties are liberated to serve their more important social functions of housing human beings, growing food, and providing common space from which to build community.

Further, organizing those properties democratically—instead of consolidating them in the hands of an individual or family—advances the cause of social transformation by fundamentally redefining the meaning of ownership and power in the tradition and reality of the collective African experience in the South.

In this society, property ownership is an overwhelmingly individualistic concept. A business has at least one owner in whom power is concentrated and profits or rewards disproportionately appropriated. This setup is bad enough in the broader society, but inside an exploited and oppressed Black community, mimicry of structures of power often leads to confusing, if not disastrous, results.

Following the end of legal segregation, Black communities, understandably, rallied behind the idea of building Black-owned versions of businesses traditionally dominated by whites, as a means of advancing the race. As Black-owned magazines, restaurants, radio stations, cable television stations, and even hotels came into their own, the limitations of the "Black-owned" version quickly became evident. In spite of the obvious benefit of a business that did not discriminate based on race, the decision-making power and the distribution of wealth associated with the business was concentrated in a few hands, albeit Black ones. There was little accountability to, or broader benefit (aside from racial pride) for, the larger Black community.

The results were predictable on a number of levels: first, the campaigns that fought for the Black business were demobilized once the campaigns were successful as there was little else for them to do. The organizing effort dissipated with the victory instead of continuing. Second, any wealth generated by the venture was concentrated in the hands of a small number of Black families and individuals, a class which grew increasingly isolated and estranged from and even disdainful of the masses that made their wealth possible in the first place. And third, the conditions of the Black community as a whole did not improve as a result of victories of individual ownership.

Cooperation Jackson, as a Black-led force of human-centered economic development is working diligently to flip this script and create a new paradigm. As part of the legacy of the national Take Back the Land campaign, it is critical that the leadership of Cooperation Jackson has internalized the many lessons of the campaign from 2009 through 2013, and applied them in new dynamic ways in a particular grounded context. All those seeking to advance a modern program of decommodification and decolonization would do well to learn from the organizing program and strategies of Cooperation Jackson, as there is plenty to digest and assimilate in our ongoing quest for liberation.

Notes

1 See "Take Back the Land National Campaign Launch Announcement," https://www.scribd.com/document/226197384/Take-Back-the-Land-National-Campaign-Launch-Announcement-2009.

2 See Kwame Nkrumah, "What I Mean by Positive Action" (1949), World History Group, Democratic Underground, accessed May 25, 2022, https://www.democraticunderground.com/discuss/duboard.php?az=view_all&address=277x471.

For more background on Kwame Nkrumah's theory of "Positive Action," see *Consciencism: Philosophy and Ideology for Decolonization* (New York: Monthly Review Press, 1964).

3 For more information on the racial disparities in the housing market and home ownership, see "Home-Ownership in the United States," Wikipedia, accessed May 25, 2022, https://tinyurl.com/vmckjmae.

4 See Kali Akuno, "Reclaiming TARP, Reclaiming Public Housing—Land and Housing Action Group Work Group Paper #1," accessed May 25, 2022, https://www.scribd.com/document/226198635/Reclaiming-TARP-Reclaiming-Public-Housing-Land-and-Housing-Action-Group-Work-Group-Paper-1-2009; Kali Akuno, "Identifying, Occupying and Transforming 'Unidentified' Public Housing—Land and Housing Action Group Working Paper #2," accessed May 25, 2022, https://www.scribd.com/doc/226199196/Identifying-Occupying-and-Transforming-Unidentified-Public-Housing-Land-and-Housing-Action-Group-Working-Paper-2; Kali Akuno, "The Meaning of The Slogan: The Meaning of The Movement—Land and Housing Working Group Paper #3," accessed May 25, 2022, https://www.scribd.com/document/226199934/The-Meaning-of-the-Slogan-The-Meaning-of-the-Movement-Land-and-Housing-Working-Group-Paper-3; and Kali Akuno, "Beyond Foreclosure Fraud: Moving to Take Back The Land Through Strategic Action," accessed May 25, 2022, https://www.scribd.com/document/226201216/Beyond-Foreclosure-Fraud-Moving-to-Take-Back-the-Land-through-Strategic-Action.

5 Akuno, "The Meaning of the Slogan."

A Long and Strong History with Southern Roots

Jessica Gordon Nembhard

African Americans, as well as other people of color and low-income people, have benefited greatly from cooperative ownership throughout the history of the US, similar to their counterparts around the world. My recent book, *Collective Courage: A History of African American Cooperative Economic Thought and Practice* (2014), documents these experiences, and particularly the efforts—successes as well as challenges—of African American–owned cooperative enterprises, and analyzes the lessons learned. I explore a variety of cooperative economic models for contemporary community economic development, particularly in communities of color.[1]

The African American cooperative movement was a silent partner in the long civil rights movement. Throughout the efforts for civil rights, from when we first set foot on North American soil, African Americans have resisted enslavement and oppression and fought for their own freedom. Pursuit of economic alternatives and solidarity economic relationships were part of this struggle and resistance. Even in the face of sabotage and violence we practiced cooperative and collective economics.

African American Cooperative Economics Message

Several African American scholars and leaders have advocated for economic cooperation as an important strategy for Black economic development and increased quality of life. Some leaders have actually practiced cooperative economics in their communities. Although all of them are well known for achievements in other areas (and not for their involvement in the cooperative movement), examples include scholar/

activist William E.B. Du Bois; activist Marcus Garvey; businesswoman Nannie H. Burroughs; activist and organizer Ella Jo Baker; writer, journalist, and satirist George Schuyler; historian E. Franklin Frazier; former Jackson State College (now University) president Jacob Reddix; and Black labor leader and organizer A. Philip Randolph; and the Ladies Auxiliary of the Brotherhood of Sleeping Car Porters. Maulana Karenga included both *ujima* (the collective work and responsibility of African Americans toward their community) and *ujamma* (cooperative economics), in addition to self-determination, among the seven Kwanzaa principles. Kwanzaa is an African American holiday created by Karenga.

W.E.B. Du Bois proposed economic cooperation as the only effective and practical solution throughout his life. Du Bois argued that African Americans must become the masters of their own economic destiny. Blacks could position ourselves at the forefront of developing new forms of industrial organization that would free us from marginal economic status. He advocated using "intelligent [consumer economic] cooperation" as an important approach. He advanced the concept and strategy of "racial economic cooperation" combining cooperative industries and services in a "group economy" through which African Americans could use their sense of solidarity, gain control over their economic lives, and assert themselves as equals, even leaders, in the mainstream economy. "We can by consumers and producers cooperation . . . establish a progressively self-supporting economy that will weld the majority of our people into an impregnable, economic phalanx."[2]

George S. Schuyler (cofounder of the Young Negroes' Co-operative League) advocated similarly, "As I have pointed out again and again . . . there is only one thing that can immediately get the Negro group out of the barrel and that is consumers' cooperation, the building up of a Negro cooperative democracy within the shell of our present capitalist system of production and distribution."[3] He called on African American youth to lead the movement.

W.C. Matney, manager of the co-op store at Bluefield Colored Institute, West Virginia, was articulate about how cooperatives offer a solution to "the economic riddle confronting the Negro."[4] President of the Ladies Auxiliary to the Brotherhood of Sleeping Car Porters, Helena Wilson, reminded that: "No race can be said to be another's equal that cannot or will not protect its own interest. This new order can be brought about once the Negro acknowledges the wisdom in uniting his forces and pooling his funds for the common good of all. Other races have gained great wealth and great power by following this simple rule, and it is hoped someday that the Negro will do the same."[5]

Philip Randolph argued that cooperatives are "the best mechanism yet devised to bring about economic democracy."[6] Three decades later in his memoir, Jacob Reddix, cofounder of Consumers Cooperative Trading Company (Gary, Indiana) and former president of Jackson State College (now University), also concluded that a "nationwide system of [African American] cooperative businesses... could lift the burden of economic exploitation" from the backs of African Americans.[7]

African Americans often followed this advice and engaged in cooperative economic practice throughout our history. According to Clyde Woods: "Generation after generation, ethnic and class alliances arose in the [Delta] region with the aim of expanding social and economic democracy, only to be ignored, dismissed, and defeated. These defeats were followed by arrogant attempts to purge such heroic movements from both historical texts and popular memory. Yet even in defeat these movements transformed the policies of the plantation bloc and informed daily life, community-building activities, and subsequent movements."[8]

African American Cooperatives in the South

The South was well represented in the African American cooperative movement. The Colored Farmers' National Alliance and Cooperative Union officially started in Texas in 1886, and grew to establish chapters in every state in the South. By 1891, it became the largest African American organization in its time with an estimated one million members or more. The first African American association to demand reparations, the National Ex-Slave Mutual Relief, Bounty and Pension Association, was founded in 1896 in Tennessee as a mutual aid society. The Colored Merchants Association, a marketing cooperative of independent African American grocery store owners, was founded in Montgomery, Alabama, in 1925. Chapters of the Young Negroes' Co-operative League, cofounded by George Schuyler and Ella Jo Baker in 1930 and headquartered in New York City, were organized across the country, including: New Orleans, Columbia, South Carolina; Portsmouth, Virginia; and Washington, DC.

After the Civil War, Blacks in Baltimore, Maryland, turned to cooperation to try to improve their lot in life. One cooperative was formed in 1865 to hire Black shipyard workers and stevedores. White workers in the shipyards agitated to get free Blacks fired, and so they formed their own shipyard, the Chesapeake Marine Railway and Dry Dock Company, which operated successfully for eighteen years, until the owner of the land used by the shipyard doubled the rent.

In August 1918, a "Mr. Ruddy" returned home to Memphis, after attending a meeting of the Negro Cooperative Guild called by Du Bois to discuss ways to spread the adoption of cooperatives among African Americans, and organized a study group. In February 1919, the group incorporated as the Citizens' Co-operative Stores to operate cooperative meat markets. They raised more equity than expected, selling double the amount of the original shares they offered. By August 1919, five stores were in operation serving about 75,000 people. The members of the local guilds associated with each store met monthly to study cooperatives and discuss any issues. The Citizens' Co-operative Stores planned to own their own buildings and a cooperative warehouse. The editor of *The Crisis* magazine who reported this (presumably Du Bois himself) notes: "Colored people are furnishing their own with work and money for services received and the recipients are handing the money back for re-distribution to the original colored sources."

The Commercial Department of the Bluefield Colored Institute in Bluefield, West Virginia, formed a student cooperative store probably in 1925. The store's mission was to sell supplies the students and school needed and be a "commercial laboratory for the application of business theory and practice."[9] A share of stock in the Co-operative Society sold for less than $1. After two years in business the cooperative paid all its debts and owned its own equipment and inventories. The store began to pay dividends of 10 percent on purchases made. The student members voted to use profits to pay for scholarships to the secondary school and junior college. Members of this cooperative were the first African Americans to attend the National Cooperative Congress, when they attended the one in Minneapolis in 1926. They had become members of the Co-operative League of America in 1925.

There was extensive cooperative activity among African Americans in rural areas of the State of North Carolina in the 1930s and '40s anchored by Bricks Rural Life School and Tyrrell County Training School. These schools sponsored cooperative economics education and developed co-ops that joined together to organize the Eastern Carolina

Council Federation of North Carolinian Cooperatives. Nathan Alvin Pitts documents that as interest increased among Blacks in North Carolina about cooperatives, speakers from the Bricks and Tyrrell co-ops were asked to speak. Efforts by the Eastern Carolina Council eventually led to the establishment of the North Carolina Council for Credit Unions and Associates (shortened to the North Carolina Council). The North Carolina Council was an organization of credit unions and cooperatives operated by Negroes to promote new credit unions and other cooperatives throughout North Carolina and to aid existing credit unions and cooperatives. As a result of this activity to promote, develop, and support credit unions and cooperatives among African Americans in North Carolina, the number of credit unions and cooperatives among Negroes increased dramatically. According to Pitts, in 1936 there were three Black credit unions in the state, and by 1948 there were ninety-eight and forty-eight additional cooperative enterprises: nine consumer stores, thirty-two machinery co-ops, four curb markets, two health associations, and one housing project.

The 1964–65 Black voter registration drives and the Selma to Montgomery March for Freedom contributed to the formation of the South West Alabama Farmers' Cooperative Association. The cooperative association was formed in 1967 by a group of African American farmers whose families had farmed the same land for more than two centuries. The goal was to keep Black farmers and former sharecroppers in the region, on their land. The means was to diversify their crops, create a marketing cooperative, and at the same time advocate for their political rights. The co-op was able to secure federal funding which allowed it to expand. Within a few years the cooperative association included 1,800 families, making it the largest agricultural co-op in the South.

In the first year, the cooperative association had saved its members an average of $2.00 per ton on fertilizer and enabled them to sell their crops for a total of $52,000. The cooperative association worked with the Farmers Home Administration (similar to what Freedom Farm did in Mississippi) to help their members qualify for mortgages and loans. While the organization achieved significant marketing successes, despite white opposition, there were challenges with its management, cooperative education program, and access to markets. Overall, the cooperative increased members' economic security by working with them to reduce operating costs, encourage diversification, and raise incomes. Originally eight of the families were white. But due to harassment by racist politicians and businessmen, banks and suppliers refused to deal with them until the whites withdrew.

The Poor People's Corporation was organized in 1965 in Jackson, Mississippi, by a former field worker of the Student Nonviolent Coordinating Committee. Within four years they were running thirteen producer cooperatives and a marketing co-op, producing sewing, leather, and wood crafts, and candles. They had over eight hundred members, mostly former sharecroppers.

Freedom Quilting Bee was established in 1967, in Alberta, Alabama, to help sharecropping families earn independent income. Some of the women in Alberta and Gees Bend, Alabama, came together to produce and sell quilts. In a few years they made enough money to buy land and build a sewing factory. They also provided day care and after-school services (for members' children and others). The cooperative was a founding member of the Federation of Southern Cooperatives and is an example of women's leadership and control over their own work conditions and company, as well as an example of community solidarity in terms of the ways this cooperative supported and helped its community and members in its community.

Federation of Southern Cooperatives

Founded in 1967 by civil rights groups to consolidate co-op development in the South, the Federation of Southern Cooperatives is a not-for-profit organization of state associations that promotes cooperative economic development as a strategy (and philosophy) to support and sustain Black farmer ownership and control, economic viability of farm businesses—especially small, sustainable, and organic farming—and stewardship of Black land and natural resources in rural low-income communities in the southern United States. After merging with the Land Emergency Fund in 1985, the organization became the Federation of Southern Cooperatives/Land Assistance Fund (FSC/LAF). FSC/LAF is a network of rural cooperatives, credit unions, and state associations of cooperatives and cooperative development centers in the southern United States. The FSC/LAF provides technical assistance, legal assistance, financial support, education, and advocacy for its members and low-income populations in the South. In addition, the organization promotes and supports policy changes and legislation favorable to small farmers and low-income rural populations. In its almost fifty years in existence, the organization has helped to create and/or support more than two hundred cooperatives and credit unions mostly in the seven states where is has state offices. Examples of cooperatives in the Federation are Freedom Quilting Bee, North Bolivar County Farm Cooperative, Panola Land Buyers Association, and Shreveport Credit Union. The federation owns and runs a rural training and research center that showcases sustainable forestry, provides co-op education, and helps to develop Black youth–run co-ops. FSC/LAF also engages in cooperative development in Africa and the Caribbean. The organization has an important reach throughout the South, is connected to the larger US cooperative movement, and has successfully advocated for important measures in US farm bills to support Black farmers, Black land ownership, and Black co-op development.

Fannie Lou Hamer moved from advocating for voting rights to advocating for and creating cooperatives in her home county in Mississippi in the late 1960s and early 1970s. She began by working with Dorothy Height and the National Council of Negro Women in 1967 to establish a "pig banking" program in Sunflower County, Mississippi, to help women farmers put meat on their tables and earn some extra income. She then raised money to buy a farm and then more land. Hamer biographer Chana Kai Lee summarizes that:

> In 1969 Hamer laid the groundwork for an elaborate project to make poor folks economically self-sufficient. That project became the Freedom Farm Corporation. Through her work with the farm, Hamer broadened the meaning of civil rights activism to include addressing the economic needs of Black poor folks. Freedom Farm was to institutionalize a structure and process for low-income and destitute rural people (Black and white at first, and then with a focus on women and Blacks) to feed themselves, own their own homes, farm cooperatively, and create small businesses together in order to support a sustainable food system, land ownership, and economic independence (which would allow for political independence).[10]

Hamer argued that "Cooperative ownership of land opens the door to many opportunities for group development of economic enterprises which develop the total community rather than create monopolies that monopolize the resources of a community."[11] She had found that voting rights were not enough. White racists use economic retaliation, fire people from their jobs, and/or evict people from sharecropping or housing for their civil rights activities. Without economic independence—owning our own land, growing our own food, owning our own homes—we can't gain political independence. Cooperative ownership allows a people to control their own economy and protect people from economic retaliation.

John Lewis, past president of the Student Nonviolent Coordinating Committee, former organizer for the Southern Regional Council's Community Organizing Project, and longtime member of the US House of Representatives for Georgia, provides a similar analysis in his autobiography. "The civil rights movement was old news," with press coverage moving North to cover the Black Panthers, riots, campus unrest, and the Vietnam War, according to Lewis, when he started organizing in Alabama in the mid-1960s. People could vote but did not have enough to eat. "My job was about helping these people join together, helping them help one another to fill those needs. It was about showing people how to pool what money they had to form a bank of their own, a credit union. Or how to band together to buy groceries, or feed, or seed, in bulk amounts at low prices—how to form cooperatives."[12] John Lewis's main focus then was to establish "cooperatives, credit unions and community development groups" throughout the Deep South.

Concluding Remarks

In sum, African Americans have used cooperative economics for survival but also to gain economic independence. African American cooperatives throughout history have provided livelihoods, land ownership, home ownership, savings opportunities, and other mechanisms for economic independence for their members—however modest. Many of the cooperative businesses emerging in health care, childcare, and temporary services, for example, are leading their sectors in changing the nature of work and increasing the returns to such work and ownership—for African Americans, women, and youth.

They address market failure and racial discrimination. Cooperative businesses stabilize communities because they are community-based and locally owned. They distribute, recycle, and multiply all kinds of local resources, capital, and expertise within a community. Co-op members pool limited resources to achieve collective goals. Co-ops generate income and jobs and accumulate assets; provide affordable, quality goods and services; and develop human and social capital, as well as economic independence for their members. In addition, co-op enterprises and their members pay taxes, and are good citizens by giving donations to their communities, paying their employees fairly, and using sustainable practices.

Cooperatives have longevity. Cooperative businesses have lower failure rates and higher survival rates than traditional corporations and small businesses, after the first year of start-up, and after five years in business. In addition, evidence shows that cooperatives both successfully address the effects of crises and survive crises better than other types of enterprises. Cooperatives enable their members to stabilize and increase their incomes and accumulate assets. Cooperatives also provide more stable employment levels than investor-owned firms, which tend to adjust employment levels in contrast to worker cooperatives that adjust pay or compensation to safeguard employment. As local businesses, cooperatives increase community economic development and sustainability and recirculate resources. Cooperatives provide economic benefits but also social and health benefits. Cooperative ownership enables affordable housing and worker ownership. Cooperative enterprise ownership also enhances community relationships (community-business partnerships), well-being, leadership development, and women's and youth development.

Notes

1 This essay is based on Jessica Gordon Nembhard, *Collective Courage* (University Park, Pennsylvania: Pennsylvania State University Press, 2014); Jessica Gordon Nembhard, "Cooperative Ownership in the Struggle for African American Economic Empowerment," *Humanity and Society* vol. 28, no. 3, (August 2004), accessed June 25, 2022, https://community-wealth.org/sites/clone.community-wealth.org/files/downloads/paper-nembhard04.pdf.

2 W.E.B. Du Bois, "The Right to Work," in *W.E.B. Du Bois: Writings,* ed. Nathan Huggins (New York: Library of America, 1986): 1237.

3 George S. Schuyler, "Views and Reviews," *Pittsburgh Courier,* November 15, 1930.

4 W.C. Matney, "Exploitation or Co-operation?" *Crisis*, February 1930, 49.

5 Wilson letter to Lucille Jones, January 26, 1942, BSCP Collection, box 27, folder 3, Chicago History Museum.

6 Quoted in Lizabeth Cohen, *A Consumers' Republic: The Politics of Mass Consumption in Postwar America* (New York: Knopf, 2003), 49.

7 Jacob L. Reddix, *A Voice Crying in the Wilderness: The Memoirs of Jacob L. Reddix* (Jackson: University Press of Mississippi, 1974), 119.

8 Clyde Woods, *Development Arrested: The Blues and Plantation Power in the Mississippi Delta* (London: Verso, 1998), 4.
9 R.P. Sims, "Co-operation at Bluefield," *Crisis*, December 1925, 92–93.
10 Chana Kai Lee, *For Freedom's Sake: The Life of Fannie Lou Hamer* (Urbana: University of Illinois Press, 2000), 147.
11 Fannie Lou Hamer, "If the Name of the Game Is Survive, Survive," speech given in Ruleville, Mississippi, September 27, 1971, Fannie Lou Hamer Collection, box 1, folder 1, Tougaloo College Civil Rights Collection T/012, Mississippi Department of Archives and History, Jackson.
12 John Lewis with Michael D'Orso, *Walking with the Wind: A Memoir of the Movement* (San Diego: Harcourt Brace, 1999), 399.

Freeing the Land, Rebuilding Our Movements: Reflections on the Legacies of Chokwe Lumumba and Luis Nieves Falcón

Matt Meyer

Obituaries typically are written to commemorate the dead; this essay seeks to resuscitate the living. Two titans of modern-day movements for liberation—Chokwe Lumumba of New Afrika and Luis Nieves Falcón of Puerto Rico—passed away within weeks of one another in two entirely different places. That those locales are both currently within the territory geopolitically understood to be belonging to the US should be little more than a historic footnote. Their lives had some interesting synchronicity, but their social and cultural realities were hardly similar to, say, the people of the Dominican Republic and Zambia. This note on their deaths and lives is intended to review how those differences and similarities still need to impact global movements for lasting social change and how our continued failures to recognize their contributions could cost us the Earth.

Revolution (and a Nation) in a Southern Town

When the shock waves spread quickly around the world announcing the unexpected passing of sixty-six-year-old Jackson, Mississippi, Mayor Chokwe Lumumba, it was hard not to be filled with disbelief and wonder: What could we have done to make this unfinished story a happier one? It is not so much that there is no world of joy and accomplishment in the heroic story of Chokwe Lumumba. He was a beloved lawyer, a well-respected organizer and founding member of several prominent Black liberation movement formations, and a legendary public speaker who inspired countless thousands over decades of public service. His funeral "homecoming" ceremony included both former political prisoners and the former governor of Mississippi, both devoted children and grandchildren as well as political comrades who clearly were also part of the family, both civil rights flag-bearer Myrlie Evers-Williams and the militants of the Malcolm X Grassroots Movement (MXGM).[1] All testified to a life well-lived.

The burning questions, hard to confront directly, are: What is still left to do? What is needed to complete the "people's platform" as Lumumba envisioned it? Perhaps the more nagging question—especially for ecosocialists, environmentalists, peace activists, anti-capitalists, and all manner of progressives (especially those of non-African or "less recently direct" African descent)—is this: Why has our presence in support of and solidarity with Lumumba and his comrades been so limited, so meager, so slow? What about our understanding of leadership and social change can explain such disconnect with this clear and powerful leader? These questions could also be asked in ways social historians and political enthusiasts would feel driven to pose: If you were alive at the time of Dr. Martin Luther King or Minister Malcolm X, would you have worked by their side? More to the point, how do we locate and commit ourselves to the Martins and Malcolms of today, before they have been eulogized, sanitized, and iconized?

For a young pacifist learning about the Black liberation movement in the early 1980s, someone being brought into the leadership of the War Resisters League, which sought to end all wars, the button worn by many who called themselves New Afrikans was more than a little curiosity. The distinct red-on-black statement had two simple but powerful words describing a current and constant condition in need of urgent remedy. The badge worn by many of Lumumba's leading supporters read: "At War."

There could be little ambiguity that the New Afrikan People's Organization (NAPO)—a vibrant part of the historic, Malcolm X-inspired tendency of the Black liberation movement, which sought to form a people's Provisional Government of the Republic of New Afrika—were revolutionaries of the first order.[2] Not only were their ideas radical on the structural and conceptual level, challenging to the imperial, so-called "United" States, but they were also equally challenging to the widespread "common" sense of ingrained imperial teaching.[3] Very few on the left, outside of their diehard supporters (including some non–New Afrikans), thought they were anything other than crazy. The same, of course, could well be said of Ben Franklin, Thomas Jefferson, and others who were far less radical in the 1750s and were all thought to be crazy before enormous changes happened that only the visionary could expect.

It is perhaps most noteworthy, then, that the major force used to describe Lumumba—whose organization's leading catchphrase exhorted making change "by any means necessary," after Malcolm's warning—was the force of love. As Déqui Kioni-Sadiki, cochair of New York's Malcolm X Commemoration Committee put it (in a personal note to this author), "Like Malcolm, Chokwe didn't just talk the talk, he walked the People's walk, making it plain in the courtroom, the City Council, City Hall, anywhere and everywhere we needed him. Chokwe fought with and for us, speaking truth to power about Amerikkka's crimes against the Black Freedom struggle." Award-winning author Asha Bandele, speaking at his funeral, expressively summarized Lumumba as "a committed soldier of love." For Bandele and a multigenerational mix which spans from South to North and beyond the borders of the Americas, "To know him was to enter into a Black dream state.... In his presence we could love ourselves."

The war fought with love and tenacity was against the subjugation that Malcolm X himself described as "America's nightmare"; the nightmare is evidenced by the US governmental designs to transform those they had previously designated property to a post-Civil War status of citizen-servant. Malcolm X asserted that those of African descent were more the victims of Americanism than inheritors of an American dream. As NAPO, MXGM, and others maintain, those for whom centuries of collective time on these shores had forged a "new" identity of "Afrikan" origins deserved self-determination as opposed to a forced status of a second-class nature.

It stands to reason that the land mass where untold millions had died, the region most directly built on the backs of slave labor, which still housed a majority of people who descended from the near-genocidal horror, be designated a free territory where those on the land could choose their future fate and relationship to the US government. Louisiana, Georgia, Mississippi, Alabama, and South Carolina could form a new nation based on truly equal power relations. As radical as it sounds, it would be but a fraction of the reparations received by others similarly wronged, from pre–World War II Jews in Germany, Poland, and Eastern Europe, to Japanese Americans interned during the more universally acknowledged war.[4]

Lumumba may have been memorialized for the deep love he demonstrated for his people and remembered for his powerful public speaking and organizing skills, but he was perhaps best known for his unique skills as a lawyer, fighting without fear or hesitation on behalf of clients such as (to the FBI) "public enemy number one" Assata Shakur, her godson Tupac Shakur, former Black Panther political prisoner Geronimo ji jagga Pratt, and countless other less-known survivors of discriminatory legal practice.[5] One such client, current political prisoner Sekou Odinga, noted this (in a private note after Lumumba's passing): "I never saw a lawyer fight any harder or more unconventional than brother Chokwe. Not only did he accept the prosecutors as adversaries, but also the police, the FBI, and even the judge. He took them all on and won.... May the undying love and commitment to his people that brother Chokwe always showed be a guiding example to us all, especially our youth."

Throughout his life, Lumumba's tactical understanding may have evolved, but his root politics and his exceptional skills at articulating and communicating them did not fundamentally change. Mighty white governor William Winter may have been famously quoted as being surprised by how accommodating Lumumba was, once he won the mayoral election in Jackson. Unlike the "splitter" he expected, Lumumba led with a "spirit of inclusiveness and reconciliation."[6] But NAPO cofounder Ahmed Obefemi noted that like the cayenne that was used as part of a deeply moving, multisensory, elemental ceremony of reflection on his life held at his funeral, Lumumba had a bit of a kick, especially in getting over hard times, getting down to collective work, and building for collective responsibility and leadership.

In many ways, it seems clear that Chokwe Lumumba was never supposed to be able to win a popular election for a major seat in city government in the South. This is especially true given his consistent politics and the consistent repression he experienced at the hands of dismissive judicial and electoral systems. That Lumumba took his decades of grassroots organizing and base-building and turned them into a hard-won political victory showed in part the maturity both of the New Afrikan movement and also the people of Jackson who had at least beginning understandings of what Lumumba as mayor could offer them. Neither the state nor the Left is particularly used to signs of growth and development.

It is vital, therefore, that we understand how these experiences suggest an advance. Settler colonialism informs most power dynamics relating to capitalist expansion, especially for countries such as the US, which have long been imperial aspirants with colonial subjects inside of their borders. A true people's history of the US must strikingly note how "race" (or the intensification of racial categorization) has always trumped and facilitated class in the US. It must recognize how the maintenance and upkeep (reconstruction) of an African-built South was just one area of domestic colonialism and a key to understanding the fate of later subjugated nations of northern Mexico and Puerto Rico, and the prior takeover of numerous Native nations.[7] Until we build movements informed by a recognition of the centrality of settler colonialism, we will continue to disconnect land from its people and miss the structural issues underlying race and class.

As Saed and others have begun to note, contemporary socialist and environmental analysis must be grounded in a recognition that the prison industrial complex is more than simply a business rooted in the containment and destruction of human life; it is the center point required to maintain ever-weakening capitalist expansion, as dying empires fight hard to extinguish people's movements, eradicate their histories, and live another day.[8] By powerfully combining courtroom skills, designed to abolish the very structures of judicial, police, and prison power, with community-based organizing, designed to empower grassroots groupings of the most dispossessed with economic self-determination skills, Lumumba's work cut to the core of imperial and capitalist planning. Taken in select, bite-size pieces, Lumumba's efforts might have appeared reformist in nature, but as a whole they were revolutionary, with a sharper knowledge of the nature of the US nation-state than most avowed "socialist" or "communist" groups inside the imperial beast.

Solidarity and a Global View in a Puerto Rican Context

Dr. Luis Nieves Falcón was nothing short of Puerto Rico's leading public intellectual—sociologist, educator, lawyer, author, organizer, and *independentista*. A world-renowned authority on colonialism, repression, and Puerto Rican history, Dr. Nieves Falcón was founder/director of the University of Puerto Rico's Department of Latin American and Caribbean Studies, founder of the Committee on Human Rights, president of the

International PEN Club, and International Advisory Board member of the Peace and Justice Studies Association and countless other groups.

When one reflects on the legacy of Dr. Luis Nieves Falcón from the context of solidarity and camaraderie, there are five areas of struggle that are important to keep in mind. These attributes should be taken as signposts of how to develop effective leaders of the future.

Coalition-Builder

Nieves understood like few others in modern times that all great united fronts must be broad enough to reach large and diverse sectors and masses of people, while still being controlled and coordinated by a clear and principled center. This concept is different from old-fashioned democratic centralism and more complicated than social democracy; grassroots initiatives must be allowed to spring up, take a shape of their own, and develop organically in ways appropriate to different communities. In this way, Nieves Falcón took a page from the book of Dr. Martin Luther King, who noted that "true leadership is not the search for consensus, but the molding of consensus." Nieves Falcón taught us how to provide strong leadership while allowing large coalitions to flourish.

Internationalist

Without for one moment giving up an inch of his proud Puerto Rican identity—his passion for his homeland and the beauty of its people—Nieves Falcón was a true man of the world. He could and did converse with leaders from every continent, earning respect for the cause of Puerto Rican freedom and recognition for the great Puerto Rican sociocultural contributions to world history. He did this with great knowledge and appreciation of global dynamics past and present, centering Puerto Rico in an internationalist perspective that rejects empire, militarism, capitalism, and greed.

Master Strategist

Few could argue that, as the architect of so many successful campaigns—bringing prisoners home, working against the US Navy in Vieques, working for expanded higher education and legal rights—Nieves Falcón was one of our greatest experts at sizing up situations and figuring out how best to achieve victories. That success might take more years or more money than we could ever imagine was no excuse or deterrent.

That we would have to work harder than we ever imagined was a given, but together and focused, we would find a way to win. Reforms were understood in a calculated fashion as part of the larger efforts for more radical and revolutionary social change. And Nieves Falcón's eyes, and all of the campaigns he led, were always set on the goal of full freedom and liberation for the Puerto Rican people and for all people.

Master Teacher

The way in which Luis told stories, with his whole body and with every nuance of every language he so expertly crafted, one was bound to listen and learn. Whether talking to a group of young women and men with little consciousness, or to experienced professionals, Nieves made you want not just to comprehend, but to act. His teaching was always in the service of social justice and action, with an aim to move forward in new ways that would enable each of us to fulfill the best of our potential. Education, for Professor Falcón, was based on the need for collective understanding to lead to lasting change.

Defender of the People

In San Juan, it is the stuff of legend that noted scholar Luis Nieves Falcón, at a time when all of his colleagues were preparing to retire, decided to leave his comfortable position at the University of Puerto Rico and work to obtain a law degree. He did this for the sole purpose of defending the imprisoned Puerto Rican independence activists who were languishing in the US jails with lengthy sentences served under torturous conditions typical of the treatment of political prisoners. Over a dozen had been found guilty of the "thought crime" of seditious conspiracy: planning a world where basic Puerto Rican rights, culture, and policy would not be under foreign control.

Legal Counselor

Nieves Falcón knew he had a new key to get into the jails and converse with his fellow patriots. More importantly, he also understood that he had only earned a one-way key: he could get in, but his legal skills alone could not get his compatriots out. Nieves Falcón was the type of lawyer who always comprehended that in working for freedom, legal and political struggle must be coordinated. No courtroom or negotiated maneuver could substitute for the door-to-door, grassroots campaigns that would mobilize a nation to call for the freedom of its prisoners, to call now for the immediate release of Oscar López Rivera.[9] Nieves Falcón was much more than a lawyer; he was a true defender of the people.

Conclusions

Twenty-first-century socialist, environmentalist, and peace movements centered in communities of largely European origin often work within a paradigm that assumes their own central role in the eradication of economic tyranny, the diminution of war, the causes of war, and the saving of the planet. Without a paradigm shift away from self-aggrandizing Eurocentrism, however, the US and European Left's work will continue to be ineffective, stuck in a vacuum of talking to and fighting with itself.

As the global "new left" only began to explore, the first steps away from these discredited models include action and ideological development informed by the realities of settler neocolonialism inside the metropole.[10] They include a deepening grasp of the role of prison, security forces, and the judicial arena as loci of struggle. And they require an understanding of organizing that reaches far beyond the structures of current mobilization, essentially replacing mass work with intellectual pursuits. If alternatives to capitalism and the destruction of the earth are to win victories and grow the ecosocialist vision some have begun to articulate, we would do well to look for inspiration from many initiatives taking place in the Global South. Representing the Global South "up north," with a keen and advanced analysis and effective practice of combating the threats to humankind, lay Mayor Chokwe Lumumba and Dr. Luis Nieves Falcón. Though their personal work must be counted as done, their examples remain for us to build upon.

Former Black Panther spokesperson and political prisoner Dhoruba bin Wahad, now a leading Pan-Africanist intellectual, summarized it all this way (in a note to this author):

> As we witness the transition of a generation of freedom fighters, one by one, each loss should give those of us who still remain serious pause for thought. We should seriously contemplate the mortality of revolutionary thought when reactionary forces dominate our society and therefore underscore the urgency for radical change in what remains of our lifetime. With each funeral,

memorial service, and tribute, we should appreciate that as Mao once said, about the disease of complacency, "as long as one remains a Monk, one will go on tolling the Bell." It's past due time for those of us still alive to cease pontification, promoting social niche work within the system as a path to radical change. It's time to readdress an alternative platform, an alternative force with which to reconcile our otherwise powerless existence. To survive today, we must systematically abolish the racist/reactionary controls that restrict our development, neutralize the powers that ill define our collective interests as symmetric to the interests of national-security-state and master the immediate environment in which we find ourselves, by any means necessary. In short, anyone over the age of sixty that is still advocating reformism rather than abolitionist politics is either too old and politically senile or so broken in mind and body that they think fascist life-support systems are meaningful! It's not just about the plan we make, it's about the stand we take.

Originally published in *Capitalism Nature Socialism* 25, no. 2 (2014): 118–25.

Notes

1 MXGM, founded in 1990 as a mass association committed to the politics of New Afrikan independence, has chapters in eight cities in the North and South, and programs focused on "taking back the land," cop-watch monitoring of police brutality, "housing is a right" projects, and a women's caucus. They have a web presence, accessed May 26, 2022, https://freethelandmxgm.org.

2 NAPO was founded in 1984 as an expression of revolutionary national liberation movement politics with a commitment to building a New Afrikan nation. With close ties to the Republic of New Afrika (RNA), NAPO relates as a nongovernmental organization in relationship to those who work directly with the Provisional Government of the RNA.

3 Imari Obadele, *Foundations of the Black Nation: A Textbook of Ideas behind the New Black Nationalism and the Struggle for Land* (Baton Rouge, LA: House of Songhay, 1975).

4 Nkechi Taifa and Chokwe Lumumba, *Reparations Yes!* (Baton Rouge, LA: House of Songhay, 1983).

5 Obadele, *Foundations.*

6 Dustin Barnes and Terricha Bradley-Phillips, "Mourners Laud Jackson Mayor Lumumba," *USA Today*, March 8, 2014, http://www.usatoday.com/story/news/nation/2014/03/08/mourners-laud-jackson-mayor-lumumba/6220679.

7 J. Sakai, *Settlers: The Mythology of the White Proletariat* (Boston: Morningstar Press, 1983).

8 Saed, "Prison Abolition as an Ecosocialist Struggle," *Capitalism Nature Socialism* 23, no. 1, (2012): 1–5.
9 Luis Nieves Falcón, ed., *Oscar López Rivera: Between Torture and Resistance* (Oakland, CA: PM Press, 2013).
10 Francis Boyle, *Foundations of World Order: The Legalist Approach to International Relations, 1898–1922* (Durham, NC: Duke University Press, 1999).

Atlanta 2021: Radical Futures

Yolande M.S. Tomlinson

The Organization for Human Rights and Democracy (OHRD), in cooperation with our partners and residents, is forging a new way for Atlanta, for economics, for queer, Black, working-class, and oppressed peoples, for anyone who shares our values, our analysis of power, and our commitment to intersectional human rights. Our work is responsive, mission- and values-driven, and determined to walk fully in its articulated principles and vision. We are grounded in some of our members and ancestors' wildest dreams of freedom, pleasure, joy, and liberation, while honoring the most robust possibilities for our communities, our children, and ourselves. We are also committed to working through the challenges that this work poses from building deep relationships to securing needed resources without compromising our values. This new Atlanta way is rooted in an analysis of our local environment, the conditions we experience as marginalized and oppressed peoples, and an understanding of power grounded in a radical queer Black feminist ethic and politic.

The "Old" Atlanta Way

Billed as the Black Mecca, Atlanta masks a sinister reality for Black and brown folks. Atlanta was the seat of the Confederacy with a deep history of segregation. In response to the infamous, white-led race riot in 1906, Black and white business and political leaders made a conscious decision to share power at the exclusion of the Black masses. Although later coined as the "Atlanta Way" by city leaders such as former mayors Maynard Jackson and William B. Hartsfield, this grand compromise has its roots in post–Civil War efforts to build the economy of the city. This agreement has kept the city's political structure in place but at a considerable cost to poor and working-class Black Atlantans. This elitist biracial patriarchal pact sits as the foundation of the massive transfer of public wealth to private hands, operating under the guise of "development." It places business interest over and above the human needs of people suffering under multiple forms of oppression in the city.

Amid the celebrity and wealth, Atlanta continues to lead the nation in several human rights violations. The city leads the nation in income inequality, where the gap between those earning the highest and the lowest incomes is the widest of any US city. Among US cities experiencing higher levels of gentrification, Atlanta ranks fifth in the nation. Nearly 40 percent of Atlanta is made up of "food deserts," or food apartheid zones more appropriately, where poor and working-class Black and brown communities lack access to healthful, fresh, and affordable foods, leading to poor health outcomes. In the pandemic, this fact alone tops the list in explaining Black folks' vulnerability to, and high rates of infection of, COVID-19. Graduation rates for Black and Latino students in Atlanta Public Schools are 57 percent and 53 percent respectively, compared with 84 percent for white and 94 percent for Asian-American students. The unemployment rate for Black Atlanta residents (22 percent) is almost twice the city's overall rate (13 percent) and more than three times higher than the rate for their white counterparts (6 percent). Despite Mayor Keisha Lance Bottoms's assertion that more than 50 percent of the business owners in metro-Atlanta are minorities, the average Black-owned business is valued eleven times less than the average white-owned Atlanta business ($58,085 versus $658,264). Citing more statistics will only reveal that Black and brown communities, and vulnerable identities within them, experience a disproportionate share of violence from all angles.

The "old" Atlanta Way serves a small elite set of Black folks and, increasingly, other racial groups at the expense of the interest and well-being of the predominantly Black, working-class, and immigrant populations in or around the city. This contradiction of Black suffering and the myth of shared Black success makes it challenging to organize in the city. Many new organizers and pop-up organizations unknowingly and knowingly perpetuate these dynamics, attempting to bolster themselves and their organizations. They form relationships with gatekeeping institutions and organizers that make it difficult to build authentic partnerships and relationships. It is hard to call out former mayor and United Nations ambassador Andrew Young for his role in expanding the Atlanta Way when he is celebrated as a giant of the civil rights movement, Atlanta politics, and the city's economic development. One of the biggest transfers of public wealth to private hands happened under the leadership of Mayor Shirley Franklin, who is celebrated as the first Black female mayor of the city, when she diverted money from the struggling Atlanta Public School system to the private development of the Atlanta Beltline, a multibillion dollar project to repurpose a twenty-two-mile corridor around the city to create light rail, green space, and walking/biking paths through forty-five communities. The money diverted from the public school system still has not been paid back in full, while teachers and administrators caught in a test cheating scandal have lost their lives, lost their jobs, and served jail time. Meanwhile, the Beltline continues to drive massive speculation, aggressive investments, racist policing, and mass displacement of poor (primarily) Black residents.

The Organization for Human Rights and Democracy

Unwilling to perpetuate the "old" Atlanta Way or to follow the trodden path of many social justice organizations, where we chase philanthropic dollars to pay personnel, OHRD has focused instead on building alternative models of key institutions that are people-centered and democratically governed in the areas of education, food, economic development, health, and housing. We shy away from civic engagement and mobilizations because those gains are temporary and do not lead to systemic change—even as they bring in money. It means that since our founding we have operated with an unpaid and underpaid "staff."

Our vision of the world is one where all people can govern their own institutions, steward the resources, and perform the cultural practices to safely pursue our full potential, in harmony with Mother Earth. Founded in 2015, our mission remains engaged in multi-issue, grassroots, radical, intersectional human rights organizing to transform our communities and the world, using Metro-Atlanta as our model. We are guided by the lived experiences, the activism, and the knowledge of Black feminists and women of color. We prioritize working-class people of color and the conditions we experience to build movements and an institution for change. Essentially, OHRD aims to be a model of the change it wishes to see in the movement and the world.

In our organizing work, we are modeling, mapping, researching, cooperating, transforming, and dreaming of new possibilities and new futures simultaneously. We are focused on meeting our people's basic and immediate needs (e.g., food, housing, education, work, safety, community) as we are building long-term infrastructure, institutions, and practices (cooperatives, community assemblies, consensus-decision-making, accountability processes) of the future we are bringing into being. We are doing this through practices of mutuality, cooperation, solidarity, and communality rooted in a deep commitment to a radical queer Black feminist ethic, politic, and framework. We are seeing differing results based on our metric of success—the relationships we build, our commitment to healing ourselves, the values we hold, how we are able to survive in the pandemic, the various types of people in our ecosystem, what resources we provide to community, how much of our needs are still being met by the current system, how much surplus we generate as a cooperative, how much resources are needed to move the work, and so forth. We are imperfect in this work. And what we have learned through doing the work is that we must set our own metrics, move in the spirit of abolitionism, and embrace contradictions as integral to the work. None of it is without struggle, but it is the principles and politics we hold and our commitment to each other that will ultimately determine our success.

Radical Queer Black Feminist

Our primary commitment at OHRD is to an intersectional or radical queer Black feminist (RQBF) politics. It means that what we have been struggling with in the work (and movement more broadly) is how to put race, gender, sexuality, ability, and economics in transformative conversations with each other. Early in our formation as an organization, we had to confront patriarchy in our leadership and organizing approach. While our colleague was able to articulate a vision of intersectionality and quote eloquently key texts and theorists, their approach lacked appreciation for the full range of human vulnerabilities, ways of knowing, and knowledge of how women of color, and Black women in particular, build communities and networks. For them, intersectionality was a buzzword and a tool for organizing, but not an analysis of power and way of being. This was a glaring contradiction of OHRD's statement of grounding in radical, Black, transnational feminisms, our politics, and our vision.

Our formulation of a radical queer Black feminist praxis (theory and action) is borne out of our lived experiences as directly and multiply impacted folks ourselves, our organizing, research, and cooperative development work in Metro-Atlanta and beyond. It is also grounded in the histories, activism, and institution-building of Black feminists and liberators such as Nanny of the Maroons, Anna Julia Cooper (after whom our learning cooperative is named), Harriet Tubman, Ida B. Wells, Claudia Jones, Ella Baker, the Gullah Geechee women of Combahee River Settlement, the Combahee River Collective, Audre Lorde, Kimberly Crenshaw, and extraordinary women such as our grandmothers, Meliana, Bernetha Day, and Rose Jones. Our approach is dynamic and flexible without compromising its integrity and core values. What follows is not exhaustive but is certainly representative of how we think, carry out the work, and ask others to show up and what we encourage them to work toward.

A radical queer Black feminist approach is conversant with rather than antagonistic toward or competitive with other formulations of intersectionality and Black feminist praxes. Like those formulations (e.g., Black queer feminism introduced by Charlene Carruthers and Black Youth Project 100) we reflect the people and places that give rise to this approach. We sit in a genealogy of Black feminist thinkers and practitioners who have given name to their experiences and their historical moment. We are also a product of our moment, in which intersectionality has gained currency and controversy, and we are attempting to reclaim its history and legacy from liberal discourse and politics that seek to unmoor the term from its herstory, peoples, politics, and power. Radical queer Black feminism is our effort to re-root and reclaim intersectionality and its liberatory power.

A radical queer Black feminist approach is first and foremost grounded in an analysis of power, which asserts that those who are directly and multiply impacted understand most profoundly the workings of structural violence through their lived experiences. Second, those who share this lived experience of structural oppression must lead and be centered in the solutioning. Importantly, it is through our liberation that we all become free. At its core, RQBF, and the work of OHRD, is a politics of abolition.

RQBF begins at the root, with the word radical to underscore our commitment to the total transformation of current structures of violence. As Dr. Angela Davis teaches us, radical simply means "grasping things at the root." Further, in the spirit of Audre Lorde's invocation to abandon hierarchical jockeying within categories of oppression, we embrace queerness as a marker of vulnerability and possibility and as a disruptor of normativity. It comes before (but not above) Blackness to unsettle the hierarchy of oppression that exists in Black liberation organizing, whereby Blackness is treated as a sine qua non of oppression. We queer race and Blackness specifically as *the* dominant marker of suffering without minimizing its significance as a central factor in how folks experience oppression. We affirm the importance of race as a signifier and marker of oppression, but we are disloyal to its dominance as the primary marker of difference and oppression. We embrace Black here as a marker of Third World identity and solidarity rooted in the abolition of all forms of racism and racial discrimination. We further embrace queerness as a site of alternative possibilities, both known and yet to be known. Likewise, we lift up "Black feminist" as a pairing to honor and amplify the continued contributions of Black women, feminists, womanists, queers, and nonbinary folx; and the analytical framework of intersectionality that it has blessed us with. We also recognize that Black feminism as a practice, tradition, and theory is expansive and has always called for holistic transformation in its insistence on moving from margins to center and recognition of the multidimensional nature of oppression and identities.

RQBF as a practice of intersectionality is a collaborative framework that aligns with our solidarity economy work. In this framework, we center collective leadership, decision-making, and visioning. We promote multigenerational space building, knowledge sharing, and leadership. This is true inside our organizing collective, across our programs, and within the projects we anchor. We take a nonpunitive, accountable approach to harm. The work we do with our children in our learning cooperative is not unlike the work we do with adults across our ecosystem. It moves away from violent, carceral models to embrace life-affirming ones. We hold folx accountable in loving, transparent, and just ways. We invest in building new relationships to ourselves, each other, and among other peoples/communities. In the spirit of Audre Lorde and the work of Regan De Loggans, we reconnect with our Indigenous and ancestral lifeways, "thrivance," and power. We believe we all have a moral imperative to do better once we know better.

And the Children Shall Lead

Perhaps our most radical institution, the Anna Julia Cooper (AJC) Learning and Liberation Center is a child- and learner-directed cooperative learning community grounded in the principles and politics of radical queer Black feminism. We were founded by a collective of Black and Latinx mamas deeply committed to liberation work. A play on bell hooks's "hurt people hurt people," AJC's motto is "free people free people." It is grounded in the belief that children are born into the world free, whole, and self-determining. It invites folks to commit to creating a liberatory ecology in direct resistance and opposition to all that is oppressive in our society. We offer a space where folks of all ages can live as their whole authentic selves and in their full dignity, while being affirmed in their worth and held in a community of comfort.

Consent is a core value for how we engage children at AJC and how we assess and acclimate to our roles as adults in community. AJC challenges parents and caregivers to accept that our role is to listen, to guide, and to nurture children's brilliance, not manufacture it through prescribed curricula, coercion, or violence. We have a strong practice of making consensus decisions with learners and facilitators, who are adult supporters in the space. When COVID-19 hit, we made decisions almost instantly about how to proceed and how we support our members who need ongoing learning facilitation for our children. We tried to re-create the learning co-op online and our children told us, "No!" We had no choice but to listen. Instead, they organized themselves through online Roblox and Minecraft gaming sessions, socially distanced meetups, coding lessons, guitar lessons, virtual role-playing, and whatever else they found interesting. Further, they deemed it important to maintain ongoing relationships with the facilitators, who they welcomed as extensions of their community and who provided a sense of familiarity and stability in an otherwise wild year.

AJC's vision and mission are liberatory but only insofar as parents and caretakers are willing and able to take leadership from children and to honor them in their wholeness and full dignity. We know, for example, that motherhood for Black, Indigenous, and other women of color is deeply devalued in the US. It is also devalued in movement. As oppressed women, how we parent our children is often very much tied to our own value, which can make it difficult for some folks to step outside of those parenting and education norms. In truth, some (movement) parents' radicalism does not go as far as their children. They only want to get free if adults are the ones leading the way.

AJC is a place for families, individuals, and communities to detox, unlearn normative ideologies by sharing power with their children. It asks us to center pleasure-based learning, self-direction, and neurodiversity. It asks parents to love and nurture their children in all their vulnerabilities and possibilities and to trust that a radical queer Black feminist politic will not "turn [their] children gay." Rather, if a child comes to identify as queer or any nonnormative identity, they will be held and supported in a community of love. In a nutshell, AJC is not (yet) for everybody. It is an invitation to be in conversation and community with other parents to decolonize both their parenting and their understanding of learning, as well as to divest from multiple systems simultaneously. It is an opportunity for parents, guardians, caregivers, facilitators, and learners to practice liberation together—now.

Metro Atlanta Mutual Aid Fund

In movement, the best currency we have is our relationships with each other. The trust we have built and the bonds we have forged. The laughs, tears, and joys we have shared. At the outset of the pandemic, we got to experience the importance of this currency through the operation of Metro Atlanta Mutual Aid (MAMA) Fund, which OHRD anchors by providing fiscal sponsorship, coordination, facilitation, and strategic direction.

Early in the MAMA Fund organizing process, we stepped in with our most trusting selves. We were raw, hopeful, ambitious, and talented. In this rawness, we were trusting of each other, we were vulnerable with each other, and we shared stories of ourselves and families. We grieved with each other, and we dreamed with each other. Some of our organizing collective even birthed new humans into the world during our time together. Alongside the beauty we have built in the MAMA Fund, we struggle with some of the same challenges we had prior to the pandemic. How do we engage in principled struggle to hold each other accountable to the values we have named and the politics we have all agreed to uphold? How do we take in enough money to support our communities without sacrificing our principles? How do we use the moment as an opportunity to hold funders accountable to the communities upon which they have built their wealth now being offered as charity? How do we as unpaid organizers honor the collective spirit of the project by being intentional about how and when we promote our work with the fund?

Across the OHRD ecosystem, we are asking questions about fundraising and philanthropic giving. From whom do we take money? What is a just amount to accept given the history of the foundation or corporation? What reporting or publishing requirements do they have for the fund and are they aligned with our values and how we want to hold our dignity, our people, and our communities? How will our name be used by donors in this moment and toward what end? Do our communities or the funder benefit more in this moment? Are we being given pennies as a public relations campaign, or is the money being given in an effort to make a deep and lasting impact in our communities? These are hard questions. MAMA Fund has turned down money from Amazon and Google, among others, because they violate workers' rights, contribute to capitalism-induced climate disasters, and actively cooperate with the state in selling or sharing our data while offering a few thousands. How do we turn down money when our people are suffering? Yet how do we take so few dollars when they get to brandish our name and image only to continue to violate our peoples' human rights locally, nationally, and globally? We are interested in meeting our people's basic needs, and we are also interested in challenging toxic institutions as we build self-determining, sustainable infrastructure to nourish ourselves and each other. And we are unwilling to compromise our dignity, our people, and our principles in the process.

Conclusion

As members of our own communities experiencing the deepest and harshest forms of violence, we understand the interconnectedness of the systems of oppression and the strategic necessity to center and prioritize our peoples and communities. We also know from experience and study that the systems of violence that oppress our communities are multiple (racism, heteropatriarchy, capitalism, imperialism, ageism, ableism, etc.) and they collude against our interests—not unlike those upholding the old Atlanta Way. Because of this fact of our reality, we utilize a radical queer Black feminist framework and praxis for understanding and shifting power to the collective; for nurturing deep relationships based in mutual trust and vulnerability; building solidarity across peoples, communities, and places; and, for modeling alternative institutions and futures.

Our members and partners across our ecosystem are clear about the work it will take to birth a new Atlanta Way. We know money will not flow easily for this work, yet we move with a spirit of abundance. We know the work is both immediate and long term, so we offer mutual aid funds now as we build a time bank to connect communities. It is messy and beautiful, so we utilize accountability processes to transform conflicts. We know that what we practice we become, so we engage in liberation as a constant practice.

V
MOVEMENT EXPANSIONS

Community Movement Builders

Kamau Franklin Interviewed by Kali Akuno

Kali Akuno: How did you come to the politics of the New Afrikan Independence Movement?

Kamau Franklin: I think for me, it was a slow process of getting politicized. My mom would tell me stories about growing up during Jim Crow, in Charleston, South Carolina. When she was young, she was in a whites-only playground with friends. They got chased out by a white cop, and because she was slower than some friends, she got hit in the back with a billy club. She has a scar to this day on her back some seventy years later from that incident. Her stories about her mom working for white families and her wanting to get out were captivating. My mom is a very honest woman about her feelings, so even as a dark-skinned Black woman who lived through that experience, she still looked at whiteness as something to envy or aspire to. So when she had children (my sister, whose father was a light skinned black man, and my father's a white man) that was part of her idea, her calculus, around what would give her kids a better shot or chance at life. Hearing that kind of story got me thinking about how the world worked, growing up mostly in the projects in Brooklyn, New York, and I began to think more and more about not only my place in the world, but my neighborhood, my block—why my block didn't have resources, when other places in New York had plenty.

In my late teens and twenties, I got to reading and watching documentaries on the civil rights movement. Then I started reading Malcolm. Reading the autobiography was a seminal moment for me. Hearing his views around what it would take for us as a people to liberate ourselves was transformative. Malcolm spoke about the fight for power, the struggle for land, the struggle for independence. In some of his speeches, like the "Message to the Grassroots," he laid out a clear nation-building framework breaking down the need for us to control the institutions in our communities and creating economic enterprises, that kind of stuff. In the last chapter of the autobiography, he talks about taking over states in the South. And slowly reading, taking that stuff into account, by the mid-1990s I came into contact with folks in the Malcolm X Grassroots Movement (MXGM). I had already joined a whole bunch of different organizations, which were specifically Black nationalist organizations. At that particular point, MXGM was talking about the Black Belt, about New Afrikan independence, Black liberation, all that resonated with me. The idea of self-determination resonated with me. Even though some of that seemed to not necessarily be attainable, the idea gave me a framework for the ideological path that I wanted to walk down.

The path of revolutionary nationalism, anti-capitalism, and anti-imperialism. This means establishing an independent nation-state built on a socialist economy. My journey along this road began by thinking about: What does it mean to own and control the means of production? To redistribute wealth and resources? I began thinking about markets differently. I still to this day consider myself part of the New Afrikan independence movement and I definitely consider myself to be a revolutionary nationalist. Those are the core ideological belief systems that I still practice, still believe in, and still drive my work even though I am no longer in that formation.

KA: One of the major intellectual organizing initiatives of the New Afrikan independence movement of the last twenty-five years was the Jackson-Kush Plan. Tell us about your role in helping to develop and execute this plan.

KF: Though I was an early proponent and supporter of the Jackson-Kush Plan, I feel like the hard writing goes to you. We had some organizational precursors that I worked on like our five-year plan, but I think your work on the Jackson-Kush Plan brought it to its natural conclusion and focus. As an organization at that time, MXGM was in a transition period. Obama had just won the 2008 presidential election. There were all these ideas around; could a Black person be the US president? What does this mean for nationalism and nationalist thought? What will that mean with Black folks who will be more married to the Democratic Party than ever? The Jackson-Kush Plan was something of a reset: How do we use this moment to advance our politics? How do we do something that combines the different elements of our politics in the electoral arena and outside the electoral arena, regarding the dual power philosophy where we really establish organizational structures and infrastructures? How do we advance the ownership of land, institutions, and productive facilities? How do we broaden out our distinct ideological perspective and work that helped us create distinct campaigns against the police (like Copwatch or the New Afrikan Militia), event planning (like Black August, the Malcolm X Festival, or Kwanzaa), and some organizing around political prisoners, etc., to a point where we are actually showing the way, a concrete path or a project that could be a model project for others to implement and emulate on creating self-determination?

The Jackson-Kush Plan became this specific idea that brought together some key strengths, which we thought we had at the time: a well-established organization and, of course, Chokwe Lumumba, who was a noted and important figure in the Jackson community. At first, Chokwe was opposed to the plan in terms of running for any office! It was me and yourself and some others that convinced him that running for office was key to this plan working—running and not even necessarily winning office. Only through a lot of back and forth with him and the Jackson chapter, did he and the chapter decide to run for city council, not for mayor.

The thing that I give the chapter in Jackson the most credit for was the successful run for city council. At least for me, from the outside looking in, given the support which I helped with, it gave me and many folks extra confidence that we could win the mayorship later. Later on, several of us as organizers became more confident following through with moving to the South as the elders had and propagandizing the work of the Republic of New Afrika (RNA) and the New Afrikan People's Organization (NAPO). Individually, as you know, we raised money to start the project in Jackson. My family, we moved to Jackson, we had our daughter in Jackson. The idea was to go down and to help fill out what we could in terms of implementing the Jackson-Kush Plan.

I think I was early among the folks who strove to implement the different aspects of the plan, including the electoral work, but also the work of economic development. At the time, it wasn't as developed as cooperatives, it was more around us owning land and property and housing. We had to facilitate other organizers coming down there. In that way, I was sort of like an early guinea pig for going down, moving to Jackson and helping to see what we could get accomplished. When I first came down, I became Chokwe's first campaign manager for mayor. My real role as facilitator, as I have been most of my life as a general organizer, was to get folks to come down and begin implementation of the plan and to organize with people in Jackson.

KA: One of the things I really want to highlight is the longer view of how we got here—you leading the charge in 2001 in Alabama—to have people buy land in the South. We learned from those experiments and sharpened things.

KF: There was a time when we, as an organization, were probably the leading Black nationalist and young adult formation in the United States—the mid-1990s. But this was still a bit of wheel spinning, right? You and I even got into some debates around if what we were doing was really organizing. When we talk about the ideology of New Afrikan independence and a revolutionary nationalist ideology, what did we have besides some organizing collectives but no models of development? Obviously, our history goes back to the formation of the Republic of New Afrika and the folks who moved to the South to do that kind of work.

But frankly, some people got settled and others would come and go within the organization. As an apparatus, things really seemed thin in terms of what we were going to accomplish, how we would meet our larger goals. At that time also, we were just beginning to scratch the surface of what grants might look like, we were a volunteer group gathered around because of ideology but not with a lot of resources. We based a lot of organizing along a 1960s and 1970s Black Power model that one joined based on ideology and then you figured out resources in a very hand-to-mouth way—what you can get from the collection plate!

I did step in and started constructing a smaller version of a larger idea around five-year plans, around bringing in resources and purchasing land. How can we call ourselves an organization for independence and the freeing of land when we own no land!? Along with a fellow attorney in the New York chapter, I started leading the call to raise money to purchase land. And we raised enough for a good amount of property, about twenty-five acres in Lowndes County, Alabama, that was purchased under my name/credit. The idea was that we would use that land and develop it, as home for our camp and/or retreat center. To be honest, it should have exposed for me some cracks and weaknesses in our formation, because part of the idea about buying this land was that we were going to purchase and then build the structure—but we had a limited time to convert the mortgage from a land purchase to a conventional thirty-year mortgage. Eventually, unfortunately, the land was foreclosed on because promises to raise additional resources were not realized.

I think we developed two five-year plans before we actually developed the Jackson-Kush Plan, and we built off some of the work that the Selma chapter was doing to create an independent party. We examined classic ideas around socialist and communist development, including readings of what happened during the Soviet Union. We began to better understand that dual power was something we needed. We could try to develop power from the outside, knowing that the state could use its apparatus to destroy you at any second. We realized that we couldn't just try to go after the resources of the state, because the state is so powerful it would make us play their game and dance to their tune. Organizers like to think they are making changes within the state when the state is making changes on you, making us fit our politics within what they need to keep their status quo going.

Dual power meant for us that we had to build some power outside of the state—an idea which became important for building the people's assemblies. Creating a political power bloc, with broader politics than MXGM, which could put pressure on any state apparatus, whether or not it was "our" person in an elected office. It wasn't about being chummy with a given candidate that we helped get into office. The focus would be on what the demands of the people were, which we were suggesting was needed whoever was in power. The outside pressure we were beginning to build was there to use as we needed it: to say to elected officials or state apparatuses "we are going to force your hand if we need to."

KA: What lessons from your time in Jackson are you applying to your work now as part of Atlanta's Community Movement Builders (CMB)?
KF: There are numerous ones, but one basic lesson is to know more about the people you're working with—know their politics, their motivations, etc. This is particularly true when dealing with mass-based organizing. I'm probably still a little careless in some of the ways in which I operate in terms of that! I offer a lot of trust upfront, in terms

of getting people involved in activities then later finding out, through the activities, they may not be so suited to a particular project. But when you're moving yourself and your family to a particular new location, it behooves you to really dig deep in finding out the full extent of who you will be working with. When I moved to Jackson, there were some people whom Chokwe trusted who simply were not interested in organizing on a day-to-day. There are some who are down today with Chokwe Jr., who did not even want to embark on the electoral work at the time. So Chokwe really tapped me to support that work and others seemed only interested in the possibility of government contracts if Chokwe Sr. won.

Another lesson is that ideology matters. People may say that they're revolutionary nationalists or New Afrikan nationalists and may turn out simply to be "race men." They're interested in what happens to Black people, but not in a radical or anti-capitalist way: "It's okay if I can get Black people more contracts or get Black people a couple of more jobs—that's what progress is!" But that wasn't how we were supposed to be measuring progress in terms of the Jackson-Kush Plan. Progress was supposed to be about "power, power, power!" Progress was supposed to be about resource distribution, about creating entities which brought in more folks to the People's Assembly. It was the dual power concept that not only were we creating some electoral power by running candidates (who had either similar ideologies or who we thought we could work with), we were also supposed to be creating a strong base of operation through having a larger chapter and/or through a people's assembly. But we weren't necessarily ready or equipped to do that kind of work.

Through an evaluative process of where we were at, we could have made a big difference in deciding the right moves at the right time at the right place. I think there was a willingness, particularly on my part, to engage in wishful thinking that we could solve whatever problems we worked on together. Those were real lessons learned. In my estimation, folks definitely wanted to see Chokwe win, obviously. They wanted to work to make Chokwe the mayor. But for some people, I think the ideas around building power stopped at that. That's where that work ended.

Applying them to CMB, even in the five years that we've been operating at a really slow pace of building up an organizational apparatus, we haven't been engaged in voting rights, in voting for candidates or supporting candidates. We felt like, as a new organization, we needed to establish some power on the ground, we needed to work with everyday people. We needed to figure out what are the mechanisms to reach people—whether it's through mutual aid survival programs, organizing cooperatives, or on a different set of tactics and strategies that we could use to spread our message. Particularly here in Atlanta, it's only up until this last year (2021), that we've even started to consider going down that road in terms of electoral power. What are we going to do at the neighborhood association level before we get to talking about the mayoral level?! We're working deeply in the southwest area of Atlanta, known as Pittsburgh.

Another lesson that was learned is the need for far more mandatory political education to make sure that we trust the people who are overseeing our resources. It sounds like it should be elementary, something that everybody should know. But after many years, it's not always something that people have figured out.

KA: Give us the background on when you started CMB: why you started it, the politics and principles of the organization.

KF: I was working in what I considered my retirement job for the Quakers, the American Friends Service Committee (AFSC), as the southern director—a well-paid nonprofit job. I was contacted by a trust fund guy who I guess contacted a lot of organizers around giving resources, and I was silly enough to respond. It turned out that he seemed to be serious, and I told him what I was working on. This was at a time when Black Lives Matter was really taking off, post-Ferguson.

There was a lot of energy on the ground, and we had different youth service groups—in Atlanta, DC/Baltimore, and New Orleans. I gave them an idea of combining them and making a community-based organization. And this guy offered to buy houses in those areas. But there was a lot of conflict in that process, and ultimately AFSC did not want the kids to be working with the property and fired me because I would not accept their final judgment on not proceeding with the idea. I stopped working for AFSC, but worked to retain the property and continue doing the local work in Atlanta. After many months of back-and-forth discussion, we decided to sell the property in New Orleans and in Baltimore, split the proceeds with the trust fund dude and give them back those resources, and started to build a chapter of whatever this organization was in Atlanta. And all we knew at the time was that we had a house and we had some young kids who might still be interested in doing some stuff!

Little by little, I and others made that house into a community center and started working with different people—as a space for folks to do events and with a community garden right next door (that was in disrepair but that we spent whatever little resources we had on getting it back together even though it was a city-owned property). We are now in year six, and CMB has expanded to approximately six chapters. In Atlanta in particular, we do anti-gentrification work, work against police brutality, and do what we call sustainability work, including mutual aid, which includes a community stabilization fund. We have a sea moss cooperative, an aquaponics cooperative, a food cooperative/food buying group... still working on a kale cooperative! We also have a security cooperative, which does a cop watch and a safety patrol. Those are our areas of work.

As a Black organization, we are fighting for self-determination, fighting for control of resources, and anti-capitalism. We work with those who don't necessarily have the same ideology but have some similar ideological positions and are willing, ready to learn from one other, to do political education, to mobilize in the streets, and to take on some tasks. We're overwhelmingly still volunteer at this particular stage, and relatively speaking, we're still a small organization. But that's how we get the work done!

KA: Give us a breakdown of CMB's principles.
KF: Our principles are basically:

- *Self-determination*: We subscribe to the theory that we are a colonized people, a colonized nation within a nation, and that we have a right as a people to fight for self-determination. We believe that we have a right to fight for freedom to own and control any and every institution and/or organization that has control over our lives.
- *Sustainability*: We believe in cooperative economic systems, in systems that work for us, which must be rooted in our history of cooperatives and Black communities. This is obviously something that I pulled from not only the Jackson-Kush Plan, but also from the work that you folks are doing in Cooperation Jackson. We need to create alternative economic systems so that we as a people can build some sense of economic power.
- *Leadership development*: We understand that our work has to be centered not strictly around young people, but centered around the

political education of our people so that we don't fall into the traps of trying to build things but falling victim or prey to big institutions and organizations whose job is "movement capture"—whether it's the Democratic Party or any liberal institutions whose job it is to pull us back into the fold of the American elite.

- *Human rights*: We say "we respect everyone's humanity"—so we're careful that we staunchly oppose any practices which devalue human life. Then we do a list of things—racism, capitalism, classism, sexism, homophobia, xenophobia—oppressions that we believe people have a right to be free of.
- *Solidarity*: This is a way of saying that we are an international people. We're obviously Pan Africanist, so we're in solidarity with ourselves, but also in solidarity internationally with people who are working to free themselves in different places around the world.
- Lastly, *Black love*: At first, I thought it was kind of corny. But folks convinced me that it's important to say that we are expressing our work in a way that shows our love. We're not doing this work out of an opportunity to get famous. We're doing it because we love our folks!

There are also other principles that we have around creating liberated territory. Since we're a relatively new and a small organization, we may not be doing "real nation-building," but we are organizing to build the institutions that we need to have some control over our own daily lives. Black organizations which have succeeded the most within Black communities are those that have shown Black folks that they can get things accomplished, that they can have an influence in people's day-to-day lives. Whether or not I agree with all of their ideologies, I think about the Garvey movement, the Nation, even the Panthers to a degree, who showed Black folks that we can make some progress by creating institutions outside of the apparatus of the state. Relying on the state to do the work will not be the way in which we as a people begin to free ourselves, we have to create models of organizing that are effective and helping to meet the needs of our people.

Cooperation Humboldt: A Case Study

The Cooperation Board and Staff Collective:
David Cobb, Ruthi Engelke, Marina Lopez, Tamara MacFarland, Tobin McKee, Sabrina Miller, Oscar Mogollon, Argy Munoz, and Ron White

It is no exaggeration to say that Cooperation Humboldt exists because Cooperation Jackson exists. The founders of Cooperation Humboldt began as a study group, and the original *Jackson Rising* book was a central part of our curriculum. We were—and still are—inspired by the fact that the Jackson-Kush Plan is not merely a plan to use existing political institutions to "govern better" but is a revolutionary commitment to transform existing social, political, and economic relationships.

Since our founding in 2018, we have engaged with the leadership of Cooperation Jackson as collaborative partners to assess what is happening in this historic moment of global conjuncture and to learn from each other. We have been honored to be pushed by them to be better. As Maya Angelo urges: "Do the best you can until you know better. Then when you know better, do better."

We adapt and apply the Cooperation Jackson strategy to our own unique local conditions and encourage you to do the same in your community. A few key lessons we have learned from them include:

- the need to be aware of and rooted to the history of the place where you are organizing;
- the need for a clear theory that is applied in the real world with ordinary folks;
- the importance of deep, authentic political education and struggle;
- the powers—and dangers—of engaging in electoral politics;
- the power of internal democratic decision-making.

This chapter is an attempt to share our experiment and to invite dialogue with others. Ultimately, we think of ourselves as a local node of resistance and revolutionary struggle. We are eager to connect with and confederate with other nodes to create a rhizomatic network of global change.

Wigi (Humboldt Bay)

Cooperation Humboldt is located in far Northern California on the Pacific Coast. This is the traditional homeland of the Wiyot people, who have stewarded this land since time immemorial.[1] We honor and recognize them as the rightful and original inhabitants of this place. Land acknowledgments are important, but they often remain a mostly symbolic statement. We are fortunate and grateful that the Seventh Generation Fund for Indigenous Development initiated a more powerful tool—the Honor Tax.[2] This is a self-imposed tax paid directly to the Wiyot Nation by people who are living on their ancestral territories.

It is important to note that the Honor Tax was *not* requested by the Wiyot Nation, although they have formally agreed via their Tribal Council to accept the support. Michelle Vassel, Wiyot tribal administrator says:

> Tribal governments provide essential services to their citizens. Other governments tax property, land, and income in order to provide these services. We cannot tax our own people because they are already paying local, state, and federal taxes. The Wiyot Tribe operates primarily on grant funding. That places us in a position of being subject to the whims of the federal government and nonprofit foundations which often dictate how funds must be spent. For me, the Honor Tax is a really important tool to develop economic sovereignty, because it allows us to choose how we spend funds with no strings attached.

The amount of Honor Tax paid is decided by the individual or organization. Cooperation Humboldt pays 1 percent of our annual gross income as an Honor Tax, and we actively promote it to individuals, businesses, and municipalities. We encourage you to learn which Indigenous people are the original stewards of the land you now inhabit and to explore how you can build authentic and right relationships with them.[3]

Our Vision

Another lesson we have learned from studying the Cooperation Jackson experiment is the importance of being clear and unambiguous about what we are fighting against and what we are struggling to create. As Kali Akuno often says, "Break it down without dumbing it down."

At Cooperation Humboldt we know with unshakable conviction that it is possible to meet all our needs without exploiting others or being exploited ourselves—and that this can be done in a manner that does not merely sustain the existing natural world but helps to regenerate it. It is not enough to merely survive; we want—and deserve—to thrive.

In order to do that, we recognize that we must acknowledge and dismantle the interconnected power-over dominator systems of heteropatriarchy, settler colonialism, capitalism, and white supremacy. We must intentionally create new systems of power-with—cooperative systems based on gender inclusivity, decolonization, solidarity economy, and explicit antiracism.

What We Believe

Another example of our shared clarity is the use of a collectively created "What We Believe" statement. Cooperation Humboldt cofounder David Cobb worked with Kali Akuno during the US Social Forum process, and witnessed the power of collective struggle for clarity in building genuine alignment and unity. That experience inspired us to write a document that clearly and publicly states our beliefs:

- We believe that our current institutions are fundamentally racist, sexist, and class oppressive. This is a result of social, political, and economic systems that incentivize domination and exploitation of women, people of color, and poor, homeless, disabled, queer, undocumented, and Indigenous people.
- We believe that capitalism is an economic system based upon exploitation and oppression, and that it will destroy the planet if we do not shift to a cooperative and sustainable economic system.
- We believe it is possible to create new institutions that incentivize cooperation, love, compassion, and kindness. This new system will be capable of supporting every person with a good quality of life.
- We believe in lifting up and supporting groups that are doing grassroots organizing with working-class people and people of color, and

people who are training organizers and building relationships and developing long-term strategies to resist fascism and create new models for a joyous and collaborative new future reality.

- We believe we can work with you (or your organization) even if you do not believe these things, but we want to be explicit and clear about who we are and what we believe.

The Characteristics of Capitalism

Some people believe economics is too hard for ordinary people to understand. We profoundly disagree. We think this is an intentional effort by the owning class to obfuscate how they undemocratically and unjustly rule the world. The wealthy and elite use transnational corporations not merely to exercise power, they are literally ruling over us.

So we recognize the importance of understanding—and teaching—the basics of economics. We are deeply indebted to our friends at Movement Generation and the seminal booklet they wrote titled "From Banks and Tanks to Cooperation and Caring: A Strategic Framework for a Just Transition."[4] From them we learned that the word economy comes from the Greek word *oikonomia*, which simply means *management of the home*. As they so eloquently observed: "The primary purpose of the dominant economy—what we call the *Extractive Economy*—is the accumulation, concentration and enclosure of wealth and power. If the purpose of a *Regenerative Economy* is ecological restoration, community resilience, and social equity, then resources must be acquired through regeneration."

We also acknowledge the work of the Center for Popular Economics which helped us with the following simple and accessible definition and framework for understanding capitalism.[5]

- *Private ownership of the means of production*: The materials, raw materials, facilities, machinery, and tools used to create and distribute goods and services are owned by private individuals.
- *Commodity production*: Goods and services are not created based on need, but for sale and exchange in the market. People originally bartered one product for another, but now a particular commodity—money—is treated separately.
- *Profit maximization*: The idea that people mostly take actions that

will result in them making money (profiting). In economics, it is about selling things at the highest price the market will accept.

- *Wage labor*: Human labor (physical, mental, and social effort) is treated as just another commodity to be used to produce goods and services, and is bought and sold via the market.
- *Market allocation*: The decisions about what goods/services are produced, how they are distributed, what they cost, and how finance and investment decisions are made are determined by "supply and demand" with little democratic control.

Taken together, these characteristics are why capitalism creates inequality, market failure, destroys the environment, cultivates excess materialism, and creates boom and bust economic cycles. More dangerously, capitalism is the ideology of the cancer cell, because it is premised on unlimited growth on a finite planet. We are consuming the resources of Mother Earth faster than she can replenish herself. Like cancer, capitalism will kill its host if it is not stopped.

The Principles of a Solidarity Economy

We also read and studied the seminal essay "Solidarity Economy: Building an Economy for People and Planet," by Emily Kawano.[6] Emily helped to cofound the US Solidarity Economy Network, and from her essay we learned about—and explicitly and publicly embraced—these five principles of a solidarity economy.

- *Pluralism*: The solidarity economy framework is not a dogmatic and fixed blueprint. It acknowledges that there are multiple paths to the same goal.
- *Solidarity*: This includes a broad range of social interactions grounded in the collective practices of cooperation, mutualism, sharing, reciprocity, altruism, love, compassion, caring, and gifting.
- *Equity*: This framework opposes all forms of oppression and discrimination whether it is based on ethnicity, gender, religion, sexual orientation, or anything else.
- *Sustainability*: This framework understands that all life is interconnected and interdependent. We embrace the concept of *buen vivir* (right living or living well).

- *Participatory democracy*: The solidarity economy framework is premised on the notion that decision-making should be as local as possible, to empower communities. If a decision affects you, then you should be allowed to participate in making that decision.

Theory of Change

In order to accomplish these broad and deep goals, we understood that we needed to be grounded in a theory of change. Some folks romanticize theory, while others dismiss it. But a theory is simply a foundational set of beliefs about how the world works. It is a set of interrelated concepts, ideas, and definitions that explains and predicts events and situations.

Whether we realize it or not, we all live our lives according to our own personal, internalized theory. Our personal theory is an assortment of beliefs and assumptions that come from a multitude of places—experiences, conversations, media, advertising, teachers, family, friends, and foes. These beliefs are often contradictory.

So theory matters. A lot. But theory without action is mere contemplation. Action without theory is merely "doing stuff." At Cooperation Humboldt, we are intentional about developing a shared theory of how the world currently operates in order to develop concrete actions to create a new world. We do this through study. Our theory of change is an interconnected commitment to *resist*, *build*, *empower*, and *inspire*.

Resisting the dominant system means fighting against oppression, exploitation, and inequality. This alone does not bring about systemic change, but it protects individuals and the overall health of our community. It prevents things from getting worse and demonstrates the power of "We the People." Resistance is necessary.

While we are resisting, we must also work to shift power away from corporations, the wealthy elite, and entrenched politicians, and toward local communities. We can do this by shifting both law and culture—for example, by crafting ordinances, passing ballot initiatives, or enacting legislation that asserts our basic human rights and protects our rights over corporations. Ultimately, we believe we must establish that nature itself has legal rights.

We must also create and nurture alternatives to the dominant system that meet our needs. Without alternatives, we remain dependent upon the existing system. Corporations, corporate culture, and the predatory class encourage this level of dependence. At Cooperation

Humboldt we build working models that foster a culture of local sovereignty, autonomy, and control. We know that people need opportunities to opt out of the corporate capitalist system, the space and opportunity to think differently, and the agency to build a new system that meets our social and economic needs.

But building alternatives alone is not enough. That leaves the rest of the society in the hands of the 1% and means only those lucky enough to participate in the alternative can avoid exploitation and oppression. Even worse, we know that unless we restructure society, the predatory owning class is going to destroy the ability of Mother Earth to replenish herself.

So we must also empower ourselves with practical organizing skills and deep political education. History illustrates the importance of strategic community organizing in creating lasting and meaningful social change. We must build a vibrant and powerful movement for democracy. In collaboration with other groups and individuals in our community, we are committed to learning how to actually "do democracy."

We are learning by doing the art of facilitation, messaging, coalition building, and campaign development. We freely and enthusiastically share that knowledge and experience, so we can help each other build more effective organizations and citizen's groups. We are committed to building trust, interdependence, and deep and authentic relationships with one another.

And when we do these things, we begin to shift culture. We know that the most dangerous threat to democracy is the mistaken belief that the US is a functioning democracy. A 2014 study confirmed what ordinary people implicitly know—a small group of obscenely wealthy people actually control the US government. The US government is an oligarchy, not a democracy.[7]

People and communities need to understand that we not only have a right to resist corporate rule—we have a responsibility to do so. As our friends at Movement Generation say, "If it's the right thing to do, we have every right to do it."

At Cooperation Humboldt we believe a democratic world is not only possible—it is necessary for the survival of life on earth. So our work always includes an historical and analytic framework for understanding the mechanisms ruling elites have used to manipulate our laws, our government, and our culture in order to maintain their power. Our work also always includes a commitment to change those rules. We recall the admonition of Amílcar Cabral: "Always remember that the people are not fighting for ideas. The people fight and accept the sacrifices demanded by the struggle in order to gain material advantages, to live better and in peace, to benefit from progress, and for the better future of their children. National liberation, the struggle against colonialism, the construction of peace, progress and independence are hollow words devoid of any significance unless they can be translated into a real improvement of living conditions." To that end, our day-to-day organizing is built around meeting basic human needs, acknowledging that if something is a need, it should never be subject to commodification. Our existing work is grouped into program areas, and each program administers multiple specific projects.

Arts and Culture

We know that cultural shift manifests itself through artistic expression across mediums. In fact, one way you know that you have an actual movement is that the principles, values, and ideas of the movement begin appearing in songs, dance, music, poetry, theater, paintings, and sculpture.

One of our main projects is the annual "Artists Dismantling Capitalism Symposium," where we bring together artists, culture workers, organizers, and scholars to explore the use of artistic and creative practice in reimagining and creating a new society based on a solidarity economy. For the past two years we had representatives of Cooperation Jackson as presenters: Abrianni Perry, Kwame Braxton, and Shambe Jones.

We also facilitate ongoing sessions titled "The Whiteness Within: Challenging White Supremacy Culture," which is a workshop that uses story sharing, reflection, and physical expression to give participants the opportunity to recognize and shift away from racism.

Field Guide to a Crisis is a project that recognizes that folks in recovery are experts in survival, and we help prepare them to be teachers in resiliency using the skills they learned in their own recovery.

Regenerative Theater envisions a theater free from a capitalist extraction model.

Cartographic Somatics helps artists and body-based practitioners racialized as white, or biracial with white skin passing privilege, to explore and examine the construct of race.

Care and Wellness

Health, wellness, and care are fundamental human rights. Our Care and Wellness team educates, provides direct services, and nurtures community partnerships to remove the profit motive from health care and empowers people to care for others and to actively participate in their own well-being.

Our Community Health Worker (CHW) Collaborative fosters the development of worker self-directed nonprofits created by and for underserved communities in Humboldt, Del Norte, and Trinity Counties. The CHW Collaborative includes Open Door Community Health Centers, College of the Redwoods, Wiyot Tribe, Yurok Tribal Wellness Court, Native American Pathways, Arcata Police Department, All Are Welcome, AJ's Transitional Living, and the Humboldt Area Center for Harm Reduction. Our current collaboratives are New Rising Hmong Association, Comunidad Unida del Norte de Arcata, Peer Community Health Worker Street Outreach Project, and the Yurok Women's GED Study Group.

Disaster Response and Community Resilience

This program area builds community power through disaster relief and creates long-term resilience for communities. Our ultimate goal is to restructure our local economy to guarantee that everyone's basic needs are always met, both during and after disasters. The work of this team includes disaster mitigation/preparedness, disaster response, immediate recovery, and resilience.

When the COVID-19 pandemic first hit, our entire organization shifted into coordinating a community-wide response. This work was mostly ad hoc, and Cooperation Humboldt team members coordinated mask making, sanitation supply procurement and delivery, grocery shopping and delivery, and hot meal distribution. We were also instrumental in creating an entire Community COVID Response Coalition that coordinated the delivery of mutual aid across eighteen different local organizations.

In response to the 2020 California wildfires, we worked closely with the American Red Cross, the Office of Emergency Services, and other local government agencies and social change organizations to support hundreds of fire evacuees.

We are currently exploring the creation of local "resilience hubs" across the community, which are sites that aim to be "ready for anything" and better prepared for natural disasters, climate change, and other stresses in our community. During nondisaster times, these sites will serve as gathering and learning spaces for the community, providing inspiration and knowledge to empower us all to adopt more sustainable ways of living.

Economic Democracy

We know that to have a functioning democracy ordinary people must control the fundamental decisions about how our society is structured. That means we must democratize all aspects of the economy. Our two main economic democracy projects are advancing public banking and nurturing and supporting worker-owned cooperative business through our Worker Owned Humboldt (WOH) initiative.

WOH collaborates with the North Coast Small Business Development Center to provide new worker-owned businesses with essential business training. We also collaborate with Project Equity to provide feasibility studies for existing businesses considering converting to worker ownership. WOH participants receive free peer mentorship and technical assistance from our partners at the US Federation of Worker Cooperatives. We are currently incubating ten new worker-owned businesses in our community.

We are also leaders in the California Public Banking Alliance. A public bank is operated in the public interest. They invest in Main Street not Wall Street, and promote a transparent, publicly governed finance system. Costs of public infrastructure projects can be literally halved, saving taxpayer money and doubling community investment power. In 2020 we helped to draft and lobbied for California Assembly Bill 857, a historic law that enables the creation of local and regional public banks in California. We are currently working with the California Department of Financial Protection and Innovation to promulgate the rules for the creation and oversight of local public banks.[8]

Last, we are exploring participatory budgeting for our own organization and also for local municipal and county budgets. At this moment this is mostly aspirational, but we are collaborating with the Participatory Budgeting Project and the "Democracy Beyond Elections" effort.

Education

Everyone has the right to education, and we know that we are all both teachers and learners. Collective education empowers us as organizers and is critical to our success. Education is a central component of everything that we do.

We provide internal educational opportunities for both our core team and to the broader community as well. We host free twelve-week study group cohorts to explore solidarity economy theory and practice, white supremacy, heteropatriarchy, and the local history of settler colonialism. These sessions not only increase participants' individual understanding of the topics discussed, they also build social solidarity and a shared analysis of where we are, where we want to go, and how we can get there. In 2020, we facilitated eight study groups with over eighty participants.

We also conduct public workshops about all our projects and program areas, as well as skills building in nonviolent communication and facilitation, speculative fiction book clubs, and more. We are especially proud that we have done numerous educational forums on understanding emerging fascism, the COVID-19 pandemic, and the George Floyd Rebellion.

Food

Access to nutritious, culturally appropriate food is a fundamental human right that should never be dependent on wealth or income. As the climate crisis worsens, connecting with and learning traditional food cultivation skills is critical—not only to our happiness and well-being—but to our very survival. Our food team's activities in 2020 focused on empowering new gardeners to grow food and strengthening neighborhood-scale sharing networks. We are intentionally, deliberately, and strategically attempting to recreate the noncommodified food forest that existed here before European settler colonists arrived.

Over the last few years, we have helped to plant more than 150 fruit trees in public places. We have also installed twenty-five Little Free Pantries in our community—where anyone can donate nonperishable foods or personal care items and anyone can take what they need—twenty-four hours a day, no questions asked.

After helping to convert about twenty front yards to organic vegetable gardens, when the pandemic hit, we shifted to get food resources to the most vulnerable people in our community. Our volunteers delivered and installed over 250 free mini gardens for our low-income neighbors. We also provide simple educational resources to empower the recipients of these gardens to make the most of their new setup, and provide ongoing support with replacement starts and/or other materials as needed.

Our food team has also agreed to take on production of an annual local food guide, a publication that is distributed all across the community. We are working with underserved and under-resourced populations to make the guide even more useful, engaging, and accessible. We are explicitly focusing on taking a food sovereignty/food justice lens to this publication.

Housing

Access to safe, secure, and affordable housing is a human right. No one should ever be without a home, and yet there are approximately twenty-nine empty properties per homeless person across the US. This is a direct function of the dictates of capitalism and what happens when housing is a commodity.

To make our vision of housing as a human right a reality, we are exploring several cooperative housing projects.

We are providing staff support to a group of local folks who are interested in developing and living in a multigenerational eco-village of ten to twenty-five people. The current founders group envisions tiny homes and shared common facilities, a makers' space, gardens, and an arts and media production center. Over time, we hope to nurture a network of eco-villages across our region, each with its own unique design and culture created by those who live there.

We are also exploring the development of housing cooperatives, in which property is collectively owned and/or managed by residents. It might be a large house with multiple rooms or an entire apartment building.

We are also on the verge of creating a community land trust with the Wiyot Tribe, under their direct control. This has been the result of an intentional, collaborative process of reimagining what regenerative development means. We have committed to a transformational process, guided by Indigenous wisdom, that will culminate in community control of the wealth and resources of this place. We intend to attract capital from "impact investors" and solicit money for the Gouts Lakawoulh Hiwechk Fund (meaning "money that makes us well" in the Wiyot language). This will be the entity through which investments flow. The

Wiyot Tribe will have the ability to approve or reject any of the projects in which the fund invests.

Electoral Politics

Although "electoral politics" is not a program area, how we engage electorally deserves a mention. As a 501(c)(3) organization, Cooperation Humboldt cannot legally use staff time or resources to support or oppose any candidate running for public office. However, we are allowed to engage in nonpartisan advocacy and election related activity. This includes lobbying, working on ballot measures, educating candidates on public interest issues, criticizing elected officials, conducting nonpartisan public education and training sessions about participation in the political process, and preparing candidate questionnaires and voter guides.

More importantly, we know that the kind of systemic change we advocate for will never be led by politicians. Only a broad, deep, and politically educated mass movement can do that. In that spirit, we insist that the movement drives the process. So even though we do engage in electoral politics, we are not electoral fetishists.

We are proud that we have organized multiple candidate forums (at both the municipal and county level), bringing together fifteen local groups to help develop a "movement of movements" community voice. Those events included organized labor, racial justice groups, immigrant rights organizations, and advocates for health care, youth, and houseless persons.

We were instrumental in getting ranked choice voting adopted for Eureka city elections.[9] We educated and lobbied the Eureka City Council, staff, and Humboldt County Elections Office, and helped to run a campaign that resulted in a win with over 60 percent of the vote.

We supported a countywide ballot initiative to make Humboldt a sanctuary county, which was the first time this was done by a popular vote anywhere in the country. We want to be crystal clear that this effort was conceived, organized, and led by Centro del Pueblo, an amazing immigrant rights organization.[10] We worked hard to ensure that we took leadership from Centro del Pueblo at every step of this process. In a county that is over 75 percent white, they won this groundbreaking initiative with over 55 percent of the vote.

We also supported the successful effort to remove the statue of President McKinley from the Arcata Plaza. This was also done by a ballot initiative process that passed with over 67 percent of the vote. No other city has removed a presidential monument for misdeeds.[11]

Core Team/Distributed Leadership Model

The forces of capitalism, white supremacy, heteropatriarchy, and colonialism are deeply ingrained in each of us, whether we are members of an elite or an oppressed class. Regardless of our good intentions, and regardless of our criticism of the problems that institutionalized oppression causes, we bring that oppression with us into our social change work. Whether it be the metrics by which we measure our "success," the means by which we achieve our "productivity," or the attitudes that we consider to be "acceptable," our structures of governance within those structures trend toward capitalist, white supremacist, patriarchal, and colonialist behaviors.

In response to that undercurrent of deep conditioning, at Cooperation Humboldt we use an iterative, deliberately developmental, distributed leadership model that includes consistent and integrated self-checks to identify and dismantle the products of our conditioning as they arise, or at least, when we recognize them. It is iterative because we make mistakes, and we learn.

It is deliberately developmental because we study what others have done and choose to build the foundation of our movement informed with the wisdom of those who have come before us. And our leadership is distributed among an ever-growing group consisting of our community participants, our core leadership group, our paid staff, and the board of directors. The model makes it possible for our community members to take active leadership roles in the programs that are deeply meaningful to them as individuals, while collectively supporting the broader mission of the organization.

To become a member of the core leadership group an individual must agree to participate in a twelve-week study group cohort in which we examine solidarity economy theory and practice, the objective reality of white supremacy, heteropatriarchy, and the local history of settler colonialism. There is no test at the end of the process, but this study group process builds social solidarity and a shared political and strategic analysis that helps to ensure a common orientation.

We commit to the organizers' adage to take people where they are. And with a hat tip to long-time racial and social justice organizer George

Friday, to get on the Cooperation Humboldt core leadership team "you must be this tall to ride that ride."

Conclusion

We are in a moment of interconnecting ecological, political, and economic crises. It is not hyperbole to say we are in global systems collapse. We know that taken alone, none of the programs, projects, or strategies described above are sufficiently revolutionary, or even commensurate with the magnitude of the crisis we face or the task before us. But taken as a whole, each project is designed to "live into" a new world.

We are attempting to create a truly transformational "liberated zone" in this community and to create new social, political, and economic systems. We are doing our best, and attempting to teach as we fight and learn as we lead.

We end this essay as we began—a call to others who are doing similar place-based work. Let's connect, conspire, and confederate.

Notes

1 Gratitude to Wiyot tribal chair Ted Hernandez who taught us to say and think about it this way; see Wiyot Tribe, accessed June 1, 2022, https://www.wiyot.us.

2 The Honor Tax Project, accessed June 1, 2022, http://www.honortax.org.

3 A great place to start that exploration is Native Land Digital, accessed June 1, 2022, https://www.native-land.ca. It is not authoritative, so you will need to invest the time and energy in learning from the Indigenous people living in your community.

4 Movement Generation, "From Banks and Tanks to Cooperation and Caring: A Strategic Framework for a Just Transition," accessed June 1, 2022, https://movementgeneration.org/wp-content/uploads/2016/11/JT_booklet_Eng_printspreads.pdf.

5 Center for Popular Economics, accessed June 1, 2022, https://www.populareconomics.org.

6 Emily Kawano, "Solidarity Economy: Building an Economy for People and Planet," August 16, 2022, accessed June 1, 2022, https://cooperationhumboldt.com/wp-content/uploads/2018/02/Kawano.pdf.

7 Martin Gilens and Benjamin I. Page, "Testing Theories of American Politics: Elites, Interest Groups, and Average Citizens" *Perspectives on Politics* 12, no. 3 (September 2014): 564–81, accessed June 1, 2022, https://doi.org/10.1017/S1537592714001595.

8 "AB-857 Public banks," California Legislative Information, October 2, 2019, https://leginfo.legislature.ca.gov/faces/billNavClient.xhtml?bill_id=201920200AB857.

9 Ranked choice voting empowers voters to fully express their opinion and frees us from "lesser of two evils" choices. Instead of just choosing who you want to win, you fill out the ballot saying who is your first choice, second choice, or third choice (or more as needed) for each position. The candidate with the majority (more than 50 percent) of first-choice votes wins outright. If no candidate gets a majority of first-choice votes, then it triggers a new counting process. The candidate who did the worst is eliminated, and that candidate's voters' ballots are redistributed to their

second-choice pick. Research shows more women and people of color run and win with this reform.

10 See Centro del Pueblo, accessed June 2, 2022, https://www.measurek.org.

11 Jaweed Kaleem, "First It Was Confederate Monuments: Now Statues Offensive to Native Americans Are Poised to Topple across the US," *Los Angeles Times*, April 1, 2018, accessed July 1, 2022, https://www.latimes.com/nation/la-na-native-american-statue-removal-20180401-story.html.

The Principles and Practice of the Afrikan Cooperative Union

Adotey Bing-Pappoe

Afrikan Cooperative Union Prehistory

Stanford Dyer, the current chief executive of the Afrikan Cooperative Union (ACU), says that the idea of an initiative to help people of African descent to empower themselves arose from discussions between himself and Kyeswa Ssebweze based on observations about how ants act for the common good. As he put it, "We organised a meeting of the willing and a group of Africans held the first meeting in April 2010 to develop the story of the ants and how that applied to us. We decided then that the way forward was to become self-sufficient and create a cooperative union for Afrikans, where we would all have shares and the money collected would be invested for mutual benefit." This statement of objectives proved to be somewhat harder to achieve than appeared to be the case on first inspection.

The first meeting, in 2010, was the start of a series of meetings that culminated in the launch of the Afrikan Cooperative Union on June 22, 2013. Between these two dates a number of thorny issues had to be addressed. Among the foundational issues that had to be dealt with were three that were central to the task that the putative organisation was confronted with: Who was the organisation for, what would it do to achieve its objectives, and how would it do this?

The debate then was around what we needed to do to create a collective of soulmates that would inspire Afrikan people to build an economic giant that would uplift us all. Note that we started as "Afrika Umoja," we then changed the name to "Black International Co-operative Union," but later settled on "Afrikan Cooperative Union," the name we registered as. These name changes are a manifestation of discussions reflecting common themes that African people face across the world. The choice of "Black," "African," or "Afrikan" in the organisation's name represents a decision about whether to attract or educate the members of the community that has been identified as the target of the organisation's efforts. In the end, the name "Afrikan" was settled on as a way of recognising that the target audience are people of African descent, but also people who were "conscious," or in current parlance, perhaps "woke."

Who For?

Initially the members that began to design the organisation were adamant that it should be only for people of African descent, and no others. Among the issues discussed was whether or not the non-African spouses of members could inherit their deceased partner's membership. The view of many, if not most, members was that they should not be able to. They would be paid back the investment their deceased partners had in the collective, but they would not be able to inherit their stake in the organisation. However, the laws of the land no longer permitted such discriminatory regulations and after a number of increasingly tense exchanges with the regulator they settled for the principle that while there would not be any discrimination with respect to who could be members, there could and would be discrimination with respect to who the organisation was intended to benefit. So they decided that they would have to accept any and everybody into their organisation, even as they sought to make it an instrument to empower African people. This, no doubt, is a journey that many African organisations in the diaspora have had to travel, in their quest to achieve some rebalancing of the socioeconomic scales. Many find it bewildering and irksome to be told that overt discrimination is no longer allowed, even as they experience it almost every day of their lives still! In this instance they were even informed that only thirteen out of their fifteen-member executive committee could be of African descent, the other two had to be non-Africans.

Doing What?

The founding members of the ACU had lofty goals. In the words of the founding declaration: "In 20 years from now it should have a minimum of 10 million members with teeth and commitment to deliver to our people. That in 50 years it should have 200 million members and growing. That it will forever remain a one-man-one-vote regardless of how many shares one may have in the organisations." As Stanford Dyer often says, the idea was to create the largest business organisation the world had ever seen. There were however some differences of opinion on how this was to be achieved. Some members envisioned the ACU itself setting up its own business ventures. Others saw the initiative as one where the ACU would take the accumulated funds of its members, and invest these in profitable and ethical ventures, so that they generated income for the members. Members were initially expected to be willing to wait five years, if not more, before they could expect to receive any dividends. Yet others saw the ACU as an organisation that would assist its members to start their own businesses. None of these alternative and competing models was able to claim the support of all of the founding members, and so none was exclusively implemented for any period of time. That was partly because the ACU had not worked out a clear mechanism for accumulating the funds that were to be brought together from within the community. Only when such funds had been accumulated would the ACU be in a realistic position to discuss what to do with them. Some attempts were made for the ACU to sell goods imported from Africa by one of its members, or donated to the organisation by one of them. However, there were also instances of the ACU being in a position where it was selling goods on behalf of its members, in a manner that did not take into account the costs to the ACU of organising itself to trade in this way. This was clearly not sustainable, and the founding members soon put a stop to such practices. There is little evidence of any prolonged period of study about cooperative organisation before the ACU was created. It is possible that had there been such a prolonged period of study, some of these teething problems might not have materialised. But almost certainly there would have been different kinds of problems.

How?

The founders of the ACU wanted the organisation to be self-reliant. A reflection of the way they wanted African people to be, both in Africa and in the diaspora. To that end they wanted the ACU to operate with funds that came from the community itself. They therefore rejected the idea of borrowing the funds the ACU might need to advance, because "that would make the Union dependent on others who could decide whether or not the Union survives." The initial idea was to get members to pay £200 per share, but by the time that they were ready to launch, the cost per share had been set at a more reachable £50. This was in addition to an annual membership fee of £30. However, there was no built-in mechanism for members to regularly buy a certain number of shares, nor to reach a target number of owned shares. There was however an upper limit of four hundred shares that any one member could own. The founding members agreed to, but in the end did not manage to implement, a plan whereby each member of the executive committee would buy a number of shares each month, so as to help bolster the number of paid-up shares held by the organisation. They also did not support the idea of lending to businesses, because they saw that as the way those with funds used their power to supposedly "support" people, but in effect shift all of the risk onto the business owners. So they intended to engage in joint ventures, where there would be a sharing of the risk between the businesses the ACU supported and the ACU itself. Finally, they were determined that as many members of the community as possible would benefit from the activities of the ACU. In the words of Kyeswa Ssebweze, "We should have a vision that is inclusive of the disadvantaged and less able amongst us." The founding members were sure that they were not trying to set up an organisation that was intending to produce some wealthy individuals whose presence would distract from the poverty and lack of assets of the remaining majority.

Although the idea of a cooperative is an old one, mobilising the spirit of renewal and self-help these days is a challenging one. The Afrikan Cooperative Union was born out of the spirit of renewal of what they saw that the ancestors did best: uniting, struggling, and surviving. African people, whether inside or outside Africa, are faced with almost insurmountable odds. So what the founding members wished to build was a solid cooperative for Black people, by Black people wherever we live. A cooperative that will engender enterprise, hard work, self-reliance, and success, and leave behind a legacy and example for coming generations. As they stated: "We will undertake all avenues of enterprise, especially those that serve our own needs." In addition, they wanted to stop the exploitation of African people and their resources. To stop buying their food, clothing, children's toys, and household goods from others, thereby enriching them and consolidating their own poverty and lack of ownership. "An earning must be turned around in our community at least 5 times before we spend outside our community," they wrote.

The Launch and Programming

By 2013 the talking had been done and it was time to launch the organisation. In the afternoon of June 22, under the theme "Investing in Our People—An Investment for Posterity and Prosperity" the ACU was launched. Among the speakers and their presentations were the following:

- Kyeswa Ssebweze, the interim chair, spoke about the ACU's vision, background, administration, and membership.
- Stanford Dyer (Akram), talked about why he had originally proposed the idea of forming such a body.
- Lorna Campbell, a local government councillor, who has championed the idea of credit banking, gave a motivating talk titled "In Numbers We Can Make a Significant Difference."
- Khalid Rashard gave a paper titled "In Unity the Afrikan Must Find His Feet."
- Mandingo's paper touched on the history of Afrikan pride and philosophy.
- Alex Paulini's paper was titled "The Potential against Lack of Funding."
- Petronilla Mwakatuma led a discussion on investing in rural women.
- Greg Morris from the Black Fathers gave a paper that proposed that we should create discussion groups that nurture unity.
- Herukuti from Galaxy Radio spoke on the spirit of the Afrikan and self-help.
- Leader Bandaka of Alkebulan gave the rallying call on the Pan-Afrikan umbrella.

The organisation began by holding a series of regular meetings, presentations, and discussions on Galaxy Radio, one of the significant voices in the community. The membership grew, but not as fast as the founding members had envisaged. But what societal issues led the founding members to set up the ACU?

Justifications and Precedents

In the UK it has long been known that African people suffer from the criminal justice system. They are more likely to be stopped, arrested, and charged by the police than other groups. They are also more likely to suffer from police brutality. When they appear in court, they are more likely to be found guilty. When found guilty, they are more likely to be sentenced to a period of imprisonment, and their periods of imprisonment are likely to be on average longer than those to which other groups are sentenced. Studies that have been done on employment practices have showed that certain kinds of names (African and Muslim for example) reduce the likelihood of the applicant securing an interview, and when interviewed, to be employed. All these were injustices that the founding members would have experienced in some shape or form, but they were concerned to address the issues at a deeper level, the level of the economy. In 2008, the Runnymede Trust published a report titled "Financial Inclusion and Ethnicity," and in so doing exposed the anatomy of the economic disempowerment of African people in the UK.

Race and Class

Beginning with education, the report tells us that in the UK around 44 percent of school leavers achieved five or more A* to C.[1] However, for Africans directly from the continent, only 38 percent reached this critical level of achievement, and for Africans from the Caribbean, it was 30 percent who achieved this benchmark. This relatively poor performance with respect to education impacted on employment possibilities. As a result of this, African people displayed high levels of economic inactivity, as well as unemployment. They were more likely to be employed in low-paying jobs, such as in the public sector, and the restaurant, catering, and transport sectors, as well as being in relatively low-paying self-employment such as painters and decorators, electricians, plumbers, and carpenters. Africans were also more likely to be living in social housing. With low incomes people are only able to afford low quality housing. So we find that 47 percent of Black Africans lived in social housing, slightly more than the 42 percent of those from the Caribbean that did so. At the start of the 1980s, Margaret Thatcher initiated what was termed a "property owning democracy," which encouraged people to buy their own houses, but also stopped local authorities from being able to use the proceeds from the sale to build any more houses. The result was a steady and steep rise in house prices. This was initially experienced as a bonanza, as those who had houses found themselves owning properties whose values continued to rise and rise. But the many Africans who did not own their own houses were excluded from the wave of capital gains, which significant sections of white society were enjoying. Some people realised that merely by possessing and holding capital people could become quite rich for doing almost nothing. Those that were able to borrow to buy houses did whatever they could to get "on the housing ladder." But they often found that their mortgages were more expensive than the average, and that what they were expected to pay each month could fluctuate by quite a large amount. In truth, given people's financial positions it would have been better for the poorest among them not to have taken out these mortgages. Such mortgages came to be known as subprime mortgages. The effect of having these mortgages meant that the owners' hold on their houses was weak and uncertain. The study also found that 8 percent of all mortgages were in the subprime category, where a majority of low-income people could be found. Overly represented in this group are people of African descent. It is here that we find the highest interest rates in the mortgage market, and where 70 percent of all foreclosures take place. The Runneymede study quoted a study done by Her Majesty's Treasury in 2004, which found that 68 percent of those financially excluded lived in the 10 percent most deprived areas of the country. These figures showed that people of African descent were disproportionately represented in social housing and also in the subprime mortgage market. As a result, they were likely to experience a high level of financial exclusion, and greater costs of exclusion. That is, not only were they living in the most deprived areas of the country because they were financially excluded, but were also paying the highest prices, for being financial excluded.

When the Runnymede study turned its attention to the savings that people had, it found that while only 3 percent of UK households do not have a bank account of any kind, 10 percent did not have a current account. Of the white-headed households, some 12 percent did not have a current account, while among Black-headed households, some 23 percent did not have a current account. Of those in the bottom 20 percent of income earners, this number rose to 25 percent. That is, one-quarter of the poorest people in the UK did not have a current account. This fed into another financial exclusion figure, which is that 7.8 million people (approximately 16 percent of the population) in the UK could not access mainstream credit. Those in this position were found to be paying £129 a month—or 11 percent of their income—on servicing high-cost borrowing. People who were receiving some kind of social benefit were found to have borrowed some £330 million and to be paying £140 million interest, or a rate of 42 percent. These are normal statistics in very unequal societies. The poor are locked out of the mainstream financial system, and then are made to pay above the odds to access substandard financial services. The UK has a system of individual savings accounts (ISAs) which allow people who hold them not to pay income tax or capital gains tax on what they own or gain from them. Among the white population some 34 percent were found to have ISAs, but among the Black only 14 percent had them. A number of people in the UK do not hold their money in banks but instead had accounts with building societies—organisations that made it their business to provide relatively safe and secure funds to allow people to purchase houses. It was found that 55 percent of white households had either bank or building society savings but that only 36 percent of Black households did.

When attention was turned to the ownership of businesses, it was found that 23 percent of white households owned stocks or shares, but that only 8 percent of Black households did. It is perhaps important to note that owning stocks and shares is a way for their owners to reap some of the wealth that those who worked in these businesses had produced. This wealth manifests itself as profits, a portion of which were then paid out in the form of dividends to the shareholders—just for owning the shares. The businesses of the self-employed in low-paid occupations more often than not do not have any shares to issue, and their owner/workers certainly are very unlikely to own shares in anybody else's businesses. Finally, we find that when it came to protecting their property, only half of the poorest fifth of society were insured or had protected their property. And people of African descent were disproportionately represented in this poorest 20 percent of the population.

A follow-up study also published by the Runnymede Trust in 2017 as "Race and Class in post-Brexit Britain" found that so far as people of African descent were concerned, Britain had not changed a great deal in the intervening decade.

The authors of the first report in making their recommendations spoke to policy makers and the establishment. The founding members of the ACU, who were almost certainly not aware of the minutiae of the findings of the Runnymede study, nevertheless would have experienced it at the micro level in their day-to-day lives. Their response as we have seen was not to address the establishment but to seek to mobilise the community, of which they were a part, to overcome their situation.

This approach was not all that novel, for less than fifty years before, a generation of Africans arriving in the UK from the Caribbean had been instrumental in bringing about a major transformation in financial services in England.

African Origins of Credit Unions in the UK

Credit unions are traditionally instruments for the less wealthy members of society so that they could provide themselves with a financial foothold. The commonest form of credit union originated in Germany and spread to the rest of Europe. But the concept of reciprocal support in production, trade, and finance is something that Africa along with people from all cultures had independently practiced.

The first credit union in the UK or Ireland was set up in Donore by Irish people in 1958. This was followed by one in Derry, Northern Ireland, in 1960, then in England in 1964, followed by Scotland in 1970, and finally in Wales in 1980 in the form of the St Theresa's credit union. What was distinctive about the credit union set up in England, however, was that it was set up by African people who had arrived in England from the Caribbean. Two were set up in London, one in Wimbledon, and the other in Hornsey in 1964. The latter was registered on April 7 as the Hornsey Cooperative Credit Union by ten members of the Ferme Park Baptist Church led by an African from the Caribbean called Blair Greaves and another called Bentley Hines. It had started out in 1964 as an informal savings club and was registered under the provisions of the Industrial and Provident Society Act with the common bond being that its members were all residents of Haringey. According to Bentley Hines, the registrar when informed that they wished to set up a credit union had asked, "What is a credit union?" This was fifteen years before credit unions gained legal status in the UK, which happened as a result of the Credit Union Act of 1979. Bentley Hines played a leading role in running the Hornsey credit union. He had worked in the engineering sector in the Caribbean before arriving in England in 1961, but he had failed to get the kind of job he thought he would find in the UK and had settled as an assembler of televisions. Somewhat less is known about the credit union, which had been set up in Wimbledon involving among others Ted Sammons, except that it closed around 2005.

Around this same time the National Federation of Savings and Credit Unions was set up by the Wimbledon credit union in collaboration with two other credit unions in Highgate (London) and Hove (Sussex) as a support organisation for credit unions. This suggests that there were a number of credit unions set up around this time by people of African descent. According to Blair Greaves, the reasons for setting up these organisations was because "racial discrimination was open and widespread, and there was a real need for a credit union to serve the needs of the many people the banks refused to help." Blair Greaves himself used the funds borrowed from the credit union to put down a deposit on a house and also to furnish it. Without it he maintained he and others would have been forced to use loan sharks. Some used the funds to pay for trips back to the Caribbean. The Hornsey credit union was so successful that by the time of its first annual general meeting it reportedly had over one hundred members. Over time many other members used their credit union membership to secure the loans to become homeowners. What unfortunately did not happen, because until 2012 it was forbidden by UK credit union law, was the use of credit union funds to establish or grow businesses. The African origins of English credit union formation may be glimpsed by the fact that according to information provided by the Association of British Credit Unions—the umbrella body of credit unions in the UK—by 1998, 38 percent of Caribbean British adults were members of credit unions. Today the overall level of penetration of credit unions in the UK is around 5 percent. Unfortunately, these and other credit unions in England did not flourish as they might, and by 2012, Hornsey Co-operative Credit Union had one active loan and an aging board. In that year the remaining 250 members voted to join a more active and thriving credit union nearby, the London Capital Credit Union, and in 2013 a merger was effected between the two credit unions. In 2014, Elaine Greaves, daughter of Mr and Mrs Blair Greaves, founders of Hornsey Credit Union, was co-opted onto the board of London Capital Credit Union.

The Restructuring

In recent years the ACU has been conducting a revaluation to see how best if can move forward. It asked it members to help to identify some key projects that it should engage in. The results identified four key projects: a bank, a shop, a school, and a community centre. However, the

ACU was lacking one or other of the crucial resources necessary to fulfil these requirements. Over time it became clearer that its best bet was to try to mobilise the financial resources from the community for clearly stated purposes. However, it was also clear that successfully mobilising these funds would only be possible if members felt that the challenge was achievable and if along the way they could expect to experience some benefits. Further thinking led to the current four-part programme that the ACU has adopted.

The ACU now sees itself as an organisation that exists not to itself directly engage in business, but an organisation that exists to support its members to engage in various forms of cooperative business, including procurement, marketing, supplier, consumer, and producer cooperatives. To this end it will act as a financial and knowledge cooperative pooling together the finances and knowledge from within the community to harness and channel these into projects that will enable members of the community to themselves manage them. By joining the ACU they will be able to establish collaborations with like-minded members of the community. The ACU therefore seeks to provide a framework that will enable the creation of an eco-system of mutually supporting cooperative enterprises in the UK owned and democratically managed by people of African descent. In so doing the ACU will act as a big tent within which businesses led by people of African descent will be able to form their own cooperative structures such as procurement, marketing, supplier, consumer, or producer cooperatives.

The Community Investment Fund

The first pillar in the programme is for its members to agree to pool resources to create an independent fund. They should then alongside this fund establish a well-managed system for assisting members who need to access finance to start or grow their own businesses. The process of financial support should go hand in hand with knowledge sharing. The independent source of financing is being called the Community Investment Fund. It is created from the revenue generated when members purchase shares, each of which costs £50. These are different from the annual membership fee. The funds generated from the sale of shares cannot be used to run the organisation, they have to be used to pursue the ACU's business objectives. The ACU is now requiring that each member buys at least two shares every year. Together with the membership fee, that means that each member is expected to contribute £135 per year. To simplify matters further, members are being asked to agree to a monthly payment of £11.25. This way going forward the ACU will be able to continuously accumulate funds and so stand a better chance of reaching the target it needs to commence the next phase of operations, which is to make business loans to members.

Business Loans

Once the community investment fund has reached a critical level, the accumulated funds will be available to be lent to members. The loans made are intended to help ACU members start or develop their own businesses. Because business finance is one of the things that people of African descent in the UK find the hardest to get access to, this initiative should make an important contribution to the well-being of members. There will be various criteria that members will be expected to fulfill including length of membership, the amount of the loan, and the viability of the proposed project. It is the intention that the application will be assessed by an assessor appointed by the ACU. The assessor will be expected to act impartially and independently, not just to provide a reject or accept recommendation. For a successful application will be expected to provide information that will assist the ACU to take measures to help the applicant do better next time, in the event of a rejection. They will then be expected to suggest what needs to be done to improve the application. Such information may form the basis of business training that will be made available to the applicant. In the event that the community investment fund is not fully utilised, then the intention will be that these funds are used to purchase African or Caribbean government bonds so that ACU members can help support these governments to meet their social and economic development objectives, while generating a return from these resources.

Business Training

Since July 2020 the ACU has instituted regular business training sessions which are currently for members as well as the general public. They have been designed to cover the main business functions such as financing, human resources, operations, marketing, and business law. In addition, each session has included a short exposition on various aspects of cooperative economics as well the ACU's four-part programme. As the ACU hopefully, grows, it will be able to run increasingly specialised sessions to cater for the needs of a particular section of the community.

Credit Union

The idea of a credit union was something that was discussed by the founding members of the ACU, but it did not get acted upon in the heady early days of the organisation. That idea has now been resurrected and forms the fourth pillar of the ACU's four programme areas. However, the proposed ACU credit union is intended to be a development of the early credit unions. First of all, the intention is that it should be a nationwide credit union. Credit unions in the UK have conventionally been defined by place of work, occupation, domicile, or worship. This has tended to make them small and local. The idea is that having the ACU as the common bond will allow people anywhere in the UK to become part of the proposed credit union. Second, it is the intention that it should make as part of its core remit, the making of loans for business development. This was not possible until 2012 when the law was amended so that loans from credit unions could be legitimately used for business purposes. Even so, many credit unions have shied away from taking the steps necessary to make this possible. Finally, the proposed credit union will be used to promote cooperative formation. Since its members will be part of the ACU, they will be able to tap into the ACU's expertise in cooperative development and gain support not just for their businesses, but for cooperative business development.

Multi-Stakeholder Cooperative

The final element of the ACU's restructuring is that it has recently gained permission from the regulator to become a multi-stakeholder cooperative. This means that it will be able to have different categories of members, so that individuals, business, nonbusinesses, organisations, employees, and users can all now become members. It is the ability to have many different kinds of members that will allow the ACU to provide the big tent within which African organisations will be able to make their own cooperative connections and formations.

There is a lot that the ACU will have to contend with as it seeks to realise the potential that it sees in cooperative organisation within the community. There are many forces that encourage people to try to build wealth as individuals, but inevitably by employing others, so that they can become masters of their own business empire. But there are also many within the community who feel drawn to the idea of collective upward movement, without leaving people behind. In these times when people of African descent are telling the world that Black lives matter, it is important that there are organisations like the ACU that are acting to mobilise Afrikan people to mobilise at the level of the economy and build their own economic foundations by building Black livelihoods that matter.

Note

1 Students are graded on an A through E, O, and Fail spread, with A* indicating that a student scored an A in all courses.

VI

RADICAL MUNICIPALISM

Cooperation and Self-Determination—Not Middle Management

Kana Azhari and Asere Bello

We are presently living within the context of the war on "poverty," the war *with* drugs, and the ever-expanding nonprofit industrial complex. Collectively, they represent the counterinsurgency. Our revolutionary forces are trying to stay alive and not to get incorporated into the system as another number/body. The pandemic is forcing the white world to contend with 2.5 million deaths as *our* communities continue to face the genocidal realities that capitalism/colonialism has reproduced daily, hourly, and by the minute over the last five hundred years *and* the pandemic.

Our protracted struggles are revisiting radical solutions and formations and are also experiencing an influx of newly politicized radical thinkers and organizers. This essay is dedicated to you. It's critical that we be grounded in the study of land-based self-determination movements, revolutionary New Afrikan nationalism (New Afrika), queer Black feminism, Pan-Afrikanism, Black cooperative economics and economic solidarity, Afro-ecology, self-defense, and the culture of healthy, sustainable, and equitable relationships. The neoliberals and nonprofit industrial complex have many would-be revolutionary organizers trained to manage and design more humane systems for extracting and exploiting land and labor from the melanated masses. This is considered progress or victory to many of this managerial class and yet the working poor see little to no material gains. This consciousness is violent and replicates structural oppression. It must be resisted.

We are not here to manage the contradictions of capitalism. As revolutionary formations, we are here to highlight the contradictions of capitalism and colonialism to our people. We are here to organize ourselves in ways that disrupt and ultimately dismantle the extractive and predatory systems that oppress us; all the while creating and sustaining our own (more advanced and equitable) institutions, relationships, and land-based self-determined movements.

> "We are clear that self-determination expressed as national sovereignty is a trap if the nation-state does not dislodge itself from the dictates of the capitalist system."
> —Kali Akuno, "Build and Fight: The Program and Strategy of Cooperation Jackson" (2017)

The Nature of Capitalism, Colonialism, and Neocolonialism

Colonialism is a system of oppression involving foreign regime(s) violently seizing occupied lands, committing genocide on the human and nonhuman living beings of that land, and extracting labor and natural resources from that land to the sole benefit (wealth and power accumulation) of the foreign regime. Settler colonialism is when a foreign regime physically settles themselves (people and culture) on currently occupied land through violence, renames it, and simultaneously operates its extractive and genocidal projects (without end or until nothing is left). The "United States of America" is the most successful and violent settler colony. "South Africa" and "Israel" are a couple of others. Its offspring, neocolonialism hires new and/or diverse management teams and trains them to administer, defend, and propagate colonial systems and institutions. Capitalism is the socio-political-economic operating system used to militarily grow and sustain global genocide, i.e., the exploitation of Black/Indigenous bodies, labor, and lands for the benefit of the few at the expense of the eventual all (ecological collapse).

What Does It Mean to Manage the Contradictions of Capitalism and Why Is It Dangerous and Ineffective to *Attempt* to Do So?

Managers of capitalism engage in social and political activities that legitimize the state apparatus such as gatekeeping, overseeing, reformism, and the professionalization (leading to the co-optation, dilution, and absorption) of revolutionary political power by nonprofits, the bourgeoisie, and the electorate.

It's foolish and misguided (at best) for Black/Indigenous peoples to attempt to manage the contradictions of capitalism. Yet worse is the mindset that it's our responsibility and honor to do so. You know, "make America great again," "not in *my* America" and so on. These mentalities and practices are far too common among the masses of our people and hold within them the seeds of internalized oppression, trauma, misdirection, respectability politics (tokenism), and unsustainability. False and distractive dichotomies like: good protesters versus bad protesters, slavery versus mass incarceration, colonialism versus gentrification are allowed to live unchecked in the open by "progressive" policy makers, nonprofits, and "politicized" celebrities. Instead of crying "Free 'em All" and "Free the Land" with the masses, they are busy filing the proper documents or waiting for the *right* platform for which they can perform revolution. These polarities isolate and target people in our communities that are most vulnerable and in the greatest need of support. Black capital driven managers and opportunists require the same extractive labor and natural resources as traditional capitalism. Historically poor Black/Indigenous bodies and lands are slated for labor and held in trust intergenerationally through military occupation (policing) and enslavement (mass incarceration). Thus, that slice of the devil's pie (the Black middle-class dream) can never truly be secured (defended) under capitalism when Black bodies and lands represent capital itself. Think Tulsa, Harlem, West Oakland, Durham.

We Must Focus on Building Sustainable Self-Determined Institutions, Spaces, Groups, Formations, Organizations, Campaigns, and Movements

History has proven that Black self-determination is *not* in the best interest of the US empire and its subsidiaries. According to international law and the UN Charter, self-determination is the right of autonomous peoples (or formerly colonized people) to separate from their colonizers and to control their own political and economic destiny. Yet, all efforts to liberate ourselves are criminalized, punished, and thwarted. Our political prisons and prisoners of war demonstrate this reality. Nonetheless, we must be clear that any destiny tied to the US empire and its multifaceted power structures will inevitably result in our physical and cultural genocide, enslavement (mass incarceration), rape, and new bigger, better laws designed to control our very existence. Focusing on our self-determination and locally controlled land-based movements is the only way for New Afrikan people (Afrikan-Indigenous) to center our long-term transformation and end our codependency on the very systems that kill, weaken, and oppress us.

Cooperative Institutions and Economic Solidarity Are Useful Tools in Supporting Our Recovery/Healing from the Internalized Impacts of Capitalism/Colonialism/Neocolonial Programming

The principles and practices of *ujima* (collective work and responsibility) and *ujaama* (cooperative economics) are at the core of Black/New Afrikan culture. Our collective survival has always depended on our ability to cocreate sustainable relationships and cofacilitate our own healing. American adventurism and rugged individualism have historically been out of reach for everyday working people, much less the masses of the Black working poor. Over the last few decades through limited access to media and technology, Black millennials and tech babies have gained a curated version of power and wealth based not in land or access to the means of production, but in online influence (Black Twitter), tech jobs, and purchasing "power" (consumerism). We are in a moment, however, where the contractions of capitalism have temporarily interrupted the regularly scheduled programming of this African American dream world and its sleeping followers.

Capitalism seems momentarily unable to reconfigure itself *and* effectively and efficiently window dress the deplorable conditions highlighted by the global health crisis, mass uprisings, genocidal prison conditions, violent transphobia, and economic collapse (the American nightmare). Now is the time to reclaim ground and reground ourselves in our culture and histories of collectivity and family-community living and advance our relationship to mutually beneficial economics.

Our personal and intimate relationships are where we play out our traumas, conditioning, and values. Here is where we need to draw on the principles of solidarity and healing the most. Solidarity places importance on interdependence, shared struggle, and collaboration. From school age we are trained to compete, stand out while blending in, rise above and receive rewards or consequences as individuals: perpetually training self-minded adults and societies to still seek after that golden star. Again, the culture of capitalism is ever present, permeating and infiltrating our relationships and values. The spirit of working toward the collective good (cooperation) opens space for self-reflection and intentional efforts to dislodge ourselves from our toxic relationships with multilayered systems of oppression, i.e., patriarchy, misogynoir, sexism, heterosexism, homophobia, transphobia, colorism, classism, ablism, and agism. Without working to eradicate all forms of oppression within us (our colonial and precolonial programming), we will continue infighting and aid in our own oppression, all the while suffering from all external forms. Housing, childcare, and health/healing collectives, youth, nonbinary and women's groups, and food growing and land cooperatives are ideal spaces to focus on engaging these dynamics and building more equitable practices. By prioritizing the basic needs of our most marginalized, we will continue to shift stale power relationships at the center of daily family and community life. As queer Black feminists, we refuse to take up the unprincipled role of patient peacekeepers, sacrificed on the altar of so-called Black unity, while facing violence, repression, and genocide within our own communities and outside of them. We charge genocide. And we demand power, land, and equity!

Cooperative businesses and institutions offer consistent accessible spaces to heal from our collective trauma with extractive economic institutions, systems, and culture while striving to cocreate more equitable relationship dynamics via revolutionary cooperative culture.

Revolutionary cooperative culture is the distillation and consolidation of a collective's most radical and sustainable relationship dynamics cocreated by its members. Worker-owned cooperatives and self-determination movements from below are of particular interest as they explicitly embody sharing and balancing power relationships. Sharing and shifting power is critical to ensure that the principles and collective good of the people are prioritized over personalities. Additional values and best practices of revolutionary cooperative culture should include: transparent accountability processes and shared governance structures, independent community funding, consensus building processes, skills sharing, radical self-care, body positivity, political education, self-defense, and a sustainability model. The equitable participation, collaboration, leadership, and lived experiences of youth, women, queer and trans, disabled, formerly incarcerated, and worker-led organizing must be prioritized.

As workers, we spend most of our productive hours at work. Within a cooperative business model, we have many great opportunities to develop healthier and more equitable dynamics with others and enhance our relating practices through participating in the development of self-governance and autonomy. Self-governance and autonomy move our people closer to the tangible aspects of self-determination and fulfilling their intrinsic need for power/control over their own destiny. The more our self-determination muscles grow the more we are able to trust in ourselves to fulfill our own needs. The more these muscles remain in a state of stagnation or atrophy the further we are subjected to the trauma of dependency on a society that has proven to be violent and abusive to us. In order to raise the capacity of our liberation movements we must heal ourselves by reclaiming our minds, bodies, energy, time, and labor... while freeing the land! Rest, recovery, pleasure, love, nourishing ourselves, and having more equitable working lives must also show up in our practices.

We Strive to Disrupt and Abolish Capitalism through Organizing and Sustaining Our Own (Self-Determined) Institutions, Organizations, Campaigns, and Movements

> "Every practice produces a theory, and that if it is true that a revolution can fail even though it be based on perfectly conceived theories, nobody has yet made a successful revolution without a revolutionary theory."
>
> —Amílcar Cabral, "The Weapon of Theory" (1966)

The New Afrikan Independence Movement teaches us that land is the basis for self-determination and independence. Revolutionary New Afrikan Nationalism and Afro-communalism are the most accessible political legacies that center Black liberation and land-based self-determination as well as revolutionary cooperative culture.

If it was not for our legacy of Afro-communalism, revolutionary nationalism, and radical organizing around mutual aid, cooperative education, and resilience, the conditions we find ourselves in during the COVID-19 crisis would be even worse. While state/capital-led education, food, housing, and other systems failed, community members and families stepped in and held down alternative forms of being that supported people before profits, like folks on the ground always do during a "crisis." We have always been our own "saviors" and liberators. Through sustaining our own autonomy, we lessen our dependence on oppressive systems/institutions, reclaim control over our lives, and design the tools for effectively and efficiently dismantling the matrix of extractive and oppressive systems. Maintaining our own institutions also prepares us to confront the unavoidable violent repression and backlash from our oppressors, right now and right around the corner.

The Jackson-Kush Plan was developed by the Malcolm X Grassroots Movement and the New Afrikan People's Organization in 2008. It *still* remains one of the most comprehensive visions for Black liberation and self-determination of this era. While there have been many hard lessons and departures from the original plan in practice, it is still ideologically relevant and valuable (particularly in the South, but also as a model elsewhere). The Jackson-Kush Plan consists of four key components that require significant work, coordination, and accountability structures and processes. These components are people's assemblies, community organizing institutions, building a solidarity economy, and taking over *strategic* seats within the local government. For the past decade of its existence *too many forces have attempted to dilute, isolate, and dissect components from the* Jackson-Kush Plan. The most notable is the seduction of engagement in electoral politics, without deeply examining the inherent contradictions and limitations of doing such, while underemphasizing or disappearing the other three components of the plan that are absolutely necessary to offset and push back on these contradictions. The continued emergence of ecosocialism, Afro-ecology and Afro-veganism as practiced through community gardening/growing, land-based cooperative development, and zero-waste practices must find its way back into the limelight among students, organizers, and cocreators of the Jackson-Kush Plan and vision.

Because of the context of the larger project in which this paper is housed, we shall focus on solidarity economies, however, it's our position that a complete analysis and coordination of all components of the Jackson-Kush Plan are critical whether they coalesce or remain independent.

On Building a Solidarity Economy

> "Solidarity Economy when pushed to its limits as a means of heightening contradictions within the capitalist system we believe is a transitional strategy and praxis to build 21st century socialism and advance the abolition of capitalism and the poverty and oppressive social relations that it fosters."
>
> —Kali Akuno, *The Jackson-Kush Plan* (2017)

> "Solidarity Economy as a concept describe a process of promoting cooperative economics that promote social solidarity, mutual aid, reciprocity and generosity."
> —Kali Akuno, *The Jackson-Kush Plan* (2017)

Our historical political and economic relationship with the US colonial project has always been one of extraction, torture, and genocide. Unfortunately (and at times unknowingly), we replicate these traumatic dynamics within traditional Black-owned businesses and institutions through the exploitation of bodies and natural resources via low-wage labor and other profit- over life-driven practices. Solidarity and cooperative economics are steps toward centering the transformation of these dynamics (private property ownership versus collective land use) and investing in sustainable relationships throughout the production process. This requires dedicated time, research, institution building (co-ops), physical engagement, political education, creative funding practices, and resources. Cooperatives often dedicate a percentage of the surplus (profits) to engaging in these activities in order to actively participate in expanding the struggle for cooperative economics (not simply to benefit from it). Other cooperatives are heavily dependent on grants and foundation funding making them less sustainable and potentially limited in their ability to fully align with radical organizing efforts. Turning toward microlending and independent community-based funding should be the aim.

Cooperatives are charged with scaling sustainably to protect the needs of workers and propagate revolutionary cooperative culture in order to grow and defend our land-based self-determination movements. To raise Black worker-owners' collective capacities to sustain themselves and eliminate the negative consequences of participation in broader strategic activity beyond those directly impacting their livelihoods (i.e., life beyond labor unions) cooperative businesses must scale sustainably. This would also involve more accessible cooperative education and recruitment of youth, the disabled, the formerly incarcerated, and other historically segregated workers. Focusing on these workers offers the greatest potential to transform and organize with the elements in our community most impacted by lifestyles and livelihoods that are criminalized, marginalized, and militarized. Offering meaningful and dignified work and the practice of autonomy have a great impact on improving Black workers' material needs (quality of life) as well as their intrinsic need for collective power and self-determination.

Cooperative culture is formed through cooperative education, training, and daily work life. Radicalizing that culture requires the incorporation of radical political analysis and commitment to self-determination. We can observe the expression of revolutionary cooperative culture throughout governance structures, operation procedures, labor conditions, buying practices, power dynamics/relationships, community support and alignment, and distribution of the businesses' surplus. Scaling while proliferating this culture means Black people will have more opportunities to be exposed to and engage with equity. Mass education and increased exposure to revolutionary cooperative culture leads to transforming, healing, and revolutionizing relationships within our community and throughout our institutions.

Cooperation Jackson is currently spearheading solidarity economic projects with a focus on scale in Jackson, Mississippi. Inspired by the Jackson-Kush Plan and rooted in revolutionary New Afrikan nationalism, their land projects, cooperative institute, coalition work, and cooperative business incubator are bringing forward the legacy of southern land-based cooperatives and our relationship to mutual aid. They are influencing the work of emerging organizations like Cooperation Richmond, Repaired Nations (Oakland, California), and others. In Brooklyn, Crystal House has been cooperativizing Black and brown housing/land liberation work for the last twenty years and offers one of the best living practices of revolutionary cooperative culture. Mandela Grocery Cooperative is a beacon for Black culture, radical self-care, food justice, and Black-led institution building. Their model is currently being used to cocreate a grocery cooperative in East Oakland with support and inspiration from organizations like Acta Non Verba Youth Urban Farm Project and Repaired Nations. *Beyond groups, land-based economics has long been a part of the Black/Afrikan/New Afrikan cultural repertoire. From mutual aid and community gardening to rideshares and the Susus, working in collaboration is our history, reality, and our future.*

The dominant economic system remains segregated and exclusionary. Unemployment, underemployment, low-wage work, and underground economies are the baseline for the masses of Black people. Our aim must be to permeate, disrupt, and transform these spaces by advancing a culture of revolutionary cooperation and equity. By propagating our culture everywhere Black workers exist, we strengthen our relationships with each other, shift and take power, and grow our faith in our ability to live and subsist independent of the system. Self-determination will always guide us toward what we can control and collectivize everywhere we exist and everywhere we plant our seeds in soil. Free the Land!

First, We Take Jackson: The New American Municipalism

Kate Shea Baird

As the US hurtles toward the November midterms, there's much excitement about the victory of insurgent candidates in the Democratic primaries, and the rise of democratic socialists in particular. These results may signal a realization that building genuine political alternatives requires, not just beating the Republicans, but also taking on and kicking out establishment Democrats.

Yet, in the midst of all the commotion, some are asking: What comes next? Is it enough to just replace corporate Democrats with candidates with a better policy platform? It's in this context that a powerful, bottom-up movement—*municipalism*—is taking hold among activists, organizers, and local electeds.

More practice than ideology, municipalism sees the local sphere as having unique transformative potential, thanks to its more human scale. Municipalists believe that the local level is the ideal site to carry out direct democracy through popular assemblies and to dismantle all forms of social hierarchy, particularly those based on race, ethnicity, or nationality.

While socialism and municipalism are by no means irreconcilable, municipalism offers distinct advantages compared to the traditional socialist quest for state or federal power. *Municipalism recognizes the limits of electoral politics and representative democracy.* It understands that power doesn't solely reside in elected institutions; it's also wielded in the economic, social, and cultural spheres. For municipalists, then, transformative politics can't just be about getting more radical candidates elected, it must also involve building an ecosystem of social movements, economic initiatives, and community institutions that can support these candidates' agendas from outside city hall and hold them to account when necessary. This inside-outside strategy, which implies blurring the border between electoral and movement politics, can be done most effectively at the local level, where institutions are closest to the people and grassroots organizing is most effective.

Right now, municipalism is gaining momentum in the US, with trailblazing examples in Jackson, Seattle, Chicago, and Richmond, and new initiatives emerging across the country. This July, I had the chance to attend the Local Progress annual convening in Minneapolis and the Fearless Cities North American summit in New York City, where I got an insight into the challenges and debates being grappled with by folks at the forefront of the movement.

This Can Work Here: Digging Up a Lost History

As is the case in many countries, doubts remain in some quarters about whether municipalist ideas will work in practice in the US. But this country actually has a rich tradition of assembly-based, direct democracy on which to draw. It's vital to demonstrate that municipalism isn't a utopian theory or a foreign import; it can work, and has worked, in American towns and cities. Restoring this history in the popular imagination was one of the concerns of municipalism's preeminent philosopher, Murray Bookchin, back in the 1980s. Though Bookchin was an avid student of international examples, including the Paris Commune and Spanish anarcho-syndicalism, he was aware that creating a mass municipalist movement in the US meant "speaking in English." By this he referred not to linguistic translations but to the need to use culturally familiar examples with which Americans would be able to easily identify.

Bookchin pointed to the example of New England town meetings, a form of direct democracy stretching back to the 1600s, but these traditions are in no way exclusive to white colonialists. The contemporary movement can also draw on the stories of the "sewer socialists" who governed Milwaukee during the early twentieth century; the Freedom Farm cooperative, founded by Fannie Lou Hamer in Mississippi in 1967; community organizations like CHARAS, run by Puerto Ricans in *Loisaida* (Manhattan's Lower East Side) until the late 1990s; and, most recently, the Occupy movement.

Indeed, going full circle, the rediscovery of the works of Bookchin, himself a New Yorker, is also part of this process, through initiatives such as the republication of his key writings in the book, *The Next Revolution*, edited by his daughter, Debbie Bookchin.

Such domestic examples of thought and practice demonstrate that municipalism responds to a deep vein of American political culture and, indeed, to the country's understanding of itself: explicitly confederalist, antiauthoritarian in impulse, radical but pragmatic, and with a commitment to self-government.

Moving Beyond Representation: In Search of a Model

Some of the most lively and impassioned debates I witnessed during my time in the States related to the electoral and organizational models that should be favored by municipalists in the US. This includes the question of whether to run candidates within Democratic primaries, what kind of relationship to build with third parties like Democratic Socialists of America (DSA) and Working Families, and how to create organizations that can go beyond election campaign machines and continue to work with candidates once they reach city hall.

This last point is particularly salient, as it relates to a defining characteristic and goal of municipalism. Building a strong, independent organization is not just about having mechanisms to hold electeds to account (though that's necessary). It's also about being able to build a movement that can supersede the limits of institutional action through an inside-outside strategy. While a single elected or group of electeds may not be able to immediately revolutionize local institutions and instigate direct democracy, they should at least start to put these ideas into practice within their own movements.

The question of how to do this won't be resolved by theory or debate, but through experimentation and practice. Fortunately, this process is already underway in a number of neighborhoods, towns, and cities.

In Jackson, Mississippi, activists have spent over a decade creating new popular, democratic institutions: a People's Assembly and Cooperation Jackson, a federation of worker-owned cooperatives. While the ultimate goal of the Jackson-Kush Plan is to create an independent political party capable of winning political power, activist Chokwe Antar Lumumba stood for, and won, the Democratic nomination for mayor in 2017. That same year, the Seattle People's Party candidate, Nikkita Oliver, came third in the city's nonpartisan mayoral primaries. The People's

Party has since continued its work from outside city hall, campaigning on issues from policing reform to housing and immigrant rights.

In Chicago, the independent political organization, United Neighbors of the 35th Ward was formed off the back of the successful campaign to elect Carlos Ramirez Rosa, a DSA member who ran on the Democratic ticket, to the city council. Since the elections, United Neighbors has continued to work with the alderman, campaigning on a range of city issues, including lifting the statewide ban on rent control in Illinois, and participating in a grassroots citizen defense network to defend immigrant families from deportation.

The Richmond Progressive Alliance in California uses a similar model. The alliance, which is registered as an unincorporated not-for-profit organization, works on the principle of "run by organizing, organize by running." Since 2004, it has run coordinated slates of independent candidates for city council and for mayor (and won!), as well as campaigning, providing training, and participating in issue-based coalitions to build power between elections.

Munici-what? Creating a Shared Identity

Finally, municipalists in the US also face the task of generating a sense of collective identity. The movement currently exists as a scattering of isolated local electoral projects alongside better-networked housing and racial justice and precarious labor movements and the cooperative economy. Many of the people already doing municipalism—from local councilors to tenant unions and activists from the Movement for Black Lives and Fight for 15—don't necessarily identify with the word or, more importantly, with one another. Building the movement will depend on the capacity to replicate and link up organizations working along municipalist lines around a sense of common purpose.

The process of building a collective identity will require a shared language to refer to the movement itself and the people and organizations that belong to it. At present, anglophone municipalism is drowning in vocabulary, with multiple words describing more or less the same thing, from "radical municipalism" to "communalism," "municipal socialism," and "social ecology." It will also require a common narrative about what municipalism is and why its time has come.

But it's not just a communication challenge, it's about creating a real community through network building between individuals and organizations. The Fearless Cities Summit in New York this July was an important milestone in this regard, bringing together activists, political campaigners, and local electeds from across North America for the first time under the banner of municipalism. Other initiatives in the pipeline designed to strengthen the network in the US include improved internal and external communication channels, a book titled *Fearless Cities* to be published by New Internationalist in early 2019, and further gatherings to be convened by Cooperation Jackson and the Symbiosis network.

The municipalist movement in the US has a lot of work ahead of it: organizing, campaigning, and proving it's capable of achieving change in the real world. But the fact that these issues are being debated in diverse contexts across the country is incredibly promising. The US's history and political culture, together with the current national political context, make it a fertile ground for the municipalist seeds that have been planted to take root and thrive.

Looking Beyond Electoralism: The New Radical Municipalism in the UK?

Daniel Brown

Now that the dust has settled after the disastrous results of December 12, it's time to seriously reconsider the approach of the Left in the UK. The electoral defeat of Corbynism has opened up a space for such analysis. As someone who has been somewhat involved in activism both outside of and within the Labour Party, I am keenly aware that this is a painful and arduous process for activists who poured a great deal of time and energy into fighting for Corbyn's Labour. However, the election laid bare serious flaws with electoralism as a strategy for radical change in the UK. Many on the left have laid the blame for defeat at the door of Brexit and whilst I broadly agree with this, it's imperative that we also examine why Brexit became such a central issue and why the Left was incapable of addressing that issue.

This failure to address Brexit in part stems from a failure to get a left-wing narrative out to the general public. This issue may be caused by an increasingly monopolized media, but there needs to be more work done about this problem. Without work in this area, the Left will never be able to address anti-immigration narratives that have been building for decades nor will it be able to change a general feeling of pessimism that surrounds radical or transformative politics.

What we desperately need to be doing then, is looking at forms of organizing, particularly new municipalist movements, that are gaining traction in post-industrial contexts. For example, the municipalist movement, Barcelona en Comú, focuses on local grassroots organizing to build support for radical politics through "small victories that prove things can be done differently, from both inside and outside local institutions." This grassroots politics is already starting to take shape with tenants' unions, militant unions, and municipalist groups such as Cooperation Kentish Town gaining traction across the country. If the massive energy and large network of energized activists mobilized by Labour and Momentum could be channeled into such politics, there is perhaps a chance of building a radical infrastructure capable of providing radical change.

What Went Wrong? Looking Beyond Brexit

The most striking feature of Labour's defeat in the general election was the loss of working-class areas across England and Wales who were traditionally loyal to Labour and voted overwhelmingly for Brexit. So far, this narrative is fairly conventional and for much of the Labour Left this implies a need to fully embrace Brexit or at least wait until it "blows over." This is, however, too simplistic and fails to get to the root of why the Left has been unable to address Brexit with any real confidence. Kim Moody's detailed analysis of the election provides a very useful view of the complexities of such failings. For the purposes of this essay, however, we can focus on to two key issues which caused such failings; first, the Left has lost the anti-globalization narrative to the right and second, a failure to address head-on the right-wing anti-immigrant rhetoric which has been used as an explanation for why globalization has decimated working-class communities.

Decades of mostly uncontested (in the mainstream at least) narratives about immigration, which grow more intense and delusional by the day, are a reality that we must face head-on. Undoing this is no easy task and cannot be sidestepped without having to face it again at a later date. Letting the wound fester is not going to save us. We need to face this challenge head-on in a way that recognizes how big a hurdle these ideas are to the left. It can't be ignored, and it will be a difficult and uphill struggle. This is partly an issue with electoralism. Undoing decades of anti-immigration narratives isn't a task suited to the fast-moving world of parliamentary politics, especially when faced with a hostile press.

It is also important here to ensure that such analysis does not fall into the trap of classism. These anti-immigration narratives are just as prevalent among the middle classes and elites, but they are unlikely to be convinced by left-wing alternatives. It is not that the working class is more prone to such arguments but that these arguments are prevalent throughout British society.

Rohini Hensman provides a strong counterargument to assertions that Brexit was not necessarily predominantly concerned with racism or anti-migrant politics. For example, she highlights the right-wing media's focus on Turkey joining the EU and a possible influx of Muslim migrants during Brexit as exemplary of the kind of narratives which drove Brexit. Importantly, she notes how Corbyn's Labour made some attempts to discuss globalization early in 2017, but often failed to emphasize the importance of anti-racism and pro-migrant politics in such discussions.

Hensman also provides a compelling argument that Labour should have "launched a powerful anti-racist campaign depicting immigrants as friends and neighbors, teachers, doctors, nurses and care workers, people whose work benefits society and whose tax and National Insurance payments contribute to Britain's economy," whilst also promoting "compassion for refugees and attempts to help them in their home countries." Such an approach would undoubtably have been better in going some way toward challenging the far-right narratives behind Brexit and much of the discussion on immigration.

However, the Labour Left, and the Left more generally, lack the kind of platform needed to get such messaging out to the public quickly and consistently enough to win electoral victories. Such a campaign would also need more focus on the kinds of exploitation faced by migrant workers. Focusing on migrants' contribution to the economy is unlikely to be convincing to those who feel left behind by the very same economy. Instead, it would be better to challenge the way that racism and migrants' precarious status are used to break solidarity and increase exploitation. The focus should be on blaming bosses and businesses for this and promoting more solidarity and labor union work that unites all workers in challenging such exploitation.

Confronting Nationalism and the Monopoly of Right-Wing Media

To counter this pervasive nationalism then, there is an urgent need to build a new left-wing internationalism which is staunchly anti-globalization and capable of presenting a convincing narrative against the rising tide of far-right nationalism.

Such an internationalism needs to grapple with a nationalism that preys on very real concerns about globalization, the cost of living, low wages, and the housing crisis by falsely laying the blame for such issues at the feet of migrants rather than the powerful corporations and political elites who manufactured post-industrial decline and imperialist wars. The free-trade deals and deregulation pushed by such politics reveal that such nationalism is simply globalization by another name. Instead of paying lip service to progressive values it is openly racist and xenophobic. Addressing this head-on and unmasking its contradictions is the only way we can begin to challenge its stranglehold over politics.

This challenge is difficult because of an increasingly monopolized media which effectively drowns out any narratives other than the old "progressive" neoliberalism or the new far-right politics gaining traction globally. The left's inability to challenge these narratives (in countries like the UK at least) can be explained by our post-industrial context. With major defeats of the labor movement by politicians like Margaret Thatcher, one of the key means of information distribution for the Left was left severely weakened. Unions provided both a key means of providing alternative narratives to people across the country and a force for political change which could limit the encroachment of the Right.

With their defeat, the UK has seen its media monopolized by an increasingly small and influential group of billionaires closely tied to corporate power and political elites. A similar process can be observed in countries like the US or Australia and closely follows the model laid out by Noam Chomsky in *Manufacturing Consent*. This is all something that the Left is keenly aware of but telling the world about this media bias is not enough. Even if such narratives can gain traction, they have to fight the effect of mere exposure. People are physiologically more likely to believe something they have been exposed to repeatedly.

New left media in the UK has done some important work in trying to challenge this monopoly and this saw some positive results in the 2017 elections, but these efforts clearly aren't enough. This is partly because such outlets rely on the preexisting Left for much of their audience; expanding your audience beyond this is difficult. Building a bigger and more receptive audience is clearly key then. It is also important to note that 2017 managed to evade Brexit, so the Left could bring in new narratives around austerity fairly effectively. However, such narratives did not necessarily challenge Brexit or anti-immigration sentiment head-on. What's needed then is a new approach to building the kind of internationalism and organizational power that can challenge this rampant nationalism.

Toward a Municipalist Internationalism

At first glance municipalist movements' focus on direct democracy and the local might seem at odds with such internationalism. However, a key aspect of such movements' strategies has been an internationalism premised on the need to confederate communities not just nationally but across borders. As Debbie Bookchin and Sixtine Van Outvyre argue, "By themselves, these democratic popular assemblies will not be strong enough to build a counter-power able to confront the power of capitalism and the state, or to eventually replace them." Instead, they must work to be mutually reinforcing sharing both resources and knowledge, but for this to function these movements need to be strong at the local level.

This process of international solidarity is already one that is taking place globally. In North America, the collective umbrella group Symbiosis represents a move by such movements to share their local successes and escalate such strategies "toward a strong network, or confederation." Meanwhile, the Fearless Cities initiative, supported by organizations like Barcelona en Comú, has worked on similar networking for municipalist movements globally to share knowledge and enter dialogue with each other.

There has also been a great deal of dialogue between these movements, democratic confederalists in Kurdistan, and the Zapatistas. For example, with expressions of solidarity between the Zapatistas and the revolution in Rojava. It is no surprise then that movements like Barcelona en Comú are explicit in identifying their politics with the revolutionary movements of the Zapatistas and Rojava. A radical municipalist internationalism then is not just a possibility but a process that is already under way. Such politics then might hold the key to uniting local democracy with the ability to address the global threat of international capitalism.

An internationalism built on these municipalist politics might go some way toward a more nuanced and engaging vision of international solidarity than what Hensman terms the "pseudo-anti-imperialism" of Corbyn's foreign policy. Hensman correctly identifies the simplistic analysis of Corbyn's team, especially over the Syrian conflict, as a fatal flaw. The difficulty of course is that international conflicts, especially ones as multifaceted as the Syrian civil war, are complex affairs. This makes them unsuited to the simplistic and fast-paced news cycle surrounding electoralism and difficult to explain to a public who understandably have more immediate domestic concerns.

Hensman's analysis does however elide the important role of democratic forces in the majority Kurdish region of northeastern Syria. As an explicitly leftist movement which played a key role fighting ISIS, focusing solidarity on supporting them would make more sense. This is especially true with the Free Syrian Army having many within its ranks who are more closely aligned to jihadist groups and the Turkish regime than they are to democratic politics.

Moreover, supporting the Kurds more explicitly would have allowed for a strong narrative on security by highlighting the West's hypocrisy in opposing ISIS whilst supporting states like Turkey who have links to ISIS and other jihadist groups. Similarly, the UK turning a blind eye to jihadists fighting Mu'ammar al-Gaddhafi in Libya might add to a narrative that could successfully challenge the Conservatives' image of being strong on security. Instead, the Left could build a narrative suggesting that the right-wing and corporate interests are more interested in selling arms and maintaining regional control than providing security and stability.

In this regard then a radical municipalist internationalism could provide a strong avenue for a more complex and nuanced approach to anti-imperialism and international solidarity. The slower localist politics enable more in-depth discussions around such issues, whilst the global network of such movements teaching each other about new challenges and approaches to building a better world is a powerful example of why internationalism is important to people's everyday lives and not just a distant concern. Municipalist politics then could imbue internationalism with more than just the simplistic moralist approach often espoused by Labour. The movement's connections to the Kurdish freedom movement would also strengthen its ability to produce more nuanced and convincing arguments around security, foreign policy, and the Syrian conflict.

The Challenge of Fighting for Utopia in the Age of Capitalist Realism

To get to the point where such internationalism is possible, we clearly need new models for organizing that can address this post-industrial landscape in a way that reaches people across the country. If radical municipalism is to do this successfully it will have to articulate a new internationalism whilst also addressing challenges at the grassroots level. Such modes of resistance will also need to address a pervasive cynicism about the prospects of radical change. Despite strong levels of support for many of Labour's more radical economic and social policies, there was an also a sense that such ideas were unrealistic or too expensive. It is imperative then to confront the specter of what Mark Fisher referred to as *capitalist realism*. This deep anti-utopian cynicism is a major barrier to the kind of support the Left needs to make genuine progress toward transformative politics.

In some sense this pessimism reflects the country's post-industrial context. No longer the heart of capitalist production, the UK's economic model instead relies on the financial sorcery which controls and profits from productive and extractive forces in the Global South. It is no surprise then that the most fertile grounds for resistance have been against the property market and service industry. This is not to say that manufacturing is nonexistent or irrelevant to the UK, but it clearly does not play the central role it did sixty or seventy years ago.

With a diminished need for a large workforce of manufacturers, miners, or shipping workers many working-class communities became "surplus to requirement." Rather than a sense of being an integral but exploited part of the economy, whole swathes of the country became vilified as a drain on resources. Without the traditional leverage of industrial action to resist this, it is no wonder that a deep-seated sense of pessimism developed.

Persuading people of the possibility of real change is not going to be as easy as having a socialist Labour leader telling them such change is possible. Firstly, the message is unlikely to filter through a hostile media and, secondly, people are (understandably) cynical about such claims. This was something many activists encountered whilst canvassing. Even amongst Labour voters in working-class areas of London there was a sense that Labour only turned up every four years to garner votes. The Left isn't going to win by turning up on doorsteps once every few years and convincing people about electoral candidates when this goes against the lived experiences of many marginalized people.

This is where radical municipalism's ability to produce "small victories" focusing on the everyday needs at the local level is instrumental in rebuilding confidence in the possibility of genuine social transformation. People are more likely to get involved with a political movement that offers immediate support in the face of rampant landlordism, gentrification, and miserable working conditions, as well as a broader long-term vision for a better society.

The radical municipalist approach for winning these "small victories" is through building local institutions, like popular assemblies, community land trusts, and cooperatives, alongside running for elections in local municipalities. Cooperation Jackson in Mississippi is a good example of this. Through democratically run cooperatives and community land trusts, they have become an important political force in the City of Jackson able to push back against gentrification whilst promoting economic and political self-determination for marginalized communities. Meanwhile, Barcelona en Comú exemplifies the localist electoral approach of some municipalists. Founded by members of the 15-M protest movement and housing activists in Barcelona, the movement ran for city council elections on a municipalist platform based on proposals heard in public meetings across the city. With housing activist Ada Colau elected as mayor, and a minority government in the city council, Barcelona en Comú is undeniably a significant political force in Barcelona.

How a municipalist politics might look in the UK is uncertain and would need to be based on listening to the needs of local communities. The examples of Cooperation Jackson and Barcelona en Comú, however, show that such movements have a great deal of potential for gaining traction and creating real change at the local level. There is a great deal that can be learnt from such organizations but crucially it's important to remember that there is no "formula." The power of such politics is their ability to adapt to local contexts and reflect the needs of communities.

Toward Dual Power and Grassroots Organizing

The forms that such radical municipalism might take in the UK are difficult to pinpoint exactly, given the need for political projects which respond to specific local needs. The economic disparities and political differences between different regions of the UK mean that a municipalist movement in London is likely to be focusing on different issues or approaches than one in Manchester or Cornwall for example. Similarly, a municipalist movement in Scotland would obviously have to address questions of Scottish independence. The key strength of municipalism in such a context would be an ability to address such economic and political differences on the local level, whilst still being able to form networks and even confederations at national and regional levels.

There are however key similarities across the UK's post-industrial context which might make for fertile grounds for resistance and organizing. Firstly, Tenant's unions like ACORN, London Renters' Union, or Living Rent have seen a great deal of success by organizing tenants to take collective action against landlords. In the wake of the general election defeat, there has been a noticeable increase in activists getting involved with such organizations. In an economy where the property market is king, it makes sense that one of the most effective unionizing strategies focuses on fighting landlords. The localized and communal nature of such struggle also makes it a powerful way to build resilient communities. Whilst tenants' unions are not automatically municipalist in nature, their potential to form a part of building dual power is clear.

Another area of remarkable success has been in attempts to unionize the gig economy and outsourced workers. Smaller more militant unions have seen a great deal of success in organizing cleaners, delivery drivers, and others to take militant strike action. Given the economy's increasingly service-orientated nature this makes sense. The precarious nature of such work especially within the gig economy means that municipalist politics could play an important role in providing some stability and community for syndicalist work.

Such organizing then can form the basis for resisting and even going on the offensive against post-industrial capitalism. However, they need a broader political movement to tie them into a coherent and resilient network of communities. So whilst this is certainly a time to seriously consider what needs to change about how we organize this doesn't necessarily mean throwing away a great deal of important and successful work being done by activists across the country. Tenants' unions and new militant unions can play a key role here in supporting and being supported by such communities.

A relatively new but promising example of how such radical municipalism in the UK might look is Cooperation Kentish Town. Inspired by the successes of Cooperation Jackson, their work creating a community food center is based on hundreds of conversations with the local community and built on pre-existing activists' work in the community. People are more likely to get involved when they see people from their community, or at least those who have shown themselves to be involved in it, working to produce real tangible change whilst listening directly to the concerns of the community. This isn't an easy thing to do, but it's vital for creating a political movement with mass appeal.

How far such movements should engage in electoralism is another important issue to consider. Whilst movements like Barcelona en Comú have seen successes stemming from local elections, others like Cooperation Jackson are warier after supporting elections of local candidates who failed to live up to the organization's principles. Even at a local level, such electoralism can be a drain on resources and energy that could be better spent creating radical infrastructure. This doesn't preclude such electoral strategies, but they should be viewed with a healthy dose of skepticism.

At the national scale, organizations like Momentum have been making moves toward grassroots organizing outside of electoral politics. While it's true that the energy and resources the Labour Left could bring to municipal movements would be significant, we should be cautious about the possibility of such movements being subsumed into a centralized national electoral politics. Building a mass movement through radical municipalism would likely increase the possibility of electoral victories at a national level for left-wing parties, but this shouldn't be the end goal or the focus of such work.

There is a real need then for much of the energy mobilized by the Labour Left to shift into this kind of work which can make a real difference to peoples' lives over the next few years. Crucially, such work is much more convincing and powerful than trying to go toe-to-toe with a hostile media. This will only work if such grassroots organizing and democracy is given the resources and respect it deserves. Moreover, even if people feel a need to continue placing some resources in electoral politics this needs to be done with a healthy skepticism about parliamentary politics and respect for the crucial role grassroots organization should play. Such organizations could form a network that allows the Left to get people to listen to (and have a say in) narratives which defy both neoliberalism and right-wing populism. People will only start to believe that another world is possible when they see it being built before them. Only then will the potential for radical change seem realistic or worth fighting for.

Libertarian Municipalism and Murray Bookchin's Legacy

Debbie Bookchin in Conversation with the Editors of *Green European Journal*

From the US to Spain and beyond, the last decade has seen a surge in municipalist and local democracy citizens' movements. Many have been influenced by the ideas of American writer and thinker Murray Bookchin (1921–2006), which envisaged a new left politics based on popular assemblies and grassroots democracy. We sat down with Debbie Bookchin to discuss how these movements are implementing her father's ideas and what the potential challenges are for libertarian municipalism.

***Green European Journal*:** How do you explain the expansion of municipalist and local democracy citizens' movements and assemblies in the last decade? How far are they a realization of your father's ideas?
Debbie Bookchin: Municipalism is taking various forms today as it evolves in practice. For my father it was part of a profoundly revolutionary project to abolish capitalism, hierarchy, and the state. He believed neighborhood assemblies were an essential building block for true grassroots democracy and began urging the Left to develop a radical municipalist politics fifty years ago. In his 1968 essay, "The Forms of Freedom," he said, "There can be no separation of the revolutionary process from the revolutionary goal. A society based on self-administration must be achieved by means of self-administration." In these statements you see an early iteration of what we today call "prefigurative" politics—the idea that we must create a new society in the shell of the old by living and practicing the ideals of the society we want to bring into existence. If we want to put power in the hands of everyday people

in their cities and towns, we must begin by organizing this kind of face-to-face radical democracy now on the local level.

My father observed that there were many historical antecedents for this, from the ecclesia of ancient Athens to the revolutionary sections of Paris in 1793 to the anarchist collectives of 1936 Spain. And we can add the Kurdish communes in Rojava, Syria, today. I think municipalism is catching on for several reasons. First, it's become clear that the Marxist notion of seizing state power is bankrupt—centralized power invariably corrupts those who claim to speak in the name of the people. At the same time, decades of organizing in the interstices of capitalist society, as anarchists have traditionally done, have failed to produce foundational changes, even as it has created spaces for more holistic types of community. Municipalism offers a third pole in this debate. It allows people to actually practice politics as it should be: an art in which every interested member of a community participates in the governing of the community. Municipalist politics is also very satisfying—it allows people to come together and experience empowerment and community. And it can begin to achieve substantive changes, as it has in Barcelona, where Barcelona en Comú has reined in AirBnB, municipalized the electric department, and made it more difficult for banks to foreclose.

***GEJ*: From the Occupy Movement to municipalist platforms, what is your assessment of the radical democratic and left initiatives of the last years in the US?**

DB: The Left has been weak in the US for many years, ceding local political organizing to the Far Right. The municipalist movement is still nascent in the US, but it is beginning to grow. In part because of the size and diversity of the country, it has taken very different forms in different places. In Jackson, Mississippi, which is in the American South and where 80 percent of the population is African American, Cooperation Jackson has been working for two decades to build a cooperative economy that empowers Black and working-class residents. In other parts of the US, like the Pacific Northwest cities of Portland, Oregon, and Seattle, Washington, municipalism has gained steam more recently in part because of the 2016 presidential election. There is an effort now to tie many of these municipalist movements together through gatherings like the Fearless Cities summits held in New York and Warsaw last summer and by the Symbiosis Research Collective, which is helping to organize a convergence of municipalist activists that would result in an organization spanning North America.

***GEJ*: What is libertarian municipalism?**

DB: At the age of nine, my father became a Young Pioneer with the Communist Party USA. So he was essentially raised by them. But over the years he became troubled by the economic reductionism that had historically permeated the Marxist Left. After working in a steel foundry, where most workers were interested in a higher wage and not much else, he became disenchanted with the revolutionary potential of the "proletariat" and sought to expand the idea of freedom to be more than mere economic emancipation. Freedom, he felt, should address all manner of oppression: race, class, gender, ethnicity, as well as freedom from mindless toil. In the late 1950s and early 1960s it also became increasingly clear to him that the grow-or-die ethos of capitalism was on a collision course with the ecological stability of the planet and that ecological problems cut across class lines and had the potential to radicalize all segments of society.

He began to elaborate the idea that he called social ecology, which starts from the premise that all environmental problems have their origin in social problems. This means that we can't solve the ecological crisis until we eliminate every form of domination and hierarchy: of the old over the young, men over women, cisgender over trans, as well as economic oppression and a myriad of other social stratifications. In social ecology he was both critiquing current social and ecological crises and also articulating a coherent reconstructive vision. The question for him was how, concretely, do we bring a new egalitarian society into being? As a historian he was aware of this rich history of direct democracy and self-government—the idea that local communities could chart their own futures and then confederate to address regional and even national problems without the need of a centralized state. He called this idea libertarian municipalism or communalism.

***GEJ*: Your father emphasized the role of the city in leading to social ecological politics. Why are cities so important and is there not the risk of further polarizing cities and countryside with its smaller towns?**

DB: There is no question that cities are Janus-faced. On the one hand, cities are noisy, polluted, and overwhelming. They have been the engines of capitalism. On the other hand, historically, they have also been the places where tribal affiliations were superseded by the emancipatory idea of citizenship—the right to be a fully participating member of society regardless of one's origins. We need to reclaim this liberatory potential of municipalities by empowering people in their neighborhoods and decentralizing cities. We can also employ decentralized technologies like solar and wind power and promote ecological values like unity in diversity and social stability as a function of complexity, variety, and diversity—values that foster mutual aid and community building. My father understood both the oppressive and liberatory potential of cities and felt that they did not need to be placed in opposition to the countryside. The reality is that more and more people are living in cities and that a politics that is based on community, that indeed must be *embedded* in the community, could provide a vehicle for organizing that the Left has lacked.

GEJ: In the book, *The Next Revolution: Popular Assemblies and the Promise of Direct Democracy*, that you edited on your father's writings, the "future of the Left" and the urgent need for unity are a recurring theme. Why and what exactly was his call?

DB: In the essay in "The Future of the Left," my father traces the historical failings of the classical Left. He suggests that capitalism remains an ever-evolving, remarkably resilient system whose ability to degrade not only the natural world but the human psyche continues unabated. He says that a future Left must mobilize people on issues that cut across class lines, and that a politics based on protest is no politics at all. In rather prescient observations (given the rise of right-wing populist politics today), he urged the Left to focus on issues that have trans-class appeal, understanding matters such as gender discrimination, racism, nationalism, and even global warming as evidence of the ills caused by hierarchy. He believed that the Left had to consciously explain to people the wider significance of individual issues, connecting them to the ravages of capitalism, hierarchy, and domination, and that one of the best ways to do this was on the neighborhood level.

For my father, municipalist politics was about much more than bringing a progressive agenda to city hall. For him it was very much an educational process in which, during the practice of meeting or "communing," we develop the character that enables us to restore politics to its original definition as a moral calling based on rationality, community, creativity, and free association. At a time when human rights, democracy, and the public good are under attack by increasingly nationalistic, authoritarian centralized state governments, it seems more important than ever to engage in face-to-face meetings with our neighbors, to reclaim the public sphere for the exercise of empathy, understanding of our commonalities, authentic citizenship, and freedom.

***GEJ*: Beyond crisis periods, how do we sustain the real political engagement from citizens that libertarian municipalism requires? While libertarian municipalism and the feminization of politics tend to reject institutionalization and leadership, both may be necessary to take the political project further.**

DB: People become involved and stay engaged when they see results in their communities. They want to see change on their doorsteps—whether better housing and schools or improved air quality—and municipalism offers people a means for addressing those issues. The next step is to tie those issues to bigger ones like racial justice, ecological degradation, and capitalism, but everything starts with the community. We have been conned into the idea that politics is going into a voting booth once every two, four, or five years and pressing a button. Municipalist politics allows us to reclaim this very essential part of being human, to become transformed into new human beings through its practice and to in turn transform society. Municipalism seeks to change the very nature of politics as something that people do for themselves, rather than something that is done for them, or more often *to* them.

I don't think that libertarian municipalism and the feminization of politics are antithetical to institutionalization or leadership. There will always be leaders, people who are better informed or rhetorically gifted. And libertarian municipalism is actually calling for the institutionalization of political power in the form of bottom-up, directly democratic neighborhood assemblies; this is what distinguishes municipalism from other progressive movements. The important element is that politics and political institutions be transparent and accountable. Specifically, a municipalist politics demands that those elected to city councils view themselves as delegates of the local assembly and are 100 percent accountable to their assemblies; they are recallable if they fail to represent the wishes of those who have placed them in a position of power. It requires that they abide by a code of ethics, and that they rotate. This transparency is designed to transform politics into something that everyone can do and that is fundamentally based on assembly forms of organization.

***GEJ*: In the early 2000s, the Kurdistan Workers' Party's (PKK) imprisoned leader, Abdullah Öcalan, decided to infuse the Kurdish political project with communalism, popular assemblies, and confederalism. How is Rojava (the Democratic Federation of Northern Syria) implementing your father's ideas?**

DB: Rojava, now home to about four million people living in a swath of land along Syria's northern border with Turkey, has been a tremendous living example of libertarian municipalism, or what the Kurds call "democratic confederalism." Built on the pillars of ecology, direct democracy, and women's liberation, the Kurdish people have implemented a system in which women hold a minimum of 40 percent of all elected offices, cochair all administrative positions, and have a separate committee system that adjudicates all issues relating to women. People meet at the "commune" level of about forty to a hundred families to collectively make decisions about every aspect of life, from traffic control to which municipal cooperatives they wish to open; they send delegates to the neighborhood level, which in turn sends delegates to the city level and finally the "canton" level. They are able to make even regional decisions across a fairly large territory, about the size of Belgium, without resorting to a centralized state, by using a delegate system that reports back to the local communes. In addition, a corresponding committee system addresses things like education, youth, women, economy, and health. It's a testament to the Kurds' commitment that they have implemented this system during a fierce civil war and while losing thousands of their young women and men fighting the Islamic State.

***GEJ*: What do you know of the Rojava experience and how do you support them? How is this radically democratic and municipalist project perceived in the US?**

DB: In the US, as in Europe, there are pockets of solidarity in the form of local groups that try to build consciousness about Rojava. Alas, the American solidarity effort is far weaker than its European counterpart.

The American media does a fairly poor job of conveying the nuances of overseas affairs and the larger American public is myopic and insular. Meanwhile, from the Left we are often confronted by anti-imperialist, anti-interventionist politics, which argues that the US must stay out of all international conflicts and that villainizes the Kurds for accepting coalition air support for their battle against ISIS. I must say that I find this argument extraordinarily narrow-minded. To hear those on the left who claim to stand for freedom, women's rights, and economic equality be willing to let the Kurdish movement be defeated rather than accepting Western air support is the privilege of armchair leftists who have no idea what it means to fight on the ground for a democratic socialist society. I've found it profoundly disturbing that the broader Left hasn't done more to make solidarity with the Kurdish people in their struggle. It's not as though we have so many examples of egalitarian, multiethnic, nonsectarian, grassroots democratic societies that we can afford to let it be crushed.

***GEJ*: You are carrying the flame of your father's political work. How do you proceed? What are the difficulties you've encountered?**
DB: Most of my adult life has been spent as an investigative journalist, but since my father died in 2006, I've increasingly felt that it's my job to help project his ideas forward. My father developed his social theory for sixty years, in constant engagement with the Left, arguing that we had to do more than go into public office, protest, or live alternative lifestyles—we had to build alternative institutions of political power. And I think that as well-intentioned as, for example, the German Green Party has been, its trajectory—which I followed very closely, including while living in Frankfurt in 1984 to 1985—shows how easy it is to start out as a "nonparty party" and, when you run for national office, become assimilated into existing power structures where you ultimately have relatively little influence and cannot rehabilitate society, much less transform it. In the US, there is no question that we would have been far better off with a Bernie Sanders presidency than with Donald Trump and I'd certainly vote for democratic socialist candidates like Sanders and Alexandria Ocasio-Cortez from the DSA. But we will never win under the current system. It forces compromise after compromise until we settle, gratefully, for pathetic tidbits, like a carbon tax, when the entire planet is going up in flames.

After my father died, the association of his ideas with the Kurdish autonomy movement brought a new generation of activists into contact with his work. I feel compelled to press forward with his vision because today, we are living in a time when the need for political change has never been greater, and his work has a major contribution to make to the Left. When global warming has placed us at the brink of ecological suicide far sooner than even my father predicted fifty years ago, we *must* build alternative institutions of political power that will contest the power of global capitalism and the nation-state. The future of the planet depends on it.

The Concept of Democratic Confederalism and How It Is Implemented in Rojava/Kurdistan

Ercan Ayboga

The Emergence of the Kurdish Freedom Movement and Resistance

At the end of the 1970s, the revolutionary Left in Turkey was relatively strong and a socialist revolution seemed possible. But much of the Turkish Left was steeped in the neocolonial chauvinism and anti-Kurdish racism propagated by Kemalism, the Turkish state ideology. As a result, many revolutionary-Left Kurds and also some Turks concluded that a separate organization was necessary. So in 1978, a group of revolutionaries, among them Abdullah Öcalan and Sakine Cansız, founded the Kurdistan Workers' Party (PKK) in North Kurdistan (the occupied part in the Turkish state) as a national liberation movement based on Marxist-Leninist organization principles and also theories.

The third military coup in Turkey in 1980 did not destroy the Kurdistan Workers' Party, like the other leftist/revolutionary organizations, because it was more prepared and retreated at an early stage to Syria and Lebanon. There it got support from leftist Palestinian militants. A few years later, the Syrian Ba'ath regime tolerated the Kurdistan Workers' Party as well, knowing it could use the group as a lever against Turkey with which it had conflicts about a number of issues. However, the relationship between the Kurdistan Workers' Party and the Syrian state was challenging because the Syrian regime was authoritarian and repressed the Kurds and denied their rights. But as the main goal of the Kurdistan Workers' Party was to liberate North Kurdistan, revolutionary organizing would get under way in Syrian Kurdistan (called Rojava) only later.

On August 15, 1984, after years of preparation, the Kurdistan Workers' Party initiated a guerrilla war against the Turkish state in North Kurdistan. In the following years it became the strongest Kurdish political organization in North Kurdistan. Tens of thousands of young Kurds joined the Kurdistan Workers' Party guerrilla army, men and women alike. Women participated even in the first armed actions.

During the Cold War, the Kurdistan Workers' Party struggled with the goal of establishing a socialist, democratic-centralist, and united Kurdistan. But at the same time, in the middle of the 1980s the first critique came up against real/state socialism, and the Kurdistan Workers' Party tried to act differently. At that time, the approach toward religion, which was not simplified as the "opium of the masses," was important. The Kurdistan Workers' Party analyzed religion deeply and emphasized its democratic elements while rejecting the reactionary parts. This led to the situation that the Turkish state could not use religion against the Kurdistan Workers' Party. Consequently Kurds, belonging to different faiths (Sunni, Alevi, Shia, Yezidi), supported the Kurdistan Workers' Party while overcoming their prejudices against each other.

When in 1990–91, with the collapse of the Soviet Union, real socialism came to an end, liberation movements around the world disintegrated. But the Kurdistan Workers' Party became a mass movement, and with new organizations it evolved into the Kurdish Freedom Movement, and it led to a searching critique of statism and began pondering other models. More than ever, it regarded the Kurdish question not solely as a national or ethnic issue but as a matter of the liberation of society, of gender, and of all people. The Kurdistan Workers' Party analyzed political and social dynamics and developed programs toward a liberated society.

One crucial step in the development was in 1993, when the Kurdistan Workers' Party created a women's guerrilla army with a strong autonomy and its own headquarters. Also, the participation of thousands of young women who came from feudal social structures to the Kurdistan Workers' Party was a factor for this step. With new self-confidence, women who became guerrillas rejected women's traditional patriarchal role and slipped into the new role of freedom fighter, because they had so much to win and so little to lose. One of the goals was to overcome the traditional socialization of feudal society and prevent its reproduction in the guerrilla army. There in the mountains, over the years, the female fighters developed principles of autonomous women's organizing, dual leadership, and the minimum of 40 percent participation of women in all political and social areas—principles that now apply to the Kurdish Freedom Movement in all four parts of Kurdistan.

In the 1990s, the Kurdistan Workers' Party started clandestinely to organize significant numbers of the Kurds in Rojava, which was economically the poorest area within the Syrian state. The population set up councils and committees on justice, women's active participation, and education in the prohibited Kurdish language. Many thousands of young Syrian Kurds left to join the Kurdistan Workers' Party guerrillas.

By the mid-1990s, the military conflict between the Kurdistan Workers' Party and the Turkish military seemed to be at a stalemate. The state's approach was characterized by war crimes: three million Kurds have been displaced, four thousand villages destroyed, and ten thousand civilians murdered. The Kurdistan Workers' Party declared several unilateral cease-fires with the aim of achieving a political solution within Turkey, but the Turkish state never demonstrated a real interest in a political solution and sabotaged peace efforts.

In 1998, Turkey, which controlled the water supply to Syria at the Euphrates River, threatened to go to war in Syria unless it expelled the Kurdistan Workers' Party. After Öcalan left Syria on October 9, 1998, Turkish and Syrian officials secretly met in Turkey. Syria increased its repression of the Kurds and started to have better relations with Turkey.

After an international odyssey of four months, Öcalan was abducted from the Greek consulate in Nairobi, Kenya, by the CIA and brought to Turkey. Millions of Kurds in North Kurdistan, in Rojava, Iranian Kurdistan, and Europe protested for weeks.

A New Concept Evolves

In summer 1999, Öcalan was initially sentenced to death, but later he was placed in solitary confinement on the prison island of Imralı, in the Sea of Marmara, as its sole inmate. This was the moment when he critically and systematically engaged with Marxist-Leninist theory and practice and intensively studied the writings of the libertarian theorist Murray Bookchin and historians and social scientists like Immanuel Wallerstein, Fernand Braudel, and Michel Foucault. He analyzed again the social revolutions of the past and the new political/social movements around the world, including the Zapatistas as an important source of inspiration. He carried out an intensive study of the history of the

Middle East, of Neolithic society and ancient Sumer, of Attic democracy and contemporary tribal organization. He discussed intensively and publicly over years his ideas with the political activists of the Kurdish Freedom Movement and others through his lawyers. From all these sources and discussions, in 2005 he declared the model of democratic confederalism that the Kurdistan Workers' Party and the whole Kurdish Freedom Movement would adopt as a paradigm shift, and that would become foundational for the revolution in Rojava, the Western/Syrian part of Kurdistan.

Drawing on communalist traditions of so-called primitive societies, Öcalan oriented himself toward "natural society," which he thought existed some ten thousand years ago. It had a communal, egalitarian social organization. It was matricentric or matriarchal, but also with a sense of gender equality. "During the Neolithic period," he wrote, "a complete communal social order, so called 'primitive socialism,' was created around woman, a social order that saw none of the enforcement practices of the state order." This idea of "natural society" clearly resembles the concept of "primitive communism" developed by Lewis Henry Morgan, Friedrich Engels, V. Gordon Childe, and others.

In Öcalan's view, the emergence of hierarchy, class rule, and statism was not inevitable but forced: "Hierarchy and the subsequent rise of the state was enforced by the widespread use of violence and fraud. The essential forces of natural society, on the other hand, tirelessly resisted and had to be continually pushed back." Against the Marxist principle of a necessary passage through stages of development, Öcalan posed the concept of building up radical democracy in the here-and-now.

In late Neolithic ages, a matricentric, communal society ultimately gave way to a statist, patriarchal society. Patriarchy, in his view, was the basis for the emergence of hierarchy and state repression, which also pursued hegemony over nature. State centralism, capitalism, and nationalism are all consequences of patriarchy.

To study this transition, Öcalan used discourse analysis to examine mythology, as well as sociological methods. From Sumerian myths, he collected information on how hierarchy, patriarchy, and the enslavement of men and women came about. They tell of the reduction of the prestige of the female elements in life and society, their destruction, and the ordering of society into female and male identities in the form of a hegemonic man and "his wife."

Today in the statist societies of "capitalist modernity" (defined by a capitalist economy and social hierarchy), Öcalan claims that commodification and assimilation wreak destruction on people, isolating them from one another, and defining them as amorphous masses to be ruled under the tutelage of elites in nation-states. But linking people together in councils and creating an active and activist citizenship is a base on which the alternative to the nation-state and capitalist modernity can be built.

For Öcalan, the concept of "democratic civilization" is a permanent subtradition of resistance to statist civilization. It opens new possibilities beyond classical historical materialism. Indeed, it criticizes historical materialism as Euro- and androcentric for requiring colonized societies to develop an industrial proletariat; moreover, it is subject to ecological critique, as capitalist industrialization is not sustainable for this planet and its inhabitants. By contrast, the Kurdish Freedom Movement's approach proposes to strengthen democratic civilization and develop a "democratic modernity."

The modernist ideology of Kemalism agrees with classical Marxism in regarding the Middle East as an underdeveloped region and disparages the Kurdish areas as "less advanced." But if capitalism has not yet totally absorbed the social fabric of the Middle East, that is an advantage. The Kurdish areas in particular are not a feudal society that must be overcome by capitalism in order to reach socialism and communism. On the contrary, the Kurdish democratic approach regards it as positive that the Middle East has not yet been fully submerged by the alienation and atomization of capitalist modernity, since it means that opportunities for development beyond modernist lines remain—that is, a different approach to tradition and society. So the area in which Kurds live now is a relatively fertile ground for development along nonmodernist lines.

We thus have two traditions: the tradition of democratic civilization and the tradition of statist civilization, which in political and social terms we can express as "democratic modernity" and "capitalist modernity." These traditions are classified according to their emancipatory content. Those that have established themselves by statism and patriarchy are to be criticized, while traditions of collectivity, that embrace the social role of women, that solve social conflicts through compromise, and that further the coexistence of diverse social singularities are to be strengthened. Power is not to be conquered; rather, an alternative is to be constructed at this historical moment. By connecting people to each other in councils and by empowering people through self-administration, the Kurdish approach resists capitalist modernity and the nation-state and constructs a practical alternative.

From Council Democracy to Democratic Confederalism

> "Peaceful coexistence between the nation-state and Democratic Confederalism is possible as long as the state does not interfere in central matters of self-administration. Any such intervention would require the civil society to defend itself."
> —Abdullah Öcalan

Since the nineteenth century, organization by councils has been an integral part of the European and Russian socialist movements. Councils were the main institutions in the Paris Commune in 1871, in the October Revolution of 1917, and in the German uprisings of 1918/1919, when workers' and soldiers' councils were established. But in all cases, the council movement was neutralized, either because the revolution was consolidated (in the case of the Soviet Union), or because the counterrevolution defeated it. Hannah Arendt called the council movement the "lost treasure of democracy." Councils, she argued, allow for political participation by the people, whereas representative systems structurally exclude people from power. Council movements have been a spontaneous part of every revolution and an alternative to representative systems. The revolutionary process of spontaneous council formation, in her view, stemmed from the heterogeneity of society. After the American Revolution, she reminds us, Thomas Jefferson criticized the US constitution-making process, saying the revolution had brought the people freedom but had created no place where they could exercise it.

But Arendt condemned the inclusion of the social question in self-administration. On this point, the German thinker Jürgen Habermas accused her of failing to understand revolution as the emancipation of oppressed social classes. Rosa Luxemburg, by contrast, saw revolutionary councils as attempts to endow the producing classes with legislative power. They were institutions of the working class that should also represent the "totality" (that is, the whole of society). Luxemburgian thinking can be considered a counterweight to authoritarian tendencies in socialist movements. In her view, a socialist revolution should be carried out not through the conquest of power by political actors but by the masses organizing radical democratic self-governance.

In the tradition of Luxemburg, democratic confederalism extends the concept of democracy to economic conditions—that is, the economy, as part of society, is to be democratized. Democratization or socialization of the economy must be distinguished from nationalization. Socialization means the administration of free economic resources by the councils and communities and the establishment of affiliated cooperatives—that is, it is communal rather than statist or private.

But Luxemburg's notion did not include women, families, or unemployed people. In the 1970s, discussions began aimed at developing a politics beyond government, political organization, and party, and a political subjectivity that went beyond class. In the West, an alternative to liberal democracy evolved that inspired international liberation movements and the anti-globalization movement. Michael Hardt and Antonio Negri proposed overcoming representative systems by means of direct participation, in which each "singularity" among the "multitude" would be represented through a process of radical democratization.

Democratic confederalism is a concept for the radical democratization of society. "In contrast to centralized administrations and bureaucratic exercise of power," Öcalan writes, "democratic confederalism proposes political self-administration, in which all groups of the society and all cultural identities express themselves in local meetings, general conventions, and councils. Such a democracy opens political space for all social strata and allows diverse political groups to express themselves. In this way it advances the political integration of society as a whole. Politics becomes part of everyday life."

In order to achieve a radical democracy, Öcalan writes, the role of women is of primary importance: "the reality of the woman determines social reality to a large extent.... Therefore, no movement has a chance of creating a real and lasting, free society unless women's liberation is an essential part of its practice." If we are to build a stateless society, Öcalan argues, we must overcome patriarchy. In Kurdistan it is the motor contradiction to change society toward liberation, emancipation, freedom, and solidarity. After years of discussion and practice this idea is deeply rooted in the Kurdish Freedom Movement and is being implemented at all levels of local government, through both the autonomous women's institutions and mixed-gender institutions.

The Kurdish Freedom Movement summarizes the concept of democratic confederalism with the paradigm of the three pillars: radical democracy, gender liberation, and ecological society. The way of implementing this is called "democratic autonomy." It can differ in its details from one region/area to another one. So the democratic autonomy concept for North Kurdistan is a bit different from that of Rojava.

In order to create democratic autonomy, communes need to spread into the whole society, councils are not enough for radical democracy. Communes are, in particular, an anti-centralist and bottom-up approach. The commune is the political center of democratic self-government, the unit that integrates the people and households. At an upper level the councils bring together the communes in a bigger area. There is theoretically no limit for more upper councils, in practice this depends on the autonomous region, which can be quite small or large. The neighboring communities themselves have to decide which areas belong to one democratic autonomy.

A few years after the declaration of democratic confederalism, Öcalan developed the discussion about a "democratic nation." With this definition, he aims to deepen and broaden the theoretical basis of the targeted society. To make it more understandable he said: "While the Democratic Nation is the spirit, Democratic Autonomy represents the body."

The concept of the democratic nation is distinct from the nation-state—a term that might be irritating if one knows the anti-nationalist and anti-statist paradigms of the Kurdistan Workers' Party. The democratic nation is more a sharing of the values of emancipation and liberation than a place with borders around it. The democratic nation is growing within the existing nation-states as an alternative form of society sharing common moral, democratic, and emancipatory institutions of democratic autonomy and aiming at transforming the nation-state and defending itself against attacks from capitalist modernity, nationalism, and statism. It is oriented along the principles of radical democracy, gender liberation, ecological society, communal economy, people's diplomacy, the right to self-defense for all living beings by themselves, bottom-up justice, health for all, a place for people with different ethnic identities, and communality/solidarity in the whole of life. These principles are also described as the sectors of society to be self-organized in autonomous organizations (also called civil society organizations or social movements) and may change in its categorization according to the democratic autonomy.

If there is an agreement between the organizations of a democratic-autonomous region and the existing state for each to accept mutually the existence of the other one, a "democratic republic" can be the result. As the remnant of the nation-state, it has the role of guaranteeing the rights that make possible democratic autonomy for certain regions. In the case of the Kurds, a democratic republic presupposes a democratization of the existing states of Turkey, Syria, Iran, and Iraq.

Democratic Autonomy in North Kurdistan

After the declaration of democratic confederalism in 2005, a new broad discussion among the organizations within and close to the Kurdish Freedom Movement about the reorganization and new orientation in the political work evolved more than ever. Since 1999, the repression by the Turkish state has decreased, but has not disappeared. At the same time the Turkish governments did nothing to resolve the Kurdish question, they just ignored it and hoped that over time the Kurdish Freedom Movement would become weaker. In 2007, the Democratic Society Congress was initiated. Since then, the Democratic Society Congress has brought together all forms of organizations within the Kurdish Freedom Movement on a democratic basis. Although the Democratic Society Congress follows the same political concept, it stayed organizationally independent from the Kurdistan Workers' Party due to the political repression.

It took some more years until the Democratic Society Congress could unfold itself broadly. Since 2007, so-called people's councils have been established in neighborhoods where for two decades the Kurdish Freedom Movement was present through clandestine and legal organizations as well the legal party. The latter had to change regularly its name due to bans (today it is BDP, Democratic Regions Party, which is the strongest member party in the internationally known umbrella party, the People's Democratic Party). As a grassroots organization the people's councils include large parts of the bases of the society. In committees oriented along the main sectors it embraces up to hundreds of activists in the daily political work; often thousands join the general assembly of one council. They send their delegates to the next level at the district level which includes a city and surrounding villages. In the councils at the second level 40 percent of the members come from civil society organizations, political parties (actually, it is only the People's Democratic Party), municipalities (if won by the People's Democratic Party), smaller ethnic-religious groups, and a small number also of some well-known persons or intellectuals. The balance of 40 percent civil society and 60 percent delegates is valid also for the upper level of the province and finally for the highest level of the Democratic Society Congress for North Kurdistan, which meets under normal conditions every six months with 501 delegates. Among civil society organizations are included social movements and political organizations from the main sectors of the society, which increased over time from nine to fourteen. The increase of the sector numbers is an expression of the development of the Democratic Society Congress as a whole.

In 2014 and 2015, when the Democratic Society Congress was strongest, it had councils in almost all Kurdish cities at the neighborhood level interacting with the majority of society. It is imperative that the stronger the councils at the neighborhood level are, the stronger and more democratic the whole structure is.

In 2010, the first communes have been developed in two dozen villages of the province of Çolêmerg (Hakkâri in Turkish). This was the first experience of bringing the self-governing structures down to the bases of the society. In the beginning of 2015, with the experience from the Rojava revolution, a campaign was started to set up communes in several provinces. The result was around three hundred communes, which were destroyed that summer when the Turkish state started its war against the Kurdish guerrillas and Kurds in general.

The political party has no dominant role within the Democratic Society Congress, it is one of the many actors in a diverse structure that reflects the diversity within the society. Rather, all organizations within the congress have a strong right to decide who will be the candidates for the local or parliamentary elections; The party alone does not decide on this issue. In the same manner, the municipalities ruled by the People's Democratic Party have to follow the decisions of the Democratic Society Congress and cannot do whatever they want. This system allows better control against hierarchy and the development of strong power relations—in the political party and municipalities—which function along the laws of the hegemonic capitalist system. Although it is not enough alone, it is a crucial mechanism against corruption by power in the "representative democracy."

It is intended that within the Democratic Society Congress, no one can dominate others and that real consensus or compromise is the basis for common decisions. Like the economic sector, the youth sector can bring issues to the Democratic Society Congress to be discussed at different levels. It took years for the Mesopotamia Ecology Movement to bring crucial concerns to the agenda of the congress. The critical approach of the People's Democratic Party–run municipalities, as a special example, had its impact only after years of being expressed publicly.

The development of the Democratic Society Congress and democratic autonomy were important steps to strengthen again the Kurdish Freedom Movement in North Kurdistan after several years of stagnation that started with the kidnapping of Öcalan. A well formulated political idea—which gives a new democratic perspective and offers space for all parts of society without allowing the domination of some over others and the development of a strong hierarchy—made this possible despite the Turkish Justice and Development Party government of Recep Tayyip Erdoğan. Consider that these were the years when Erdoğan's party was considered by many in both the West and Muslim world as a model for the combination of democracy and Islam. That this was a misleading view became clear in recent years with the growing political repression in Turkey, which meanwhile launches military attacks against other countries.

Nowadays due to the extreme repression with fascist methods, the absolutely illegal forced occupation of the People's Democratic Party–ruled municipalities by state commissioners (done in 2016 and 2019) and the arrests of up to ten thousand activists, many civil society organizations do not work well, including the people's councils, but the people resist and the Democratic Society Congress continues to exist. There are always new people who replace the arrested ones. As was the case in the last decades, when the extreme dictatorship in the Turkish state is broken (hopefully soon), the Democratic Society Congress structures will spread quickly again.

Revolution in Rojava and Democratic Autonomy

Rojava is the smallest part of Kurdistan with almost three million people. It consists of three regions (called from east to west Cizîre, Kobanî, and Afrîn) with a mostly flat geography disconnected from each other, which is a disadvantage for organizing and defense.

The idea of democratic confederalism in Rojava has been spread by the Party of Democratic Union, founded in 2003 by leftist Kurdish activists. But it needs to be mentioned that already in the 1990s some clandestine autonomous structures had been implemented at the initiative of Öcalan, who was at that time in Syria, including many women's committees of the Kurdish women's movement, Kongreya Star; peace committees; language initiatives; and common labor groups which organized voluntary working days for the Kurdish Freedom Movement.

When in 2011, the uprising in Syria started and the state weakened, this experience of the Kurdish Freedom Movement in Rojava was crucial for a rapid self-organization starting in spring 2011. Within months, in the most neighborhoods of Rojava's cities and Aleppo, people's councils, Kurdish language courses, and social centers had been founded. In July 2011, the umbrella structure Movement for a Democratic Society had been established and committees for the main nine social sectors initiated. The Party of the Democratic Union, the women's movement Kongreya Star, the people's councils, and other groups of the Kurdish Freedom Movement took the Democratic Society Congress from North Kurdistan as a model. So for example, 60 percent of the members of the Movement for a Democratic Society's broad assembly (called the People's Council of Western Kurdistan) came from the neighborhood councils while 40 percent were composed of the civil society organizations, political parties, and others.

Since spring 2011, the Syrian government has not oppressed the Kurds as much because it did not want the Kurds as direct enemies in the growing uprising. The Kurds benefited from these new liberties as they stood at a distance from the nationalist, Islamist, and reactionary opposition, but there was also no cooperation with the Syrian regime, only some talks. In Rojava (and Aleppo) the Movement for a Democratic Society was much more active and successful than the other nationalist-liberal Kurdish parties, which came together in the Kurdish National Council of Syria, and soon the majority of the Kurds supported it while the council became weaker and even hostile to the revolution.

When the Syrian government was at a very crucial moment due to the attacks of the armed reactionary opposition, the Movement for a Democratic Society, together with the recently founded People's Protection Units (YPG) started to liberate the cities and villages of Rojava. It started with a popular uprising on July 19, 2012, in Kobanî and was some months later completed. The Syrian regime could not resist much and gave up within a few days in each city, except in the two big cities Qamişlo and Hesekê where it remained in a few neighborhoods. If this had not been done the reactionary opposition could have occupied Kurdish cities.

Since this liberation, there was no state presence in Rojava, which posed huge challenges to the Movement for a Democratic Society, which was now in charge of this territory where many Arabs, Assyrians (Christians), and other identities also lived. The Turkish state acted with great hostility, immediately closed border gates, and few months later organized Islamist armed groups like Al Nusra to attack Rojava. Also, the globally known terrorist organization Islamic State (IS) was encouraged by Turkey to attack the Kurds; Turkey supported and still supports IS militarily and economically. That's why since the beginning of the revolution, the YPG and the Women's Protection Units (YPJ), founded in spring 2013, had to show a huge effort to defend their own land in close coordination with the Movement for a Democratic Society. Nevertheless the movement stated that it is essential to organize the society in a radical democratic way, even under conditions of ongoing threats, war, and embargo.

The Movement for a Democratic Society, with its economics committee, successfully avoided an economic crisis from which the most would suffer, and few would benefit. It strictly controlled the prices in the markets in the weeks after the liberation, ensured the basic services like bread production, drinking water supply, and wastewater removal, and founded associations for economically acting individuals and small companies. As the electricity supply stopped because the big power plants were outside of Rojava, the Movement for a Democratic Society encouraged people to organize common diesel generators. It also avoided new conflicts over land by prohibiting its sale (because the Syrian regime created many land categories with much confusion and injustice) until a new inclusive commission develops proposals to resolve the problems.

Economically, there was the advantage of having large amounts of wheat, olives, and oil wells, and an acceptable level of groundwater. Also, the fact that there were neither very rich people or companies or very big landowners (only 7–8 percent of the agricultural land belongs to them) nor people in extreme poverty offered some opportunities for a more balanced share of economic outputs.

From the very beginning in Rojava, women were part of the revolution and present in each developed political, social, and self-defense structure. With the gender quota of 40 percent among the leadership as well as through intensive public discussions and political education, the sustainability of all this could be ensured. Without a doubt, to this date, it is a strategic goal to implement the women's liberation theory in Rojava and beyond. It is no exaggeration to say that the social revolution first happens in gender relations, then spreads from there to other sectors of the society.

Building inclusivity without giving up the principles of radical democracy, women's liberation, and an ecological society was and is the subject of much discussion. So apart from the Party of the Democratic Union, four other Kurdish parties joined the Movement for a Democratic Society immediately after the liberation; they had in the councils the same votes as the Party of the Democratic Union. The Chaldeans, ethnically like the Assyrians but fewer in number, joined in large numbers the Movement for a Democratic Society. Also, in all cities, democratically thinking Arabs joined the structures of the movement.

Despite these positive steps, the Movement for a Democratic Society was not satisfied because the broad majority of the population did not support self-administration, particularly in the Cizîre region. Around 40 percent of the population was not part of it. So a new process was started in fall 2013 with almost fifty social and political organizations. As a result, the majority of the Assyrians and a significant portion of the Arabs approached the Movement for a Democratic Society. In January 2014, a collectively prepared social contract, approved by the broadly composed Democratic Self-Administration and the Democratic Autonomy was declared. The formation of three cantons with legislative, executive, and judiciary institutions was set up. The new political structure has been a combination of direct democracy represented by Democratic Self Administration, and representative democracy, which was requested by all the new organizations in the Democratic Self-Administration.

The Democratic Self-Administration, as the motor of the revolutionary process, had more than ever an emphasis on building communes, the bottom-up structure of radical democracy. Including usually fifty to two hundred households in cities and villages, the communes spread as elements of an organized and engaged political society. The bases of other political parties joined them too. The communes are the political structures where a large number of people from the same location have to meet with each other. They have to overcome differences and contradictions in order to make social, economic, and cultural progress as a community. In the communes, the big issues are political education, which is understood as an ongoing process; basic health care; and women's autonomous organization and self-defense, which is organized with the support of the academies and social movements of the main sectors. With the economic committee, the basic needs of the society are met on a common ground and not individually. The communes also organize justice in their streets with the peace committees, which usually solve 80 percent of the conflicts, which are decreasing with the spread of self-governed structures.

In 2016, a new process began to reorganize the political system when large areas, populated mainly by Arabs, were liberated by the Syrian Democratic Forces, which is a coalition of YPG/YPJ and the self-defense structures of Arabs, Assyrians, and others aiming at a democratic society. So in 2017, with a broader social contract, the Democratic Federation of North Syria, composed of a growing number of cantons, was established. In September 2018, Raqqa and Eastern Deir-ez-Zor were added and there have been some small modifications to this system, like the change of name to the Autonomous Administration of North and East Syria. Ethnic and religious diversity, decentralization in governing territories, human rights, freedom of speech, the liberation of women, the role of youth, and the right to asylum have all been highlighted. In addition, the prevention of monopoly in the economy and the role of communes are strong elements of the social contract. With the acknowledged role of communes, it is ensured that direct democracy is also part of the political system.

In recent years, the communes have also spread to regions outside of Rojava in North and East Syria. The number should be around four thousand. The idea of self-organization and trusting people to their own power and capacities is spreading slowly but steadily in all the liberated territories. At the next level of direct democracy are the neighborhood councils, which are composed by the delegates of the communes and have social centers called people's houses where the communes meet and decide together. The highest political structures at the district level are also called people's councils, but the difference is that 60 percent of their members are elected, usually in general elections every second year, while 40 percent come from the neighborhood councils and civil society organizations, which is an important reason that no single group gets the majority of votes. So the approach of consensus remains in effect and the inclusion of all parts of society is ensured. The people's councils at the canton level are formed in the same way. Their delegates establish the Autonomous Administration of North and East Syria.

In the economy, the number of cooperatives grows slowly but significantly. Around two hundred cooperatives with several tens of thousands of members act on the basis of a statute which says that only an economic entity that maintains a gender quota of 40 percent, adheres to ecological principles (like refusing chemicals in agriculture), and that does not exploit the labor of others, is a cooperative, otherwise it is a private company. The majority of cooperatives operate on land that has been socialized by the state in 2012. The cooperatives of a district (the level between neighborhood and canton) have upper common associations, which coordinate among each other and are part of the economic councils. These exist in each district and canton and are part of the autonomous administration. For the cooperative movement it is crucial that the idea of solidarity economy is internalized and members stand fully behind the cooperative idea before new cooperatives are spread broadly. The failures of real socialism are not to be repeated and there is a search for a solidarity economy. Only then cooperatives could dominate in the long term the economy of North and East Syria, which nowadays has a mix of solidarity economy, capitalism (small and some middle scale companies usually), and a public sector economy (for example, the oil sector is ruled by the autonomous administration).

Conclusion

When in October 2019, the Turkish Army and its proxies attacked North Syria and occupied two districts, despite the military imbalance the people defended their land. The Turkish state aimed to break the alliance between Kurds and Arabs. But they, together with Assyrians and others, fought successfully together against occupation and massacres which is a result of the set-up of a bottom-up political system adapted to their own conditions (democratic autonomy), which goes beyond known representative political systems. Democracy is when all people are requested continuously to discuss, share, and make decisions, not only to vote every four years. Real (radical) democracy is very challenging and needs an organized, political, and ethical society. To develop it at first usually a social and/or political movement is necessary, which does not require a centralized and small political structure as we had in East Europe in real socialism and nowadays have with elected governments in parliamentarian (representative) systems.

However, there are many ways to achieve a society free of exploitation and oppression that cannot easily be corrupted by the lobbies of private companies or small groups in the society. Kurdistan, with its democratic confederalism, is an interesting and important example. It is sharing actively its experience in North Kurdistan and particularly Rojava/North and East Syria. The latter place is special because there is no state presence, despite pressure from war and embargo. Thus, it invites people from around the world to come; but at the same time, the revolutionaries from Kurdistan are in search of more experiences of similar practices, like the Zapatistas in Chiapas, Cooperation Jackson in the US, and Brazil's Landless Workers Movement. When connecting with others, the principles of radical (direct) democracy, women's (gender) liberation, and ecological life (anti-capitalism) are fundamental.

VII

TOWARD THE GENERAL STRIKE AND DUAL POWER

Building the Commune

George Ciccariello-Maher

The only possible saviors of the Bolivarian process are those who have saved it on every other occasion—and who today coalesce around the horizon of the commune.

Have you heard about Venezuela's communes? Have you heard that there are hundreds of thousands of people in nearly 1,500 communes struggling to take control of their territories, their labor, and their lives? If you haven't heard, you're not the only one. As the mainstream media howls about economic crisis and authoritarianism, there is little mention of the grassroots revolutionaries who have always been the backbone of the Bolivarian process.

This blind spot is reproduced by an international Left whose dogmas and pieties creak and groan when confronted with a political process that doesn't fit, in which the state, oil, and a uniformed soldier have all played key roles. It's a sad testament to the state of the Left that when we think of communes, we are more likely to think of nine arrests in rural France than the ongoing efforts of these hundreds of thousands. But nowhere is communism pure, and the challenges Venezuela's *comuneros* confront today are ones that we neglect at our own peril.

"Revolutions Are Not Made by Laws"

What is a commune? Concretely speaking, Venezuela's communes bring together communal councils—local units of direct democratic self-government—with productive units known as social production enterprises. The latter can be either state owned or, more commonly, directly owned by the communes themselves. Direct ownership means that it is the communal parliament itself—composed of delegates from each council—that debates and decides what is produced, how much the workers are paid, how to distribute the product, and how best to reinvest any surplus into the commune itself.

Just as the late Hugo Chávez did not create the Bolivarian Revolution, the Venezuelan state did not create the communes or the communal councils that they comprise. Instead, the revolutionary movements that "created Chávez" did not simply stop there and stand back to admire their creation—they have continued their formative work in and on the world by building radically democratic and participatory self-government from the bottom-up.

Before the communal councils existed on paper, *barrio* residents were forming assemblies to debate both local affairs and how to bring about revolutionary change on the national level. And before the communes existed on paper, many of these same organizers had begun to expand and consolidate communal control over broader swathes of territory. After all, as Marx, among others, insisted, "Revolutions are not made with laws."

But what the state *has* done has been to recognize the existence of first the councils and then the communes, formalizing their structure—for better and for worse—and even encouraging their expansion. Within the state apparatus, the communes found no greater ally than Chávez himself who, knowing full well that his days were numbered, dedicated the last major speech before his death to the expansion of what he called the "communal state." And since his death, grassroots revolutionaries have seized upon his words for the leverage they provide: insisting that to be a Chavista is to be a *comunero* and that those who undermine popular power are no less than traitors.

Communes against the State

And traitors there are plenty. Not only did the state not create the communes, but the majority of the state apparatus is openly hostile to communal power. This is especially true of local elected officials—Chavistas very much included—who positively loathe these expressions of grassroots democracy that cut into their territory and resources and threaten their legitimacy as leaders. Thus, while many local leaders wear Chavista red while mouthing the words of popular participation and revolution, in practice they routinely attack, undermine, and obstruct the most participatory and revolutionary spaces in Venezuelan society today.

Ángel Prado, a spokesperson for the sprawling El Maizal commune in the central-west of the country that today cultivates 800 hectares of corn, explains how the history of the commune is a testament to the tense relations between communal power and the state. It took grassroots pressure for Chávez to throw his weight behind these *comuneros* by expropriating the land, but even when he did so, the lands passed into the hands of the state agricultural corporation.

Organizers were left wondering, why is the state here if this belongs to the commune? and had to undertake a second struggle against the "revolutionary" state. By organizing themselves and nearby communities and by proving they could produce even more effectively than corrupt bureaucrats, El Maizal eventually gained the support of Chávez to take over the land for themselves. But even today, Prado argues that local Chavista leaders and United Socialist Party of Venezuela represent their "principal enemies," and are actively attempting to "extinguish the commune." "We *comuneros* share very little with the governing party," he insists.

For some—like the longtime militant Roland Denis—this clash comes as no surprise. The phrase "communal state" is "a camouflaged name for the communist state," and even an outright oxymoron. If Marx had described the Paris Commune as "a revolution against the state itself," Denis wonders: "*What* state, if we are actually talking about a non-state? The communal state is a non-state, otherwise it's a bureaucratic-corporative state." Ideally, "the communes could create a productive capacity that begins to compete with capitalism, with its own internal rules and logic, and this could really progressively generate a non-state. There are some very interesting communes moving in this direction."

Free Socialist Territories

Alongside the political antagonism of local leaders, the communes face a daunting economic challenge that is, in fact, their *raison d'être*. Since the discovery of oil in the early twentieth century, the Venezuelan economy has been almost entirely reshaped in its image: cheap imports and a lack of support for the peasantry saw an exodus from the countryside into the cities, making Venezuela simultaneously the most urban country in Latin America—93.5 percent of the population lives in cities—and the only country in the region to import more food than it exports (nearly 80 percent of food by the 1990s).

The communes are an ambitious attempt to reverse this trajectory by encouraging self-managed production geared toward what people actually need on the local level, and what the country needs as a whole. It is therefore no surprise to find the bulk of Venezuela's communes in the countryside—the entire communal project requires reversing this migration, decentralizing the Venezuelan population and its production. Toward this end, the communes are producing—directly and democratically—millions of tons of coffee, corn, plantains, and bananas annually, and straining upward for increased regional and national coordination.

Groups of communes are coming together from below to form regional structures known as "communal axes" or "political-territorial corridors." According to Alex Alayo, a member of the El Maizal commune, the goal is to develop what he calls "free socialist territories" in which communes exchange directly with one another, cutting out the global economy and the domestic capitalists entirely. Through this broader integration, the communes will be able "to communalize or even communize" entire territories not from above, but as an expansive form of self-government from below.

This expansion has led to a tense dual power situation, the uncomfortable and even antagonistic coexistence of the new with the old. On the one hand, there is what Alayo considers a popular government in a bourgeois state structure, and on the other hand, this expanding network of communal territories "building a new state" from below. Tensions and "frictions" are inevitable and will only increase as the communes expand: "Here we are fighting an outright war against the traditional, bourgeois state. Chávez invited us to build the communal state, and that's going to have a lot of enemies. Chávez may even have been the *only* public functionary who agreed with it completely."

Producing the Commune

If there is a single most important contradiction internal to the communal project, it is this: not all communes produce goods. While Venezuela's urbanization saw the rural population abandoning potentially productive lands, the other end of their journey saw them congregating in *barrios* where little production has ever taken place. *Barrio* residents have been the spearhead of the Bolivarian Revolution since they set it into motion by rebellion against neoliberal reform in the 1989 Caracazo, but without production there is no hope for communal autonomy and sustainability.

Where the terrain is unproductive, however, communes have responded creatively and in different ways. Some have developed a productive apparatus where none had existed with the support of government loans or the demand of state companies for specific goods. Others have sought to adapt to the economic terrain of the *barrios* themselves by establishing communal mechanisms for the circulation of people (transport collectives) and goods (distribution centers). Still others have developed communal linkages that bridge the urban/rural divide by establishing barter exchanges between urban and rural communes.

Most ambitiously, some communes have demanded control over local urban industries. When a beer factory in Barquisimeto, previously owned by the Brazilian transnational Brahma (now a subsidiary of Anheuser-Busch), was closed, workers took over the factory and began to bottle water for local distribution. Today, the workers continue to resist court orders to remove them, and are demanding the factory be expropriated and placed under the direct democratic control of the nearby Pío Tamayo commune.

Producing goods is not everything, however. Former commune minister Reinaldo Iturriza argues that while communes need to produce, "the commune is also something that is produced." In other words, especially amid and against the atomization of urban areas, producing communal culture is a primary and very concrete task. For example, I spoke with young *comuneros* in Barrio Los Sin Techos, in the violent area of El Cementerio in southern Caracas, for whom establishing a commune meant producing something very tangible: a local gang truce and a vibrant and cooperative youth culture.

Crisis and Counterrevolution

The Venezuelan communes are emerging against the daunting backdrop of sharpening economic crisis. The plummeting price of oil, the government's ineffective response to a currency devaluation spiral, and the continued reliance of a "socialist" government on private-sector importers have all conspired to pull the rug out from under the stable growth of the Chávez years. Economically, this has meant periodic shortages and long lines for certain, price-controlled goods, as importers would rather speculate on the currency than fill the shelves.

But every crisis is also an opportunity. Venezuela's communes today are struggling to produce, but there is good reason to believe that they are more productive than either the private or state sector. In this case, the crisis itself and the corruption and treason of the private sector might be enough to force the Bolivarian government to throw its weight behind the communes as a productive alternative. And while the sharp decline in oil income has hit the communes hard, it has also forced a long-overdue national debate about the country's endemic oil dependency.

Politically, Venezuela's oil dependency has also meant reliance on cheap imports—a reliance that has become the government's Achilles' heel, and we have all seen the result. Shortages and long lines have whittled away at popular support for *Chavismo*, while providing a pretext for first right-wing protests (in early 2014), and more recently, a landslide opposition victory for control of the National Assembly (in December 2015). While the government continues to blame the crisis on an "economic war" carried out by opposition forces, this disastrous defeat shows clearly enough that many Venezuelans are not convinced.

The consequences of the opposition victory in the National Assembly are very real: right-wing forces are already strategizing how best to remove Maduro from office before his term is up, and planning to roll back many crucial gains of the Bolivarian process. The communes are directly in the crosshairs, with the National Assembly threatening to revoke communal rights to land expropriated under Chávez and Maduro. This first major defeat for Chavismo at the polls immediately galvanized revolutionary ferment at the grassroots, sparking street assemblies and sharp public debates about what had gone wrong.

But it remains to be seen whether the "whip of the counterrevolution" will provide an alibi for continued government inaction or a foothold for new qualitative leaps. As is so often the case, the biggest challenge of all lay precisely on the political level: if Chavismo united can't even defeat the opposition in elections, then what hope is there for a Chavismo divided—communes against what is called the "endogenous right"? Reversing a century of perverted economic development while simultaneously confronting the opposition, right-wing *Chavistas*, and the machinations of US imperialism might seem an impossible task.

But no one ever said communism would be easy...

The Communal Wager

The time has come to bet it all on the communes. The wager may seem a risky one, but according to one estimate, 2013 alone saw some $20 billion simply disappear into a black hole of fake import companies—imagine what the communes could do with $20 billion! The middle class, the *ni-nis* (neither-nors) in the center, the parasitic bourgeoisie, the state bureaucracy, a socialist party incapable of even winning elections, increasingly corrupt military sectors—the alternative to the communes is no alternative at all.

For Ángel Prado of El Maizal commune, the only possible saviors of the Bolivarian process are those who have saved it on every other occasion—and who today coalesce around the horizon of the commune: "It's radical Chavismo that participates in the commune, hardline Chavismo, those who have been Chavistas their entire lives... the grassroots sectors that withstood the *guarimba* protests [of 2014], that withstood the coup d'état and oil strike [of 2002–2003], that resisted all of these and neutralized the right wing."

If the government doesn't embrace this hard core of Chavismo, it can't possibly hope to survive. "And if the government—with all of the challenges of imports, hoarding, and prices—is fucked, who else can solve this? We can, the communes... because we don't depend on the state." The wager today is the wager of always, one best expressed by the late Venezuelan writer Aquiles Nazoa: "I believe in the creative powers of the people."

As the crisis deepens and divides the state against itself, setting the opposition-controlled National Assembly against the Maduro government, anything is possible. The only certainty is that the tipping point is rushing forth to greet us, and Chavismo will either move decisively to the left or retreat to the right. But retreat would be as cowardly as it is naive—as goes the commune, so goes the Bolivarian Revolution as a whole. As Chávez himself often put it, the choice on the table is increasingly between *la comuna o nada*, the commune or nothing.

Dual Power and Revolution

Symbiosis Research Collective (John Michael Colon, Mason Herson-Hord, Katie S. Horvath, Dayton Martindale, and Matthew Porges)

A Prologue by Mason Herson-Hord

Reflecting back on this piece of our writing from fall 2016, I find it extraordinary to see how much has changed in the movement landscape in the United States—and despite the extent of these changes, how much in this essay still rings true.[1]

In our essay we described a world in a state of intractable crisis, a diagnosis far truer today than in the time it was written. The entire Trump presidency was a time of escalating militancy and popular mobilization. Independent grassroots labor action coincided with terrifying new expansions of far-right paramilitary force; the nativist brutality of the new administration met unprecedented levels of political action by the previously uninvolved and disconnected. Fittingly, it was the final year that was most rocked by crisis and mass resistance. Between the pandemic, the domestic rebellions in cities across the country following the murder of George Floyd, the multiple ecological catastrophes of the summer and fall, and the general madness of the election and its aftermath, 2020 in the United States left nothing untouched.

Abandoned by our government, with hope for a livable future slipping away before our eyes, we in the millions stepped onto the pavement to fight for the dignity and lives of the most oppressed among us against the murderous forces of the most powerful. A majority of these participants experienced the thrill and the power of collective action for the first time in their lives, and in multiple cities they learned through the unrivaled teacher of direct experience that it was actually possible to challenge American police forces and physically expel them from a given space. The political confidence of the masses, the tactical sophistication of street militants, and the number of politically conscious youth coming of age in a time of turmoil all dramatically exceed the state of things less than five years ago.

The movement also experienced the limitations and exhaustions of struggle by street action alone, of mobilization absent deep organization. In the places where the anti-police struggle burned hottest, local movements found themselves on that cusp between abolition as confronting the police state and abolition as enacting a new social order where it had been driven out. This took the form of multiple temporary direct seizures of urban land and buildings, repurposed to communal ends. Experiments in assembly democracy grew out of these spaces by the very necessity of their administration by the people. But here our essay was prescient in a negative sense as well: cobbled together in the moment of struggle, these institutions lacked the time to learn-by-doing the practices of democratic self-governance, as well as the majority participation necessary to secure much in the way of popular legitimacy. Absent such preformation of the postrevolutionary society, as we put it in 2016, the cop-free occupations could hardly sustain themselves, much less pose a serious threat to the state. In the summer of 2020, it was clearer to me than ever why the Zapatistas took for their symbol the humble snail, *el caracol*. Revolutionary democracy is a project of decades, not of days, involving more listening than street battles.

All of this is new data in the annals of the social laboratories of our movements, which must be reread and rewritten in each passing generation. Even in their failures, political experiments like the Capitol Hill Autonomous Zone can—and must—inform our strategic thinking for the future. Defeats that we learn from, that sharpen our vision and steel our resolve, are not defeats but victory deferred. For me these illustrate the necessity of a mass politics that is not merely oppositional but reconstructive, not merely acting in response to the demands of the present moment but taking upon itself the slow and steady work of building institutions of self-determination and autonomy for the many moments to come. If there is any key insight in our reprinted essay that I would insist on repeating in our new era of struggle, it is this. We cannot wait until the iron is hot to build our anvils.

Nearly five years of additional political experience behind us, it has become clear that the greatest weakness of this essay was its drafting in political isolation. Occupy was dead and gone, though its ghost shadowed much of what was to follow. Most left-wing political energy in the United States was coupled to the failed Sanders presidential bid and focused on readying itself for resistance to the incoming Trump presidency. The Movement for Black Lives and the Standing Rock occupation had heated up and served as major entry points for political radicalization, but to much of the Left in the United States, radical democracy as a political project seemed like something to be in solidarity with from afar, that Americans only learned about through the struggles of Rojava and Chiapas. Being ourselves disconnected from other emerging local struggles and the rethinking of revolutionary strategy that accompanied them, we thought of the essay project as crafting a new synthesis out of our own studies of movement history, the ideas of an array of dead theorists, and the piecemeal elements of a potential dual power we saw through our own inexperienced, embryonic organizing work in Detroit. This sense of being politically alone was reflected in our naive initial plan to focus on building a replicable model of this dual power strategy in Detroit over a period of many years, after which a wider network of local movements elsewhere could be assembled based on that model's successes.

When this essay—originally published as "Community, Democracy, and Mutual Aid: Toward Dual Power and Beyond"—was announced the winner of the Next System Project's essay competition, we were thrown into contact with far more readers and fellow organizers than we ever anticipated and found ourselves facing a far more exhilarating reality.

The piece resonated not because its ideas were unique or new but because it articulated a convergence of revolutionary thought that was actively underway from a diverse set of starting points. Between entering the orbit of the Institute for Social Ecology alongside a number of other young assembly democracy organizers, helping found the Libertarian Socialist Caucus of the Democratic Socialists of America, and taking part in other face-to-face gatherings of similarly minded activists and thinkers in Montreal, New York City, and Vermont, we were able to share in an exchange of ideas and organizing experiences with a wide array of people committed to the project of building a genuinely democratic society from the ground up. For the first time we met our comrades in Cooperation Jackson and read their theoretical and practical work laid out in *Jackson Rising: The Struggle for Economic Democracy and Black*

Self-Determination in Jackson, Mississippi—which we were woefully unfamiliar with at the time of our own writing but now use as a principal text for political education in our organizations.

Over the course of 2018 and 2019, out of these new relationships we stitched together Symbiosis, a network of various radical projects putting these core ideas of direct democracy, solidarity economy, and dual power into practice. We sought to learn from each other's experiences in our different local contexts, discuss our shared principles, and plan how we could work together into the future. In September 2019, we gathered in person in Detroit as the Congress of Municipal Movements. Over a hundred people—most of them elected delegates representing organizations such as Cooperation Jackson, Radio Fogata Cherán, Asamblea de los Pueblos Indígenas del Istmo en Defensa de la Tierra y el Territorio, Carbondale Spring, and dozens more—spent five days together in shared meals and discussion. We hammered out the beginnings of a North American federation of revolutionary grassroots organizations committed to building dual power in our own communities.

The congress was not without conflicts and challenges. Most related in some way to the central problem of any self-constituting process: deciding how to decide. Many of our organizations were interacting in person for the first time, and we faced major differences in organizational culture with respect to how exactly we practice democracy, which were only ultimately overcome through relationship and humility. The accumulated wisdom of the Indigenous assembly democracy movement in Oaxaca, brought to the rest of us by their delegate Bettina, was indescribably valuable for breaking through. At the time when frustrations and tensions were at their highest, Bettina stepped up to speak not on what she thought we ought to do, but on how challenging and slow, yet in due time successful, La Asamblea's attempts to bring together various community organizations and assemblies in the Isthmus of Tehuantepec had been. She said that even to be in this room together was a victory, and to build on it requires only patience. *El caracol* extends from his spiral shell again. Months later, as we finished gathering consensus on our final draft of our shared principles, the last point of unity channeled her as it concluded: "The road is long, and we must walk it together."

The matter of time, of the pace of democracy and of revolutionary struggle, is one that has hovered at the edge of my conscious thoughts over the past several years. There is no question that 2020 was a turning point, but turning to what, and on what timescale ought this turn be imagined?

Indeed, in the aftermath and aftershocks of 2020, many revolutionary organizers in Symbiosis and elsewhere that I have spoken with are in a process of reflection, regrouping, and recovery. We have all learned much over the past two years of street action, mutual aid disaster response, and mobilization, and we must also reorient ourselves to a new terrain of struggle. Whether or not we have any respite from the crises that will likely continue to punctuate the 2020s, a deepening and a maturation of our movements will be necessary to meet the challenges ahead: to shift, in the language of Grace Lee Boggs, from the sporadic outbursts of rebellion to the sustained social transformation of revolution.

I believe this deepening is underway, in the theoretical clarity of our radical democracy movements most of all. Nonetheless there remain a number of thorny questions before us.

What does robust internal democracy in our organizations look like? How are differences in degree of participation, experience, proximity to a given project's founding, and available time managed in cultivating a participatory, nonhierarchical mode of movement organization that does not replicate the oppressive dynamics of our wider society? Hardest of all, how can this best operate at scale, for initiatives like Symbiosis?

Further: How do we build political spaces that are not self-selected? What kinds of organizing practices can break a revolutionary minority out of such self-imposed social isolation and into building mass organization of ordinary people? How do we navigate the democratic tensions between such mass organizations' role as directly democratic expressions of popular power and the role of ideological cadres in organizing them, when it comes to their political content? Is political education really a means of bridging such gaps, and if it is, how concretely do we build it into our mass organizing? How, in other words, do we go to the people?

And, for the long haul: How do we take seriously the conquest of political power by these institutions of direct democracy? What do we even mean by political power in such a context, and what avenues might exist to secure it? How do mass disruption and defensive violence relate to the establishment of revolutionary democracy? How can the use of force be prevented from strangling the free and equal democratic participation that is the very foundation of our political project?

Some of these are explored (if not answered) in our original essay. Others have seen serious attempts to think them through in the more recent writings of our comrades, some of which are collected in this very volume. All of them will require deep consideration within our movements: not by individual thinkers at their keyboards but in the spaces of mutual reflection and deliberation we foster between us, and in the spaces of political experimentation we seed in our communities.

Above all else, however, the question occupying my mind is this: when the time comes, when the next crisis descends, will we be ready? That one may be answered only in deed. We snails have a long, meandering journey ahead. So long as we follow it together, we may yet arrive.

Introduction

Five years ago, the Arab Spring reclaimed public spaces across the Middle East and North Africa, demonstrating to a new generation the possibilities for creative resistance and political imagination under even the most repressive circumstances. They sparked a Movement of the Squares that swept the world, from the anti-austerity movement in Europe to Occupy Wall Street in the United States.

Adopting the slogan, "Another World Is Possible," Occupy offered one of the fiercest rebukes in a generation to the dominant narrative that ours is the best and only possible system. It demanded new forms of radical democracy outside the state and an end to unfettered capitalism—indeed, many Occupy offshoots attempted to create such a world in miniature.

Yet the utopian spirit that swept the globe in 2011 hasn't yielded comprehensive alternatives to the present political and economic system. Occupy and the movements it inspired have failed to answer the question of what that other world—the "next system"—should look like and how we can possibly get there.

Our aim in this essay is to channel our struggles against oppression and domination into a strategic approach toward building real utopias—to transform the poetry of Occupy into the prose of real social change. Both concrete and comprehensive, our proposal is to organize practical community institutions of participatory democracy and mutual aid that can take root, grow, and gradually supplant the institutions that now rule ordinary people's lives.

By meeting communal needs and channeling our communities' collective action through organs of radical democracy, we aim to develop institutions that can both build popular power against unresponsive oligarchy and be the very replacements for capitalism that the Left is so frequently criticized for failing to envision. This next system we imagine is a libertarian ecosocialism grounded in the direct participation of citizens rather than the unaccountable authority of elites; in the social ownership of the economy rather than exploitation; in the equality of human beings rather than the social hierarchies of race, gender, nationality, and class; in the defense of our common home and its nonhuman inhabitants rather than unfettered environmental destruction; and in the restoration of community rather than isolation. Above all else, our aim is to lay out a framework for crafting such a society from the ground up—to, as the Wobblies declared, build the new world in the shell of the old.

Karl Marx famously criticized utopians as trying to "write recipes for the cookshops of the future." By this, he meant that utopians imagine they can design a new society from scratch and bring it into being by sheer force of will. When they inevitably fail, they are doomed to disappointment and disillusionment. By contrast, Marx's method of analysis grapples with the complex and dynamic process by which societies change. He believed that only by carefully examining the social relations, incentive structures, and class dynamics of a society can we understand its path going forward. In Marx's view, every social system is a complex process rather than a static essence, and each system contains the seeds of its successor, which need only be encouraged to grow for change to come about.

In our view, the answer to political change lies between the utopians and Marx. There is some truth to Marx's claim that describing a desired future is a waste of time; devising complex utopias does little to guide us politically or strategically if it is divorced from the process through which such ideas could feasibly come about. Yet neither can we sit by critiquing the current economic and political landscape while we wait for "inevitable" revolution. The next-system vision spelled out here can and must be enacted in our communities today as an essential, intermediate step toward realizing a revolutionary vision for the planet.

The next system is more likely to succeed and endure if we steadily transform existing institutions, modes of production, and ways of relating to one another rather than try to conjure up a whole new system out of thin air. The heart of our argument is that building networks of radically democratic, cooperative institutions can sustain our communities and our collective struggle in the near term, organize our base to win fights with the state and private sector, begin eroding public support for the current dysfunctional system, and, in time, become the dominant institutions of tomorrow's world. Our proposal integrates process and objective, with democracy and community as both the means and the ends of social transformation. Filling in the gaps between "scientific" socialist analysis and utopian imagination, we have attempted something the Left has always struggled to create: a realistic transition model to a postcapitalist world.

Our Democratic Crisis

Today's political situation hangs in a limbo of crisis, in which nothing fundamentally changes despite a seemingly endless series of catastrophes. Capitalism's structural imperatives for endless growth and privatized gain for externalized costs have pushed our global climate rapidly toward the brink of total destabilization. Habitat destruction, overexploitation of resources, and pollution have eroded the ecological base of (human and nonhuman) communities the world over, driving the worst mass extinction event since an asteroid wiped out the dinosaurs. A tiny transnational ruling class leverages its position in the global economy to extract extraordinary amounts of untaxed wealth and keep billions in poverty. Divided global working classes compete for survival in a race to the bottom. Even the middle classes in rich countries have been hollowed out and robbed of political power as postwar social democracy has morphed into neoliberalism.

"Democratic" institutions, supposedly designed to secure the common good through the power of an enfranchised public, seem powerless to stop any of this. The power of ordinary people over their own lives has eroded from the 1970s onward as capitalist elites have recaptured the state and returned us to an era of privatization, deregulation, and austerity while nationalist and neofascist movements scapegoat the vulnerable in response. Meanwhile, imperial adventurism continues to displace millions through ever new wars and conflicts. The likelihood of further economic crisis and the looming ecological cliff all promise to intensify the global trend toward suffering, violence, and tyranny beyond anything seen yet.

Underlying this systemic crisis is a deficit of democracy. The European Union and global financial institutions (which exert considerable control over the policy decisions of indebted developing nations dependent on investment and trade from the Global North) are managed by an unelected technocracy beholden to transnational capitalist interests. A rigorous quantitative study of American politics recently demonstrated that the policy preferences of the lowest earning 90 percent of Americans have no independent effect on government policy decisions; instead, lawmakers respond exclusively to the interests of corporations and the wealthiest 10 percent. As the authors conclude, "America's claims to being a democratic society are seriously threatened."[2] Even in allegedly democratic nations, the institutions that channel national decision-making are structurally incapable of staving off ecological and economic collapse and securing a decent life for everyone. What we face is a colossal collective action problem.

Our Theory of Social Change

The German American political philosopher Hannah Arendt argued that intolerable situations such as ours could be cast aside by the public's revolutionary withdrawal of support from governing institutions. As a prominent theorist of totalitarianism, political violence, and direct democracy, Arendt developed important concepts that help disentangle the problems humanity currently faces and indicate a way forward.[3]

Power is conventionally understood in politics as the ability to make others do things, often through violence or coercion to enforce obedience and domination. In *On Violence*, however, Arendt demonstrates that power works quite differently in actual human societies. She defines "power" as people's ability to act in concert—the capacity for collective action, and thus a property of groups, not individuals. Leaders possess their power only because their constituents have empowered them to direct the group's collective action.

Arendt argues that all power, in every political system from dictatorships to participatory democracies, emerges from public support. No dictator can carry out his or her will without obedience from subjects; nor can any project requiring collective action be achieved without the support, begrudging or enthusiastic, of the group. When people begin to withdraw their support and refuse to obey, a government may turn to violence, but its control lasts only as long as the army or police choose to obey. "Where commands are no longer obeyed," Arendt writes, "the means of violence are of no use.... Everything depends on the power behind the violence."[4] The understanding that power emerges from collective action, rather than from force, is a key component of our transitional vision.

As a revolutionary political strategy, however (rather than a mere description of certain past political events), Arendt's theory of power requires several modifications. First, without preexisting mass organization, the public has no way to collectively withdraw its support.

Individuals acting alone have no impact on the state's power. This is why Arendtian revolutions (Hungary in 1956, Czechoslovakia in 1989, and Tunisia in 2011) occur only in exceedingly rare moments of crisis.

Second, most people will never even consider retracting support for governing institutions if they don't see viable alternatives. As Antonio Gramsci explained a century ago, the ruling class's cultural hegemony can be undermined only by what he called a "war of position"— developing a material and cultural base within the working class to craft an oppositional narrative and to organize oppositional institutions.[5] The organization of unions, worker-owned firms, and housing cooperatives is what makes socialism a real, lived possibility around which greater movement-building can occur.

Third, withdrawal has serious costs. Even absent violent repression (a feature of even today's most liberal democracies), we are made dependent on capitalist and state institutions for access to basic survival needs and avenues for collective action. Transcending capitalism and the state thus requires having alternative institutions in place to meet those needs and organize people to act powerfully in concert with one another. Retracting support without engaging in such oppositional institutions is hardly distinguishable from apathy.

Fourth, we cannot neglect the preformation of the postrevolutionary society—the need to actively create institutions to replace the ones we have now. Arendt has somewhat romantic notions of the forms of organic democratic politics that emerge in the vacuum following a mass public retraction of support for governing institutions. To a certain extent, history is on her side.

The Syrian Kurds' democratic confederalism in Rojava; the workers' councils of revolutionary Russia, Germany, and Hungary; the Paris Commune; Argentina's factory takeovers; and Catalonia's anarchist revolution all exemplify community-rooted participatory politics emerging out of revolutionary crisis. More complex institutional arrangements to manage and coordinate society as a whole, however, are beyond the reach of spontaneous face-to-face democracy. Far from expressing public will, such institutions are usually seized or assembled by whichever party or faction is best positioned to capitalize on the conditions of vacuum and uncertainty (as Arendt herself notes and criticizes).[6] A revolutionary transfer of authority to popular organs of radical democracy requires the preexistence of such participatory institutions, not a naive faith that they will be conjured into being out of a general strike, mass retraction of public support, or insurrectionary upheaval.

Arendt's analysis of the sources of state power, we contend, generally applies to capitalist institutions too (though they are, of course, shored up by the state). These can be supplanted only by creating sustainable, egalitarian alternatives to sap their public dependency and approval. An effective political strategy for the present must combine the best of Arendt's intuitions about the workings of power in society and possibilities for popular revolution, with an organizing vision of community institution building. With such dim prospects for sufficient progress through existing institutional channels, new democratic and cooperative institutions must be built from the ground up.

In early stages, crafting the political infrastructure of radical democracy and libertarian socialism will be mainly local, through outgrowths and codifications of existing social processes that can be expanded into mainstream practice and incorporated into a broader strategy. The community institutions proposed here are modular. They can stand alone as individual projects, fine-tuned to solve specific problems created by the current system's failures, but they are designed to be organized as a network. By working together and mutually reinforcing one another, these institutions can qualitatively change the power relations of a city or neighborhood and lay the groundwork for new macro-structures of self-governance and civil society. Through engineering and managing new institutions of their own, communities can cultivate a creative and communal spirit that will empower them to take control of their lives, connect to one another across cultural and geographic distances, and develop the egalitarian foundations of a new society. Only such a process serves as the basis of a truly democratic ecosocialism.

Most of the community institutions discussed here are not new inventions but have been developed through generations of popular struggle all over the world. The challenge taken up here is to synthesize them into a unified anti-capitalist strategy at every level of society.

Particular institutional arrangements will likely depend on local needs and conditions, but possibilities include worker-owned cooperatives, neighborhood councils, community land trusts, local food distribution systems, mutual aid networks, community-owned energy, popular education models, time banks, childcare centers, community health clinics, and more. Specific institutions will be discussed as illustrative examples of political possibilities, but the understanding is that radical democracy means ordinary people possess the power to innovate, modify, discard, or replace them as they wish, as part of a global conversation of open-source experimentation. Underpinning this strategic vision is a spirit of pragmatism. If what a community builds works, it can be exported elsewhere with local adjustments—much as the goals and protest methods of the Movements of the Squares were rapidly adopted and adapted by social movements around the world.

Our organizing vision has roots from across the history of revolutionary movements for freedom and justice. We draw our inspiration and intellectual development from, among others, autonomist Marxism, Zapatismo, the alt-globalization movement, the new anarchists, the civil rights and Black power movements, the Alinskyist community organizing tradition, asset-based community development, anarcho-syndicalism, council communism, social ecology, and the movement for a social solidarity economy. Using the following proposal as a starting point, our goal is to synthesize these wide-ranging currents of thought into a movement organization engaged in community institution building and organizing work spanning housing, energy, food, healthcare, technology, labor, education, ecological restoration, and other issues. Here, we will further explore the precursors to this sort of organizing, how we can build on those political traditions through community institution building, and how such institutions can be integrated into a revolutionary framework for social, political, economic, and ecological transformation.

Lessons from the Past

In 1917, between the overthrow of the tsar in March and the October Revolution, Russian society saw a division of political authority into two oppositional forces governing society in parallel. The soviets, a network of radically democratic, autonomous workers' councils, operated alongside an official parliamentary Provisional Government that they were attempting to displace. The Petrograd Soviet in particular, which represented the city's workers and soldiers, competed with the Russian state for popular legitimacy. It incorporated delegates from other soviets around the country and refashioned itself as the All-Russian Congress of Soviets.

At the time, many Russian socialists referred to this political situation as *dvoyevlastiye*, or "dual power." Leon Trotsky wrote about dual power in his *History of the Russian Revolution*, and Vladimir Lenin argued that this bifurcation of authority was fundamentally volatile and could give way to a revolutionary overthrow of the republican Provisional Government. At the time, however, "dual power" was essentially descriptive. The American anarchist theorist Murray Bookchin was the first to flesh out the concept into a strategic framework for transformative politics. In his political blueprint, called "libertarian municipalism," confederations of directly democratic assemblies would be forced into conflict with the nation-state, making continued coexistence impossible.[7] We advocate a somewhat more flexible approach than Bookchin's—engaging with liberal democratic governments wherever possible to restructure them in a participatory and ecosocialist direction. Even so, his theoretical work on dual power is central to our strategy. The sections below explore how to build dual power in the here and now by modifying and transcending current approaches to community and labor organizing to create radically democratic community institutions. As North Americans, our focus will be primarily on the United States, but our proposal should be understood as a transnational project, inspired and guided by visionary organizers the world over.

Building On and Beyond Current Approaches to Organizing

Participatory democracy is at the core of our vision for organizing and institution building. When a community can decide for itself what its needs are and how to address them instead of receiving "solutions" from on high, the benefits are many. While the fields of organizing, social service provision, and international development are full of well-intentioned organizations and individuals who fail to understand this, a more positive illustrative example comes from Young Shin, the founder of the Asian Immigrant Women Advocates (AIWA).

In the early 1980s, Shin set out to organize Chinese and Korean immigrant women workers in the Oakland garment, hotel, and high-tech factory industries to fight rampant wage theft. When she spoke with these women, however, time and again they told her that their top priority was to learn English, not to organize. Shin was confused—as she tells it, most of the women worked, shopped, and did laundry without a word of English, and rarely had time to venture outside their immigrant enclaves. Why was learning English so important then? Were the women just looking to assimilate and individually ascend the social ladder?[8]

Shin trusted the workers, however, and the English classes she organized turned out to be pivotal. For starters, they allowed the women to stand up to their oppressors in the workplace.

One group of women told Shin that they wanted to be able to tell their boss to stop yelling at them and to treat them with respect. They recognized what Shin had not—that learning English was "a form of self-defense and self-affirmation."[9] The classes also helped the women learn their labor rights, situate themselves in all working women's historical struggle for justice, and push back against oppressive cultural norms regarding gender and the family.

Eventually, as they gained new skills and confidence, the women did take on wage theft and many other battles for labor justice. For Shin and for anyone who seeks to organize, it was an all-important lesson: the community knows what it needs better than anyone else does. Building directly democratic, cooperative institutions creates buy-in at an early stage and ensures that a community can make decisions in its own best interest. Direct democracy is also a form of popular education. Through it, people can develop political consciousness and practice living the ethic of horizontal collaborative democracy.

Murray Bookchin writes: Those forms of association where people meet face-to-face, identify their common problems, and solve them through mutual aid and volunteer community service.... serve, to greater or lesser degrees, as schools for democratic citizenship. Through participation in such efforts, we can become more socially responsible and more skilled at democratically discussing and deciding important social questions.[10]

Bridging divides of race, class, and gender can also be facilitated through a deliberative, democratic process, so long as that process is structured toward eliminating those inequalities.

Across all sites of organizing—workplaces, neighborhoods, and more—a genuinely transformative politics can be ushered in only through a framework of radical democracy. This means building up a network of neighborhood councils from the community level that can create and manage these institutions themselves. With that as our starting point, let's next consider the main currents of progressive organizing in the United States and ways that an ethic of participatory democracy for decision-making and a strategy of cooperative institution building can take those traditions to the next level.

Labor and the Cooperative Movement

Since the rise of industrial capitalism, worker struggles have cultivated a progressive politics voicing demands from survival to liberation. At minimum, labor movements demanded higher wages and a decent living standard for the average worker. At their most ambitious, they demanded the abolition of the wage system, the common ownership and democratic administration of key productive infrastructure, and a society where the people themselves determined the goals and exertion of their own labor. It is this latter, more radical labor movement that must be revived and expanded. Bargaining for a better share of economic surplus without transforming the ownership structure of the economy itself is not a strategy that can succeed in the long term.

Despite the temporary successes of mid-century social democracy—"successes" that inadequately addressed matters of ecology, race, gender, and internationalism—the present neoliberal consensus has driven unionization to an all-time low. Unions have been curtailed by mass unemployment, the casualization of work, anti-labor laws in developed countries, and violent political repression in industrializing ones. The traditional industrial proletariat is no longer well defined or large enough to be the single revolutionary agent, and perhaps never was.

Now, though, there is an opportunity to situate the industrial proletariat as a prominent wing within a broader democratic struggle, not just against wage labor but against racial and sexual oppression, hierarchy, ecological destruction, the state, and perhaps even work itself. A better socioeconomic system can only be won by a cross-class international coalition among peasants, proletarians, social movements beyond labor, and progressive elements of the middle classes. The labor movement should be conceptualized as a central pillar of that struggle but not equated with the struggle itself.

Workers have already begun to organize outside the boundaries of traditional industrial unionism. Innovative methods include creating cross-class alliances and unionization drives at such labor hubs as hospitals, airports, and universities; defying union bureaucracies to advocate for union democracy; and creating nonprofit organizations, worker centers, and other autonomous working-class institutions.

One of the most promising worker institutions for achieving workplace democracy is the worker's cooperative. Since worker ownership of the means of production is socialism's central demand, transforming individual workplaces into sites of democratic worker self-management is a crucial step for creating direct democracy and socializing the economy at large. By giving workers direct control over firms, cooperatives provide democratic control over sectors of the economy and an escape from wage labor, free of state intervention. But cooperatives also suffer from important problems—some borne of their failure as firms, others from their success.

Studies have shown co-ops to be even more competitive than oligarchic capitalist firms of the same scale once they get started—but "once they get started" is the key phrase. The major weakness of co-ops, and the reason for their scarcity, is the enormous difficulty of financing them. Unlike wealthy entrepreneurs, typical workers at median wage have very little capital to proffer, making whatever small initial investment they can raise essentially an all-or-nothing risk for them.

Absent venture capital, worker-owned firms must turn to banks. In today's for-profit credit system, banks are inherently skeptical of firms with an experimental structure that allows production to be structured around goals besides maximized profits, such as the livelihood of workers or the common good. Thus, most lenders demand either a significant amount of capital as collateral or a role for their agents in the start-up's decision-making processes, up to and including a potential ownership stake (which compromises the very workplace democracy that is a co-op's fundamental goal).[11] Given these constraints, a huge number of cooperatives fail before ever being given the chance to succeed. Even those that do jump the hurdles are often limited to relatively small-scale activities (supermarkets, restaurants, bike shares, etc.).

On the flip side, co-ops that do succeed face other problems. Mondragon—a network of cooperatives in Spain with over 74,000 worker-owners and €12 billion in assets—supports a wide range of industries and programs and has implemented some degree of internal democracy. Yet it also demonstrates many of the limitations of even successful cooperatives. One of Mondragon's first problems (as early as the 1960s) was that its worker-owners became concerned primarily with their own prosperity and neglected participation in the broader anti-Franco struggle.[12] More recently and perhaps more distressingly, the cooperative's internal democracy has slowly eroded amid reforms meant to keep it competitive with capitalist firms. Between 1985 and 1991, the component worker-owned co-ops of the Mondragon network ceded most of their decision-making power to the Mondragon Cooperative Corporation, a centralized holding company whose elected upper management was largely unaccountable to the worker-shareholders except in largely symbolic annual general assemblies. At about the same time, Mondragon began hiring legions of wage workers (nonowners) in its foreign subsidiaries. By 2014 only 40 percent of Mondragon's employees were worker-owners who had voting power in the cooperative.[13]

The lesson here is that an institution beyond the worker-owned firm is needed to provide an incentive against self-exploitation as co-ops come under pressure to adapt to survive within capitalism. Macroeconomic structures that would help a cooperative economy thrive—such as a large-scale nonprofit credit system and limits on corporations' use of sweatshop labor—are largely beyond what cooperatives themselves can create.

And insofar as cooperatives are part of a capitalist society, they also face pressures to exploit the consumer or commodify things that should not be commodified (such as health care or artistic creation). Even a democratically run power company, for example, could exploit its monopoly over electricity to price gouge consumers should its workers decide to make a higher profit—unless energy, along with other necessities, were taken off the market altogether and its provision coordinated some other way. It is not enough, then, to make a single workplace democratic (though it's a start). Cooperatives can achieve their potential only as parts of a more comprehensive struggle to remake the entire capitalist economy.

The Common Fund

How do we fund cooperatives, incentivize cooperation over competition, and tie these member institutions to an explicitly socialist politics? We propose a common fund, which would absorb the profits from a network of community-run cooperatives and pool money that communities could reinvest for economic development. It would be under the democratic control of the networked cooperatives' member-owners and would initially finance additional cooperatives to further grow that network. As it grows, the fund could invest in such profitless purposes as building new infrastructure, establishing other independent socialist institutions, and financing political movements to take over and reform local government along radically democratic lines.

Credit streams through nonextractive finance from organizations such as the Working World are a particularly good starting point for worker ownership. The Working World fund's initial capital was raised from donations, investment capital, and the profits of the successful workers' cooperatives that control it. The organization uses this mixed capital stream to offer zero-interest loans and educational support to newly founded worker co-ops or existing firms transferring ownership to workers. Uniquely, the fund accepts no loan repayment until the co-op begins to turn a profit, and even then, it gets paid back strictly as a percentage of profits. (In months without profit, the firm pays nothing.) The Working World has funded over two hundred worker-controlled companies around the world, and it has been so successful that it is now spearheading the development of a network of local funds for cooperatives.[14] The fund currently needs local organizers to set up local credit institutions and incubate new co-ops; and answering that call would be a powerful addition to the labor organizing and grassroots cooperative development proposed here. Such a network of funds—if democratically controlled and funded from the bottom-up—can form the basis of a new cooperative economy and a new communally engaged labor movement.

There is no doubt that an organized worker's struggle is important. But the union movement of the past developed institutions primarily to leverage their collective action within capitalism. Now these proletarian institutions must replace capitalism.

Rules for Radicals Are Made to Be Broken

Community organizing in the United States has historically been dominated by a model known as "institution-based community organizing" (or "broad-based community organizing"). This model evolved mid-century out of Saul Alinsky's work in Chicago neighborhoods and the Southern Christian Leadership Conference's civil rights organizing across the South. The legacy of the civil rights movement is obviously central in the progressive political imagination, and Alinsky's *Rules for Radicals* is still used as a foundational handbook for organizing. The central idea of this model is that such community institutions as labor unions and religious congregations are already internally organized and already have community buy-in, making them the perfect vehicle for more powerful organizing in the community's interest. The civil rights movement, for example, was organized through the existing strength of the Black church. Major organizing networks based on this legacy continue to use the methodology of institution-based, largely faith-based organizing across the United States, and public-interest advocacy organizations draw upon the Alinskyist tradition in their campaigns on many issues.

Institution-based organizing relies on two premises that we question, however. One is that community institutions already exist, ripe for organizing. The other is that representative democracy can still be made to work for the people if only they are engaged enough and apply enough pressure.

In recent decades, community institutions in America have crumbled under the advance of the neoliberal state, the dismantling of organized labor, the privatization of public space and public schools, the closing of recreation and community centers, and the waning importance of organized religion to many people, especially younger generations. Simply put, working through today's community institutions does not get us very far if there is a dearth of them and if the surviving ones are less important than they once were to many citizens.

Using existing institutions to demand concessions from power also fails to achieve the full potential of Alinsky's own "iron rule of organizing"—never do for others what they can do for themselves. In institution-based organizing, the iron rule means that professional organizers should emphasize training and leadership development in the community, rather than running campaigns on behalf of the community. The former method builds power and grows the organization or movement; the latter stifles it. Although the philosophy behind the iron rule is sound, institution-based organizing does not take it far enough. Training people to apply pressure to the levers of power in a (barely) representative democracy still means ultimately relying on others—mostly unresponsive "elected" officials and undemocratic institutions—to make changes on behalf of a community, rather than initiating those changes oneself.

Institution-based organizing networks and the sprawling ecosystem of public interest advocacy groups also subscribe to another core Alinskyist principle: that the issues they take up must be concrete, immediate, and winnable. In our experience, these strictures have limited the scope of what such organizations consider possible and the extent to which they can change the basic structures of society.

As community organizers Francis Calpotura and Kim Fellner ask: Do fights for incremental changes necessarily contain, or even lead to, a critique of prevailing social and economic structures, or do they only redivide the same pie in other ways? Increasingly since the 1960s, we are also asking: Do organizations that engage in these fights—purportedly to alter relations of power between the powerful and the dispossessed—build more just and equitable internal structures or do they merely replicate the patterns and culture of the larger society?[15]

The model proposed here does focus on the concrete practices of meeting community interests and does involve taking immediate winnable steps—but the focus is always on a larger vision of systemic transformation.

Although it must draw upon this legacy of community organizing, the transition to our next system must prioritize building up new communal institutions of democratic self-governance and self-sufficiency rather than working through the traditional organizing model that eschews service provision. Creating and organizing these institutions are means for building the community's power, preparing it to wage more traditional organizing campaigns when needed to force the government or private sector to act in the community's interest. At the same time, these democratic cooperatives can be ends in themselves, filling in the gaps of the shrinking welfare state through networks of mutual aid and direct action where and when the state and private sector fail to respond to citizen needs or demands.

The best American precursor to this aspect of the model is the Black Panther Party. Even so, the full radical potential of its organizing model was left unrealized. Founded in 1966, the Black Panthers articulated a vision of Black power and revolutionary socialism in opposition to American militarism, the impoverishment of Black communities, and police violence. Their "Serve the People Programs" included free breakfasts for hungry schoolchildren, a cooperative shoe factory, community health clinics and education centers, and cooperative housing for low-income people.[16] They often illustrated the programs' function with the metaphor of being stranded on a life raft—the community must take practical steps to stay alive in the present, but never forget that the real goal is to make it to shore, to revolution. The Panthers understood these programs as "survival pending revolution"—a means of sustaining their communities until they could achieve liberation.

Survival programs proved to the community that the Black Panthers were serious about improving Black people's lives. This approach let the Panthers build power where revolutionary rhetoric alone would have failed, and membership swelled. Even so, such programs could have been structured toward building power even more than they were. If they address more than mere survival, by building the structures of a society autonomous from and in opposition to the state and capital, survival programs can become liberation programs as well. By meeting basic community needs, such institutions rupture capitalism's control over people's lives, allowing oppressed people to carve out space within capitalism, defend it, and thus transform the world around them. This relationship between "survival work" and "liberation work" is a core theme of the political vision developed here.

The Black Panther Party's successes and failures have much to teach us about winning real victories in the present. We intend to draw upon the Black Panther tradition while taking their model to the next level.

Revolutionary Institution-Building in Practice

How can these moving parts in our strategic framework work together as a powerful revolutionary force? Below we use the First Palestinian Intifada to demonstrate that integrating institutions of mutual aid and participatory democracy can mobilize all of society into an effective resistance movement. Then we lay out a blueprint for scaling up this sort of organizing to a revolutionary transition in an American city.

Organizing for the First Intifada

The First Intifada broke out in late 1987 as a mass uprising against the Israeli occupation of the Palestinian territories. It was one of the most powerful popular mobilizations in recent history, largely responsible for the Oslo Accords and the formation of the Palestinian Authority as a framework for achieving Palestinian independence. The flaws of this framework notwithstanding, this popular struggle upended the previous consensus around the de facto annexation of the occupied territories and the impossibility of a Palestinian state, changing the course of the conflict forever.

Most discussion of the First Intifada focuses on the role of mass protest in making Palestinian society ungovernable for Israeli occupying forces. Less discussed is the role of community organizations of mutual aid and confederated participatory democracy in making such mass protest possible. The brief overview below shows how these institutions laid the groundwork for and sustained a revolutionary upheaval against one of the most totalitarian political orders of that time.

Organizing within the prison system was a political incubator of the Palestinian resistance movement and offers a microcosmic example of the development of dual power in the much larger prison of the occupation. With hunger strikes, political prisoners eventually won concessions for their own self-administration within the prisons. They assembled structures of political organization and representation, forced prison authorities to recognize those representatives, and developed a division of labor around hygiene, education, and other daily tasks. Palestinian prisoners described this arrangement as *tanthim dakhili* (internal organization), similar to the concept of dual power. Even in the least free of circumstances, these prisoners carved out space for self-governance and created the preconditions for revolutionary struggle.

Prisoners taught and studied everything from Palestinian history to Marxist political economy, often for eight to fourteen hours per day.[17] As these freshly educated and trained political activists were released back into society, the resistance movement was galvanized. Illiterate teenage boys arrested for throwing stones reentered the fray months later as committed, competent organizers who had studied movement building, strategic civil resistance, and dialectical materialism.

Meanwhile, the organizing context outside of prison transformed dramatically. Saleh Abu-Laban, a Palestinian political prisoner from 1970 until 1985, stated, "When I entered prison there wasn't a 'national movement'; there were only underground cells that performed clandestinely. When I got out I found a world full of organizations, committees, and community institutions."[18]

Central to this new world of community organizing was the Palestinian labor movement. Unions were formed out of workers' places of residence rather than workplaces because migrant labor was prevalent and Palestinian unionism within Israel had been criminalized. Unions then formed strong alliances with local organizations in the national movement. With rapid growth in the early 1980s, labor unions found it necessary to decentralize and democratize their structure to become more resilient as Israeli repression intensified against union leaders and organizers.[19] These local unions were networked together through the Palestinian Communist Party and the Workers' Unity Bloc, creating a web of labor organizers and community groups that linked their class struggle to the larger project of national liberation.

Young people also played a vital role. They organized student associations at high schools and universities. There, they assembled demonstrations, set up volunteer committees serving refugee camps and poorer villages, and funneled youth into the national movement. Youth cultivated solidarity practices that were crucial during the uprising, including the formation of a largely student-run national mutual aid network to coordinate service delivery among dozens of local committees.

The Palestinian women's movement was perhaps the most important of all in laying the groundwork for the First Intifada.[20] These feminist organizers started by addressing their members' real material needs, but deliberately oriented these projects toward the higher goals of women's liberation and Palestinian national liberation.

The women's committees they formed brought together housewives and working women in cities and towns throughout the occupied territories. They set up classes and cottage industry cooperatives (managed along roughly anarcho-syndicalist lines, with one vote for each worker-member) for women looking to generate supplementary income.[21] Organizers went door-to-door in the poorer villages and refugee camps to reach women who were illiterate, economically dependent on men, and largely confined to private domesticity. Free cooperative childcare allowed these poorer women to join the co-ops, take literacy and vocational classes, and participate in women's committee politics.[22] The women's committees were a confederal system, with webs of individual committees democratically operating local projects. Each women's committee nominated a member to represent its members at a district/area committee, which in turn nominated representatives for the national body. These national women's committees built strong ties with labor unions, expanded mutual aid supply lines, and developed community leaders.

Such activities served multiple purposes. They made the conditions of military occupation more livable, sustaining Palestinian families in the face of relentless colonization. They provided individual women with greater economic independence, allowing them to slowly stretch the boundaries of patriarchal control and participate more actively in public life and the national movement. They laid the early foundations of the "home economy," which fostered Palestinian self-sufficiency and later provided the sustaining material support for economic resistance against the Israeli occupation, in forms such as boycotts and strikes. Finally, these women built up the community's organizational capacity to wage a broad-based social struggle drawing on all segments of Palestinian society.

These various local community institutions overlapped with one another cooperatively. Women's committees and voluntary work committees joined forces for many of their charitable projects, feminist organizers ran labor unions for garment workers, and political parties helped link different labor groups together. The labor, student, and women's movements eventually coalesced in the Intifada's most important political institution—*al-lijan al-sha'abiyya*, the popular committee—and gave birth to radically democratic council management of the community.[23]

When an Israeli military truck killed four Palestinians in the Jabalia refugee camp on December 8, 1987, a mass protest movement rapidly ignited across the territories. Huge demonstrations sprang up in every camp and city, demanding justice for the victims and an end to the occupation. By January 1988, popular committees had formed out of the social infrastructure of local unions, women's committees, student associations, political party organizing, and friendly neighbors across the West Bank and Gaza Strip. Committees carried out tasks for every social function imaginable: collecting garbage, determining local strike dates, collecting donations through an "alternative taxation system," distributing food and medical aid, repairing damaged buildings, organizing barricade building, developing local economic self-sufficiency, and more.

Like the women's committees, the popular committees coordinated with one another through a confederated structure. Local committees nominated delegates to represent them at area/municipal committees, which coordinated resistance activities among neighborhoods, camps, and nearby villages. These committees in turn elected representatives to a district committee, and district committees sent representatives to al-Qiyada al-Muwhhada, the secret Unified National Leadership of the Uprising (UNLU).[24] The UNLU first began distributing pamphlets in January 1988 detailing strike dates, boycotts of Israeli goods, marches, and other guidance for individual popular committees—such as calls to develop the "home economy," to withhold taxes from the occupying regime, and to resign from posts in the occupation government.[25]

This structure acted as a democratic confederalist shadow state, parallel and in opposition to the repressive and undemocratic military government, with enthusiastic nationalist legitimacy and organizational effectiveness to make up for its lack of monopoly on violence. It carried out a three-part strategy of resistance to the occupation: undermining the hegemony exercised by the occupation and its institutions, out-administering the occupation with parallel institutions to meet human needs, and creating a new nationalist hegemony to supplant the occupation.

This organizational structure also proved essential for coordinating local actions into territory-wide coherence. It gave ordinary Palestinians a voice in the direction of the struggle and the formation of their new society.[26] Building dual power from the ground up is what enabled the mobilization of the entire Palestinian public against its collective disenfranchisement and dispossession.

For those of us inspired by the rise of horizontalism in today's social movements, the First Intifada has much to teach us about the organizational conditions necessary for this ideal to be truly realized in a practical and powerful way.

Eventually, the scale of repression became too much for even this highly resilient model to bear. The imprisonment of the most experienced organizers and the paranoia about the wide network of paid or coerced informants in Palestinian society eventually fractured and then crumbled the Intifada's organizational capacity, and the movement collapsed. How the Palestinian liberation movement could have done better to overthrow the occupation regime is another discussion; the movement nonetheless illustrates how this form of grassroots democratic institution building can channel collective action on an incredible scale and empower participatory democracy and mutual aid as the guiding forces of a society. The end goal of the First Intifada was not to build libertarian socialism or radical democracy, but to replace the occupation with a democratic Palestinian state. Even so, a similarly structured movement with different goals could trace an analogous path, with greater success in a freer society like the US. For the Palestinians, libertarian socialism and radical democracy were means to national liberation; for us, they will be both means and ends.

Toward an American Dual Power

The First Palestinian Intifada proves the potential strength of putting the pieces of dual power organizing together. What would this organizing model look like transposed to an American context? As our example, we will use Detroit, Michigan—the city we know best and the one where we first intend to begin putting the ideas outlined here into practice. It is also one of the harder-hit cities in the current neoliberal crisis. Detroit's conditions of undemocratic governance, depressed property values, depopulation of the urban core, high point source pollution, tremendously powerful developers, high poverty rate, and racial segregation are more extreme than in most other cities, though not exceptionally so. Postindustrial cities across the Rust Belt and elsewhere present similar challenges and opportunities, and what works in Detroit will likely have cross applications.

What follows is an inexact blueprint of how organizers starting from present conditions can build dual power and libertarian ecosocialism in Detroit and, through parallel organizing work around the country and the world, scale up from there. To keep our overview concise and comprehensible, we confine this discussion of the envisioned evolution of democratic cooperative institutions to housing, food justice, energy, and neighborhood democracy—rather than attempting to outline a similar trajectory for every possible issue. These and many other institutions will be coordinated in a network and approached through the framework of strategic escalation. In other words, we start small with what we can do now, but simultaneously calculate each project and action to build power for the future and carry the struggle to multiple fronts of economic and political life.

Housing Equity

In this era of rapid urbanization worldwide, housing and real estate are central battlegrounds for class struggle. The power of developers and landlords over tenants and the public at large lets them extract wealth and resources, enforce artificial scarcity, expel poor residents from their communities through gentrification and "urban renewal," deprive human beings of their basic right to shelter, and suppress approaches to urban development that could uplift the common good. Yet it is the urban commons that gives prime real estate much of its value—through the infrastructure, culture, and humanity clustered around it. This social value that we all create is captured by a tiny rentier class at the expense of the rest of us.

Detroit is well situated for pioneering methods of fighting back against this social order. Most of the city has severely depressed property values but sits on the cusp of a major wave of gentrification (likely over the next twenty years). Low property values do not mean an absence of real estate capitalist interests and exploitation; since 2005, more than a third of all homes in Detroit have been foreclosed on due to mortgage default or tax delinquency. Concentrated development in downtown and midtown Detroit has simultaneously seeded a process of non-inclusive "comeback," carving out a white and middle-class pocket in an overwhelmingly Black and low-income city.

Rising property values drive the expulsion of poor residents in two ways. As demand rises in an area, landlords increase rents, and tenants who cannot afford those increased costs are evicted. At the same time, as appraised home values increase, so do tax burdens. If homeowners cannot afford their new property taxes, they will face tax foreclosure, have their home sold at auction, and be evicted. Many tenants who have paid rent are also evicted because their landlords failed to pay property taxes.

Organized efforts to keep foreclosed families in their homes are already underway.

Formed in 2014, the Tricycle Collective buys occupied homes at the county auction, often for considerably less than the back taxes owed, and signs ownership back to the occupants.[27] Although this form of temporary tax relief for such families is essential, it leaves them vulnerable to future tax delinquency and does nothing to change the structural forces of the real estate market that drive eviction, residential segregation, and gentrification. The only solution that guarantees housing for low-income citizens is socialization: removing housing from the market altogether.

In the short term, the institution best suited to creating an anti-gentrification bulwark of socialized housing run by the community is the community land trust (CLT). A CLT is a nonprofit legal entity entrusted with property management in the community's interest—ensuring affordable housing, preserving environmental assets, and driving cooperative neighborhood development. The leadership structure of a Detroit CLT, designed along radically democratic lines, would have recallable board members accountable to housing cooperative members and would subject policy changes to democratic approval.

Through this CLT, organizers would raise funds to purchase both abandoned and (with the homeowner's or renter's consent) inhabited properties, restore them, and secure them for income-adjusted affordable housing outside of the market. Like Habitat for Humanity's model, those who receive housing through the CLT would commit a certain number of labor hours (by themselves or someone else on their behalf) to future projects of home restoration to expand the cooperative housing system.[28] We would also assemble a tool library, cutting costs for both home renovation teams and the library's community members.

A CLT could create a varied landscape of housing aimed at fostering intentional community while meeting a diverse population's need for shelter. In essence, the housing system would maximize resident choice and create opportunities for experimentation in a variety of forms of cooperative living. Understandably, many individuals and families have no desire to live in communes, and an emphasis on expanding the cooperative sphere of daily life should not be a barrier to entry. However, many other people feel constrained by the alienation and limitations of current housing options. Revitalizing community and pushing back against our social atomization is an important aspect of all projects in this organizing model—rethinking living arrangements most of all.

Housing arrangements in this system would vary on two axes: duration of anticipated residence and degree of communality. On the first axis, housing options would range from emergency temporary shelter for those currently on the streets, to transitional housing for victims of abuse and domestic violence seeking refuge and those coming from temporary shelters as a starting point for receiving other social services (the housing-first model), to short-term housing for up to a year for university students or long-term visitors, to semipermanent housing from one to five years with extension available if needed, and, finally, to permanent housing for those planning to stay in a house or apartment indefinitely.

On the second axis, options would range from individual apartments and single-family homes to a variety of communal living situations. Some apartments would be redesigned so that residents have private living spaces connected to common spaces for recreation, cooking, and eating. Close-knit neighborhood blocks would be integrated with a food co-op, so that one building would house an expansive kitchen and dining room where everyone on the entire block gathers for meals, taking turns with weekly cooking and cleaning shifts.

Other large houses and residential complexes might become the sites of even more closely connected intentional communities. Common management of the home, shared rituals of belonging and deepening relationships, and collective child-rearing are all features of current intentional communities that such a housing system would nurture and expand. Some houses or apartments would also adopt the model of the Camp Hill and L'Arche communities, with people of varying physical and mental ability living in community alongside able-bodied and neurotypical people, or of mixed-age housing as an alternative to the segregation and pervasive abuse of the elderly in assisted living facilities.

Developing affordable cooperative housing options outside of the destabilizing real estate market is a meaningful stride toward preempting the expulsion of poor communities of color in Detroit. A CLT used in this way would foster community while laying groundwork for the liberated society.

Food and Environmental Justice

CLTs are also of use in building power to bring food justice to neglected communities. In many sites around the country, these institutions have been used to steward community gardens. Developing a cooperative, sustainable local food system is of utmost importance for both urban communities and the biosphere. Urban community gardens can simultaneously reclaim public space, expand civic participation and community social ties, and provide for people with little access to healthy food. In Detroit, where huge swaths of the city are food deserts, many parts of the city have already given rise to community gardens, but for the most part they aren't coordinated with one another or the people who need food the most. As with housing, the community land trust could partner with this dual power organization's social work arm to connect individuals and families to a mutual aid network supplying fresh produce from community gardens.

Even if radically expanded from their current small-scale, patchwork level, these gardens couldn't meet all of Detroit's food needs. But they would begin to replace an unsustainable and unhealthy industrial food system and to develop an informed food movement that can push for radical change in food production everywhere.

The capitalist food system, to put it mildly, desperately needs an overhaul. It is among the leading drivers of habitat destruction, climate change, and dangerous levels of soil and water pollution. By draining aquifers, poisoning environments with pesticides and herbicides, replacing complex ecosystems with industrial monocultures, and destabilizing the global nitrogen cycle through overreliance on petrochemical fertilizers, it erodes the ecological base that all agriculture (and life itself) depends on. Furthermore, the food this system produces is poorly distributed by the market. Eight hundred million people worldwide are undernourished, including 15 percent of American households and one in five American children. The worst offender is animal agriculture, with its inefficient land use and harm to water, air, soil, climate, wildlife habitat, and human health. Our farms and fisheries horrendously exploit human workers, inflict unconscionable abuse on the animals themselves, and wreak havoc on local ecosystems.

By making produce affordable and accessible, community gardens are an important step toward a plant-based food system.

This role for community gardens is not only material but ideological. Just as parent-run childcare co-ops both empower working-class women and challenge patriarchal norms, and just as restorative justice practices both reduce the power of police and prisons and challenge the dehumanizing and often racist beliefs underlying those institutions, so too would sustainable community gardens both feed people and challenge the rapacious logic of conventional agriculture. By adopting the principles of permaculture and agroecology in urban gardens and housing—that is, by integrating human society and food production within our ecosystems, rather than wiping them out—people become more conscious of their role in the food web and less alienated from the nonhuman world.

Community gardens should welcome everyone to contribute, regardless of ideology.

However, organizers should also work to pass on green and post-humanist ethics—deep respect for the interconnected living world of which we are a part—through the shared practice of cultivating the food that sustains us all. Without nurturing and transmitting these values, any socialist project is unlikely to succeed in the long run, as declining biodiversity threatens every society.

The ecological effort must ultimately go beyond food, impacting all aspects of society from clothing to scientific research to transit to recreation to resource extraction to waste management. Nonhuman interests must eventually be represented in structures of participatory democracy too, through human proxies to give them a voice and enshrined norms that make certain activities off-limits, analogous to current initiatives to provide legal rights to ecosystems and to individual nonhumans. But to get here, studies suggest, we need to help people develop an emotional attachment to nature.[29] A great place to start is in the garden.

Energy Democracy

Energy production, distribution, and consumption is another critical site of environmental and class struggle in the urban landscape. As in most US metropolitan areas, Detroit's energy grid is controlled by a state-backed private monopoly. The energy company (DTE) secured a 10 to 15 percent return on all infrastructural investments through price setting by state regulators. This is an especially exploitative and (as shown below) vulnerable model of energy capitalism. Effective, visionary organizers can help their communities bypass the corporate monopoly's price gouging and pollution through a community-owned grid of renewable, distributed generation supplying affordable electricity to all.

Since the Industrial Revolution, energy production has been complex and capital intensive, requiring technology and expertise that lent itself to elite-controlled centralization. In *Fossil Capital: The Rise of Steam Power and the Roots of Global Warming*, Andreas Malm argues that the switch from hydropower to coal power for industrial manufacturing was actually driven by a capitalist need to intensify control over the workforce.[30] Textile mills using cheap hydropower could be built only where water flowed reliably. Even though steam power was more expensive, it could power a mill anywhere that coal could be delivered. The resulting capital mobility allowed capitalists to set up in urban centers, which—unlike rural riverside sites—had an abundant reserve army of labor to serve as scabs and a strong state to punish striking workers. Centralized control over energy sources was—and continues to be—a form of social power. Social ownership over new forms of distributed energy production, like wind and solar, potentially threatens that power.

Community energy has already begun to take root in Detroit. In 2011, DTE repossessed all of Highland Park's more than one thousand streetlights due to unpaid electricity bills.[31] In response, Highland Park residents formed a group called Soulardarity to install community-owned solar streetlights. Members pay annual dues to keep up and expand the program. Soulardarity is a very young organization, but its model has the potential to expand into solar arrays, wind generation, and efficient battery systems to power member homes, especially if integrated into a wider multi-issue strategic framework. Solar arrays could be managed by community land trusts, community-owned wireless routers could be combined with streetlights for affordable public Internet access, and housing cooperatives could collaborate on weatherization and energy-saving measures.

As with community gardening, organizing for energy democracy presents an opportunity for popular environmental education. Without taking steps to meaningfully improve people's lives, Soulardarity would have no credible platform from which to raise ecological consciousness. But by grounding its education work in a concrete program in which community members are invested, Soulardarity can communicate effectively about climate change and environmental justice.

The ownership structure of the energy economy is an essential part of halting greenhouse gas emissions. As Naomi Klein argues in *This Changes Everything*, democratic management (rather than for-profit management) of the grid is often necessary to transition away from fossil fuel dependency.[32] By placing control over energy systems in community hands, and by upscaling those systems into the public sphere, we would improve neighborhood economic conditions while staving off climate catastrophe.

Neighborhood Councils

At the center of all of this mutual aid and participatory social service work is the creation of organs of radical democracy. Like the Palestinians in the First Intifada, the Kurds in revolutionary Rojava, and the Catalonians in the Spanish Civil War, American communities should both actively organize local assemblies in which free citizens come together to make decisions and empower those institutions politically. Detroit has several good starting points.

Detroit has a long history of block clubs on which neighborhood councils could be built. During the worst of the recession, block clubs and more informal networks of neighbors proved vital in preventing the total collapse of many neighborhoods. Indeed, the neighborhoods that weathered the downturn best were the ones with organized block clubs already in place. They mowed vacant lots and lawns, chased off would-be looters, and communicated with the city when basic services were delayed or absent. Block clubs are typically apolitical, however, and almost always focused hyperlocally, with little aspiration or ability to influence broader city politics. Still, as incubators of participatory democracy, they can coordinate with other cooperative institutions and take on more ambitious community projects, gathering strength as they do so.

Another starting point is tenant organizing. "Community syndicalism" or "community unionism" is a strategy for organizing renters to bargain collectively with landlords. A tenant union is, in essence, a neighborhood council organized around an apartment building or residential complex. Tenant organizing overlaps with both cooperative housing work and the proliferation of democratic councils. Take Back the Land organizer Shane Burley discusses community syndicalism in the context of exporting anarcho-syndicalist labor organizing methods to struggles outside the workplace.[33] He notes that, just as unions in that tradition work to become the very structures that can replace the boss-worker relationship when capitalist modes of production are overthrown, so too can the tenant community union fight to take over management of the property. Burley does not, however, carry over this aim of worker and tenant organizing—to form the institutions of the liberated society—into the self-governance of a community in political terms. This is a serious oversight. Developing such councils is about restructuring democratic governance rooted in community participation, not just autonomous management of a few buildings.

A confederation of neighborhood councils would oversee the management of community cooperatives and mutual aid networks. The next step would be to integrate these councils into city governance itself. In Detroit, recent amendments to the city charter allow residents of a city council district to form a community advisory council (CAC); their city councilperson must then regularly confer and host public meetings with these councils. Establishing or taking over these CACs might be a place to start on the road to radical democratic governance. In other cities, the specific mechanisms will differ. Some cities have run pilot programs of participatory budgeting, following the lead of Porto Alegre in Brazil.[34] Pressuring the city to adopt such modes of governance would be a major step toward empowering the neighborhood councils and instituting a democratic confederal system.

The levels of civic engagement sustained by neighborhood councils and other projects would also allow this revolutionary community organization to seize municipal power directly through elections. The city charter could then be rewritten, restructuring city governance toward radical participatory democracy. It is at this stage that the institution-building strategy described here would begin to create a cascade effect of municipal transformation.

Upscaling Radical Democracy

Municipal authority provides a powerful new lever to advance all other movement work. Public backing for cooperative credit streams and community common funds would vastly expand the postcapitalist economy. Once cooperative housing is extensive enough to demonstrate proof of the concept and weaken developers' power, the new political base and city council support could be leveraged toward further municipalization of land and housing. So long as the central role of participatory democracy in the governance of the cooperative housing system is legally enshrined, municipalizing it would vastly expand the community's available resources and legal powers (such as eminent domain). The City of Detroit could guarantee shelter as a human right.

Municipal authority would also allow citizens to municipalize the entire energy grid to be managed in the public interest as part of the urban commons. The voting public could then force a complete drawdown on fossil fuel use. With enough preexisting social and physical infrastructure around community ownership of energy, this shift toward energy democracy is entirely feasible. In Michigan, state regulators set the price of electricity to guarantee DTE an exorbitant return on investment within a certain range. If demand for electricity decreases beyond projections, they recalculate and raise the price to maintain a similar level of return. This pricing structure could drive a downward spiral of energy monopoly insolvency: as more people switch to cooperative renewable power, the price of electricity that DTE sells will rise and the average capital costs to community ownership will fall. Eventually, DTE would be forced into a fiscal crisis by its obligation to maintain such high returns for shareholders. At that point, the city government would be well positioned to municipalize the grid and buy up any productive infrastructure that would be in the public good (such as DTE's solar arrays).

Leveraging democratic power for control over municipal policy making would mean an entirely new direction for Detroit's redevelopment. Non-reformist reforms like a location value tax, expansive public transit, and restorative justice practices would all be within reach. So would many other crucial policies that this essay lacks the space to discuss. This approach to radical organizing could build a universal health-care system rooted in community clinics. It could vastly reduce the police force's scope of activities and bring all public security services under direct civilian control through police-monitoring neighborhood patrols and community-based teams of trained mental health professionals and conflict de-escalators. It could help us reimagine the public school by integrating mixed age popular education models and community-based learning into the public sphere to be available to all. We could devise citywide bike shares, recycling and composting syndicates, community centers, and time banks.

Conclusion: A Next System beyond the City

Suppose we can reconfigure a series of large municipalities like Detroit along libertarian municipalist lines—making city officials report directly to a confederation of decentralized neighborhood councils and using the new city governance structure to encourage development of the socialist institutions in civil society that made such reform possible in the first place.

Cooperatives, common funds, community land trusts, collective housing, social services, urban agriculture networks, and other such innovations would spread. What comes next?

Local action is not enough by itself to actually transform capitalist society. Capital and state violence are organized regionally and globally, and so must their replacements be. Once we have established dual power, we can turn to the larger-scale reforms necessary to transition out of capitalism. The question is how to go from local and municipal institutions to a global network of economic cooperatives, mutual aid organizations, and democratic decision-making bodies that can challenge and ultimately overturn the existing power structure.

The key to this lies in what Kurdish revolutionary Abdullah Öcalan calls "democratic confederalism," a version of Bookchin's libertarian municipalism. This political system has local deliberative democracy at its core but is networked to allow regional and, eventually, global collaboration.[35] For example, Detroit's appointed delegates might attend a regional congress—perhaps initially a network of Midwestern cities, though ultimately an assembly including every rural, suburban, and urban community in a given area. As the number of represented communities grows, so would the number of confederated levels—from the neighborhood to the city, the county, the state or province, the region, the nation, the continent, and at last the planet.

While superficially this may resemble US federalism, the difference is that in democratic confederalism the key locus of power is at the grassroots. Delegates must be subject to instant recall and be accountable to the neighborhoods' wishes, while higher-level bodies focus mainly on coordination and leave politicking as much as possible to local communities.

In some ways, regional collaboration works the same as within the city—the confederations engage in shared struggles, create autonomous institutions to coordinate and democratize their economies, and undermine the state by making its authority ever more obsolete in daily life. These regional democratic bodies would also connect the economies and civil societies of their respective communities. A network of midwestern cities would pool and redistribute resources when necessary, exchange goods and services, and plan political action in concert. Such joint political action will be critical as the tensions of dual power come to a head. The strategy for dealing with these tensions will vary greatly by country, depending on whether the state is sympathetic or hostile to the transition or, more likely, somewhere in between.

In the sympathetic case, as under a leftist or social democratic government, cities where democratic confederalism has taken root would push for meaningful progressive reforms.

Confederations would pool resources to create political alliances and win policies ranging from a universal basic income to stringent environmental protections to tax incentives for cooperative businesses. Such policies would give cities additional time and space to continue building up their alternative, postcapitalist institutions. Of course, coexistence with even a sympathetic state will be impossible in the long run—even relatively democratic states are unlikely to willingly cede much political power to local organizations and can't be expected to wither away on their own.

But this movement should be willing to work with them and pressure them for beneficial reforms, even as it ultimately aims to replace all their functions—and, when the time comes, following Arendt, to suffocate their authority by withdrawing public support.

More difficult is the hostile case, as under an authoritarian or right-wing government. Such a state may use violence to quash any local uprising, as the example of the First Intifada illustrates. Or they may close off a community's legal right to determine its own future.

Numerous American state governments in the pocket of the fossil fuel industry have forbidden townships and cities from banning fracking, for instance. A Trump administration will likely attempt mass deportations, necessitating oppositional unity by sanctuary cities.

An isolated revolution is a fragile one, so amid hostility confederation and regional alliances are even more important. It is harder to quell a geographically dispersed revolution, and, should the state try, sympathetic cities—especially if networked with communities outside the country—can launch their own political campaigns against a hostile government or aid their besieged allies. Progressive social movements of every sort would be strengthened by channeling their efforts through permanent community institutions instead of becoming flashes in the pan, as so many protest movements are. The existence of a widespread and powerful alternative is the only hope for sparking enough Arendtian noncompliance to weaken the state.

We can all take comfort from the fact that embryonic forms of this radical democratic strategy have popped up in many countries, and a global conversation among the libertarian Left can bring such transnational alliances into being. The Greek base of mutual aid organizations that launched Syriza to power, the Zapatistas of Chiapas, the Kurdish revolutionaries of Rojava, and the Sahrawi refugee communities of western Algeria all exemplify an international shift in leftist politics rooted in "community before party," with a growing understanding that the state is not the only political tool we have to work with. Organizing across borders, we can together build these prefigurations of the egalitarian and ecological society we wish to usher into being.

No matter what, we can expect the private sector to be hostile, hastening the need for unity and confederation. The cooperative economy must be networked among cities to grow large and resilient enough to be a viable and stable replacement for capitalism. Regional political bodies are also better positioned than local ones to successfully rein in capitalist power, simply by virtue of their scale. Larger-scale institutions are also more visible, and thus better suited to serve as a model to communities across the globe.

One by one, entire governments and capitalist industries will dissolve as their democratic communal alternatives spread. And what will this leave us with?

It is important not to presume the precise contours of the future society since no static blueprint can predict changing circumstances, and the very point of the new system is that the people will design it democratically. That said, a democratic successor to statism and capitalism must address certain big-picture problems: labor arbitrage and the flight of capital, the industrial development of nonindustrialized nations, and the global ecological crisis. We can surmise from these global socioeconomic problems at least the outlines of what the next system will have to be to survive.

The solutions are interlinked and require new global institutions to administer them. These institutions would need to bring multinational corporations under control through an international agreement like a new Bretton Woods—likely with strict capital controls and redistributive taxes on the international finance market. This global network would also need to codify universal labor rights (through a global minimum wage, universal union rights, and globally agreed upon mechanisms to transfer control of production to workers and communities) and administer them through an international labor organization. Finally, a great deal of collaborative economic planning will be needed to develop nonindustrial countries while transitioning into an ecologically sustainable economy—Green New Deals in the rich countries and Green Marshall Plans for the developing ones.

Clearly, these goals are best accomplished by international or even global decision-making bodies. From our point of view, these decision-making structures ought to consist of a global representative body with fairly limited power held accountable to regional bodies that in turn answer to more powerful local bodies run via participatory democracy. Only democratic confederalism at the local and regional level can hold the institutions that emerge to tackle global issues accountable to the people of the world, not distant elites.

These political organizations would be sustained by cooperative economic ventures managed democratically by their workers and the public. The community itself would determine production and allocation of (at least) the essentials—food, shelter, and health care managed as core public goods. All co-ops would be accountable to community councils to ensure that they meet social and environmental needs.

If we can meet these goals, a better future is ours for the taking.

Work hours would shrink drastically, and leisure time would skyrocket. Less resource-intensive forms of recreation, such as the arts and hiking, would keep our bodies, minds, and the biosphere healthier. Nearly everyone would subsist on plant-based foods grown in urban hydroponic systems or permaculture farms nestled symbiotically in local ecosystems. Energy would come primarily from wind and solar, incorporated into the built environment rather than displacing wildlife. Waste would be reused, composted, or broken down into new materials, eliminating the need for landfills and mining.

When we have established bottom-up democratic governance, eliminated private profit, and begun to restore Earth's devastated ecosystems, does that mean we've reached the "next system?" Well, maybe—but that doesn't mean politics is over. The central ethos of the vision articulated here—community control, local experimentation, and radical democracy—means that we cannot predict precisely what the future will look like; nor do we want to. Even the authors of this essay don't agree on all the particulars—should some semblance of money, the market, and private ownership remain for nonessential goods? Or should all economic activity be fully communal? To what extent can or should the Internet reduce the need for face-to-face deliberation in democratic decision-making? But these details are for people in communities now and in the future to discuss and try out; attempting such political sorcery ourselves would be self-defeating. The only certainty is that change should be guided by egalitarian principles—beliefs that might be called libertarian or anarchist, socialist or communist, ecological or posthumanist—but adherence to these principles still allows for pragmatism and diversity.

There are no perfect worlds, only better ones. Even our vision of the next system, if we can achieve it, will not be homogenous or static. Less than an end goal, the path and the system described here is a framework, a way to ensure that the systems to come can represent and respond to the needs and desires of the people who inhabit them. Actually building that world, then, is up to all of us. In this we have followed the Zapatistas, whose defiant revolt at the precise moment when history was said to have ended sparked a revolutionary wave—a global movement for ecological consciousness, radical democracy, and libertarian socialism—that we are riding still. They emerged from the Mexican jungle to demand a world beyond neoliberalism, a world of true democracy and justice, a world where all worlds fit. Their advice to the international volunteers who wanted to help was simple, and resonates even louder today: Build Zapatismo in your own communities. Twenty-three years later, it's not too late to start.

Notes

1 This is a production of the Symbiosis Research Collective, accessed June 2, 2022, http://symbiosis-revolution.org/research-collective.

2 Martin Gilens and Benjamin I. Page, "Testing Theories of American Politics: Elites, Interest Groups, and Average Citizens," *Perspectives on Politics* 12, no. 3 (September 2014): 577, accessed June 1, 2022, https://doi.org/10.1017/S1537592714001595.

3 Hannah Arendt, *The Origins of Totalitarianism* (Cleveland: Meridian Books, 1951).

4 Hannah Arendt, *On Violence* (New York: Harcourt Books, 1970), 48–49.

5 Antonio Gramsci, *Selections from the Prison Notebooks*, ed. and trans. Quentin Hoare and Geoffrey N. Smith (New York: International Publishers Company, 1971).

6 Some examples: the political opportunism of the Bolsheviks in the Russian Revolution, Ayatollah Khomeini's faction in the Iranian Revolution, and the Muslim Brothers in the Egyptian Revolution.

7 Murray Bookchin, "Thoughts on Libertarian Municipalism," *Left Green Perspectives*, no. 41 (January 2000), accessed June 28, 2022, https://social-ecology.org/wp/1999/08/thoughts-on-libertarian-municipalism.

8 Young Shin, personal communication, 2016.

9 Nilda Flores-Gonzalez, Anna Romina Guevarra, Maura Toro-Morn, and Grace Chang, ed., *Immigrant Women Workers in the Neoliberal Age* (Urbana: University of Illinois Press, 2013), 214.

10 Murray Bookchin and Dave Foreman, *Defending the Earth: A Debate* (Montreal: Black Rose Books, 1991).

11 Ben Craig and John Pencavel, "Participation and Productivity: A Comparison of Worker Cooperatives and Conventional Firms in the Plywood Industry," Brookings Papers on Economic Activity (1995), 126–127.

12 Sharryn Kasmir, *The Myth of Mondragon: Cooperatives, Politics, and Working-Class Life in a Basque Town* (Albany: State University of New York Press, 1996), 86–87.
13 Anders Christiansen, "Evaluating Workplace Democracy in "Mondragon,"" undergraduate thesis, University of Vermont, 2014.
14 The Working World, accessed July 1, 2022, http://www.theworkingworld.org/us; Oscar Abello, "Closing the Funding Gap for Worker Cooperatives," NextCity, July 8, 2016, accessed June 2, 2022, https://nextcity.org/daily/entry/red-emmas-working-world-nyc-financial-cooperative.
15 Francis Calpotura and Kim Fellner, "The Square Peg Finds Their Groove: Reshaping the Organizing Circle," H-Urban Seminar on the History of Community Organizing and Community-Based Development, COMM-ORG Papers Collection, vol. 3 (1996), accessed June 9, 2022, https://comm-org.wisc.edu/papers96/square.html.
16 David Hilliard, ed., *The Black Panther Party: Service to the People Programs* (Albuquerque: University of New Mexico Press, 2008).
17 Maya Rosenfeld, *Confronting the Occupation: Work, Education, and Political Activism of Palestinian Families in a Refugee Camp* (Stanford, CA: Stanford University Press, 2004), 252; Avram Bornstein, "Ethnography and the Politics of Prisoners in Palestine-Israel," *Journal of Contemporary Ethnography* 30, no. 5 (2001): 546–74.
18 Rosenfeld, *Confronting the Occupation*, 218.
19 Joost R. Hiltermann, ed., *Behind the Intifada: Labor and Women's Movements in the Occupied Territories* (Princeton: Princeton University Press, 1993), 7, 34, 57, 64.
20 Joost R. Hiltermann, "The Women's Movement During the Uprising," *Journal of Palestine Studies* 20, no. 3 (Spring 1991): 48–57.
21 Hiltermann, *Behind the Intifada*, 52; Philippa Strum, *The Women are Marching: The Second Sex and the Palestinian Revolution* (New York: Lawrence Hill Books, 1992), 74–78.
22 Strum, *The Women Are Marching*, 53.
23 They were also called "neighborhood councils" (or, in rural areas, "village councils").
24 In older sources, the UNLU is commonly mischaracterized as a command structure with political parties at the center. More recent interviews with veteran organizers in the popular committees provide little to no evidence for this framing. Rather, the UNLU was dependent on and democratically embedded in the popular committee network. See Mazin B. Qumsiyeh, *Popular Resistance in Palestine: A History of Hope and Empowerment* (London: Pluto Press, 2011); Mason Herson-Hord, "Sumud to Intifada: Community Struggle in Palestine and the Western Sahara," undergraduate thesis, Princeton University, 2015.
25 The "home economy" included community gardens, cottage industry cooperatives, food and medicine distribution networks, and other forms of economic self-sufficiency that provided subsistence for neighborhoods so they could both provide for all members of the community and participate fully in strikes and boycotts.
26 One First Intifada veteran interviewed in Beit Sahour in 2014 said that he was jokingly accused of being in the UNLU because the suggestions his popular committee had given him to present to Beit Sahour's town-wide committee appeared in a UNLU leaflet two weeks later. This model was extremely effective at disseminating strategies for popular resistance. The idea of a tax strike, deployed so effectively by the people of Beit Sahour, was actually first proposed by the popular committee of a small village near Nablus and ended up in a communiqué printed and distributed by popular committees throughout occupied Palestine. See Herson-Hord, "Sumud to Intifada."
27 Those being foreclosed upon are prohibited by law to bid on their own homes.

28 Most uninhabited homes in Detroit are in need of serious repair to become habitable again. A cooperative labor pool would vastly reduce the costs of each renovation.
29 Jill Suttie, "How to Raise an Environmentalist," *Yes! Magazine*, September 24, 2016, accessed June 2, 2022, https://www.yesmagazine.org/environment/2016/09/24/how-to-raise-an-environmentalist.
30 Andres Malm, *Fossil Capital: The Rise of Steam Power and the Origins of Global Warming* (New York: Verso Books, 2016).
31 Highland Park is a small, three-square-mile city entirely surrounded by Detroit.
32 Naomi Klein, *This Changes Everything: Capitalism vs. the Climate* (New York: Simon and Schuster, 2014).
33 Shane Burley, "Ready to Fight: Developing a 21st Century Community Syndicalism," Institute for Anarchist Studies (January 23, 2015), accessed June 10, 2022, https://anarchiststudies.org/communitysyndicalism.
34 Marion Gret and Yves Sintomer, *The Porto Alegre Experiment: Learning Lessons for Better Democracy*, trans. Stephen Wright (London: Zed Books, 2005).
35 Janet Biehl, "Bookchin, Öcalan, and the Dialectics of Democracy" (lecture, Challenging Capitalist Modernity conference, Hamburg, Germany, February 3–5, 2012), accessed July 1, 2022, http://new-compass.net/articles/bookchin-%C3%B6calan-and-dialectics-democracy.

"A Deeper Understanding of What We're Trying to Accomplish"

A People's Strike Dialogue with Kali Akuno, Sacajawea "Saki" Hall, Rose Brewer, Wende Marshall, and Matt Meyer

Wende Marshall and Matt Meyer: What is the relationship and the connection between Cooperation Jackson and People's Strike. Why was Cooperation Jackson the logical space for People Strike to emerge?

Kali Akuno: Two things I think really gave us direction. The first is the memory and passing of a dear comrade who died of SARS in 2008. That and the rising tide of Ebola put epidemic on my radar screen and the radar screens of many people within the Malcolm X Grassroots Movement. So for me in particular, every time I've heard about some novel disease, I've paid very close attention, despite the limits of what you can find in in the Western press. COVID-19 first got on my radar screen in November. And I remember telling Saki and a couple of other folks that there was some weird new virus that was emerging in China that they didn't quite understand. And there were actually two things that were going on at the same time. There was a major outbreak of the plague, although that contagion was largely subsumed in the media by COVID.[1] Hearing about the toll it was beginning to take, I could sense that this was going to be serious.

The second thing relates to how Cooperation Jackson came about through our collective understanding and knowledge around Hurricane Katrina in 2005, which developed as core parts of our program.

Cooperation Jackson grew from that experience as a response to the growing number of ecological, political, and economic crisis that we both predicted and knew were coming down the pipeline.

People's Strike emerged at the end of February 2020 when we did our first collective assessment of things. We decided to shut down our operations like fairly early in the first week in March. We were learning and listening, especially to comrades in Italy, and elsewhere around the world. First, they were saying, "Oh it's just like a bad flu." But the next week they said, "No, no this is much more, we were wrong." Comrades outside of the US warned us that we didn't know enough about the virus and there was not enough PPE (personal protective equipment) out there. We heeded that lesson and shut everything down.

By mid-March, it became clear that there was a dire need for a political response based on how the State of Mississippi was reacting and how the Trump administration was just ignoring the situation in order to keep the economy open, in clear contradiction to how fast this deadly virus was spreading.

The Trump administration, according to a report, knew how deadly the virus was but refused to respond.[2]

Paying attention to the impact of COVID on Black people in particular made it clear that we had a role to play in developing a collective political response and raising awareness. Initially, we made an effort to combat a lot of misinformation that was out there, like the false notion that Black people couldn't get COVID. That was coming out of particular anti-vaccine forces. We knew that Black folks were getting COVID in other parts of the world, so we knew that this was misinformation.

Saki Hall: COVID was very personal to me by mid-March. By that time two of my kinfolk had gotten sick, even before anyone even thought this was a threat, and my mind immediately went to the politics of public health, and the sorry legacy of racism in this country, and the politics of class because these were both working-class women, who at that early stage obviously didn't know what was what, but it became strikingly clear that we were going to be confronting unequal access to health care and knowledge about the threats that were posed. Now, I didn't link that particular response to Cooperation Jackson because I didn't get pulled into People's Strike until around May 1, but the politics of COVID were already pretty clear to some of us, and the Left wasn't really responding in any kind of responsible way. It made a lot of sense to me, to try to get connected to some information that was seeing this and treating this quite seriously.

Wende Marshall: I started being worried about COVID in like November or December just because I read the paper. And I remember in December, talking to a comrade about it, who was like, "Oh, that's no big deal since 80,000 people die of the flu each year." And I said, "Yes and it's us who died more than everybody else from the regular flu." I was alarmed and startled by the way people on the left were ignoring the threat of COVID, implying that it was manufactured, right-wing propaganda.

Saki Hall: It is disturbing that people are okay with hundreds of thousands, if not more people dying, very disturbing. I think that like, somehow, people have gotten accustomed to the loss of life...and do not necessarily think that there is something that could be done to avoid it. People just accept it as inevitable.... I think that that is even more so among a younger...generation that's socialized in totally different ways than previously and has become desensitized—leading to the idea that there's not that much that you can do.

I think that from the onset, having a void of political leadership that asserts that every life is precious and any number of deaths is too many, and there are ways to protect ourselves and each other and to make care and protection a collective responsibility. And yeah, it's deeply disturbing.

Wende Marshall: What is the Black and Indigenous wisdom that shapes our conception of socialism and our understanding of revolution? What is the basis of our relationship with one another and with the land?

Saki Hall: The political world view of capitalism is resigned to not taking care of people and to letting millions die, but People's Strike is flipping that script into positive Black and Indigenous wisdom. People's Strike is Black- and Indigenous-led, Black woman–led, which ties into broader questions about conceptions of socialism and revolution.

My understanding from an early age of what I later understood to be socialism came from growing up in a multicultural, multinational neighborhood of poor and working-class folks on the Lower East Side of Manhattan and Alphabet City. I think the wisdom and culture of people taking care of each other and sharing resources was something that made me constantly question, at an early age, the levels of inequality and injustice that I saw. This rampant economic inequality never really sat well with me, when I could clearly see that there were enough resources, that there were people that had extra, more than they needed. And it didn't sit well with me that people can have a whole lot more than what they need and then there are people who don't have what they need. That was my experience growing up in New York City. I also learned from my experiences of being in Haiti when I was younger. That taught me about being in a community where people don't have everything they need but still figure out how to survive right and how to live and how to make do. The women in the one building that I grew up in literally shared food stamps.

I think my undergraduate education in political science, coupled with real life, real world political development, after school, taught me to focus on how we care for each other, how we share with each other, how natural resources are seen as having life and giving life, how it is not about every individual person but, rather, about community, and how resources and skills are shared and bartered.

I do want to say that without romanticizing it or clumping everybody into this essential idea of what African and Indigenous wisdom is; I think that there are important ideas and practices around how you relate to Earth, how you relate to land, and how that mirrors how we relate to each other, that I think is important for us to reclaim, even though the context is so different with where we are now in 2020. We have to both reclaim and redefine our relationship to each other, and our relationship to the land, and ask how we repair those relationships. And that really cannot be done without there being a transformation and a revolutionary movement toward socialism. At Cooperation Jackson we are focused on shifting the economy and working toward ecosocialism and a complete break from capitalism. But at the same time there's still heteropatriarchy that I think we have to recognize existed previously. That's one of the reasons why I think that it's not only like reclaiming; it is definitely looking to wisdom in the practices that correct our relationships. But then at the same time, what were the things that our folks didn't have right, and how do we address those systems of oppression and the institutions that perpetuate them so that we can actually think about and realize, and practice, better ways of relating to each other when it comes to gender.

Rose Brewer: Riffing off of Saki's observations, so much of what she lifted up is really deeply materially rooted, even though there is a Black value structure that intertwines with material realities to promote survival. In the neighborhood that I grew up in, if you didn't share, the refrigerator was probably going to be pretty empty.

So there's a real material grounding about how Black people in this country, in particular, have had to move with one another just to live, to struggle another day, and a lot of that had to be collective. A lot of this depended on earlier systems of wisdom, like the African concept of *ubuntu*. And that goes back to the continent, whether that's explicitly socialist, it certainly is collectively rooted as a logic that any kind of society that values humanity would have to have infused within it.

And, of course, you know there's the history of anti-colonial struggles that intensely attempted to imbue within them a socialist ethic, and to practice a form of African socialism in the context of this global capital system that didn't work out too well. Samora Machel, Amílcar Cabral, and others, all of them had at least a notion of feeding the people, sharing the produce, living collectively, and drawing on the best of those traditions, as well as what it takes to struggle.

Those are things that we can draw upon.

And I like Saki's point not to romanticize, but to be very clear about what Indigenous wisdom represented. There certainly was a different material relationship to the land which shares a lot in common with African peasants who understood that you had to rotate the land, that you couldn't use it up. The individualism rooted in the white Eurocentric mindset is opposed by a through line of African and Indigenous thinking about the world that existed and that we want to create again.

Wende Marshall: I want to add that I think this abomination called capitalism is based on the dead bodies of our ancestors, on the theft of our bodies and our lands. This entire disgusting white supremacist capitalist patriarchy was enabled by the murder and degradation of our people. Now we can take that a step further, it is not just historical, it's ongoing. I just read a very profound article today around how the expropriation and death of the land is catalyzing the millions of people who are hungry. Either you can produce your food on land that you can grow or—under conditions of corporate agriculture—you have to be able to buy it or you don't eat. So the extractivism continues into the current moment and, as you said, the abomination of it and the death of humanity, because of it continues aggressively and will continue. Some kind of change has to happen: transformation, revolution. Yes!

Matt Meyer: So what's changed? What is the nature of this moment that offers new possibilities? And how do we best respond to what we see coming up in the next year or two?

Wende Marshall: COVID has ripped any illusions we may have had that this abomination of a capitalist system is reasonable. Black people are dying of COVID and getting sicker from COVID more than white people. And then scientists say things like obesity is a causal factor in who gets COVID, but four out of five Black women are fat, or obese, and many Black people do not have access to or resources for enough nutritious food. We have to acknowledge the way that white supremacy, capitalism, and heteropatriarchy fuck us up physically, spiritually, and psychologically. There's also just the reality of all the people that can't feed themselves now. And all the people that are suffering and who are addicted to lessen their pain, or all the people who have lost their jobs or have been deemed essential and forced to go to work. All of this has been clarified in the era of COVID. It is part of our work in People's Strike to keep all that in the forefront, to help folks understand the purpose of competing narratives from the Dems, in particular.

Rose Brewer: It also reveals something that we knew was true: that there is a fascist base underneath this capitalist system that has revealed itself, very prominently, and has struck a chord in folk who are trying to struggle and organize.

Kali Akuno: I think COVID, coupled with capitalist economic crisis, has presented the opportunity for developing mutual aid and trying to figure out how to expand on some informal survival practices. This is definitely a growing desire for folks, to create and expand on solidarity economy practices so that people, neighborhoods, groups, are able to put into practice some mutual aid. And I think this is an opportunity for us to lift up those stories of mutual aid in a broader narrative so that people can see that the state continues to fail us and not only fails us but is putting us in a position where the survival of the state is at the cost of our lives. It's important to be able to juxtapose that and have people make the connections about the importance of mutual aid.

But we must be careful that the practice of mutual aid doesn't end up shifting into charity. There's got to be analysis and strategy that underline and strengthen these practices, these types of experiments that folks are doing, because it can easily shift into charity and away from supporting revolutionary movement.

If we do not recognize the imperative of taking ownership and control, of being able to produce what we need to live, then we are brought into the nonprofit charity model, which posits a certain elite group as providers and takes the agency away from community folks to collectively forge survival. The nonprofit charity model is really limited, right, and does not end up building the type of power that we need to move beyond capitalism. Nonprofit charity models preclude the blossoming of a solidarity economy and keeps the power in the hands of nonprofit staff.

Matt Meyer: What do you think has changed over the past year, and where does that leave us today in terms of obstacles and opportunities?

Kali Akuno: One of the things that we've learned is that, with political will, it is possible to stop the world economy immediately. In terms of climate change talks, governments walked out saying that there was no way we could halt production and shift to a greener economy. But in one month we learned that wasn't true. If there is a need for it, the whole global economy can be shut down. That is the critical lesson.

People's Strike perspective is that the decision to shutter the economy shouldn't be a bureaucratic decision. It shouldn't be a decision left up to multinational corporations, or capitalists on Wall Street. Ultimately, we have to build the collective power that we need to make that decision to shut down the economy and transform it. Capitalism is facilitating the extinction event we are living through, and things will get much worse if we don't make some critical changes. So the lesson we learned about how quickly the economy can be shut down is crucial.

Second, from April through October, we saw the first wave of strikes, mainly wildcat strikes, from workers in meatpacking houses, Amazon distribution centers, Instacart, and the like. People joined forces in the interest of defending their lives against COVID-19, since they were being forced to work without any personal protective equipment or hazard pay. That was a beautiful thing, that folks built collective power. But then, unfortunately, that energy and collective power was surrendered to electoral politics aims. In September, October, November more energy was spent getting Biden elected than figuring out how we regroup to regain our autonomous motion so that we do not have to rely on a philanthropic benefactor.

The work of stimulating the radical imagination of folks is critical work that People's Strike is committed to. We saw that radical imagination in August and September in inspiring and hopeful ways in occupations in Portland and Seattle, in people's assemblies occurring in parts of New York, in Atlanta. In Jackson, through our work in Cooperation Jackson and the work of others, we began to see new ways of relating and new ways of governing. We have to combat the lack of imagination stemming from deep indoctrination in bourgeois democracy, and parliamentary and electoral politics. We must move people to build up their confidence and believe that a different world is possible.

This last year shows the potential of what can happen, but also the constraints that we need to overcome on a much deeper level than I think sometimes we want to admit, in part because it involves so many forces. Some of the folks with limited imaginations are forces that we work with... that we are being comrades with, or in some relationship with, and trying to move folks beyond the limitations of the system and the limitations of our own imagination is a critical piece of what I think we still have to do.

Wende Marshall: What is the relationship between a strategy of dual power and a revolutionary conception of nonviolence? How can we build mutual aid into revolutionary processes and concrete revolutionary projects? What are the lessons of the Black Panther Party and post-1960s movements, especially in terms of mutual aid, self-defense, and community ties? How do we balance militancy and militarism, the idea that nonviolence is always reformist, that "by any means necessary" equals armed struggle? How do we understand and deal with the violence generated by this white supremacist capitalist patriarchy, and ours?

Kali Akuno: I think we have to do a lot more work of dispelling this notion that nonviolence is inherently reformist, because it's not. Now we know that many of examples which people cite, or the ones that they know best, those narratives tend to lean in that direction. But in actual practice, both from a theoretical and a practical standpoint, the powerful unarmed strategy we can use, to the extent that we can organize it, is a general strike. When one organizes all those who labor in one form or another, primarily for the means of livelihood and survival, to act in accord with one another, you have a formula for massive and radical social change. In this scenario, we could first shut the system down, but then also move away from the existing system. Transformation of society could actually be done, and in some cases has been done, through nonviolent means.

There are just some conceptions, which have come down, particularly within the Black liberation framework, in terms of dichotomies. "Malcolm is the revolutionary and Martin was a reformer." These actually don't fit our own history in the larger narrative. They play into a particularly dangerous narrative that we see in the here and now between "the good protester" and "the bad protester," which only benefits our enemies.

That type of thinking doesn't help us form a deeper understanding of what it is we're trying to accomplish and what it will take. We always need to have clarity that those who own the means of production, those who control the state, are not going to give up their power without a struggle and are not going to accept even the most basic of democratic practices without a struggle. At the end of the day, we can and should control all strategies and tactics, but not do so blindly. I think there's more of a merging of those two past dichotomies. Those issues have to fit into a larger context around strategy and what it will take to get to that point of mass insurrection and general strike.

Our strategic analysis of the moment is what should dictate and determine tactical considerations. When our enemies strike back, and we know at some points that they will strike back, they will surely use the violent apparatuses of the state. The question for us, then, is: What should be our collective response?

And if there's a limited response, it's typically going to mean more of a self-defense kind of struggle. If it is a more collective response, then we could use more of the nonviolent tactics. It is important to understand that when we talk about some of the dynamics of a general strike, we must be prepared for the fact that the opposition is always going to be exacting penalties and making life unbearable. The people's power is in making it so that nothing can move, no production or work or schooling or business as usual can proceed, because there's a heightened sense of universal solidarity that everybody would act on the same core principles and frameworks. That general strike scenario is going to take a whole hell of a lot of political understanding and unity building over an extended period of time. But I think it's something that we should always keep in mind.

This also goes back to the piece which Saki raised and elevated, about the sanctity of life, which must remain our aim and objective. We understand that not everybody is going to come along or want to come along with that viewpoint. There are fascist elements who would much rather see the planet burn and everything be destroyed than see life preserved. We shouldn't walk into anything blindly. We need to be clear about all our articulations about the sanctity of life.

At the same time, we must also be clear that half measures are not going to do it. We can't mediate our way to liberation through a series of compromises with capital or the institutions of reaction! Thinking that this is possible will actually be a barrier to the change that we're trying to seek. We must constantly and strategically reflect upon how we build within an overall dialectic of where we will make compromises and where we won't. And that's a big piece because that is where our enemies best utilize divide and conquer tactics. They push to know what our breaking points are.

Following the summer 2020 Black liberation uprisings, we saw a trend very illustrative of this point, in how much money was being pumped into a certain kind of social justice reformism. We have to really figure out how to move those who are within that kind of reformist orbit so as not to get lost in their narratives or their games. We do need to do the work of actually reaching out to the large mass of the people in this country who are not in formal organizations, but who are feeling the pain. And there are still tons of spaces to reach people to build bases within the US, building an infrastructure and relying on our own resources.

That's where I think that this larger piece around mutual aid fits in, because there's a level of mutual aid that revolutionaries in the US context really have to reinvent.

Saki Hall: I think we have to figure out how to bring together people who see themselves as revolutionaries, especially those who are tied and connected to organizations or projects. There are disconnects even just between people who are paid organizers and unpaid deep community organizers with ties to the grassroots. There are lessons here from the post-1960s era, with mutual aid and self-defense work and the deeply rooted relationships that directly engaged people to be able to develop strong ties.

Unfortunately, part of what makes the gap is folks who are doing paid organizing work conforming to the very nature of the nonprofits. They create a certain dynamic that's different; the conversation is more about how people get paid to do the work, compared to how we get back to a voluntary responsibility and something we're doing to sustain ourselves. I think we've seen that gap widening instead of decreasing, but now—dealing with mutual aid—we may be coming back to thinking about "how do you build the new society," while also increasing accountability, and fightback, and community defense work.

Another big issue around balancing militancy and militarism and the violence that is meted against us is how our own relationship to violence repeats within our communities. I advocate for us paying great attention to the problem, which we fuel just by repeating militarized thinking even in language we use and how we talk about strategy. There is a repetition of military thinking and language that is deeply patriarchal and violent and lends itself to perpetuating (or at least leaving the door open) to the kind of tactics which have repeatedly been used against us.

Kali Akuno: [Gently laughing] Saki's on a campaign to change movement language! She doesn't want anything referred to based on military roots; and this is a long-standing battle between us!

Matt Meyer: There are echoes here of contemporary Mozambican reflections on their postindependence conflicts with apartheid and US-supported counterrevolutionaries. FRELIMO militants have been consistent in their self-critiques of how militarized their education and propaganda was, and how that propaganda did not do well to prepare the next generation of revolutionaries. As Amílcar Cabral of Guinea-Bissau warned, "We must be militants but never militarists."

Saki Hall: I don't see how we can want to shift away from how we relate to one another, and how we struggle for change, while still maintaining these ideas and concepts and language which has successfully put us at odds with each other! Because the language does impact our practice!

So yeah, I am an advocate for changing how we speak to one another, and I've even questioned the way we've used the language of having "enemies." People aren't always clear about who the enemy is, and there is a spectrum right now as we deal with tactical and strategic differences within the movement. But those differences don't necessarily mean that you're my enemy, compared to people who actually are at odds with our entire Black community attaining self-determination!

Notes

1 "Plague in the Democratic Republic of the Congo: Nearly 300 Cases in Ituri since August," Outbreak News Today, January 2, 2021, accessed June 9, 2022, http://outbreaknewstoday.com/plague-in-the-democratic-republic-of-the-congo-nearly-300-cases-in-ituri-since-august-25381.

2 "Trump Knew Seriousness of the Coronavirus Early On, New Book Says," *All Things Considered*, November 9, 2020, accessed June 9, 2022, https://www.npr.org/2020/09/09/911188322/trump-knew-seriousness-of-the-coronavirus-early-on-new-book-says.

VIII

GOING FORWARD: ECOSOCIALISM AND REGENERATION

Red, Black, and Green Destiny Weapon: Cooperation Jackson and the Ecosocialist International

Quincy Saul

> "The only way we'll get freedom for ourselves is to identify ourselves with every oppressed people in the world."
> —Malcolm X

> "In the ongoing struggle to improve our practice, enhance our capacity, broaden our reach, and form strategic alliances to build power, the Executive Committee of Cooperation Jackson made the commitment to join the emerging FIRST ECOSOCIALIST INTERNATIONAL in November 2017"
> —*The Cooperative Way: The Newsletter of Cooperation Jackson* (April 2018)

On October 31, 2017, in a town called Palmares—in the municipality of Veroes, near the birthplace of Andresote, in the Bolivarian Republic of Venezuela—Black Panther veteran Charlotte Hill O'Neal was handed a torch from the local *maestras cimarronas.*[1] She led the Maroon multitude through the night to the assembly hall. The next day, over a hundred delegates from nineteen countries and five continents—including Cooperation Jackson—made the commitment to constitute the First Ecosocialist International. This is the story of the ecosocialist international: its ancestors, its birth in a Maroon cradle, how it came home to Jackson, Mississippi—and where it's headed next.

The story begins over five hundred years ago—centuries before there was any serious revolutionary internationalism in Europe, it was in the Americas, North and South. The Great Dismal Swamp in what's now the USA was a Maroon stronghold from the seventeenth century until the end of the US Civil War. The great *quilombo* of Palmares in what's now Brazil controlled more territory than Portugal, and lasted longer than the Soviet Union.[2] For three hundred years, the Maroon international, composed of Africans, Native Americans, and renegade Europeans, with communication and trade throughout the Western hemisphere, was a force to be reckoned with.[3] At one time or another, it outfought all the colonial governments on land and sea. It is still alive, and its fight is not over. "The war we fought, it's not finished yet.... Those times shall come again," say the elder oral historians of the Saramaka Maroons.[4]

The Maroon international kept no written records—its history is in the infinite archive of ancestors, locked and unlocked by the spirit of struggle.[5] Its members were the first proletarians—who had nothing to lose but their chains, and labored in satanic mills as early as the sixteenth century. Pirates were their foreign agents.[6] Its message traveled the clandestine yet popular "common wind," its essence was smuggled in dances and recipes across borders, and transmitted in myth and legend across generations.[7] It survives in bloodlines more than books, in the land more than in literature. It survives in song and in polycultures. But mostly it is found not in mere ink on paper, nor statues in museums, but engraved in something sturdier—the material and cultural everyday life of its descendants.

It won its first decisive victories in Suriname and Haiti. It participated decisively in the wars of independence of every country throughout Central and South America and the Caribbean. It scored again with the defeat of the South in the US Civil War. The tides turned against it, but when the enemy wins, it goes underground—whether in the mountains or the municipalities, the swamps or the slums. It is capable of hiding for generations and blossoming again when the time is ripe.

The same lineage which built international Maroon societies continued with leaders like Marcus Garvey and W.E.B. Du Bois and C.L.R. James who gave another name to the old practice—Pan-Africanism. At the end of the twentieth century it was carried on by Malcolm X and the Black Panther Party. Today, Cooperation Jackson is the tip of the same spear.

The internationalist dimension of the Black liberation movement in the US is illustrious, but receives less attention than it deserves. As pillars to hold up the bridge of the story—how ancestral internationalism culminates today in the participation of Cooperation Jackson in the First Ecosocialist International—we will call upon some powerful ancestors: Malcolm X, George Jackson, and Frantz Fanon. Malcolm X:

> This is why the man doesn't want you and me to look beyond Harlem or beyond the shores of America. As long as you don't know what's happening on the outside, you'll be all messed up dealing with this man on the inside.... When you understand the motive behind the world revolution, the drive behind the African and the drive behind the Asian, then you'll get some of that drive yourself. You'll be driving for real. The man downtown knows the difference between when you're driving for real and when you're driving not for real.... Today, power is international, real power is international; today, real power is not local. The only kind of power that can help you and me is international power, not local power. Any power that's local, if it's real power, is only a reflection or a part of that international power. If you think you've got some power, and it isn't in some way tied into that international thing, brother, don't get too far out on a limb. If your power base is only here, you can forget it.... No, you have to have that base somewhere else. Don't put it in this man's hand.... We would be out of our minds, we would actually be traitors to ourselves, to be reluctant or fearful to identify with people with whom we have so much in common. If it was a people who had nothing to offer, nothing to contribute to our well-being, you might be justified, even though they look like we do; if there was no contribution to be made, you might be justified. But when you have people who look exactly like you, and you are catching hell, to boot, and you are still reluctant or hesitant or slow to identify with them, then you need to catch hell, yes. You deserve all the hell you get.[8]

A few years later, George Jackson echoes the same tough internationalist love:

> There are other peoples on this earth. In denying their existence and turning inward in our misery and accepting any form of racism we are taking on the characteristic of our enemy. We are resigning ourselves to defeat. For in forming a conspiracy aimed at the destruction that holds us all in the throes of a desperate insecurity

> we must have coordinating elements connecting us and our moves to the moves of the other colonies, the African colonies, those in Asia and Latin Amerika, in Appalachia and the southwestern bean fields.... We must establish a true internationalism with other anticolonial peoples. Then we will be on the road of the true revolutionary. Only then can we expect to be able to seize the power that is rightfully ours, the power to control the circumstances of our day-to-day lives.... The entire colonial world is watching the blacks inside the US, wondering and waiting for us to come to our senses. The problems and struggles of the Amerikan monster are much more difficult than they would be if we actively aided them. We are on the inside. We are the only ones (besides the very small white minority left) who can get at the monster's heart without subjecting the world to thermonuclear fire. We have a momentous historical role to act out if we will. The whole world for all time in the future will love us and remember us as the righteous people who made it possible for the world to live on. If we fail through fear and lack of aggressive imagination, then the slaves of the future will curse us, as we sometimes curse those of yesterday.... We must build the true internationalism now.... If there is any basis for a belief in the universality of man then we will find it in his struggle against the enemy of all mankind.[9]

And Frantz Fanon's theory and practice of internationalism is legendary. He warned in detail about "the pitfalls of national consciousness," insisted on "the reciprocal bases of national culture," and thus invoked internationalism:

> The consciousness of self is not the closing of a door to communication. Philosophic thought teaches us, on the contrary, that it is its guarantee. National consciousness, which is not nationalism, is the only thing that will give us an international dimension.... If man is known by his acts, then we will say that the most urgent thing today for the intellectual is to build up his nation. If this building up is true, that is to say if it interprets the manifest will of the people and reveals the eager African peoples, then the building of a nation is of necessity accompanied by the discovery and encouragement of universalizing values. Far from keeping aloof

> from other nations, therefore, it is national liberation which leads the nation to play its part on the stage of history. It is at the heart of national consciousness that international consciousness lives and grows. And this two-fold emerging is ultimately the source of all culture.[10]

But which international program should we be part of? The decision of which international alliance to join has big implications; in previous generations this was even the criterion by which individuals and organizations were judged on the local level.

Ho Chi Minh explained how he confronted this question in his youth:

> After World War I, I made my living in Paris, now as a retoucher at a photographer's, now as a painter of "Chinese antiquities" (made in France!) I would distribute leaflets denouncing the crimes committed by the French colonialists in Viet-Nam.... The reason for me joining the French Socialist Party was that these "ladies and gentlemen"—as I called my comrades at that moment—had shown their sympathy toward me, toward the struggle of the oppressed peoples. But I understood neither what was a party, a trade-union, nor what was Socialism or Communism. Heated discussions were then taking place in the branches of the Socialist Party, about the question of whether the Socialist Party should remain in the Second International, should a Second-and-a-half International be founded, or should the Socialist Party join Lenin's Third International? I attended the meetings regularly, twice or thrice a week, and attentively listened to the discussions. First, I could not understand thoroughly. Why were the discussions so heated? Either with the Second, Second-and-a-half, or Third International, the revolution would be waged. What was the use of arguing then? As for the First International, what had become of it? What I wanted to know—and this precisely was not debated in the meetings—was: Which International sides with the people of the colonial countries?[11]

Ho Chi Minh's predicament as a young man will resonate with many today who wonder which international alliance to join, but are confused about all the different factions. (Wait a minute, is "international" a noun or an adjective!?) Nobody teaches this stuff in school. To understand we have to braid another strand into this story.

Better late than never, the Europeans were developing a revolutionary internationalism of their own. From the late nineteenth century through the twentieth, this anarchist, socialist, and communist lineage stretches from Karl Marx to Rosa Luxemburg to V.I. Lenin—from the International Workingmen's Association to the Communist International—from the Paris Commune to the Soviet Union. As Ho Chi Minh found, the Third, or Communist International, was the first in these to take sides firmly with the people in Africa, Asia, and Latin America. The Third International has an extensive history in relation to Africa and the African diaspora, which still a subject of study and debate.[12]

But it was not until October 2017 that this lineage was interwoven with the much older tradition from the other side of the Atlantic. Delegates and descendants of the anarchist, socialist, communist, anticolonialist, feminist, environmentalist, internationalist traditions were welcomed into in the *quilombo*. They were adopted, converted, and redeployed. The result is a route of struggle, stretching five hundred years to the horizon of the future: The combined strategy and plan of action of the First Ecosocialist International.

The First Ecosocialist International

As Kali Akuno said, "It's ecosocialism or death."[13] Catastrophic climate change and the sixth mass extinction no longer need any introduction—it's there on the tip of our tongues, and the only options are denial, disavowal, or revolution. As Joel Kovel wrote, it's "the end of capitalism or the end of the world."[14] This unprecedented crisis, like nothing humanity has ever seen since the late-Pleistocene, draws a line in the revolutionary tradition on both sides

The First Ecosocialist International emerged from a convocation process that was imagined in the early 2000s, meandered in Europe for a couple decades, was reenergized at the World Social Forum in Belem, Brazil, and came home to roost in Venezuela in 2015. From 2015 to 2017, a formal convocation process was kicked off, spreading from nine countries to nineteen, from one continent to five.

It has been constituted and centralized in a "Combined Strategy and Plan of Action," and coordinated around a "Route of Struggle." It was written collectively in groups and assemblies by two hundred hands over three days in liberated territory: Veroes, Yaracuy, in the Bolivarian Republic of Venezuela. It's no coincidence that two veteran Black Panthers were among its founding members. Here are their testimonies:

Charlotte O'Neal aka Mama C, Black Panther Party (Kansas City Chapter) and United African Alliance Community Center (Arusha, Tanzania): "'The Plan of Action' reads like poetry from the heart, something which is revolutionary in itself! The result of this work is phenomenal.... It's perfect in its understanding and execution, and should be put into action immediately. I hope that the rest of the world will have the opportunity to absorb its lessons and plans soon. I have no doubt that the seeds which have been sown are going to change ideas and conclusions and the paths ahead. What a blessing!...I am very excited to organize meetings here in Tanzania, between schools and artists who I work with there. I am honored to be a small part of this revolutionary movement that will be an example to change the world, community by community."[15]

Dhoruba Bin Wahad, Black Panther Party (New York Chapter), Community Change Africa (Ghana): "I'm impressed by the welcome of the people of Veroes in the state of Yaracuy, for their attention, their humility and their beauty, with whom we stayed for several days discussing the problems which affect our Mother Earth. I'm very proud to belong to the First Ecosocialist International, and I hope we can continue with this social movement.... We concluded that we must build an international movement, made up of progressive governments, activists and ordinary people, to save the planet from the devastation of the imperialist capitalist system which destroys the environment."[16]

As the saying goes, while bad news travels fast, good news travels slow. There hasn't been much fanfare or glossy publicity for the Ecosocialist International. But is has resonated where it counts most, for instance in the US prison system. One politicized prisoner wrote when he heard the news:

Ghani aka Kempis Songster: "The First Ecosocialist International in history; a hundred delegates?! From FIVE continents?! 19 Countries?! 12 indigenous nations?! And it all happened in Maroon communities?! Damn. We enter into a new era of hope and possibilities. Beautiful, brothers! The Ecosocialist International is pulsing with promise. I look forward to its translation to [E]nglish and to all the reports."[17]

These reflections continued into 2018. A continental tour of the US announcing the founding of the Ecosocialist International, with events from Los Angeles to Vermont and New York to New Orleans, culminated with a national convergence hosted by Cooperation Jackson in April 2018.

Jackson, Mississippi

The April 2017 edition of *The Cooperative Way* tells the story in real time:

> We are hosting an ECOSOCIALIST CONVERGENCE IN JACKSON from Friday April 20th through Sunday, April 22nd, in partnership with Ecosocialist Horizons and various adherents of the recently founded First Ecosocialist International.... The convergence will be a strategy and plan of action development session. A primary practical aim will be to start identifying, recruiting, uniting, and mobilizing the strategic forces necessary to build a political force that can unite around building a coherent Ecosocialist program and practice to emancipate oppressed people and the working class, save our species, halt the sixth extinction event, and liberate our Mother Earth from the terrors of capitalism and imperialism.[18]

Over the weekend, participants traversed principles and practices, peoples and programs, all of which were grounded in the rich soil of struggle upon which the City of Jackson Mississippi rests and rises. Colia Clark, civil rights movement veteran and Medgar Evers's field secretary, led a tour of historic Jackson, connecting the dots between the birth of Black Power and the emergence of ecosocialism. This history was complemented by Kali Akuno and Gyasi Williams, who guided participants on a tour of Cooperation Jackson's ongoing work, which ranges from fighting gentrification to building worker-owned cooperatives. From *kazi* (an African word for "work") to *trueke* (the Venezuelan concept of barter and trade), participants engaged in ancestral African and South American practices of collective labor and exchange, and hatched plans to spread the good news; developing strategies for communication and curriculum design around the practice and theory of ecosocialism.[19]

Participants recognized that the new international and its "Plan of Action" are only just the beginning, and began to outline additions and complements to its program, based on rereading its program and synthesizing it with the "Jackson Just Transition Plan" and the "Jackson-Kush Plan." Here we'll share only five of them, one for each of the elements on the Ecosocialist International's plan of action:

1. *Earth:* New stops were planned on the Route of Struggle—from Haiti to the Congo. And as these internationalist radicals gathered in Mississippi discussed Congo, the words of Malcolm X reverberated:

   > When I speak of some action for the Congo, that action also includes Congo, Mississippi. But the point and thing that I would like to impress upon every Afro-American leader is that there is no kind of action in this country ever going to bear fruit unless that action is tied in with the over-all international struggle. You waste your time when you talk to this man, just you and him. So when you talk to him, let him know that your brother is behind you, and you've got some brothers behind that brother. That's the only way to talk to him, that's the only language he knows.... As long as we think.... that we should get Mississippi straightened out before we worry about the Congo, you'll never get Mississippi straightened out. Not until you start realizing your connection with the Congo.... You can't understand what is going on in Mississippi if you don't understand what is going on in the Congo. And you can't really be interested in what's going on in Mississippi if you're not also interested in what's going on in the Congo. They're both the same. The same interests are at stake. The same sides are drawn up, the same schemes are at work in the Congo that are at work in Mississippi.[20]

2. *Spirit:* The program of the Ecosocialist International promises to "continue the struggle for the liberation of political prisoners," but the Jackson convergence went a step further. Attention was refocused on the general prison population of the United States, and the words of George Jackson resounded:

   > Only the prison movement has shown any promise of cutting across the ideological, racial and cultural barricades that have blocked the natural coalition of left-wing forces at all times in the past. So this movement must be used to provide an example for the partisans engaged at other levels of struggle. The issues involved and the dialectic which flows from an understanding of the clear objective existence of overt oppression could be the springboard for our entry into the tide of world-wide socialist consciousness.[21]

3. *Water:* Connecting the dots between the watersheds of the world, participants compared notes from struggles over water, from Flint to Buffalo to Los Angeles to New Orleans to New York. While strategizing to work together, they made plans to support the "First International Encounter of Sowers and Guardians of Water,"—the first stop on the Ecosocialist International's Route of Struggle—which was successfully carried through in November 2018 in the Plurinational State of Bolivia.[22]
4. *Air:* A video was produced to build greater solidarity between Venezuela and grassroots movements in the United States, who share a common position: "We are a threat because we resist."[23]
5. *Fire*: The year of this national convergence was also the 150th anniversary of the birth of historian and activist W.E.B. Du Bois. Participants reflected on his legacy, and in particular on the comment in his seminal book *Black Reconstruction*, about how the First International of Marx and Engels never took root in the US: "The international movement, however, took no real root in America.... The main activity of the International was in the North; they seemed to have no dream that the place for its most successful rooting was in the new political power of the Southern worker."[24] Today this power is best expressed and represented by the diverse ecosystem of cooperatives and assemblies and farms and popular schools and electoral politics that Jackson is heir to. That there is fertile soil for ecosocialism in the lands of the Choctaw and the Republic of New Afrika was summarized by the exclamation of one local participant: "George Washington Carver was an ecosocialist!"

Cooperation Jackson's newsletter celebrated both the future and the past, grounding its discussion of ecosocialism in the legacy of struggle in the US South. The newsletter reminded us that 2018 was the fiftieth anniversary of development of the Provisional Government of the Republic of New Afrika out of the Black Government Conference organized by the Malcolm X Society in Detroit, and also the fiftieth anniversary of the assassination of Martin Luther King Jr. in Memphis, Tennessee, at a sanitation workers' strike for dignity. "Both of these developments," they wrote, "were critical to the formulation of the Jackson-Kush Plan, which Cooperation Jackson is a vehicle of."[25]

If anyone is wondering how to connect the dots between the big picture and the local struggle, the answer is clear. Get involved with Cooperation Jackson. As John Clark, one of the participants in this convergence, wrote in his latest book, in a chapter on the legacy of the Black Panthers: "Paradoxically, it is by becoming more radically local that a movement is likely to spread far beyond its boundaries."[26]

Red, Black, and Green Destiny Weapon

At the end we go back to the beginning: the threat to all life on earth. *¡Planeta o muerte!* Ecosocialism or death! This talk of internationalism and Maroon history is all very well—but how will it help us to navigate the storm? For our conclusions we'll be guided by a far-sighted strategist whose life story—from Black Liberation Army to Maroon to ecosocialist—represents all three braids of our story. "I'm writing these words from a prison," Russell Maroon Shoatz explains. "Don't get bent out of shape about that, because I'm actually freer than many of you."[27]

> The global capitalist economic contradictions, along with the ecological devastation that is the product of centuries of unbridled misuse of the Earth's ecosystems, are propelling the rapid disintegration of societies across the planet. In such communities, we are witnessing something that resembles the Mel Gibson *Mad Max*, *The Road Warrior*, and *Beyond Thunderdome* movie trilogy. The forces that still "control" whatever state power functions in these territories are themselves entrenched in a struggle with other forces that are attempting to independently satisfy the survival needs of those around them. In many of these communities there is a three-way struggle between the truncated state, struggling subsistence elements, and a welter of warlord-style drug gangs and cartels.[28]

He goes on to discuss Libera, Sierra Leone, and Colombia. But then he brings it all home to Philadelphia, where conditions are different only by degree. The *Mad Max* scenario he predicts is not a matter of speculation. As George Jackson said, "It's predictable as nightfall."[29]

And so we get to the point—what we're going to do about it—the Red, Black, and Green Destiny Weapon. In the last chapter of his book, Shoatz puts his readers through a "training module"—a theory of history and revolution based on a well-known, popular movie:

A Prefigurative Matriarchal Interpretation of *Crouching Tiger, Hidden Dragon* (CTHD). From our point of view CTHD serves as a perfect training module, because this movie is centered on an epic struggle between patriarchal forces and an aspiring matriarchal womyn, who risks everything to seize the tools she needs to overcome male violence and control. To follow our reasoning you too must view CTHD.... Sometime after our shero returned home, this patriarch is summoned to retrieve the legendary Green Destiny sword that had been stolen from the local ruler's home, the ruler being our shero's father.... Our young shero believes that by possessing the Green Destiny she will solidify her effort to destroy patriarchy.... In our interpretation of CTHD our shero and her mentor are using the captured Green Destiny and their stolen martial arts skills to destroy the patriarchal "men's house," then to usher in a new matriarchal order—which we assume the Green Destiny's "magical" powers will allow them to accomplish.... We too need our own version of a special weapon.... [N]o matriarchal/ecosocialist order has any real chance of standing up to any serious effort by those who have these weapons and skills, unless that matriarchal/ecosocialist order does as our shero did: capture the Green Destiny weapon. This is what the African Americans who joined the Union forces during the US Civil War did, and what the deserters and mutineers did during the Russian Revolution.... A lesson learned from these examples—of the United States Civil War and the Russian Revolution—is that both groups of oppressed people would have found it extraordinarily difficult to reinvent the commons without the Green Destiny weapons they forged. In both cases those weapons were the products of a massive prefigurative project to help people see the necessity of obtaining positions in their societies that would provide them with opportunities to become professionally trained, and to win over others to join them in those highly trained arenas.... The primary problem is that the old Chinese, Vietnamese, African, and other anti-colonial struggles relied on space, time, and will in order to forge their Green Destiny weapons.... The establishment of a panopticon, however, has circumscribed that old method.... Only by establishing a core of professionally trained, matriarchal, ecosocialist, conscious, and

> fully committed individuals, can an effective foundation be laid to reinvent the commons in a world where the potential for overwhelming violence on the part of others is ever-present. Such a professionally trained and committed formation will be able to develop twenty-first-century ways to utilize space, time, and will to forge and wield its own Green Destiny Weapon.

To survive the gauntlets of climate catastrophe and world war, mass extinction, and mass incarceration—we need a Green Destiny Weapon. One that can overcome the panopticon of the interlocking directorates of National Security States (CIA-M16-Mossad-KGB-RAW, et al.). The politics of the armed lifeboat and isolated survivalism in the face of a global enemy is suicide. We need to preserve and propagate intercontinental unity—for islands to become archipelagoes and at last continents. We need an organizational form and a program of action which connects the immediate demands of the moment to the distant needs of the seventh generation. We need a global coordinating, deliberating, and decision-making vehicle that can coordinate the exodus toward and around the foundations of a future ecosocialist world-system. In this context, the First Ecosocialist International may be understood as a Red, Black, and Green Destiny Weapon: a tool to reclaim our own humanity, redeem our ancestors, and save our children.

To get there, the network of adherents of the Ecosocialist International, formed in Jackson, will have to evolve. In the sudden light of the global pandemic which hit the world this year, the following theses may serve as a guide:

- This crisis is the crucible in which we will forge the postcapitalist order.
- Just as the empire's nakedness is revealed, so too is its antidote and antithesis.
- The resolution of the world crisis hinges upon the emergence of ecosocialist leadership.
- The threshold we are crossing requires an overdue transformation of our tactics.
- Our task is not to introduce ecosocialism, but to bring the production of ecosystems and the distribution of essential goods and services under the control of freely associated workers.

- Representative social democracy as we know it is dead.
- We are on the crossroads of world war, just when global cooperation is most necessary.
- Now is the time to call for assemblies and congresses at every level, and to prepare for organizational and ideological struggle.
- International solidarity has been in hospice—now it must be reborn.

A new world is struggling to be born and indeed will be, for better or worse. Its best hope is in a global strategy and plan of action, with a route of struggle conceived to reweave Pangaea. Its mission is to not only transcend capitalism as a mode of production, but to resolve the most ancient lesion in the history of our species: our alienation from the rest of nature and thus from our own true nature. Ecosocialism or extinction! Now's the time to join with Cooperation Jackson, with the new International, and help forge a Red, Black, and Green Destiny Weapon.

Postscript—Colombo, September 2020

Research Agenda toward a Pan-African Ecosocialist Summit

The Route of Struggle of the Ecosocialist International connects dots between hot spots of decolonization. Collective actions in Bolivia, Puerto Rico, and Iraq have already been carried out.[30] Pending is "a panafrican summit to facilitate the interconnection between Our America and Our Africa [*Nuestramerica y Nuestrafrica*]." But every revolutionary practice requires its revolutionary theory. Therefore, the articulation of an Afrocentric ecosocialist theory is a priority. I can only begin to suggest its outline as a point of departure.

On the continent, Samora Machel (Mozambique), Julius Nyerere (Tanzania), Govan Mbeki (South Africa), Léopold Sédar Senghor (Senegal), Patrice Lumumba (Congo), Thomas Sankara (Burkina Faso), Amílcar Cabral (Guinea-Bissau), Mu'ammar al-Gaddhafi (Libya), Cheikh Anta Diop (Senegal), and Kwame Nkrumah (Ghana). In the diaspora, C.L.R. James (Trinidad), Walter Rodney (Guyana), Édouard Glissant (Martinique), Aimé Césaire (Martinique), and Frantz Fanon (Martinique/Algeria).

It is deeply important that a research agenda in Afrocentric ecosocialism drinks from the springs of not mere political theory but also of literature and music. The novels of Ngũgĩ wa Thiong'o, Ousmane Sembène, Chinua Achebe, and Patrick Chamoiseaux, among many others, are all full of material for Afrocentric ecosocialist theory. The music of Fela Kuti and Bob Marley, to name only two, are of high revolutionary ecosocialist caliber.

And for those alive now? Well, that's for us to know and you to find out. To the defeat of their enemies, and the defense of Mother Earth, we dedicate our lives.

Notes

1 "*Maestras cimarronas*"—female Maroon teachers; an active grassroots organization in the municipality of Veroes.

2 Glenn Alan Cheney, *Quilombo dos Palmares: Brazil's Lost Nation of Fugitive Slaves* (New London: Librarium, 2014).

3 For more about Maroons, see Quincy Saul, *Maroon Comix: Origins and Destinies* (Oakland: PM Press, 2017), which includes a "Maroon Library" listing hundreds of sources.

4 Richard Price, *First-Time: The Historical Vision of an Afro-American People* (Baltimore: John Hopkins University Press, 1983), 15, 17.

5 "In a sacred grove beside the village of Dángogó, shaded by equatorial trees, stands a weathered shrine to the Old-Time People (*Awónêngè*), those ancestors who "heard the guns of war." Whenever there is a collective crisis in the region—should the rains refuse to come on time or an epidemic sweep the river—it is to this shrine that the Saramkas repair. As libations of sugar-cane beer moisten the earth beneath newly raised flags, the Old-Time People are one by one invoked—their names spoken (or played on the *apínti* drum), their deeds recounted, their foibles recalled, and the drums/dances/songs that they once loved performed to give them special pleasure.... All history is thus: a radical selection from the immensely rich swirl of past human history." (Price, *First-Time,* 5).

6 For more on piracy as marronage, see Peter Linebaugh and Marcus Rediker, *The Many Headed Hydra: Sailors, Slaves, Commoners, and the Hidden History of the Revolutionary Atlantic* (Boston: Beacon Press, 2013); and Peter Lamborn Wilson, *Pirate Utopias: Moorish Corsairs and European Renegadoes* (New York: Autonomedia, 2003).

7 Julius Scott, *The Common Wind: Afro-American Currents in the Age of the Haitian Revolution* (London: Verso, 2020).

8 Malcolm X, *Malcolm X Speaks: Selected Speeches and Statements*, ed. George Breitman (New York: Grove Press, 1966), 121, 128–30.

9 George Jackson, *Soledad Brother: The Prison Letters of George Jackson* (Chicago: Lawrence Hill Books, 1994), 263–66.

10 Frantz Fanon, *The Wretched of the Earth*, trans. Constance Farrington (New York: Grove Press, 1963), 247–48.

11 Ho Chi Minh, *Ho Chi Minh on Revolution: Selected Writings 1920–66*, ed. Bernard B. Fall (New York: Signet Books, 1967), 23–24.

12 The dialectic of this ongoing debate is represented by the titles of two books: *Pan-Africanism or Communism* by George Padmore (1972) and *Pan-Africanism and Communism* by Hakim Adey (2013). For the history of the Third International and Black liberation in the United States, see Mark D. Naison, *Communists in Harlem During the Great Depression* (Urbana: University of Illinois Press, 2005), Robin D.G. Kelley, *Hammer and Hoe: Alabama Communists during the Great Depression* (Chapel

Hill: University of North Carolina Press, 2015), and Harry Haywood, *Negro Liberation* (New York: International Publishers, 1984).

13 See Kali Akuno, "Ecosocialism or Death," in this volume.

14 Joel Kovel, *The Enemy of Nature: The End of Capitalism or the End of the World?* (London: Zed Books, 2007).

15 "Testimonios sobre la primera Internacional Ecosocialista," quoted in *Lucha Indigena* no. 137 (January 2018).

16 Quincy Saul, "From the Plan of the Homeland to a Plan for the Planet," Telesur, December 8, 2017, accessed June 24, 2022, https://www.telesurenglish.net/opinion/From-the-Plan-of-the-Homeland-to-a-Plan-for-the-Planet-20171208-0010.html.

17 "Testimonios sobre la primera Internacional Ecosocialista," quoted in *Lucha Indigena*, Number 137, January 2018.

18 "Eco-Socialism: An Idea and Movement Whose Time Has Come," *The Cooperative Way: The Newsletter of Cooperation Jackson* 4, no. 3 (April 2018).

19 For more about *trueke*, see Quincy Saul, "Venezuela Farmers Fight Monsanto Seed Imperialism—and Win!" Telesur, October 14, 2016.

20 Malcolm X, *Malcolm X Speaks*, 90, 125.

21 George L. Jackson, *Blood in My Eye* (New York: Random House, 1972), 109.

22 See the documentary "Sowers and Guardians of Water," February 2, 2019, accessed June 24, 2022, https://www.youtube.com/watch?v=3PCI85YpBPo. Read the "Declaration of "K'oari" on the website of Ecosocialist Horizons (www.ecosocialisthorizons.com). And for a report, see Quincy Saul, "The First International Gathering of Sowers and Guardians of Water," *Counterpunch*, March 1, 2019.

23 See Kali Akuno's interview of Livio Rangel, "Venezuela: We Are a Threat Because We Resist," Reel News, April 23, 2018, https://www.youtube.com/watch?v=NoA3MYqV7yc.

24 W.E.B. Du Bois, *Black Reconstruction in America, 1860–1880* (New York: Oxford University Press, 2014).

25 *The Cooperative Way: The Newsletter of Cooperation Jackson* 4, no. 3 (April 2018), http://oldandnewproject.net/Essays/The_Cooperative_Way_Vol_4__Issue_3_web_FINAL.pdf.

26 John P. Clark, *Between the Earth and Empire: From the Necrocene to the Beloved Community* (Oakland: PM Press, 2019), 159.

27 Russell Maroon Shoatz, *Maroon the Implacable: The Collected Writings of Russell Maroon Shoatz*, ed. Fred Ho and Quincy Saul (Oakland: PM Press, 2013), 40.

28 Ibid. This and all the following quotes from Russell Maroon Shoatz cited below are from his book's last chapter, "The Question of Violence."

29 Jackson, *Blood in My Eye*, 79.

30 Community of K'oari, Tiraqu, "Convocation! To the First International Gathering of Sowers and Guardians of Water," Ecosocialist Horizons, August 15, 2018, https://ecosocialisthorizons.com/2018/08/convocation-to-the-first-international-gathering-of-sowers-and-guardians-of-water. Ben Barson, "Report from the Mesopotamian Water Forum," Ecosocialist Horizons, May 14, 2019, https://ecosocialisthorizons.com/2019/05/report-from-the-mesopotamian-water-forum. "The Boriken Declaration: January 2020," Ecosocialist Horizons, February 8, 2020, http://ecosocialisthorizons.com/2020/02/the-boriken-declaration-january-2020. All accessed August 1, 2022.

Countering the Fabrication Divide

Kali Akuno and Gyasi Williams for Cooperation Jackson and the Community Production Cooperative

The third digital revolution, a revolution in cyber-physical integration and personal fabrication, is changing the world, and changing humanity, culturally and physically, in the process.[1] The third digital revolution is marked by technological and knowledge breakthroughs that build on the first two digital revolutions, and the three industrial revolutions that preceded them, which are now fusing the physical, digital, and biological worlds—including the human body. The main technologies of this revolution include advanced robotics, computer numeric control (CNC) automation, 3D printing, biotechnology, nanotechnology, big data processing, artificial intelligence, and of course these autonomous vehicles we've been hearing so much about of late. As a result of these developments, soon millions of people will be able to make almost anything with their personal computer or smartphone and fabrication technology in their own homes. Truly, a new era of technological innovation is upon us. One that could enable many of the social freedoms envisioned by scientists and science fiction writers for over a century.

As we have painfully learned from the previous industrial and digital revolutions, technology is not entirely value neutral, meaning neither good nor bad. Under the social and economic system of capitalism, most technological innovation has been driven by the desire to maximize profits, reduce space/time limitations (i.e., how long it takes to make and deliver a commodity or service), and eliminate labor costs. So while it is true that the technology does not determine its own use (not yet anyway), its application and value have largely been determined by a small subset of humanity. We want to make sure that we change this equation with the third digital revolution. How we structure the ownership, control, and use of the technologies of the third digital revolution will either aid humanity in our collective quest for liberation, or deepen our species' inhumanity toward itself and our dear Mother Earth.

One thing is painfully clear, and that is if these technologies remain the exclusive property of the capitalist class and the transnational corporations they control, these tools will not be used for the benefit of the overwhelming majority of humanity, but to expand the profits and further consolidate the power of the 1% that rule the world. Under their control, these technologies will lead to a crisis of global unemployment on a scale unseen in human history. The end result will be a global dystopia, a social nightmare predicated on massive poverty, lawlessness, state repression, and ever greater human disposability rather than the utopia these technologies could potentially enable.

In order to make the future that we want, we have to openly confront the stark problems already at the heart of the third digital revolution, and there are several glaring problems already in plain sight. Despite great efforts toward democratizing the third digital revolution by making much of the technology "open source," historically oppressed and disenfranchised communities remain excluded. The same access gulf seen in the current "digital divide" is being replicated and deepened. Instead of a ubiquitous transformation, with equal access and distribution, what in fact is emerging is a "fabrication divide."

This divide is layered, multidimensional, and compounded. The first and obvious barrier to access is cost. Those who can afford the machines will eventually be able to produce whatever they want, while those who can't will remain dependent on the inequitable market, the forces that manipulate it, and the increasingly antiquated methods of production they employ to produce their consumer goods. While this revolution is spurred on by the dropping cost and rapid development of fabrication technology, Indigenous and working-class Black and Latinx populations will still find themselves at least a step behind as the cost of early adoption will continue to advantage the already privileged.

The issues of cost and accessibility lead directly to a discussion of class. The working class is almost always alienated from the market mechanisms that enable people to take the best advantage of emerging technology. Further still, the dismantling of society by the neoliberal project has eroded the bonds of social solidarity and eradicated the safety nets created through working-class political victories. The emergence of the third digital revolution within this sociopolitical context will only widen the inequality and access gaps that already exist. For example, the recent elimination of net neutrality combined with years of starving public schools of funding and eviscerating city services ensures that libraries and many other public services that once helped to counterbalance the technological gaps experienced by the working class during the latter half of the twentieth century are becoming ineffective or altogether nonexistent.

While there has been a great deal of public discussion about the advance of the third digital revolution and what benefits and threats it potentially poses, there has been little discussion about racial inequity within the third digital revolution. Without a major structural intervention, the third digital revolution will only exacerbate the existing digital divide. Again, here the problem is layered and compounded, for the advances in automation and artificial intelligence that the third digital revolution will advance will disproportionately eliminate many of the low-skill, low-wage, manual labor and service sector jobs that historically oppressed communities have been forced into over the last several years. Given some projections of massive job loss due to automation, there is a real question about whether the potential benefits this transformation could have will outweigh the severe pain and loss Indigenous, Black, and Latinx working-class populations will face as this technology advances.

Even less discussed than the class and race-based impacts of the third digital revolution are the gender disparities that are likely to deepen if there is no major intervention in the social advance of this development. Despite recent advances, it is no secret that women are grossly underrepresented in the technological and scientific arenas.[2] The question is: How can and will the gender inequities be addressed in the midst of the social transformations stimulated by the third digital revolution, and will the existing gender distribution patterns remain, be exasperated, or will they be eliminated?

The third digital revolution, like its predecessors, will undoubtedly make fundamental shifts not only to human society but to the planet as well, many of which have yet to be anticipated. One likely shift that must be examined is the potential of accelerated environmental catastrophe. Currently, 3D printing is all the rage, and for good reason. It inspires the imagination and hints at a future where we are able to download or create a file that will allow us to fabricate just about anything that we can imagine. The key question that hasn't been asked is how will humanity manage personal fabrication on a mass scale? The earth's resources are finite.

Nevertheless, capitalism has ingrained in us an infinite desire for commodities. While the methods of production under capitalism have been horrifically destructive to the environment, there is no guarantee that the appetites that have been programmed into us over the last several hundred years will suddenly accommodate themselves to ecological balance and sustainability if we are suddenly given the ability to fabricate what we want in the privacy of our own homes. There is a great deal of consciousness-raising and resocialization about our ecological limits and responsibilities, accompanied by major policy shifts, that must be done to prevent the resource depletion and massive fabrication waste that is likely to result from this technology becoming broadly adopted.

All of these challenging facets of the coming third digital revolution must be addressed, and quickly. The third digital revolution is emerging in a society with immense inequality and imbalance with regard to the integration of existing technology from the previous industrial and digital revolutions. As these historic developments converge into the third digital revolution, the concern is that not only will this inherited inequity continue but will be drastically deepened for all of the reasons listed above. Those of us seeking to realize the potential of the third digital revolution to help our species realize its full potential, must create the means to combat this deepening inequity, and democratize this transformation. If we can do that, we may very well be able to lay the foundation for a democratic and regenerative economic order, one that could potentially eliminate the extractive, exploitative, and utterly oppressive and undemocratic system that we are currently subjected to.

Those who seek to assist in democratizing the technology of the third digital revolution must understand that any initial investment at this time is risky. The road ahead is not clear. What we do know is that we cannot afford to leave the development of this technological revolution solely up to actors like Amazon, Google, Walmart, or the US Department of Defense. In their hands, it will only serve to further extract profits from the majority of humanity and maintain the imperial dominance of the US government through force of arms. However, finding capital players willing to make "nonextractive" investments that center on tech justice, cooperative business innovation, and production driven to fulfill human need over profit realization are hard to find. There are many organizations experimenting with getting this technology out to vulnerable populations to aid us from falling further behind the technological access gap, but none of us really know what will work initially, nor when the technology will be at a significantly advanced stage to truly replace the existing mode of production. The stakes are high, as are the risks at this stage. Nevertheless, we must struggle, as all early adopters should, to not only avoid being left out in the cold but to help guide the development in a democratic and egalitarian manner.

Creating the Future, Taking Risks, Co-constructing Solutions

Early adopter risk-taking is exactly what Cooperation Jackson is embarking upon with the launch of our community production center and community production cooperative.[3] Our aim is to make Jackson, Mississippi, the "city of the future," a transition city anchored in part in the practices of a "fab city"[4] that would transform our city into an international center of advanced, sustainable manufacturing utilizing 3D printing and other innovative tools of the third digital revolution. The only way we are going to come anywhere close to attaining anything like the utopia these technologies promise is by democratizing them and subjecting them to social use and production for the benefit of all, rather than the control and appropriation by the few.

The democratization of the technologies of the third digital revolution, both in their ownership and use, is one of the primary aims of Cooperation Jackson. To realize this aim we struggle for tech democracy and tech justice first and foremost by educating our members and the general public about the promises and perils of the technology so that people can make informed decisions.[5] We suggest this as a general framework of struggle. The next course of action we suggest is the pursuit of self-finance to acquire as much of this technology as we can, with the explicit intention of controlling these means of production and utilizing them for the direct benefit of our organization and our community.

Another course of action we suggest and are embarking upon is organizing our community for political and economic power to expand and reinforce our community production efforts. Our aim is to gradually make community production ubiquitous in our community, with the explicit intent of gradually replacing the exploitative and environmentally destructive methods of production in use at present. A related course of action is to utilize our political power to make demands on the government, the capitalist class, and the transnational corporations to remove the controls they have on the technology, like exclusive patents, in order to make these technologies publicly accessible. Another essential demand on the government is to make massive investments in these technologies to make them public utilities and/or commons and to ensure that the corporations make restorative investments in these utilities for the public good.[6]

We also think that public/community partnerships should be pursued on a municipal level to establish direct community ownership over these technologies to help ensure that vulnerable populations and historically oppressed communities gain direct access, with the prerequisite being where these communities are sufficiently organized and possess a degree of political power within the municipality. Public/community partnerships could also be essential toward capitalizing these democratic pursuits, by enabling the community to use both its tax wealth and various vehicles of self-finance to build out the necessary infrastructure in a manner that will ensure that it remains in the community commons or public domain. It is essential that these types of pursuits be public/community partnerships, with the community being organized in collective institutions like cooperatives, credit unions, community development corporations, etc., and not your typical public/private partnerships that will only remove this infrastructure from the commons or public domain as soon as possible in our neoliberal dominated world.

Further, given the steady decline in union membership, density, and overall social and political power, coupled with the ever-growing threats of automation, mechanization, big data, and artificial intelligence to the working class as a whole, we want to appeal to the various unions, in and out of the AFL-CIO, as the most organized sector of the working class in the US, to take the challenges of the third digital revolution head-on. In fact, we think organized labor should be leading the charge on the question of community production, as it is in the best position given its resources, skills, and strategic location in society to steer the third digital revolution in a democratic manner. In this vein, we want to encourage organized labor to utilize the tremendous investment resources it has at its disposal to start creating or investing in community production cooperatives throughout the US to further the ubiquitous development and utilization of the technology to help us all realize the benefits of a "zero-marginal-cost society" to combat climate change and eliminate the exploitation of the working class and the lingering social and material effects of racism, patriarchy, heterosexism, ableism, etc.[7] It is time for the cooperative and union movements, as vehicles of working-class self-organization, to reunite again, and community production units could and should be a strategic means toward this end.

Finally, we have to keep pushing forward-thinking universities, particularly public colleges and universities, and philanthropists to also provide support to community production development efforts seeking to democratize control of this technology early on.

These are the core elements of what we think is a transformative program to utilize and participate in the development of the third digital revolution for the benefit of our community and the liberation of the working class and all of humanity. We want and encourage other historically oppressed communities throughout the United States to follow this path, Jackson cannot and should not follow this path alone.

Supporting Cooperation Jackson and the Center for Community Production

If you agree with this analysis, in whole or in part, we need your help to bridge the fabrication divide. Cooperation Jackson is seeking broad public support for the development of our community production center. We are aiming to raise $600,000 to complete the purchase of the facilities, build them out, and equip them with all the utilities and equipment needed to create a dynamic production center. You can help build the center for community production by becoming a national donor or investor and recruiting others to do the same. The $600,000 figure does not have to be daunting, if we can recruit six hundred people to donate and/or invest $1,000 each, we can easily meet this goal. So let us not be swayed, but moved to organize to turn this vision into a transformative reality.

Notes

1 We draw our primary definition of the "third digital revolution" from the work of Neil Gershenfeld, particularly his recent work, *Designing Reality: How to Survive and Thrive in the Third Digital Revolution* (New York: Basic Books, 2017), cowritten with Alan Gershenfeld and Joel Cutcher-Gershenfeld.

2 For more detail on the gender gap in the science, technology, engineering, and math fields see, Lauren Camera, "Women Still Underrepresented in the STEM Fields," October 21, 2015, accessed June 13, 2022, https://www.usnews.com/news/articles/2015/10/21/women-still-underrepresented-in-stem-fields.

3 We derive our notion of "community production" from Blair Evans and Incite Focus, based in Detroit, Michigan. For more information, see Incite Focus, accessed June 14, 2022, https://www.incite-focus.org; and Matthew Piper, "Green City Diaries: Fab Lab and the Language of Nature," November 12, 2015, http://www.modeldmedia.com/features/greencity1113.aspx.

4 Fab city is a concept that grew out of the Fab Lab Network, see https://fab.city/about.html.

5 We are adopting the concept of "tech justice" from LabGov, which describes itself as the "laboratory for the governance of the city as a commons"; see LabGov, accessed June 14, 2022, http://www.labgov.city.

6 We utilize the notion and definition of the "commons" utilized within the Peer 2 Peer Network, see "What Is the Commons Transition?" accessed June 12, 2022, https://primer.commonstransition.org/1-short-articles/1-1-what-is-a-commons-transition.

7 We have adopted the notion of a "zero–marginal cost society" from Jeremy Rifkin, *The Zero–Marginal Cost Society: The Internet of Things, the Collaborative Commons, and the Eclipse of Capitalism* (New York: Palgrave Macmillan, 2014).

Fearless Cities and Radical Municipalism

Sophie L. Gonick

In 2009, the Malcolm X Grassroots Movement (MXGM) decided to run a candidate in municipal elections in Jackson, Mississippi. A radical Black organization, MXGM identified local electoral politics as one arena in which to advance liberation within the highly unequal Mississippi capital, and so proposed Chokwe Lumumba as a candidate for city council. They went on to craft Lumumba's 2012 mayoral platform, which proposed a radical municipalist agenda called the Jackson-Kush Plan. The success of this initiative led to the birth of Cooperation Jackson in 2014, which sought to instantiate the plan's proposal to democratize the economy from below through worker's cooperatives and the solidarity economy.

Similar electoral victories at the municipal scale have emerged across the North Atlantic: In 2015, progressive citizens' coalitions swept municipal elections throughout the Spanish peninsula. In 2013, Bill de Blasio was elected mayor of New York City on a platform that empowered citizens and encouraged new forms of participation (even while his tenure has been a deep disappointment to progressives). While Cooperation Jackson, the Spanish municipalist platforms, and de Blasio's win are born out of distinct histories and have uneven records of success, they have all engaged with the idea of municipalism. That idea broadly looks to the city and its institutions of rule as key sites for the instantiation of radical forms of democracy. As a rallying cry for a variety of activisms, municipalism has inspired a new generation of political leaders and organizers across diverse geographies, from Rojava's governance programs, to the emergence of democracy in postrevolutionary Tunisia, or to new experiments around land and property in the deeply unequal City of Jackson. In response to a global landscape that seeks radical urban transformation, Fearless Cities has emerged as a mechanism for sharing and learning.

In this essay, I explore some of the ideas behind Fearless Cities and radical municipalism, while delving into the material histories and shared horizons that have brought this network into being. In particular, I examine the conditions and struggles across the urban North Atlantic, with examples drawn from cases of Jackson, Mississippi, New York City, Madrid, and Barcelona.

Fearless Cities

How might we imagine the city in more just terms? What are the emancipatory possibilities of the urban and the local as key sites of struggle? Can social movements and electoral politics work together to effect radical change? And can a network of unruly cities, horizontal collectives, municipal experiments, and urban activists resist global right-wing revanchism and beat back its advances? Such questions are what animates Fearless Cities, which aims to transform the ways in which we do urban politics, configuring it as a key arena for radical change. A variety of different political projects have come together under its umbrella to explore the radical possibilities of the city as a site of struggle, but also love, community, and solidarity. Cooperation Jackson has been a central player within the network, through which they put forward a robust reimagining of institutional power. Here formal politics must engage with alternative spaces that celebrate the multiplicity of the urban experience—feminist, queer, multiracial, migrant—often left out of politics as usual. Rather than align themselves around traditional parties, the grassroots collectives and insurgent candidacies that comprise Fearless Cities seek to bring the wisdom and energy of street organizing and activism into official sites of political power.

Fearless Cities demands that city hall be accountable to the neighborhood assembly and insists that other forms of knowledge and action can inflect or even replace bureaucratic expertise. In Barcelona, for example, the insurgent mayoral candidacy of Ada Colau brought her lengthy experience as a housing activist to bear on pressing questions of gentrification and displacement. It was in the assemblies and protests, the blocked evictions, and the late-night plenary sessions where new forms of solidarity and political horizons emerged and took hold. In the process, social movement collectives imagined an alternative urban future, one predicated on collective life and commonality, sociability, and sanctuary. Barcelona en Comú and their counterparts demanded a similar symbiosis between interior and exterior, in which state institutions are no longer the bastion of the elite and instead porous—they do and must rely on their constituents, and thus in this moment there is a constant intermingling of the institutional interior with the messy, glorious audacity of the everyday. Hence new experiments with citizen participation and regular mayoral visits to seemingly forgotten neighborhoods in peripheral corners of the city.

Municipalism as both an object of study and a tool for praxis can invigorate place-based politics. As a project that engages both institutions of state rule and autonomous forms of activism, it allows for the flourishing of distinct repertoires of practice that bridge different kinds organizing. Further, as we have witnessed in our events in New York, municipalism can bring together a diversity of publics to engage with the deeply political questions of dwelling together, constructing community, and resisting the predations of capitalist development. I am hesitant to call this purely *urban* politics, because many of the locales that have both developed and could benefit from municipalist experiments fall outside the bounds of what we might consider the urban. So too does it resist the label of "local," as its conscious engagement with various scales and networks of exchange reveal that immediate specificities are bound up within much broader processes of transformation and extraction. Thus, the insistence on the municipal brings into focus how the activities of everyday are embedded in a rich landscape of politics, policy and governance, and insurgent activism.

Against the Global Right

Let us not be naive and only celebratory when considering the emergence of Fearless Cities. What hastened its creation, after all, has been the rise of virulent right-wing nationalism in many places across the globe. We know well the case of Trump and the GOP's wholesale embrace of a white supremacist, anti-urban politics of punishment. Elsewhere, right-wing populism has transformed electoral politics, often through laser-like attention to migration. In national elections in many European countries, traditional parties of both the Left and Right have faced challenges from insurgent populist groups. Many of these populist campaigns are explicitly anti-immigrant, from Viktor Orbán's government in Hungary, to the enduring pull of Marine Le Pen's National Front. These political currents have also put into doubt the future of Europe, its union, and its common currency. The postwar liberal consensus appears to be crumbling, particularly in relation to questions of borders and national sovereignty. We saw these trends reach their apogee in the 2017 drama of Brexit, which enfolded the themes of immigration, Euro-skepticism, territorial control, globalization, and austerity economics into a popular politics of dissent. We are left wondering, then, what we might build out of the ashes of liberalism and its myriad institutions.

Municipalist experiments see a way forward through a flourishing politics from below. Indeed, the Fearless Cities network makes evident another, more inclusive global politics that rebukes the hegemony of the nation-state. The drumbeat of nationalism has fixed our gaze on the nation-state, a sagging and in many ways antiquated political body. The obsession with borders in particular continues to draw our attention to questions of sovereignty writ large. Yet this obsession occludes the ways in which borders are constantly redrawn at much more intimate scales. In the neighborhood, the apartment block, the sidewalk, too, people interact with one another, struggle with the conditions of rising inequality, and articulate the terms of cohabitation. A fearless city thus insists on the municipality as a key political instrument. Here we might come together to share our vision of the good life. The Fearless Cities network draws attention to the globality of these struggles against the dangerous scourge of revanchist politics. Resisting the pull of the nation-state, it evinces a politics from below that might contest our contemporary landscape of nationalist white supremacy. In coming together, Barcelona, Paris, and New York, for example, can put forward more inclusive models of sociality and exchange that rebuke the rightward turn.

Against the anxious chatter of borders and demographic transformation, cities have become crucibles for new forms of conviviality and dwelling together. Barcelona en Comú declared the Catalan capital a sanctuary city immediately upon taking office. A new wave of Italian electoral initiatives has experimented with novel forms of governance throughout many southern towns and cities, and explicitly sought to include migrants within participatory processes. Meanwhile, from rent strikes to Black Lives Matter and Abolish ICE, many of our most exciting and transformative political struggles contest decidedly local questions that nonetheless connect with much broader terrains of action. For example, activist responses to the June 2020 police murder of George Floyd confront the vast landscape of militarized policing, the management of surplus populations through prisons, and the generalized expendability of Black life in a system built on white supremacy. But they also are hyperfocused on the local particularities of inequality as it is managed through the police, municipal finance, segregated schooling, inequitable transportation systems, immigrant detention centers, access to food and water, and the deepening fissures brought about by commodified housing.

In an interview, the late anthropologist and activist David Graeber talks about the need to coordinate these disparate efforts under a unified umbrella. For him, drawing them together under a loose confederation is a means of ensuring a lively bottom-up politics. Here the neighborhood, the unions, the grassroots collectives might participate in the daily politics of social reproduction. Constant experimentation in participation and inclusivity can offer a powerful antidote to the tyranny of authoritarianism. A confederation, meanwhile, can ensure both accountability and longevity, to resist the enervation of activism and organizing. As such, it might offer a renewed internationalism predicated on the symbiosis of local and global.

Undoing White Supremacy

To beat back the march of white supremacy, fearless cities must not only put forward an alternative international confederation to make evident a more emancipatory horizon of possibility. Rather, they must also utilize such as a structure as a key circuit of exchange. Here disparate places learn from and emulate one another in fighting for change, such that Barcelona, Spain, might learn from Jackson, Mississippi. Sharing knowledge, tactics, and repertoires of action is of particular importance in our current moment. From climate change to migration, many of our most pressing issues are felt acutely at the local level, yet require strategic coordination across a host of different scales and spaces. Of particular interest of late has been the increasingly globalized struggle for Black lives, and subsequent confrontation with the immediate manifestations of race, racism, and racialization. Indeed, the advance of white supremacy requires we elaborate antiracist praxes.

Europe in particular has not yet found the language or will to discuss the specter of race. The rise of revanchist nationalist politics has of course been accompanied by a resurgence of racism, evident in xenophobic border policy, rising anti-Semitism, and the Mediterranean's longstanding role as a mass burial ground. The problem of race in Europe has long remained a problem understood mostly in the starkest American terms, of Black ghettoes and race riots, or as the lingering vestiges of the Holocaust. The variable of class has long been paramount in understanding and analyzing urban difference, from Friedrich Engels (who nonetheless disparaged the Irish on racial terms) to more recent engagements with precarity in the face of austerity. Anything less than mass extermination is rendered largely null and void, or the spectral afterlife of long-ago colonial exploits. Antiracism efforts, meanwhile, often depict the racialized other as a subject deserving of pity, rather than a political actor enmeshed in the social fabric of the everyday.

Our futures on both sides of the Atlantic, however, are clearly multiracial. In Spain, over the course of a single decade (2000–2010), migration went from being a novel phenomenon to a fact of everyday life. Urban centers are now home to lively immigrant enclaves and ethnic mixing. In November 2019, I spent three weeks on a fellowship in Olot, Catalonia, an old industrial town still steeped in money from its heyday in the textile trade. The town is now home to over eighty nationalities that speak over sixty languages. Out to lunch with other fellows one Sunday, we witnessed an enormous Sikh parade go past our restaurant. Small floats bedecked in marigolds went by as hundreds of South Asian men and women marched through the street. Such scenes are no longer unusual; rather they constitute a facet of daily life in a small city at a distinct remove from what we might think of as a major international center (Barcelona is about two hours away).

How might places not steeped in the language of race and racism confront demographic transformations? During the first Fearless Cities in 2017, I joined a motley crew of activists, elected officials, grassroots organizers, and academics sitting under the gothic arches of an interior patio, where we had convened to discuss race and municipalism. Much of the program centered on housing and governance, urban politics, and political campaigns. This session was the lone hour devoted to the question of race and praxis. Indeed, despite dramatic demographic shifts, neither Fearless Cities nor the broader project of Spanish municipalism had taken up the question of immigration and ethnic and racial difference as a serious component of contemporary urban governance.

Yet racial pasts and presents, and fear of the ethnic other infect everyday discourse and policy directives, configuring immigrant neighborhoods across the continent, from Brussels's Molenbeek to Madrid's San Cristóbal de los Ángeles, into dangerous cancers to be excised from the greater urban polity. One participant exhorted us to remember that, indeed, "White supremacy predates America; it is a European construct." During the summer of 2020, as Black Lives Matter went global, activists in Barcelona, Brussels, and other Fearless Cities also took to the streets. Barcelona en Comú now grapples with what Black Lives Matter might mean within the Catalan and Spanish context, and a recent event asked, "Is the Left racist?" On Twitter I rebuked this formulation—it is not enough to determine whether *X* is racist. Instead, we might introduce frames of understanding that address race and racialization. In this endeavor, counterparts across the network might offer radical and trenchant examples, from Cooperation Jackson's foundational engagement with the Black radical tradition, to Wet'suwet'en opposition to oil and gas companies on unceded First Nations territories in Canada.

The Fearless Cities network exists precisely because in coming together and sharing our collective histories, capabilities, and challenges, we can illuminate similar points of struggle, even when they are not obvious at first blush. Thus, Barcelona can learn from Jackson as it grapples with how Black lives matter within the European context. A truly emancipatory municipalism must engage with difference—class, gender, age, and yes, race—in the pursuit of radical democracy.

Social Movements and the Growth Machine

While it seeks to instantiate an emancipatory international network, Fearless Cities' radical imagination responds to pressing local questions in addition to the retrenchment of revanchist national politics. Central to the various political projects under its umbrella is fierce struggle against the deepening inequalities of urban life. Indeed, while the municipality is often the site of cooperation and dwelling together, it is also where we feel and see the ravages of neoliberal rule. Thus, the municipalist project also contests the city as growth machine.

In the age of neoliberalism and austerity, cities have been forced to fend for themselves in the rush for finances. Reactionary politics across the North Atlantic have a markedly anti-urban thrust. In Spain, the Francisco Franco dictatorship espoused an ideology that celebrated the small town and disparaged the city. Its legacy, deeply rooted in the Spanish Right, is evident in national priorities and budgets, which have starved municipal budgets over the course of the democratic era. In the United States, we see a similar anti-urban bent within our politics. Yes, Trump and his minions decry the "inner city," an outdated notion of the racialized ghetto (is there any other kind?) of vice and crime. But the federal budget has long prioritized large rural swathes of the country, such that major cities pay out far more in taxes than what they receive in turn. This mismatch is echoed in our political arrangements, which accord rural voters far more political power at the national level (a framework echoed in Spain). Even while cities are the clear economic engines of the US economy, they remain a political afterthought within both political discourse and practice.

Urban development that emerges out of this political arrangement privileges elite spaces over comprehensive urban growth, and the endless spread of the private property model. Thus, we see Hudson Yards in Manhattan, which used tax subsidies meant for Harlem in order to build a luxury, privatized urban spectacle for the 0.01%. In Madrid, the municipal government sought to build 300,000 new housing units—all under the rubric of homeownership—over the course of the early 2000s, despite an estimated shortage of only 120,000–170,000. In both cases, city government predicted hefty returns on future sales and property taxes, which might finance municipal budgets in perpetuity. What they actually produced, however, was vast amounts of empty real estate.

Once again, the question of sharing is paramount. The Fearless Cities network has allowed emergent political projects to share tactics of resistance. As we see our cities transformed through the ubiquity of apps, for example, Cooperation Jackson has been in conversation with Barcelona en Comú about how to resist the inequities wrought by algorithms. Ada Colau's city hall has pushed back forcefully against the tyranny of AirBnB, which has transformed the local housing market. Where once there were homes, now there are tourist rentals, a situation that has inspired a host of new policies. So too has the regulated taxi industry seen its fortunes fall with the advent of Uber. Yet rather than submitting to what geographer Desiree Fields has termed "platform urbanism," Barcelona has used municipal law as a mechanism of containment and even disassembly. Cooperation Jackson, observing similar processes unfolding in their city, fully endorsed the strategy of building an international municipalist movement to act in solidarity with others to restrain, contain, and ultimately defeat these exploitative tech apps. As such, they have used Barcelona's techniques in order to explore how to combat algorithmic discrimination and dispossession.

Yet municipal law might not be enough to confront the growth machine and its newer, tech-based manifestations. Indeed, the municipalist turn reveals the fundamental role of social movements in forcing transformation. Institutions alone cannot do the work. In Jackson, New York City, Barcelona, and Madrid, insurgent candidates were elected on promises of doing away with urbanization as usual. But resisting the urban status quo has proved difficult. In Jackson under the leadership of Chokwe Antar Lumumba, plans continue for a hospital complex that Cooperation Jackson anticipates will lead to gentrification in historically poor and Black areas of the city. Likewise, de Blasio's affordable housing plan included rezoning parts of East New York, which activists and housing experts predicted would only raise rents and displace poor people of color. In Madrid, the Manuela Carmena administration continued with an enormous commercial real estate project on the city's northern edge, long a speculative frontier for multinational corporate interests.

Social movements thus must do the work of unmaking ongoing logics of elite urbanism and its reliance on private property. Across a number of cities, rent strikes in the face of the pandemic have demanded rent forgiveness instead of deferrals. More audacious land grabs either by stealth or spectacle have insisted on the importance of local community and sociability in the face of gentrification. During the summer of 2017, for example, a huge coalition of Madrid activists occupied an enormous historic building in the urban center. Renamed "La Ingobernable," the building had been part of a corruption scheme under the previous municipal government. It became a vibrant social center in a moment of increasing gentrification and an affordability crisis. Its occupation illuminated the ways in which the logics that propelled Madrid and Spain's dramatic crash continue to dictate the production of the city.

As revealed in this volume, meanwhile, Cooperation Jackson has not been content to observe the ongoing predations of capitalist urban development under the Lumumba administration. One key tactic has been the outright purchase of land as a stealth move to prevent gentrification and disrupt the growth machine. While deeding the land to the tribal communities that have long made the area their home, Cooperation Jackson also draws upon legacies of the Black radical tradition that see land as fundamental to liberation. Property here becomes not a tool for speculative growth, but rather a necessary precondition for radical autonomy against the market. The Jackson experiment demonstrates how land markets can also be used against themselves.

These claims to space draw attention to the limits of institutional politics. The efflorescence of Spanish political projects such as Barcelona en Comú and Ahora Madrid promised new modes of governance. At the same time, it left social movements depleted, as many central protagonists made their way into official positions of power. The results, however, have been mixed. In Madrid, the city center has emerged from urban crisis shiny and new, as old commerce has been replaced by multinational chain stores pumped full of tourist dollars. There appears little room for ordinary urban life. And so La Ingobernable issued a challenge, insisting on the need for alternative spaces and collective life organized from below. Drawing on the experience and limits of the 15-M movement, it injects new activism into the city: while squatting is not new, this effort consciously brought together diverse groups to experiment with alternative forms of inhabiting the city. The politics of ungovernability, then, is one of unruly opposition and disobedience but also constant vigilance.

In Jackson, meanwhile, Lumumba's tenure has not substantively improved the city for poor Black folk. The COVID-19 pandemic has brought home this reality: health care is spotty, expensive, and far away. Public transport is practically nonexistent. The police continue to have wide leeway. Cooperation Jackson has thus sought out new avenues to effect change. From urban farming to 3D printing, their model of economic solidarity and autonomy creates alternative institutions that operate outside official urban development policy. Engagement with the state, then, is on an ad hoc basis. As left organizations such as the Democratic Socialists of America flirt with the romance of electoral politics, Cooperation Jackson continuously calls out the limits of that model of transformation. In both Madrid and Jackson, then, everyday politics also reveals that change cannot come from new institutional blood alone. Rather, it requires agitation, insurgency, and confrontation with the past, present, and possible future of producing the city and its inequalities.

Ecosocialism or Death

An Interview with Kali Akuno by the Editors of *Jacobin*

The Green New Deal (GND) is now part of the national conversation. But for decades, social movements have been doing the on-the-ground work to resist fossil capitalism and envision a different future. Such grassroots social mobilization—but at a massive scale—is vital to ensuring the GND catalyzes transformative social change.

Cooperation Jackson is at the forefront of ecosocialist organizing to create a new society and economy from the bottom up. Cooperation Jackson encompasses a network of worker cooperatives and supporting institutions fighting to build a solidarity economy in Mississippi and beyond. *Jacobin's* Green New Deal editorial team spoke with Kali Akuno, the cofounder and executive director of Cooperation Jackson, and coeditor of *Jackson Rising: The Struggle for Economic Democracy and Black Self-Determination in Jackson, Mississippi.*

In this wide-ranging interview, we discussed the links between local ecosocialist action, national movement-building, and an internationalist orientation; tactics and strategies for interacting with electoral politics to radicalize the GND—and much more. Throughout, Akuno draws on a long history of environmental justice activism in the United States and around the world, providing key lessons about how to move forward—and quickly—to generate a militant, mass movement for a just planet.

***Jacobin*: We're in an interesting political moment where there's a lot of excitement around a GND coming from insurgent left-wing Democrats, but also a lot of pushback from centrists in the party who have a lot of power, as we saw in Nancy Pelosi's move to weaken the Select**

Committee on a GND. How can we be strategic about interacting with different representatives and power players? Looking forward to 2020, how can we orient ourselves toward the most radical GND possible?

KA: Organizing is the answer. We have to organize a strong independent base to advance the transition program we need, be it the Green New Deal or anything similar. Without that this epic issue will be held hostage to forces seeking to maintain the capitalist system as is, whether it be the Democratic or Republican variety of this worldview and its articulated interests. And we have to build this base to advance two strategies at once.

One, we have to organize a mass base within the working class, particularly around the job-focused side of the just transition framework. We have to articulate a program that concretely addresses the class's immediate and medium-term need for jobs and stable income around the expansion of existing "green" industries and the development of new ones, like digital fabrication or what we call community production, that will enable a comprehensive energy and consumption transition. This will have to be a social movement first and foremost, which understands electoral politics as a tactic and not an end unto itself.

For our part, one of the critical initiatives that we as Cooperation Jackson are arguing for is the development of a broad "union-co-op" alliance that would seek to unite the three forms of the organized working-class movement in this country—i.e., the trade unions, workers' centers, and worker cooperatives—around what we call a "build and fight" program. It would seek to construct new worker-owned and self-managed enterprises rooted in sustainable methods of production on the build side and to enact various means of appropriation of the existing enterprises by their workers on the fight side, which would transition these industries into sustainable practices (or in some cases phase them out entirely). We think this is a means toward building the independence that is required to dictate the terms of the political struggle in the electoral arena.

The second strategy calls for mass civil disobedience, as we witnessed at Standing Rock. We have to recognize that the neoliberal and reactionary forces at the heart of the Democratic Party are only part of the problem. The main enemy is and will be the petrochemical transnationals. We have to weaken their ability to extract, and this entails stopping new exploration and production initiatives. This is critical because it will weaken their power, particularly their financial power, which is at the heart of their lobbying power. If we can break that, we won't have to worry about the centrists, as you put it.

J: Cooperation Jackson is a local project, and a lot of the most exciting left projects now are local or municipal. The Green New Deal is likely to involve a lot of money that will ultimately be spent by local bodies. Yet the history of the US, including the New Deal, includes a lot of examples of local institutions actually defending inequalities and privileges from federal intervention, whereas something like what W.E.B. Du Bois called "abolition democracy" required federal back-up. How do you think about the role of decentralization and the federal government in terms of a Green New Deal, especially in the early years?

KA: Cooperation Jackson is a locally situated project, as you noted, but we see ourselves as part of an international, or more appropriately, several international movements. I say this because we don't think the answers to the questions posed are local or national; they are of necessity global. We have to build an international movement to stop runaway climate change and the sixth great extinction event that we are living through right now. There is no way around that.

One of the reasons why we have to build a powerful international movement is to fortify our national, regional, and local movements against the reactionary threats and counter-movements that exist throughout the US, but that are extremely concentrated in places like Mississippi. For instance, on a practical level, being connected to an array of international forces helps give cover to our work in Jackson. We can bring various types of pressure to bear on local reactionary forces whose constant threats against us can be mitigated (to varying degrees) by acts of economic and political reprisal by our international (and national) allies.

To the extent that the Green New Deal becomes policy, and is rooted in a radical just transition framework, it will make a significant contribution toward addressing the climate crisis as it transforms energy and consumption practices in the US, particularly those of the government, which is one of the leading carbon emitters on the planet. However, in order for the Green New Deal to be effective in its implementation, it is going to have to be extremely nuanced to address the situated racial and class inequalities that are at the heart of your question.

So for instance, barring a major radical transformation of the Mississippi government (and society), we in Jackson would need a direct relationship with the federal government to ensure access to the federal resources provided by the Green New Deal. Under present conditions, if those resources were allocated to the state government alone, you best believe that Jackson would only receive a fraction of those resources—if that. The primary reason being the ongoing structural intersections between settler colonialism, capitalism, and white supremacy that continue to define the US as a project.

Therefore, in order to be effective, the Green New Deal must not be one-dimensional in its orientation—i.e., only concern itself with reducing carbon emissions, without taking into account how to address and overcome the racial, class, gender, and regional-based inequities in this society.

J: Cooperation Jackson has been working on cooperative agricultural models. What role should food sovereignty movements play in the GND, in terms of agricultural production methods?

KA: A significant part of the sixth extinction event is the rapid loss of habitat and corresponding ecological destruction that countless species have suffered the past two hundred years. We have to, and I stress have to, figure out a way to severely restrict our habitat (i.e., land) use and engage in some major ecological restoration.

The challenge is how to produce more food, on smaller plots of land, without resorting to genetic modification. We haven't figured this out, to my mind. Not even close. I think permaculture points us in the right direction, as does some degree of small-scale agriculture to at least break the stranglehold the monopolies currently have. I also think we will need to maximize urban density, fairly significantly, to enable more habitats to be recuperated for other species and to restore ecological balance and the replenishment of the soil, which are major carbon sinks. In doing this we will have to turn our urban spaces into "living farms" to address many of our caloric needs.

The Green New Deal is going to have to address this challenge head-on and leave ample room for experimentation, but an experimentation that intentionally breaks the power of the monopolies and creates new incentives for production that are not profit driven or bound.

J: You've been very lucid on the problem of productivism that's implicit in a lot of Green New Deal proposals. One way some of us have tried

to address this issue is by emphasizing other kinds of work, like care work. Another idea out there is to transition huge amounts of the workforce toward part-time work—that is, to distribute existing work more evenly. What are some of the ways you think we should finesse a jobs guarantee to avoid reproducing capitalist and/or socialist productivist politics?

KA: The Left has to start positioning itself around improving the overall quality of life of the working class, the oppressed, and humanity as a whole. A broader distribution of work is a necessary step in this direction without question, and it's not only the right direction, but the imperative one. However, this has to be combined with forms of solidarity exchange to improve the quality of life of the majority of humanity. This is where things like time banking on a mass scale can and should come in. As well as the overall expansion of the commons.

To my mind, this will also entail transitional measures, such as a universal basic income (UBI). I say transitional because instituting a UBI without socializing the means of production would only serve to reproduce the capitalist logic of accumulation and the unequal relationships that are necessary for its reproduction.

Ultimately, I think we are going to have to develop a comprehensive and democratic planning system that equitably distributes the essential goods and services we all need to survive and thrive. And to be clear, I'm not arguing for a return to the centralized state-capitalist economies of the twentieth century, but the democratic socialization of the emergent information-based exchange economies, and that would utilize technological innovations to create a regenerative economy.

This would entail, at least in its early stages, various rules and limits, to make sure that exchanges stay within scientific and social limits related to resource extraction and energy utilization, until they become normative—which would take a few generations to undo the century of conspicuous consumption that has been advanced and promoted by late capitalism.

J: You've pointed to Indigenous leadership in stopping pipelines at places like Standing Rock and argued we need to "scale up our campaigns against the oil companies," including through direct action. Others have called for nationalizing and shutting down oil and gas companies. What does scaling-up the fight against fossil fuel companies

look like? What's the political path to taking down these incredibly rich and powerful companies?

KA: As I noted, the type of direct action that we witnessed at Standing Rock is where we are going to have to go. The march of death that the petrochemical companies are leading us on leaves us with no other choice.

There are some critical steps that must be taken before we get to that level of mass direct action on an ongoing basis. We have to do a much more thorough job of getting the masses of people to understand the severity of the crisis *and* our collective ability to do something about it. We have some hearts and minds to win; and we have to defeat the notion that capitalism can't be defeated. It's going to be hard, but it's not an immutable system.

The forces of reaction are doing everything within their power to make the direct action we've seen over the last decade explicitly illegal. They are going to escalate their brutality. Standing Rock should have taught us that. Indeed, many land, water, and sky protectors are already getting killed throughout the Global South.

We are going to have to get people to understand that preserving life on this planet is well worth the sacrifices that thousands if not millions of us are going to have to consciously make, by throwing our bodies directly on the line against the system. We are at the midnight hour, and it's ecosocialism or death. We have to be clear about what it will entail to eliminate the current system.

This type of consciousness-raising has to precede options such as nationalization as a means of liquidating fossil capital. This doesn't mean that we shouldn't introduce the idea and use it as a motivating factor, but we have to be real that it is going to take millions of people acting in accord with one another to make this option a concrete reality.

J: You've been active in the environmental justice movement for a long time. What lessons do you draw from that work? What kinds of strategies and coalitions have been most effective? What can we learn from the people who have been fighting on this for a long time about how to take on powerful industries?

KA: To be honest, the answer to this question would take a book. Let me redirect the question a bit. It is time that we seriously appreciate the insights of groups like Earth First! In terms of social movement development, they were ahead of their time. Our challenge now is figuring out how to scale them up significantly and in a very short period of time—within five years, because we only have a decade at best to get this right.

We need to reevaluate the differences in outcomes between the ecologically oriented movements of the 1960s and 1970s from those of the 1990s to the present. It is no accident that the most significant environmental legislation yet passed in the US, like the Endangered Species Act, the construction of the Environmental Protection Agency, the Clean Air Act, were passed in the late 1960s and early 1970s—and by Richard Nixon no less. These acts were passed on the basis of the strength and militancy of the social movements of the era, which posed a direct threat to the system.

The ecological movements of the 1990s to the present have not benefited from coexisting with strong, militant movements among broad layers of the oppressed and the working class. In the absence of these latter movements, the struggles against environmental racism and for climate justice have had to rely on lobbying to address their demands. This has in turn forced these movements to rely on "good politicians," rather than creating conditions that the system had to respond to—or else. We have to build movements that have the size, clarity, strength, and determination to pose clear "or else" threats.

J: Internationalism is one of the principles of Cooperation Jackson, and you've emphasized the importance of internationalism on climate in particular. What would it look like to build internationalist policies into a GND? And what examples of political projects in the Global South—of ecosocialism, just transitions, sustainable agriculture, cooperatives, energy democracy, etc.—do you find inspiring or exciting? How can leftists in the US connect to, support, and learn from those projects?
KA: Another excellent question. I will mention four critical policies:

1. Policies that create international mechanisms and institutions that work directly with Indigenous peoples and communities in the rainforest regions of Africa, Asia, the Caribbean, Latin America, and Oceania to stop the operations of multinational mining, petrochemical, agricultural, fishing, and medical corporations. These policies would need to explicitly counter the United Nations

Reducing Emissions from Deforestation and Forest Degradation in Developing Countries (UN REDD) program—not because we are haters of the United Nations, but because this program is rooted in neoliberal logic and is a reintroduction of colonial practices that threaten to displace millions of Indigenous peoples from their lands.

2. Policies that promote the development of open-source technologies to directly transfer technology and information to peoples throughout the world. This will enable communities to produce the new carbon-reducing or carbon-neutral technologies that are innovated locally, thus eliminating the need for long-distance trade that would fuel more carbon emissions.
3. Policies that will end the international operations of the US-based petrochemical, mining, agricultural, fishing, and medical transnational monopolies. This will enable local production of essential goods and services when and where needed and put a halt to the extraction and accumulation regimes that currently dominate our planet.
4. Policies that eliminate the impositions of the World Trade Organization (WTO) that negate national and local sovereignty, which has been detrimental to the introduction of major climate mitigation initiatives in the US and Canada.

There is no shortage of political projects occurring in the Global South addressing the climate crisis and the broad range of topics that you mention. I have been deeply inspired by movements in Micronesia and the Maldives to force the world to deal with the fact that their island homelands are disappearing as we speak. Their direct-action engagements at various UN and international functions have been heart-wrenching and eye-opening. There are a few explicitly ecosocialist movements in the Global South that I am aware of. The most developed in my view are in South Africa, Venezuela, and Bolivia. The critical thing about the movements in these countries is that they have put the question of climate change and the regeneration of the ecology on their national agendas.

And finally, it is imperative for our movements here in the Global North to be intentional about connecting with the movements in the Global South. In many respects, the movements in the Global South are far more advanced than those in the Global North, especially in terms of their political consciousness, organizational development, membership, and social bases. However, what many of the movements in the Global South don't possess are the resources we have at our disposal in the Global North—and I don't just mean financial resources, but varying degrees of infrastructure, like widespread access to electricity and telecommunications services.

In thinking about how to build a new international, we have to think strategically about how best to utilize our respective strengths to overcome our respective weaknesses. We need to draw on the political and organizing strengths of our comrades in the Global South, understanding that we will have to adapt them to our respective context and all the social struggle that will entail, while also figuring out how to transfer our own strengths, if only by providing them with greater resource and media access to speak and act on their own behalf to the wider world.

Conjunctural Politics, Cultural Struggle, and Solidarity Economy

An Interview with Kali Akuno by Boone W. Shear

In this expansive interview, Kali Akuno explores the current political-cultural conjuncture in the United States. Thinking through the responses to the pandemic and the Floyd Rebellion, Akuno analyzes the violence of and tensions between an escalating white supremacy, on one hand, and an intractable (neo)liberalism that is attempting to capture and channel the energies and ideas of the Left, on the other. Akuno locates direction for the Left amid the flourishing of mutual-aid projects and the possibility of a politicized solidarity-economy movement that can fight for and build practices, relationships, and institutions beyond the limitations of the market, the state, and what is deemed to be practical.

Boone W. Shear: **When we first approached you (May 2021) to do this interview, we were interested in focusing on the pandemic as part of the current conjuncture, in the United States in particular. A lot has happened since then. And responses to both the anti-racist rebellion and the pandemic made me think of some short commentary that you wrote in the summer of 2016 heading into the presidential election that I think maybe can help bring some context to where we are now:**

> The US Left must get prepared to fight on two fronts simultaneously from here on out. On the one hand, we must get prepared to fight the advance of an emergent white supremacy in its fascist form, which might in fact be even more virulent and violent if Trump doesn't win. And on the other hand, we better get prepared to fight the most aggressive and malicious form of neoliberal and

neoconservative governance Wall Street can buy, which will be fiercely averse to any resistance from the Left.

So I'm wondering if we might start by talking a little bit about that two-front dynamic in this current moment; how are these fronts functioning and what is the Left up against?

Kali Akuno: Yeah. Both of those tendencies are kicking hard right now. The latter, the neoliberal option, is much subtler. It appears in the form of Biden and the Democratic Party—and it's part of the electoral apparatus. It's posing as both a friend of the people, but also, you have no other place to go. It's walking a fine line between trying to hold a multiclass, multiracial coalition intact while recognizing that it has some clear and obvious weaknesses based on their 2016 performance. They have to reconstitute, as they call it, the Obama coalition in order to have the faintest chance of winning because they not only have to win the popular vote, just like they did in 2016, but they also have to win the electoral college, and that is not necessarily guaranteed. They may overwhelmingly win the popular vote, just on the basis of the domination of the two coastal areas, but lose everything in between. In which case the Republican Party would still be able to retain the presidency.

But here's a clear dilemma that they're posing to the people. Up to this point, in the face of a pandemic that has clearly brought out the contradictions in their health-care approach—the DNC's health-care approach—they have fundamentally denied the aspiration and demand for universal health care—given expression best by Bernie's campaign, but that's been an issue that he picked up from grassroots activists, really. So in the midst of a pandemic in April and May, the neoliberals stuck to their guns and said, "No, we're not going to offer universal health care." If anything, Biden, their representative, has been very much focused on saying we are going to fix the Obamacare plan. But there is no way of saving it, particularly in the midst of close to 50 million people newly unemployed. There's no way of salvaging it because people don't have the money to pay the premiums. And they're automatically not in the system because for most of us, our health care is tied to our employment. So you're unemployed and you can't pay. There's no way for the math that they set up to even cover that.

But they're sticking to their guns. It's the market or die. And you see the same logic playing out in the face of the Floyd Rebellion and in what has probably become the central demand, around defunding the police. In the face of that popular demand, their core leadership says: "We're not defunding the police in any form or fashion, and in fact, we want to give them more money." This is the option which has been put clearly on the table by Pelosi, by Biden, and by Clyburn—remember the role that Clyburn played in the elevation of Biden, in saving Biden, I should say.

And so they've made it clear that they're not going to bend on two core things that are at the heart of what the vast majority of their constituency are objectively demanding and objectively need. And if they don't bend—which I don't think in this period they really can—if they don't bend, then they're still leaving the door open for an extremely hobbled and extremely weakened and increasingly more isolated Donald Trump, representing a neofascist option—just acting very openly and blatantly, now, the last couple of months, and the last couple of weeks in particular. The neoliberals are giving him life and breath because, with their approach and with a program that anemic, it's no guarantee that the vast majority of folks who are considered the kind of captured audience of the neoliberals are going to turn out for a program that doesn't speak to any of the fundamental demands or aspirations of the working class.

This is the pincer move that we are really in. And it's not just that these folks are entrenched, or these sets of interests are entrenched. They are very clear. They are much more clear than the general population, unfortunately. They are clear that the only way they're going to continue on is through more austerity and more of a squeeze on the working class. There really are very few material options for a break from this to happen unless everything is changed. So that section of the ruling class is very clear: either everything changes or fundamentally nothing changes.

And they are not with the program of everything changing, in no form or fashion. And that puts them in this real weird bind, and this weird place where they can only speak to what is in their view the kind of amoral nature of the Trump administration. And the best that they really have to offer is, "We rule, more gently. We will rule, more civilly."

BWS: "We will be less openly vicious."

KA: Right! The program remains the same. They've offered no alternative. And I think too many people see through that. So we really are at a conjuncture where the center cannot hold. I think they're going to do everything they can between now and November to pull out all the stops to make sure that they can get back in office and try to sustain not only the country but the world economy as it was pre-COVID-19. But fundamentally there's no way to do that.

And that really leaves the door open, both here and internationally, for the fascist option. And I'm not saying that just tongue in cheek. If the neoliberals and what they represent are not able to really corral and contain—particularly the energy that's been unleashed around the Floyd Rebellion—if they're not able to channel that in some very particular ways which gets people off the streets, which tones down the demands, which waters down the expectations, then you could very well see a scenario in which Trump and the forces that are allied with him are able—in the midst of continued unrest, or even an escalating unrest, which I think is a real possibility and which would provide a legitimacy—to cancel the elections and to institute a program of law and order, which he's clearly invoked.

And in some respects, they [liberals] have suggested that they would support aspects of this as part of a getting back to normal: "This is all well and good, we'll make a few tweaks here and there, but we got to get the show back on the road." I mean, the Democrats, particularly Pelosi and Schumer, even more so than Biden, have given, I think, the greatest expression to this desire, if folks really listen to what they've been saying, as they're trying to push through concrete relief programs, through the House and Senate right now.

At the same time, we have had police forces all throughout the country who, during the first two weeks of the uprising, were kind of flat-footed. It wasn't clear whose orders to follow and who was giving the orders. It wasn't clear what they would do. They were very much on the defensive rhetorically and positionally. But it seems since Atlanta in particular, they've kind of regained their footing. You started to see it, I think initially, in Buffalo where they pushed an elder to the ground and cracked his skull and how the first kind of concrete action was, "Hey, if we're going to be limited in the types of force we're allowed to use, we're just going to step down off of this unit." That was the first kind of clear action, and it's been cascading since then, these kinds of symbolic actions.

But it's being met on the streets, increasingly, particularly in small towns, but also midsize towns. You know, this open fascistic violence is occurring, as we've seen. In the last two weeks, you know we've seen the kind of autonomous-zone experiments, the largest of which is the

CHAZ, the Capital Hill Autonomous Zone in Seattle. But its outskirts have been raided the last two or three weeks, by Proud Boys and other kinds of neofascist forces. That's also happened in Portland, and it's also happened on a major scale in Philly in defense of the Columbus statue and other statues.

It's not just happening in the outskirts of society or just in Trump country—that's actually not true. And we can't prove it yet, but in following the right-wing rhetoric—which is something I have to study in my political context to understand what the other side is thinking and moving, given the current proximity of forces—they're speaking of this lynching that's happening and folks being found hung as an active lynching campaign. And there've been some things that have been stated at least on the radio here, kind of instructions on how to go about doing that and pursuing that.

I see this as an active campaign. I see it as part of the kind of right-wing ideology which has been built up in particular since the 1980s. And the level of just open reception of forces in Oakland, in New Mexico, in Phoenix, and in Seattle where they've described the armed fascist vigilantes, they've been heard and recorded in many cases. Over the channels they've described them as "friendlies."

The counter rebellion is in motion now, and I think it's gaining steam. And it is my fear for those of us on the left, to be honest with you, that, in the euphoria of the moment, in seeing the kind of major actions of the Floyd Rebellion taking place now for three, almost four weeks straight, that folks are being blinded by what they want to see and are not seeing the countermotion, the counterinsurgency that is developing kind of underneath it or alongside it. And then there's the undecided middle, which I think the vast majority of the working class in this country really falls into. And I don't think we know quite yet what their appetite really is for sustained action in the midst of both a pandemic and in the midst of this uprising. It's not quite clear yet.

This is not a 1968 moment; this is different. Trump has tried to invoke that. And what makes it different is that a good portion of this "middle," I would say, are Black petty-bourgeois forces and other kinds of petty-bourgeois forces that have arisen over the course of the last fifty years, who very much feel that they are part of the system and who have something to lose, both in position and access, by a more militant hard-left orientation emerging. So it's not quite clear where they're going to bend and where they're going to break, and how long or how much of this kind of program they're willing to go with.

The future is wide open. It's unknown. It is very hard to kind of imagine where things are going to go. But the one thing is clear: almost anything can trigger events to go on in any kind of direction. And so we need to be mindful of that. Relative to the initial question, the fascist option is clear. And I think also the neoliberal option is clear. And I think the interplay between them in the course of the next four months to a year is really going to define what the future looks like, I think, for many years to come.

White Supremacy and Disposability

BWS: **I want to make sure that we further explore this struggle between neoliberals and the Far Right, and in particular what this might mean for openings for the Left. And I am wondering if we can dig in a bit toward understanding some of the forces that are not only shaping political orientations but are also implicated in the concrete violence that's being experienced, exacerbated, and further exposed by the impacts and responses to the pandemic as well as the Floyd Rebellion and that, perhaps, are shifting consciousness and relationships. The pandemic, for example, has been talked about as a sort of great unveiling that reveals the depths of inequality and oppression in our system between the elite and the masses but also within the working class itself.**

Frontline and care workers, black communities, indigenous communities, Latinx communities, incarcerated folks, the elderly, poor people, and people without homes are much more at risk then the general population, and seemingly deemed more disposable.

For example, a study done by researchers at Harvard that was recently released found that among folks aged 25–34, Black people had a COVID mortality rate 7.3 times as high as whites. Among folks aged 35–44, Black people had a COVID mortality rate 9 times as high as whites. And for those aged 45–54, Black people had a COVID mortality rate 6.9 times as high as whites. Similar inequities were also seen for Latinx and Indigenous populations, who had COVID-19 death rates that were 5 to 8 times as high as white folks (for age groups 25–54).

How do you understand what has produced these dramatically different unequal outcomes by race? And what might be done to alter these patterns of racialized violence?

KA: At its roots, it's the settler bargain. I agree wholeheartedly that this is laying bare a lot of the fundamental contradictions in this society. That's what COVID-19, basically, laid out. There's something I think, which is perhaps even more revealing, that can get at your question. In the midst of the kind of the epicenter of the pandemic in April where, by that time, almost all the states had come to the conclusion that they had to shut down. And at this time—in relation to those who could work from home and those that couldn't—white people were significantly more likely to be able to work from home than Black people. Which meant that the brunt of the unemployment went to Black workers, Latino/a workers, Indigenous workers. And it speaks to clear fractures around who's doing what work and why in the society.

BWS: Who's doing certain service work and care work, particular occupations that were thought of as low status and expendable and are now being shown as, and rhetorically supported as, being essential?

KA: Who's really doing that work? And who was in a position to do that? Who couldn't afford to stay home, or by virtue of their occupation couldn't stay home because they were deemed essential? And I think we really need to understand those relations. It helps to understand not only who got infected, who got sick, and who died, but it also speaks to the very nature of, and the lack of imagination of, the health-care response.

And, again, it points to the very real limitations of what the system was willing to do and was willing to accept at that point in time. I think everybody needs to be clear: the total response from the beginning was about saving the capitalist system. Point blank. Period. From both sides. And they were only going to bend enough to keep that system afloat. And I would argue that it was very clear from the beginning, in how they rolled out those stimulus checks and who they were rolling them out to, and the conditions that they put on them, that all of the racial factors of how this society is structured was baked into that very response. And then you saw it play out, particularly among the Right, who were saying, "We're not going to give more of a stimulus, particularly on the federal level, because it incentivizes people to stay at home, because they make more with unemployment than they do making hourly wages in their quote-unquote 'essential work.'"

If we want to peel this onion further, and to get at both the response and people's clear understanding from the beginning of who this was going to impact and why, I think we begin to understand why there's just no regard for the consequences of reopening the economy, because there's just not only a chronic belief but there are statistical facts and proven scientific fact. If this population gets it, this is what's going to happen. If this population gets it, then this is what's going to happen. Using their language, since "normal people" aren't dying... let's go. Let's get back to work. Because these Black folks, these Puerto Ricans, and these Mexicans, and Central Americans, you know, these Hondurans and Nicaraguans and El Salvadorans who are in our meatpacking factories, or are in auto plants, or who are working in these fields—if they die, fuck it. We can replace them. Let's go. Let's keep it moving.

If we want to peel this onion back, we can see it's not just, like, who is dying. We can see it's a very structured setup of who will die. That's the piece I'm getting at, the way in which this structure is channeled very clearly: this is who's going to suffer from this, and we've calculated and surmised that we're willing to accept that. And that's not just like the right-wing fanatics who are pushing that. Listen to Cuomo, he's just as eager to get the economy in New York going as Donald Trump is. Cuomo may be using a bit more, you know, sound medical reasoning and actually working in some stages and phases. But the imperative to get everything going to the point where we're not worried about eradicating COVID, we're just trying to get it to a manageable position—that's always what he's been arguing. Liberal leadership has put him out as kind of a front man, right, and helps argue, "This is the best humane response, and this is how the Democrats would do it." It's not about eradicating the disease; it's about making it manageable. That's always been the aim and objective on both sides to varying degrees.

And the other dimension to this response is that everything has been geared toward finding a cure. Now what does that mean? That means we're finding a way in which we can profit off of the response to this particular pandemic. Because the clearest, easiest, proven way is to shut the shit down and let it trace itself out. That is a no-brainer. That easily could have and should have been done. Nobody really wanted to do that. People want to talk about the contrast between Trump and the Democrats, but we've got to interrogate that further because, in some fundamental respects, they really aren't that different. We have to really tell the truth there, and really point out what the alternative is. And if we want something different, we have to be clear about how much structural change actually has to happen. Nowhere in the past couple of months, amid these discussions of talking about them as "heroes," nowhere are there serious proposals to raise the wages of these "essential" workers. We are not extending them overtime pay or hazard pay. Nowhere has that really been offered. It's been rhetorically stated, but nowhere has it fundamentally been put out there by either one of these forces and the politics that they represent that they're going to make a fundamental change.

For me, what this fundamentally gets at, it really speaks to what I've called the age of disposability, and we are starting right in the middle of it now in a way that's plain to see. I think if it wasn't for the Floyd Rebellion, we would be still very much in a deeper conversation about this. Unfortunately, I think there's some aspects of what's occurred in the last three or four weeks which has kind of pushed COVID-19 kind of way back in the background. I'm kind of holding my breath because, it's like, it's not like this wave ever stopped. If this is really like its cousin the flu, we know it's going to get worse as it gets colder. So we are in for one hell of a ride. And I know COVID-19 is not necessarily completely off a lot of folks' minds, but it has been interesting, some things I've had to point out to some comrades. I've been doing work responding to extrajudicial terror from the police all of my life, but there's a way in which the movement still has to do some groundwork to get folks to understand these dynamics. We've lost seventy thousand Black folks to this pandemic, at least; we didn't have the same level of anger or systemic response as we did to when Floyd got murdered. And we have to figure out how to get people to not just respond to the visceral but respond to the structural. And that's a major challenge we still have ahead of us.

Hegemonic Struggle and War of Position

BWS: Despite these unveilings of violence over the past few months, capital accumulation continues unabated. On Friday, it was reported that another 1.5 million people filed for unemployment that week for a total of 45 million claims since the beginning of the pandemic, and during this same time the total wealth of the nation's billionaires has increased by almost 600 billion.

The owning class seems to be doing just fine. One way to approach this challenge is by thinking through it in terms of a Gramscian "war of position." And this follows from some of what you have just described but even more so from a recent essay that you wrote, in which you discussed the potential openings for the Left: what we are up against most immediately is a sort of narrative or cultural struggle against Democrats and liberals who stifle radical politics.

We can see this in the moves calling for defunding the police rather than abolition, or the inability to give any sort of serious thought to increasing the well-being of frontline workers that you were describing earlier, or in ridiculous and awful symbolic gestures like the congressional Democrats kneeling for the cameras, wrapped in kente cloth.

KA: [Laughing] That was a moment I will forever be grateful that I got a chance to witness. That was some of the most absurd shit I've ever seen.

BWS: The architects and managers of the prison-industrial complex!

KA: Right! Like, this is bizarro world. I've lived to see bizarro world.

BWS: In addition to or as part of this struggle of ideas that the Left must engage in, you were earlier suggesting a kind of more fundamental ontological situation, a kind of reliance on or investment in the disposability of life that's just sort of baked into our dominant reality. It makes me want to think about the importance of not just struggling over the ideas and contents of what has been exposed in the dominant social order but the importance of a politics that seeks to rupture or work outside the real in order to support or create or expand other possible modes of life—so people cannot only think and act critically within the world as it is but begin to actually imagine and practice how to be together differently, as part of a shift in reality or opening of realities. I agree with you, it's pretty clear that liberals and progressives are winning the cultural struggle over the Left, for the moment.

At the same time, it is still pretty remarkable how public discourse has changed in the past few weeks and then things like systemic racism, racial capitalism, abolition, and even defunding the police—these are all new narratives and discourses to struggle over in the broad public arena. And then things like mutual-aid relationships and projects have exploded, some movements have become quite militant, acts of solidarity large and small are widespread. How might the Left engage in a struggle that doesn't just create progressive reforms that shore up liberalism and white supremacy but that begins to work toward and assemble other ways of being in the world?

I am thinking here a bit in terms of what you described as nonreformist reforms in the first essay in *Jackson Rising*, practices and policies that subvert the logic of the capitalist system, "upend its relations, and subvert its strength... [and] seek to create new logics, new relations, and new imperatives." How to struggle in and against the violence of patriarchal racist capitalist modernity and pull open and expand more fundamental ruptures or breaks so we can reorient and organize around life and relationality and autonomy?

KA: I think that there is a path already in the present, I really do. I've been trying to look at what already exists, particularly since COVID-19, in the level of mutual-aid response. We haven't seen that since the Great Depression. It's gotten hardly any attention. I think even in the movement, it hasn't received adequate attention. And it's a remarkable development. To me it's demonstrated that there is still something left of a deeper humanity in this empire, a humanity that neoliberalism as a cultural project has tried to do away with—this is actually the most successful dimension of the neoliberal project, but it hasn't broken that down completely. That's a deeply encouraging sign. And I think in some respects, mutual aid and care really are the bedrock on which we need to be thinking about how we construct the alternatives. I think that's it. We've seen mutual aid play out almost everywhere in kind of a spontaneous motion—there's been medics, there's been food pantries, and other care. And it's set up everywhere quickly.

Now why am I saying this? Because I think it speaks to some of the work in the movement, and I think in particularly the solidarity economy. And it speaks to the success of some of our advocacy, even if we didn't necessarily see it borne out as we wanted to, before COVID-19, in practice. But beyond that advocacy, now the practice of cooperation and care is here on a level I think far faster, wider, and deeper than we imagined even six months ago. It's here now. The question I think is to what degree can it be politicized, and to what end?

I think other practices and structures have to be coupled with it. Cooperation Jackson has been putting out what we are calling a "Build and Fight" program. And, you know, as fate would have it, it's broken out into a ten-point program. But we started out with that mutual-aid piece, very deliberately and on purpose, in order to say: "This is what's already objectively happening in the world." We can work on politicizing that and then linking it with the work around food sovereignty that's already happening, been emerging and deepening in a lot of our communities over the past fifteen or twenty years. And we could then tie that into all of the solidarity economy work and have this all move in a concerted political direction. The seeds of a new world are then there, and that gives us not only the social dimension of production that will be needed in a sustained conflict but the democratic, not only production, but distribution of the goods and resources that are then produced through the food sovereignty efforts, through the community production, through the cooperative piece, and the mutual aid is already there: you're laying a material foundation to be able to express a different politics. If we're able to politicize this and then organize it to reach forty or fifty or sixty million people, we can take the best practices of the Unemployed Councils' work, and, you know, there are people out there talking about a poor people's army. And if we can do that, we could objectively have it, and have it working in such a way that it is building the alternative outside of the state, outside the established capitalist market. And then it might be able to build enough strength to make a real go at it, a real challenge to not just make demands on the state, which are set up in a way in which we're asking the businesses and the managers to implement some things on our behalf but are really chipping away and building direct governance and control.

We have that ability to get us there.

I think it is going to take some hard and uncomfortable politics. And this is where a battle of ideas is really important. I do think it's not a disjuncture to say that we got to conquer this fundamental reality of disposability head-on. Because that's only going to increase, particularly as the capitalist market economy continues to worsen.

And we know now already that a good chunk of jobs are never coming back. You know, most of them are "bullshit jobs"—to use that phrase—anyway. They are never coming back. I think we have a basic recipe to do something profoundly different, but it is going to take some serious struggles with a lot of the liberal forces who want to channel things back into a position where they can manage and supervise as part of this rush to get things back to normal. So for example, it's going to be hard having a real conversation between the defund the police folks and the abolish the police folks.

The folks that want to push to defund the police are going to push for a "practical" solution and say, "Hey, this is the best that we can do given the limitations." But that's going to be a real question, and so they'll have the phrasing, and they already do, that the "abolitionists are impractical. They are intransigent and they are impractical." If we fall in and cave to that narrative and are unable to win over a critical component of the defund side, then that radical alternative will be halted, stunted, and I would argue repressed.

BWS: And then you'll have a situation where so many people are going to not be interested or energized in following a kind of middle-of-the-road liberal or progressive platform, and the Right gains momentum.
KA: Right. What the liberals are offering is not going to work.

Solidarity Economies and Postcapitalist Politics

BWS: So let's talk more about solidarity economy. In Massachusetts, solidarity economy, even just a decade and a half ago, was mostly discussed in academic circles. Lots of solidarity-economy-type stuff was and always has been happening, of course—cooperatives, land trusts, formal and informal mutual aid, and collective care—but in the past decade we've seen more visibility and more concerted action in direct relation to an emerging movement theory and framework. And this has really more recently taken hold in community- and base-building organizations, as well as a statewide network, and you've played a significant role in that for us here; you've been involved in lots of organizational and public conversations and continue to organize and educate, through the Center for Economic Democracy and ongoing workshops and meet-ups and so on. There are a lot of theoretical and political and strategic questions that are emerging for us right now, and this conversation is making me think of three areas of questions that might be important to consider as part of solidarity-economy politics—a politics aimed at creating and advancing postcapitalist ways of living.

The first is the fundamental importance and role that the cultivation of imagination and desire for other economies, for other worlds, plays in building and organizing for solidarity economies.

The second is about the importance and role of an organized Left. Where is that in the United States and how might it emerge in relation to solidarity economy? From the movement side, we have all of these really amazing and powerful base-building organizations, but they are also a pretty disparate lot and hamstrung by the nonprofit industrial complex. And a cohesive political organization: there is no viable leftist political party. How do we think about the role of an organized Left in relation to building and fighting for other economies and worlds?

And third, I'm also thinking about solidarity-economy projects themselves and how easily they can slip into a reproduction of the "world as it is"—a sort of liberal or progressive reformism like we discussed earlier, by playing an ideological and material role of filling in the gaps or by imagining and measuring solidarity economy in terms of development, growth, producing jobs and commodities, and that sort of thing—in short, a channeling of energies into a reconstitution of capitalist modernity, as opposed to radical transformation: decommodification, relationality, community autonomy, and that sort of thing.

Cultivating Imagination and Desire

BWS: So for this first area, the importance of imagination and desire: I think it resonates with something that you were saying earlier, suggesting that the contradictions of capitalism cannot be resolved through a liberal project and that everything must change. I think we have this situation where many people know on a certain level that the world as it is cannot go on—extractivism is undermining its own conditions of possibility and the conditions of life for many—but also and at the same time, a denial of this reality and seeking out of explanatory narratives that provide more practical solutions, because it's really difficult to truly imagine anything different than the reality that we are designed by and help to reproduce through our daily lives. So there is almost a resignation to the reality of capitalism and capitalist modernity. A lot of my progressive friends and many in the movement—though increasingly this is changing—and many of my students embody this kind of split subjectivity that enables a sort of realist stance: a critical opposition to violence and oppression but also a resignation to that reality. But I also see that my students and others—and myself—can begin to transform and reorient themselves and their desires when they involve themselves in, learn about, and see, or even just read about, alternative projects, for example, projects like Cooperation Jackson. I'm wondering how you—and as part of Cooperation Jackson—understand and talk about the importance of Cooperation Jackson itself in cultivating and advancing a radical imagination for members in Jackson, in the movement, and in the broader public?

KA: I would say there's a couple things that that we've been trying to be keen on in our own work. One is just constant studying and a constant exposure to other "real-time" examples of alternatives. We've been clear that things don't have to be perfect or complete, but we are asking what we can learn from each example.

About two weeks ago we did a whole conversation about the CHAZ (Capitol Hill Autonomous Zone) and had a conversation about where this whole notion of autonomous zones came from. We had a deeper conversation with our core folks about dual power and what that might look like. We tied that into the Paris Commune, which a couple of people on the core had heard about, some of the older more advanced folks had heard about it, but some were kind of like, "I heard about this, but..." And we looked at the CHAZ and said, "Imagine this but more militant." The CHAZ is still in that spirit, in that aim, through all of its contradictions. The Paris Commune had contradictions, and so does the CHAZ, and so does every one of these experiments, but that's a part of it. Democratic transformation is going to be very sloppy. You know, there really is no way around that.

But we've been able to have these exposures to and conversations about political and cultural experiments. And I think that's key here, really, because there are so many people who in Mississippi don't have access to travel, who haven't been that far out of the state. And so that's something we've been really supporting folks to do. We've sent a couple of folks to Ghana, on a year-long return program. We sent two different waves of folks to Cuba to look at permaculture and some of the work there. And that can ground people and take them out of their immediate experience and can help get people to understand that what they are seeing and learning about may be different, but it's also the same. And I think that really helps to stimulate people's imagination about what's possible, and they can start to think, "Maybe I can do that here, or we can do some elements of this over here." That's a core piece that I hope in our work, and in the best dimensions of our work here, that we've been able to kind of provide that.

To others, and I think particularly in our context, we've always tried to highlight that, even under some of the worst conditions, we can do a lot. And, you know, what we've been able to pull off in the adverse conditions in Mississippi I don't think should be underestimated. And I think, if anything, it provides an example that through the use of imagination organizations can overcome some pretty significant obstacles. But, you know, we have challenges and questions like everybody about where this is going. We see the vision. We see the dream. But will we be able to expand or get to a place where this vision is kind of ubiquitous? That's an ongoing challenge and question.

I think now, in this period, this last couple of months, I think it has done wonders for us. I can say for the political consciousness of our folks, some of the more abstract things that we've been introducing, people are saying, "Now I get it. Now I understand why we are doing this or why that's important."

But the larger question, that larger existential question remains for all of us. We've got to look it kind of square in the face and do the best we can. And the answers are with us; they're not external to us. And I see that realization is happening more and more. That's the part around this particular moment that's more beautiful than anything. The way that demands and ideas are being articulated, being framed, and being pushed; folks are kind of like, "We have to do this. Nobody's coming to save us. Nobody's coming to the rescue." I think that's becoming more and more apparent. And if there is anything that I think is going to create these ruptures in a conscious way, it's going to be that, as people continue to grapple with the failures and violence of liberalism and democratic capitalism, they'll see more, like, "Wait a minute, you know, we asked them for this. They said if we asked them and we voted in a particular way that this would be the outcome. We're not seeing the results, and you're not going to produce it, we need to do it ourselves." I think that's growing by leaps and bounds.

BWS: **So that imagination and desire is in large part cultivated through practice—through, like, actual practice and relationships made through practice—and as more people practice and see themselves in solidarity, then more people can move into and expand those ruptures.**

KA: Yeah. Yeah.

Building Power, Federation, Mutual Aid

BWS: **Okay, for this second area—and I want to make sure to talk about the People's Strike and the Build and Fight platform as part of this—what do you think about where the Left is in the US? What is the state of the Left? What do we need in order to expand and assemble solidarity**

economy? A seeming feature of solidarity economy is this sort of necessary localism—the necessary kind of community-driven, place-based nature of these projects. If this is the case, if solidarity economy and a postcapitalist politics need to emerge and be driven from and through local place-based conditions, how are we to build the level of collective organization and power necessary to expand and defend these projects? How do we think about the role of an organized Left? And maybe a more precise question to get at this: How does Cooperation Jackson think about solidarity economy as part of a revolutionary politics?

KA: We might have to do this in sections. I make the distinction between the Left we need and the Left that might be possible. And the Left that might be possible, I think, is going to work, and is going to have to work, along lines of federation. For those who don't come out of anarchic traditions: democratic associations and relationships around and through shared efforts and projects. And this is really about the tenor of the times. The vast majority of the work that is taking place—within a revolutionary framework—is not of a party orientation or nature. It's much more like small collectives, study groups, mutual-aid organizations, and so on. That is the predominant form of leftist politics all throughout the country and to a certain extent all throughout the world right now.

Part of this is just because of how eviscerated the Left has been, just literally smashed and destroyed in many places, particularly in what used to be called "the Third World" and the Global South. Just liquidated. Here in the United States, we've had elements of that with COINTELPRO and various other types of programs. But we've also had just the tremendous growth of the nonprofit industrial complex, in many respects as an intentional strategy of capital that has worked to absorb some of the uncontainable, ungovernable motion with oppressed peoples. Particularly in an era when the stable employment that you found from the late forties, fifties, and sixties—which kind of set the framework for the American Dream—that really started to disappear in the seventies. And part of what has really replaced that has been all of this nonprofit work. And you have a large sector of the folks that have leftist leanings and leftist trainings, and who have leftist orientations, who have really clustered into these nonprofits, to try and do transformative work, no question, but who are very much dependent on philanthropic cycles and their wishes and whims.

And in the last twenty years, that has kind of replaced many of the party-type structures. The nonprofits became new forms of mass work, using that framework that many of us used to orient ourselves around.

BWS: It became the scaffolding of movement politics.

KA: Right. That is what it is in this country. Not just here, this is international. It became that architecture. But I would argue, particularly since the WTO, there's been growing threads of resistance to that model. Largely led by various kinds of anarchic collectives and other kinds of collectives, some with Leninist or Maoist kinds of orientation, who refused to operate officially in a political capacity in that realm but tried to build institutions and organizations and networks outside of that.

I think we saw this really flower with Occupy, and then, since Occupy, we've just had all these assortments of loose networks and loose coalitions, loose alliances, and loose collectives. And these kind of come in and come out of existence, but they are based upon solid relationships that I think are really rooted in mutual aid. We saw this in relation to disaster relief and politics in New Orleans around Hurricane Katrina—like the People's Hurricane Relief Fund that I worked with and Common Ground—they were really flowerings of this on a pretty significant scale. And that continued with Hurricane Sandy and other natural disasters and hurricanes.

And recently we've seen another flowering of these mutual relationships and networks in March, April, and May during the beginning of the pandemic, where literally thousands of them just kind of emerged.

And we now also see efforts—that are maybe more so concentrated on the West Coast, from what I've seen, but exist throughout the country—where mutual-aid networks are the backbone of a lot of the protest activity. I think Portland probably exemplifies this the best in an ongoing way. And what people can miss in these visible protests is the kind of solidarity infrastructure that's behind them: where there's water, there's community medics, there's food, there's increasingly places for people to stay in tents and different kinds of places. There's an infrastructure of that mutual-aid work that was kind of developed in this last twenty years.

It's kind of forming that backbone of leftist political activity. And what I think we need in order to advance is for those mutual relationships and alliances to move from an informal to a more formal orientation. And as part of this, build a very intentional infrastructure, and with the knowledge in mind that the crisis that we are in now is definitely going to be a generational crisis. It's going to last for some years. If you just look at it on the level of employment, for example, we know there's going to be mass unemployment for maybe another decade. A good number of these jobs that were lost, you know, as a result of COVID-19 may never come back. As David Graeber might say, there's all these bullshit jobs. And so many of these are going to disappear, particularly as capital makes adjustments and learns from this period. And trust me, they have learned a hell of a lot; you know they're squeezing a lot of productivity out of folks from the whole digitization of work on a new level—through Zoom and Jitsi and all these other kinds of programs. There's already been some pretty decent studies saying that the folks who are in the more secure, stable, working-class jobs, or quote-unquote "middle class jobs"—these people that have the privilege to work from home—they are actually working more hours at home than when they were in the office, on top of juggling childcare and domestic work.

Going back to the question: I think we need to look at this informal infrastructure that was built, you know, autonomously by the movement over the last twenty years. And then we can take the most radical elements of it that have really been rooted in this mutual-aid work, and move that to an actual federated place, where communities and organizations democratically choose to unite and work with each other on either a limited set of goals or transitional kinds of efforts. And then, through conversation and debate, we can work toward the most maximal program.

It is time for us to connect. The pandemic has shown us that need. And the uprising has shown us the need, particularly in the face of the growing strength of the militia forces. They have been organizing. And we are just kind of seeing the results of that organizing.

And we are seeing the results of our own organizing and orientation, with the Floyd Rebellion and how it has been able to sustain itself in some places. But now we have to move to a deeper level of federation that is built upon intentionality of not only, "I'm going to come to your aid and rescue; you're going to come to my aid and rescue." We can start on that level. But then we have to ask, Well, what do we want to build together? How do we actually build the alternative? What is it? That level of dialogue and debate needs to take place, and that's where I think we need and where we can constitute a federation.

I think what Cooperation Jackson has put out through our Build and Fight program—we've articulated practices of positionality that can set up our ability to actually challenge the system and transform it. So the first is mutual aid. Which is connected to food-sovereignty work, which is basically just transforming all of the tens of thousands of community gardens and bringing together folks who've been going back to the land to do farming, or some of the folks like in your area who are doing major aquaponic or hydroponic type operations, and then linking that directly to the mutual-aid work.

You know, some of the stuff that's going on now that is called mutual aid is still more oriented to charity—let's be real—than it is toward mutual aid. The mutual aid part is, you know, "I have some skills and resources; you have some skills and resources. Let's exchange those on an open democratic basis and serve our broader communal needs—our individual needs but also our communal needs." But in order to do that, the transformative element has to be building the relationships. So it's not just you show up and I give you food or donate to a food pantry but, instead, "Hey, we need some support with the farm, or we need some support, you know, fixing up some of these abandoned houses or things of that nature. Who has some skill? Who has some time? Okay, if you don't have those skills or if you don't know how to build a house, that's okay, right? Most of us didn't know either." So at some point, we all just get together and learn.

That's the mutual aid part. That's the piece that really needs to be intentionally connected to the food-sovereignty work and to the solidarity-economy work and building cooperatives and building time banks: building those kinds of institutions and practices that we're going to need that function outside of commodity exchange and the market economy. And, you know, the reality is that most of us are already seeing diminishing returns on being able to engage in the market anyway because there's no money circulating. Nobody's getting paid.

But that doesn't mean that we don't have time, energy, and resources to put to our productive capacity to work. And I think this piece is critical when talking about federation, and we need to have open discussions about it. We are going to need to do work and try to mediate it through [noncapitalist] trade and exchange, not through monetary compensation or through commodity exchange. We are going to need to do it through exchange of labor. Because the thing that we need to elicit, I would argue, is maximum participation from as many folks as can be involved. That is where the real political education is going to come from. Yeah, we've got our books and study groups. But the real practices of transformation are going to come from folks that are actually out in the field, working on relationships and figuring out how to be both productive and accountable to the comrades that they're working with and, as part of this, work toward understanding and meeting the needs and demands of the communities that we are in.

We can see some of the limitations of some of what we have been calling mutual aid; a lot of that is really drawing on donations. It's either people dropping off food or, or, you know, doing some kind of funding campaign that asks people to make a contribution, or we go to a big warehouse and make a contribution. I think we need to redirect that and figure out: how do we produce for ourselves and build the relationships to decide among and between ourselves what we need and want? Because that's the only way that it winds up being sustainable, which is why it's necessary.

BWS: And that's also the only way that becomes political: if there's a relationality and reciprocity and learning about each other built into the exchange—

KA: That's right.

BWS: —rather than charity, or redistribution with no kind of expectation of return, where there is just a donation. No growing together or getting to know each other or building together. Charity or just simple redistribution keeps people separated and keeps the same relationships in place.

KA: Right, right. Redistribution is limited; like, this is something we have to learn from, from the failures of social democracy, because it keeps the old relationship with a capitalist exploitation in place. And it just says you should get a fair wage and, you know, we'll provide some health care, childcare, whatever. Yeah, but they're still, they're still—capital is still in place, a boss is still in place, a corporation is still in place; there's still no democracy in the workplace. So we've got to transcend that, and that's where the reciprocity and mutual-aid piece really comes in.

It is something that, again, we have to be intentional in structuring this with each other. So it is really a political dialogue, a political conversation. And that's why I would start by raising the idea that we are going to do this for nonmonetary reasons. And we do not expect monetary exchange among each other to produce this or that. If we're going to get to the point of breaking wage labor and commodity production, intentionality and actual practice to support that have to be born together. We will have to struggle through it.

This is the type of federation that I'm hoping that we can put forward and build a new Left, to be able to begin to carry a transformative program in this country. And, I think, the beauty of what we see in this year is that millions of people are already engaged in some of these practices. But we have to politicize. That doesn't mean coming in with a preset ideology. The Build and Fight program is not an ideology; it's a set of practices. So whether somebody is an anarchist or a socialist or social democratic or a communist or whatever, just get down with the practice, you know, and let's figure out how we sharpen up our ideological and political tools in the context of doing this work with each other on a mass level.

That's the federation that we need to build in this time. And that's how I think we're going to rebuild a Left that really has some strength, power, and capacity to move things.

BWS: One of the practices of the Build and Fight program is the People's Strike. Can you talk about how organized labor and a general strike fit into or relate to mutual aid and a federated politics?

KA: One of the initial principles that we laid out with the People's Strike was unity without uniformity.

We need to live into the politics of the age and try and build on that. And so there needs to be not just a diversity of tactics but there needs to be, there is going to be, a diversity of ideology. I'm one who believes that the politics of the nineteenth and twentieth centuries should be a guide for the Left, both of what worked and what we did terribly; and both of these are illustrated. We are nowhere near a place to say or decide that this particular ideology or form is the line, or this is the only way, or this is the vanguard. Let's skip all that. That's just not real.

With the People's Strike, we can think about it and practice it in the similar way and as part of a sort of federated politics. There are those of us that are connected to folks in the trade unions or folks in the workers center, or that are doing work at Amazon or Instacart or Target or Whole Foods or whatever. Or there are those of us who are doing work on the housing front, you know, trying to organize rent strikes and mortgage strikes or debt forgiveness. We all need to be in a common dialogue with each other, and at a level of a kind of shared exchange and practice of saying, "We want to move toward this particular aim and objective," because we are trying to harness the strength of as many people as possible.

That's why the People's Strike is a clear articulation of a move toward a general strike. We were under no illusion that in May 2021 there was going be some general strike in the United States. Do we believe the conditions, eventually, with the right kind of push and subjective forces coming together, we can move in that direction? Yes. But it's not along the basis of, you know, everybody has to follow this particular line. Instead, it's like, "What can you do that's going to break the domination of capital in your area?" And there's not some central committee somewhere, you know, determining that, right? Like, I don't know what conditions look like in Massachusetts. But, I think me and you and others could agree, something like this needs to happen. And now, how do we figure it out together?

That's the nature of what we're trying to build in the People's Strike and trying to follow this in a federated way. It depends upon what's going on locally, and what you can do. We can try to inspire and make some recommendations. But the point is to elevate it. And to be in dialogue, share and exchange and build power over time, collectively, through and as part of trying to figure these things out. And then, from there, build a kind of coherent strategy based upon the autonomy of folks acting on the ground, with both the freedom that offers but then also getting to a point of people asking each other to engage in and through intentional solidarity.

There is an interesting kind of dynamic with the People's Strike that kind of helped me to think about it this way. Initially, we were particularly reaching out to some unions and union activists that could help kind of consider this and argue for it. So it wasn't a totally open call, but it was sort of trusted kind of allies on the left, who were kind of embanked or embedded in certain positions. So we reached out to them as part of a coalition setup.

But then a lot of people and groups who just kind of heard about it showed up. And what I quickly noticed was that the more formal the organizations that folks were in, the less flexible they were. And the actions that actually took place on May 1 were mainly by folks who were kind of unaffiliated and just banded together loosely to make something happen. It wasn't even clear coalition politics. We had that in mind and tried to kind of construct it that way; the People's Strike was oriented as a coalition and is still kind of oriented that way, fundamentally. But the people who actually had the capacity to move and were willing to do that are much more loose and unaffiliated. So the theory and the practice aren't lining up; in this case the folks who are actually able to take the most advanced position in the work are those who are loosely affiliated and federated and just kind of say: "Hey, you want this? We agree on this. Let's work on that." And that kind of pushed me to a place of seeing that dynamic being replicated in place after place.

Look how long it took for the unions and some of the nonprofit kind of base-building organizations; it's really taking them a moment to step into the dynamic of the era. Some of it is just, you know, the dynamics of just being an organized force. You have your protocols and your processes and procedures for using a democratic method, and things take time to be proposed, and we deliberate on it. So it's not—I'm not condemning it; I understand that. But it is an interesting thing that if we look at the Floyd Rebellion during the first couple weeks, I would say the harder, the more militant side of that actually was fairly spontaneous. It's taken a while for the more organized groups to emerge in it, and I think that the more organized groups are really in a dangerous space right now, you know, in trying to shape where the Left might go. Because it's not like folks in those spaces constitute a political party; they're more like mass groups that have politics, not a political party.

What I'm seeing is, in the infusion of a certain level of kind of professionalism, they're also slowing some of the momentum down. And that also kind of hints at, I think, a more conservative tendency around how we frame demands and, you know, moving things toward, kind of, policy. Those habits of what we were doing to move things before the rebellion and before COVID-19, those habits are kind of getting in the way.

BWS: There's a liberalism endemic to the organized Left in the US.
KA: Right.

Build and Fight

BWS: A final question, and this is the third question from earlier: How do those of us involved in solidarity-economy politics—a politics that

really has the potential of creating other practices and relationships, of helping us to reimagine and rework ourselves, as not individuals, as not commodities, as not beholden to state and capital logics and imperatives—how do we steer solidarity-economy politics away from development projects and community-development projects, where those capitalist and modernist rationalities are in play? It's so easy to talk about cooperatives and measure cooperatives and think about cooperatives in terms of growth and development and "providing opportunities." How do we create a context inside a solidarity-economy politics so it's about a revolutionary politics rather than a development project?

KA: We can't without a political force to push it. Is that going to be a consolidated Left or is it going to be a federated force? That's the question. I think it's going to be more of a federated force. I think the practice of solidarity economy lends itself to a federated force at this stage of the game.

I think (a), the critical question is—going back to the mutual aid: How to build upon that foundation?

And (b), it speaks to the need to accept some of the core values and principles that we need to lean into: "You are valuable because you're human." That's at the root, and what makes it so beautiful.

And then: I'm here fighting whether I'm conscious of it or not; I'm fighting the disposability dynamic of the capitalist system itself.

BWS: And mutual aid really is animated by and animates the fundamental communist principle and logic: "From each according to their abilities, to each according to their needs."

KA: Right. Right. I think we have to build that, and I think the question—what I mean by politicizing: Are we able to engage in a federated way and link up and share in such a way so that we create our own value and supply chains? But it's going to have to come, I think, through those of us who kind of have this certain orientation and vision from being trained and being creatures of the Left to infuse it by raising questions that ask things like, "Will we be stronger in this particular way?" So I think we have to figure out how to work in a more federated way. So nothing has to be about "my" organization or any singular community that is going to lead this or develop this, but we need to get involved with the motion and raise questions and provide our training and make points of connection that need to be made.

But that's why I feel that the Left that is possible, given the real dynamics, is a federated Left. And if we can do that in a nonsectarian way, and in a flexible and nimble way, then we can politicize the solidarity economy and then move it in a concrete direction and have it be kind of a lead in the transformation. Then I think the next critical challenge would be linking that up with the more formal organized sectors, and how we democratize the rest of the economy becomes a central challenge that I think we're going to have to face.

BWS: And is that Build and Fight program—those different features of Build and Fight—would you describe that as the politicization of the Cooperation Jackson solidarity economy?
KA: Yeah, that's what the aim and objective is. And what I plan on doing, in the course of the next few weeks, is a series of thirty-minute videos that break down each one of our ten components. What I have in mind with pushing that is to help with the actual strategy that we can develop while working in a federated way to ask questions and address challenges.

IX
AFTERWORDS

Home Isn't Always Where the Hatred Is: There Is Hope in Mississippi

Ajamu Baraka

> You don't have to live next to me,
> Just give me my equality, Everybody knows about Mississippi—
> Everybody knows about Alabama—
> Everybody knows about Mississippi Goddam!
> —Nina Simone

Mississippi, the poorest state in the US with the highest percentage of Black people, a history of vicious racial terror and concurrent Black resistance is the backdrop and context for the drama captured in the collection of essays that is *Jackson Rising: The Struggle for Economic Democracy and Self-Determination in Jackson, Mississippi*.

Undeterred by the uncertainty, anxiety, and fear brought about by the steady deterioration of the neoliberal order over the last few years, the response from Black activists of Jackson, Mississippi, has been to organize. Inspired by the rich history of struggle and resistance in Mississippi and committed to the vision of the Jackson-Kush Plan, these activists are building institutions rooted in community power that combine politics and economic development into an alternative model for change, while addressing real, immediate needs of the people.

The experiences and analyses in this compelling collection reflect the creative power that is unleashed when political struggle is grounded by a worldview freed from the inherent contradictions and limitations of reform liberalism.

As such, *Jackson Rising* is ultimately a story about a process that is organized and controlled by Black people who are openly declaring that their political project is committed to decolonization and socialism. And within those broad strategic and ethical objectives, Jackson Rising is also a project unapologetically committed to self-determination for people of African descent in Mississippi and the South.

And while the end of this story is not yet written, the documentation of the social, political, and economic context and players involved in this ambitious drama is required as part of our collective learning. It is a form of bearing witness to a process of collective self-empowerment and reversing the silencing imposed on our communities by oppressors who want us to believe that "there is no alternative" to the existing order.

What we see in *Jackson Rising* is the historic task of building the new within the context of the already existing. Instead of abstract theorizing, or worse yet, despondent passivity and even collaboration that we have witnessed from some progressives and radicals in the West over the last few decades, Black activists in Mississippi are exercising agency as historical subjects.

But what is this Jackson-Kush Plan that guides *Jackson Rising*?

I will not attempt to comment on all the plan's intricacies here because that will be done elsewhere in the book. But also, because for me what is valuable about the plan is not its intimate details but what it represents broadly as the very embodiment of a decolonial project.

This audacious plan for Black empowerment and self-determination was written by Kali Akuno, one of our leading intellectuals and revolutionary theorists. But brother Kali is not just an intellectual and theoretician, as important as that is for a broad-based, mature movement, he is also a long-time practitioner whose work reflects the dialectic of theory and practice that informs praxis. So while the plan is imprinted by Kali's unique contributions, its essence was collectively formed by the broader context and congealed experiences of the Black liberation movement in general and specifically by the work of the Malcom X Grassroots Movement (MXGM) and its "parent" organization the New African People's Organization in the South.

These activists defined what they refer to as the Kush District as the areas that link Jackson within and as part of contiguous Black-majority counties along the Mississippi River in the states of Mississippi, Louisiana, Arkansas, and Tennessee.

It is therefore, a project to build Black political, social, and economic power within the heart of the Black-Belt South, recentering the issue of land, Black culture, and Black "peoplehood." It says without any equivocation that it is a project committed to building socialism unrestrained by the fear of Trumpism and in the most bourgeois society on the planet.

The plan and work represent an ethical, decolonial break with the constraints of "Northern" radical theory and practice and its myopia related to colonialism and US "domestic colonialism."

The work is informed by the baseline position that the struggle for self-determination and the liberation of Black people in the US has been undermined, not just as a result of the repression from the state, but by the reluctance of many Black activists to come to terms with the fact that for there to be authentic liberation there has to be a "critical break with capitalism and the dismantling of the American settler colonial project."

However, the value of the Jackson-Kush Plan is not just in its material/structural analysis, but the alternative ethical framework that it asserts as being fundamental to revolutionary practice and a consistent worldview that links their work to the work/struggles of people globally against neoliberal capitalism.

For me, the plan reflects an alternative ethical framework that rejects capitalist market fundamentalism in which everything, including nature itself, becomes a commodity to be bought and sold for profit.

It even rejects the left "economism" that sees production and productive relations in ways that mirror capitalist production with its emphasis on mass production and notions of "growth."

Building on the idea that economic development is rooted in the needs of the people, the Jackson-Kush Plan for economic development is rooted in its commitment to people and not objects. It is committed to community power and community-based economics that closes gap between spaces of production and consumption

The economy should serve the people, not the reverse. And the notion that economic activity is legitimate that rationalizes production in which a small group of private individuals are allowed to own and thus steal the value of what is produced by the majority for their own private use is rejected as absurd and irrational.

Politically, the Jackson-Kush Plan and the work it informs represents an unalterable commitment to the principles of democracy. Not bourgeois democracy that is reflected in five minutes of voting, but democratic participation and accountability in every aspect of social life.

The Jackson-Kush Plan reflects an understanding that *authentic* liberation cannot be achieved without creating independent structures, but it does not automatically reject engagement with bourgeois electoral processes and state structures. However, it recognizes the absolute necessity of relating to those structures from an organized and independent base.

The popular base that grounds their relationship to those structures are the people's assemblies. From that base the Jackson organizers believe that "engaging electoral politics on a limited scale with the express intent of building radical voting blocs and electing candidates drawn from the ranks of the assemblies themselves is important. As we have learned through our own experiences and a summation of the experiences of others, we ignore the power of the state at our own peril."

Understanding the complex and delicate line that must be walked when participating in bourgeois processes from a radical base with the intention of exploiting these spaces to alter power relations, the analysis represented in the plan demonstrates that the activists are aware of how easily these kinds of engagements can be co-opted by the state and used to prop up the hegemony of the state and system. The plan states:

> It should be clear that we do not engage the electoral system of the settler colony that is the state of Mississippi because we aim to legitimize its existence or its claims to being a democratic institution... we struggle to engage it as means to create political openings that provide a broader platform for the struggles to restore the "commons," create more public utilities (i.e., universal health care and comprehensive public transportation), and the democratic transformation of the economy to be waged. As we are struggling against a state apparatus that is an edifice of white colonial supremacy and neo-liberal in its orientation of governance, we are clear that this combination of defensive and offensive struggles must be given equal attention. If this perspective of critical struggle against the state is not maintained, our initiatives could easily turn opportunist and fall victim to becoming the latest Black-faced trend in the neo-liberal administration of austerity.

What these activists are engaged in is important not only to the people of Jackson, Mississippi, or the territory that is at the foundation of the Jackson-Kush Plan for self-determination, but also for peoples throughout the world still caught in the rapacious grip of the 524-year-long racialized, predatory colonial capitalist experience.

By situating its struggle for self-determination and socialism within the context of the dynamics of global struggle against neoliberal capitalism but informed by the specificities of Mississippi, it is a project that has a transnational relevance for Black people in the US and across the "Americas."

Like the innovative work of the "Black Community Process" in Colombia that integrates culture, territoriality, the people-centered development that they refer to as *buen vivir* (the good life), mass direct democracy, and the right to be recognized as a people, *Jackson Rising* decenters US/Eurocentric assumptions as the foundation and source of knowledge production and revolutionary praxis. Jackson *is* rising and emerging as a model for resistance and visioning beyond the challenges of the present. It stands as the dynamic counter to economic redundancy, political marginalization, and systematic state violence.

Resist and Fight!

Hakima Abbas

In 1601, African freedom fighters established the village of Palenque de San Basilio in what is now Colombia and in so doing broke the imperial logic of enslavement. From this village, African people established their own cultural, social, and political systems in the Americas, including their own language, in counter position but also independently from the genocidal hegemony of the rapidly expanding European colonialism of the territories. For decades, the growing community of people of Palenque de San Basilio launched attacks on the nearby port of Cartagena where ships arrived carrying kidnapped African people, vowing to free all enslaved Africans arriving there. The Palenqueros at once resisted and built.

Between 1959 and 1974 the African Party for the Independence of Guinea and Cape Verde (the PAIGC) created liberated zones on the territory it had taken back from Portuguese colonial forces. By the end of colonial rule in 1974, this liberated area constituted two-thirds of the territory of Guinea-Bissau on which half of the population lived. On this territory, during the bloody war of independence, the PAIGC and the peoples of Guinea-Bissau and Cape Verde began to construct the decolonized society they were seeking to create. They formed village committees, to deepen direct democracy in each cantonment, elected from and by the people with at least two of the five positions on the committee being held by women. They also established people's courts, health clinics, and schools and began to develop the basis for solidarity economics through People's Stores in which an exchange, rather than purchase, system was established for goods and products. In these liberated zones, the PAIGC and people of Guinea-Bissau were able to build counterhegemonic realities despite being faced with the direct assault and wrath of fascist colonial forces. They resisted and built.

The world in 2017 is marked by a global fascist surge: from the reactionary religious or ethnically based southern fundamentalisms, to white supremacist populism in the North. These right-wing forces are gaining traction out of the systemic collapse of liberal democracy and neoliberal capitalism. Often couched in anti-globalization or even anti-imperialist language, these fascisms are led by classed elites uninterested in shifting the super-exploitation of the last decades of capitalist voracity but cementing divisions among the working classes. In the global Black world, colonial patronage and an internal comprador class have been maintained in the economic relationships established by globalized capitalism. Ecocide has given an ever more desperate twist to the struggle of peoples to protect land and territory.

Black people across Africa and the diaspora live outside of hegemonic imperialist logic because our very survival counterposes our disposability in the system. Our cultural expressions are by their nature thus counterhegemonic, but like Benkos Biohó and the Palenqueros, we are surrounded, impacted, and affected by the imperatives of globalization's engulfment. Without counterhegemonic intention, we become mere pawns to be used, dismissed, and discarded at the will and necessity of colonized interests: Black communities pose little threat as territories of resistance and militarized murderous police are established to ensure even the menace of Blackness is quelled. But when Black territories are organized, when we call to action our collective survival, when we split with the crumbs of the state, end our collaboration, resist and build—then our territories become liberated zones: epicenters of rebellion, posing clear and present threats to the logic of patriarchy, capitalism, and white supremacy. If effectively engaged to build Black futures outside of the logic of domination, we can begin to realize radical queered, decolonial, crip, feminist, Black realities: liberation practice.

Autonomous or liberated Black territory is space where the relationship of people to land, exchange, life, and value is torn away from the logic of capitalism, white supremacy, patriarchy and domination, and where self-determination and direct democracy mean that people are able to shape realities in the image of their freedom dreams. Cooperation Jackson attempts to create economic democracy and self-determination within the oppressed Black nation inside the belly of the imperial beast itself. It is a star in a constellation of African autonomous zones throughout the Black world, with self-determining communities being built across Africa and the diaspora.

As you have read, *Jackson Rising* is an attempt to document the theoretical foundations, practical applications, and hard lessons learned from this emerging African liberated zone. What the success of the Jackson-Kush Plan demonstrates is that we, as our ancestors, can develop and execute effective liberation strategies through organizations of struggle like the Malcolm X Grassroots Movement and Cooperation Jackson and democratic experiments like the People's Assembly. But, one *palenque* or *kilombo* or autonomous zone is not enough. We need thousands of autonomous zones, and we need them to link on the basis of mutual aid and solidarity to break the back of imperialism and move us toward collective liberation and eco-regeneration.

In this moment, the lessons of this book are essential reading to all people interested in saving this earth from the devastation of capitalism and building a world free from oppression where many worlds are possible. So wherever we are, wherever we are situated, let us develop our plans to resist and build!

Further Reading

The Chokwe Lumumba Administration

Dee, Jim, "Mayor Looking for Radical Change in the Deep South," *Belfast Telegraph*, July 1, 2013, accessed June 24, 2022, https://www.belfasttelegraph.co.uk/opinion/news-analysis/mayor-looking-for-radical-change-in-the-deep-south-29384680.html.

Garrison, Ann, "Jackson, Mississippi, Mayor-Elect Chokwe Lumumba on Economic Democracy," *San Francisco Bay View*, June 20, 2013, accessed June 24, 2022, https://sfbayview.com/2013/06/jackson-mississippi-mayor-elect-chokwe-lumumba-on-economic-democracy.

Hales, Larry, "The Political, Historical Significance of Chokwe Lumumba Mayoral Win in Jackson, Miss.," *Workers World*, June 25, 2013, accessed June 24, 2022, https://www.workers.org/2013/06/9664.

Mayor Chokwe Lumumba and His Legacy

Biko, "Chokwe Lumumba Be Like Him: Dare to Struggle, Dare to Win," Black Workers for Justice, March 7, 2014, accessed June 24, 2022, http://blackworkersforjustice.com/chokwe-lumumba-be-like-him-dare-to-struggle-dare-to-win.

Buchsbaum, Herbert, "Jackson Mourns Mayor with Militant Past Who Won Over Skeptics," *New York Times*, March 9, 2014, accessed June 24, 2022, https://www.nytimes.com/2014/03/10/us/jackson-mourns-mayor-with-militant-past-who-won-over-skeptics.html.

Carr, Greg, "Chokwe Lumumba (1947–2014): Long Distance Runner," Dr. Greg Carr (blog), February 26, 2014, accessed June 24, 2022, https://www.drgregcarr.com/blog/2014/2/26/chokwe-lumumba-1947-2014-long-distance-runner.

Eaton, Susan, "A New Kind of Southern Strategy," *Nation*, August 10, 2011, accessed June 24, 2022, http://www.thenation.com/article/162694/new-kind-southern-strategy.

Flanders, Laura, "Remembering Chokwe Lumumba" Yes!, February 27, 2014, accessed June 24, 2022, https://www.yesmagazine.org/economy/2014/02/27/remembering-lumumba.

Goodman, Amy, "Mayor Chokwe Lumumba: A Life of Struggle, A Legacy of Progress," Truthdig, February 27, 2014, accessed June 24, 2022, https://www.truthdig.com/articles/mayor-chokwe-lumumba-a-life-of-struggle-a-legacy-of-progress.

Hales, Larry, "Honor Chokwe Lumumba," Workers World, March 11, 2014, accessed June 24, 2022, http://www.workers.org/articles/2014/03/11/honor-chokwe-lumumba.
Hawkins, Eljeer, "The Election Victory of Chokwe Lumumba," Socialist Alternative, December 12, 2013, accessed June 24, 2022, https://www.socialistalternative.org/2013/12/12/the-election-victory-of-chokwe-lumumba-part-one-of-two.
Luckett, Robert, "Remembering Chokwe Lumumba: A Revolutionary Politician," The Root, March 6, 2014, accessed June 24, 2022, https://www.theroot.com/remembering-chokwe-lumumba-a-revolutionary-politician-1790874839.
McCauley, Lauren, "Chokwe Lumumba (1947–2014): Activist and Revolutionary Mayor of Jackson, MS," Common Dreams, February 26, 2014, accessed June 24, 2022, http://www.commondreams.org/news/2014/02/26/chokwe-lumumba-1947-2014-activist-and-revolutionary-mayor-jackson-miss.
Meyer, Matt, "Freeing the Land, Rebuilding our Movements: Reflections on the Legacies of Chokwe Lumumba and Luis Nieves Falcón," *Capitalism Nature Socialism* 25, no. 2 (2014): 118–25, accessed June 24, 2022, https://doi.org/10.1080/10455752.2014.916954.
Mitter, Siddhartha, "Chokwe Lumumba, Radical Mayor of Jackson, MS Dies at 66," Al Jazeera America, February 26, 2014, accessed June 24, 2022, http://america.aljazeera.com/articles/2014/2/26/chokwe-lumumba-radicalmayorofjacksonmsdiesat66.html.
Moberg, David, "After Chokwe Lumumba's Death, Mississippi Auto Workers Mourn Ally," *In These Times*, February 28, 2022, accessed June 24, 2022, http://inthesetimes.com/working/entry/16363/with_chokwe_lumumbas_death_mississippi_auto_workers_lose_a_union_ally.
National Conference of Black Lawyers, "Chokwe Lumumba: A Legal Biography," *Africology: The Journal of Pan African Studies* 9, no. 7 (September 2016): 180–86, accessed June 24, 2022, http://www.jpanafrican.org/docs/vol9no7/9.7-15-Lumumba.pdf.
Nichols, John, "The Legacy of Chokwe Lumumba Must Not Be Buried with the Man," *Nation,* February 26, 2014, accessed June 24, 2022, https://www.thenation.com/article/archive/mayor-who-brought-economic-democracy-vision-mississippi.
Sunkara, Bhaskar, "Chokwe Lumumba: A Revolutionary to the End," *Nation*, February 26, 2014, accessed June 24, 2022, https://www.thenation.com/article/archive/chokwe-lumumba-revolutionary-end/.
Sunkara, Bhaskar, "Waltz for Lumumba," *Nation,* March 5, 2014, accessed June 24, 2022, http://www.thenation.com/article/178691/waltzlumumba.

Jackson Rising Conference Mobilization

Bandele, Asha, "Why We All Should Care about the Mayoral Race in Jackson, MS," HuffPost, April 3, 2014, accessed June 24, 2022, https://www.huffpost.com/entry/jackson-mississippi-mayor-election_b_5086812.
Bartley, Aaron, "Realizing Mayor Lumumba's Promise," HuffPost, updated June 21, 2014, accessed June 24, 2022, https://www.huffpost.com/entry/realizing-mayor-lumumbas-sustainability_b_5185933.
D, Davey, "Jackson Rising: The Bold Agenda of Mayor Chokwe Lumumba for 2014," Davey D's Hip Hop Corner, January 16, 2014, accessed June 24, 2022, http://hiphopandpolitics.com/2014/01/16/jackson-rising-bold-agenda-mayor-chokwe-lumumba-2014.
Flanders, Laura, "After Death of Radical Mayor, Mississippi's Capital Wrestles with His Economic Vision," Yes!, April 2, 2014, accessed June 24, 2022, https://www.yesmagazine.org/economy/2014/04/02/mississippi-capital-jackson-wrestles-economic-vision.
Flanders, Laura, "After Jackson Loses its Radical Mayor, a Movement Spreads in the South," *Nation*, May 14, 2014, accessed June 24, 2022, https://www.thenation.com/article/archive/after-jackson-loses-its-radical-mayor-movement-spreads-south.

Jackson Rising Conference Reports

Black Organizing Project, "The Dream that Lives in our Hearts: Reflections from Jackson Rising 2014," accessed June 24, 2022, http://blackorganizingproject.org/dream-lives-hearts/.

Davie, Grace, "A Radical See Grows in Jackson, MS," Waging Nonviolence, May 17, 2014, June 24, 2022, http://wagingnonviolence.org/feature/radical-seed-grows-jackson-miss.

Dubb, Steve, "Will Co-Op's Spark a New Civil Rights Movement?" Shelterforce, May 6, 2014, accessed June 24, 2022, https://shelterforce.org/2014/05/06/will_co-ops_spark_a_new_civil_rights_movement.

Editors, "Jackson Rises to Face New Challenges," Solidarity, May 12, 2014, accessed June 24, 2022, http://www.solidarity-us.org/site/node/4175.

Flanders, Laura, "After Jackson Loses its Radical Mayor, a Movement Spreads in the South," *Nation*, May 14, 2014, accessed June 24, 2022, https://www.thenation.com/article/archive/after-jackson-loses-its-radical-mayor-movement-spreads-south.

Kemble, Rebecca, and Hannah Nyoike, "Mississippi Rising," *The Progressive*, May 14, 2014, accessed June 24, 2022, https://progressive.org/latest/mississippi-rising.

Nuñez, Ricardo, "Free the Land! Jackson Rising," Sustainable Economies Law Center, May 13, 2014, accessed June 24, https://www.theselc.org/jackson_rising.

Scission, "Jackson Rising, Black Mutual Aid, Cooperatives, Mondragon, and All That," Scission, May 7, 2014, accessed June 24, 2022, http://oreaddaily.blogspot.com/2014/05/jackson-rising-black-mutual-aid.html.

The Struggle Continues: Cooperation Jackson and the Road Forward

Aronoff, Kate, "Bringing Solutions to COP21," Truthout, December 8, 2015, accessed June 24, 2022, http://www.truth-out.org/opinion/item/33948-bringing-solutions-to-cop21-a-conversation-with-cooperation-jackson-s-brandon-king.

Flanders, Laura, "After Death of Radical Mayor, Mississippi's Capital Wrestles with His Economic Vision," Yes!, April 2, 2014, accessed June 24, 2022, http://www.yesmagazine.org/commonomics/mississippi-capital-jackson-wrestles-economic-vision.

Green, Marcus Harrison, "COP21: What Paris Can Learn from a Mississippi Co-op," Yes!, December 3, 2015, accessed June 24, 2022, https://www.yesmagazine.org/economy/2015/12/03/cop21-what-paris-can-learn-from-a-mississippi-co-op.

Johnson, Cat, "How Cooperation Jackson Is Transforming the Poorest State in the Union," Sharable, August 6, 2014, accessed June 24, https://www.shareable.net/how-cooperation-jackson-is-transforming-the-poorest-state-in-the-u-s.

King, Brandon, "Building Power in a Frontline Community: The Cooperation Jackson Model," *Socialism and Democracy* 30, no. 2 (2016): 219–24, accessed June 24, 2022, https://www.tandfonline.com/doi/full/10.1080/08854300.2016.1195180.

Nave, R.L., "Chokwe Lumumba Center Opens with Ferguson Talk," JFP.ms, November 20, 2014, accessed June 24, 2022, https://www.jacksonfreepress.com/news/2014/nov/20/chokwe-lumumba-center-opens-ferguson-talk.

Savali, Kirsten West, "Chokwe Antar Lumumba Doesn't Need City Hall to Lead Jackson, MS into a New Era," Ebony, April 25, 2014, accessed June 24, 2022, https://www.ebony.com/news/chokwe-antar-lumumba-294.

Schneider, Nathan, "The Revolutionary Life and Strange Death of a Radical Black Mayor," Vice, April 17, 2016, accessed June 24, 2022, https://www.vice.com/en/article/5gj7da/free-the-land-v23n2.

About the Contributors

Hakima Abbas is a revolutionary. When she closes her eyes, she can see, taste, and feel the warmth of liberation in the breeze. She aspires to tending the land, dancing with the ocean, and being surrounded by the laughter of children.

Kali Akuno is a cofounder and codirector of Cooperation Jackson. Kali served as the director of special projects and external funding in the mayoral administration of the late Chokwe Lumumba of Jackson, Mississippi. He also served as the codirector of the US Human Rights Network, the executive director of the Peoples' Hurricane Relief Fund based in New Orleans, Louisiana, after Hurricane Katrina, and was a cofounder of the School of Social Justice and Community Development based in Oakland, California.

Ercan Ayboga is an environmental engineer and activist. Formerly living in Germany and cofounding the Tatort Kurdistan Campaign there, he now he lives in North Kurdistan and is politically involved in the Mesopotamian Ecology Movement, particularly in water struggles.

Kana Azhari is the executive chef at Healing Kitchen. Chef Azhari is a Bay Area native and is passionate about sharing her love for healthy food and lifestyle.

Kate Shea Baird is based in Barcelona where she works in international advocacy for local governments. She has written on Catalan and Spanish politics for Novara Media, *Red Pepper*, Open Democracy, Indy Voices, Planeta Futuro, Sentit Critic, and Media.cat. Kate has participated in the municipal platform Barcelona en Comú since June 2014.

Ajamu Baraka is an internationally recognized leader of the emerging human rights movement in the US and has been at the forefront of efforts to apply the international human rights framework to social justice advocacy in the US for more than twenty-five years. Baraka was the founding executive director of the US Human Rights Network from July 2004 until June 2011. Ajamu served as the Green Party's nominee for vice president of the United States in the 2016 election. He is currently an editor and contributing columnist for the Black Agenda Report and a writer for Counterpunch.

Asere Bello is program director of the Center for Alternative Sentencing and Employment Services, Inc., Brooklyn Justice Corps, serving Bedford Stuyvesant, East New York, Brownsville, Bushwick, and Crown Heights.

Adotey Bing-Pappoe is a Ghanaian economist who has worked as an economist in Zambia, edited reference books on Africa, and been director of London's Africa Centre. He currently serves as secretary of the Afrikan Cooperative Union, where he is focusing on the development of credit unions.

Debbie Bookchin is a journalist, author, and coeditor with Blair Taylor of *The Next Revolution: Popular Assemblies and the Promise of Direct Democracy* (Verso, 2015), essays by her father, Murray Bookchin.

Rose Brewer is a sociologist and the Morse alumni distinguished teaching professor of African American and African studies, and a graduate faculty member in American studies and gender, women, and feminist studies at the University of Minnesota-Twin Cities. A life-long organizer, she is a founding member of the People's Strike National Organizing Committee, the Black-Left Unity Network, and many other groups.

Daniel Brown is a freelance researcher in the UK focusing on autonomy-based struggles. He is a contributor to the journal *New Politics*.

Thandisizwe Chimurenga is a Los Angeles–based writer who is the author of *No Doubt: The Murder(s) of Oscar Grant* (CreateSpace, 2014) and *Reparations…Not Yet: A Case for Reparations and Why We Must Wait* (Ida B. Wells Institute, 2015). Thandisizwe is committed to infusing radical Black feminist/womanist politics within revolutionary nationalism, which she believes is key to destroying capitalism, patriarchy, and white supremacy. She has been informed by the political thoughts and/or practice of Aminata Umoja, Assata Shakur, Pearl Cleage, bell hooks, Angela Davis, Queen Mother Moore, Gloria Richardson, Fannie Lou Hamer, Ella Baker, Claudia Jones, Ida B. Wells, and the "Amazons" of Dahomey.

George Ciccariello-Maher is an organizer, writer, and radical political theorist. He has been visiting scholar at the Hemispheric Institute in New York and the Institute of Social Research at the Universidad Nacional Autónoma de México (UNAM), and has taught previously at Drexel University, U.C. Berkeley, San Quentin State Prison, and the Venezuelan School of Planning in Caracas. His first book, *We Created Chávez: A People's History of the Venezuelan Revolution* (Duke University Press, 2013), is a history of revolutionary movements in Venezuela.

Cooperation Humboldt helps to build a solidarity economy on California's North Coast, empowering residents to meet their collective needs in harmony with nature, without exploiting anyone. Their contribution for this book was developed by the Cooperation Board and Staff Collective, including David Cobb, Ruthi Engelke, Marina Lopez, Tamara MacFarland, Tobin McKee, Sabrina Miller, Oscar Mogollon, Argy Munoz, and Ron White.

Carl Davidson is a national cochair of the Committees of Correspondence for Democracy and Socialism and a national board member of Solidarity Economy Network, advocating a mixture of market socialism and worker ownership.

Bruce A. Dixon was managing editor at Black Agenda Report, and a state committee member of the Georgia Green Party. He served seven years on the board of a 480-unit housing cooperative in Chicago.

Kamau Franklin has worked as a community activist for over fifteen years in New York City and is now based in the US South. In addition to his work as an activist attorney, he is a leading member of the Malcolm X Grassroots Movement, an organization dedicated to human rights advocacy and building grassroots institutions in the Black community. The organization works on various issues including youth development, fighting police misconduct, and creating sustainable urban communities. Kamau has helped develop community cop-watch programs, freedom school programs for youth, and alternatives to incarceration programs.

Katie Gilbert lives in Chicago. She has written for Al Jazeera America, the *Atlantic*, *Pacific Standard*, and others.

Sophie L. Gonick is assistant professor of social and cultural analysis at New York University with an emphasis on global urban humanities. A scholar of urban planning and history, poverty, and race and gender, Gonick was educated at Harvard and the University of California, Berkeley, where she earned both an MA in city planning and a PhD. She is author of *Dispossession and Dissent: Immigrants and the Struggle for Housing in Madrid* (Stanford University Press, 2021).

Sacajawea "Saki" Hall is a radical Black feminist activist, mother, birth-worker, educator, and journalist who loves crafting. She sees her life's work as engaging in the collective struggle for African liberation, human rights, and social transformation. She is a native Lower East Side New Yorker who migrated to Jackson, Mississippi, in December 2013 to help advance the Jackson-Kush Plan. She is a founding member of Cooperation Jackson.

Matt Meyer is an internationally recognized author, academic, organizer, and educator recently reelected secretary general of the International Peace Research Association (IPRA). Based in New York City, Meyer works with both PM Press and Africa World Press and serves as Africa Support Network Coordinator for War Resisters' International as well as chair of the International Fellowship of Reconciliation Financial Advisory Committee. The author/editor of over a dozen books, Meyer is senior research scholar at the University of Massachusetts Amherst Resistance Studies Initiative.

Wende Marshall was born in Connecticut at the height of the civil rights movement and worked as a student and community organizer in Central Harlem, New York City, during the 1980s. With degrees from Union Theological Seminary and Princeton University, her scholarly work centers on the study of race/class, medicine, science, and social change, topics covered in her book *Potent Mana: Lessons in Power and Healing* (SUNY Press, 2012). Marshall is also a leader of Stadium Stompers, a movement of North Philadelphia–based community members, students, and workers fighting to stop Temple University's proposed football stadium, and serves on the National Organizing Committee of People's Strike.

Ajamu Nangwaya, PhD, is an educator, organizer, and writer. He is a lecturer in the Institute of Caribbean Studies at the University of the West Indies, Mona Campus. Ajamu is coeditor with Dr. Michael Truscello of the anthology *Why Don't the Poor Rise Up? Organizing the Twenty-First Century Resistance* (AK Press, 2017).

Jessica Gordon Nembhard, PhD, is professor of community justice and social economic development in the Department of Africana Studies, John Jay College, City University of New York, and author of *Collective Courage: A History of African American Cooperative Economic Thought and Practice* (Penn State University Press, 2014).

Max Rameau is a Haitian born Pan-African theorist, campaign strategist, organizer, and author. He works at the Center for Pan-African Development, Positive Action Center.

Quincy Saul is a writer, organizer, and musician. He is a columnist for *Capitalism Nature Socialism*, where he is also a senior editor. He is the author of *Reflections of Crisis: The Great Depression and the 21st Century* (Lambert Academic Publishing, 2010). More of his writings can be found on his blog, "Yo No Me Callo." After a decade of participation in different social justice movements, he cofounded Ecosocialist Horizons, for which he is an organizer. Saul is a composer and performer on the clarinet, specializing in improvisation and fusion.

Boone W. Shear's work involves critical investigations into the violence and limits of patriarchal capitalist modernity, as well as efforts to uncover, cultivate, and organize around hidden, suppressed, and emerging projects that advance other selves and other worlds. He is a professor of anthropology at the University of Massachusetts Amherst and lives with his daughter in Easthampton, Massachusetts. Shear works with community organizations and networks across the state in formal and informal ways, including as a board member of Worcester Roots, a board member of Wellspring Cooperatives in Springfield, a board member of Stone Soup Cafe in Greenfield, and a member of the organizing committee of the Massachusetts Solidarity Economy Network (MASEN). Shear is also associate editor of the journal *Rethinking Marxism* and a member of the Community Economies Collective.

Symbiosis Research Collective is a network of scholars engaged in a collaborative process of knowledge production embedded in struggles at the grassroots.

Yolande M.S. Tomlinson is a radical queer Black feminist philosopher and organizer, who brings a lifetime of experience, passion, and learning to her role as the codirector, and director of education and applied intersectionality for the Organization for Human Rights and Democracy. She is a native Jamaican, an avid gardener, and a lover of people and all species of flowering plants, including dandelions.

Gyasi Williams is a Jackson, Mississippi-based amateur musician and aspiring engineer/creative who is part of the team building a community fab lab–based organization called the Community Production Cooperative.

Richard D. Wolff is an American Marxian economist, known for his work on economic methodology and class analysis. He is professor emeritus of economics at the University of Massachusetts Amherst, and currently a visiting professor in the graduate program in international affairs of the New School in New York.

Index

"Passim" (literally "scattered") indicates intermittent discussion of a topic over a cluster of pages.

ABOUT PM PRESS

PM Press is an independent, radical publisher of books and media to educate, entertain, and inspire. Founded in 2007 by a small group of people with decades of publishing, media, and organizing experience, PM Press amplifies the voices of radical authors, artists, and activists. Our aim is to deliver bold political ideas and vital stories to people from all walks of life and arm the dreamers to demand the impossible. We have sold millions of copies of our books, most often one at a time, face to face. We're old enough to know what we're doing and young enough to know what's at stake. Join us to create a better world.

PM Press
PO Box 23912
Oakland, CA 94623
www.pmpress.org

PM Press in Europe
europe@pmpress.org
www.pmpress.org.uk

FRIENDS OF PM PRESS

These are indisputably momentous times—the financial system is melting down globally and the Empire is stumbling. Now more than ever there is a vital need for radical ideas.

In the many years since its founding—and on a mere shoestring—PM Press has risen to the formidable challenge of publishing and distributing knowledge and entertainment for the struggles ahead. With hundreds of releases to date, we have published an impressive and stimulating array of literature, art, music, politics, and culture. Using every available medium, we've succeeded in connecting those hungry for ideas and information to those putting them into practice.

Friends of PM allows you to directly help impact, amplify, and revitalize the discourse and actions of radical writers, filmmakers, and artists. It provides us with a stable foundation from which we can build upon our early successes and provides a much-needed subsidy for the materials that can't necessarily pay their own way. You can help make that happen—and receive every new title automatically delivered to your door once a month—by joining as a Friend of PM Press. And, we'll throw in a free T-shirt when you sign up.

Here are your options:

- **$30 a month** Get all books and pamphlets plus a 50% discount on all webstore purchases
- **$40 a month** Get all PM Press releases (including CDs and DVDs) plus a 50% discount on all webstore purchases
- **$100 a month** Superstar—Everything plus PM merchandise, free downloads, and a 50% discount on all webstore purchases

For those who can't afford $30 or more a month, we have **Sustainer Rates** at $15, $10, and $5. Sustainers get a free PM Press T-shirt and a 50% discount on all purchases from our website.

Your Visa or Mastercard will be billed once a month, until you tell us to stop. Or until our efforts succeed in bringing the revolution around. Or the financial meltdown of Capital makes plastic redundant. Whichever comes first.

Look for Me in the Whirlwind: From the Panther 21 to 21st-Century Revolutions

Sekou Odinga, Dhoruba Bin Wahad,
Jamal Joseph
Edited by Matt Meyer & déqui kioni-sadiki
with a Foreword by Imam Jamil Al-Amin,
and an Afterword by Mumia Abu-Jamal

ISBN: 978-1-62963-389-3
$26.95 648 pages

Amid music festivals and moon landings, the tumultuous year of 1969 included an infamous case in the annals of criminal justice and Black liberation: the New York City Black Panther 21. Though some among the group had hardly even met one another, the 21 were rounded up by the FBI and New York Police Department in an attempt to disrupt and destroy the organization that was attracting young people around the world. Involving charges of conspiracy to commit violent acts, the Panther 21 trial—the longest and most expensive in New York history—revealed the illegal government activities that led to the exile, imprisonment on false charges, and assassination of Black liberation leaders. Solidarity for the 21 also extended well beyond "movement" circles and included mainstream publication of their collective autobiography, *Look for Me in the Whirlwind*, which is reprinted here for the first time.

Look for Me in the Whirlwind: From the Panther 21 to 21st-Century Revolutions contains the entire original manuscript, and includes new commentary from surviving members of the 21: Sekou Odinga, Dhoruba Bin Wahad, Jamal Joseph, and Shaba Om. Still-imprisoned Sundiata Acoli, Imam Jamil Al-Amin, and Mumia Abu-Jamal contribute new essays. Never or rarely seen poetry and prose from Afeni Shakur, Kuwasi Balagoon, Ali Bey Hassan, and Michael "Cetewayo" Tabor is included. Early Panther leader and jazz master Bilal Sunni-Ali adds a historical essay and lyrics from his composition "Look for Me in the Whirlwind," and coeditors kioni-sadiki, Meyer, and Panther rank-and-file member Cyril "Bullwhip" Innis Jr. help bring the story up to date.

At a moment when the Movement for Black Lives recites the affirmation that "it is our duty to win," penned by Black Liberation Army (BLA) militant Assata Shakur, those who made up the BLA and worked alongside of Assata are largely unknown. This book—with archival photos from David Fenton, Stephen Shames, and the private collections of the authors—provides essential parts of a hidden and missing-in-action history. Going well beyond the familiar and mythologized nostalgic Panther narrative, *From the Panther 21 to 21st-Century Revolutions* explains how and why the Panther legacy is still relevant and vital today.

A Soldier's Story: Revolutionary Writings by a New Afrikan Anarchist, Third Edition

Kuwasi Balagoon, edited by Matt Meyer and Karl Kersplebedeb

ISBN: 978-1-62963-377-0
$19.95 272 pages

Kuwasi Balagoon was a participant in the Black Liberation struggle from the 1960s until his death in prison in 1986. A member of the Black Panther Party and defendant in the infamous Panther 21 case, Balagoon went underground with the Black Liberation Army (BLA). Captured and convicted of various crimes against the state, he spent much of the 1970s in prison, escaping twice. After each escape, he went underground and resumed BLA activity.

Balagoon was unusual for his time in several ways. He combined anarchism with Black nationalism, he broke the rules of sexual and political conformity that surrounded him, he took up arms against the white-supremacist state—all the while never shying away from developing his own criticisms of the weaknesses within the movements. His eloquent trial statements and political writings, as much as his poetry and excerpts from his prison letters, are all testimony to a sharp and iconoclastic revolutionary who was willing to make hard choices and fully accept the consequences.

Balagoon was captured for the last time in December 1981, charged with participating in an armored truck expropriation in West Nyack, New York, an action in which two police officers and a money courier were killed. Convicted and sentenced to life imprisonment, he died of an AIDS-related illness on December 13, 1986.

The first part of this book consists of contributions by those who knew or were touched by Balagoon. The second section consists of court statements and essays by Balagoon himself, including several documents that were absent from previous editions and have never been published before. The third consists of excerpts from letters Balagoon wrote from prison. A final fourth section consists of a historical essay by Akinyele Umoja and an extensive intergenerational roundtable discussion of the significance of Balagoon's life and thoughts today.

"We have to get our jewels where we can, for this is how we carry on from one generation to the next—it's revolutionary cross-pollination. To paraphrase Che, we need one, two, three, many more Kuwasi Balagoons in order to get free of the chains that bind us."
—Sanyika Shakur, author of *Stand Up, Struggle Forward*

For All the People: Uncovering the Hidden History of Cooperation, Cooperative Movements, and Communalism in America, 2nd Edition

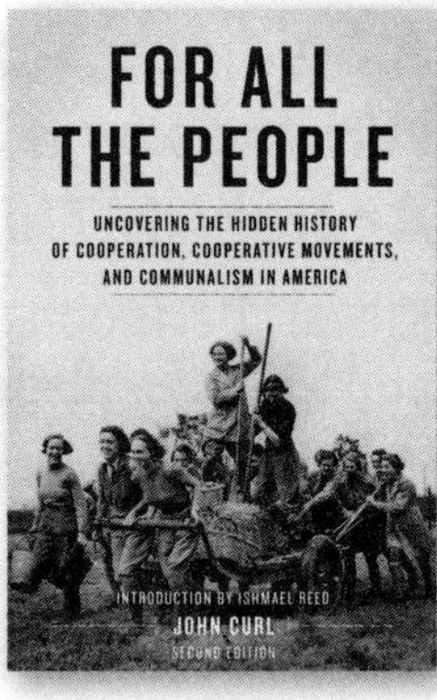

John Curl with an Introduction by Ishmael Reed

ISBN: 978-1-60486-582-0
$29.95 608 pages

Seeking to reclaim a history that has remained largely ignored by most historians, this dramatic and stirring account examines each of the definitive American cooperative movements for social change—farmer, union, consumer, and communalist—that have been all but erased from collective memory. Focusing far beyond one particular era, organization, leader, or form of cooperation, *For All the People* documents the multigenerational struggle of the American working people for social justice. While the economic system was in its formative years, generation after generation of American working people challenged it by organizing visionary social movements aimed at liberating themselves from what they called wage slavery. Workers substituted a system based on cooperative work and constructed parallel institutions that would supersede the institutions of the wage system.

With an expansive sweep and breathtaking detail, this scholarly yet eminently readable chronicle follows the American worker from the colonial workshop to the modern mass-assembly line, from the family farm to the corporate hierarchy, ultimately painting a vivid panorama of those who built the United States and those who will shape its future.

This second edition contains a new introduction by Ishmael Reed; a new author's preface discussing cooperatives in the Great Recession of 2008 and their future in the 21st century; and a new chapter on the role co-ops played in the Food Revolution of the 1970s.

"It is indeed inspiring, in the face of all the misguided praise of 'the market,' to be reminded by John Curl's new book of the noble history of cooperative work in the United States."
—Howard Zinn, author of *A People's History of the United States*

"John Curl's book For All the People *is a one-of-a-kind gem. He has done what no one else has by exploring the various permutations of 'cooperation' as a value system and as a movement throughout American history. He also makes clear that the cooperative alternative to wage-labor and exploitation still offers hope to those of us who want to see democracy permeate the world of work."*
—Steve Leikin, author of *The Practical Utopians: American Workers and the Cooperative Movement in the Gilded Age*